ECONOMIC HISTORY

of

GREAT BRITAIN

By

W. STANFORD REID

ASSOCIATE PROFESSOR OF HISTORY
MCGILL UNIVERSITY

THE RONALD PRESS COMPANY　　　NEW YORK

Library of Congress Catalog Card Number: 54–6973

PRINTED IN THE UNITED STATES OF AMERICA

DEDICATED TO MY WIFE

PRISCILLA LEE REID

WITHOUT WHOSE AID THIS BOOK WOULD
NEVER HAVE BEEN COMPLETED

PREFACE

THE PURPOSE of this survey is to provide a factual basis upon which the student of economics and history can build an understanding of the economic development of Great Britain. Primarily designed for college students in the United States and Canada, it sets forth the facts in a manner intelligible to those with no specialized knowledge of Britain or her history.

While the book gives an account of the economic growth and development of Great Britain from prehistoric days down to the return of the Conservative party to power in 1951, more than half of it is devoted to the period since 1715. This emphasis is felt to be in accord both with the facts of history and with the interests of the majority of modern students. Great Britain became uniquely important in the world economy only with the beginning of the Industrial Revolution. Until 1715 she was merely one among a number of growing nations. But from that point on she gradually became the dominant economic power, a position which she retained until the first World War. What is more, much of the explanation of Britain's present economic position can be traced, not to the second World War, but to a sequence of events starting well before 1870. It is of vital importance for the student of international economics today to have these facts at his disposal. These considerations have led the author to lay special stress on the modern period. But the events which led up to this period cannot be passed over in silence. It is hoped that in the present volume a proper balance has been achieved.

This is a history of the economic development of the whole of the United Kingdom, not of England alone. While England has undoubtedly been the most important area economically, Scotland, Ireland, and Wales have all played important parts which cannot be ignored. This is particularly true of the period since the Industrial Revolution, in which Welsh and Scottish natural resources, as well as the natural aptitudes of all the peoples of the British Isles, have had a very real influence on the growth of the British economy.

If a well-rounded picture is to be achieved, the whole complex of islands must be considered.

Whenever possible the author has pointed out the relation of economic development, in particular economic thinking, with its cultural environment. To this end an attempt has been made, within the limitations of available space, to appraise the climate of opinion of different periods as expressed in political, philosophic, and religious thought. And references to contemporary political events place economic changes in their proper perspective in relation to the whole moving panorama of history.

Throughout this account the author has endeavored to avoid value judgments as far as possible. Any attempt to give an ultimate explanation of historical events is bound to pass from the field of history into that of speculation. It has seemed best to present a balanced treatment of the established facts as a foundation upon which instructor and students can build their own interpretations of specific problems. On some controversial issues between Britain and the United States the author, as a Canadian, has tried to take an impartial position which would be less easily achieved by a native of either of the two countries concerned.

The author has been deeply indebted to many people for their help and interest in the preparation of this book. To Dr. F. Cyril James, Principal and Vice-Chancellor of McGill University, he expresses his thanks for first suggesting that he take up this work and for his continual encouragement. Of his colleagues at McGill University he is particularly grateful to Professor F. Kenneth Hare, Chairman of the Department of Geography, for his guidance in the writing of the first chapter and his kindness in reading the proofs; to Rev. E. Clifford Knowles, University Chaplain, who also read the proofs; and to Assistant Professor Murray Kemp of the Department of Economics and Political Science for reading certain sections dealing with economic theory. He would also like to acknowledge the faithful work of Miss Audrey Kinnear, who typed the manuscript. Finally, he can never express his gratitude to his wife for her help in many ways, and for her unfailing encouragement.

W. Stanford Reid

Montreal, Canada
January, 1954

CONTENTS

CONTENTS

MAPS

ix

A NOTE ON MONEY AND MEASUREMENTS

The British monetary system does not follow the decimal system but has its roots in the Middle Ages, when there was no great interest in working out the numerical values of one unit relative to another except in terms of weight. The basic units of money are:

$$12d. \text{ (pence)} = 1s. \text{ (shilling)}$$
$$20s. \qquad = £1 \text{ (pound)}$$

The standard value of the pound prior to 1931 was usually $4.86⅔ (U. S.), but it now (1954) stands at $2.80.

It is impossible to estimate in modern values the worth of money in the Middle Ages owing to our lack of knowledge, but Professor G. G. Coulton in 1931 felt that to obtain the modern psychological equivalent, the medieval money value should be multiplied by 40; so after World War II the multiplier should be approximately 60 or 65. In attempting to compare the present value of money with that of the eighteenth and nineteenth centuries there are even greater difficulties, since during these centuries there were periods of rapid fall and rise in prices. To determine even an approximate value one must know the actual period for which he is attempting to make an estimate. However, if one takes a rough average for the nineteenth century as a whole, perhaps multiplying by the figure 5 will give a faint approximation. The author would emphasize, however, that this is exceedingly rough and completely useless for periods of boom or depression.

When giving measurements of weight, tons are "long tons," or 2240 pounds, and for measurements of capacity the gallon is the Imperial Gallon, which is one-fifth larger than the standard U. S. gallon.

ECONOMIC HISTORY OF GREAT BRITAIN

Chapter 1

THE GEOGRAPHICAL BACKGROUND

In STUDYING any history, there are always two types of forces which must be taken into account: the cultural and the physical. The cultural forces, which include man's religion, his philosophy, his science, and similar phases of his thought and activity, tend to change and alter with time. Religions rise and wane, science changes and adopts new hypotheses, philosophers contradict each other and compromise. Consequently, cultural forces are by no means always the same, and, for this reason, they do not always exert the same type and same kind of pressure. Thus, as one studies any long period of history, the cultural factors must ever be assessed anew if one is to understand the changing scene. In fact, the history itself is part of the cultural picture, whose components act and react upon each other.

As a relatively constant background to all the historical action, on the other hand, remains the physical environment, the geography of the country. While the culture has changed gradually and continuously during man's sojourn the physical aspects of the British Isles have remained very much the same, except for cataclysms such as earthquakes and landslides. Hence, one must have a grasp of the geographic essentials of the islands before he can understand many of the events which have taken place upon them.

While at first it may not appear clear why one should have to know something of the geography of the British Isles, a moment's thought should make it obvious that the very fact that man's economic goods come, for the most part, from the physical environment gives it considerable importance. If man would produce steam engines, he must mine the necessary iron and coal. If he would eat, he must grow wheat, raise cattle, and obtain water. All these processes and activities are dependent upon the use to which he can put his land. Moreover, the exchange of goods is very frequently controlled by the facility with which one part of the coun-

3

try can communicate with another. Therefore, although by means of science man very often overcomes geographic obstacles and can change the face of the earth with irrigation, drainage, railways, and the like, geography still remains a constant influence upon a country's economic history.

The Physiography of Great Britain

Although Great Britain was in its earliest days attached to the Continent by land across the present North Sea and English Channel, it was at the same time divided into two distinct areas which might now be indicated by a line drawn from the mouth of the River Exe on the southwest to the mouth of the River Tees on the east. The Highland Zone, which lies to the northwest of the line, consists largely of the stumps of two mountain ranges: the Caledonian, running through Northern Ireland and the Highlands of Scotland; and the Hercynian, which covers the south of Ireland, Wales, Cornwall, and Devon and then turns across the English Channel to reappear in Brittany. These ranges were worn almost flat by erosion, but during the later upheaval which brought the Alps into existence their roots were lifted up to form the present mountains. The rocks which appear in the Highland Zone therefore are extremely old and, owing to their toughness, very resistant to the processes of weathering. The Lowland Zone, to the southeast of our line, is composed of much newer rocks. It has also at different times been under the sea, which has left deposits of sediment. During the period when the present Caledonian and Hercynian Ranges were being formed, the surface of the Lowlands was warped and gently folded,[1] producing such phenomena as the chalk Scarplands and the Sussex Weald. In this way the British Isles gradually took shape.

Besides earthquakes and volcanoes, ice also played its part in molding the surface of Britain. Apparently, toward the end of the up and down movements of the earth the northern hemisphere had four periods of extreme cold. The result was four great glaciers which seem to have covered everything in Britain except the part lying south of the Thames-Avon line. This ice and its movements radically changed the surface of the country. Gradually, through melting, the great masses broke up into smaller, or

[1] "In geology, a fold is a bend or curvature in the stratified rocks of the earth's crust, whereby they have been made to take up less horizontal space . . . a certain amount of buckling up or sagging down of the crust being continually in progress in one region or another." "Fold," *Encyclopaedia Britannica* (11th ed.; 1910).

local, glaciers. As these moved, they swept the mountain tops clear of soil, which they carried into the valleys. They plugged rivers, making them seek new courses, scoured out valleys, and dug holes which are now lakes. They even carried large rocks, moving them long distances and leaving them piled up in the most unexpected places. Not infrequently in Ireland or Scotland such collections of rocks are attributed to the work of either giants or the Devil.

Following the period of glaciation there took place what seems to have been the last general movement, the tipping of the land from northwest to southwest. The North Sea Basin was at this time finally submerged completely, to a depth of about 300 feet, although it varies greatly from place to place. Following this, the sea flowed into the present location of the English Channel. In this way the animals and men who had previously crossed over the valley between Dover and the French coast were cut off. Britain had become a series of islands.

It was all these movements of the earth's crust, resulting in the upheaval of different types of rocks and soils, along with the varied relief of the land, which gave Britain its ever-changing scenery. "The frequent contact and the repeated contrasts of highland and lowland must be regarded as characteristic of the country. By giving rise to differences in topography, the relief multiplies the number of little natural regions and local peculiarities." [2] It is the differences between these little regions and their local peculiarities which have been so important in British economic history. For this reason it is necessary to gain some general idea of the country's various areas if one would grasp the physical environment of Britain's economic development. In glancing over the Lowland and the Highland Zones we shall start, as would an invader, in the southeast corner.

The Geographic Areas of Britain

The Lowland Zone. At one time the southeast part of Britain, including the Weald, the county of Kent, and parts of Surrey and Sussex, was all under chalk. During the Alpine earth movements the chalk was broken open by the upheaval of substrata, with the result that, owing to subsequent erosion, next to the south coast one finds chalk hills, the South Downs, sloping to the sea, and to the north, just south of the Thames, another line of chalk hills, the North Downs, sloping northward toward the river. Between these is the Weald, a domelike area extending from west to east. The

[2] A. Demangeon, *The British Isles* (London, 1939), p. 24.

center is sandy with woods, while on either side of the axis are other soils, clay and greensand, the latter being so called because of the greenish color which it obtains through the presence of iron and potassium. The clays are usually quite damp and unsuitable for arable farming, while the greensand forms a good soil for that type of agriculture.[3] The Downs have rather steep faces, caused by the breaking of the surface toward the center of the area. They are cut transversely by a number of river valleys and are also breached at the east end by the sea. At one time the section between the Downs was heavily forested, its wood being employed throughout the Middle Ages for the smelting of local iron ore.

To the north of the North Downs, on both sides of the River Thames, lies the London Basin, almost surrounded by chalk hills. This area has a great variety of soils: sand, clay, loam, and gravel terraces. It is very similar to the Hampshire Basin, which lies south of the point west of the Weald where the North and South Downs come together. The Hampshire Basin was at one time completely surrounded by chalk hills, but the sea has broken through at both ends of the Isle of Wight to form one of the best harbors in the British Isles: Southampton. The basin has a variety of soils capable of supporting a considerable amount of mixed farming.

To the west of the Weald lies the unbroken chalk plateau of Salisbury Plain. Thence the chalk lands stretch northeastward, forming a line of hills known as the chalk scarps with steep slopes to the west and long gradual slopes to the east.[4] To the northeast, they decrease in height until they reach the sea southeast of the Wash, reappearing again northwest of it in Lincolnshire and Yorkshire.[5] The chalk scarps are not very suitable for arable farming, as their soil is a thin mixture of clay, sand, and flints. Because of the inability of trees to grow in their light soil, they formed some of the earliest sites of human occupation in the British Isles.

Farther to the east of the chalk hills and north of the Thames lies East Anglia, comprising Norfolk, Suffolk, and most of Essex.

[3] There are three main types of farm land: (1) "Arable land," which is suitable for plowing and cultivation. In earlier days arable was a term applied only to land upon which food crops were grown, i.e., wheat, barley, etc. Now, however, it may include land temporarily sown in hay for cattle. (2) "Permanent grassland" is usually, though not always, enclosed with fences or hedges and is without coarse herbage or shrubby vegetation. It is kept for top grade pasture or for the raising of hay, in modern times not infrequently being seeded. (3) "Rough grazing" is land without trees, but it is usually covered with shrubs and bushes and neither enclosed nor cultivated. In Britain heathland or moorland, particularly in the Highland Zone, is of this type, being used only for the grazing of animals.

[4] These hills form the Marlborough and Berkshire Downs and the Chiltern Hills.

[5] They are known as "wolds," having the same meaning as "weald" or "wild."

In the center is a loamy soil excellent for arable farming, while on the west and the east the land is inclined to be sandy. The clay land of the northeast is excellent for dairy farming. The northern part is low-lying, being wet and in need of drainage. East Anglia, whose coast line is much like that of Holland, has a number of small ports looking across the North Sea to Flanders.

Turning west from the highest levels of the Scarplands one looks out over the Midlands. This is a V-shaped area, extending from its point in Somerset north to the Pennine Range. Here it divides, one arm going to the west of the mountains and forming the Lancastrian Plain, the other going to the east, forming the Vale of York. The area south of the Pennines is largely covered with clay and marls,[6] out of which rise islands of older rocks. There is relatively little good arable land in this area, but it is excellent for grazing. Until the time of the Normans much of it was under forest.

While the Midlands have been important for their grazing lands, even more valuable were the large supplies of coal and iron found under the northern two thirds of the plain.[7] It was because of the close proximity of coal and iron that Sheffield, along with its neighboring towns and cities, became the great center of British iron and steel production, the whole district to the south being dubbed "The Black Country." Today industry here tends to overshadow the agricultural pursuits of the surrounding countryside, for this is one of the most important manufacturing areas of the British Isles.

To the northwest lies the left arm of the "V": the Plain of Lancastria, including part of Lancashire, all of Cheshire, and the northern half of Shropshire. It is connected with the central plain by the Midland Gap, which has on its eastern side the Pennines and on its west, the sea. Heavily covered with glacial deposits of boulders and clay (boulder clay), it is well suited to grazing. North of the River Mersey, however, there are more easily worked soils which are eminently suitable for arable farming.

The Vale of York, the other arm of the "V," lying east of the Pennines and west of the Yorkshire and Lincolnshire Wolds, is composed mainly of glacial drift and sedimentary soil, much of which was originally marshy but has been reclaimed. The slope of the Pennines to the east at this point is very gradual. The northern end of the area is good for arable farming, while in the center and south grazing holds the place of importance. A noteworthy feature of the Vale is that on the eastern slopes of the Pennines there are

[6] A soil consisting of clay and carbonate of lime, valuable as a fertilizer.
[7] South Staffordshire, East Shropshire, Leicester.

large coal measures, which are the foundation of Yorkshire industrial development.

The Vale of York is drained to the south by a number of rivers which eventually link up with others coming from the Midlands to form the Humber River system, which empties into the North Sea. To the south of this system, lying around the Wash, is the area known as the Fens. Marshy lands at one time flooded by rivers and the North Sea, the Fens have been reclaimed, so today they form one of the best areas for arable farming in the whole of the British Isles. They have rich black soil where there were formerly river mouths and lighter silt where there were sea marshes. This area is particularly suitable for the production of grain.

Thus, on looking back over the Lowland Zone, one sees a section of England which is possessed of no little wealth, both agricultural and industrial. Although the chalk lands have never been very valuable, the rich soils of East Anglia and the clays of the Midlands, as well as the fertile Plain of Lancastria and the Vale of York, have formed the basis of the country's agriculture. At the same time, it must be remembered that in the early days none of these areas were really accessible, since they lay either under water or heavy forests. The high, unwooded chalk lands were the earliest scenes of economic activity. Once the forests had been removed, however, not only did agriculture begin to improve, but coal and iron also became important economic assets. Out of this has grown much of Britain's prosperity.

The Highland Zone. The Highland Zone actually starts in Cornwall and Devon, the most southerly of the three rocky peninsulas which form the west coast of England. This section was untouched by the glaciers, the soil being left undisturbed. However, owing to the climate, the mountains of the area, which are part of the Hercynian uplift, have been so worn down that the whole peninsula is a high undulating plateau, with outcrops of hard granites forming the highest part of the land. Moorlands (Dartmoor, Exmoor) are very extensive. The higher lands are not good for agriculture, but in the early days the area possessed extensive deposits of copper and tin, which made it economically very valuable. The peninsula ends in cliffs reaching at times to a height of almost 800 feet.

To the north of the Cornwall-Devon Peninsula, across the Bristol Channel, which is the first great break in the mountain chain making up the Highland Zone, lies Wales. This forms the second of the highland peninsulas. The center of the zone is mountainous, the highest peak being Snowdon in the northwest (3,560

PHYSICAL ASPECT
OF THE
BRITISH ISLES

100 MILES

SHETLAND ISLANDS

ORKNEY ISLANDS

ATLANTIC OCEAN

LEWIS

WESTERN ISLES OR HEBRIDES

N. UIST

S. UIST

SKYE

LOCH NESS

SCOTTISH HIGHLANDS

BEN NEVIS

SCOTLAND

NORTH SEA

SCOTTISH LOWLAND VALLEY

Glasgow Edinburgh

TWEED R

SOUTHERN UPLANDS

CHEVIOTS

HIGHLAND ZONE LOWLAND ZONE

NORTHERN IRELAND

BELFAST LOUGH

Belfast

LOUGH NEAGH

DONEGAL BAY

MAYO MTS.

CLEW BAY

GALWAY BAY

IRISH CENTRAL PLAIN

Dublin

WICKLOW MTS

EIRE

ST GEORGES CHANNEL

ISLE OF MAN

IRISH SEA

LAKE DISTRICT

TYNE GAP

TYNE R.

TEES R.

YORKSHIRE WOLDS

PENNINES

ENGLAND

HUMBER R.

LANCASHIRE PLAIN

Liverpool

Manchester

MERSEY R

TRENT R

LINCOLN WOLDS

THE WASH

WALES

MT SNOWDON

Birmingham

Coventry

SEVERN R

AVON

COTSWOLD

BERK-SHIRE DOWNS

CHILTERNS

London

THAMES R.

NORTH DOWNS

THE FENS

OUSE R

EAST ANGLIA

Cardiff

Bristol

BRISTOL CHANNEL

EXMOOR

DARTMOOR

SALISBURY PLAIN

SOUTH DOWNS

WEALD

EXE R

ISLE OF WIGHT

SCILLY ISLANDS

ENGLISH CHANNEL

FRANCE

ELEVATION ABOVE SEA LEVEL MORE THAN 500 FEET

COALFIELDS

TRM

feet). Although around Snowdon there is much hard volcanic rock, the central mountain ranges, lacking it, have been worn down. To the southeast of the mountains are some of the wildest moorlands in the British Isles. No part of this region is suitable for arable agriculture, but it is good for sheep raising.

The principal industrial area of Wales is to be found in the lowlands surrounding the mountainous center. While there is little of such lowland in the north and northwest of Wales, it increases as one moves south along the west coast. The south coast, facing Bristol Channel, which is probably part of a drowned plain, is of immense importance. There the climate is too wet for anything else but the growing of oats and the raising of cattle. Of greater moment, however, in and around the Vale of Glamorgan are the large coal deposits which have been so influential in modern British economic development. Fairly extensive coal deposits are also located in the northeast, where Wales faces the Lancastrian Plain. These supply fuel for the industries of Lancashire.

To the north of Wales, across an arm of the Irish Sea, lies the third of the peninsulas: the Lake District. It includes Cumberland, Westmoreland, and north Lancashire, being made up of a central core of very hard rocks surrounded by newer and softer types. It is generally held that the original formation took place with the uplifting of the Caledonian Range. The rivers radiate from the center like the spokes of a wheel; the glacial action has denuded the upper lands of soil, leaving many lakes. The damp uplands can be used primarily for grazing, while in the leeside valleys arable and mixed farming is carried on successfully. This area forms one of the principal barriers between England and Scotland.

The remaining part of the Highland Zone in England is formed by the Pennine Range, the so-called backbone of Britain. Extending north from Derby to the Scottish Border, it is linked to the Southern Uplands of Scotland by the Cheviots. Flat-topped uplands, the Pennines present a steep high edge to the west and a long rolling slope to the east. As they are composed mainly of sandstone, with interspersed limestone outcrops, and are flanked on both sides by coal measures, they are useful only for pasture and for supplying water to towns in the lowlands. Although something of a barrier to communication from east to west, they are cut by three major valleys: the Tyne Gap, Stainmore, and the Aire Gap. These valleys, which enter into the Pennines from the east, are quite fertile and well watered. Extending east from the Pennines somewhat north of the Vale of York is an undulating plateau reaching to the North Sea, and draining into the River Tyne. This area is particularly rich in easily worked coal deposits and is also valuable for grazing. To the south of the plateau is the Tees valley, fertile and rich in phosphoric iron ores.

North of the Scottish Border one moves deeper into the Highland Zone. Here the first section with which one comes in contact is the Southern Uplands, formed by the denuded remains of a great mountain chain which extended from Northern Ireland. The rocks, being softer than those farther to the north, have been worn down and then round tops with moors and wide glaciated valleys have been formed. The uplands are useful for grazing only, while the dales spreading north, northwest, and south, southeast are very fertile, particularly in the Tweed Valley to the east and, to the west, in the counties of Kirkcudbright, Wigtown, and Ayr along the Irish Sea. In the Uplands sheep raising is most common; on the west coast, cattle raising and dairy farming; and on the east coast, arable farming.

North of the Uplands, with its axis extending from Edinburgh to Glasgow, lies the Scottish Lowland Valley, formed by a subsidence of land when the mountain ranges to the north and south were raised. Since that occurrence, the seas have flowed in and out a number of times, leaving sedimentary deposits; forests have grown up, later being turned into coal measures; and still later, volcanoes and glaciers have played their part in moulding the terrain. The valley is entered by three arms of the sea: the Firths of Tay, Forth, and Clyde, the two latter narrowing Scotland's middle to a width of 25 miles. The eastern end of the valley is fertile, except for the poor soil of central Fife. Although throughout the valley mixed farming is common, toward the west the damper climate requires different types of crops. At one time underlying part of the area were rich coal measures, which at the western end of the valley lay in close proximity to considerable deposits of black band ironstone. Except in Fife, these have both been almost completely worked out.

To the north of the Lowlands are the Scottish Highlands, divided in two by Glen More, which runs from southwest to northeast. Although the land lying southeast of the glen has the highest peak in Great Britain (Ben Nevis, 4,406 feet), it is not as rugged as that on the northwest, since its softer rocks have been worn down. Despite this difference, however, all the Highlands are poor for agriculture, almost 95 per cent being moor. To the northwest of Glen More, the Highlands increase in ruggedness and bleakness, ending on the west coast in a range of high cliffs. The islands off the west coast are of the same character. On the eastern seaboard

of the Highlands lies a low fertile coastal plain of varying width.
Here pastoral farming and the raising of barley is carried on. The
Orkney Islands off Scotland's northern tip resemble the coastal
plains, but the Shetland Islands north of the Orkneys, which are
similar to northern Scotland, do not favor agriculture.

Included in the Highland Zone is Ireland, which has been
likened to a saucer with a rim of mountains around a central plain.
The mountains, generally speaking, are related to those of England
and Scotland. In the north there are the ranges of Antrim, Derry
and Donegal which originally formed part of the Caledonian system. In earlier days there was also a central valley like that of
Scotland stretching from Belfast Lough to Lough Neagh, but now
it is covered by lava and glacial deposits. On the east coast south
of Belfast are hills originally connected with the Southern Uplands
of Scotland. Further down the east coast, south of Dublin, are the
Wicklow Mountains, very similar to those of Wales and cutting off
from the rest of Ireland a small but very fertile coastal plain around
Wexford. Along the south of Ireland, extending east and west, is
another range of mountains. Part of the Hercynian uplift,[8] it is
traversed by various rivers from the interior as it continues to the
most southwesterly tip of the island. On the west coast are the
mountains of Connemara and Mayo, linked with those of Donegal
and breached by the River Shannon and by Clew and Donegal bays.
In general the western mountains are barren and bleak, usable only
for pasture. In the east and south, however, particularly around
Wexford, where the area is protected from the Atlantic storms, the
land is more fertile, arable farming being carried on on the eastern
slopes and in the valleys. The uplands, however, are usually covered
with moor or peat bogs.

The bottom of the saucer, the Central Plain, is limestone covered with extensive glacial deposits, and here drainage is extremely
poor. Where drainage is possible, as in the north along the Foyle
and Bann rivers and around Lough Neagh, the land is very fertile,
so both arable and pastoral farming are common. Farther south,
however, the story is different. The east is only moderately well
drained, while the Shannon, to the west, does not succeed in its
slow and turgid course in carrying off nearly enough water. The
result is bog and wet pastures, except where the mounds of glacial
deposits above the marsh level are sufficiently dry for the growing
of hay and oats and the grazing of sheep. To the south the Central
Plain is broken up by many hills. Although they are of themselves
of little agricultural value, the valleys, if drained, are usually quite

[8] See pages 4 and 8.

fertile. The best of these valleys, lying to the west and south of the Shannon, is the Vale of Limerick, probably the most fertile region in the whole of Ireland. In general, however, because of the difficulty of arable agriculture, except in certain limited areas, grazing is the principal form of Irish farming.

The Highland Zone is a rather poor area, however one looks at it. With its rough terrain, poor soil, and wet climate, it does not offer very much to the farmer. At the same time, it is not rich in minerals, except in the Scottish Lowland Valley. Added to all this, it is farther from the continent of Europe than is the Lowland Zone, its orientation being out into the Atlantic, rather than towards Europe. Consequently, of the two principal geographic areas of the British Isles, although the Lowland Zone, confined to England, is smaller, it is by far the richer of the two. This goes a long way to explain why England has always been the economically predominant part of the British Isles, and it also explains why, out of every seven people in the islands, six live in the Lowland Zone.

Rivers and Coastal Waters

Glaciation had an important effect upon the whole river system, blocking river valleys, carving out lakes, and changing the direction of the flow of water. Today the rivers flow generally east or west, with the longer rivers on the east coast. The eastward drainage of the Lowland Zone is by three main systems: the Thames to the southeast, the Ouse emptying into the Wash, and the Humber. To the west, drainage, centered on the Severn, rises in Wales and flows into the Bristol Channel. These river systems have been of immense importance not only as means of drainage, but also as means of communication. The same is true of the main rivers of Scotland, the Clyde, the Forth, and the Tay, which drain the central Lowlands. In Ireland, on the other hand, rivers such as the Shannon and Foyle, flowing over wide beds with relatively little fall, are of no great help for either drainage or transportation.

Another important function of the rivers has been the provision of estuaries which can be used as ports. A number of the rivers' mouths are really submerged valleys, which have gradually been filling up with silt. Man has done much to stop this by dredging, while in other places, where there is perhaps a bottleneck through which the tide flows, the water itself scours the channel and keeps it clean, as in the case of Southampton Water. If one glances at the map, one can immediately see how closely connected ports are with rivers' mouths on the east and west coasts of both Britain and

Ireland. Of the greatest importance, however, is the fact that the east coast of England and Scotland, particularly in the early days, had the best ports, which provided points of entrance for both invaders and traders from the Continent.

The seas surrounding the British Isles are influenced by two main currents. One carrying warm and salty water flows from the Atlantic into the North Sea between Scotland and the Faroe Islands and thence to the coast of Norway. The other comes probably from the warm Mediterranean, moving up the Iberian coast and through the English Channel. In this way the submerged land around the British Isles known as the Continental Shelf has warm water brought to it from two directions. Somewhat like the ocean currents, the tide moving in from the Atlantic divides in two off the west coast, one part going around the north of Scotland and the other part up the Channel, the two waves finally meeting off the Thames estuary. In the narrow waters such as one finds around the Western Isles, the powerful tidal currents make navigation difficult, while in other places they help, as mentioned above, to keep channels clear. The eventual meeting of the tidal waves at the Thames mouth causes considerable submarine disturbance, resulting in the dangerous sand banks off the southeast coast.

The coastal waters of Britain, particularly in the North Sea and off Cornwall, are plentifully supplied with fish. When the fish rise to spawn, they are easily caught, and for many centuries fishing has formed one of the most important industries of the coastal areas. Herring, mackerel, and cod are the principal varieties in the catch, which is larger in the North Sea than in any other area in Europe. The causes of this superiority are, first of all, the abundance of food and, secondly, the fact that warm, relatively shallow water covers the continental shelf. This industry has always been a factor in British economic life.

The Climate

The mild, moist climate of the British Isles has also wielded a very great influence on its economic development. Generally speaking, the weather comes from two directions: either from the southwest in the region of the Azores, a high pressure area where clear weather prevails, or from the north near Iceland, an area of low pressure with fogs and rain. Added to these two conflicting types of weather is a third, resulting from the Continental climate, which is a center of low pressure in the summer and of high in the winter.

The British Isles lie at the crossroads of the weather movements from Iceland and the Azores. During winter the influences of Iceland and the Continent are stronger, thus making for cold and rain or snow. However, in the summer, since the high pressure areas move northward, the influence of the Azores is greater, bringing warmer weather. When the warm winds from the southwest strike the cold edge from the north, they rise. Condensation takes place, resulting in rain. A further complicating factor is the appearance of what are known as secondary cyclones or minor storms, usually from the direction of Iceland and also bearing rain. These atmospheric disturbances travel in various directions, thereby increasing the general uncertainty of the climate.

Apparently for the purpose of adding to the weather prophets' difficulties, other influences are at work. There are the mountains, valleys, lakes, and coastal waters; and even the difference in the conductivity of the rocks has its part in determining the weather.

That the mountain area lies on the western side of the British Isles is probably one of the dominant influences on the climate. The first effect of this is that as the winds come in off the Atlantic, they rise, become cool, and deposit their rain just to the east of the highest points, giving the northwest of Scotland and Wales a rainfall of as much as 200 in. a year. The precipitation decreases gradually from that point eastward, until it reaches its smallest amount near the Thames estuary, where it stands at about 20 in. Since little of the land receiving more than 40 in. can be used for agriculture, the western rainfall helps to prevent the development of arable farming in the already rather barren area of the Highland Zone. Although Essex has about 150 days of rain in the year, the west of Scotland has 225, and Ireland receives a similarly liberal allowance. Yet, despite this, we are assured by some British geographers that few places in the British Isles have rain for more than 14 consecutive days.

A somewhat different pattern is followed in matters of sunshine and temperature. In Orkney, at 60° latitude, the possible daily sunshine varies from over 18 hours in June to 5 hours in December. But, on account of fog and haze, the sun is visible each year for only 26 per cent of the daylight hours. In southern Cornwall (50°) the variation is between 16 and 8 hours a day, with the sun's visibility being annually about 40 per cent. The brightest part of the country is along the south coast and the dullest in the northwest. In January the warmest place is in the southwest, with the temperature falling as one goes northeast, while in the summer also the south continues to be warmer than the north. The average temperature for the British Isles in January is 40° and in July, 60°. This means that the British climate, though relatively damp, is mild. Fog is actually not quite as common as is usually supposed. This generally temperate climate has wielded a considerable influence on Britain's economic development.

The Geographical Position of Britain

In the Middle Ages the British Isles were at the end of the world. More than one bishop of Caithness, in writing to the Pope, declared that to be the case. At that time the Mediterranean was the center of western civilization, as well as the principal water trade route of Europe. As medieval economic life tended to move northward, however, the picture gradually changed. The inhabitants of the British Isles found themselves closely linked with the markets of Flanders, France, and Germany, but they were still dependent upon the Venetians and the Genoese for their eastern goods such as silks and spices. At the same time, Ireland developed contacts with southern France, Spain, and Portugal, which lay to the south and the southwest. Yet Britain as a whole still lay on the periphery of the European world.

The situation was suddenly and drastically changed with the discovery of the New World and the opening up of the sea routes to the East. Britain, formerly on the outskirts, now found itself at the very heart of the world's trade routes. The shortest route from America to northern Europe was via the British Isles. This made Britain a natural port of call, and a natural point for transhipment of goods for distribution on the Continent. If a Channel Tunnel should ever be dug, Liverpool would form a natural terminus for all European rail lines. Thus, Britain since 1492 has been located in an enviable position: next to Europe, yet not joined to it; looking out upon the broad Atlantic not merely to America, but to all the world. Combined with her physical characteristics, her central location has helped to make her one of the most important economic areas on the globe.

As one tries to grasp the general picture of the physical scene upon which the economic history of Britain has been acted, it must always be kept in mind that there is tremendous geographical variation in these small islands. The islands differ from each other and even have great differences within themselves, facts which have done much to mold British economic, political, and social development. Therefore, to understand Britain's economic history, it is necessary to refer back continually to the character and nature of the islands themselves, for an explanation of many of the economic customs, habits, and practices which have appeared from primitive times down to the present.

Chapter 2

THE BEGINNINGS OF BRITISH ECONOMIC DEVELOPMENT

To UNDERSTAND fully the economic growth of Great Britain, it is necessary to go back to the seed from which it has sprung. This is to be found in man's search for food and shelter in the British Isles long before any written record had made its appearance in western Europe. It was only after a very considerable length of time that man gradually developed even the most primitive form of economy. Glaciers, followed by the appearance of dense forests, tended to make human life difficult, so for some thousands of years man's economic development was slow. Down to about 6000 B.C. man could usually cross what is now the North Sea or the English Channel on foot, but after that time he had to use boats. The consequence has been that since the islands were formed the inhabitants have tended to develop their own special form of civilization. Yet, at the same time, it must be kept in mind that between 6000 B.C. and 48 A.D. most of the changes in Britain's economy came not as a result of internal development, but rather as a consequence of invasion. One group of invaders superimposed its way of life on that of the preceding group, to form pre-Roman British culture.

The Waves of Invasion

After the land connections of the British Isles disappeared beneath the waters of the North Sea and English Channel, there remained three main routes open to newcomers. One was from Holland and Belgium across the North Sea to the east coast. The second and shortest was across the English Channel from France to the southeast tip of England, only some 21 miles away. This has been one of the primary foci of invasion since prehistoric days. The third route lay from southern France and the Iberian Peninsula to Cornwall; thence north, through the Irish Sea and up the Scot-

18

tish coast as far as Orkney, Shetland, the Faroes, and Scandinavia. While this route is not used for travel so much today, it was one of the great prehistoric waterways which effectively bound together Ireland and western England and Scotland. These were the three primary routes that invaders or traders followed to Great Britain after the dawn of British history. In the Lowland Zone, once the newcomers had landed, they tended to avoid the low-lying heavy soils covered with forests. Instead, they kept to the sparsely-wooded, high-lying, light, chalky, and sandy soils which cross the country in various places. In the Highland Zone, however, where the high areas were wind-swept and boggy, the tendency was to cling to the leeward sides of the mountains or to move into the glens where the soil was light and protected from the winds and rain coming off the Atlantic Ocean.

To understand the way in which prehistoric economic life developed, one's first consideration must be the various invasions which took place before the coming of the Romans.

The earliest men to reach Britain came, apparently, thousands of years ago, between the first and second glacial periods. Of these visitors there are only scanty remains, but what they have left behind would indicate that their economy was extremely primitive. Paleolithic (Old Stone Age) people, as they are called, had few tools and lived mainly on easily obtained food such as shellfish.

Some time later came Mesolithic or Middle Stone Age invaders. Here one is on firmer ground, for the remains are more plentiful. After the British Isles had really become islands, the Mesolithic people arrived by the three routes already mentioned. It was at this point that the cultural inbreeding began and Britain started to develop a specifically insular way of life. The people of the Mesolithic period spread gradually across the south of England, up the east coast, and also into Ireland and the west of Scotland. As the climate of the islands became somewhat modified over a long period, there was a considerable expansion of population. The woolly rhinoceros, the great auk, and other animals common to arctic areas began to disappear, while bears, wild oxen, and animals accustomed to a warmer climate took their places. Thus man found his environment demanding change and adaptation.

The first real revolution in the prehistoric economy came, however, only with the arrival of Neolithic groups. Between 2500 and 2000 B.C. these invaders, made up of people who seem to have come in the first instance from southern France and Spain, appeared on the scene. It has even been suggested that they may have been related to the predynastic Egyptians. They probably landed first on the western coasts of Britain, thence extending their culture northward as far as Orkney. They are particularly noted for their building of monumental tombs and shrines made of tremendous stones, spoken of as Megalithic (Great Stone). Because of the labor involved in handling the stones, they must have been well organized, possessing a rather complex society. In a sense they can be regarded, therefore, as introducing the first major advance in British economic life.

The beginnings of another era are to be seen, however, with the advent of a new race, the Beaker people, so known because when they buried their dead, they always left, among other things, a beaker, or pottery drinking mug, in the tomb with the corpse. They differed physically from the Neolithic people, who were "long-headed," by being a "round-headed" race. Two branches seem to have struck Britain first about 2000 B.C. One group, starting from Spain, had moved into central Europe, whence, after mixing with other peoples, they came to the east coast of the British Isles from the region of Holland and Belgium. The other group, coming more directly from Spain, invaded the islands via the western route. They seem to have concentrated mainly on western England, Wales, and Scotland, avoiding Ireland. With these peoples began the Bronze Age invasions, which lasted roughly for the next 1500 years. During this period the use of bronze largely replaced that of stone throughout the country. In the Highland Zone bronze continued in use until the time of the Romans.

The appearance on the English Channel of a new people, the Celts, brought the Bronze Age officially to a close. Coming from eastern Europe, they reached the Atlantic between 600 and 500 B.C. Instead of their weapons being made of bronze, they were of iron. Some Celts (*Gaels*) had already come to Britain from Holland about 750 B.C. as late Bronze Age invaders, settling in Ireland, Man, and Scotland. The iron-using Celts, however, known as Brythons, arrived on the south coast around 500 B.C., to be followed some 150 years later by another wave of invaders of the same racial group. To add to the complications, from about 150 to 45 B.C. the pressure of population in north central Europe and the impetus given by Roman imperialism caused further migrations, this time of a mixed Teutonic and Celtic group known as Belgae. These people began to arrive in southern England in ever-increasing numbers, driving the earlier arrivals out of the southeastern region. Better organized than their predecessors, they set up a number of kingdoms which were well developed and functioning when Julius Caesar made his raids on the southern coast.

Thus, when we come to the beginning of the Roman period, we find that the British Isles were inhabited by a very complex ethnological group. Invaders had entered from practically every side, although the main pressure had usually come from across the Channel, particularly upon the Kentish coast. The Lowland Zone was largely dominated by Brythonic peoples who had fused with the earlier Stone and Bronze Age inhabitants. At the same time, they were gradually spreading northward and westward, dominating and mixing with the Gaelic inhabitants of the Highland Zone. Although from time to time new strains have been added, it is this basic mixture of peoples upon which Britain has built her history. Even at that early date a culture really different from those of the Continent was beginning to appear. The "British," if one may so call them, were by now truly an insular race.

The Matter of Tools

While man's hands are extremely clever, Providence has not armed them with the claws of the animal. Consequently, as far back as one can trace human history, man appears as one who invents and uses instruments. Whether it be a wooden club, a hoe, or a micrometer, he has to employ a tool to achieve his ends. Consequently, the question of tools will be emphasized repeatedly during this account of Britain's economic history. Indeed, tools are so important in the early stages that the various epochs are named after the materials from which they were made. Before one can understand, therefore, the development of either farming or industry, he must obtain some idea of the way in which prehistoric man progressed in the use of such aids to his welfare.

The earliest weapons and tools were merely natural objects which came readily to hand. Most often they were of wood and have long since perished, but those made from two other materials —stone and bone—have remained. The most ancient tools which have been discovered are stones or flints slightly chipped in order to make them more useful. As the years rolled by, men began to work harder at the business of shaping these natural objects. One method employed was to chip away all the parts of the stone, leaving only the core, which was then shaped into the desired tool. Another was to knock off a large flake and then trim it to the proper dimensions. These two techniques, originating outside of Europe, are both found during the Mesolithic period in Britain. Bones of animals were also employed, since they were relatively plentiful and more easily worked than flint. Consequently, knives, picks, hammers, clubs, and daggers were fashioned out of stone and bone to give man an advantage over his animal and human enemies.

Up to this time implements and weapons were relatively rough, although some belonging to the later Mesolithic period are very well made, considering the tools with which craftsmen worked. The Iberian Neolithic invaders, however, introduced further improvements in the methods of chipping, as well as the practice of grinding. With this greater knowledge many other types of stone less easily chipped than flint could now be used also, while holes could be bored in the stone to allow the fitting of hafts to hammer- and axheads. Spearheads shaped like laurel leaves appeared, knives and daggers improved not only in appearance but in efficiency as well, and arrowheads made of stone became common. Thus man was advancing his economic position by subduing his environment.

The gradual introduction of bronze into Britain was the next step. Compounded of copper and tin, it was one of the earliest known metals which man could employ in the making of tools. Whether the formula for making bronze was worked out independently in Britain or whether it was first imported we do not know. It is certain, however, that Cornish tin and Irish copper were early exploited in the making of this important commodity. The Beaker people were the first to employ it, but they did not do so to any great extent, and only with some difficulty did it replace the well-made stone and flint tools.

At first the patterns of the bronze tools and weapons followed the lines of neolithic products. For instance, knife blades were fastened into handles by means of tangs, and axheads were usually set into pieces of split wood. By the Middle Bronze Age, however, because of the ductility of the metal, men had learned to make axes and spearheads with sockets. They also found that by making a rib down the center of a knife or sword blade they could give the implement much greater strength. As a result of increasing supplies of bronze, swords, knives, chisels, and gouges all came into use. Man now had instruments which could cut wood more easily and effectively; he also had weapons which enabled him to kill animals, as well as his fellow men, with less difficulty. Thus bronze gradually replaced stone, remaining in the Highland Zone the dominant material for tools down into the Christian era.

Before the Bronze Age had come to an end in Britain, on the Continent a new age had begun with the introduction of iron. It quickly became important both because it was easily obtainable from the earth and because it was fairly plentiful. Even more important, it was stronger than bronze and could be tempered to hold a sharp edge. This meant tools of greatly increased efficiency. It was during the period of transition from bronze to iron on the Continent that the first iron-using invaders (the later Gaels) reached British shores. Shortly afterward (about 500 B.C.) another group, whose culture had been even further developed by the influence, first of Greece and then of Rome, the Brythons, arrived. They brought final destruction to the Bronze Age civilization.

While many claim that it was because the Celts carried iron swords that they easily conquered their enemies, much more important for our purposes is the fact that they carried iron axes and used iron plowshares. The iron ax meant that men were now in a position to overcome the forests which dominated the river valleys and the Midland Plain of the British Isles. Furthermore, with an iron plow they were able to break up the woodlands' heavier and more productive soils. Thus an even greater revolution than that made by bronze took place. Through the advent of iron and the knowledge of its use, the ground plan was laid for the development of British economy down to the present time.

From the foregoing it is easy to see that even during prehistoric times great economic changes were taking place in the British Isles. Over a period of many thousand years man had gradually acquired knowledge which enabled him to improve the control of his environment. New methods of facilitating his efforts to preserve and make life more comfortable were either discovered at home or introduced from abroad. These changes, largely brought about by improving tools and implements, make up the economic history of the period.

Prehistoric Farming

The problem of obtaining food was for Early Stone Age man even more important than it is for us, since he had much more difficulty in acquiring the minimum necessary to keep body and soul together. We could perhaps understand his problems only if we were placed on a deserted south sea island, without even such supplies as were available to Robinson Crusoe from the neighboring wrecked ship. In the Lowland Zone settled along the sparsely wooded chalk ridges or along the sea shore, and in the Highland Zone confined to the mouths of rivers or beaches, earliest man had to depend upon what he could pick up; consequently, nuts, fruits, and the like formed a large part of his diet. He also spent much time hunting. In the earliest days, when part of the British Isles was either under ice or was at least subject to very cold weather, his quarry was the mammoth, the woolly rhinoceros, the auk, and other arctic animals. When the climate was warmer, he had the elk, red deer, and wild pig for food. Along with these, he also ate shellfish which he found on the beaches and the fish which he speared or hooked in the sea. He was fundamentally a food gatherer, rather than a food producer. He had no agriculture, depending entirely on what nature itself might provide.

The beginnings of farming in the British Isles took place with the advent of the Neolithic peoples. Agriculture, developed in the Middle East, had gradually spread north and west until it reached the western isles. The migrants who arrived in Britain about 2500 B.C. engaged in both arable farming and grazing. Usually settled along the sparsely wooded chalk ridges of the North and South Downs or the scarplands, they cultivated small plots with a hoe or with some sort of digging stick. When one plot was worn out, they moved on in order to keep up the output of their crops. They also had domesticated such animals as long-horned cattle, sheep, and pigs. By this means, for the first time in the history of the British Isles, man gained some freedom from the vagaries of nature. He could now do something toward "laying up against a rainy day." Man was, in fact, beginning to develop something of an economy, for he was indulging in actual production. What is more, he was commencing to take thought for the morrow, for he had found a means of providing against its possible disasters.

The Early Bronze Age saw relatively little improvement in agricultural techniques. At first the Bronze Age people had been almost entirely pastoral, so when they turned to arable farming, they continued to stress animal husbandry as an important part of their system. Mixed farming was the usual type. The methods employed were Neolithic, but the introduction of metal prepared the way for improvements. Sickles, hoes and similar instruments could now be made increasingly efficient. A great advance came toward the end of the period, with the appearance of the first Celtic invaders. They used the horse harnessed to wheeled wagons and added to that two types of iron-tipped plows, which, although not very good, were considerable improvements upon the old hoe system. Along with these changes, and largely because of them, a more settled system of farming began to appear, and farmsteads surrounded by fields were actually becoming common.

The Celtic farmer did not think in terms of big fields, for his tools were too light for the extensive plowing required. The more primitive of his two types of plow, that called the *caschrom* and still in use in the Western Isles, was probably very common. It had a head of metal, with a long handle fastened at right angles to the butt. At the side of the handle, close to the head, was a projection upon which the foot could be placed. The point of the head was thrust into the ground, and by means of pressure from the foot and a pulling of the handle it was forced up, breaking the sod. This would be a tedious way of plowing a large field, but where the plots were small, as was frequently the case in the Highland Zone, it was a satisfactory instrument.

The other plow, called by the Romans *aratrum*, was horse-drawn but did little more than scratch the earth without turning a furrow. It was thus suitable only for light soils, and, because of its ineffectiveness, cross-plowing was necessary, resulting in fields which were usually square. What is more, since light soils were sought, the fields most frequently cultivated were on well-drained hillsides. The slant of the field caused the earth on the upper part of the field to slide down to the lower side, making a bank, which was usually faced with stone. Thus the hillsides became "stepped." These steps are known as "lynchets" and are often discoverable today by aerial photography. Celtic farming methods, although very primitive, were a step forward, for they meant that men could substantially increase the quantity of their food production. Population could grow, and the search for food would become less pressing.

The final episode in the history of prehistoric agriculture took place with the appearance of the Belgae about 250 B.C. This tribe brought with them a much heavier iron-fitted plow which operated on two wheels (Latin, *caruca*). Originally developed on the heavy lands of the German plain, it could be employed to cultivate both the heavy loam lands of the English river valleys and the clay of the Midlands. The outcome of this was that, aided by some artificial drainage in the valleys of the southeast, grain production increased considerably. When Caesar landed in Britain in 55 and 54 B.C., he testified to the great crops of wheat on the farms, an improvement made possible by the new plow. At the same time, the need for a large number of oxen to pull the plow tended to make it a rich man's implement. This may be one of the reasons for the appearance of large farms under the Belgae. Later these establishments frequently became Roman villas. However, the important thing to remember is that the Belgic plow remained standard in the Lowland Zone until nearly the nineteenth century, while the lighter plow and even the digging stick continued in use in Ireland and the Highlands of Scotland.

By the time of the Roman Conquest farming had become the chief occupation in Britain. The main center of arable agriculture was the southeast, while through the rest of the islands the more important activity was grazing. This dominant position of farming over all other economic activities continued until the Industrial Revolution.

Britain's Earliest Industries

Having already obtained some idea of the development of tools from wood, stone, and bone, through bronze to iron, we must now look at the whole industrial picture. Were there any real industries? How did they operate? In answering these questions one must realize that there are always two types of industry possible. There is, first of all, the domestic type, in which each individual produces what he needs for his own use or for barter. Then there are the industries in which there is some form of cooperative organization. The workers in the latter concentrate entirely upon a single product, depending upon others to provide the capital or other necessary goods which they do not supply for themselves. Although one might think that domestic industry would be the only type possible in prehistoric Britain, even the Stone Age had its industrial organization.

One might naturally expect that each person would attempt to chip out his own stone tools, but as that was no easy task, when a man attained a special proficiency in this work, he might devote himself entirely to stone chipping. Moreover, certain areas provided better stone or more flint than others, and the fortunate inhabitants of these areas concentrated upon their natural resources. On the chalk South Downs, for instance, prehistoric flint mines containing the miners' tools and lamps are still in existence, indicating some sort of cooperative mining organization. When the flints were brought to the surface of the earth, skilled workmen roughed them into the shapes of various tools. In northern Wales a primitive factory has been discovered, where prehistoric man made axes in large quantities from the local stone. Some of these have been found as far east as Essex.

One type of production which seems to have commenced as a domestic activity but may have developed by Roman times into an organized industry is cloth making. It is probable that cloth was first worn in the British Isles in the Neolithic period. Weaving of both flax and wool was common in the Bronze and succeeding ages. While it undoubtedly began as the work of the wives and

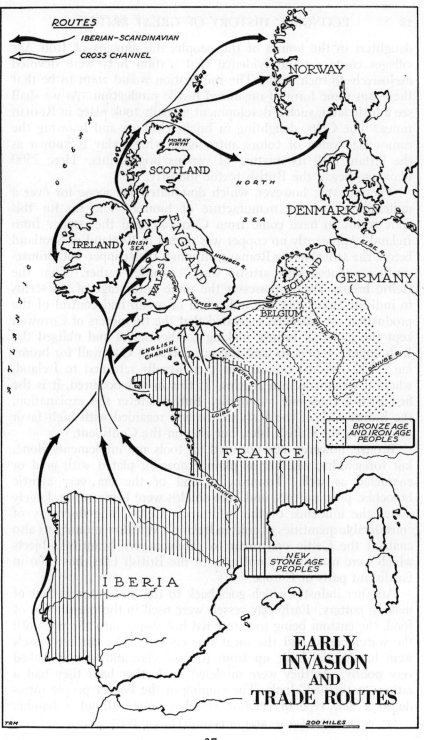

daughters in the homes of the people, the remains of Iron Age villages contain some evidence that certain huts were devoted exclusively to such work. The implication would seem to be that there was some form of organized textile production. As we shall see a little later, such a development actually took place in Roman times. The Celts, delighting in bright clothing and knowing the camouflage value of colors, introduced what today is known as the tartan, with its mixture of various bright tints. Here 2500 years ago began the British textile industry.

The industry, however, which dominated the scene for over a millennium was the manufacture of bronze. The tin for this alloy seems to have come from Cornwall, and the copper from Ireland. Apparently no copper was mined in England or Scotland before the arrival of the Romans, although Irish copper- and bronze-smiths produced very artistic work centuries earlier. That the Celtic bronze always possesses the same percentage of tin seems to indicate that some one individual or group had control of the production. It has been suggested that the tin miners of Cornwall kept the secret of bronze making to themselves and obliged the Irish copper miners to send the raw metal to Cornwall for bronz-ing.[1] The finished bronze was then usually returned to Ireland, where it was made into articles. If this in fact occurred, it is the first British economic monopoly. But, whatever the explanation, the bronzework of the Irish smiths was regarded with high favor not only in the British Isles, but also on the Continent.

Bronze, however, was not used for tools and implements alone, but for jewelry, whether as plain bronze or plated with gold or enameled as well. Toward the end of the era very artistic brooches, pins, mirrors, and even shields were being made, largely under the influence of the infiltrating Celts. The discovery of considerable quantities of gold in Ireland's Wicklow mountains also enabled the Celtic craftsman to produce very beautiful objects which were used widely not only in the British Isles, but even in far distant parts of Europe.

Another industry which goes back to the Stone Age is that of making pottery. Early clay vessels were used in the preparation of food, the custom being to throw red hot stones into the pot until the water boiled and the meat was cooked. The earliest vessels were handmade, built up from rolls of clay and usually baked very poorly. As they were modeled on leather bags they had a rather "potbellied" look. The coming of the Beaker people intro-duced a new type of ceramic vessel—a mug without a handle.

---

[1] C. P. Martin, *Prehistoric Man In Ireland* (London, 1935), p. 103.

From the appearance of different types of pottery in tombs and ruins it is often possible to determine the type of culture which was predominant at a certain time or place. During the Celtic period, particularly after the Belgic invasions, the potter's wheel came into common use, making pots of greatly improved shapes. The firing also was usually better, and the ornamentation at times became quite beautiful. It may have been through the influence of the Belgae that this manufacture tended to become a large-scale industry. In any event, the ceramic industry was of very great economic and social importance, for it affected deeply the way in which the people lived, thereby contributing much to their standard of comfort.

Until the invention of metal tools, wood had not been an easy material to work. Only when bronze became common did saws, axes, gouges, and chisels make it possible for man to take advantage of the wood which grew all around him. He was soon engaged in the making of wooden vessels, the hollowing out of logs to make canoes, and the employment of wood for the more efficient hafting of tools. The Celts further improved the woodworking industry by introducing the iron ax, which could cut down the biggest trees, while at the same time they brought in the pole lathe, which has left some very beautiful specimens of Celtic turned work. The mortise and tenon and the dowel were also known.[2] Consequently, both small wooden objects and large structures could be made.

Other industries no doubt existed, but those mentioned will give some idea of the amount of economic activity in prehistoric Britain. It has been suggested that in Ireland whole tribes devoted themselves to one craft or another. The early Irish records speak of "the wheel people," "the sword people," and others, perhaps indicating that certain groups in a tribe specialized or excelled in specific types of manufacture. All this assembled evidence would indicate that even before the Roman conquest industry had become important.

The Beginnings of Trade

Fundamentally, trade is simply the exchange of goods. We find someone who has what we need; then, if we can produce something he wants, we arrange an exchange. Such barter undoubtedly formed the basis of early trading operations. If, however, some particular commodity, say bronze, was very much in demand, some

---

[2] Mortise: a hole in a framework designed to receive the end of some other part; tenon: end of piece of wood fitted for insertion into a mortise; dowel: headless pin of wood, metal, etc., to fasten together two pieces of wood, stone, etc.

enterprising person might gather together a supply and travel around the country exchanging his bronze for other commodities. He would then be a peddler. He might even store the goods which he obtained by barter in a certain place to which people could come when they desired to make a purchase. If they then paid him for the goods in pieces of bronze, this would be the beginning of money, the trader becoming the modern middleman or retailer. It was in some such manner that trade originated in the British Isles.

The first real traders were the Mesolithic Peterborough people who were partially submerged by the Neolithic invasions. Having been forced to retreat north and west to the foot of the Pennines, they continued to hunt for their livelihood but found also that in their travels they could profitably trade flint implements. Taking advantage of their opportunities, before long they became noted as middlemen. For instance, they seem to have been responsible for the distribution of Welsh stone axes in eastern England. The Celts who arrived during the latter part of the Bronze Age were also much interested in commerce, largely owing to their close connection with the Continent. Consequently, ever since the middle of the Stone Age trade has always been a matter of some importance in the British Isles.

To carry on trade in those days was not easy. For one thing, lines of communication were few, the main external trade routes being the same as the invasion routes mentioned at the beginning of this chapter. The sea was the principal highway for the early merchant, while inland transportation was provided by the rivers along which canoes could travel. These two highways joined at the mouths of rivers which provided good harbors. Such waterways as the Thames, the Clyde, the Severn, and others, therefore, were at a very early date important as trade routes. The lines of travel on land were, on the other hand, largely confined to the higher, lightly-wooded areas. A quick glance at the physical map will make clear where such routes would run. In the south of England the chalk lands along the south coast, which linked with the scarplands lying as far north as York, furnished the chief arteries of travel. These ridgeways were also joined, through the Mendips, to the west and Wales. A further incentive to use the highlands was that along these ways the main settlements were established. To the north, in the Pennines the Aire Gap opened up one line between modern Lancashire and the east coast, while, further north still, the Tyne Valley provided a route from what is now Carlisle to Newcastle. In Scotland one traveled from Galloway on the west along the ridges of the Southern Uplands, by the rivers over to the east coast, or from the mouth of the Clyde, along Glen Mor, to Moray Firth. In this way the merchant could, although with considerable difficulty, traverse a large part of the country. The forest-covered midlands, however, were practically untrodden by man.

The earliest trade within the country was no doubt in flint and stone implements. The peddler would go along the summit trackways with his pack, bartering his goods in the various villages. With the coming of bronze, trade experienced a further expansion. As copper was not found in England or Scotland, the art of fashioning bronze articles was not practiced to any extent by their craftsmen. Instead, bronze articles were brought from Ireland, certain routes across the country being followed by traders from the west coast ports to the eastern communities. Quite frequently these men combined the work of middlemen and bronzesmiths, taking in part payment for new wares old articles, which they melted down and made over. With the arrival of the Celts, trade seems to have increased once again. It is possible that actual markets where people could gather on certain days to exchange their goods were set up. By these means the exchange of commodities throughout the country gradually became more common.

The British Isles had not only an internal trade, but also exported to and imported from the Continent. This was natural, considering that throughout the whole period there were repeated invasions. Moreover, trade was not merely with near points on the coast of France, but seems to have ranged far and wide. Bronze was carried through England and Scotland for export across the North Sea to northern Europe, as well as being sent directly from Ireland to southern France and the Iberian Peninsula.

With the coming of the Iron Age, exports of bronze goods fell off, but raw materials took their place. The Roman historian Strabo records that grain, cattle, gold, silver, iron, tin, leather, slaves, and dogs were the principal items sent abroad: Jewelry, particularly inlaid and enameled work, was also sold to the Continental peoples. In return, quantities of goods were brought into the British Isles. There was amber from the Baltic area, blue segmented faience, or earthenware, beads, probably from Egypt (ca. 1400 B.C.), and ornaments from central Europe. During the Celtic period in particular, the imports consisted of wine and probably oil from Italy, pottery, chariots, iron goods of various sorts, and textiles. Thus the foreign trade of the British Isles, even at this early date, was of considerable value.

The conduct of external trade, at least as far as we can trace it, seems usually to have been in the hands of Continental peoples.

During part of the Celtic era the Greeks from Massilia (Marseilles) had a virtual monopoly. Later, about the time of Caesar, a Gaulish tribe, the Veneti, was the principal mercantile power until the Romans smashed its navy. After this the Belgae in Britain itself may have played a more important role.

Commerce, however, could not develop if it were forced to depend entirely upon barter. Some system of setting values and of providing a medium of exchange which would have common currency was necessary. Early in the Iron Age the first coinage appeared, consisting of bars of iron, resembling those from which swords were fashioned. These bars were of different sizes but were related to each other mathematically and doubtless represented the first real attempt to set up some common system of value and medium of exchange. They were, however, rather awkward to carry, particularly if one had a large bill to pay. Consequently, when Roman influence began to be felt, coins usually copying the *stater* of Philip of Macedon came into use. The copying was weird and wonderful to behold but served its purpose, and the Belgic kings issued a considerable number of such coins between the time of the landing of Caesar in 54 B.C. and the actual conquest one hundred years later. From the distribution of these historians can very frequently trace the political influence of the different Belgic kingdoms. It is safe to assume, therefore, that by the time of Caesar, while barter was no doubt still common among the ordinary people, it had disappeared in the general realms of trade. Britain was developing a money economy.

The Life of the People

While we have been talking about farming, industry, and trade, we must realize that these are the activities of human beings. But how did they live? This is something at which we can take but a passing glance.

In trying to understand the pre-Roman way of life one is faced first of all with the matter of political and social organization. It would seem that until the appearance of the Belgae, the tribe was the usual unit. Ruling over this body was the chief, surrounded by the free warriors and their families. Under these were poorer but free people, while on the lowest stratum was a relatively numerous body of slaves, usually made up of the conquered inhabitants. That there must have been considerable organization of power even in the Stone Age is apparent from the huge stone tombs and forts which have been left. It has been estimated that in one great stone tomb in Scotland there is enough material to build six parish churches. Later, in Iron Age times, a fort such as Cissbury in west Sussex was built with walls consisting of 35,000 cubic feet of chalk taken from the surrounding ditch, while the timber uprights numbered between 8,000 and 12,000. Equally great efforts were made to meet man's spiritual needs. When one considers some of the Bronze and Iron Age religious monuments, such as Stonehenge on Salisbury Plain, where stones weighing some tons have been raised twenty feet in the air and placed across equally large slabs of rock set up on end, he cannot but marvel. These examples indicate no little economic power and organization as well as large supplies of human labor. This is true for all parts of the islands, for there are Megalithic tombs and places of worship as well as forts of different periods to be found as far north as the Shetlands. While in the north of Scotland some of the forts are relatively small and suitable only for tribal use, all these remains point to an increasingly complex culture.

There is no doubt that the standard of living was generally rising throughout this whole period. The improvement in tools and weapons would help to make this certain. What is more, the development of agriculture, and particularly the advent of the plow, would assure a more continuous food supply. There were, of course, cultural and economic recessions, but, in the long run, the average inhabitant of Britain in the days of Julius Caesar was much better off than the cave dweller of the Old Stone Age.

Perhaps the change in living quarters gives us the best idea of the advance which had taken place. In the early part of the Stone Age the usual type of house was merely a hole sunk into the earth and covered with sods or branches. Later, a certain amount of wood was used for the walls which rose above the level of the earth, while in the Highland Zone beehive stone huts were the most common type of shelter. During the Bronze Age these continued to be the usual forms of housing. Toward the end of the period we find "wattle and daub" (walls of woven osiers or reeds covered with clay) coming into general use. Moreover, both villages and individual permanent farmhouses were beginning to appear in greater numbers. By the time the Iron Age was well underway various other improvements, such as individual rooms in the small houses, had been introduced. When Caesar landed in 54 B.C. real towns, influenced by Roman fashions and ideas, were standing. This trend increased during the one hundred years after Caesar's invasions. No doubt the houses, villages, and towns would seem very poor affairs to us; nevertheless, they were an enormous improvement over what had gone before. During the Iron Age some villages had been built on marshes with foundations of brush and clay. While there are traces of only two remaining in England: Glastonbury and Meare, there are many others, known as *crannogs*, to be found in both Ireland and Scotland. They often reached quite a high level of civilization, some having been occupied into the Middle Ages.

Thus, by the close of the prehistoric period the British Isles had developed a rather active, if primitive, economic life. During the century following Caesar's short-lived invasions, the Britons, as we shall now call them, increased in wealth and also became more Roman in point of view. It was these two factors, coupled with dynastic squabbles within the country, which persuaded the Romans to come over and take possession in 43 A.D.

The Romano-British Economy

The Romans, while they stimulated British economic activity for a time, really added very little which was absolutely new. Almost their only contribution to British economic life was the improvement of organization. In the techniques of production there was little or no change. Moreover, whatever effect they did have was wiped out by barbarian invasions within some four hundred years of the conquest.

Another reason for the relative unimportance of the Romans is the limit of their actual occupation. They did not touch Ireland, and while they made inroads into Wales and Scotland, they exerted no real economic influence on those areas. Thus, the Roman impact was largely confined to the Lowland Zone, and in particular to a horseshoe shaped area surrounding the forest-covered clay lands of the Midlands. The area extending south from Chester through the Mendips and the Cotswolds, along the south coast downs, and up the chalk ridges to York was the principal region of occupation. In this section of the country they attempted to Romanise the natives, but the adoption of the conquerors' customs was not more than skin-deep. When the Teutonic barbarians struck in the fifth century, the influence of Rome very quickly departed, while in Gaul, where it had taken real root, it remains even to the present.

Roads were the one contribution of the Romans which survived the occupation for many centuries. Built primarily for military purposes, they were solidly constructed of stone slabs laid on a firm foundation, and ran straight across hill and dale. With London as the hub, they spread out like the spokes of a wheel toward the frontiers and sea coasts. Both the merchants of those days and their successors for many centuries afterward followed these routes, vestiges of which remain in some places to the present day, many of the principal highways following, even now, lines laid down in that far-off time.

The social and economic organization most characteristic of the Romans was the town, with its expensive public buildings, its baths, and its forum. Consequently, the Roman authorities tried to persuade the natives to follow their example by developing urban life. In this they were partially successful, although even at its height London, the largest town, had probably no more than 15,000 inhabitants and occupied about three hundred and thirty acres of land. The other towns were little more than tribal capitals. Simply places for the exchange of goods, they were industrially almost negligible. They prospered, however, until the fourth century, when the Emperor Septimius Severus began to exploit and tax the middle class. The outcome of this policy was that the urban communities declined and within a hundred years fell into ruin.

A much more pleasing part of the picture is that of the villas. These were large farms, almost self-supporting, owned by Roman officers or by Britons who adopted Roman customs but who continued to farm as had their forefathers. Usually the villa properties were laid out in large fields which were cultivated with the *caruca*, or heavy Belgic plow. This had probably been the agricultural system in use before the Romans came, but the owners also attempted to follow Roman customs by building houses with porticoes, central heating, and large rooms. Toward the end of the Roman occupation some of the villas were tending to specialize in wool growing, and in some areas, such as Wiltshire, where villages had been quite numerous, the people were being cleared out to make room for sheep. This is a preview of what was to happen in Britain at the close of the Middle Ages.

The villages, concentrated largely on uplands such as Salisbury Plain and the Marlborough Downs, were inhabited by natives, probably of Bronze Age stock. Their remains are usually found quite separate from those of the villas in geographic location. While the villas were typically Roman, the villages were only very slightly influenced by the conquerors. They seem to have continued on their Bronze Age or Early Iron Age ways without paying much attention to the newcomers. It is possible that they were under direct imperial control or that they were leased to imperial favorites to whom they would have to pay taxes. But apart from that, the average peasant continued to cultivate his small square field with the light plow, raising relatively sparse crops of grain.

In industry there was again little change. During the early years of the occupation the Romans and their imitators imported from Italy large quantities of Samian and Arretine pottery as well as wine, jewelry, and the like from various parts of the Continent. The British workman, however, soon began to copy the pottery and metal goods with such success that a considerable decline in imports resulted. Sometimes, as in the case of the Castor potteries, located in what is now Northamptonshire, large companies produced goods en masse, while in other areas small individual craftsmen hawked their wares around the countryside. The Romans made a real contribution in the field of exploiting mineral wealth. Under their aegis the tin mines of Cornwall were revived, iron production was increased, and the lead deposits of the Mendips were worked. Textile manufacture also became important, for the increasing popularity of British cloaks on the Continent stimulated that industry. Some of the villas were actually turned into fulling mills, probably to finish the cloth woven by peasants or slaves in their own homes. Generally, however, it would seem safe to say that while industry prospered, it did not experience any startling advances.

Trade also seems to have continued much as usual. Exports consisted primarily of raw materials: minerals, hides, oysters, dogs, slaves, and a certain amount of cloth. The imports, on the other hand, were, as already stated, much greater at the beginning of the period than after the British workman got into his stride. Trade with Scotland was also carried on both by sea and land, British goods being found as far north as Orkney. Internal trade was aided greatly by the use of Roman coins and by the military roads radiating from London by which merchants were able to visit the various town markets with ease and safety. But once the towns collapsed in the fourth century, the merchants disappeared, leaving traveling peddlers as probably the only distributors of goods. Thus, Britain's trade continued under Roman rule, but without much change of character.

Although during the first and second centuries A.D. Britain prospered economically, the seeds of dissolution were even then beginning to sprout. The continental Empire was breaking up from both internal rot and external pressure. As mentioned above, after 250 A.D. the towns began to decline owing to taxation and exploitation. The villas, on the other hand, continued to flourish for another hundred years, but gradually they too began to feel the effects of the imperial dissolution. For one thing, raids along the east and south coasts by barbarian pirates who specialized in sacking the wealthy farmhouses were becoming common. Then too, the rural lower classes were placed in an increasingly unpleasant position by the government's taxation and oppression by local landlords. Poverty-stricken, with no means of protecting themselves against virtual, if not actual, slavery to the neighboring wealthy land owner, they were ripe for revolt. As a result of all this, both industry and trade withered away. Even the farmer found it unprofitable to raise crops which might be destroyed or taken from him.

The final blow came when the Romans evacuated the country in the middle of the fifth century. The Britons, who for three hundred years had depended upon imperial legions to protect them, were left defenseless, without leaders or arms. As the barbarian invaders from the north and east swept in with comparative ease, the Roman civilization crumbled. So did the whole economy of the country. Little was left of Roman civilization except towns such as London, which may have continued to harbor a few inhabitants. Generally speaking, Britain reverted to the cultural condition of the early Iron Age or even earlier. For the next two hundred years the barbarian conquest went on. When the British Isles next emerged into the light of history, they were a new entity with a considerably changed way of life. Yet despite the changes, the old substrata of prehistoric civilization remained to form the foundation of the new economy.

Chapter 3

THE TEUTON MAKES HIS CONTRIBUTION

THE FIRST chapter in Britain's economic development came to an end with the withdrawal of the Romans. During the latter days of the fourth century the Empire had begun to fall to pieces. Civil war was chronic, with various military leaders fighting each other for the imperial crown. Even in faraway Britain the Roman generals were not without such ambitions, and a number of them took the garrison troops to the Continent to support their claims. At the same time, the pressure of Germanic invasions along the Rhine and Danube forced the imperial authorities to draw on the British garrison to bolster the home defenses. Thus, gradually more and more of the Romans disappeared from Britain until finally in the first quarter of the fifth century the last Roman soldier left the country.[1]

The Anglo-Saxon Conquest

Probably for more than a hundred years before the final Roman evacuation, Britain had been faced with a barbarian menace from outside her borders. For one thing, the Celtic peoples to the north and west, the Picts in Scotland, the Britons in Wales, and the Scots in Ireland, which was called Scotia, had never been reconciled to Roman domination of the Lowland Zone. They continually raided the coast or the border fortifications, plundering, robbing, and killing whenever they could find opportunity. At the same time, piratical adventurers, known as Saxons, came from around the mouths of the Rivers Elbe and Rhine and the districts now known as Frisia and Schleswig. The Romans did everything they could to protect the east coast from their depredations, and, as in the case

---

[1] The actual date of the evacuation is uncertain. Some believe that it was 407, but others feel that Celtic tradition is correct when it says that on petition of the Britons the garrison later returned for a short time.

of the Celtic marauders, the Saxons never accomplished very much while the legions were in Britain. But once the Britons were left to defend themselves, they could do little against either their brother Celts on the northwest or the Saxons on the southeast.

In order to meet the Celtic threat it seems that around 449 A.D. a king in Kent invited two Saxon leaders to help him, promising them a reward of land. This was the beginning. The Saxons, turning against their employer, proceeded to take over the country. They were followed by others of their own people and also by related folk such as the Angles and the Jutes.[2] Generally speaking, in their invasions of the country the Anglo-Saxons concentrated on three areas. The first was the Thames Valley and the south coast as far west as what is now Southampton. The second was the district commencing at the Wash on the east coast and extending through the East Midlands to the River Severn. The third included most of the area lying along the east coast between the Humber River and the Firth of Forth. The invaders of all three areas killed, drove out, or enslaved the Celtic inhabitants, and pushed gradually westward until by 900 they had reached Devon and the Welsh borders. The conquest slowed up as it went farther west, with the result that in that area the Celtic people survived in larger numbers. From the Firth of Forth south to the Channel and from the east coast west to the Pennines, Wales, and Cornwall the land became largely Anglo-Saxon.

While the original settlements were at first primarily along river valleys and in areas of loamy soil, gradually they spread out and began to fill the intervening spaces. The settlers, much like those in America in the early days, had to clear the land of forest before they could start farming. Step by step this was accomplished, kingdoms appearing in the three areas of original settlement. Meanwhile the westward movement continued until the King of Northumbria, defeating the Celts in 613, finally reached the Irish Sea. The country experienced little political stability, however. The seven states which eventually appeared fought among themselves for sovereignty until about 850, when the Kingdom of Wessex, situated on the upper waters of the Thames, at length gained the hegemony. By this time Britain was experiencing the greatest economic development since the beginning of its history.

One of the aids to this advance was the coming of Christianity in the persons of Roman missionaries. Although there were already

[2] The relationships between these peoples are by no means clear, and historians are not entirely agreed on the subject. They are usually lumped together simply as Anglo-Saxons.

Celtic missionaries in the country, from an economic point of view
they represented the tribal, pastoral civilization of the Highland
Zone. The Roman monks who landed in Kent under Augustine's
leadership in 597, however, came from a different background, one
which was more urban and advanced technically. By 714 the whole
of the British Isles was at least nominally within the fold of the
Roman Church. This unity of religious allegiance tended towards
political unity, while the moral teachings of the Church also had
a pacifying effect upon the individuals. Both these influences
helped to stabilize society. More directly influential on the economy, however, were the monastic orders. Often seeking the wildest
and most deserted areas of the land in which to set up monasteries,
by hard work they made the desert "rejoice and blossom as the rose."
They cleared the land, sowed crops, and established large flocks of
sheep, frequently becoming the leaders in the development of
agricultural techniques. Moreover, as they grew in wealth they
imported foreign goods and workmen for the adornment of their
buildings, thus stimulating trade and immigration. Benedict Bis-
cop, for instance, in the eighth century brought glass, vessels of
precious metal, and workmen to England to improve the appearance of the monasteries of Jarrow and Monk Wearmouth in Northumbria. In these ways the church played an important part in the
early economic growth of the country.

The New Agricultural Methods

Before one can understand the new methods of farming introduced by the Anglo-Saxons, another question must be considered.
Who owned the land? In the later period this is not a difficult
problem, for the king came to be regarded as the lord of all the
land. In the beginning, however, when there were widely scattered
settlements with no king, there seems to have been no established
theory on the matter. At best one can deduce from practice what
seems to have been a general point of view.

When a raiding band came to England to settle, it seems to
have been led by a chief, to whom all the members of the group
were bound by an oath of obedience. The chief, therefore, would
probably be regarded as the ruler of the section of land occupied.
He might, in a general way, even be regarded as the owner of all
the territory, although in the beginning at any rate the question of
title was not of great importance. The settlers might have to help
farm some of the land for the chieftain and give him military
service, but, apart from that, the land seems usually to have been

held "in common." This does not mean that there was any "communism," for each peasant was regarded as having a right to part of the land for his own use. He did not, however, own it outright, nor could he sell it or give it to someone else. The fact that he held some land meant also that he was responsible to the community to help in the land's cultivation. Not that he would want to leave, for he would probably have nowhere else to go; nor was there any available market in which his land could be sold. Thus while he owned land, it was not the type of ownership which we know. His ownership depended upon his being a member of the community, which was ultimately in control. This was to exercise a great influence upon English farming down into the eighteenth century.

The actual farming methods employed by the Anglo-Saxon were considerably different from those of the Romano-Celtic system. While the Anglo-Saxons undoubtedly allowed many British villages on the lighter soils to continue cultivation under the old methods, they did not, on the other hand, take over the Roman villas. These were left deserted. Instead, the newcomers tended to settle along the river valleys in villages surrounded by farm lands. Usually the village settlement or township consisted of a long strip of land, perhaps ten by two and one-half miles, extending back from the river bank and including different types of soil. There would be a wet area to provide meadow for the winter's hay, with a section of dryer and more easily worked soil for the crops of grain. There would also be a large amount of rough woodland and waste which would provide both firewood for the people and pasture for the animals, particularly the pigs and cows. In this way the village, as far as possible, would attempt to be self-sufficing and independent. In outward form many of the townships, like those of the early American settlers, must have been mere clearings in the forest.

When one comes down to the actual methods of farming, it will be remembered that in the last chapter reference was made to the Celts' light plow, which did little more than scratch the surface of the ground, and to the heavier Belgic plow, which seems to have been used only in the southeast in Kent. The Anglo-Saxon version of this latter instrument used an improved plowshare which dug underneath the sod and a moldboard which turned the sod over. A much more thorough implement than that employed by the Celts, it was effective in soil such as loam or clay. This meant that the Anglo-Saxons could cultivate heavier lands, which settlers in Britain had hitherto avoided. The new plow, however, was not such an easy instrument to operate. Because of the depth of its furrow it was harder to turn or pull than the light Celtic plow, requiring heavier draft animals and more skill in operation. All these factors along with the general social organization were influential in forming and developing the Anglo-Saxon method of agriculture.

As mentioned above, the sense of "community" seems to have been strong among the Anglo-Saxons, but this was not so much a matter of mere tradition as of absolute necessity. The inhabitants of a village were obliged to cooperate in order that they might keep body and soul together. The plow, for example, might be owned by one man or by the village, but since some six or eight oxen were required to pull it, every villager who owned one would be expected to furnish a beast, receiving as his payment a part of the plowing. The first day's labor would go to the plow owner, the second to the owner of ox number one, and so forth. These "lands" usually were plowed in oblong strips in the direction of the contour of the land to facilitate drainage. Sometimes they would be long and thin, sometimes short and broad. But whatever their shape, they seem to have been dealt out in rotation until all the men in the plow team had been supplied. The process then started over again. In this way a man's holding consisted of a number of strips interspersed among those of the other villagers. The boundaries of each strip were marked only by a double furrow which provided drainage, or by a piece of unplowed turf. There were no permanent fences. The size of the strip in the field varied according to the type of land, but often it was 220 yards long (a furrow long, or *furlong*) and twenty-two yards wide. The length of the furlong was apparently the distance that an average team could normally pull a plow without stopping. The width of twenty-two yards (one chain) was determined as the maximum size of a "land" which could profitably be plowed as a unit. These lands may have been regarded from the very beginning as the permanent property of those to whom they were assigned, or they may have been reallotted annually. Which was the custom is not known, and it may have varied from place to place.

One of the fundamental problems of any agricultural community is that of soil exhaustion. If land is cultivated continuously for any length of time without its chemicals being replaced, it will soon cease to bear crops. This is one of the causes of the present day dust bowls in western America. Very early in Old Testament times farmers learned that if the land was occasionally allowed to rest for a year, its fertility would be partially restored, and the Anglo-Saxon

TEUTONIC
SETTLEMENTS

200 MILES

SHETLAND
ISLANDS

ORKNEY
ISLANDS

LEWIS

HEBRIDES

SKYE

SCOTTISH
PICTS
(CELTS)
HIGHLANDS

DALRIADA

FORTH R.

CLYDE R.

STRATHCLYDE

GALLOWAY

CUMBERLAND

ISLE
OF
MAN

IRISH SEA

KINGDOM OF
NORTHUMBRIA

YORKSHIRE

York

SAXONS
ANGLES

HUMBER R.

GAELS
(CELTS)

IRELAND

SHANNON R.

Dublin
Clontarf

Limerick

Waterford

Wexford

Cork

Chester

MERSEY R.

Derby

Leicester

Nottingham

Lincoln

WASH

Stamford

EAST
ANGLIA

ST. GEORGES CHANNEL

BRITONS
(CELTS)

WELSH
MASSIF

WALES

KINGDOM OF
MERCIA

Droitwich

SEVERN R.

Gloucester

ESSEX

ANGLES
SAXONS

London

THAMES R.

Rochester

Canterbury
KENT

Wedmore

KINGDOM OF
WESSEX

Southampton

Sussex

JUTES

DEVON

BRITONS
(CELTS)

SAXONS

VIKINGS

ENGLISH CHANNEL

DANELAW AND
VIKING AREAS

ROUTES

VIKINGS

ANGLES, JUTES, AND SAXONS

TRM

43

farmers understood well the need for such treatment of their fields. Consequently, they early devised the plan of leaving half of their strips untilled every year to enable the free or fallow land to regain its strength. Little manuring was done except on the small garden plots sometimes attached to the houses of the village. The land under cultivation would be planted partly in the autumn, with wheat, winter beans, or rye, and partly in the spring, with barley, oats, spring beans, or peas. Thus, only half the land was under cultivation at any one time. By virtue of having two crops a year raised on the cultivated portion, the farmer soon began to think of his arable land as divided into three rather than two parts. Out of this there grew up a system of triple (summer crop, winter crop and fallow) instead of double rotation. Only one-third of the land would then be left fallow, and the other two-thirds sown and cropped each year. This increased the possible food supply by one-sixth, which in days of scarcity was important.

In the cultivation of his soil the peasant could not do just as he pleased. He was not only dependent upon his fellows for their oxen and plow, but he had to work together with them at all times. The lack of permanent fencing would ensure this if nothing else did. All of the farmers, therefore, had to follow the same procedure for their lands in the same village field; otherwise disaster might come, for instance, by cattle eating the farmer's unprotected crop. In the field to be cultivated the seed was sown broadcast, which often meant uneven patches and considerable waste. Temporary fences might be placed around the crops as they grew to protect them from marauding animals. Then when the time for harvest arrived the villagers would gather to cut the grain, probably doing it in very much the same order as they had plowed. After the advent of Christianity (597-717) one-tenth of the sheaves would go to the village priest and the rest would either be taken home to small barns or threshed and stored in a granary. Once the crops were off the fields, the fences were taken down and the cattle allowed to graze on the stubble. The next year the fallow field would be treated in the same way.

Quite as important as the arable fields were the meadows and waste lands which were the source of food for the livestock. Since there was no idea of cultivating artificial grasses such as clover, alfalfa, or timothy hay, the only source of hay for the winter was the meadow, usually the land lying next to a river or stream, which was divided up like the arable fields into individual plots. The wild grass was cut and stored, and along with straw and leaves (in Scotland, broom), was fed to the cattle during the winter months.

Since, however, this did not provide enough sustenance for all the cattle, most of the herd had to be slaughtered before the snow began to fall, the meat being salted for future use. The animals kept for breeding purposes merely existed on their insufficient diet until the spring, usually having to be carried to the field when the grass commenced to grow. Cattle raised under such conditions were thin and scrawny, with tough meat, satisfactory neither as draft nor beef animals. The waste land provided firewood for the villagers and also summer grazing for their cattle, sheep, and pigs. It was only by the use of all these resources that the early English farmers were able to exist.

The size of a peasant's holding differed greatly throughout the country. The area of arable land considered necessary to support the family of a peasant or *churl* was called a hide, but it varied in size from forty acres in the Midlands to one hundred and twenty acres in the south, while the land of a cottager, or *cotsetla*, might consist of only a plot of between five and ten acres. Along with this, each villager had also certain definite rights in the meadow and waste land. This arrangement enabled the churl to live more or less comfortably, while the cotsetla by selling part of his time to his wealthier neighbors could manage to keep body and soul together. In many cases a few of the villagers, perhaps one or two of the cottagers, were craftsmen, such as blacksmiths, providing services in return for part of the village produce. In this way the community was largely self-sufficient.

Up to this point we have been speaking as though the common field system of cultivation was universal. It must be kept in mind, however, that the lighter soils continued to be cultivated in the more primitive manner by the Celtic peoples. The Anglo-Saxons had turned first to the loamy soils; once they had accumulated capital in the form of plows, slaves, and experience, they started on the heavy clays. The Anglo-Saxon strip field system, therefore, was concentrated in the Midlands, on the east and south coasts, with the exception of parts of East Anglia, Kent, and Surrey.

The areas untouched by the common strip field can usually be linked to the Celtic inhabitants. In the west of England from Cumberland to Devon and probably in Ireland and Scotland the Celtic type of agriculture seems to have prevailed with its individual farmsteads and small square fields. In Wales and Scotland the land near the hamlets, which was plowed up continuously, was kept at least partially fertile by manuring through the folding of cattle and sheep. This land was known as the "infield." The "outfield" consisted of patches of waste land cultivated for a few years without fertilization and then allowed to return to weeds. The strips or "rigs" in both the infield and outfield were scattered as in the three-field system.

In Ireland the method followed was that of intermingling the strips throughout the arable land without division into fields, whether "in" or "out." With inheritance in "gavelkind," particularly common in Wales and Ireland, when a peasant died each strip was divided equally amongst his various heirs, making the individual pieces successively smaller and smaller. This practice was harmful, for it made the holdings unprofitable, since they were liable to become so small that they were not worth the labor they required. Annual reallotting of the strips also tended to make a man careless about the cultivation of his land, for he would not hold it for more than a year or two. To this was added the poverty of the soil and the very large amount of rainfall, all tending to make agriculture difficult. The result was that arable farming in the Highland Zone was usually very poor, and grazing continued to predominate.

In the southeast, in Kent, the compact individual fields were universal. Some attribute this to the fact that trade crossing the area between London and the coast made money so plentiful that opportunities were provided for the consolidation of strips. A truer explanation, however, seems to be that the area was already well cultivated under Romano-British methods when the first Jutish settlers arrived, and since they apparently came by treaty, they simply followed the existing system. That they would be prepared to do this is probable, since they came from the mouth of the Rhine, where there have been discovered traces of a similar form of agriculture. In East Anglia also the strips were concentrated in certain sections of the village lands. However, they all seem to have been worked on the usual cooperative plan.

Thus, in summary, there were the Midlands and south, with their Teutonic nucleated villages surrounded by arable fields and other farmlands. In the Highland Zone the Celtic hamlets were cultivated on the "infield" and "outfield" system; and in the east and southeast there were individual compact fields within the village fields, indicating the development of compact farms.

The Revival of Trade

While we have said that the Anglo-Saxon village was *largely* self-sufficient, it was not entirely so. One thing it lacked was metal, from which it could make scythes, plowshares and other implements. Moreover, the tribal chiefs, and later the kings and nobles, desired to have fine clothes, expensive armor, and Continental wines. Therefore, commerce probably continued even during the devastation of the invasions. The Anglo-Saxons had for many years traded along the coast of France, and there is no reason to believe that at this time they suddenly stopped. It would seem likely that as soon as settlements were established, traders, as in American colonial days, appeared in the villages with goods for sale or trade. What is more, merchants from Gaul or France began to visit the courts of the petty kings with jewelry, clothes, arms, and wine to tempt the Anglo-Saxons to buy. Peace restored, trade would again begin to develop.

While there is little direct information on the early growth of trade, the marriage of Ethelbert of Kent, the first Anglo-Saxon king to accept Christianity, to a Frankish princess shows that there was considerable interchange with the Continent. There are also early laws relating to commerce, which date back to the seventh century. Although reflecting very primitive conditions, they nevertheless indicate that trade was being carried on. In 796 Charlemagne of France guaranteed to Offa, King of Mercia, protection for the English merchants who came to sell goods and requested in turn that the English cloth sold by them should be of a fixed standard length. More important than all this evidence, however, is the fact that towns were beginning to grow up. Here we have direct proof that commerce was reviving.

Merchants, in order to carry on their business, require certain things. They need security for their goods, they need security of bargain, i.e., when they purchase a product they must be sure that it is truly theirs, and they need a place where people can come to see their wares. To provide these necessities the first towns, frequently known as burhs in Anglo-Saxon England, arose in the south, on the sites of such old Roman towns as Canterbury and Rochester. There the earliest urban form seems to have been that of a number of self-contained plots, surrounded by a wall. The owners lived inside the wall but cultivated fields outside. These primitive settlements probably first grew up around a court, a fort, or, by 600, around a monastery. But however they originated, they appeared early, and while at first their primary interest was in agriculture, they were also important as trade centers. Usually regarded as possessing special royal protection, they had at their head a royal appointee known as the reeve. This man's chief duties seem to have been to witness business transactions, to make sure that they were properly carried out, and to see that the goods bought and sold were not stolen property. He also governed the town, with the advice and assistance of the most important inhabitants, who were probably the leading traders. Thus, while towns had not developed very far, they were beginning to provide market facilities. A new class of men who were more interested in trade than agriculture was making its appearance, although even by 800 it was neither numerous or powerful.

In summary, the period from 450 to 800 was the time of settlement and consolidation. Despite their continued expansion into the southwest even after 800, by that date the Anglo-Saxons' territory was pretty well delimited. At the same time the pattern of their economy was also fixed as primarily agricultural, although some trade was also being carried on, and towns were beginning to develop. They had become a peaceful people contented with their lot, having little desire to expand or extend their economy. How long they would have continued in this way we cannot tell, but the arrival of the Vikings changed the whole situation.

The Scandinavian Contribution

While what was now coming to be known as England was slowly recovering from the destruction and wasting of the Anglo-Saxon invasions, a new storm was brewing to the north among another branch of the Teutonic people. In Scandinavia, particularly Norway and Denmark, a movement of population was beginning, similar to that of the German peoples some centuries earlier. There were a number of causes for this. For one thing, the inhabitants seem to have been increasing, thereby putting a pressure on the amount of land available for cultivation. The practice of polygamy among the upper classes meant that there were large numbers of younger sons who had to be provided with land and occupations. A trend toward political centralization with the rise of kings who endeavored to bring the nobility under their control made the more turbulent members of society seek an outlet for their energies. And finally, the migrants were enticed by the prospect of trade and piracy in the wealthier and more peaceful lands of western Europe. As a result of all these factors, there was a great outburst of combined raiding and trading east into Russia, south into northern Germany and along the North Sea Coast, and west to the British Isles. Since the raiders eventually settled in the areas which they attacked, a new wave of Teutonic peoples entered European history.

The raids on the British Isles came from two different directions.

One group, following the old prehistoric trade route from Norway via the Shetland and Orkney Islands to the north of Scotland, moved down the west coast through the Sudreys: the Hebrides, Skye, Islay, and the Isle of Man, until they reached Ireland and Wales. Meanwhile, from Denmark came another group of adventurers who sailed along the west coast of Europe to attack France and the south of England. Others sailed directly from Denmark to East Anglia and Northumbria. A little later Norwegians and Norse-Irish from Ireland landing in Lancashire and Cumberland pushed across the Pennines into Yorkshire. For a time the Norwegian kingdom of Dublin was even united with that of York. Finally Danes from England began to appear around 900 in Dublin and in the port towns of Ireland, where they formed an influential commercial element. In this way Britain was almost swamped by the Scandinavian invaders.

In the Celtic areas of the British Isles, particularly at first, the Vikings faced relatively little opposition. Scotland was divided into four warring kingdoms, Ireland into seven, and Wales into even more. The disunity and strife which was common to these countries aided the attackers. Having overrun the Shetland and Orkney Islands, they settled there first. They then attacked the north of Scotland, bringing a large part under their control. Others meanwhile had been doing the same in the Hebrides, Uist, Skye, and Lewis. In Ireland, their greatest impact was on the coastal ports of Limerick, Waterford, Wexford, Cork, and Dublin; in the last named a Viking kingdom was even established for some time. Some also settled in the Isle of Man and southwestern Scotland. While they had few colonies in Wales, they caused that country untold trouble by their raids.

The effect of these attacks was first of all to force the Celtic countries to seek greater unity within themselves. Under Kenneth MacAlpine (844-875) Dalriada and Pictland in Scotland were united and even northern sections of Northumbria were taken over. In Ireland much the same story was told. A large part of the country was eventually brought under the rule of Brian Boru who, in 1018, defeated the Norse at Clontarf near Dublin, thus finally forcing them to settle down as peaceful inhabitants. Wales had much the same experience under the leadership of Rhoderi the Great (844-878) and his descendants. Economically, in the Celtic areas the Scandinavians had their greatest impact on Ireland, where by their interest in trade, they stimulated the growth of the port towns which they occupied. Ever since their day, Dublin, Wexford,

Waterford, Cork, and Limerick have been southern Ireland's principal centers of commercial activity.

In England the Viking inroads commenced about 787, and until 865 they continued to be nothing more than raids. As in Ireland and Scotland, they were very destructive of property and life, monasteries, because of their wealth, being particular objects of attack. From 865 on, however, the raiders' interests changed; they began to settle the country. For some twenty years a great Danish army roamed the land, overthrowing the Anglo-Saxon kingdoms and dividing up the territories among its people. York was seized in 875, Northumbria in 876, Mercia in 877, and East Anglia in 880. An effort was also made to conquer the kingdom of Wessex, but the Danes were brought to a standstill through the efforts of Alfred the Great. He effectively put a stop to their expansion, and from his day on the Scandinavian invasions grew weaker, although for a time in the eleventh century (1004-42) the Danes, under Sweyn Fork-beard, Canute, and Canute's sons, ruled the country. They did not, however, revive the Danish attempts to colonize.

The area of Danish settlement in England was fixed by the Treaty of Wedmore (878) in which Guthrun, leader of the Danes, agreed to accept Christianity and to remain north of a line drawn roughly from London to Chester. This area was called the Danelaw. Here, where the Danes probably formed about fifty per cent of the population, they did not kill off the English, but instead usually reduced them to slavery. If the Danes, however, hoped to remain independent of English rule in this area they were sadly mistaken, for as time went on, Alfred and his descendants achieved considerable success in their attempts to bring them to submission. During the whole of the tenth century this aim dominated English history, becoming an actuality only when Edgar (973) became King of England. Then, for the first time, the whole of England acknowledged one ruler. In 980, however, a new wave of Viking attacks began, leading to further conflicts and anarchy, which continued until the unscrupulous Canute the Dane was crowned King in 1013. Henceforth there would be only one King of England.

The Danish settlements were primarily military in character. The soldiers in the armies took over land, an oxgang of 15 acres being the average holding. There was the toft, a homestead with surrounding land, and the common fields cultivated on the same plan as that of the Anglo-Saxons. There were also commons and hedged fields for the grazing of cattle. The peasant continued to be a soldier liable to service, and paying to the military leader an annual sum which eventually became a rent. He, however, remained personally free and was also recognized as the real owner of his land. Thus, throughout the Danelaw there was a large body of free peasants known as *sokemen*, amounting in some regions to more than half of the population.

As in Ireland, the important contribution of the Vikings was the stimulus which they gave to towns and trade. The Danes were not merely raiders, they were also merchants. What they stole in one country, they sold in the next. This interest in commerce continued to influence their whole way of life. Very early in their settlements they began to set up trading centers at mouths of rivers or at fords and bridges. Often in these locations they found Anglo-Saxon villages or towns, whose growth they stimulated by their activities. Then, too, even when they settled down as farmers, they were frequently concentrated around a fortified town or burh, which was in a sense the capital of the district. For instance, in the heart of the Danelaw was the district of the Five Burhs: Lincoln, Leicester, Derby, Nottingham, and Stamford, the main strongholds of the Danish power. Later, when Canute was king, Danes and Norwegians came to London where they formed a very important part of the commercial population. The same was true of the other towns in southern England. In this way the Danes wielded a great direct influence on the growth of English town life.

Almost as important was their indirect influence. One of King Alfred's principal means of holding back the Danish attacks upon the country was the small fort or burh, which was erected at strategic points along the borders of his Kingdom of Wessex. Later, when his successors were endeavoring to subdue the Danelaw, they followed the practice of setting up burhs to hold down newly conquered areas. The country around the burhs had to provide garrisons for the forts, and had to supply them with the necessary food and arms. In a great number of cases these burhs were situated on important routes, or at river crossings, so that it was natural for them to become places of trade. The invasions likewise indirectly stimulated English interest in foreign countries and travel. All of these influences played their part in encouraging the growth of commerce and the rise of towns.

The Later Development of Commerce

The tenth and eleventh centuries saw a resulting increase in the volume of England's trade both foreign and domestic. The Viking invasions naturally stimulated commerce with Scandinavia. Probably in Sweden, English goods were exchanged for those of Russia and the Near East; amber and furs were bartered for English cloth. Merchants traveled to other parts of the Continent also, some going as far as Rome, while from Rouen, Lorraine, Flanders, and southern France traders brought their goods to England. Similarly, there was considerable traffic between England and the Celtic areas of the British Isles, marten skins being imported from Ireland and probably wool from southern Scotland. All this coming and going tended to increase further the demand for foreign goods, so that the period from the death of Alfred down to the Norman Conquest was one of continually expanding business activity.

This in turn tended to develop the towns and set them aside as different from the surrounding country. The townspeople, although continuing to be largely agricultural, began to show an increasing interest in the more profitable exchange of goods. Chester became noted for the import of Irish products; Gloucester specialized in iron and Droitwich in salt. Other towns, particularly on the south and east coast, devoted themselves to the fishing trade. London was the chief entrepot, a colony of Danish traders having been established there at an early date. This emphasis on commerce soon gave the town a particular status. It was no longer merely a fort, but was also "a port." The latter title signified a place of trade, as shown by Athelstan's (925-40) law which forbade trading outside a port to the value of more than 20d. The purpose of this restriction was to make sure that, with the exception of minor transactions, all dealings should be carried on before witnesses, thereby preventing fraud. Government recognition of the burh's status took another form also. The principal townspeople, usually merchants, were beginning to organize to obtain privileges and assume corporate responsibilities. In one or two instances the towns took corporate control of their own common lands. Apparently this corporation at times even assumed responsibility for burh dwellers' taxes owed to the crown by paying a lump sum, which was then collected from the individual inhabitants. Finally a few towns, particularly London, seem to have obtained the right to hold courts which could deal with petty crime and which could pass regulations and bylaws. In this way the towns were beginning to obtain some powers of self-government.

The inhabitants of the burhs also began to change their way of life. Known as burgesses, the commercial element in the towns was by 1000 turning from agriculture and becoming interested in trade alone. They continued to pay their "burh customs," which included the land tax to the king, and to perform various services to the town such as helping with the police work or repairing the

walls. But, unlike most of the peasants, they often owned only
the land upon which their houses were built, having power to sell
or mortgage it as they pleased. This was known as "burgage right."
What is more, in some of the towns they seem to have formed
themselves into organizations, called gilds, for common action.[3]
While there is no evidence that such developments were general,
the fact that they occurred even in a few places shows that the
early merchants were beginning to assert themselves as a distinct
class with special privileges. Even more important, being the one
class with ready money, they were very necessary to the kings, who
were often in dire financial straits. The burgesses, therefore, by
1066 formed a small but very important part of the community.

The Economic Importance of the Government

Although the Anglo-Saxons laid the foundations for subsequent
political organization, they did so only very tentatively and crudely.
Nevertheless, it is necessary to understand something of the governmental institutions which they established.

Before 850 there was usually more than one kingdom in England, but from the middle of the ninth century on there seems to
have been only one King of England, the kings of Wessex being the
first to hold that position. Although with the passage of time the
king was accepted as the lord of all the land, he was by no means
an absolute monarch, for he had to rule with the assistance of the
Witanagemot, or council of wise men, made up of leading ecclesiastics and laymen. The former were usually bishops and abbots
who because of their education did much of the clerical work, while
the laymen were probably the leaders in wealth and power and also
the king's special servants. Such laymen were usually divided into
two groups: *athelings*, or members of the royal family, and *gesiths*
or *thanes*, who were the nobility. The *witan* advised the king,
helping him to decide what the law was, acting as judges in disputes, and, most important of all, deciding on the succession to
the crown by choosing a new king from the members of the royal
family. Such was the Anglo-Saxons' form of central government.

Local government was carried on by two different councils, or
moots. The hundred moot was the lesser of the two, supposedly
being made up of the representatives of 100 families. The shire
moot was attended by the free men of the shire, which included a

---

[3] The name "gild" is derived from "gelt," meaning money, apparently referring to
the fact that the members paid fees. The later spelling "guild" is a corruption of
the original form. For a full description of the gilds see pp. 96 ff.

number of hundreds. The shire was sometimes the remnant of one of the earlier kingdoms and was the most important territorial division in the country. Its moot was presided over either by the local bishop or the local earl, or *ealdorman*. This latter official was an appointee of the crown, usually from the most important family in the shire, and although the office was not supposed to be hereditary, it very frequently became so, especially if a weak king occupied the throne. Under the earl was the shire-reeve (sheriff) who dealt with financial matters relating to the king. Both these moots were courts and places of discussion where cases, criminal and civil, could be tried as well as laws enacted and taxes raised. All freemen had a right to a voice in proceedings, although with numerous nobles in attendance it is doubtful whether the system was very democratic. Nevertheless, such was the form of Anglo-Saxon government—the government which at this period influenced the economy of the country.

If trade is to be conducted properly and expeditiously there must be some medium of exchange such as money. In this respect the Anglo-Saxons had progressed beyond prehistoric man, for very early they appear to have had a well-developed coinage based, after 750, upon the Frankish monetary system. Offa, King of Mercia (757-796), struck a finer and heavier silver penny than had been used before, and this remained standard into the twelfth century. The kings, who reserved to themselves the right to control the coining of money, designated the number of coiners who could work in each port and also the number which nobles and bishops might have in their employ. Thus they succeeded in maintaining the coinage at a proper standard and facilitated the trader's business. Consequently, when the Normans took over, they found that in the matter of money they had little improvement to make.

The state also played an important part economically through the expansion of its system of taxation. As the government became more centralized, particularly in the tenth and eleventh centuries, it required a greater income. A growing body of officials meant increasing expenditures. Along with this, some kings, instead of fighting the Danes when they raided the country, had tried to buy them off. This led to the institution of a tax known as *Danegeld* (Dane money). It was not a fixed yearly impost, but was raised whenever the enemy had to be persuaded to leave. In one twenty-five-year period during the tenth century it amounted to over seventy tons of silver. From this one gathers that the country had considerable financial resources which the crown tapped in times of need. The most troublesome problems were those of collecting the taxes and of preventing tax evasion or misuse.

Besides the Danegeld, which was a special levy, other revenues were collected. One was the *feorm*, a tax supposed to consist of enough provisions to keep the king and his court for twenty-four hours. It was usually assessed upon a definite area, some think, of a 100 hides of land which was known as a "hundred." The goods were originally collected in kind and paid to the king's shire-reeve, who took them away. Before very long, however, the custom grew up of commuting this tax to a money payment.[4] Other payments consisted in services known as the *trimoda necessitas*. These were the obligations to provide cartage for the king's goods, to work on the burh defenses and to serve in the *fyrd*, or national militia. While the king might allow others to collect the feorm, since they were of national importance, he could not alienate the services. In this way the possessors of the land helped to pay for the government.

The townspeople also had their financial responsibilities to the crown. The burh lands were regarded as belonging to the king, or sometimes to nobles to whom he had sold or given them. These lands had to pay the *landgable*, which was a rent or tax. Usually the amount for the town was a fixed one, and even if some individuals obtained relief from the obligation to pay, the town still had to furnish the original sum. In addition, as mentioned above, the burgesses had to serve as police and had to maintain the burh walls. Then too they were under obligation to pay tolls. Since the markets in the towns were owned by the king, he charged for the right to buy and sell goods at these markets, thus obtaining a direct share of the profits of trade. In most cases one third of the revenues so collected went to the earl, the official who was usually in charge of the defenses of the shire and who was supposed to employ this money for the upkeep of burh fortifications. The other two thirds, which went into the royal coffers, were very soon furnishing an important part of the government's revenues.

Another source of revenue was court fines. Each one of the moots could try criminal and civil cases. As there were no prisons and capital punishment was not always practiced even in criminal cases, a system of monetary penalties was used. Different grades of men had different worths. For instance, a thane or noble was rated

[4] One feorm was as follows: 2 tuns full of clear ale, one "cumb" full of mild ale, one "cumb" of British ale, 7 oxen, 6 wethers, 40 cheeses, 30 "ambers" of rye corn and 4 "ambers" of meal. F. M. Stenton, *Anglo-Saxon England* (Oxford, 1943), p. 284.

at six times the value of the churl. A bishop was equated in value with an earl at some 40 times a churl's rate. Besides this, even parts of the body were valued so that compensation could be properly calculated. Whenever these fines were levied, part would go to the king, or to someone such as a thane or bishop who held the right to the *wite*, and the other part, the *bot*, to the injured person. Courts thus became valuable sources of revenue in days of considerable lawlessness. Even crime was made to pay.

The collection of the crown revenues was in the hands of the king's reeves. The shire-reeve, or sheriff, was the financial officer for the shires, and the port-reeve held the same position in the burh. It would seem that it was not unusual for the income to be farmed out to the officials, who paid to the king a lump sum, in return for which they obtained the right to collect and keep the royal revenues. They were able to make a profit by the fact that their lump sum payment was considerably below the total amount expected. This system ensured the extraction of every last penny from the taxpayer.

Fundamental to the whole fiscal system was the view that all the land belonged to the king. It was on this basis that the people paid feorm. The king however might grant to a faithful follower (gesith, thane), or to a church, the right to collect the feorm from some specific area. In such a case the villagers paid the feorm, not to the king's reeve, but to the church or gesith. Likewise the king might grant someone the right to the judicial revenues of a hundred or a shire court. The court became then the grantee's property, which was called the right of *soke* and *sake*. As this practice grew, in order to make the grant formal and binding the king and his council, or witan, used to issue a charter to the recipient. The charter or *boc* (book) set forth the privileges involved, and the land in question was then known as *bocland*. The grantee no longer made the usual payments to the king, although, on his death, such possessions as a spear, a helmet, and a horse were given to the king to indicate that he was still theoretically the owner.

The lands which continued to pay the feorm to the king's reeve were known as *folkland*, as they were still liable to old folk levies. With the development of bocland we see the beginnings of feudalism. If bocland were heritable it remained in the family to which it was granted; if not, it reverted to the king on the death of the grantee. By the tenth century the practice of making such grants was becoming very important, for by this means individuals were increasingly obtaining large slices of the king's revenues which they kept for themselves.

The Social Classes in 1066

Economic developments from the seventh to the eleventh centuries wielded a great influence on the social organization of the country. At the top was the king and the royal family, while next in rank came the thanes. Both members of the royal family (*athelings*) and the thanes usually held bocland. At first this had been granted as a *reward* for military or administrative services, but by 1050 it was being given as a *condition* of service. These grants, in turn, brought the common people on this land under the thanes' control. As most of the peasants usually lived close to the border of starvation, a crop failure could mean disaster. If unable to pay their feorms for some such reason, they could promise to pay off their debt to the thane by rendering him services, or they might surrender their property to him and receive it back on a rental basis. The land was no longer theirs, but they would probably have to promise to stay and cultivate it. Danish raids also played their part in bringing the peasants, whether through debt or for protection, to surrender their land to the thanes.

In return for help and protection the churl promised to pay rent and services, an obligation from which he could never escape, and was thus bound to the land. This process was known as "commendation," and by it the nobles began to grow in power and influence. Those who received larger amounts of bocland than they themselves could exploit, in turn made grants to men who became their thanes. In this way the social structure of feudalism began to develop on English soil.

As a result of these changes, by the year 1066 a general decline had taken place in the economic and social position of the peasant class, although there were still personally independent peasants owning their own lands and paying money tax. These latter were the Anglo-Saxon *geneats* and the Danish *sokemen*. The fact that there were larger numbers of Danish sokemen than free Anglo-Saxon peasants would seem to indicate that the Danish invasions had been one of the main causes of the Anglo-Saxon peasants' decline. In increasing numbers below the free peasants came the *geburs*, or *churls*, those who had ceased to be owners and might be bound to the land. The usual holdings were about 30 acres, or a *virgate*, for which they paid a rent in goods and gave to the thane two days' work a week with an extra *(boon)* day at harvest. Not infrequently the thane supplied seed, stock, and implements. Below them were the *cotsetlas* or *bordars*, holding at least five acres and giving work one day a week with extra, or boon, work at harvest. The lowest class of all was that of the slaves who were the property of their lords.

Here were the beginnings of what came to be known as the manorial system. One man had been given the right to receive the revenues from the land. For this reason and also because of commendation, he was regarded as the owner of the land and sometimes of part of the stock kept by the peasants. In return for the use of the land and stock, a rent in goods and services was paid to the lord. This was part of the income which he derived from the land, the other part coming directly from the soil which his personal servants tilled for his own use. By 1050, because of the revenues which he received, the lord was responsible for a fixed amount of service to the crown. This usually consisted of service in the field as a soldier, the length of time required being determined by the amount of land. In this way the Anglo-Saxons, even before the coming of the Normans, had gone a long way toward the establishment of a form of society which the Normans were to crystallize into a fixed political organization.

So far we have spoken only of the people who were attached to the land. The church, with its monasteries and cathedrals, often held lands in much the same way as did the thanes. These properties were received as a reward for praying for the soul of the king or some particular noble. Then too, there were the burgesses, who by 1066 were really outside the growing feudal organization. While they were at this time of no great political importance, they formed the basis of the class which was eventually going to help in the overthrow of the medieval social structure.

This, then, was the contribution of the Teutonic element to Britain's economic evolution. When William the Conqueror landed in England in 1066, he found an economic organization which he adopted and adapted to suit his own purposes. It was this Anglo-Saxon-Scandinavian economy which not only formed the basis for the Anglo-Norman development, but which has also been the foundation of Britain's economic rise and growth down to the present time. It laid the groundwork for the agricultural system which endured until the eighteenth century, it saw the beginning of British commerce, and it commenced the erection of a system of national finance. True, they were but rudimentary beginnings, but all succeeding centuries have built upon their accomplishments.

Chapter 4

ECONOMIC LIFE BECOMES REGULATED

From a study of Anglo-Saxon Britain one receives the impression that economic life and institutions developed in a haphazard fashion. Since the needs of the moment rather than any developed philosophy or theory governed economic practices, there could hardly be much discussion of economic theory. With the coming of the Normans to English shores in 1066, this state of affairs changed. The Normans were much more economically minded. In closer touch with intellectual developments on the Continent than the Anglo-Saxons, they had adopted many of the current philosophical views on such matters. Coupled with this, the duchy of Normandy was probably one of the most thoroughly organized feudal states in eleventh century Europe. It is not surprising, therefore, that the Norman Conquest meant not only a political but also a social and economic revolution in Britain. The Normans added another story, and a very important one, to the British economic structure.

Norman Social and Economic Reorganization

One of the reasons for the success of the invading Norman armies was that they had been welded into a single unit by the genius of Duke William. Having successfully devoted almost the whole of the first half of his life to bringing the Norman nobility into submission to ducal authority, by 1066 he was, in fact as well as in name, the real ruler of the duchy. In imitation of the French pattern whereby all land was held of the king on condition of service, William established a feudal government with certain Norman improvements. The military services due to him by the knights were carefully defined and applied to the knights' lands. All castles were ultimately under the duke's control. Private war was strictly limited, so that peace generally prevailed. Justice, the coinage, and

59

the church, even in its purely ecclesiastical aspect, were all under
the central authority. Politically, William was supreme.

In the economic organization of the duchy the same condition
prevailed. The common feudal idea was that the king was the
owner of all the land, an idea with which William, who adopted
the style of a king, was in full accord. As he could not, however,
farm all the land himself, he granted it out in parcels to his knights
who promised to furnish him certain services, usually of a military
nature. Each grant of land was supposed to furnish the duke with
from one to ten mounted knights to serve for at least forty days'
fighting each year. It was considered a rule that a knight's *fief*, or
holding, consisted of one or two manors which would provide him
with a suitable income. One man might, of course, hold quite a
large number of manors, but this meant that he had to provide a
correspondingly large number of mounted warriors. The whole
system was based upon agriculture as the primary source of the
people's wealth, the manors being the unit of farming organization
of the time.[1]

The consequences of the imposition of such a system upon
Anglo-Saxon England were in some respects momentous. Many
of the old ways of looking at land and its revenues disappeared. To
a large extent a definite theory enforced by law took the place of
haphazard custom. All those who had fought for Harold or who
later rebelled against William lost their lands as traitors to their
rightful sovereign. Even those who submitted were soon after the
Conquest deprived of considerable portions, if not all, of their
property. These holdings were then granted by William to his own
followers. As he traveled through the country, he would give one
manor to one man and the next to another. Nowhere except on the
Scottish and Welsh borders does he seem to have granted lands
in large blocks. It is probable that he was mindful that a vassal
with a large consolidated block of land, such as he had been in
France, might later cause trouble. Only where border defense was
a problem were large, virtual principalities given to vassals. One
was granted to a clergyman, the Bishop of Durham, who could not
leave the land to a son; the other went to the Earl of Chester, who,
along with the earls of Shrewsbury and Hereford, had the duty of
defending England against the Welsh. The reason that William
found it relatively easy to allot lands in conformity with the feudal
system would seem to be that the Anglo-Saxons had already developed an organization very similar to that of the Normans. Although
the Anglo-Saxon manor was not completely organized by 1066,

[1] See Chapter 5.

most of its later components were in existence when William and his forces arrived. Thus he completed what had already begun.

· Just as the Norman agricultural and landholding system was more advanced than that of the English, so also was their commercial organization. The Vikings, as mentioned in the preceding chapter, had always been interested in trade, so when they settled in Normandy in the ninth century, they kept up business as usual, trading with the Baltic, with the British Isles, and southward along the French and Portuguese coasts. As a consequence, towns began to appear in Normandy on the banks of the Seine and in the hinterland. Rouen dominated the scene, but Caen, Barfleur, and Dieppe on the coast all became important. Another of the Norman towns, Breteuil, became famous for its laws and constitution, many of the English and Scottish towns later basing their form of government upon its Norman pattern. Over all these towns the Duke maintained a careful surveillance. They were his, and the revenues derived from their trade came to his coffers. Thus trade and traders, as well as agriculture, were always carefully controlled by Duke William.

Once England had submitted to William's army, there was an immediate influx of Norman merchants and businessmen. Since they had helped to finance his expedition, they were now going to reap the profits. Their advent meant alterations in the tempo and direction of English trade. For one thing, instead of being turned towards the Baltic and the Scandinavian countries, England was now oriented toward France and the Mediterranean. She had moved into France's economic as well as her political orbit. What is more her trade began to expand. The Norman merchants were aggressive and pushing, while Norman nobles expected to have the same goods in England as those which they had used at home. The Norman interest in trade is manifested in the fact that shortly after he arrived, William, in typical Norman fashion, gave London a charter containing numerous economic provisions. Towns were not only a means of holding the country down; they also provided market places for the merchants. At this point the Duke's political needs became an aid to commercial interests.

The royal interest in the country's material prosperity arose also from William's desire for revenues. The old system, still followed by the kings of France, had been that of the ruler traveling from royal manor to royal manor and consuming their produce. Similarly, servants, rewarded by grants of royal revenues, often received payment in goods which they collected from the royal lands. In Normandy, however, money was more commonly used, thus making possible a real system of taxation. What is more, the Norman dukes, particularly William, made very sure that they received from the lands everything which was their due. It was for this reason that William in the years 1085-86 had an economic census taken of the whole country. Known as the "Domesday Book," it enabled him to determine accurately what he should be receiving from his subjects in terms of money and produce. There was to be no more haphazard Anglo-Saxon tax collecting. His revenues, especially the Danegeld, were to be collected in a businesslike manner.

From the foregoing it is easy to see the important changes resulting from the coming of the Normans to England. Instead of a somewhat loosely organized nation, with local differences based upon the old Anglo-Saxon and Danish divisions, there was to be a centralized state controlled by the duke. Moreover, as he kept the administration of justice and the control of the armed forces in his own hands, he could make his authority effective. Even those who held lands from William's immediate followers were obliged to recognize that the King was to have their first loyalty. As expressed somewhat later, he was their "liege lord." All this meant that the regulation of the economic life could now be much more easily attained. True, it was by no means as easy as it is today, with our speedier means of communication and greater military power, but, compared with the Anglo-Saxon organization, it was a distinct advance towards centralized control.

Medieval Economic Theory

When one thinks of the control and regulation of economic life, he is immediately faced with the problem of the principles involved. By what rules should economic activity be governed? It was obvious to the Normans that control merely for the sake of state revenues was not all. There was the question of right and wrong economic practices as defined by the medieval church in accordance with its beliefs. Since the Normans had by the eleventh century become loyal sons of the church, they were quite prepared to pay attention to these ideas and to put them into force. Therefore, while William the Conqueror always kept in mind the idea of his own control over his duchy and kingdom, he seems also to have given full play to the church's moral teachings as applied to economic activities.

During the ninth and tenth centuries the church had been very seriously weakened throughout western Europe. There were various reasons for this decline, but toward the end of the tenth century a reform movement began, centering around the French Abbey of Cluny. The stress upon strictness of monastic life and a return to Christian morality soon brought important changes in the church. The lives of the clergy were purified, learning began to flourish once more, and the spiritual health of the church began to improve. This movement was so welcome in Normandy that the reformers were able to wield a wide influence from their monasteries, such as that at Bec. Although Duke William, who favored the movement, insisted on retaining control over the appointment of bishops, he was quite prepared to do anything he could to strengthen and cleanse the church.[2] Such, however, had not been the attitude in England despite the work of Dunstan, Archbishop of Canterbury, during the preceding century. To put it mildly, the English church was lax. Because of this, one of the important consequences of the Norman Conquest was the introduction of the reform movement to England. It was the hope of cleaning up the church that persuaded Gregory VII, one of the greatest of the reforming popes, to give his blessing to William's expedition. Once the Normans had gained the control, therefore, they endeavored to bring the English church up to Continental standards, which included adherence to the church's ethical standards in economic matters.

Altogether apart from this secular support, however, the church itself possessed in the sacraments enormous spiritual power over the individual. The coming of the Norman ecclesiastics with the spirit of reform meant that the church regained its former important position in the life of the ordinary man. Claiming to speak for God to men, the church insisted that this world was primarily a preparation for the next. This was important to most men during the Middle Ages, for the world around them was not too pleasant or happy a place. Consequently, they were more prepared than they are today to listen to the church's views regarding belief and conduct. In this realm the church exercised considerable influence on medieval economic life, by subordinating economic practice to ethical principles. It stressed the fact that economic activity, as much as specifically religious observances, must come under the control of Christianity and Christian teaching. Economics in this

[2] The theory of episcopal appointment was that the bishop, elected by the cathedral clergy, did homage to the crown for his feudal lands, but received his "ring and crozier" as signs of the spiritual authority from the pope. In practice, however, the theory had frequently been ignored, the king, when powerful, controlling the appointments. The matter was not finally settled in England until the reign of Henry I (1107) when the king seems to have gained the right to choose the bishop. Cf. W. P. Hall and R. G. Albion, *A History of England and the British Empire* (New York: Ginn & Co., 1953), p. 88.

way were to be governed by morals, for economics were made for man, not man for economics. This view of production, distribution, and consumption must continually be kept in mind, or one can never really understand medieval economic theory or practice.

Medieval economic thinking was never abstract. It attempted to base itself firmly both upon the Scriptures of the Old and New Testaments and upon the teaching of the Canon Law. To the economic theorist all social activity had to be subject to the rules: "Thou shalt love thy neighbor as thyself," and ". . . all things whatsoever ye would that men should do to you, do ye even so to them." Fair play and equality were the aims of the church in its attitude toward commercial activities. In the early days such ideals were not hard to apply. With the collapse of Roman economy and the return to a system of virtual barter, it was fairly easy to determine what was truly just and fair in economic dealings. The only danger was, however, that as prosperity returned and business revived, an attempt would be made to deal with much more complex problems in the same simple manner. The solidifying of the economic theory might hamper economic growth and cause trouble to both the merchant and the church. This was what ultimately happened, although its consequences were not really seen until some time after the Middle Ages had ended.

Fundamental to the thinking of the time was the concept of status. There were three main classes of men: those who worked, those who fought, and those who prayed.[3] They formed these groups by the will of God and held their various positions in them according to the Divine plan. In this way every individual in society had his status, a position which not only laid upon him certain responsibilities, but also guaranteed him a certain degree of economic well-being. Each had the right to enjoy a certain proportion of the earth's produce. The result was a tendency toward fixed social and economic stratification. While this was so, the idea of status also guaranteed the individual a certain amount of security, for to live according to one's status was a natural right. This was an important fact, for one finds that the Middle Ages really thought more of security than of abstract freedom, a situation parallel to that of the present time. When there is a possibility, as there always was in the Middle Ages, of a famine or of a devastating war, economic security is of prime interest. Thus one of the chief

[3] This fitted in with, although it did not cause, the feudal system which originated in Britain through the economic and social needs of the time and was finally made effective by the Norman Conquest.

purposes of economic activity was to enable a man to live in the estate to which he had been called by God.

From this, one must proceed to ask what the medieval thinker had to say about property. When dealing with this question, he usually based his ideas on the teaching of the Bible, the Church Fathers, and Aristotle, the last mentioned being especially important after the time of Thomas Aquinas (1225-1274). Without attempting to trace the complicated history of the thinking on this subject, one must keep in mind that a distinction was made between "nature" and "convention." By this was meant that man as originally created held all things in common, which was natural. But with man's fall into sin, he became avaricious, wanting to have everything for self. What is more, he was also unwilling to work for the common good. Consequently, for the restraint of the effect of sin, private property was morally necessary. Aquinas, following Aristotle's view that man was naturally a "social animal," held that property was not merely a concession to sin but that under the present circumstances it was actually beneficial. Further, what each person owned was, for practical purposes, to be determined by the law of the land. For these reasons private property was not only to be tolerated but to be regarded as absolutely necessary for man's continued social existence.[4]

How was this property to be used? While the right to possess property was recognized, there was no idea of an absolute ownership. Aquinas, along with all the other medieval writers, insisted that a man who owned property had the right to use it to supply himself with that which was needful for the maintenance of his own and his family's status. An accumulation over and above what was necessary for this was not considered charitable. After all, the individual held the property ultimately for the benefit of the community. Consequently, he was responsible to the community to be liberal with any surplus which he might acquire. Almsgiving was an important part of the activities of life, for it was the giving of justice to others who had a right to share in one's wealth. The purpose of developing such a point of view was to make people realize that after all wealth is not man's real objective in life. If one thinks too much of money, he is inclined to forget that the true purpose of life is one's preparation to see God. This point of view dominated most of medieval economic theory.

The next question that arose was: which is the proper form of economic activity? To most writers in the early part of the Middle

[4] For a full discussion of this, see Bede Jarrette, *Social Theories of the Middle Ages 1200-1500* (London, 1926), chap. v.

Ages, agriculture was the only true work for man. When working on the land, he was truly earning his bread by the sweat of his brow. He was not exploiting someone else, but was actually earning his and his family's livelihood. Moreover, the farmer was not considered to be in danger of becoming avaricious, for he did not have a great temptation to accumulate wealth. He saw too little of it for that. Consequently, throughout the Middle Ages the agricultural class was regarded with the greatest favor.

The attitude toward trade and commerce was somewhat different. In the early days the merchant was viewed with suspicion, since it was felt that he did not really earn his profits but rather took advantage of other people's needs. What is more, as he was not attached to the land in any way, he was not regarded as possessing any particular status. And finally, he made his money too easily, exploiting someone else's labor. As trade developed, this attitude was obliged to change. The church itself, requiring incense for its services, eastern cloths for its vestments, and similar commodities, began to realize that the trader had his place after all. By the time of Thomas Aquinas the merchant was regarded not as a necessary evil, but as an important person in the community. Moreover, his profits were quite legitimate if they were used for the support of his family or for charity and public service. Yet, at the same time, it was realized that the merchant was in very grave danger of seeking money merely for money's sake. This was condemned roundly, the businessman being continually reminded of the danger of such an attitude.

The church attempted to keep business in hand by insisting that there was a "just price" for every economic good. The just price represented what the article, whether a physical commodity or labor, was actually worth. Only by buying and selling at this price could equality between purchaser and vendor be attained. Supply and demand, or even personal desire, should not determine price. It would seem that Augustine of Hippo had first set forth this idea, and it continued to be held, albeit somewhat vaguely, until the days of Thomas Aquinas. He taught that labor was the determinant of price. A man had to be given a price for his article which took into consideration both the time spent in production and his status in life. As business developed, becoming more complex, other factors in price were seen to exist. Later medieval economic writers added industry, risk, and scarcity. "Common estimation" was also regarded as sharing in the determination of price, and eventually the idea of a maximum and a minimum just price developed, the just price oscillating between the two extremes.

Once the just price had been generally determined, it was often felt that it should be established by law. Thus national governments as well as municipal and gild authorities attempted to set the just price of an article. Standards of quality were also fixed and maintained in order that no one might be cheated.

Another question which arose was whether real profits could legitimately be taken by the merchant. At first this was regarded as very doubtful. But as commerce developed it was realized that a man might add to the price which he paid if he transported the goods to another place or if he took any risk in handling them. The motive for trading, however, was the principal thing. If one were in business merely to earn a livelihood, then a modest profit was lawful, but if his purpose were the accumulation of wealth, it was improper. Such an attitude seems natural when one remembers that in most local trading the craftsman sold directly to the consumer. A middleman was unnecessary. It was really only for goods brought from a distance that the merchant was required. But as the economy of Europe expanded and specialization of function began, a change took place. The retailer became more important, and the idea that the producer was of more importance than the consumer began to grow. All this loosened the restrictions upon profits. Moreover, the church's view that one had a right to receive a rent from land, as well as the position that if one shared in the risk of a partnership, he had the right to a share of the profits, might be very broadly interpreted. Consequently, by the middle of the fifteenth century, most of the medieval restrictions had been modified according to a better understanding of trade and its needs.

Another problem which interested medieval economists was that of money. In the early years of the Middle Ages money was scarce, and what there was of it was poor in quality and standard. With the gradual growth of trading, however, particularly from about 1100 on, it came increasingly into use. Since all countries did not have the same coinage or adhere to the same standards, when a merchant went to foreign parts he was faced with the necessity of exchanging one lot of coin for another. The person performing this function for him was a professional money-changer, who would require payment for the service. It might be that instead of carrying the actual coin, the merchant would simply take with him a letter from a money-changer in his own country to another which authorized payment of a sum equivalent to that deposited at home. For this service a charge was also made. In both these cases the medieval economist felt that since actual service was rendered, such charges were quite justified. This was entirely in accord with the idea of the just price.

There was, however, another side to the question of the use of money: the matter of charging usury or interest for loans. The earliest views of the church on this question were rather vague, but they crystallized during the economic decline which took place during the latter days of the Roman Empire. Loans at that time and for the following 500 years were usually made because of the desperate need of the borrower. To charge for the use of such a loan, therefore, was regarded as being contrary to charity. Charlemagne forbade laymen to charge interest, and the second Lateran Council in 1139 declared usury to be contrary to all law, both natural and divine. Forty years later the fourth Lateran Council ordered usurers to be excommunicated, while in 1311 Pope Clement V classed them with heretics. Usury was held to consist in making loans of either goods or money, but particularly the latter, and in receiving back more than the amount lent.[5] In the early days this prohibition was certainly justified, since the unrestrained charging of usury would work hardship upon the poor. As economic conditions changed, other arguments were sought for the law's justification.

The main reasons given for the banning of usury were three in number. First, there was the Scriptural injunction to "lend hoping for nothing." Then there was Aristotle's view that money was barren, incapable of reproduction. Finally, there was the view that a loan was really a sale of goods. The man who formulated these views most clearly was, again, Thomas Aquinas. He held that since money could never beget money unless someone's labor went along with it, the person doing the labor, rather than the one lending the money, should receive the profit. His chief reason for opposition to usury was that, to his mind, a loan was a sale. He made a distinction between goods which could be consumed, such as food, and those which could not be consumed, such as a house. If one loans food, he does so for consumption; otherwise there would be no point in food lending. What is more, both use and ownership are transferred by the loan, and only the just price should be given in

<hr/>

[5] W. J. Ashley, *Introduction to English Economic History and Theory* (London, 1931), Vol. I, pp. 152 ff., points out various transactions which were regarded as usurious: (1) To lend goods for consumption, expecting to receive more; (2) to pay a sum to be repaid in goods which one knew would rise in price before repayment; (3) to receive back the value loaned in kind, and then to demand the capital in money, i.e., the case of land held as a pledge and the crops harvested, although the money had to be paid back in full; (4) to receive back increased price for goods because of delayed payment.

return. Money is of the same nature, for its use consists in being spent. Therefore, when one loans money he should receive in return only a just price—the equivalent amount of money. To say that the lender should be compensated for the time during which he is deprived of the use of the money is to charge for time which is God's, not man's, possession. Consequently, the loan of consumable goods for a profit was forbidden, although a charge for the loan of nonconsumable goods was permitted since ownership was not lost to the lender.

One might point out, of course, that the borrower could spend the loan on nonconsumable goods, which would seem to be equivalent to obtaining a loan of such goods. Would not the title of ownership then properly rest with the lender? Or, since the price of anything was determined primarily by labor, the money borrowed represented human labor. This would mean that the borrower was using the labor of the lender without giving him anything in return. It was inevitable that these and other doubts would gradually begin to cross people's minds.

Once trade began to expand and the opportunities for profit began to increase, it was impossible to maintain a strict prohibition of usury. Various methods were employed to modify the regulations. One was the introduction of the *poena conventionalis*, whereby in the contract of the loan, the borrower promised that if he failed to reimburse the lender within a set time he would pay a penalty. *Damnum emergens* was somewhat similar in form. It was not included in the contract, however, and required the lender to prove that he had suffered actual injury because he was deprived of his money. If he could do this, the debtor then had to pay damages. Finally, there was *lucrum cessans*, which required the payment of damages because the lender had lost a chance of profit while the money was on loan. Aquinas was opposed to the last mentioned because he felt that the possibility of gaining a profit was merely speculative. Still, as opportunities for investment increased this was taken as a normal reason for paying back more than the sum borrowed.

Expanding trade and chances of making money eventually forced a general change in attitude. By 1400 businessmen were usually in need of loans, not for consumable goods, but for the purpose of financing transactions out of which they could make a profit. Consequently, they found that lenders would not give them money except for a price. Even the church's efforts to found cooperative credit banks for the poor were unsuccessful because it was necessary to make a charge for administration. Consequently, it became the usual thing to pretend to loan a sum for a very limited time, after which interest was to be paid, or it was taken for granted that profit always would be lost, damages having to be given by the borrower. Similar fictitious leases were also arranged, whereby both the original sum and the rent were given to the lender. Or fictitious partnerships were established, in which the lender was supposed to take equal risks with the borrower. By these means medieval financiers avoided the church's regulations. What is more, the church itself was doing the same thing, usually borrowing at high rates of interest, with the result that it had some difficulty in trying to make the average businessman conform. At the same time, those in the church who were thinking about such matters began to see a difference between usury and interest. The former was money taken for a loan to one who needed it for consumption. Interest, on the other hand, was a return for lending in order that the borrower might make a profit. In this the lender had a right to participate. Although such a distinction was not always easy to make, by the end of the Middle Ages both the church's theory and the practice had been considerably modified, laying the groundwork for the modern point of view.

Before leaving this matter of economic theory we must take a look at one more of its facets, the matter of coinage. During the latter part of the fourteenth century there appeared a work written by Nicholas of Oresme, who attempted to deal with coinage scientifically. Taking his stand on the idea that all property was ultimately for the community, he taught that even the prince could not count the coinage his own. Therefore, he could not debase or adulterate it for his own profit. Nicholas was of the opinion that a sound coinage was necessary for sound business, for when a country had bad coinage the good money would be exported. Like those who preceded him, he insisted that usury was wrong and should not be permitted. His importance, however, lies in his insistence upon the need for a sound coinage, particularly since the years which followed saw numerous attempts to change the various European coinages to the advantage of the rulers.

As one glances over the economic views of the medieval thinkers, he cannot but feel that they were trying to formulate principles for a society more static than that which actually existed. Most of the economic theorizing had attained a set form before the year 1300, when trade and commerce, particularly in Britain, were as yet quite unimportant. Agriculture still occupied the attention of the majority of the people. Therefore, with rapid commercial expansion after 1300, changes were bound to come. While the church did succeed, at least partially, in adapting its views to new situations the general decline of its influence tended to make its views appear irrelevant. The outcome was a gradual fading of the medieval Christian economic ideals and the beginning of the worship of money as an end in itself.

Enforcement of the Theory

Theory has little use unless it is put into practice. While the Anglo-Saxons knew a certain amount about the church's teachings as applied to economic affairs, they paid little attention to them in everyday life. It remained for William and his successors to enforce the medieval economic theories. Although William commenced by assuming that he was the lord of all the land, from very early days it was also held that the king was subject to law. Because of this King John was forced to sign the Magna Charta (1215). The nobles insisted that they should not be obliged to give the king special "aids" or taxes without their consent being obtained, for the "aids" were their property. To a very considerable extent this point of view lay at the basis of the origins of parliamentary institutions. By 1295 both the smaller nobility (knights of the shire) and the businessmen (burgesses) were being called to parliament whenever they were expected to make direct contributions to the royal revenues. These groups soon developed the idea that they spoke for the common people not only on financial matters, but on others as well. They therefore claimed the right to a voice in the affairs of the state. Much the same development took place in Scotland after 1326, although the "Estates" never succeeded in obtaining as much power as did the English parliament.

The outcome of this was that the government, whether it was "the king-in-council" or "the king-in-parliament" issued laws controlling and regulating the country's economic affairs. The enforcement of the just price was particularly important. No man was to meet merchants or farmers on their way to market and buy up their goods (known as "forestalling"); nor was he to come early, before the market opened, and purchase commodities so that he cornered the market ("engrossing"); nor was he to buy goods and attempt to resell them at a higher price ("regrating"). All such practices were really attempts to force prices up beyond that which was just. Another law, enacted in the same year (51 Henry III [1267]), also established machinery for keeping the price of bread tied to that of grain. Later the same thing was done for ale. These statutes were known as the Assizes of Bread and Ale. Other laws were enacted to see that proper weights and measures were used, while still others strictly controlled the minting of money, which was held to be a royal monopoly. In this way the crown and Parliament endeavored to make effective the current economic ideas.

The church also took a part in the effort to make men behave in a manner both ethically and economically correct. First and foremost, there was the church's formal teaching, contained in the works of such men as Aquinas and Oresme as well as in the decrees of councils. In the popular preaching of the day the clergy never tired of pointing out the ultimate dangers of such sins as avarice and greed. Morality plays and other devices were also used to bring home the same lessons. Although there is considerable evidence that the clergy themselves were at times not entirely free from these sins, the important thing is that the church was endeavoring to reach the individual conscience and keep the faithful from undue concern about the material things of this world.

Teaching, however, was not enough. Since man seems to be naturally greedy, the church was obliged to do what it could to enforce the law by censures. For instance the enforcement of the laws against usury was placed in the hands of the Inquisition. It was also declared that the wills of usurers were not to be recognized and that the guilty man himself was not to be buried in consecrated ground. Such stringent regulations may have had a certain amount of influence, but probably not much.

The only bodies which could really enforce obedience to the law were local organizations. Even before the Norman Conquest associations or gilds of merchants and craftsmen had grown up in the towns. After 1100 these gilds came to have a considerable amount of power and authority, and since they usually had a religious basis, they were under the direction and influence of the church, whose rules they attempted to enforce. Through their governing bodies and their gild courts they were able to maintain a common price and a common standard of workmanship. The members were also supposed to make loans to each other without charge. The state had no police, and the church had no compulsive power apart from the civil authorities, but the gilds were on the scene, and their officials could see that the rules were enforced. The only difficulty was that the gilds in the later days tended to become restrictive, falling under the control of a few who used them for their own enrichment. This meant that they lost their reason for existence and finally fell to pieces.

Municipal authorities also attempted to see that the economic rules and regulations of the day were obeyed. In consultation with the gilds concerned, they might set up regulations for various trades. They also supervised the markets and kept a close check upon the foreign merchants who came to sell their goods. Yet despite the fact that they were on the ground and armed with considerable authority, they were by no means successful. The sheer force of economic circumstances was too much for them, and ultimately regulation failed.

That there never was much hope of enforcing the law can be gathered from the fact that throughout the Middle Ages groups existed virtually immune from the regulations on usury. The earliest group, and one which continued to do business in England until 1286, was that of the Jews. They felt no compunction about taking interest from non-Jews and since, from the medieval point of view, unless they became Christians they were already without hope for the next world, the church and state allowed them to carry on business under certain restrictions. The English crown actually permitted them to receive up to 33⅓ per cent per annum, but frequently much of this went into the royal coffers in the form of forced loans. For the protection of Christian debtors the Exchequer of the Jews was established to deal with suits arising between them and their creditors. Finally, in 1286 Edward I banished them from the realm. In the thirteenth century French merchants from Cahors also entered into the money lending business. They were able to circumvent the law, often receiving interest as high as 60 per cent. They were followed a little later by Italians, who were the principal financiers of the crown until 1351, when Edward III defaulted on his payments. Lombard Street in London was the quarter in which they lived. Thus, despite church anathemas and government regulations, even from the days of William the Conqueror exceptions to the common economic ideas had to be made in order that the economic wheels might turn.

The Rise of Individualism

As can be seen from what has already been said, the great tendency of medieval thinking was toward cooperation. Competition was opposed. While this was probably not a bad idea when economic opportunities were limited, it might have had unfortunate results in the long run. The mediocre man could become the standard of craftsmanship or business accomplishment; consequently, those who were more energetic or more far-seeing would be held back. This was not the necessary outcome of the regulations, but they could be accused of unwarranted restrictions and, in actual fact, it would seem that not infrequently they did tend to curtail initiative and circumscribe activity. To a certain extent they were a brake upon the progress of economic development.

It soon became apparent, particularly after the Crusades, that the restraints imposed by the church could not be maintained indefinitely. The growth of towns resulted in greater potential markets. This in turn brought an increase of trade, and the possibilities of accumulating large fortunes became more numerous. In these circumstances it is not surprising that the individual began to forget that the highest good was not to be found in this world. What is more, as philosophic skepticism became more influential man began to doubt the need for bothering about the next world at all, feeling that he should take advantage of every opportunity to accumulate this world's goods. Only then could he really enjoy life. To do this successfully he needed money and so was obliged to take risks. When he was successful the result was usually large profits, of which, if he had borrowed the money, his creditor or partner would expect a corresponding return upon the investment.

The idea of Christian brotherhood which had been preached by the church now fell into discard. It was a case of every man for himself. The church's moral teachings regarding economic activity gradually came to be regarded as outdated and impractical. Even the church itself began to find out that it was not easy, particularly if it was to continue as a secular as well as a religious power, to stand by its earlier views. By 1500 practices which would have been roundly denounced by Aquinas were quite common, no one thinking them wrong. Even the gilds' attempts to maintain their controls were gradually being given up. The old order was changing, giving place to the new. Individualism was taking the place of corporatism, competition supplanting cooperation.

This trend was further strengthened by the attitude of the secular rulers. The contemporary rise of prices, coupled with an ever growing demand for armaments and a greater need for a civil service, made it impossible for the state to subsist upon the old feudal revenues. Taxation of a modern type was increasingly necessary. As this was to come from individuals, the more money they had, the better for the state. Consequently, efforts were made to help the merchants enlarge their fortunes. At the same time, restraints were laid upon the giving of land to the church, for that removed it from the realm of taxable property. Consequently, individualism received support from the state in the form of monopolies, charters, and grants of privileges in order that gold and silver might come into the country. In this way the state would grow in wealth and power.

By the end of the Middle Ages, which can be dated as about 1485, economic thinking had changed very greatly from what it had been in 1066. While the church's views on just price, usury, and other such matters might still be acknowledged in word, in deed they were more often ignored than obeyed. Even though the church had in some ways modified its theories to meet the changing economic situation, the economic change itself had been much more drastic and radical. The new wine of commercialism was bursting the old bottles of an agricultural economy. The individual was coming to a position of greater importance. Out of this was born a different, and in some ways a more modern, type of economic philosophy.

Chapter 5

THE DEVELOPMENT OF
MEDIEVAL FARMING

W<small>HILE</small> William and his Norman followers did not immediately conquer all of England, within some twenty years of the initial invasion they had achieved a large measure of control which enabled them to rule and exploit the country. From that time on the Norman policy was one of steady and gradual expansion. In Wales during the twelfth and thirteenth centuries, piecemeal encroachment took place at first, culminating in direct action under Edward I, who in 1284 brought the whole of the country under his rule. In Ireland frontal attack by the feudal nobility, aided and abetted by the crown, was the method employed from 1169 on. The Irish, however, were never really conquered, not infrequently absorbing and "Irishing" their would-be masters. Still, a Norman conquest did take place, for the eastern parts of the country were brought under Norman control and forced to conform to a Norman pattern of organization. In the case of Scotland there was a somewhat different outcome. An infiltration of Norman-Flemish elements, which soon became Scottish in outlook, provided a foundation for resistance to Anglo-Norman imperialism. Thus, the attempts of Edward I and Edward II to subdue the Scots failed. Nevertheless, the influence of Norman ideas, both legal and social, north of the Tweed, was noticeable at that time. Institutions containing a mixture of Celtic and Norman concepts soon appeared, making Scotland a distinct national entity.

Partially because of such differences in the strength of the Norman influence, medieval agriculture in Britain showed a wide variety of forms. These were further developed by other forces. Geography had no little influence, the nature of the soil and the climate both being important factors. For instance, the decision as to whether an area was to be under arable or pastoral farming was probably determined, particularly in early days, more by the physical surroundings than by whether the population was Celtic or Anglo-

Saxon. The pressure of a growing population also had its influence. Although vital statistics are very indefinite during the Middle Ages, A. P. Usher has estimated that numbers in England increased from 1.8 million in 1086, to 2.2 million in 1327, to 2.5 million in 1377, and to 4 million in 1570, with mean density per square mile rising correspondingly: 26 (1086), 44 (1327), 49 (1377), 76 (1570). Although we have little information concerning Scotland, it has been reckoned that in 1350 its population was around 470,000.[1] With this growth in the English population it is not surprising that there was a migratory movement from the east and southeast to the west and northwest. It is against this background that one must examine medieval farming in the British Isles.

The Organization of the Land

As has already been pointed out, the land of the subdued country was distributed by William the Conqueror in individual manors, and sometimes blocks of manors, frequently according to the already established Anglo-Saxon pattern. Between 1066 and 1086 the political situation, owing to a series of rebellions and uprisings, was rather unstable, causing a number of vassals both Saxon and Norman to lose their lands. Since peace had settled upon the Kingdom by the latter year, however, William instituted a survey of the country in order that he might ascertain what was due him in services and taxes. Representatives of the King were sent to every manor, where the priest, the reeve, and a number of the inhabitants were obliged, on oath, to tell the value of the manor in Edward the Confessor's day, its value when granted, and its value in 1086. In this way the King gained an exact knowledge of both the feudal services owed to him by the barons and the revenues which he should receive from his own fiefs. The survey also helped to fix the division of the land, making the manors permanent and crystallizing the already established form of organization.

The real economic basis of this system was the Anglo-Saxon village. While in many cases a village and its lands constituted a manor, just as frequently a village might be divided among a number of manors. For the two hundred years after the Conquest the villagers or *villeins* (Anglo-Saxon geburs) were generally in servile condition. The villein's average holding, according to the

[1] See: A. P. Usher, *Introduction to the Industrial History of England* (New York, 1920), chap. iv; I. F. Grant, *The Social and Economic Development of Scotland before 1603* (Edinburgh, 1930), p. 351.

Domesday survey, was a virgate (30 acres) of land scattered in strips through the two or three fields. As in pre-Conquest days, he had to give week work and also boon work, which was labor at harvest and sowing, according to the lord's need, and usually to the neglect of his own crops. Holding between five and ten acres, the *cottars* or *bordars* had fewer services to render to the lord, supplementing their slender incomes by hiring themselves to the wealthier villeins or to the lord. These men were all obliged to attend the lord's court, to pay him fines on inheritance of the land, and to receive his permission to sell cattle or to marry their children outside the manor. What is more, if they left the manor, the lord could bring them back by force. At the same time, they were guaranteed possession of their land, so they could not be sold as slaves.

Living alongside the villeins and cottars, in the same type of one-room clay-walled houses, were freemen. They might hold land in the common fields like the villeins, or they might have separate fields, known as *assarts*, cut out of the waste lands. While it is often hard to differentiate between the freemen and the villeins, there seem to have been one or two ways in which they were dissimilar. For one thing, the freeman was not bound to the land, and what is more, he could initiate suit in the king's court against the lord, an action from which the villein was inhibited. It is possible that the freeman might actually own his land, simply being subject to a lord's soke, or court jurisdiction. He was then known as a sokeman. On the other hand, he might be merely a tenant who paid a rent and was obliged also to help with boon works at harvest. Sometimes his rent was paid in money, but probably more often in produce during the early years. From what we can learn from the Domesday survey it would seem that many freemen, particularly in the Danish areas, were reduced by the Normans to the position of villeins, the villeins, at the same time, being depressed even further. In this way the Norman Conquest brought about a most effective and ruthless exploitation of the small people.

The method of landholding employed in East Anglia and Kent continued, as in Anglo-Saxon days, to differ from that of the Midlands. From Norman records one receives the impression, however, that there had been some changes. In Kent there was still no organized village with its common land. Instead, there were hamlets made up of scattered dwellings, the farm lands being divided into *iugae* through which the peasants' property was scattered in small parcels. This system seems to have developed from the earlier form, in which the iugae were compact fields which had been, as in Ireland, increasingly subdivided through inheritance in gavelkind. To the Norman lord the inhabitants of the hamlets paid heavy rents in the form of both money and food and performed such services as carting, but were free of week work. North of the Thames in East Anglia and Essex, much the same system prevailed, although the people lived in large villages. Thus, despite its difference from the Midlands, the east and southeast of England had the same manorial system imposed upon it, with manor houses and castles erected at strategic places.

In the Celtic areas the Normans found a third type of organization. The Celts, not much interested in arable farming, specialized in cattle raising, the principal reason for this being, as mentioned earlier, the climate and soil of the Highland Zone. Their original form of land tenure had been tribal, all the land belonging in common to the tribe. Before long, however, chieftains and other important tribesmen succeeded in obtaining land for themselves. On their deaths the property was divided equally among all their heirs, (gavelkind), which usually resulted in a great subdivision of holdings. Those not fortunate enough to obtain land soon became dependent upon the chief, tending his cattle or receiving from him property and cattle on loan, for which services were rendered. Because of this predominance of pastoral farming, the population usually lived not in villages, but in small hamlets scattered over the countryside. Here the Normans tried to impose the manorial system, their greatest successes being obtained in the fertile arable valleys of Wales and in certain sections of Ireland. Where lands, however, were unsuitable to arable farming the old Celtic system prevailed, the Norman noble taking the place of the chief but defining the services of the *betaghs* more exactly.

In Scotland manorialism never gained control. On the other hand, Celtic custom was very greatly modified both by Anglian influences from the north of England and Lothian and by Norman ideas. There is little information as to the status of the villein, although it is certain that he existed and was bound to the land. The people were usually settled in hamlets surrounded by what was known as the infield. Divided into strips (*run-rig*) it was cultivated in common, as in the three field system. The strips, however, were often reallocated each year. There was also the "outfield," which was land taken out of the waste, cultivated for a number of years until it lost its fertility and then allowed to revert to waste. It too was held in run-rig. The land of the hamlet as a rule amounted to a plowgate of 104 acres, being let out to four, six, or eight tenants. If each of the eight tenants provided an ox for the plow, he would hold 13 acres, or an oxgate, the unit by which was reckoned the size of a man's holding. This method of land-holding was known as "commonty," the obligations being a rent, along with such dues to the lord as heriot by which the lord received the tenant's best beast on his death, and the requirement to pay a fine on inheritance. In some cases the lord might provide the tenant with stock, a system known as "steelbow." Little real legal stability existed in this scheme, since it was largely based upon personal relationships between owner and tenant. In fact, it was a modification of Celtic tribalism.

Thus, in attempting to summarize the system of landholding in the British Isles, one finds two main types: the manorial and the Celtic. The Anglo-Norman manorial organization dominated the Midlands, was imposed on the east and southeast, and had representation in Wales and Ireland. In the two latter countries, however, despite superficial attempts to introduce the manor, the Celtic form predominated. Scotland, owing to both its geographical and racial characteristics, came closer to a compromise between the two systems. Thus, generally speaking, the manorial system in the British Isles was limited to the Lowland Zone, while in the Highland Zone, where land organization was less stable and uniform, the Celtic form prevailed. The differences between the two areas can be linked to the different kinds of agriculture followed. In the Lowland Zone arable farming predominated, while in the Highlands grazing of both sheep and cattle was the chief form of agriculture.

The Cultivation of the Land

If today one were able to visit a medieval English village or a Scottish hamlet, he would not be very impressed with the way in which the people lived. The village might have from twenty to one hundred houses, the hamlet only six or eight. The buildings were usually beside a road or by a river, probably at a ford or bridge. There was always a church with its steeple rising high above the surrounding country, and on a nearby height there might be a manor house, perhaps even a castle. The manor houses and the castles varied greatly as to size and construction, but the peasants' houses were always the same. They were one-roomed affairs with clay walls, thatched roofs, no windows, and only a hole in the roof to let out the smoke. The people themselves wore very rough clothing, drank ale or beer, and ate bread and meat, the latter in the winter frequently being in a state of decay. They had relatively few amusements, although on the village green they indulged in games resembling football and cricket, while weddings and funerals were the principal occasions of jollification. The real business of life was that of cultivating the land around the village.

Although the system of cultivation was still that of the Anglo-Saxons, the farmer in the Norman period had advanced somewhat in his techniques, particularly in the matter of preserving the land's fertility. Not only was fallowing of the fields continued, but manure and plowed-in stubble were also employed to this end, while lime was used to kill moss, and marl, a heavy clay, was spread on sandy soil. By following these practices productivity could be maintained and even improved.

In studying the Anglo-Saxon economy we saw that there was a system of fields, either two or three, attached to each village. In these were scattered the strips of the peasants' virgates or yardlands which by Norman times totalled thirty acres, all being cultivated in common. When a Norman lord took over a manor he did not alter the methods of farming, but merely claimed a part of the arable land as his own possession. Upon this the villeins had to work for two or three days a week, while during sowing and harvest they often had to work for a week or so at a time. Even freemen were occasionally obliged to give such boon work. This was usually carried on under supervision of the lord's bailiff, who was in charge of the manor, and under the immediate direction of the reeve, one of the peasants elected by his fellow villagers.

In East Anglia, Essex, and Kent also the Normans made little change in the method of cultivation. The customary tenement in East Anglia and Essex was about twelve acres, although in Kent it seems to have been considerably larger. All these holdings were worked, as in the open-field villages, on a cooperative plan, and the villeins were also obliged to give week and boon work to their manorial lords. In East Anglia and Kent there were also many sokemen who held large parcels of land and who paid rents. In the Celtic areas the earlier forms of agriculture continued as they had for many centuries earlier. Thus, while the system of landholding had changed somewhat, the methods of farming throughout the later Middle Ages were fundamentally the same as those which had been employed prior to the Norman Conquest.

The only instance of improvement is the appearance of some new farming implements. While the plows saw little or no advance, other instruments were being introduced. There was, for example, the harrow. At first little more than a bundle of thorns dragged over the land by the oxen, it soon developed into an instrument fitted with teeth. Hoes of various shapes and uses were also invented, as well as mallets or mauls used to break up sods. For the harvesting of grain the sickle was still the common instrument. The farmer frequently cut off only the heads, leaving the straw standing, part to be used later for thatching roofs, the rest to be plowed in or left for the cattle. Hay was cut with a straight handled scythe. The earliest threshing was done with a beating stick, but later a flail consisting of two pieces of wood joined together by leather thongs was introduced.

Although one might consider the methods of farming employed in the Lowland Zone during the middle period of the Middle Ages primitive, they were quite advanced compared with those in use in the Highland Zone. The farming of the Midlands and the eastern part of England was relatively more efficient, although it never produced enough to remove completely the fear of starvation. On the other hand, the Celtic areas seem to have lived in constant fear of insufficient food, Scotland being continually obliged to import grain from England or the English cultivated areas of Ireland. The difference was due to the climate, the soil, and also to the different traditions of the farmers.

The Production of the Land

The principal crops raised in the Lowland Zone were wheat, barley, and rye. All these grains were ground into flour, and barley was also used for brewing. Wheat and barley required well-tilled soils, while rye could be grown on poor soil and even in small holdings. Usually the wheat and rye, and sometimes peas and beans, were sown in the fields at the amount of two bushels to the acre, giving a yield for wheat and rye of eight to ten bushels and for beans and peas, six to eight bushels. Barley was sown at the rate of 4 bushels to the acre and would produce anything from 12 to 16 bushels. The common grain of the ordinary peasant was rye, which, with wheat, was sown between August 12 and November 1, beans and peas being sown between February 2 and March 31.

In the Celtic areas, particularly in Wales and Scotland, the crops were somewhat different. Because of the wet climate wheat was not popular. On the other hand, oats was the most important crop. It was sown usually in the spring, producing 12 to 16 bushels from 4 bushels of seed. Barley and a similar type of coarse grain known as "bear" were also common. Barley bread and oatmeal porridge were the customary food of the Celt, a fact which has sometimes been blamed for his peculiar characteristics.

Fortunately for the medieval peasant, he was not dependent

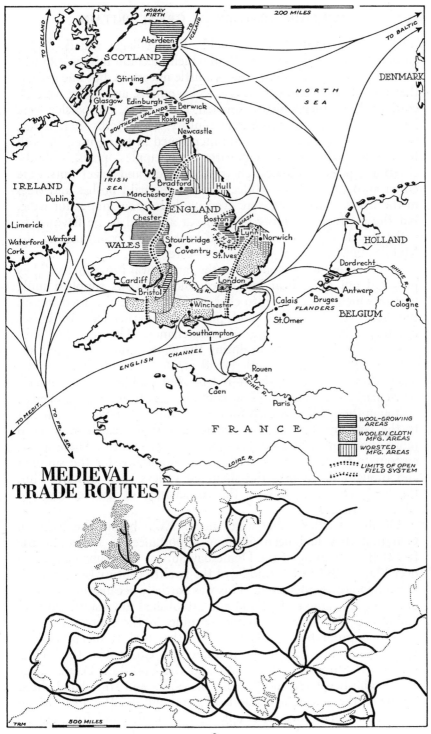

MEDIEVAL
TRADE ROUTES

WOOL-GROWING AREAS

WOOLEN CLOTH MFG. AREAS

WORSTED MFG. AREAS

LIMITS OF OPEN FIELD SYSTEM

200 MILES

SCOTLAND

MORAY FIRTH

TO ICELAND

TO ICELAND

Aberdeen

TO BALTIC

DENMARK

NORTH SEA

Stirling

Glasgow Edinburgh Berwick

SOUTHERN UPLANDS

Roxburgh

Newcastle

IRISH SEA

Bradford Hull

IRELAND

Manchester

Dublin

Chester ENGLAND

Boston

THE WASH

Limerick

Lynn Norwich

HOLLAND

Waterford Wexford

WALES Stourbridge

Cork

Coventry

St.Ives

Dordrecht

RHINE R.

Cardiff

THAMES R.

London

Antwerp

Bristol

Calais Bruges

Cologne

Winchester

St.Omer

FLANDERS

BELGIUM

Southampton

ENGLISH CHANNEL

Rouen

TO MEDIT.

Caen

SEINE R.

TO FR. & SP.

Paris

FRANCE

LOIRE R.

TRM

500 MILES

83

solely on the products of his field. Each villager usually had a garden, known as a *toft* or *croft*, in which he could raise vegetables. What vegetables he would grow is a little uncertain, but one gathers that peas, beans, lentils, cabbage, leeks, onions, and garlic were all cultivated. Lettuce, chicory, spinach, beets, cress, and parsley were known as early as the fourteenth century, while herbs such as rue, sage, clary, hyssop, and mint are mentioned as being used in both food and medicines. Along with these, apples, pears, walnuts, chestnuts, plums, peaches, cherries, quinces, and hazel nuts were either cultivated or were collected from the wild bushes and trees in the woods. Attempts were even made to grow grapes for wine, but the product was more like vinegar and had to be flavored to make it palatable. Bees were also kept, honey being one of the Middle Ages' principal sources of sweetening.

Another important concern of the farmer was his animals. They provided not only meat but hides, and the cows supplied milk, part of which was made into cheese. Cattle were also used to pull the heavy carts, sledges, and plows, being preferred to horses because of their lower costs of maintenance. They did not have to be shod nor fed on grain during the winter and were much less liable to disease. Besides, they had greater strength and docility. They worked more slowly, it is true, but rapidity of movement, particularly in a medieval plow, could be disastrous. Consequently, although the horse was used for cavalry, farm work was usually left to the cow and the ox. In Ireland and Wales cattle were even more important, being the principal form of wealth. There it was customary for them to be sent to the mountains for the summer and brought down into the sheltered valleys each winter. Thus the lowly cow and ox were the cornerstone of the economy of Medieval Britain.

Of almost equal value were sheep. Even before the Norman Conquest they had been of some importance, as shown by the fact that at the time of the Domesday Survey, Ely Abbey possessed over 13,000. But by the middle of the twelfth century the country's flocks had greatly increased. This was partially because of monastic orders which came to England and established monasteries in wild and waste places. Since arable farming in these areas was frequently unprofitable, if not impossible, they took to sheep farming. In England they had flocks roaming the Cotswolds, the rolling country of Shropshire, the Fens, and the Yorkshire Dales. They also established large sheep farms in Wales and stimulated sheep raising in the southern Uplands of Scotland and the area around Aberdeen. Their success, coupled with the demand for wool on the continent, particularly in Flanders, encouraged the nobles to follow suit. The result was the rise of a new type of farming. It has been estimated that during the fourteenth century England alone had about 8 million sheep.[2] Most people kept at least a few, which grazed on the manorial commons. Manorial organization, however, soon disappeared where large-scale sheep farming was introduced. This was particularly true in Lincoln and York, which produced the best long-haired wool, and in Wales, home of the short but very fine Ryeland wool. Although sheep were rather susceptible to disease, cures were discovered which gave the flocks adequate protection, while at the same time selective breeding, which considerably improved the grade of wool, was introduced. By 1350 wool growing was becoming the most profitable part of agriculture.

From the point of view of the small farmer, of even greater value, though not as important commercially, was the pig. It was in a sense a universal animal, providing its owner with an effective scavenger while alive and, when dead, not only with meat, but also with leather, lard, and bristles. As the pig cost practically nothing to feed, living as it did on refuse or on such things as beech mast and acorns in the forest, it was an economical animal to raise. The Anglo-Saxons had always relished a meal of pork, and the Normans were no less attracted to the succulent flesh. Consequently, the pig was both common and popular in England, Scotland, and Ireland. It was a very important member of any agricultural organization.

Other elements in the medieval farmer's livestock were poultry: chickens, geese, ducks, swans, and even peacocks, although the two latter were usually possessed only by the nobility. Then too, there was always the manorial dovecote, or pigeon house, containing feathered marauders who were protected even though they stole the peasants' grain. Conies or rabbits were also eaten, and it was during this period that they were first domesticated. Very frequently rents were paid in poultry, eggs, or rabbits, making them important not only as food, but also as a medium of exchange.

From the foregoing it can be seen that medieval farming in Britain was at no time static, nor was it everywhere the same. Various influences were always at work upon it, changing and modifying it from time to time. As one looks at the period from 1066 to 1350, however, one finds that there was a relative stability which tended to disappear during the next century and a half. It

[2] H. C. Darby (ed.), *Historical Geography of England Before 1800* (London, 1936), p. 239 ff.

was this change which was to lay the groundwork for the rise of the modern type of farmer.

The Changes in Medieval Farming

One of the characteristics of the century from 1250 to 1350 was the growth throughout western Europe of a money economy. Trade, stimulated by the Crusades, by the rise of industry in Italy and the Netherlands, and by an increased production of silver in Austria, began to expand. This, in turn, meant the rapid rise of towns as markets. England, and to a lesser extent Scotland and Wales, felt the impact of the contemporary economic development. The result was that the position of farming in the economic organization began to change. It was now expected to provide not merely subsistence, but also a surplus which could be sold for cash in the market. Even in the days of Henry I there had been an interest in landholding from the purely financial point of view, but from 1250 on it became of even greater importance, dominating the scene by 1350. The possibility of one's acres providing money profits stimulated men to seek ways of obtaining greater returns from their land.

The easiest method of obtaining an increased yield was to establish a general increase in efficiency. Efficiency, however, was hard to obtain when one's labor force was composed of villeins who preferred to work on their own land. There was always a certain amount of unwillingness to give time to the lord's demesne, with the result that the work was not done properly. If, therefore, the lord of the manor could obtain money, it would pay him to hire workers, leaving the villeins to attend to their own farms. This would be satisfactory to the villein, who could now devote himself entirely to his own land, and to the lord, who could engage help when it was needed, without having to bother with the laborers when there was nothing to do.

No sooner had this decision been reached than there appeared the practice of "commutation." At first it began somewhat spasmodically. Some summer the lord would not need all his villeins to help with the harvest, so he would permit some of them to remain at home, with the condition that they would pay a penny for every day that the others were obliged to work. The next summer they might have to give services once again. Before long, however, some lords became increasingly interested in commutation as a permanent institution. To make this effective, a lord might grant a lease, or he might declare in the manorial court that a certain villein could hold his land on condition that he paid a penny for so many days' week work. Although he was still required to give boon work and other services, such as cartage, later on he was permitted to pay for all services. This agreement would be recorded in the manorial court roll, a copy being given to the peasant, who soon came to be known as a "copyholder." From then on the conditions of tenure were regarded as fixed and unalterable.

In Scotland, owing to the system of holding land in oxgates for rent and boon services, commutation was introduced at a very early date. A peasant paying rent was either given some form of lease or was allowed to remain on the land through the kindness of the owner. Quite properly, the latter type was called a "kindly" tenant, but by custom he soon gained a form of prescriptive right to his land. In this way villeinage began to disappear earlier in Scotland than in England, the last Scottish reference to villeinage being dated 1364.

In England the practice of commutation was becoming common by 1345, although it was never uniform. Sometimes rents were paid in produce, sometimes certain services continued, and on occasion whole manors were rented out to the villeins, who simply paid a fixed sum each year. There is an example of such a lease dating back to 1183. Consequently, there was a wide variation in practice between manor and manor, between county and county.

The process of commutation would seem to have been considerably speeded up, particularly in some parts of England, by a disaster which then struck the country. Bubonic plague was by no means unknown in Medieval Europe, but a particularly virulent type called the "Black Death" swept the Continent in the early part of the fourteenth century, reaching England about 1348. The resulting epidemic was, for some parts of the country at least, ruinous. A large part of the population died. The Scots, seeing the English thus weakened, felt that it was a good time to attack their "auld enemy" and carried the plague back home with them. It is very probable that outlying districts may not have been seriously affected, but in the urban areas, in the monasteries and in the larger villages the death toll was undoubtedly heavy. While some historians have denied that there was any great depletion of the population, others have estimated that the country lost between one third and one half of its inhabitants. However that may be, there is little doubt that there was a considerable decline of numbers in the Midlands and the south of England.

The first consequence of this sudden increase in the death rate was that a considerable number of villein lands fell into the hands of the manorial lords, who had to obtain new tenants. At the same time, there was a corresponding decrease in the amount of labor available for the cultivation of the lord's demesne. In order to meet the problems caused by this shortage, the lords tried to re-establish the old system of services due from the villeins. The latter, however, knowing that labor was scarce, demanded high wages without increased rents. If their terms were not met, they simply threw up their land and went to other lords who might agree to their demands. The result was dislocation of the manorial economy. The government attempted to mitigate the difficulties by passing the Statute of Labourers (1351), requiring villeins to work at the rates of pay current before the plague. This law may have been partially successful, but it caused smoldering discontent, which, in 1381, broke into open rebellion when an attempt was made to impose universal taxation. The Peasants' Revolt was smashed with considerable cruelty, but, in spite of all the efforts to curb the demands of labor, increased wages had to be paid, thereby forcing other changes in the economic organization.

Prior to the Black Death manorial lords had been separating their demesne strips of land from those of the villeins and concentrating them in one part of the manorial property. They had also been fencing off assarts, or individual plots, from the rest of the waste. These consolidated and enclosed arable lands, which were becoming more and more numerous, were often rented to the peasants. With the increase in the cost of labor, the peasants also, by agreement with their fellows, were frequently allowed to combine their strips. The land was then leased, sometimes with stock, for a period of years, so that by 1400 the leaseholding or copyholding of farms was quite common. Sometimes the tenants' farms were consolidated, and sometimes they continued to lie in the intermingled strips. The important thing was, however, that the old services were rapidly disappearing, rents taking their place. The manor of Forncett is perhaps a good example. Between 1348 and 1379 more than half the week works disappeared, and by 1400 of 73 holdings only 16 were occupied by villeins, the other holdings having been rented. Thus the old economic organization was disintegrating.

Along with this change went a second. During the fourteenth century the continental market for English wool expanded greatly. What is more, with the advent of foreign workmen there was a considerable increase in the domestic production of cloth. This meant that there was an ever-greater demand for wool. It is not difficult to understand, therefore, why the lords of manors turned to sheep raising. With farms becoming vacant and labor costs rising, it was easy to turn the farming land into sheep runs. Not only was the cost of employing a few shepherds to tend the sheep relatively small, but what was more, the product was easily sold, bringing in a high cash return. It was not long, therefore, before sheep farming became very popular. In fact, a good number of landlords even attempted to clear their tenants and copyholders off the land in order that they might profit from the new source of income. This was another phase of the agricultural change.

In the Highland Zone, particularly in the west of England, Wales, and Ireland, similar alterations were taking place. Sheep farming became the prevailing type in all these areas. Western England and Wales saw the spread of sheep farms to such an extent that one might say that manorialism had pretty well disappeared by 1500. Where there was good arable land, however, the tendency was for it to be enclosed and rented out to tenants. In the arable areas of Ireland there was a parallel increase in renting, although consolidation and enclosure was not so common. The trend was in the direction of the increased subdivision of the individual strips, until they became practically useless for arable farming. At the same time, cattle farming and sheep raising continued to be of the very greatest importance for Irish economy.

In Scotland also, from 1300 on, there were numerous changes. For one thing, leaseholding became more common, although the leases were usually for a short term of only five to seven years. This meant that there was no incentive to improve the land, since the tenant might have to leave at the end of his term. Coupled with this there was the fact that he was still liable for various types of uncertain services such as boon work, fencing, ditching, and cartage, as well as heriot. By 1350, however, a new type of lease began to come into existence. This was the *feu*. Land was feued when it was rented to an individual for a fixed sum and for certain services over a long period, sometimes two or three generations. In order to obtain a feu the tenant frequently had to pay a large amount of money down and a higher rent, but he did have a long lease. Some-times the feus increased rents as much as 400 per cent, a rise often disastrous to the small tenant, who was pushed off the land in favor of the larger landowner. Sheep farming also increased rapidly, and one of the principal exports by 1500 was wool, woolfells (skins with the wool still attached), and hides. Coupled with these alterations, there began to develop a tendency toward large farms with subtenants, who held land at a rent and did most of the work. The "chief" tenant, however, obtained the largest share of the profits. In this way most traces of manorialism finally disappeared from Scotland before 1500.

While these changes in agriculture, and particularly in the method of landholding, were taking place, modifications were also occurring in the position of the peasantry. For one thing the smaller farmers were being divorced from the land. Cottars in England and crofters in Scotland were being deprived by enclosure and renting of their small plots, and even of their houses. Increasingly their only source of income was their labor. While at first this was quite valuable, with the general change in the system and organization of agriculture agricultural laborers became less necessary, resulting in a social revolution. There is not much reference to it prior to 1500, but it was beginning as early as 1400 and by 1550 it was a very real problem.

As the natural outcome of all this change, villeinage was disappearing. In Scotland it had gone by 1400, and it is probable that in practice, although not in legal theory, it had disappeared from England by 1500. The reason for the transformation was that villeinage, owing to the use of money and the development of leases and rents, was unprofitable. What is more, the rise of the borough also helped. From the earliest days, if a runaway villein could live in a borough uncaught for a year and a day, he automatically became a free man. With the growth of trade, bringing with it a rise in borough population and increased opportunities for work, this became an easy thing to do. Although the ecclesiastical landlords, such as monasteries and cathedrals, were slower to change their methods of cultivation and of landholding than were the secular landowners, even they were forced to make concessions to the new spirit. Thus by 1500, the relative positions of the peasants and the landlords had been changed radically.

Farming in 1500

As one looks back over the vista of medieval agriculture, one important fact stands out: while agriculture in some areas and in some ways had deviated considerably from what it had been in the ninth and tenth centuries, in other places and ways it was still much the same, for the changes which had taken place were by no means general nor uniform. Some areas, owing to the proximity of markets or to certain types of soil, climate, and even tradition, had developed in one particular way, while others, if they had changed at all, had followed another route. Nevertheless, one can make certain generalizations which may perhaps sum up the history of farming since the advent of the Normans.

For one thing the status of the people who did the actual cultivating had changed. Generally speaking, villeinage, if not in law at least in fact, had disappeared. In Scotland even the law knew it no longer. The servile status which was based upon services of the villein to the lord had been destroyed by the development of the money economy. In Scotland, Ireland, and Wales land was held either by some form of lease or simply at the will of the lord. In England the leasehold or the copyhold was practically universal. This meant that manorialism, wherever it had been planted or developed by the Normans, had virtually disappeared as a system of land holding and agriculture. As it was no longer profitable, both lord and farmer were prepared to forget it.

This change meant that, instead of villeins, tenants or small freeholders were now the principle cultivators of the land. In Ireland and to a certain extent in Wales, owing to the practice of inheritance by gavelkind, the farms so held were usually quite small. In Scotland and to an even greater extent in England, on the other hand, the appearance of the substantial rented or freehold farm became quite common. In England the rising "yeoman" class, for a long time the backbone of English rural society, lived upon these farms. It was this group of tenants and yeomen who were among the chief beneficiaries of the disappearance of the manor.

The other side of the picture is not so pleasant, for many people whose forefathers had been villeins possessing at least a small plot were now entirely divorced from the land. While those who were still in possession of land were better off than before, those who had been dispossessed were in a much worse condition. Nor was there any great expansion of industry, as was to take place in the eighteenth century, to provide employment. Consequently, these landless folk simply took to the road, coming under the penalties of the law which punished those who did not work. For the peasants who did find work the situation was not much better, for they were now entirely dependent upon their wages. True, the government had long ago given up the attempt to enforce the Statute of Labourers; instead, the Justices of the Peace had been authorized to fix wages in accordance with the scarcity of food. Yet sickness, a bad harvest, or some other disturbance of the usual routine would bring great suffering upon these people. Had it not been that victuals were relatively cheap compared with the level of wages during the latter part of the fifteenth century, the rural wage earner would have been in a serious plight.

One of the principal reasons for the cheapness of food was the increase in production. This, in turn, was largely the outcome of the new system of landholding. Although there was relatively little improvement in technique, when a man owned his land on freehold or on a long-term lease he was prepared to spend time and money improving it. Since this was true even when the land remained in scattered strips, how much more would it be the case when the land was held as a consolidated lot! Throughout the last 200 or 250 years of the period men had been enclosing land from the waste, the lords had been consolidating and enclosing their demesnes, tenants had been laying field to field, and those interested in sheep farming had been evicting the peasants to give the flocks more room. Although toward the end of the period sheep farming seems to have declined somewhat, the enclosure movement had nevertheless become increasingly important. Yet extensive as it was, it affected only a small percentage of the country. A hundred or two hundred years was too short a time for the process to be accomplished. It was to continue at varying speeds in various areas until the middle of the nineteenth century, by which time it would be virtually complete.

Thus, in summary, one may say that while the Middle Ages saw a considerable change in the method of holding land in Britain, it saw relatively little change in the method of production. Few if any new implements were introduced, although there may have been some improvement in crop rotation and the use of fertilizers. The real improvement came in the increased incentive to bestow more care upon the land and its produce. In this, the foundation was laid for the introduction of modern agricultural methods.

Chapter 6

MEDIEVAL TOWNS AND TRADE

A<small>T THE TIME</small> of the Norman Conquest the towns in the British Isles, when compared with Continental cities such as Rouen or Paris, were small and unimportant. Before 1066 the inhabitants had done relatively little to develop trade and industry, so, while the towns were usually in favorable trade locations, that is about all one can say. In Scotland and Ireland they were mere villages. Even the largest settlements in Britain could have had no more than 7,000 or 8,000 inhabitants. How "urban" they were can perhaps be best estimated by the continued connection of most of the inhabitants with agriculture. Even by 1150 they were more often than not as much farmers as they were merchants and craftsmen, and in Scotland the burgh lands, often cultivated by burgesses themselves, were very important down to modern times. Yet, at the same time, there was apparently a clearly felt town consciousness. There was little thought of the townsmen being English, Scottish, or Irish; instead they were citizens of London, Norwich, Aberdeen, or Armagh. Only in England, where the strong Norman government of William the Conqueror and his successors could never be completely ignored, did they experience any real central control. Scotland was very much divided, the king's authority being recognized only in certain limited areas. In Ireland and Wales, where the political organization was primarily tribal, the villages were either the capitals of tribes or were settlements of tradesmen and laborers who had settled around a monastery.

The Beginnings of Town Life

In towns such as these one could hardly expect very much industry or trade. There were, of course, craftsmen, such as the carpenter and blacksmith, in most centers, but their work was done chiefly for the local market. Luxuries and exotic goods, usually of foreign origin, were imported by foreign merchants[1] who were always treated with very great suspicion, if not hostility. They could stay only 40 days, during which time they usually had to live with a local citizen and might sell only to native merchants. The native merchants, in turn, made their profits by traveling about the surrounding country and selling these foreign imports, or locally produced goods which were scarce elsewhere. As can be well imagined, under such circumstances trade was not very great or profitable.

When William the Conqueror set up his government, English towns were of two types: those on royal and those on baronial land; the same was true of Scotland. Since the inhabitants, as tenants or even serfs, were obliged to pay dues to their lords, the royal boroughs, which were by far the more important, came directly under the control of the King's representative—in England the local sheriff and in Scotland the royal chamberlain. Both these men had the duty of collecting the king's feudal revenues. Even in Anglo-Saxon days there had been a representative of the burh inhabitants who collected the feudal dues and saw that the town obeyed the lord's orders. Really a manorial official known as the reeve, he continued to fill the same office after the Conquest. Although the sheriff tried to extend his financial and legal authority over the towns in England after 1066, the trend was really in the other direction. Before long certain individuals began to "farm" the borough revenues, paying down a lump sum in cash and receiving in return the right to collect the town taxes owed to the king or baron. These revenues had been considerably increased after 1066, some by 300 per cent. The profit of the farmer came from the discount which he obtained in return for the advance cash payment. By 1130 the wealthier citizens of some of the larger towns began to feel that they might do the same thing as a group. Although occasionally practiced before 1066, this became increasingly common in the twelfth century. What is more, the wealthier traders could offer to buy such special privileges as freedom from paying tolls when they went to trade in other towns or freedom from suit in any court but their own. The result was that London, Lincoln, and a few other towns received special grants which even included a borough court. Yet while these freedoms were very important, the king, through his sheriff, still supervised the towns for his own profit. Even by 1200 most towns were still predominantly manorial in form.

---

[1] The term "foreign" denoted anything or person from another town, a merchant from Southampton being as much a "foreigner" in London as one from Rouen.

At the same time, the twelfth century marks in England, Scotland, Wales, and to a certain extent in Ireland, the beginnings of the town as something more than an extension of the manor. Both the English and the Scottish kings were finding that they required a more efficient collection of the produce of their royal lands for purposes of government. What is more, in times of emergency they needed all that the lands could give. Consequently, they were sometimes willing not only to let the towns' representatives take over the collection of the royal taxes from the townspeople, but in return for special aids or contributions they were prepared to give special corporate privileges. Such rights, setting town apart from country, were at times incorporated in charters to make sure that the towns' freedoms would be clearly understood. In England Henry I (1100-1135) granted London the privilege of electing its own magistrates. Fifty years later in Scotland, William the Lion began the practice of granting charters to his towns. Other monarchs, however, were not so favorable to the idea, since it meant that the towns began to achieve a certain amount of independence. Henry II refused or abrogated charters whenever he could, while both barons and churchmen were very loath to give their boroughs any freedom. Towns were not popular in feudal society.

The Merchant Gild Stimulates Development of The Town

One of the primary reasons for the growth of burghal independence was the rise in the towns of an organization known as the merchant gild (or gild merchant). At first this seems to have been composed of the wealthier citizens, who banded themselves together in the interests of trade and who also assumed certain financial obligations for the community. While there are a few traces of burh gilds before 1066 the first to be known with certainty appeared about 1093 in England and slightly later in Scotland. Many others came into being in succeeding years, according to the economic and political development of the town. In places such as London and Norwich, where there seems always to have been some borough government, there is no evidence that a merchant gild ever existed. Although the merchant gilds did not become the town government, in most cases they wielded a great influence over it. In England the "alderman of the gild" often became a civic official, and before long the Scottish "dean of gild" was a part of the burgh government. The reason for this was simply that since the most influential burgesses were in both organizations, the two bodies would tend to coalesce. Moreover the gild's authority usually went back, in the final analysis, to the town charter in which the privilege of having a merchant gild had been granted.

No two gilds were exactly alike. At first, however, they seem to have been composed of most of the businessmen in the town, including craftsmen. The latter, working in their little shops, and selling their goods directly to the consumer, were regarded as merchants. But before long the specifically trading element, particularly in Scotland, tried to force the craftsmen out of the gild. The association was usually governed by an alderman and two or four assistants, who, along with twelve or twenty-four gild members, formed the gild court. Possessed of authority to enforce gild regulations, this body usually directed the whole of the town's business life.

While, in theory, all burgesses were not required to belong to the gild, it seemed to be the sensible thing to do if one wished to carry on business. This organization existed primarily to enforce economic privileges, the most fundamental being a monopoly of all the town's trade. Members alone could buy from and sell to foreigners coming into the town. What is more, they sought absolute control of the foreigner by saying where he could lodge and how long he could stay. In Scotland this exclusive policy was carried even further, large areas around the towns being subordinated to the gild authority. For instance, the gild of Aberdeen was given the monopoly of all finished cloth made in the shire. This greatly hampered the rise of rural industry, probably being one reason for the relative scarcity of villages in Scotland. To prevent monopolies within the gild itself, however, when a member made a purchase, a fellow gildsman usually had the right to share in it if he wished to buy for his own use. Members were under oath to maintain the price and quality of goods, to share in the gilds' financial obligations, and to support each other in case of indebtedness or suit at law. Sick benefits were provided by the gild for its members, and they also participated in common religious observances and pageants. In this way the merchant gild dominated the economic side of the borough life.

Mention has already been made of borough charters.[2] With

[2] A distinction must be made between a burh and a borough. A burh was an Anglo-Saxon term which denoted a town which served primarily as a fortress, although it might also be a marketplace and the chief town of a shire. The term "borough," a derivative of "burh," is later and denotes not so much a military post, as a municipality with certain rights of self-government and also well-defined economic privileges. The Scottish equivalent of "borough" is "burgh."

the appearance of these documents began the growth of the idea of borough incorporation. Generally speaking, until the end of Henry II's reign, the people in the royal towns were regarded as merely a group of "king's men." They could not act as a single body or legal personage. With the economic difficulties of Richard Coeur de Lion and John Lackland, however, came their opportunity. The result was that the merchant gild, or the merchants as a group, began to negotiate for incorporation. In return for a cash consideration they obtained a charter, which enabled them to elect their own mayor, aldermen, and bailiffs, and to have their own courts and merchant gild (often already in existence). Above all, they gained the right to collect the payments due by them to the crown in "fee farm." That is, they were to pay over their royal taxes to the crown in a lump sum, not just as long as the king wished, but in perpetuity. This meant that from 1200 on town corporations rapidly increased in number throughout the British Isles, their privileges being not infrequently based upon those of some other town whose charter had been copied. The Scots imitated Newcastle; the Irish, Bristol; and many of the baronial towns in both Wales and Ireland, the Norman town of Breteuil. Here was a new nonfeudal form of social organization rising to a place of influence.

Once the towns began to achieve incorporation their authority necessarily began to expand. Those who had the right to take part in the town government varied from place to place, according to the charters. In some towns it was those who owned land, in others it was those who were members of the merchant gild. But however the body of burgesses was constituted, the scope of the town's authority was gradually extended so that by the fifteenth century the local urban governments were endowed with very large powers. The town fathers had the responsibility of seeing that prices were what they should be, that quality was up to standard, that there was no cornering of the market nor buying of goods before they came on to the market, that weights and measures were honest, and that markets and fairs were properly conducted. What is more, in conformity to the example of the continental town, a number of communities required all members of the corporation to take an oath to defend the privileges of the town. This involved the creation of a "commune," a political unit separate from the shire and prepared to resist all encroachment.

In this way the merchant gild was gradually supplanted during the thirteenth century by the town government. In Scotland as well as in England, the gild was, to a large extent, absorbed by the corporation, while in other cases the merchant gild just dropped out of sight. The next step was that in many larger centers the various crafts and trades began to organize for their own particular interests. Craft gilds and trading companies appeared. Thus, with the increase of trade and industry as well as the development of borough authority, the merchant gild had no longer any reason for existence, and by 1350 it seems to have lost most of its importance.

The Rise of the Craft Gilds

Industrial methods employed after the Norman Conquest did not advance very much beyond those of Anglo-Saxon days. The manufacturer was a shop worker, making his goods by hand. Whether he was a goldsmith, a spinner, a weaver, a cordwainer or a bowyer, he was primarily a craftsman. It was only at the end of our period that machinery driven by waterpower came into use. From about the middle of the fourteenth century the process of fulling woven cloth, that is, of beating out the woolen fibers, under water, to make a "felted" type of material, was done by water-driven fulling mills. Water power was also applied to iron production. Around the year 1400 water operated bellows came into use, and by 1500 mechanical hammers, also driven by water, were making their appearance. Machinery was just starting to take its place in industry at the end of the period. Even by 1500, however, most of the industrial workers were still hand craftsmen who sold their products either directly to the consumer or to a merchant, who, in turn, would sell them to foreign traders or send them abroad.

It was natural that these small craftsmen should eventually get together in some form of organization. They tended to live in the same district, to worship in the same church, and to have the same patron saint. Consequently, religious fraternities developed, sometimes without any trade connection, the members taking part in certain common religious observances and wearing a common uniform or livery. It could not be long before men who belonged to both the same fraternity and trade would begin "to talk shop." The outcome might be the organization of their own fraternity, or even a fraternity of all related trades, such as metalworkers, if there were only a few craftsmen. This frequently meant the withdrawal of the fraternity members from the merchant gild. At the same time, they would begin to enter into agreements regarding quality and prices of goods. The next step was the acquisition of a charter enabling them to enforce their agreements. Because the merchant gilds and the towns were usually hostile to such a move, the crown would then be petitioned, and a considerable sum paid for the grant of the privilege. In this way the craft gilds came into existence.

The earliest examples of such organizations appeared in London at the beginning of the twelfth century. There the weavers were the first to organize, probably because theirs was the most important craft. They obtained a royal charter which made them virtually independent of town control, while at the same time they tried to force all weavers into their organization. However, alien weavers from Flanders and Brabant, who began to settle in London in the fourteenth century, refused to enter the London weavers' gild and obtained the right to organize their own. This was another way in which gilds came into existence, although the natural growth just described was much more common.

The organization of the craft gild was very similar to that of the merchant gild. Usually at its head were four wardens, chosen on a quasidemocratic basis by the gild masters or its wealthier members. There was also the council or court, frequently made up of twelve of the older members, which had the duty of judging in disputes or punishing those who broke the gild regulations. In nearly all cases, however, the town court remained the final court of appeal, to which an aggrieved craftsman could carry his case. Then there was the assembly, where all the craft members met together at different times for business, religious observances, or jollification. Everyone who practiced the craft in the town was obliged to be a member; and where there were but a few craftsmen in each trade, all those working in one type of material might be lumped together. At one time or another Norwich had some 147 crafts, but most of them were practiced by less than five persons. Consequently, leather workers, whether shoemakers, cobblers, pursemakers or saddlers, all belonged to one gild. The same was true of loriners (bitmakers), spurriers (spurmakers), and cutlers (knifemakers). In this way the gilds could perform their duties more effectively.

What were these duties? First and foremost, there was the supervision of the craft within the town. The wardens had the right to make sure that the goods offered for sale were of the proper quality and fairly priced. In this way they enforced the prevalent idea of the "just price." Owing to the limited market, much policing was necessary, for dishonesty and rigging of the market were by no means uncommon. Along with this, there was the regulation of wages of the workmen, who not infrequently, particularly in the later days, might threaten to go on strike. There was also the participation in religious observances and in the pageants for which each gild was responsible. Usually the pageant or play was performed on the feast of Corpus Christi, the type of performance being in accordance with the craft's occupation. The carpenters, for instance, played "Noah's Ark," for Noah in this instance was a carpenter. These were known as "mystery plays," since they were performed by some special craft or "mystery" (métier). Last of all, the gilds were organized to see that all members of the craft had the opportunity to make a fair living. No one was to take advantage of the other or to entice away his servants. If misfortune came upon a "brother," the gild gave him aid and assistance.

When they first appeared, the craft gilds were apparently quite unpopular. The merchant gilds did not like them because, in the beginning, they did not have to help to pay the borough "farm" to the crown. What is more, some of them obtained royal charters making them free from town control, while others did not bother with a charter, but still continued to function independently. The result was a conflict, which was particularly violent in Scotland, between the craft and the merchant gilds. In England, with the gradual breakdown of the latter, it was the borough government which offered the opposition. But as industry was expanding, particularly in the larger towns such as London, Norwich, Bristol, and Coventry, it was difficult to restrain the crafts' desire to organize. By 1450 London had over 100 gilds, Norwich 26, Winchester 20, and Coventry 23. As these bodies had by this time been made to contribute to the borough expenses they were gradually recognized. The towns, however, usually saw to it that they were carefully controlled, strictly limiting the powers of their courts. Craftsmen, however, could be members of the borough council. Finally, in 1437 an English act of parliament placed the gilds completely under the municipal authorities, even though they might possess a royal charter. This was the beginning of the end of craft gilds' power and influence.

The gilds were also heading for disintegration because of their own internal structure. As originally organized, they had been composed of small craftsmen and their helpers, known as apprentices and journeymen. The helpers who worked by the day (journée) may have had at first little training, but by 1300 the tendency, particularly in England, was to insist that they should go through a definite time of preparation or apprenticeship. They commenced their education at an early age, usually when in their

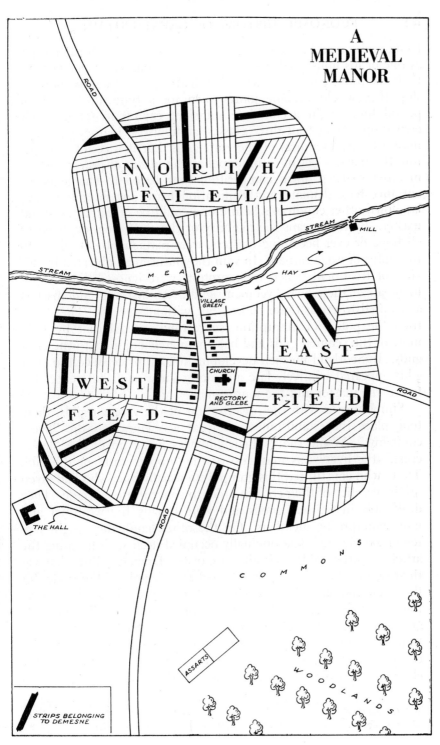

A
MEDIEVAL
MANOR

ROAD

NORTH
FIELD

STREAM

MILL

STREAM

MEADOW

HAY

VILLAGE
GREEN

EAST

CHURCH

RECTORY
AND GLEBE

FIELD

WEST

FIELD

ROAD

FIELD

ROAD

THE HALL

COMMONS

ASSARTS

WOODLANDS

STRIPS BELONGING
TO DEMESNE

teens, and served for as many as seven years, living with the master as one of his household but receiving little or no payment beyond their food and clothing. After they had fulfilled their apprenticeship they would become journeymen for a time, during which period they might accumulate sufficient capital to set up their own shop. At first all three classes, apprentices, journeymen, and masters, were members of the craft gilds, but it was not long before the masters began to monopolize the places of power. Then, in order to keep down competition they began to charge heavy entrance fees, demand costly initiation feasts for the gildry, and lay down other conditions before one could be admitted as a gild master. By this means the majority of the craftsmen, deprived of all hope of ever becoming masters, were permanently confined to the status of wage earners. In vain the journeymen objected to this kind of treatment; when their protests were ignored, they began to organize their own "yeomen" gilds. At first the gild masters attempted to crush these bodies, but without success. They then tried the policy of absorption, succeeding so well that by 1500 most of the yeomen gilds had become merely adjuncts to the craft gilds. In Scotland no such development took place since the craft gilds appeared relatively late and never knew such differences between the master and the journeyman.

Simultaneous with the organization of the yeoman gilds, there took place the establishment of what was known as the "livery company." While the yeoman gild was made up of the "lower crust," the livery was made up of the "upper crust" of the gild. Those who constituted this group were usually men who had given up the practice of their craft in order to concentrate on trade. They dealt only in finished goods and were usually the wealthier and more enterprising members. On the other hand, they might represent a gild which had originally occupied itself with finishing the articles of other gilds, as in the case of the Drapers.[3] But whatever their origin, they frequently obtained a monopoly of the trade, for they were the ones who sold outside the local market. They therefore could set prices and could determine quality. Like the craft gilds, they organized themselves under a charter of incorporation from the crown and were governed by a master or mayor and a court of assistants. In London the twelve livery companies not only chose the mayor of the city but also wielded considerable political

---

[3] The Drapers probably commenced as shearmen, who finished cloth by raising and cutting the nap. Very soon they gave up the actual work, leaving it to hired labor, while they devoted themselves to marketing the finished article.

power by virtue of their ability to lend money to the crown.[4] They were therefore able to bring industry under their control, virtually putting the craft gilds out of business. The gild system thus tended to break down from internal economic and social divisions as well as from external (municipal) pressure.

It was not, however, merely these local influences which tended to cause the gilds' disintegration. Their collapse was a symptom and a result of much greater changes which had been taking place since the beginning of the fourteenth century. A rise in prices which, owing to the expansion of trade, had commenced before 1300 had been greatly accelerated by the Black Death. Craftsmen were demanding higher wages to meet the greatly increased cost of living, thus accentuating the conflicts within the gilds. The price rise had, on the other hand, also acted as a stimulus to trade, and as trade expanded the old order could not but change. The gild methods of production, based upon the concept of a small potential market, were simply out of date. Gild restrictions and limitations had to be ignored if the possibilities of the rapidly expanding economy were to be exploited. Thus, while at first meeting a real economic need, the gild system by 1500 was on the way out, for it was no longer suitable to the new state of affairs.

The Growth of Trade

Trade before 1400 was generally interurban. Merchants who traveled abroad always conducted their business as merchants of London, Winchester, Rouen, Caen, or Antwerp, not of England, France, or Flanders. The reason for this was that each town was an economic unit in itself. Since the local market was limited and privileges were obtained only on payment of money, anyone not a native of the town was regarded as a potential interloper. This was true not only of the French or Scots coming to Norwich, but also of men from Southampton trading in London or Bristol. From about 1350 on, however, this attitude began to break down. The national state was developing. In Scotland's fight for her independence (1296-1328), the merchants, who had taken a considerable part in the struggle, had arrived at a deeper realization of their common Scottish nationality. What is more, from early times Berwick,

---

[4] The twelve companies were: Mercers, who dealt in merceries, such as linen, canvas, and silk; Grocers, who dealt in wholesale imports of spices and drugs; Drapers, Fishmongers, Goldsmiths, Skinners, Merchant Tailors, Haberdashers, Salters, Ironmongers, Vintners, and Clothmakers.

Stirling, Roxburgh, and Edinburgh had formed the Court of the Four Burghs, becoming a sort of central organization for the Scottish towns. Out of this court had come a set of laws which were regarded as binding for the Scottish burghs in general. These laws were national rather than local. In Ireland, largely owing to the fact that they were inhabited by people of English descent who were inclined to be anti-Irish, the towns formed some sort of a league. In England, the Hundred Years' War, the extension of royal authority, and the growth of trade, all tended to have the effect of unifying the interests of the towns so by the end of the Middle Ages national rather than local patriotism was dominant. Thus, generally speaking, by 1500 trade had become international rather than interurban.

The principal places of trade apart from the craftsmen's shop were either the market or fair. The market was usually held weekly, when people from the surrounding country brought their produce into town for sale. They were carefully watched by the town authorities, who made them pay tolls and forced them to do business with none but burgesses. Only those towns granted in their charters the privilege of holding a market could do so. In Scotland this successfully limited legal markets to royal burghs until the middle of the fifteenth century. Not infrequently market towns were required to pay a special farm to their feudal lord for this profitable perquisite.

More important, although less common than markets, were fairs, probably originating accidentally in the gathering of people together to celebrate a saint's day. But by the time that there are records of their existence, they appear to have been rather well organized. Their existence was usually sanctioned by a royal charter, although the owner might be a lord, a cleric, or a church. They were as a rule held once a year, opening on some saint's day and continuing for a fixed length of time, up to one, two, or three weeks. The town at which a fair was held, ceased all ordinary business during its activities, even the municipal government being surrendered to the fair's owner. Outside the town's precincts were set up stalls and booths which were assigned to the various crafts and traders. Certain fees were charged for the use of the facilities, for the use of the fair seal to guarantee bargains, and also for the right to buy and sell. When these had been paid everyone could carry on his business freely. A special court, known as "pie powder" court, from the name *pied poudré* ("dusty foot") applied to traveling merchants, was set up to deal quickly with any disputes according to the universally accepted principles of merchant law.⁵ By this means trade was facilitated, for it protected the traveling merchant from abuse, guaranteed his transactions, and even provided security for the payment of debts. The fair was thus an enormous help to commerce in days of no little public insecurity.

In England there were numerous fairs, bringing in varied sums to their owners. In 1282 the one at Manchester yielded £6 13s. 4d. Bradford in 1311 brought in £6, while in 1190 St. Giles paid £146. The principal English fairs were: St. Ives, founded in 1110 and lasting eight days after Easter Monday, dealing mostly in hides, wool and cloth; St. Giles, Winchester, founded about 1090 and taking place from August 31 to September 15, retailing cloth, wool and French goods; St. Bartholomew, Smithfield in London, founded in 1133, dealing in cloth; Stourbridge, founded by King John, dealing in costly cloth of gold, embroidery, and other continental produce; St. Botolph, founded in 1200 and selling primarily cloth and food. Thus England from quite early times possessed a mechanism by which she could exchange her goods for those of foreigners, although by 1500 other means of trade were causing the fairs to fall into disuse.

In the early part of the period (1066-1300) the foreign trade of the British Isles was largely in the hands of continental merchants. They visited mainly the port towns, especially those lying along the east and south coasts from the mouth of the Thames north to Aberdeen and west to Bristol and Cardiff. There was also a certain amount of continental trade with the Irish towns of Cork, Wexford, Waterford, and Dublin.

One of the earliest racial groups to trade in England was that of the Jews. Sir Walter Scott's picture of the Jewish merchant in *Ivanhoe* gives us a description of his position in the community. Being also money lenders, Jews were extremely unpopular so that they were expelled from the country by Edward I. They never showed much interest in Scotland. From the beginning of the reign of Richard I the Italians gradually grew in importance, their power reaching its highest point early in the fourteenth century. Since 1170 they had been collecting papal revenues, usually in wool, which they exported to Italy for manufacture. They also became financial advisers to the crown, frequently lending the king money. When, however, Edward III refused to honor his obliga-

---

⁵ Merchant Law was a body of mercantile law common to the nations of western Europe in the Middle Ages. It was founded on the customs of the merchants and was set forth in a number of different codes, the most famous being the Laws of Oléron. The matters dealt with included the collection of debts, the sale of goods, and the transfer of money by means of bills of exchange.

tions, the Bardi, Peruzzi, and Frescobaldi and other Italian financiers were hard hit, some of them even being forced into bankruptcy. Another group of Italians then took over. These were the Venetians, who began to send trading galleys from Venice to Flanders, one being dispatched to Southampton, Sandwich, and London on the way. This practice continued until 1532.

More important than either Jews or Italians, however, were the merchants from northern Europe: Germany and Flanders. The German merchants came at first from Cologne, but later from the Baltic cities of Lübeck and Stralsund. In the beginning they came as individual merchants, but before long they established an organization of North German cities known as the Hanseatic League which carried on business until the time of Elizabeth. The League had factories or depots at such places as Bergen in Norway, Bruges in Flanders, Novgorod in Russia, and also in London. The London factory, known as the "Steelyard," was a veritable fort, with the merchants in it living more like soldiers than men of commerce. Other groups of Hanseatic merchants were settled in such east coast ports as Lynn, Boston, and Hull, while still others, even prior to 1290, were carrying on trade with Scotland. Traders from northern France had an organization in London similar to that of the Germans. Both these groups were able to obtain privileges from the crown because of their wealth. They loaned money to the kings, paying in return reduced customs duties and obtaining the freedom to retail throughout the country along with the right to reside anywhere they pleased. These were considerable privileges for that time. By such means foreign merchants dominated the medieval foreign commerce of the British Isles.

Despite the need for the aliens, they were not popular with the native merchants. The towns, particularly London, placed every possible obstacle in their way. It was partly because of this that the Germans and Flemings set up their fortified factories for protection. Although the foreigners had powerful allies, such as the king, who before 1350 was dependent upon them for loans, and the feudal aristocracy, who were their customers, they still had to fight the native merchants. The latter attempted to take a profit from all foreign wares, insisted that foreigners could sell only wholesale, and endeavored to limit a foreigner's residence in the country to forty days. As a result of baronial support, however, the foreign merchants received from Edward I the *Carta Mercatoria* (1303), which guaranteed them personal freedom, exempted them from municipal taxes, promised quick action before the courts, and partially opened up the retail trade. Customs duties on exports were later reduced, so the Hansards, for instance, paid less than natives.[6] As the English merchants increased in wealth, however, they also increased in political influence and were gradually able to force a limitation of the foreigners' privileges. By the middle of the fifteenth century aliens were being severely restricted, while a century later, during the reign of Elizabeth, even the Hanseatic League lost its special rights. Royal dependence on their wealth gave the native traders ever-increasing power to curtail their foreign competitors' activities.

In Scotland the story was somewhat different. Disturbed political conditions between 1300 and 1450 had caused the foreigners to lose interest in the country's trade, leaving it to be carried on almost entirely by natives.

Mention has been made a number of times of the rise of native merchants. Throughout the Middle Ages there were always traders who were Scots, Irish, or English. William of Doncaster, an early merchant of Cheshire, is a good example. He sold wool to Flanders, imported grain from Ireland, and was customs collector for the king. There were likewise Scottish merchants trading with the Continent as well as with England and Ireland. While these men dealt on a limited scale at first, as commerce expanded they became increasingly important. During the fourteenth century the English merchant so increased his wealth and power that when the crown found itself in need of funds to carry on the Hundred Years' War it turned to him for help. As early as 1256 the towns' representatives had been called to take part in the English Parliament, in order to grant special taxes beyond stated feudal requirements. The same class of men first appeared in the Scottish Estates in 1326, after they had played a considerable part in the War of Independence. It is not surprising, therefore, that by the beginning of the fifteenth century merchants such as the de la Pole family were rising into the ranks of the nobility. A century later the English merchant, with increasing political influence, was pretty well in control of the situation throughout England, Wales, and

[6] The Hansards were particularly favored, being required to pay customs duty of only 1¼ per cent ad valorem and being given complete freedom in the country. The customs duties required on cloth were:

	English Merchants	Hansards	Other Merchants
Dyed cloth	28d.	24d.	66d. (12d. subsidy)
Half dyed cloth	21d.	18d.	49d. "
Undyed cloth	14d.	12d.	33d. "

E. Lipson, Introduction to the Economic History of England (London, 1926), Vol. I, p. 466.

Ireland, while in Scotland his economic counterpart was rising to a similar place of power.

To understand how he attained this position it is necessary to know something of the goods he exchanged. The imports were of two types. There were, first of all, raw materials unobtainable in the British Isles. From the Baltic came wood, amber, iron, furs, and naval stores, such as tar. From the Mediterranean area came spices, some wines, particularly from Greece, and fruit, such as figs. The spices were especially important, as they were needed to preserve and also to disguise the taste of the meat, which by spring had often begun to putrefy. The second class of goods was made up of manufactures, among numerous other items being fine cloths, jewels, glass, and iron and steel products, such as knives, armor, and Spanish swords. French wine, particularly claret from Bordeaux, was also imported in large quantities. In return for such goods there were exported fish, particularly from Scotland, some tin, alabaster, coal, and even butter and eggs. Scotland also seems to have built ships to sell abroad. Most important of all, however, was the export of wool, woolfells, hides, and from England after 1350, cloth. It was upon these latter commodities that the wealth of both the English and Scottish merchants was built. The Scots, however, although their wool exports were extremely important in the country's commerce, never attained either the opulence or the organization of their English competitors.

The wool trade, which goes back to pre-Norman days, was very important, for wool was the principal material from which clothing was made. From 1200 on England and Scotland were the main sources of supply, both large and small farmers as well as many monasteries being engaged in raising sheep. At first the large farmer might buy up the smaller peasant's wool to sell to an exporter, perhaps to a Fleming or an Italian, but once the small farmer began to interest himself seriously in wool production, merchant middlemen appeared. Usually Englishmen or Scots, they would travel around the country, buying up the wool in small quantities to sell later in bulk to the foreign merchant. Many of these woolmen became very wealthy, and not a few began either to export for themselves or to enter into partnership with aliens. It has been estimated that by 1273 the English merchants controlled about 35 per cent of the trade. A large part of the Scottish wool probably was included in this, for the Scots seem to have found their biggest market in England. By 1300 wool exports had reached their peak.

Meanwhile certain changes had been taking place in the wool

trade itself. For one thing, there grew up in London a group of wealthy English wool exporters who obtained a virtual monopoly of the trade. They, along with some foreigners, were becoming the bankers of the crown. Not infrequently parliament would grant the king a subsidy or tax *in* wool, which would have to be sold. The king would commit the business of disposing of the wool to these men, who were sometimes known as "the King's Merchants" or the Merchants of the Staple (market). Before long taxes *on* wool had also become common, but they were hard to collect when wool was being exported from more than a dozen ports. Therefore, in 1294-97 Edward I, to facilitate the collection of customs and to raise a forced loan, tried to have all wool shipped to Dordrecht, and later to Antwerp. It was not compulsory, but those who complied with the king's wishes were given various privileges, among which was the right to organize into an association called the Merchants of the Staple with a mayor and a court. In 1313, to help collect revenue and to prevent goods from going to the Scots during the Anglo-Scottish wars Edward II established a compulsory staple at St. Omer. Thereafter the Staple was the usual organ of wool export, sometimes located at home, sometimes in a continental city, and from 1392 to 1557 at Calais, a French city in English possession. In this, its final location, the merchants were organized into the Company of Merchant Staplers of Calais with a monopoly of the nation's wool export, paying in return heavy taxes. The Scots after 1500 tried to imitate the English plan, but were not so successful, since their trade was not as great.

While the English Staple, through its monopoly and price fixing, made it easier for the crown to collect taxes, it undoubtedly restricted the wool trade. This, along with the fact that England was beginning to manufacture her own cloth, caused, as early as 1300, a decline in the amount of wool shipped abroad. Even by 1100 woolens were being made in Yorkshire, Gloucester, Somerset, and Hampshire, while in Norfolk and the surrounding shires the finer worsteds were the staple manufacture. In 1197, a law known as the Assize of Cloth had laid down regulations for the maintenance of proper standards of workmanship, and before 1200 cloth was being exported in small quantities. Since, however, it was not the best grade of cloth, it was at this time of no great importance.

The fourteenth century saw a considerable change in the organization of the industry. Owing to the desire to have English cloth instead of the less valuable wool sold on the Continent, English kings began to encourage in various ways the immigration of European weavers and cloth finishers. In 1331 John Kempe, a Fleming, arrived with a group of workers, and others soon followed. The coming of these foreigners, who refused to join the native gilds, began to break down the old craft system. The country people also, wherever wool was easily obtainable, were beginning to weave in their own homes. But they did no fulling or shearing, processes carried out by professional cloth finishers who purchased their product. Unprotected by gild regulations, these weavers soon came under the control of the finishers, or clothiers, who required them to make their cloth according to specification and usually to sell it at a fixed price. Before long the clothiers began to provide the wool as well as to collect the finished goods. Then, having had the cloth fulled and sheared, they took it to London or some other center, where, usually in a hall set apart for the purpose, they would sell to foreign merchants or more often to the town cloth merchants or drapers. Not infrequently the drapers also were in the habit of going around the country purchasing cloth which they themselves finished. This all meant that the town craftsmen were losing business to their country competitors, the old gild being gradually supplanted in the cloth industry by what was known as the domestic or "putting-out" system.

The drapers, who were also the exporters, really controlled the industry, for they handled the ultimate sale of the goods, which enabled them to regulate the export trade. Some think that the drapers were originally Merchant Staplers, but this is not certain. They dealt only in such nonstaple goods as cloth, both white and colored, and at times in hardware. When they organized is unknown, but by 1360 the London cloth exporters were called the Merchants Adventuring to the Low Countries, and there were apparently similar organizations in other towns, such as Bristol. Because the London group tried to control the cloth export of the whole country, its members came into frequent conflict with the "out-port" merchants, who insisted either on their freedom or on a voice in the conduct of the London company's affairs. By 1500 the London Adventurers, having admitted out-port traders, had a virtual monopoly of the trade and were also being used by the crown to collect the 2 per cent customs duty on cloth, levied since 1347. Their rise to power can perhaps best be seen in the increase of the export of cloths from 5,000 in 1355 to 85,000 in 1509, while the wool exports decreased from 30,000 to 7,500 sacks in the same period. Cloth instead of wool was now the master.

The Development of Capitalism

Parallel to and stemming from the development of trade were the beginnings of the accumulation of money for investment, or capitalism. The earliest capitalists seem to have been foreigners: Jews, then Italians and Flemings, who had made their money elsewhere by means of commerce and loans. Although the taking of interest was considered unlawful, Jews were permitted to do so, since it was not contrary to their religion.[7] The Italians, on the other hand, invented ways of getting around the church's prohibition. These businessmen invested not only in English goods, such as wool, but also loaned money to the crown, to nobles, and to ecclesiastical institutions. Sometimes they would buy up all the wool of a monastery for the next fifteen years, paying cash immediately. This was, of course, risky, but the conditions on which they purchased usually covered every possibility of crop failure.

By 1250 the native businessmen also began to accumulate capital. Their appearance in parliament to provide special taxation from their own class shows their growing wealth. Among these men were two types of capitalist: the industrialist and the merchant, although lines of demarcation are not always clear. The first type was either a gildsman or someone involved in cloth production. The members of the goldsmiths' gild, for instance, from the nature of their business accumulated substantial amounts of bullion in their coffers. They were willing also to keep on deposit, for a fee, other people's money. Soon they discovered that it might be profitable to loan this money out at interest. Here was the beginning of banking based upon industry or trade and bringing large profits. On the other hand in the country districts the entrepreneur, or "enterpriser," was hiring weavers to work for him in their own houses. Under this capitalistic plan, for example, one clothier at Barnstaple produced 1080 and another 1005 narrow cloths in a year. All this required, but it also increased, capital. In the same way the masters in the town gilds, by bringing all retail selling into their own hands, were gaining a greater monopoly of town industry. In these ways industrial capitalism had its medieval beginnings.

Trade, however, was the most important source of accumulated wealth. Therefore the masters of the gilds who had obtained control of their industries tended to give up working themselves in order to become merchants. In Scotland before they could take

[7] See Chapter 4.

this step they had publicly to surrender their craft tools. Out of this group came the livery companies already mentioned. The members were primarily interested in trade and, in fact, often belonged to two or three livery companies at the same time. Allied with them were the wool and cloth merchants. By 1350 they had all become involved in private and public finance through the granting of loans to nobles, ecclesiastics, and kings. In Scotland, although the merchants were not nearly so wealthy, by 1500 the same thing was taking place through the activities of such traders as Robert Barton of Over Barnton. Some of the leading English financiers were William and Richard de la Pole from Hull, Roger de Conduit, Sir John Pultney of the London Drapers' Company and Henry Picard of the Vintner's Company. In the fourteenth and fifteenth centuries many of these men, through loans to the crown, made great fortunes rapidly, but when on occasion the kings failed to repay, they lost them just as quickly. To protect themselves from such misfortunes the merchants organized as companies, giving loans in return for privileges. This was one of the reasons why the Merchants of the Staple developed such political power after 1350 and why, a little later, the Merchant Adventurers became important. Thus by 1500 through the growth of industry, the expansion of trade, and the increased opportunity for investment in Britain, particularly in England, one finds a well-developed capitalism.

The Government and Economic Affairs

As mentioned at the beginning of the chapter, the state never completely lost its control of the town. Instead, as the kingdom developed and as trade increasingly became national rather than urban, so commerce became more and more a matter of state concern. In England even by the reign of Richard I (1189-99), laws were enacted regulating the sizes and qualities of cloth, and shortly afterward, to see that they were enforced, an official known as the *aulnager* was appointed. Although the merchants who did not like such controls sometimes succeeded in having them suspended, they were usually reimposed, the last being reintroduced in 1411. While endeavoring to control the native workmen and merchants, Parliament was also continually trying to attract to the Kingdom foreign merchants and artisans. To further this plan, some of the English kings favored staple ports in England, and one of the Scottish kings even forbade his own merchants to go abroad. The *Statute of Merchants* (1283) and the *Carta Mercatoria* (1303) both granted large privileges to alien businessmen. The purpose of these laws was to entice merchants who would buy goods, especially wool. As the cloth industry grew, however, and as native capitalists emerged, policies changed. Alien textile workers were still encouraged to settle in the country, but the export of wool was discouraged, and at length even forbidden, since the sale of cloth was more profitable than the sale of wool. At the same time, the state discouraged the purchase of competing foreign goods, especially cloth. Coupled with this, to prevent foreigners receiving profits from freight charges Richard II forbade foreign goods to be imported in any ships but those of England or the country of the goods' origin. The point of this was that the English kings were striving to bring gold and silver into the land by having the country sell more goods and services than it bought. In this way the store of treasure would be increased, and the government, so they thought, would find it easier to finance its operations.

The difficulties of national finance caused the government to think that a large store of bullion was necessary. Originally the king had been the greatest landowner in the country and also the owner of its mineral deposits. It was expected that, supported by income from his own lands and aided by his chief feudal vassals along with their armed retainers, he would be able to rule the country without difficulty. By the fourteenth century this was not true. As industry and trade developed, money became more plentiful, and prices began to rise. Among other things, this made wars more expensive. To meet this situation Henry II, instead of accepting military service from his knights, had found it more profitable to take payments of *scutage* (shield money), with which he hired soldiers who were directly under his control. But this was not sufficient, for in the fourteenth century both the kings of England and Scotland fell into serious financial difficulties. Robert the Bruce was practically beggared by the War of Independence, while somewhat later Edward III of England found it a real problem to supply men, ships, and the "new-fangled" cannon for his fighting in France. The kings, therefore, were forced to seek large increases in their revenues.

The original revenues of the crown consisted, first of all, of the produce of the royal manors. There were also "casualties," made up of certain aids and fines which the king could claim on specified occasions. He could, for instance, demand that his vassals help pay his ransom if he were captured. When his eldest son was to be knighted another present was expected. If a vassal died his heir had to pay a sum for the right of inheriting the land, and if the heir were a minor the king could take over the land and draw the revenues for his own use until the child came of age. The royal boroughs in both Scotland and England were supposed to pay similar dues to the crown, but usually these were commuted at the granting of the town charter to a fixed yearly sum. During the latter part of the Middle Ages these sums, established at twelfth or thirteenth century levels, declined rapidly in value.

The collectors of the royal revenues were still the sheriffs. In the early days they would gather the produce from the royal manors and boroughs, pay off any royal bills in the shire, and either reserve the balance until the court came and ate it or ship it to the king. As this was all very inconvenient, even in William I's reign, the sheriffs were given the job of selling the produce and paying the revenues in money. Sometimes they themselves would "farm the tax." They would contract with the king to pay a prescribed sum, usually less than the estimated return, so that if the sale of the produce came to more, they made a large profit. In such transactions, capitalism often had a beginning. The sheriffs' position gave them very great power over the towns also, until the granting of charters made the municipalities directly responsible to the Exchequer. This latter body was the accounting department of the royal treasury. Before it the sheriffs and town representatives appeared twice a year, and across a table covered by a checkered table cloth with squares denoting pounds, shilling, and pence, they paid their money or showed receipts for sums expended on behalf of the king.

While the government's disbursements, particularly in time of war, increased, the amounts paid in by the sheriffs became gradually smaller and smaller. The result was that direct taxation began to take the place of aids and dues in an effort to augment the royal revenues. Thus Richard I, in order to pay the expenses of a crusade, obtained from the pope a grant of a tithe of all movable goods. Later, on his way home from the East he was captured, and his people had to pay for his ransom a quarter of the value of their movables. Edward I (1336), following the idea of Richard's "Saladin tithe," obtained the consent of Parliament for the permanent establishment of a tax of $\frac{1}{15}$ on movables in the country and $\frac{1}{10}$ in the towns. At first the goods taxed were evaluated anew each time the taxes were granted, but soon the estimated income was calculated at £38,000, a fixed proportion being assigned to each shire. Thereafter, when Parliament voted taxes, it always did so in multiples or fractions of tenths and fifteenths.

A second source of increased state revenues was customs duties.

The king, by the right of "prise," could take a portion of every cargo which came into his country's ports. By 1215 it also had been computed into a regular set sum of money. Whether imported or exported, ½ mark was paid on every sack of wool, 1 mark on a last (a gross) of hides, and 3d. on a pound of lead or tin, while the prise of one or two casks per cargo of wine was continued as before. In Scotland much the same method was followed. The goods were stamped to show that the duty had been paid. Edward I tried to increase the duties, even imposing as much as 40s. per sack of wool. But to do so he was forced to obtain Parliament's consent, a procedure which gave that body considerable power over the government's revenues. These "customary" charges were known as the *antiqua custuma*, while special customs, applicable after 1303 only to foreigners, were called the *nova custuma* and brought considerably higher returns. Naturally, as trade increased, so customs revenues rose, providing another way in which the crown could obtain more money.

A third method of augmenting revenues was the use of the crown's legal power and jurisdiction. Henry II discovered how to employ this profitably. His courts, which used the jury system, usually gave fairer trials than did the feudal judges. Citizens therefore desired to take cases to the royal justices, a proceeding which the kings favored, in return, of course, for a consideration.[8]

Another, and much less respectable, way in which the royal prerogative was employed to increase income was in minting coin. If people brought silver or gold to the minters for coining, they had to pay for the privilege, the fee going to the crown. After 1300, however, the crown began to decrease the amount of silver in what was originally Canute's silver penny, until by 1527 it had dropped from 22½ to 10½ grains, although the face value remained the same. This meant that the crown, to its own profit, succeeded in doubling the amount of coin in circulation. Normally prices would have skyrocketed, but because the production of goods was steadily climbing and trade was expanding there was an increasing demand for coinage. As a result, this devaluation did not have any great effect upon the price level until the sixteenth century, but it did enable the crown to obtain more funds.

A fifth means by which the crown obtained money was through loans. As already pointed out, in the early days of the Norman régime Jews and Italians had been the principal sources of such income. As the English merchants increased in wealth, however, they were able to perform the same services. After the "stop of the

[8] G. B. Adams, *The Constitutional History of England*, p. 105 f.

'Chequer' " in 1343, when Edward III's failure to pay ruined his
Italian creditors, English merchants took over, and by 1350 they
had become the crown's principal bankers. But they did not loan
money merely out of the goodness of their hearts. They usually
received certain taxes or customs duties in pledge. These "securities" always brought in sums larger than the original loans themselves, so the lenders were happy while, at the same time, the loans
met the needs of the crown for the moment, which was the important thing. Another type of loan employed was the "forced
loan." This was particularly common in the reign of Henry VII,
who employed two officials, Dudley and Empeson, to collect such
moneys. It was said that if any one spent much, the collectors felt
that he had a large amount out of which he could give some to the
king. On the other hand, if one did not spend much, he must be
very saving, and likewise could contribute to the king's needs. It
was, "Heads I win, tails you lose." The method was successful, for
when Henry VII died in 1509 he left a full treasury. On the other
hand, when his son-in-law the King of Scotland died four years
later he left a country in serious financial straits. He was neither
as unscrupulous as Henry VII nor did he have such wealthy merchants who could help meet his need for large sums of money.

Thus, at the close of the Middle Ages the economic situation
was very different from what it had been in 1066. Towns had
grown up, industry had developed, and commerce had increased
to such an extent that men were standing on the threshold of a
new world—the modern world. Yet one must never forget that the
principal employment of people was still agriculture. Even the
wealthy merchant, once he had made his fortune, invested it in a
manor which would bring him good returns and establish his social
position in the country. The purchase of land was still the best
and most secure investment. What is more, the large landowner
was still more common than the very wealthy merchant. The economic balance had begun to change, but the beam had by no
means tipped in the direction of an industrial and commercial
economy. It was swinging that way, but time had to pass, bringing
new ideas and forces to light, before Britain could become the
"workshop of the world."

Hand in hand with the economic changes went a change in the
balance of social and economic power. By virtue of their wealth
the merchants were increasing in social prestige, marrying into
noble families, and even obtaining titles themselves. With this
went a parallel growth in their political influence, aided by the fact
that much of the country's liquid wealth was in their hands. To

them the nobles had to turn for loans, and to them the king had to come when he needed financial aid. The new commercial middle class was in this way moving into a position of hitherto unknown power. Therein, however, lay a danger for the crown's prerogatives, for, although the relations of crown and nobles were by 1500 rather clearly defined, up to this point the question of the middle class's position had not been fully considered. With this increase in its power, however, new problems arose, for although the crown might control the situation by skilled diplomacy, if a monarch should arise who would ignore this new but powerful element, there would be great danger of a conflagration, in which the monarchy might be destroyed.

Chapter 7

THE CHANGING ECONOMIC OUTLOOK

The period between the years 1485 and 1715 is in reality one of transition. It was the time when England and Scotland both changed from a medieval to a modern form of economy. This development or evolution went hand in hand with political, social, religious and intellectual changes, so it is not an isolated phenomenon. It took place gradually, imperceptibly, and by fits and starts. The Protestant Reformation, the Reign of Elizabeth, the Puritan Revolution, the final establishment of parliamentary supremacy under William and Mary, and the eventual union of England and Scotland, all had their impact upon the economic thinking and action of the people. In turn, the economic forces which were in operation wielded a very considerable influence over the political, social, and intellectual movements of the day. Thus, it is not always easy to separate cause from effect, or the political and social from the economic forces. But in order to make some attempt to understand what happened it is necessary to see how, during the two centuries between the accession of Henry VII and the death of Queen Anne, the general economic outlook of the people in Britain was modified.

The Forces of Change

In order to evaluate the reasons for the transformation of economic thinking it is necessary to place them in two different categories. In the first place, there are what might be called general forces of change acting in noneconomic fields. These have an indirect influence upon economic activity or they enter the field of economic thought and action only at certain points. There are, on the other hand, forces of change within the sphere of economic operation acting directly upon the economic activities of the time. In order to understand the changing economic outlook of the so-called "mercantilist period" one must analyze the various influences which were exerted.

The first of the general forces of change was the Renaissance, a movement which grew out of the Middle Ages. Its great drive was an interest in man himself, as pictured in Greek and Roman antiquity, particularly in art and literature. At first the movement was inside the medieval church, an attempt being made to use classical forms to set forth medieval Christian ideals. But before very long the paganism of the Greek and Roman examples began to gain the upper hand. The classical stress upon the autonomy of man began to turn men away from the church, resulting in an increased emphasis upon the free individual and his abilities. Before long many of the Renaissance thinkers, even when they used a Christian veneer for their thoughts and were prepared to submit to the church in matters theological, were devoting most of their thought and time to the study of man and to a certain extent of physical nature. While giving lip-service to God, they for all practical purposes ignored Him. Machiavelli, Benvenuto Cellini and to a lesser extent Galileo, are perhaps good examples of such thinking. Others, such as da Vinci and Michelangelo, while probably more orthodox, were nevertheless strongly influenced by the humanism of their own day.

Another movement which had a considerable influence upon the thinking of the period was the Protestant Reformation. With its focal points in Luther's Wittenberg and Calvin's Geneva, this movement took a different direction from that of the Renaissance. Its stress was laid not upon classical paganism but upon the Bible. In the teaching of Calvin, particularly, men were told that they could have immediate fellowship with God apart from the intervention of priest, saint, or sacrament. They could hear God speaking to them in the Bible and could find forgiveness of sins through simple faith in Christ as Saviour. The organized church was necessary as a teaching and disciplinary agency, but membership in this "visible" church was not essential for salvation. The individual could, by faith, have direct access into God's presence.

The spread of these ideas was particularly rapid where there had already grown up a certain amount of individualism, as in the Low Countries, western Germany, parts of Switzerland, and the British Isles. The emphasis laid upon the individual's direct relationship to God and upon his duty to serve God in the place and work to which he was called in everyday life met a deeply felt need. In central Germany and the Scandinavian countries Lutheranism was predominant, but in the western part of the Continent, western Germany, Holland, and sections of France, Reformed or Calvinistic churches were the most numerous. Although in England the church outwardly was more closely allied with Lutheranism and even Roman Catholicism, doctrinally, as represented in the Thirty-Nine Articles, it was strongly Calvinistic. In Scotland Calvinism was very strong, producing a Reformed-Presbyterian form of doctrine and polity.

Leaving the realm of the philosophical and the theological, another influence of a general nature was geographic discovery. In 1492 Columbus discovered the Caribbean Islands and two years later John Cabot, representing Bristol merchants, landed on the American mainland. In 1497 Vasco da Gama, on the other side of the world, reached India. English interest in these efforts was considerable, although at first little was done to exploit the new lands. During the reign of Elizabeth, Hakluyt and others stirred up enthusiasm for colonies by their writings, while the search for gold and exotic goods offered tangible rewards for imperialism. As a result, during the seventeenth and eighteenth centuries England established a great empire. The building of this "Old Empire" in turn brought about great changes in economic methods, particularly in finance. At the same time it widened men's vision of the world and its products, helping to break down the regionalism of the Middle Ages.

A second type of influential discovery was in the field of the natural sciences. To this both the Renaissance and Reformation contributed. The medieval idea of the all-prevalent miracle was put aside. The world of nature was to be studied for itself, the results of the researches to be applied to the world in which man lives. As a consequence of the efforts of such scientists as Galileo, Descartes, van Huygens, Newton and others much information was accumulated concerning the physical world. Laws of mechanics, hydrostatics, optics and the like were formulated. The telescope, the thermometer, the barometer and even a rudimentary steam engine were all invented. But probably more important for economic thinking than the inventions and the formulation of physical laws was the gradual acceptance of the idea of Natural Law itself. Everything existing had a natural cause or causes which could be discovered and whose effects could be measured. This idea was applied not merely to physics and chemistry but, as time passed, it was to gain increasing currency in economic thinking until finally economists elevated their subject to the status of a science.

Besides the noneconomic factors already mentioned, there were others: wars and rumors of wars, political upheavals, and conflicts.

In fact, the whole historical development of the time influenced and was influenced by economic thought and action. But of even greater importance for our purpose were the specifically economic forces which were in operation. Here one comes down to the basic drives in the economic development.

To understand the economic history of the Tudor and Stuart period (1485-1715), it is necessary to realize that most of the economic organization and ideas of those two centuries found their origins in the Middle Ages. There was, for instance, capitalism. Some historians have felt that this was a post-Reformation phenomenon. The fact of the matter is, however, that by 1300 both capitalistic techniques and the capitalistic outlook were well developed in certain circles on the Continent, and, as has been seen, they became quite common in both England and Scotland during the fourteenth and fifteenth centuries.[1] The wool trade, and then the manufacture and export of cloth, laid the foundations. Then came the wealthy merchant looking for opportunities to invest his money. Later, with the stimulus of new-found lands, an expanding population which meant increased consumption, and a growing tendency toward individualism, a further development of capitalism was to be expected. Opportunities for investment in new and costlier ventures increased greatly, along with the hope that they would bring back larger profits. Thus, the primary factor in the economic development of the early modern period was medieval capitalism, inherited and expanded by the new generation.

But the increase of capitalism made certain demands upon business organization. Credit and banking facilities were still relatively simple and crude. While accounting had improved with the advent of double-entry bookkeeping, probably in the fifteenth century, large accumulations of funds were difficult to establish unless one hoarded treasure in gold and silver. This was difficult, since in the Middle Ages bullion was scarce. There was really too little specie to cover all the financial transactions involved in medieval commerce. Consequently, everybody was seeking gold and silver. Laws were passed to prevent its leaving a country. Even towns banned its export and required foreign merchants to spend their profits on local goods. What was needed was either more specie or a better credit system.

The immediate answer given was to provide more specie. During the fifteenth century the silver deposits of the Tyrol were exploited more fully and systematically than ever before, placing an increased amount of bullion at the disposal of the merchant and

[1] See page 111 f.

industrialist. But of far greater importance was the influx of Spanish-American gold and silver, particularly after the discovery in 1545
of the silver mine at Potosi. As prices rose in Spain because of the
importation of bullion, Holland, France, and England began selling
larger and larger quantities of goods to the Spaniards. What they
received in return was Spanish gold and silver money. The resulting
inflation meant a rise in prices in their own markets and a corresponding stimulus to business. This, in turn, tended to overthrow
many of the old concepts of control and restraint inherited from
the Middle Ages and preached by the Reformation. Instead, the
humanistic ideal of self-expression and self-enjoyment began to have
a growing number of devotees. Although the price rise might mean
virtual disaster for the man on low wages, for the man at the top,
business began to boom.

Along with these economic changes went an extension of the
power of the civil government. The rise of the national state in
the latter part of the Middle Ages meant not only the breakdown of
the old ideal of the unity of Europe under a Roman Empire, but
also the loss of urban autonomy. In the British Isles the towns had
never possessed the freedom of many of their continental counterparts. But what freedom they had possessed was drastically curtailed by both Tudor and Stuart monarchs. Throughout the islands
there appeared an increasingly national rather than an urban concept of economic policy. Since all economic activity was to be
judged by its usefulness to the state, it was to be kept under rigid
governmental control.

This policy was being forced on the state partially because of its
enlarged responsibilities. For one thing war was now a very expensive matter and could not be carried on by a few towns. Large
financial resources were needed for a prolonged campaign. Then
too, there was the problem presented by unemployment and poverty, while supervision of trade regulations also required a larger
and better paid civil service. All these things, in turn, demanded
higher expenditures by the state. No longer were feudal revenues,
supplemented by occasional taxes, enough to meet even ordinary demands on the Exchequer. A regular income had to be obtained
from other sources and in the form of money. To this end taxation
was increased, a more efficient method of collection developed, and
any other possible source of revenue exploited.

One of the "other sources" was the church, which in England,
Ireland and Scotland was regarded by impecunious rulers during
the sixteenth century as fair game. Henry VIII dissolved and expropriated the monasteries, and his son, Edward VI, did the same

to the chantries (lands held for religious purposes by the gilds). In both these cases the crown made money, Henry VIII perhaps £1,000,000 and Edward VI about £100,000. Elizabeth mulcted the bishops in every way possible. In Scotland, although the monasteries were not dissolved, all the clergy were heavily taxed, with much the same result. Besides the money obtained in this way, an important effect of the crown's action in both countries was that a considerable proportion of the church's lands was thrown onto the market just as prices were beginning to rise. Since the church owned about one third of the land in England and close to one half in Scotland, it is easy to estimate the effect of this move. The land was bought up very rapidly by people desiring to make money either from increased rents or a quick resale, so that by 1600 much of the country's real estate had been redistributed. In this way the Reformation, along with the new concept of the state and its ruler, was employed by poverty-stricken monarchs as an excuse for raids upon ecclesiastical wealth.

As a result of the action of these various forces, economic activity began to expand and to accelerate in tempo. This was further helped by a general increase in population throughout the western world, England and Wales, for instance, experiencing a rise from 4 millions in 1570 to 5.5 millions in 1700. Demand for goods, not merely in Britain but also on the Continent and in the colonies, rose with the population, causing prices to spiral upward. When compared with even such important medieval merchants as Sir Richard Whittington or the early de la Poles, the trade of the late seventeenth century merchant was simply fabulous. But this was so only because, along with enlarged demand, there had been a corresponding improvement in the understanding of the whole process of credit. Joint-stock companies had appeared upon the scene. Exchanges or bourses where men could trade in commodities without ever seeing them had also been established. Finally, banks had begun to develop some paper currency as a substitute for the use of gold and silver. It was the appearance of these credit means of exchange which really brought the transition period to a close, for by them the scarcity of money was virtually ended.

Yet the picture was by no means always clear and bright. As industry and trade increased, so less and less could countries live unto themselves, and their interrelationships grew more complex. A war in Europe might ultimately cause hardship and disaster to the Welsh shepherd on the side of Snowdon, or to the woolen weaver in a small Yorkshire dale. Overenthusiasm on the part of some "projector" or promoter might cause an increase in demand

for certain goods in England which would boost production beyond
what was necessary, bringing about a fall in prices. Or it might be
that a tariff placed on Spanish goods by the English government
would bring about retaliation in the form of a ban on English
cloth in the Spanish Netherlands, to the detriment of the home
producer. Thus by 1700 trade was not nearly as simple as it had
been in the Middle Ages. No longer were dealings merely between
two individuals, but rather between two countries or even two
empires.

To understand the development of economic thought and activity during this time of transition it is imperative to keep in view
the various forces which came into play. The people involved in
the movements of the period did not grasp the significance of what
was occurring around them, nor were they able to explain the
clearly visible changes. It is in their attempted explanations, however, that one is best able to trace the economic thinking and
outlook of the times.

The Characteristics of the Changing Outlook

When one endeavors to understand the nature of the economic
outlook of the Tudor and Stuart periods, the first thing which must
be considered is the accepted end or objective of economic activity.
As already seen, the medieval ideal had as its primary objective the
service of God and the meriting of God's favor by faithful and just
dealing. The Protestant reformers held somewhat the same point
of view. The followers of Calvin in England and Scotland believed
that the end of all human activity should be the glory of God.
That is, by faithfully performing the work which came to one's
hand, one was truly fulfilling his God-given duty. Thus, the highest end in life was to do one's duty to the best of one's ability. This
meant honesty, diligence, and justice in all dealings. Milton expressed it as doing everything "in [the] great Taskmaster's eye."
Although this view tended to drop out of sight in the latter part
of the seventeenth century, it came back in the Evangelical Revival
of the eighteenth century.

While such ideas as these might appeal to people with strong
Christian convictions, there were many who did not accept such a
religious point of view. Instead, they held, as did the Italian
Machiavelli, that the chief end of man was to provide power for
the state. The state became the be-all and end-all of life. When
they spoke of the state, however, they did not mean the nation, but
rather the government. Economic power was to be sought in order

that political power might be obtained. This was primarily an irre-
ligious economic philosophy which stemmed from Renaissance
humanism and the growing needs of the national states. The immediate objective was the increase of individual and national wealth
so that the state, by heavy taxes, could support strong armies and
navies. It was recognized that unless a country were wealthy, its
government would be poor. Consequently, national wealth must
be increased at all costs, for only then could the state gain power.
By 1650 this had become the dominant objective of all European
economic leaders and planners.

But how was all this to be achieved? How was man to fulfill his
economic obligations? Both the Roman Catholic and the Protestant churches stressed that a person's economic activity must be
controlled and guided by Christian principles. In many cases they
disagreed as to the nature of the principles, but they were at one
in holding that it was God who established these principles of economic action, whether they were revealed through the Church or
through the Scriptures. To enforce Christian teachings and make
them effective moral suasion was attempted. Many of the Protestant divines in England and Scotland dealt in their sermons with
economic problems, appealing to the consciences of their hearers.
Since, however, this method was not always successful they resorted
to the discipline of the Church and the law of the land to control
economic action. Some of these staunch Protestants were every
bit as opposed to usury as were the medieval schoolmen. Holding
to an even more thorough-going doctrine of original sin than did
the medieval church, they were not at all optimistic about man's
goodness. They felt that in economic affairs, as in most others, he
had to be closely watched and controlled if he were to be induced
to conduct his business in a Christian manner.

The humanist's point of view was somewhat different. He was
opposed, as he said more than once, to the preachers' interference
in economic affairs. Economics operated by natural law. Consequently, there was not much sense in either the church or the state
attempting to control man's economic activities directly. Instead,
man's natural covetousness and greed should be so stimulated and
guided that they would accomplish the purposes of the state. There
were various ways and means of providing such inducements. Taxation, particularly the levying of customs duties, was one. While the
Scottish government, under the influence of the Calvinists, would
ban certain imports or forbid Scottish merchants to trade with
Spain because of its Roman Catholicism, the more sophisticated
English rulers adopted a different plan. They taxed the undesirable

goods. This policy the Scots were quick to follow. Another typical method of stimulation employed in both countries was that of granting monopolies. At first these were given to individuals who were prepared to risk capital in the establishment of some new industry or trade. For a period of years they could draw all the profits from their innovation. Later, however, monopolies tended only to restrict trade and curtail other men's freedom. Trade treaties, subsidies, and the like were also employed.

Basic to all these plans and policies was the assumption that man should be given as much freedom as possible, being induced by an appeal to his greed to do what was for the benefit of the state, while morality or religion was virtually ignored. Such a point of view, while not uncommon in the sixteenth century, became dominant in the seventeenth, particularly after the restoration of the Stuarts in 1660. Hales, in his *Discourse of the Commonweal of this Realm of England* (1547), Thomas Mun, in his *England's Treasure by Forraigne Trade* (1668), and John Law, in most of his writings, expound this theory very fully.

One of the fundamental questions that always arose in connection with the increase of the state's power was that of the nature of money. Owing to the scarcity of bullion in the Middle Ages, there had been a tendency to regard it as wealth or income. Since the credit system throughout the early modern period was very crude, the lack of money strengthened the bullionist idea. Coupled with this was the fact that the state's income, in order to be usable, could no longer be collected in kind, but had to be in money, for it was only if the money was available that the military forces and the civil service could be maintained. Gold and silver in this way became the sinews of war. Now it is true that few of the economic theorists of the period held any such crude idea as that bullion was intrinsically wealth. But they did realize that it was needed if business was to prosper and the government was to pay its debts. Along with land, money was one of the factors of production, and interest was simply rent for money's use. They also held that the quantity of money available controlled the price level. If money was plentiful, prices would rise; if it was scarce, prices would fall. In most of these views they were partially right. But it was what they did not know which made their thinking faulty.

Out of their reasoning about money came a change in the prevalent attitude toward usury. As already pointed out, the medieval church had regarded the taking of usury as immoral. By the end of the Middle Ages, however, the demands of business had made a considerable gap in the surrounding hedge of prohibition. Other

names and methods were found to nullify the restrictions. The
Jesuits, faced with realities of life, approved the idea of taking
interest by means of "probabilism," holding that it would *probably*
do more good than evil.[2]

In the Protestant camp, Martin Luther was strongly opposed to
any permission of usury, but Calvin, a French lawyer living in the
commercial city of Geneva, realized that for business it was a
necessity. He stated his views in his commentaries, and particularly in a letter written in 1546. Usury or interest was lawful if the
borrower would make an equal profit from the loan. Usury, however, was never to be taken from the poor, nor was it to be above
the legally permitted limit. At all times equity and justice were to
be preserved. Calvin in this statement was not saying anything that
was new, but was simply facing the existing situation. The Calvinists in England and Scotland at first refused to go as far as their
leader. They opposed the legislation of Henry VIII permitting the
taking of usury (1545), and in Scotland the receiving of a maximum
of 10 per cent became legal only at the end of the century. Because
of Calvin's statement on usury, some have endeavored to prove
that he is the father of the "capitalistic spirit," but an examination
of the facts proves that he was not an innovator; he was only dealing with the contemporary situation realistically. Usury was being
taken long before his day. He saw its need, but he so hedged it
about that his restraints were far greater than those imposed by the
church at the end of the Middle Ages. As one writer of his own
day stated, he dealt with usury "as an apothecary dealeth with
poison."

Despite Puritan and Presbyterian misgivings concerning the
taking of interest on loans, by 1550 it was becoming common.
What is more, businessmen increasingly tried to throw off all restraints imposed by the church. Economic practice was to be determined altogether apart from the demands of morality. The Jesuit
idea of judging the propriety of usury by its effect upon trade was
all that was important. If merchants favored the limitation of the
amount of interest which one could take, making a distinction
between interest and usury, it was entirely for business reasons.
The Dutch were noted for the low rate which they charged on

---

[2] Probabilism is a system of morality, developed primarily by Jesuit thinkers who
held that when there are divergent views "as to the lawfulness of an action for each
of which solid arguments may be advanced, then, provided the lawfulness be alone
in question, we are under no obligation to follow the more probable of the two
views, but are equally free to adopt either course." G. H. Joyce, S.J., "Probabilism,"
The Encyclopedia of Religion and Ethics, ed. James Hastings (Edinburgh, 1918),
Vol. X, p. 349.

loans, and it was felt that this might have something to do with Dutch prosperity. Low rates were therefore considered good because they would help business. By 1700 interest was being taken as a matter of course. It simply represented what profit one might have made if he had employed his money himself, instead of loaning it to another. The amount of interest also was determined solely by economic considerations.

The Development of Mercantilism

Although the easing of restrictions on usury helped to develop a system of credit, the primitive methods employed tended to emphasize the continued importance of gold and silver. To England and Scotland, countries with no gold or silver mines, the question of how to obtain these commodities was always pressing. The only way open was trade. Yet as they looked at the trade of the world they felt that its amount was limited and static. If one country increased its commercial operations, then some other country or countries must suffer, for in every transaction, if one party gained, the other lost. There was no idea that there might be mutual gain through each person's obtaining something he desired. In the mind of sixteenth century economist trade was closely linked in this way to war, being really an extension of it into other fields. All trade was basically part of a "cold war."

The dominant concept of trade was, therefore, that in order to prosper commercially a nation should sell more and at a higher price to, and buy less and more cheaply from, foreign nations. By this means there would always be a balance owing to the country by others, who would have to meet their obligations in gold and silver. Some felt that this balance must be obtained on each transaction and between each country. It was soon realized, however, that it was a question of the country's over-all trade. Moreover, it was recognized that it was not merely a matter of an exchange of goods, but that the sale of services, such as the carrying of freight by ship, also brought in foreign bullion. Therefore, great efforts were made to build up the merchant navy. By establishing a favorable balance of trade it was felt that money would flow into the country, prices would rise, and business would boom, thus bringing prosperity and power to the state.

It had early been realized that when a country exported manufactured goods rather than raw materials, the balance of trade was always most favorable. Wool made into cloth sold on the Continent at a higher price than did the raw commodity. The trick, therefore, was to increase domestic manufactures and to buy abroad only the raw materials needed for industry or goods for resale to other countries. To this end, the government usually did everything it could to attract foreign artisans, who would introduce new techniques. Monopolies were given with the same object in view. By these means, it was hoped that the country would be made industrially self-sufficient and other nations would be able to buy from it only the more expensive manufactured goods. Consequently, industrial expansion was crucial in the economic thinking of the time.

With the increase of industry, however, there developed a new fear. As larger quantities of goods were manufactured and supply began to catch up with demand, the prices tended to fall. With more and more goods on the domestic market, the fall of prices in turn caused a cessation of production. There thus developed what Heckscher calls "a fear of goods," [3] leading to further attempts to increase exports while at the same time trying to maintain high prices. This was one of the basic internal contradictions of the mercantilist theory. To increase production and sales on a limited foreign market while keeping the prices high was a difficult problem. But, as one can easily see, this was demanded by the idea that the important objective of the trade was a balance of payments resulting in the import of precious metals.

Because of this attitude toward money, the question of consumption was ignored. Petty in 1662 said that a state's wealth was a large and strong population, while thirty-five years later Davenant declared that it consisted in all useful possessions. But they were both thinking of these things as basic to the acquisition of gold and silver. This is clearly indicated by the continued stress upon foreign trade. They knew that money helped to stimulate internal economic activity, that it provided income for many people who paid taxes to the state, and that, therefore, exports must be increased and extended. Domestic trade and production for home consumption was largely ignored.

It seems to have escaped the economic thinkers of the day that a country's economic position was really indicated by the population's general standard of living. As pointed out above, their whole conception of wealth was bound up with the potentials of production rather than a high level of domestic consumption. Nor did they, because of their idea of a limited quantity of available trade, feel that the general standard of living of other nations was of any importance, except where this standard of living would force these nations to purchase the manufactured goods they needed from

[3] E. F. Heckscher, *Mercantilism* (London, 1935), Vol. II, pp. 53 ff.

Britain. If only all foreign countries could be kept as agricultural producers, British manufacturers would make their country the greatest in the world. This brought them to the place where they opposed the importation of foreign industrial products, particularly such luxuries as French wines and lace, which only helped to take money out of the country, giving no economic advantage in return.

The emphasis on production appears very clearly in various situations. For instance, in connection with colonies and colonization the mercantilists were convinced that these new areas had two principal functions. First of all they were to supply raw materials for the home manufacturer. Therefore, all the colonies' surplus raw materials were to be shipped to England either for manufacture or resale abroad. What is more, in order to stimulate the ship-building industry and to prevent carrying charges from going to other nations these raw materials: tobacco, rice, sugar, lumber, etc., had to be transported in English or colonial ships. Only after much agitation on the part of the colonies were they allowed to sell such commodities as rice directly to the importing countries. In the second place, the colonies were to be the markets for home industrial goods. To achieve this end, manufacturing in the colonies was strictly limited, if not actually banned, while the export of colonial manufactures was prohibited. By this means it was thought that the home country's industry and commerce would be stimulated. The relatively backward colonies should exist to provide both raw materials and markets for the home producer. What was Britain's surprise, therefore, after the American revolution, to find that the independent and prosperous United States was a far better customer than the closely regulated thirteen colonies had ever been!

Another indication of the stress on production and of the disregard for the general level of the standard of living is given in the attitude toward poverty. Owing to the increased numbers of wage earners entirely dependent upon trade and industry, occasional unemployment and poverty were becoming more common. Since most artisans in the Middle Ages were partially connected with the land, and also because of the rather indiscriminate charity of the church, the problem of the poor had not been too pressing. The Protestant Reformers, such as Calvin and Knox, objected to the medieval church's idea of almsgiving and its advocacy of voluntary poverty as "a counsel of perfection." But at the same time they realized that poverty was a question which had to be faced. They saw it as coming from laziness or from economic or physical disability. The lazy, they believed, should be forced to work. For those who could not find work employment should be provided.

With this idea in mind, Calvin founded the weaving industry in Geneva. If work, however, could not be provided, or if the poor were unfit for labor, they were to receive charity distributed by the church. This teaching of the Reformers to a large extent laid the foundation for the English and Scottish poor laws. It was what might in view of the contemporary situation be called "Christian realism."

The humanistic-mercantilist approach was somewhat different. It recognized that there were poor people with whom the government had to deal. Usually, however, it regarded these unfortunates as a potential source of cheap labor, which could be used to produce goods at low cost. They were therefore to be integrated into the mercantilists' national industrial program. The beginnings of such an attitude may perhaps be seen in the Statute of Artificers (1563), which provided for the compulsory apprenticing of the unemployed to agriculture or to some other trade. Davenant one hundred and fifty years later pointed out that such use of the poor would enable Britain to obtain cheap industrial labor, thereby making it possible for her, because of relatively low cost, to sell her goods on the foreign market at a greater profit. It was this attitude which led to the general failure to enforce the Elizabethan Poor Laws after the Stuart Restoration (1660). The machinery for enforcement had broken down during the anarchy of the Civil War, and after Charles II ascended the throne, there was little interest in its revival.

Much the same fate befell regulation of wages. As a result of the Black Death (1346-48), attempts had been made to set up machinery to establish maximum wages, particularly in agriculture. But with the rise of prices, the real need was for a minimum wage. The Statute of Artificers (1563) endeavored not only to provide everyone with work but also to fix wages in accord with rising costs. Later statutes followed the same policy. At first the Justices of the Peace, to whom was committed the fixing of wages, seem to have fulfilled their duties, thereby alleviating the current distress. But, once the Privy Council lost its supervisory power during the Civil War and men began to forget that they were their brothers' keepers, the practice was neglected. The Quarter Sessions of the justices simply reissued old wage-rates without ever bothering to bring them up to date. By 1700 the practice of wage-fixing had become a dead letter. Wages, it was felt, should be determined simply by supply and demand. Here again, production rather than consumption was the criterion of judgment.

The same thing also applied in the matter of riches. Calvin and his followers did not believe, as some claim, that riches necessarily showed that one was being blessed by God because he was of the elect. They held that both poverty and wealth came from the Almighty. Therefore, in whatever status a man found himself, he was to be content. That was his calling, and any *inordinate* desire to get out of it was wrong. The Reformers stressed this because they were well aware of the danger of riches. The deceitfulness of wealth was continually emphasized, for riches led men to place all their desire on the things of this world. Men were to live frugally in order that they might not be led astray and in order that they might give largely to the poor. When Calvin spoke of frugality, however, he did not mean asceticism. A human being had a perfect right to enjoy all the good gifts which God gave, as well as the obligation to maintain his status in society. But he was not to set his heart upon riches, either for themselves or in order that he might make a display which would satisfy only human pride. This position was very similar to that of the Methodists in the eighteenth and early nineteenth centuries.

As the influence of the Reformation began to lose its power, another point of view took over the field. It represented primarily the humanistic attitude of "Get all you can." Wealth became the criterion of success. Money spent on domestically produced luxuries was held to stimulate manufacturing, so luxury was of benefit to the nation. Some even went so far as to favor the purchase of foreign luxuries, as this would stimulate the sale of English goods abroad. Any sense of trusteeship for one's wealth was lost. Instead, the concept of full and complete private ownership became dominant. Therefore, the ultimate economic object of every man was to amass as much money as possible and to spend it on himself. By 1700 "money-making" had become the highest end which a merchant, a manufacturer, or an artisan could pursue.

The Consequences of the Change

The consequence of the new type of thinking was that, by 1715, economists had come to regard the good of the state as the end of all economic activity. By its control of all phases of economic life, the state was to gain economic power, which meant "power" in general. The individual, whether rich or poor, tended to fall into the background. He was no longer of any great importance, but was really only a cog in a machine. Whether the state regulated trade, consumption of goods, or manufacturing, it was all done in the interests of the increase of the state's power.

Simultaneously, by the beginning of the eighteenth century a growing optimism could be noticed in many economic writings. There was a tendency to regard the individual as a rational creature who, in seeking his own ends, helped the state forward to power. Since natural law governed the individual as well as the state, it began to be felt that if the individual were allowed to seek freely his own ends, all would be well. The subtitle of Mandeville's *Fable of the Bees, or Private Vices, Public Virtues* makes this very clear. The state did not really have to legislate or impose tariffs and taxes to control trade. It could simply permit man to go his own way, and his natural selfish activity itself would settle the matter. Thus, the economic freedom of the individual was coming to be regarded as necessary for the state's economic prosperity.

From this it is not hard to see that questions of morality largely disappeared from economic thinking. The religious point of view both of the Middle Ages and of the Reformation was ignored. Economic activity was amoral, and sometimes it might justifiably be actually immoral. It was not a matter of whether a deal was fair or just, but whether or not it could be "put across." Economic motivation in this way became ultimate in man, success being the test of propriety. Utility became the final standard of whether a thing was desirable or not. Voltaire's comment that "if there were no God we should have to invent one for the benefit of the common people" perhaps gives us the best expression of this attitude. The state was to consider what would enable it most easily and effectively to achieve power. When that was decided nothing should stand in its way. Natural law would then be taking its prescribed course.

Such an attitude was characteristic of the period which lasted from the middle of the eighteenth down to the twentieth century. It was partially romantic, but very frequently purely cynical. It found its origins in the gradual decline throughout Europe, in Roman Catholic and Protestant countries alike, of religious beliefs, and in the growth of economic activity. Trade and industry, being made purely secular, were largely separated from the realm of Christianity, and even morals. This change, which had commenced in the fourteenth century, was by 1715 quite dominant, and by 1800 it had gained the day. Laissez faire now became the ideal.

Chapter 8

THE DISSOLUTION OF
THE OLD ORDER

It was in the Tudor period (1485-1603), as far as England and Scotland were concerned, that the Middle Ages died. This was the period of the Protestant Reformation, the period of the breakup of the medieval organization of society, and, most important for us, the period which virtually brought the economy of the Middle Ages to an end. Yet, at the same time, it was the age in which the groundwork was being laid for modern developments, although these do not really begin to appear until the sixteen hundreds. As we saw in the preceding chapter, during the sixteenth and seventeenth centuries men's thinking was undergoing very radical modifications. While this had its influence upon economic action, simultaneous economic conditions and necessities forced men to change their ideas. The dying of the old concepts, which was particularly noticeable in the sixteenth century, prepared the road for new theories and interpretations in the years to come. In this way the sixteenth century embraces a distinct epoch in British economic development.

The Rise of Prices

One of the chief characteristics of the economic changes in the sixteenth century was the rise in prices. One cause of this was the growth of population. By 1500 England and Wales probably had three and a half million people between them, while Scotland may have had as many as seven or eight hundred thousand. Throughout the century the numbers gradually increased, and by 1600 England and Wales had about four million inhabitants and Scotland more than 800,000. Approximately ninety per cent of these people were still rural, in spite of urban growth. By 1603 London had a population of about 150,000, although the other towns nearest to her in numbers were probably less than half that size. This steady increase caused a rise in demand for goods and services, thus helping to raise prices.

The most fundamental cause of the rise in prices, however, would seem to have been the alteration in the value of money. During the first half of the century the crown frequently debased the coinage in order to make a profit. The silver content of the penny was reduced in order to make many more coins from the same amount of bullion. Henry VIII followed this policy so thoroughly that by the end of his reign the amount of silver in the coinage had been reduced by about two thirds. At the same time the ratio of value between gold and silver was continually being altered. This uncertainty concerning the value of the money raised prices even further. Elizabeth, as soon as she ascended the throne in 1558, attempted to correct the trouble. One difficulty was, however, that silver was then coming into the country from foreign, especially Spanish, trade more rapidly than the metal could be assimilated, resulting in a dislocation of the whole economy. This state of affairs, common to all of western Europe, affected not only England but also the other areas of the British Isles. In Ireland the situation was aggravated by the introduction from England of a debased coinage, minted to prevent the export of Irish money to the Continent and to keep English money at home. Too much money could be as dangerous as too little.

As a result of these influences, prices kept rising steadily throughout the century. This was particularly true in the case of goods in most common demand, food and clothes. In 1600 they cost the average Englishman more than three times what they had cost his grandfather in 1500. In Scotland, where, owing to continual fighting, industrial production had gone backward rather than forward, the prices had probably risen five or six times. It has been estimated that during the sixteenth century the price of wheat increased in England more than six times, while in Scotland the price of oats climbed even farther. The rise in the cost of essentials very quickly forced up all other prices in spite of the government's efforts to arrest this trend by fixing prices. Money was becoming cheaper, so other goods were becoming more expensive.

The consequences of the price changes were varied. For the producer, such as the tenant farmer, with fixed medieval obligations, or for the merchant, whose income consisted of profits from his sales, or for the debtor, the change in prices was fortunate. The producer and the merchant were able to obtain increasingly greater returns from their goods. The debtor had to repay in *real* value considerably less than he had borrowed. For the man who was on a fixed income, however, the situation was very different. To the landlord receiving rents, perhaps determined in the fourteenth century, and to the crown, with fixed income from feudal revenues and tenths and fifteenths, the change was a source of great trouble. To the laborer, unorganized and unprotected, it was a real disaster, since his wages rose much more slowly than did prices. During the sixteenth century wages did not even triple, although prices were multiplied by four or five. To add to his plight were the efforts on the part of the landlord to obtain higher returns from his land by increasing rents and by enforcing all obligations. Consequently the laborer was often compelled to leave his land, and to go forth to work for wages without the possibility of having even a small garden plot for his own use. Thus the increase in prices was by no means an unmitigated blessing to the country.

When faced with these difficulties men tried to discover their causes. Many blamed the bad coinage for the trouble. This deficiency Queen Elizabeth attempted to remedy. About the same time a Frenchman, Jean Bodin, set forth the theory that the situation was caused by the change in the ratio of money to the amount of goods available for purchase. The plentifulness of money and the scarcity of goods made prices rise; therefore the solution was to increase the output of goods. This proved to be correct, for the rise of prices so stimulated production that by the end of the century in England the quantity of goods available for consumption was beginning to reach a balance with the country's holdings of gold and silver. In Scotland, on the other hand, production had improved only very slightly. What is more, the coinage was in such an evil condition that, although prices were high at home, Scottish money could buy little abroad, forcing the prices of imports even higher. Thus there was scant hope of a solution to the problem in Scotland, although south of the Tweed the end of inflation was coming into view.

When Sheep Ate Men

Although the sixteenth century saw the beginning of the end of the medieval system of agriculture, it was not until the nineteenth century that the process was completed. The sixteenth century, however, did witness a considerable change, for in it the market for agricultural products began to experience an unwonted expansion. With the increase of population and the development of towns there came a corresponding rise in demand for foodstuffs. Throughout the Middle Ages there had always been some market farming, but with the growth of an element in the population which was completely separated from the land, it became increasingly important. Coupled with this, owing to continental demand for wool, throughout the sixteenth century both England and Scotland exported considerable quantities of that product. Much more important, however, was the expanding market, both at home and abroad, for English cloth. Profits could now be made on a considerable scale by men who were prepared to invest in better methods of arable and sheep farming. The landowner saw before him the chance of greatly increasing his income, and in this prospect lay the motivation for agricultural improvement.

The greatest single landowner in the British Isles in 1500 was the Church. It has been estimated that it held between one third and one half of the islands' real estate. Although the clergy, particularly the monks, had in earlier days been the great improvers of the land, by this time they had become very conservative. Also, because the Church never alienated or sold property which had once been committed to it or to religious purposes, such land never came back on to the market. It is not surprising, therefore, that impecunious landlords and hard-pressed rulers looked at the Church with greedy eyes. When the Reformation came, religion could be used as an excuse for expropriation, moral standards being set aside for economic needs.

In England direct attacks were made upon the Church's holdings by both Henry VIII and Edward VI, the former expropriating the property of the monasteries (1536, 1538), and the latter, the lands held for religious purposes by the gilds (1549). This left only the episcopal lands intact. To these Elizabeth turned her attention and, womanlike, succeeded in making the bishops pay her large sums. This forced the sale of much of their property to meet her demands.

The Scottish kings were somewhat more "canny." James V, while remaining a good Catholic, so taxed the clergy that abbots and bishops alike were forced to feu their lands for long terms. Then when the Reformed Church was established by law, the feuars simply appropriated the lands for their own purposes. The new church, which desired to use the lands for the support of the clergy, for education, and for aid to the poor, received little.

Economically this change of ownership was extremely important, for it threw onto the market a large amount of land, which in turn was taken up by progressive landowners and middle class merchants, who introduced new agricultural methods in the hope of increased profits. In England the church lands were bought from the crown for the purchase price of twenty years' rent at the old valuation. With rising prices, the opportunity for profits was, therefore, considerable.

The transfer of ecclesiastical lands to lay hands did not, however, immediately improve agricultural production. Throughout the sixteenth century, methods, on the whole, remained medieval. Some even feel that they deteriorated. Fitzherbert's *Boke of Husbandrye* (1523) and Thomas Tusser's *Five Hundreth Good Pointes of Husbandrie* (1557) show little increase in knowledge over the thirteenth century, and as long as tillage in common was customary little improvement could be expected. For this reason, men began to think increasingly of enclosing fields for individual use. As already explained, this was not something new, but was a process which went far back into the Middle Ages. During the sixteenth century it became much more customary, in the first half of the century common fields, commons, and waste lands being enclosed for sheep runs, while from 1560 on the trend was to enclosure for arable farming.

As leases "fell in," landlords refused to renew them. When an heir desired to take over his father's farm, he was usually charged such a large amount that he could not pay. Copyholders, customary tenants, and, in Scotland, "kindly tenants" who could not prove their rights to holdings were deprived of their property. In Wales inheritance in gavelkind disappeared after 1536, the head of the family becoming the only recognized owner. Last of all, in some cases sheer force was employed to oust unwanted tenants. In these ways, some 750,000 acres, particularly in the east Midlands, were consolidated and enclosed. One must always remember, however, that the movement was not general, nor did it take place all at once, but was carried out as a lord could persuade his tenants to agree or as he found that he had the right and power to take action.

Generally speaking, the long term effect of enclosure was improvement. Under the old system the laziness of one man could hold up the farming operations of a whole village. Under the new plan each individual worked as much or as little as he liked. Moreover, dependent upon the proximity of markets and his particular type of soil, he could employ his own farm to the best advantage. With enclosure usually bringing about the amalgamation of small farms into larger units, there followed greater efficiency in operation. This, coupled with rising prices, increased income and farm values. Rents climbed steadily, not infrequently by 1000 per cent. The whole system was placed on a money basis, hired labor taking the place of villeins' customary services. Thus in some parts of the country, although not all, the old order was changing.

Yet it was not all happiness and joy which came in enclosure's train. The villein, now a mere wage earner, was pushed off the land, while the small farmer, unable to meet his obligations from the produce of his little piece of property, had to sell out. Since industry was not expanding as rapidly as the displacement of the rural lower classes, it could not provide them with work. Therefore, these unfortunates took to the road as "rogues, vagabonds and sturdy beggars," rendering ineffective the government's attempt to deal with the problem by means of legislation.[1] One must not, however, exaggerate the size of the number involved. There may have been 40,000, or 2 per cent of the total population of England and Wales, displaced from the areas in which enclosures were common, while in Scotland, on the other hand, where manpower was relatively scarce, the uprooted farmers were easily absorbed.

By the end of the century the results of higher prices and individual ownership in some parts of the country were to be seen in increased productivity. Crops continued to be much the same as they had been during the Middle Ages: wheat, rye, barley, peas, vetches, and, in the wetter areas, oats. It is estimated, however, that the wheat yield had climbed from six or eight bushels to the acre in 1500 to about 20 bushels in 1600. Hops were becoming an important crop, and vegetable gardens were increasing in usefulness with the introduction of the turnip, the Spanish or sweet potato, and from South America, the ordinary potato. Asparagus and new types of beans were also introduced. Thus, by cereals and vegetables becoming more plentiful, the effects of enclosure for sheep runs were somewhat mitigated. On the other hand, although a larger amount of food was raised, owing to improved fertility by marling, manuring, and a little scientific drainage, the labor of fewer hands was employed. This helped further to increase rural unemployment.

Animal husbandry was also expanding production. Sheep had always been very important for wool. In fact, it was a proverb that "the sheep ate men" because of the depopulation caused by the setting up of sheep runs. By the end of the century, however, as the demand for foodstuffs became greater, the raising of sheep for food instead of wool was becoming more common. Lord Ernle has estimated that the weight of the average sheep increased during this period from 28 to 40 pounds.[2] The weight of the fleece had

[1] See page 153.
[2] Lord Ernle, *English Farming, Past and Present* (London, 1936), p. 97.

also become heavier, although with prosperity the fibers had become coarser. Cattle, too, were larger, their weight rising from around 300 to close to 600 pounds. Oxen were still employed for the plow, horses being generally reserved for riding or for pulling carriages. Thus, in 1600 animal husbandry was much advanced over what it had been a hundred years earlier. This, along with the growth of cereal production, helped to keep food prices from rising completely out of sight.

In mercantilist eyes any improvement in agriculture was all to the good. Cheap food meant cheap labor, which, in turn, meant low export costs, resulting in a favorable balance of trade. Therefore, both to encourage agriculture and to keep prices within reason, the export of grain was controlled. In 1437 wheat could be exported only if the price dropped below 6s. 8d. a quarter. In 1563 the floor price was raised to 10s. and in 1593 to 20s. The only difficulty was that the market prices were usually far above the minimum. In 1597 wheat actually reached 72s. a quarter. Another way of helping arable agriculture and keeping down the price of grain was that of legislating against enclosure for sheep. Various laws for this purpose were passed throughout the century, but the Justices of the Peace, themselves usually large landowners, were not interested in enforcing them. Restrictions were also laid upon corn-dealers, who were blamed for raising prices and causing scarcities, while attempts were made by the Statute of Artificers (1563) to keep the workers on the land at low wages. The real trouble was, however, that the profits from wool were too attractive to keep land in tillage, and the influx of gold and silver was too large to keep prices down. Profits continued to rise, so enclosure continued to take place. The government could not hold back economic changes.

By the end of the century the basic differences between medieval and modern agrarian organizations were clearly marked. The modern landlord, who either farmed his own land by hired help or who rented it out to tenants, was becoming common. He was growing wealthy on rising prices and increased demand for farm products, whether foodstuffs or wool. The substantial tenant farmer, or yeoman, had also made his appearance, particularly in East Anglia and Kent. He was likewise profiting by the change. At the same time, the villein had sunk to the position of a landless laborer dependent upon relatively low wages. The small farmer in the areas of enclosure was also in none too happy a position, for he could not compete with his neighbors' large farms. On the other hand, by far the greater part of the country was still cultivating the land in the medieval way, with the same wasteful practices. The new methods were largely limited to the areas of enclosure, and it was two more centuries before they were countrywide. The important thing was that a beginning had been made.

The Change in Industrial Organization

The history of industry during the sixteenth century resembles, in one sense, that of agriculture. There was relatively little improvement in technique. Since there were few machines, hand power still performed most of the operations. Such machines as there were appeared principally in the textile and heavy industries. The gig mill for raising the nap on cloth, the stocking frame, and the Dutch loom for ribbon weaving were all introduced during this century, and the use of the fulling mill was increased. In the iron industry the blast furnace, water-driven tilt hammers, and bellows and grinders' wheels were brought into use. A good many of these machines, however, were unfavorably received as taking work from honest craftsmen. This was particularly true of the gig mill. Consequently, it was not at all uncommon for statutes to be enacted either forbidding their use or so circumscribing them with regulations that they were useless. Because of this and because demand was not yet so great as to force improvement, throughout the sixteenth century mechanical advance was very slow.

It was during this century that industries not organized into gilds began to gain prominence. The building trade outside of the towns, and also shipbuilding, seem to have been of this type. For instance, a contractor or entrepreneur would undertake to build a noble's house, employing his own workmen on a piece rate system. But more important than these were the heavy industries: coal, iron, and tin mining and brass production. In both England and Scotland the mining of coal was on the increase, since wood was becoming scarcer with the clearing of forests for settlement or enclosure and since it was being used more and more as fuel in the expanding iron industry. Contractors would lease *delves* or *heuchs* (pits) from their owners and pay men to mine the coal. In the metal industries much the same system was followed. The capitalist, for that is what he was, would own the blast furnace, the forge, and the supply of ironstone and charcoal. Much less a master than an employer, he would simply hire men to produce his iron. Tin-mining followed the same plan, although sometimes the mines were worked cooperatively by the miners. For brass production, foreigners, Flemings and Germans, were brought in. They worked as miners for the Mines Royal (established 1568) or as brass-founders under the Mineral and Battery Works (organized 1568), joint-stock companies established with a monopoly of the industry. In this way the tin of Cornwall, the lead of the Mendip Hills, Cumberland, Durham, and Derby, the coal of the Tyne Valley and Lothian and the iron of the Sussex Weald and Forest of Dean were all brought into industrial use.

Similar developments helped to complete the gild's decline. The heavy industries, because of the large capital investment required, could hardly have operated on a gild basis. At the same time, the accumulation of large fortunes through the older industries and trades tended to break down these organizations even in the towns. During the latter part of the Middle Ages, as already has been seen, there was growing up a moneyed trading class. In the sixteenth century this element became even more influential. As prices rose, and as the individual craftsman was obliged to produce for the general market rather than for an individual customer, he became more dependent upon the person who was retailing his goods. This tended to break down gild control of industry. Added to this, craftsmen were often setting themselves up outside the limits of the towns, where they could produce more cheaply than the gildsman, who had to pay fees and taxes and to perform civic duties. To these workmen, the merchant, seeking cheap goods, would give his custom. The gildsmen, feeling the loss, tried without success to enforce their regulations upon the suburban workers. Before long they found themselves in the position of piece workers or simple wage earners, taking their orders, not from the gild authorities, but from the merchant. This meant virtually the end of the gild system.

In London the development went even further. During the sixteenth century the livery companies controlled the economy of the city. Entrance could be bought into their membership, or it might be inherited. Once, however, a man became a member of one company, he was free of all the others. He might trade or not as he wished, or he might be in the Vintners' Company and deal in iron, but the important thing was that he had special social and economic privileges.[3] The yeoman companies, subordinate to the livery, were no longer made up of journeymen, but were composed of small masters who produced goods for the merchants. Very frequently efforts were made to keep these small masters from doing any retailing at all. In 1547 Edward VI further crippled the gilds when he seized all their property employed for religious pur-

[3] See page 112.

poses. Henceforth the gilds were to be merely economic and mildly social bodies. But even if the government had taken no action, by 1600 so dependent upon the merchant had the industrialist become that the gild system, even in London, was facing its dissolution.

Another factor in the breakdown of the gilds and the development of industry was the appearance of the foreign craftsman, particularly during the reign of Elizabeth. As a result of persecution and religious wars on the Continent, the stream of French, Dutch, Flemish, and German immigrants broadened noticeably. Very frequently they were unpopular because they were better workmen than their English counterparts and because they still refused to join the English gilds. But, as they brought new techniques in metal work, and particularly in cloth production, the authorities received them gladly. They introduced the "new draperies" which were lighter and finer than the English broadcloth, and also helped to improve the English worsteds. In some cases enterprising merchants banded together to finance their establishment in towns such as Norwich. Some of the immigrants even went as far as Ireland to set up their looms. With the consequent improvement in the quality of English cloth, early in the seventeenth century all export of wool was forbidden. Henceforth England would pin her hopes for foreign trade to her cloth rather than to her wool exports.

One other feature of the industrial development of the period was the gradual supplanting of gild laws by municipal regulations. Town authorities, who even in the Middle Ages had been extending the scope of their powers, now became supreme in their own areas, subject only to the crown, and in Scotland to the Convention of Royal Burghs. In London, the livery, and in other towns a similar type of merchant gild, virtually controlled the town councils, who now asserted their authority not only over the manufacture and sale of food, but even over all industrial products. Furthermore, they even obtained control over goods produced in the neighboring rural districts. This had, of course, been done earlier in Scotland, but in 1552 the Norwich council obtained the right of inspecting all worsteds produced in the county. In this way gild authority was being further undermined by the town.

The state also took a hand in industrial regulation. It had since 1193 issued rules concerning the length of cloths and had for years tried to control selling of wool and the price of food. The climax came in 1563 when Parliament, endeavoring to restore some economic order, enacted the Statute of Artificers. This law not only tried to ensure sufficient labor for agriculture, but it also laid down regulations for the government of industry. Apprenticeship was to last for seven years; only the sons of 40s. freeholders, i.e., those who owned land worth 40s. a year, could be apprenticed to mercers, drapers, goldsmiths, ironmongers, and clothiers; employment contracts were to be for a year, and minimum wage rates were to be fixed according to the cost of food. All these regulations were to be enforced by town authorities or the justices of the peace, and during the reign of Elizabeth they performed their duties efficiently under the watchful eyes of the Privy Council. But, as can be seen, this made the gilds unnecessary. While they continued to function as social bodies and also as the enforcers of some government regulations, by 1650 they had lost most of the reasons for their existence.

Concurrent with the gradual disintegration of the gild system had been the rise of domestic industry, or industry in the homes. Having begun back in the fourteenth century in the cloth industry, by 1600 it had come to full flower. A wool merchant, a fuller, a dyer, a cloth merchant, or even a weaver would go to the country areas, buy wool, have it spun and woven by the peasants, and then either sell it to the exporter or export it himself. The clothiers and the weavers in the towns, especially London, attempted to stop this. Although the clothiers demanded that finishing should be done in the towns, and the weavers even succeeded in having an act passed in 1555 forbidding weaving outside the urban centers, their efforts were ineffectual. Indeed, even factories were established. Jack Winchcombe of Newbury and William Stump of Malmesbury both set up a number of looms under one roof, where they employed weavers and finishers of cloth.

The London drapers also tried to keep the export of cloth in their own hands, fighting hard against merchants from the provincial towns, but they likewise were unsuccessful. The demand for English cloth so expanded the industry that the old medieval regulations were no longer applicable. In other industries the same thing was becoming apparent. The production of nails, cutlery, and similar metal goods followed much the same pattern. Industry was turning from the medieval system to something approaching our modern capitalistic industrial organization.

In Scotland a similar pattern was developing without the same industrial improvement. The merchant element, which controlled the situation completely, fought hard to prevent the craftsman from retailing his goods. The Convention of Scottish Royal Burghs, which had developed out of the Court of the Four Burghs, also directed the economic policy of the country for the benefit of the merchant. For this reason, since wool and other raw materials found a ready continental market, industry was not encouraged. The lack of villages and the strict enforcement of burgh industrial and commercial monopolies on the surrounding country also helped to prevent the establishment of a domestic industry. At the end of the century Scotland was little better off industrially than she had been at the beginning. James VI did entice some artisans from the Netherlands, but they, becoming discontented, soon left. The opposition of the merchants, and perhaps the climate, may have had something to do with their unwillingness to remain.

Thus, by 1600 many of the medieval characteristics of industry had largely disappeared. While much of the medieval form remained and gilds were apparently flourishing, the truth of the matter was that industrial capitalism and government regulation were putting an end to the medieval system. The worker was increasingly becoming an employee, largely dependent upon the wages paid by the capitalist, who was the owner of the raw materials and, in the case of the clothiers, not infrequently of the looms used by the weavers. Thus, although the worker continued to produce in his own home, he was being turned into a mere wage earner. It was because of the resultant breakdown of the medieval craft type of industry that the state had to step in with the Statute of Apprentices, which might be called a "national labor code." In industry, as in agriculture, the old order was disappearing.

Commercial Capitalism and Trade

The sixteenth century saw also the beginnings of an expansion of trade and commerce. Internal trade in some ways seemed to remain much as it had been in the Middle Ages, but appearances were deceptive. Although fairs at Stourbridge, St. Botolph's, Winchester, and London continued to function, and market days in the various towns and the selling of goods locally over the shop counter went on as usual, still, forces of change were at work. The improvement of roads after 1555, the development of river transportation, and the establishment of peace after the Wars of the Roses, all helped to modify the internal commercial organization. Towns with a natural advantage in some product found it profitable to concentrate on the manufacture and distribution of this commodity throughout the country. Corn and wool could move with much greater ease from place to place. Moreover, the decline of the gilds enabled citizens of different towns to buy and sell more freely on each other's markets. In Scotland the growth of burghs of barony, created by nobles within the monopoly areas of royal burghs, helped to break down the latter's controls. In this way internal trade became free and national, rather than being restricted and largely urban.

Greater changes still were taking place in foreign trade. The use in Britain of exotic goods: spices, sugar, silks, and jewels, was increasing rapidly, payment for these commodities being made by the expanding cloth export. At the same time, Spanish gold and silver were being sought eagerly. Although the principal market continued to be the Netherlands, particularly Antwerp, where the Merchant Adventurers had their staple, the English at this time began to expand their operations by trying to trade directly with the sources of supply: Russia, India, and America. To do this successfully they had to improve their organization, spread the risks, and provide for long term investment. At the same time, they were commencing to discover that extension of trade connections meant business fluctuations. Wars and rumors of wars, tariff barriers, and poor harvests might hurt the sale of cloth, which, in turn, brought trouble to the London clothier and to the primary producer. Thus, trade cycles, depressions, and booms began to play their part in the economic life of the day. No longer could England and Scotland live unto themselves.

The chief English export of the century was cloth. Broadcloths, worsteds, bays (baizes), says (serges), Irish friezes, and various other types were shipped abroad. Wool was exported, particularly from Scotland and Ireland, but the quantity leaving England declined steadily throughout the century. Lead and tin also seem to have been important, although their export in the raw state was not favored. Skins and hides, woolfells, and pewter were also included in most cargoes leaving the country. Fish were frequently sent abroad, although they came primarily from Scotland and Ireland. The lowly herring made up the bulk of the fish cargoes which were sent to both the Netherlands and the Mediterranean. By the export of these goods Britain was able to import the goods which she needed for her own welfare.

On the part of the government there was a strong desire to restrain imports of foreign luxury goods, seeing that they were of no real use to the country, and in the case of manufactured articles, might even hurt home industry. Above all else there had to be a favorable balance of trade. Despite their fond hopes, however, from all over the world there came imports in large quantities. From the Baltic came fish, wood, and naval stores; from the

Mediterranean and Portugal, spices, oil, wine, and silks; from Africa, sugar, saltpetre, dates, molasses, and carpets; and from Germany and the Netherlands, hops, linen, brass, and copper. Most valuable of all was Spanish gold, although its actual quantity was not very great, since there was frequently an adverse balance of trade, sometimes amounting to as much as £100,000. Moreover, as direct trading with the east became more common, a considerable amount of the gold imported was re-exported to purchase the costly eastern goods.

Most of the trade of England went through London. For a time Southampton became a London outport, but once methods of navigation had been so improved that ships were able to sail around the North Foreland into the Thames, Southampton was deserted. By the beginning of Elizabeth's reign London was paying about 90 per cent of all the customs duties. Leith, Dundee, and Aberdeen were Scotland's principal ports, while in Ireland, Dublin controlled most of the foreign trade. Some west coast ports, such as Bristol, Limerick, and Aire, traded directly with the south of France and with Spain, but they were far behind the others.

By reason of the expansion of trade which was taking place throughout the century, it was found necessary to improve on methods of financing. There was the problem of risk. A man might invest most of his money in one venture, which, if it were a failure because of piracy, shipwreck, or war, would be his ruin. To meet this contingency insurance had begun to appear, at first as a gamble, but soon as a regular form of protection. Then too, there was the problem of waiting for one's profit. Investment in a voyage to Turkey might not bring any return for six months. Consequently, a businessman could not sink all his funds in one voyage. Partnerships became the earliest means of meeting these difficulties. A venture involving a long wait for returns might not be possible for the average individual, but a number of men could get together, pool their resources in a common fund, and trade as a unit. As pointed out earlier,[4] this practice was often followed in the Middle Ages, but as the possibility of profits increased, it became even more common in the sixteenth century.

Toward the end of the Middle Ages another form of commercial organization known as the regulated company had been developed by the Merchants of the Staple. It was really a gild chartered for foreign trade, each member trading for himself, but under the gild regulations. The unfinished cloth exports were handled by much the same type of organization, the Merchant Adventurers.

[4] See page 70.

Composed of about 3,500 members, their export of white broad-cloths increased from 22,000 in 1500 to about 40,000 in 1600, along with another 40,000 colored cloths. Like the livery companies of London the Merchant Adventurers were autocratically controlled by the governor, his deputies and twenty-four assistants.

A medieval modification of this system was the method by which the craft gilds had sometimes bought goods and done business on shares. This method was now applied to risky long distance trade. In 1553, as a result of the activities of Willoughby and Chancellor, a trade route around Norway to Russia was opened up. To exploit this route the Muscovy Company was formed, each member contributing a sum of money which was used to purchase a common stock of goods. The goods were traded in Russia, a return cargo purchased, and when that had been disposed of, the profits were divided among the investors. Here was the partnership and company combined. In 1555 their new organization received a royal charter. The dishonesty of its agents in Russia, however, caused it, for a short time, to become a regulated company of the medieval type, such as the Merchant Adventurers; but as this was found to be impractical, it soon reverted to its joint-stock character. Other companies, such as the Eastland Company (1579), trading to the Baltic, and the Levant Company (1592), trading in Turkey, were organized on the same principle. Finally, with the year 1600 came the East India Company. The joint-stock company was becoming the recognized means of financing ventures involving great risks but bringing in high profits.

In the charters which established these companies various privileges were granted. The principal one was that of monopoly. As in the case of the medieval gilds, the company was usually granted the sole right of trading in a specified area and was frequently given the monopoly of certain goods. This enabled the companies to fix prices, control imports and exports, and generally rig the market as they saw fit. The opposition to such practices was very vocal, but was not effective until the third decade of the seventeenth century. Sometimes the charter also granted the right of establishing a staple port to which the enumerated goods were to be sent. After the capture of Calais (1557) by the French, the staple for wool moved several times, but never again became important. The cloth staple was situated at Antwerp for a long time, but as a result of wars of religion and the ensuing chaos, it was later moved to Emden and then to Hamburg, finally coming to rest at Middleburg in Holland. The Scots also established a staple, first at Bruges, but finally at Veere, not far from Middleburg. The primary purpose of the staple was not the collection of taxes, but the maintenance of monopoly and the acquisition from foreign governments of privileges for the traders. This system, however, by reason of the growth of trade, was soon to disappear.

Throughout the period both the English and Scottish governments continually worked to strengthen and develop foreign commerce. To improve ports and harbors Henry VIII incorporated the fraternity of Trinity House at Deptford, giving the members authority to supervise beacons and seamarks. At the same time, the kings were diligent in signing treaties with other nations in order to obtain privileges for their merchants. It was, in a sense, these treaties which, by helping to spread exports more widely, outmoded the idea of a staple port. They also helped to break down company monopolies. Yet the monarchs did not by any means believe in free trade. They set up customs duties, which could be used not only to produce revenues, but also to keep out foreign manufactures. During the reign of Philip and Mary (1553-58), the Privy Council produced the first rate-book of customs duties. This gave an exact statement of all taxes to be paid on goods entering or leaving the country. Home industry was also given every possible encouragement. If anyone had a scheme for developing a new industry, he was given a monopoly whereby he would be guaranteed a profit. The difficulty was that frequently these monopolies had nothing to offer and were only "rackets." But they continued to be granted, on the ground that they would supplant some foreign import or would produce a new commodity for export.

The government also tried to stimulate shipping and the carrying trade. It subsidized shipbuilding and required everybody, whether they wanted to or not, to eat fish on both Friday and Wednesday in order to give business to the fishing industry.

Furthermore, in line with the example of Richard II, statutes were enacted to force importers to bring their goods into the country either in English ships or in the ships of the country of the goods' origin. Added to this, many restrictions were laid upon foreign merchants trading in England. Down to 1550 these men had controlled a large part of English trade, but with the expansion of native capitalism, this began to change. When Elizabeth found that she could obtain money from English financiers, she began to curtail foreigners' privileges. Finally, when in 1598 the Hanseatic League was deprived of its surviving rights, the power of foreign merchants in England was virtually broken.

By 1600 trade had risen into a place of prominence much greater than it had held a century earlier. Increasing numbers of people were involved in it, either as producers or as merchants. What is more, it was increasingly becoming a capitalistic enterprise, based not upon individual but upon corporate investment and organization. While the commodities with which it dealt were much the same as those of the Middle Ages, because of the increasing risk involved, commercial structure was becoming more and more complex.

This growing complexity was accepted because of the greater profits now obtainable. These commercial gains were very frequently invested in industry and land, thus laying the groundwork for economic expansion into other fields. By the end of Elizabeth's reign medieval methods of trade were fast dying out, giving place to new techniques and modern ideas.

Finance and Taxation

The latter part of the sixteenth century was a period in which accumulations of private capital became increasingly important. As profits from trade, industry, and agriculture piled up, they created a further demand for investment opportunities. But this demand could be satisfied only if it were possible to create new needs for money or credit. Since industry or commercial ventures could take only a part of the available capital, some companies were at times prepared to follow the earlier practice of investing in loans to the crown or to municipalities. For the purpose of the small man, the goldsmith and the scrivener (the writer of documents) were more important, for they would give interest on deposits left with them. Private individuals might also make loans at interest, they might invest in joint-stock companies, or they might help to insure a ship going on a distant voyage. Since opportunities for such investment increased greatly throughout the early sixteenth century, by the beginning of the reign of Elizabeth such finance capitalism, interested not in commercial, industrial and agricultural ventures, but solely in the loaning of money, was becoming important in the economic life of the country.

The rise of native finance capitalism was particularly important to the government. As pointed out at the beginning of the chapter, prices rose steadily throughout the century. This meant rising costs for the state. While Henry VII had been careful of his resources, Henry VIII had thrown his inherited treasure to the winds. Under Edward VI things went from bad to worse. In 1550 £250,000 at 14 per cent was owed in Antwerp and the next year the government went bankrupt. When Elizabeth came to the throne, the crown was in debt to the tune of £227,000 of which £107,000 was owed abroad. In Scotland the situation was even worse, for the Scottish Kings found difficulty in obtaining loans except from their own subjects, who themselves were by no means well off. The trouble was, of course, that the monarchs of both realms were obliged to operate their governments upon income derived from old fixed feudal revenues. These had been insufficient in the days of Edward I, so they were even less able to meet the costs of sixteenth century administration.

The taxation and confiscation of church land helped to satisfy the government's needs temporarily. This, however, was soon dissipated. Elizabeth tried to stem the rising tide of prices by placing the coinage on a sound basis, but that was not enough. The government had to obtain more money, which was possible only through an increase in taxation. This took two forms. First of all, there were customs duties (tonnage and poundage) which Parliament usually granted to the crown for life. The cost of collecting these duties in England was often high, amounting to 16 per cent, while in Scotland the collection was even more inefficient. Still, with all its weaknesses, the customs brought in £102,000 to Elizabeth in 1588. Another form of taxation was the direct assessment: the tenth, the fifteenth, and the general subsidy. The tenth and the fifteenth, still fixed at £37,000, were insufficient. Consequently, in 1514 a general subsidy was levied amounting to 6d. in the pound, in 1534 increased to 1s. in the pound, on all land or goods worth £20 or more. As the machinery for assessment soon broke down, the subsidy came to be rated at £80,000. Even this was not enough. Consequently, other methods had to be employed. Henry VII had been good at collecting forced loans, which Elizabeth called "benevolences." In 1588 these netted £4,000, while prizes taken at sea brought in an added £5,000. Altogether Elizabeth received that year from all sources, including rents, feudal revenues, and the Duchy of Lancaster, about £390,000.

Although Elizabeth was unwilling to spend more than she absolutely had to, her expenses continued to increase. No longer could the crown depend upon clergy to conduct the administration, as they had done during the Middle Ages. A salaried civil service as well as a paid army and navy had to be maintained. In the event of a war further requirements had to be met. It was when such extraordinary demands were made upon the Exchequer that the crown turned to the English capitalist. By 1560 the native financier had entered the picture, making loans, giving aids, and buying government annuities. Not infrequently trading companies furnished the necessary funds, as when Henry VII borrowed £10,000 to import grain, or as when Elizabeth obtained £20,000 for the Irish war. From 1560 on, hardly a year went by without some loans being made by companies and municipalities to the crown. Elizabeth no longer asked the foreigner for help in time of need, but rather she depended upon the native financier. Yet, by the same token, she was unconsciously bringing royal power under the influence and control of the English merchants and financiers. It was the Stuarts who paid the price of this policy.

If the financial situation of the English government was unsatisfactory, that of Scotland was infinitely worse. Prior to the establishment of the Reformed Church, the economic condition of the government had been bad. Every year's operations ended with the state heavily in debt. When the church's land was taken over in 1560, it looked as though something might be done to alter this situation, but the irresponsible granting away of the land by the regents, and then by James VI, aggravated rather than improved the crown's position. In 1564 the royal debt stood at £32,698, and twenty years later at £67,000. Revenues climbed between 1513 and 1600 from £15,000 to £133,000 but this still did not meet the needs. Ecclesiastical incomes were plundered and *teinds* (tithes) were appropriated. Finally, to augment the royal revenues, in 1578 the old church's lands were all reannexed to the crown's use. But it was of no avail. The king was still in need. At the same time, taxation on the towns increased, thereby giving them some right to a say in parliament concerning government expenditures. By the end of the century both the English and Scottish crowns were in much the same condition, except that English money was worth about twice as much as that of Scotland. Thus, when James VI came to London, his poverty was even greater in actuality than in appearance.

In summary, while many individuals had accumulated large amounts of wealth during the sixteenth century, the crowns of both England and Scotland had become progressively poorer. Landowners who were entirely dependent upon their land were also feeling the pinch of rising prices. The wealthy were now the industrialists and the merchants. It was upon their riches that the crown had to depend, and should there be a conflict between the crown and the people, it would be the moneyed classes who would to a considerable extent determine the victory. By 1600 feudalism was dead, money instead of land was becoming the criterion of wealth and power.

The Problem of the Poor

The economic changes of the sixteenth century brought with them alterations in the social structure. While they raised up a wealthy capitalistic class, they also brought to the forefront the question of poverty. For one thing, there was the effect of enclosure. With some 35,000 or 40,000 peasants forced off the land with no possibility of absorption into industry, there was the problem of chronic unemployment. This was further aggravated by the beginnings of trade fluctuations. A falling off in the export of cloth reacted upon the whole country, throwing weavers, wool combers, spinners, and others out of work. A decline in the market for some other types of goods might have much the same effect. The introduction of machinery might also increase unemployment, although it is difficult to determine how accurate were many of the pamphleteers who bemoaned the use of labor-saving devices. Finally, there were the aged and "impotent poor," who could not care for themselves but were dependent upon charity. From the beginning of the century all these classes were increasingly posing a problem for the government.

The situation was made even worse by the concurrence of a numbers of factors. In the early part of the century many companies of feudal retainers which had been established in England during the Wars of the Roses had been disbanded, releasing unemployed soldiers to roam the roads. Coupled with this, the dissolution of the monasteries and the seizure of much of the gild lands in England, as well as the appropriation of church lands in Scotland, had removed one source of poor relief. True, the charity had often been indiscriminate and misused, but it had succeeded in helping many a sufferer. Then too, there was the rising cost of living, so charity which might have met some needs in 1500 was by 1575 completely inadequate.

In England the solution was sought in two ways: wage regulation and poor relief. The first wage-fixing attempt had been made in the Statute of Labourers of 1351, and during the later Middle Ages many similar statutes had been enacted. The sixteenth century law which was intended to meet this problem was the Statute of Artificers of 1563. This not only laid down conditions of labor and methods of assessing wages, but also gave power to local authorities to force the unemployed to work. Even this did not meet the need. As poverty was not always curable by orders to work, some form of charity was needed. To solve the problem of the "impotent poor," orders were issued in 1531 to the Justices of the Peace to grant begging licenses to deserving paupers. Vagrants who could work were to be whipped. In 1536 church-wardens were given the power to collect alms on Sunday so that the "impotent poor" should not have to beg. As this was not successful, in 1552 weekly collections were authorized. Three years later the wardens were instructed to make a canvass to see how much would be given throughout the year. Voluntary contributions were, however, ineffective. In 1563 the Justices of the Peace were empowered to force payment on pain of imprisonment, and in 1572 poor rates (taxes) were made binding in each parish under the direction of new officials, the Overseers of the Poor. By 1601 a full-fledged poor law was in operation. Provisions were made for apprenticing poor children to agriculture or trades, for supporting the "impotent poor" from the rates, and for supplying work to the able-bodied. In this way it was hoped that poverty would be eradicated and that national peace would be assured.

In Scotland much the same method was followed in dealing with this problem. The Scottish church, however, seems to have acted more on its own. One of the demands of the reformers was that the ecclesiastical lands should be employed partially to support the deserving poor. As this was not possible, collections at the churches as well as fines levied as church discipline were used to meet the paupers' needs.

In both countries the attitude towards the able-bodied poor was quite unsympathetic. They followed the injunction that, "if a man will not work, neither let him eat." Consequently, whipping, scourging, placing in the stocks, and even hanging were employed to discourage vagabondage. To protect efficient and conscientious parish overseers from an influx of poor seeking help, relief could be granted only in the paupers' home parishes. People who "came on the rates," whether "impotent" or able-bodied, could be shipped back to their home district. In each parish stocks of wool and similar commodities were to be provided for the work of the able-bodied and sturdy beggars. By means of this labor, goods for export would be produced cheaply. Poverty would thus be relieved, while at the same time it would help to meet the mercantilist desire for a favorable balance of trade.

In 1603 Queen Elizabeth died and was succeeded by James VI of Scotland, who united the two crowns. The sixteenth century had seen a gradual change from a medieval to the beginnings of a modern economy. The old industrial and agricultural techniques were still employed, but the medieval organization of the economy had virtually disappeared. Capitalism had become common in all phases of economic activity. At the same time, there had appeared a widening gap between the rich and the poor. Of all the problems bequeathed to the new century, however, the greatest was the declining financial power of the crown. Here lay the seed of much of the social and political conflict of the next hundred years. Thus, in 1603 one stands at the beginning of a new era, for the seventeenth century is the entrance hall to the modern age.

Chapter 9

THE PRELUDE TO MODERN
TIMES, 1600-1715

THE DIFFERENCE between the year 1500 and
the year 1700 in the British Isles is the difference between medieval
and modern times. As already indicated, the sixteenth century saw
the decay and disintegration of the medieval economy. The economic concepts and forms of the Middle Ages had begun to disappear. It is true that certain practices and types of organization
continued even down into the nineteenth century, for in history
there is never any abrupt change between periods. But despite this,
the seventeenth century and the early part of the eighteenth were
very different in spirit and considerably different in economic practice from the centuries which had preceded them. It was the period
of the Stuarts that laid the groundwork and made the preparations
for the modern economic developments. Thus it became the ante-
chamber to the present day.

In the political as well as in the economic and social fields the
period of Stuart kingship saw many changes. These, partially
caused by the economic developments, in turn exercised a great
influence on economic activity. Probably the most important innovation in the political arena was the rise of Parliament from its
secondary position in 1603 to the position where, in 1688, it could
depose a king. This acquisition of power came only after the Civil
War (1640-48) and the so-called "Glorious Revolution" (1688).
During the same period there took place the final subjugation of
Ireland to the will of England by the ejection of many of the Irish
from their lands and the "plantation" of English and Scottish
Protestant settlers. Plantations also took place in lands farther
away from home. Under the Stuarts colonies were established on
the American seaboard, Virginia, the Carolinas, Maryland, Pennsyl-
vania, New Jersey, New York, and New England, while many
Caribbean Islands were also occupied. In the Far East the first
steps were taken toward the eventual establishment of British rule

156

in India. Finally, and to sum up the whole matter, in 1707 the parliaments of England and Scotland were united. There was much opposition to this move, particularly in Scotland, but it seemed to be a case of either union or war. The former was chosen, although many since have rued the bargain, for by the Union the Scottish economy became merged with that of England. By 1715 modern Britain, at least politically, was nearly established.

While all these events were taking place, there were other fundamental but less noticeable changes. In 1700 Davenant, a contemporary student of economic affairs, reckoned that the wealth of England had increased from £17 million in 1600, to £88 million in 1688, the annual national income in 1700 being estimated at £43 million. Thinking primarily in terms of balance of trade, he calculated that the national wealth was increasing at the rate of £2 million a year. Whether his estimates are right or not, it shows that during the century England had experienced a very considerable economic expansion. What was even more important, wealth had increased while prices had not. By 1600 Spanish-American silver production was beginning to decline, and by 1650 the price revolution was over. Coupled with this was a growth of British population. By 1700 England, Wales, and Scotland had each increased their population some 25 per cent over the 1600 figure. Towns, particularly in England, were expanding, with London leading at about the half million mark, although even by 1750 not more than 20 per cent of the population were urban dwellers. Most important of all, while the monetary supply remained stable, the market both at home and abroad had experienced a marked extension.

Intellectually it was also a period of growth. In 1663 the Royal Society had been organized to study both scientific and social matters. Out of this came not only inventions, but also a stimulus toward scientific economic studies. With the growing wealth there was a spirit of adventure abroad. Men were ready to invest, to "adventure," their wealth in new projects in the hope of large returns. Thus it was no wonder that the troubled time of the Stuarts was also a time of economic expansion and development.

The Era of Expanding Trade

The dominant factor in the economic evolution of the seventeenth century was the expansion of trade, particularly with the foreigner. This accorded with the mercantilist idea that all industry and agriculture had to be geared to make profits on the world markets, a theory apparently corroborated by the concurrent increase in commerce and in national wealth.

While accurate figures are not easy to obtain, it would seem that the volume of trade did steadily become larger.[1] By 1700, the home market alone was consuming annually between £42 million and £43 million worth of goods, of which only £4 million was produced abroad. At the same time England's exports had passed the £6 million mark. It is true that trade fluctuated owing to wars at home and on the Continent and also to "booms and busts," but still there had been a steady growth. For this the mercantilist, the manufacturer, and even the farmer were glad. The merchant had now become a valued member of the community, was honored in the City and at court, and was even marrying his daughters to impoverished but well-titled gentry. Sir Thomas Mun had well named his defense of the East India Company *England's Treasure by Forraigne Trade.*

Throughout the whole period English exports continued to be dominated by cloth. In 1621 it made up nine tenths, in 1662 about two thirds, and in 1700 about one half of the total value of goods sent abroad. Although the attempt to sell woolens in India, China, and the West Indies had been unsuccessful, the Baltic, Russia, France, and the northern colonies took large supplies. As a consequence, the cloth industry was highly organized, with its principal southern depot at Blackwell Hall in London, while in the north the seventeenth century depot was at Wakefield, and the eighteenth century one at Leeds. Export of wool was unlawful, for cloth was now king.

Besides cloth, English coal was becoming an important cargo in both English and foreign ships. France, Scandinavia, and the Netherlands, all anxious to obtain this commodity, sent their vessels to Newcastle in large numbers. In 1609 the export amounted to about 250,000 tons, in 1660 to 537,000 tons and in 1700 to 653,000 tons. Wheat also was being shipped abroad in times of plenty, although between 1593 and 1663 laws were passed requiring the home price

[1] E. Lipson, *Introduction to the Economic History of England* (London, 1931), Vol. II, p. 189, gives figures as follows:

	Exports	Imports
1613	£2½ million	£2 million
1622	2⅓	2⅔
1663	2	4 (London only)
1700	6½	6
1710	6⅓	4
1720	7	6

to be below a certain level before this would be permitted.[2] In 1670 free export was allowed, and from 1673 on the production of grain was actually subsidized. This helped to stabilize tillage and to increase the amount sold abroad, which jumped from the 1660-72 annual average of 2,000 quarters to about 300,000 quarters in 1675. Along with these commodities went tin, lead, and a large part of the goods imported from the East: spices, drugs, fruits, and cottons. Thus, sales to foreigners were held to be the key to the country's prosperity.

England's imports came from three well-defined areas. There were first of all those from Europe. In times of food scarcity grain was an important commodity, usually brought in from the Baltic, particularly Russia. From the same area came iron. Between 1660 and 1715 Sweden sent a yearly average of 12,000 tons, while between 1700 and 1750 Russia averaged about 23,000 tons. The other important group of commodities from the Baltic area was naval stores: rope, pitch, and timber. When the Swedes, however, laid restrictions on the export of these products, England had to look elsewhere. After 1660 the taste for French and Portuguese wines and other luxury goods gave these countries a special place in the English import list. In fact, it has been reckoned by some that England's greatest amount of trade was with France, with whom she had a perpetually adverse balance. Meanwhile, trade with the Netherlands had lost most of its old importance.

Secondly, the East Indies and the Levant provided many commodities some of which were re-exported, while others were either consumed or processed in England. Cloves, mace, nutmeg, pepper, saltpetre, indigo, cotton yarn, raw silk, calicos, and, after 1700, coffee and tea all made up the cargoes. As the cotton and silk industry began to develop, raw cotton from the Levant and raw silk from China were imported in increasing quantities. Last of all, from the American and West Indian colonies came sugar, tobacco, and naval stores.

Scotland, who had seen her trade with Holland wrecked by the Anglo-Dutch wars, was prevented before 1707 from trading with the colonies, while she could sell to England only animals and some raw materials. In much the same situation, Ireland, treated as a colony, after 1672 was forced to send all her wool and cloth to England. Thus the English were gradually gathering the trade of the world into their hands.

Simultaneously, the commercial organization of England was

---

[2] The maximum prices were set in 1593 at 20s., 1604 at 26s. 8d., 1624 at 32s., 1654 at 36s., 1656 at 40s. a quarter (eight bushels).

beginning to change with the expansion of trade. It is true that a number of the old chartered companies, with their individual traders and their apprentices, continued to operate. Foremost among these was the Merchant Adventurers, which in 1611 finally established one staple at Hamburg, to be followed by another a few years later at Dordtrecht. The days of the regulated company, however, were numbered. For long-distance trade the necessity was the joint-stock organization. This was shown by the establishment of the East India Company (1600) on the pattern of the earlier joint-stock Muscovy Company. While this form of enterprise helped to spread the risks more widely, it came in for as much unpopularity as did the older organization. Both obtained trade monopolies in certain areas, and the fact that both were usually dominated by London meant that the monopoly was virtually a London perquisite. Consequently, throughout both the sixteenth and seventeenth centuries there was violent opposition to all such corporations, particularly in ports like Bristol and Newcastle. Moreover, since trade was expanding, it was felt that the privilege of trading freely was the right of all Englishmen. "Interlopers" became increasingly common, and the smuggling into the country of monopoly goods became an important industry. Thus, while the companies could enforce their medieval rights in certain limited areas, much of England's foreign trade throughout the century was illegal.

That the nature of commerce was changing can be shown by the modifications of government trade policies. James I, on his accession, abolished all monopolies. True, he re-established many for the profit of his favorites, but Parliament in 1624 limited monopolies to new industrial processes, to chartered corporations such as the East India Company, and to industries involved in national defense. Even this was not enough, and opposition to company monopolies continued, on the ground that those who received profits were few in number, prices at home were kept up, and bullion was exported. As a result, with the exception of the monopolies of certain long-distance trading concerns such as the Levant or Russia companies, by 1689 trade in such commodities as cloth was practically free. By 1700 many other monopolies had disappeared. At the same time, regulations relating to such things as the standardization of the length and quality of cloth had become a dead letter. It was felt that competition would take care of that problem. Finally, the protectionist attempts to control trade by import and export duties began to disappear. The idea of preventing the export of raw materials was outmoded. In 1691 export duties on many foodstuffs were removed; in 1699 woolen goods were freed; in 1703 the Methuen Treaty gave Portuguese wines special favors in return for the free import into Portugal of English cloth; in 1709 coal exported in British ships ceased to be taxed; and by 1721 practically all export duties were gone. At the same time, many import duties had been reduced. There was a growing tendency to allow trade to follow its natural channels.

One apparent exception to this rule was the English "Navigation Policy," the principles of which had been embodied in the Navigation Acts of 1651 and 1660. This, however, affected only the colonies which were regarded as part of the mother-land. It was designed to strengthen English shipping, to keep foreigners out of the colonial trade, and to make the colonies a source of raw materials as well as a market for manufactured goods from the homeland. The colonies could trade among themselves, but might trade with other countries only through England. All imports had to come via England, and by the law of 1660 certain enumerated articles: tobacco, sugar, cotton, wool, and dye woods, the main colonial products, were to be exported exclusively to the mother country. England felt justified in this, since she furnished them both with capital and with military protection. Moreover, she gave the colonists a monopoly on her own market, even going so far as to destroy her domestic tobacco crops so that there would be no competition with the colonial products. She also gave "drawbacks," or rebates on customs duties, when goods were re-exported to the colonies, thus often making them cheaper in America than in England. Then too, if the colonies objected that such products as rice were damaged by having to go first to England, restrictions were very frequently removed. There were, however, two main causes of disagreement. England refused to countenance trade between the French and English colonies in America, and she insisted that no colonial manufacturing industries should be established. Before 1751 this was no very great hardship, for little manufacturing could be done, and smuggling took care of the intercolonial trade.

Ireland had in 1660 been given the same position in colonial trade as England, but jealousy on the part of English industrialists and landlords soon brought about a change.[3] By 1691, except for the export of horses and victuals, the Irish had been prevented from dealing with the colonies. Moreover, in 1667 the export of Irish cattle was generally forbidden. The Irish thereupon began to export meat and dairy products, which in 1681 were also banned

[3] See page 167.

from England. Wool, which prior to 1672 could be sold abroad, was after that date limited in export to England, where until 1740 it paid a heavy duty of 4d. on the pound. From 1699 on Irish cloth was controlled in the same way. The only product not entirely banned was linen, manufactured mainly in the north. The English seemed to be determined to keep the Irish as poor and as wretched as they could.

During the seventeenth century Scotland was not much better off. The royal burghs still controlled trade and trade policy in their own favor, curtailing commerce and industry at will. Added to this was the damage which resulted from the union of the crowns in 1603. Scotland, whether she liked it or not, now became entangled in every war of England. In this way she lost two of her best customers: Holland and France, without any compensation from England. Under Cromwell she was allowed to trade freely with England and the colonies, but after 1660 her products were rigorously excluded. Worst of all, as she had developed only a few industries, such as the making of rough cloth, linen, and stockings, she could export little but raw materials: wool, linen, yarn, coal, salt, cattle, and fish. Since she imported nearly all her manufactures, by 1681 her trade account showed: imports £317,-930, exports £66,345. In an attempt to overcome this adverse balance and to set up colonies, she organized in 1698 a joint-stock venture, "The Company of Scotland trading to Africa and the Indies," in which some £400,000 were invested. The attempt, however, to establish a settlement on the Isthmus of Panama at Darien was mismanaged. Even more damaging was the violent opposition it met with from both English and Dutch vested interests. They virtually sealed its doom before it started. The consequent disaster might have meant war with England had not cooler councils prevailed. In 1707 the organic union of the two countries took place, with the result that the Scots were given the free run of the colonies, to which they promptly turned their attention.

In summing up the condition of trade, we find that it grew steadily between 1600 and 1715. Exports were increasing much more rapidly than imports. By 1715 trade with the colonies amounted to £2,000,000 while the amount of shipping had risen above the 200,000-ton mark. Roads, on the other hand, not much better than they had been a century earlier, formed something of a barrier to trade within the country. Nevertheless, despite difficulties of transportation and occasional slumps, commerce was laying a solid foundation for future development. At the same time, it was facilitating the accumulation of capital, which, in turn, was to be invested in industry and agriculture. For instance, in 1651 Dud Dudley, the ironmaster, had as his partners a merchant and a linen-draper. But the accumulated capital would only be invested where there was a certain amount of freedom in its use. Therefore, trade, industry, and agriculture were all looking forward to a relaxation of state control, for only in this way, it was felt, could the highest peak be reached.

The Expansion of Industry

Expanding trade meant also expanding industry, for the growth in trade provided both markets and capital. But there were additional stimuli to industrial evolution. For one thing, the seventeenth century, like the sixteenth, saw the advent of more religious refugees from the Continent. Protestants from Holland and Belgium continued to emigrate to the British Isles, bringing new techniques in the manufacture of pottery, textiles, and metals. The Revocation of the Edict of Nantes in 1685 forced the Protestants of France, the Huguenots, to leave their country. Many crossed the channel to England, Scotland, or even Ireland. Some who were silk workers set up their looms in Spitalfields, just outside of London, while others, locating in different areas, introduced new processes in the making of sailcloth, beaver hats, and paper. Concurrently with the entrance of these immigrants, natives were inventing and beginning to use new machines. The gig mill, so unpopular in the sixteenth century, became quite common after 1660. The stocking frame, the Dutch loom for ribbons, and the spinning wheel also became customary tools of industrial production. But probably most important of all was the appearance of mechanical power. To drive tilt hammers, wire drawers, and the like men were increasingly turning to water power. In 1719 the first real factory using water power was established for silk throwing. Seven years earlier, Newcomen had invented a steam engine for pumping water out of mines. Although this was not immediately important, it was to be a pivotal point in the development of British industrial production, for steam was to become even more useful than water power.

To understand how these changes reacted upon industry, a glance at woolen manufacture is necessary. From 1600 on the output of fine English woolens and worsteds was expanding rapidly, each district specializing in its own particular type.[4] This tended to

[4] The eastern and southeastern counties produced worsteds, made of combed long wool, tightly woven and not fulled. Essex produced bays (baize) made of

deal the final blow to the old gild organization, for small shop production was now not enough. As a result, the domestic system expanded widely. The clothier, providing all the material and giving piece rates for cloth production to the small producer, became the dominant and usually very wealthy figure. Middlemen for the handling of wool were also more numerous after the export of wool was forbidden in 1617. Many of these also became clothiers. They would collect the cloth and take it either to Blackwell Hall in London or to a provincial market, such as Leeds. On the other hand, they might dispatch their wares to a factor in London, who, for a consideration, would dispose of it to a London draper for export. Sometimes the London draper himself would come into the provinces to buy cloth from the small producer, but the usual result was a fight with the local clothier. The domestic system was now completely capitalistic in organization.

The outcome of this development was the gild system's complete breakdown. In the early part of the seventeenth century lip service continued to be given to the gild idea, the early Stuarts being its great advocates. But simple economic necessity administered the coup de grâce. With the small farmer and his family living far from the towns and doing the weaving and spinning as by-industries, gild regulation was impossible. What is more, the whole question of apprenticeship took on a new aspect. Men simply did not bother with the required formalities. The Civil War also played its part by destroying much of the old supervisory power of the Privy Council. After the war Cromwell furthered the process by giving permission for any of his disbanded troops to enter a trade without the necessity of apprenticeship. From then on apprenticeship was virtually at an end. The courts refused to enforce the Statute of Apprentices, and by 1700, while occasionally the form of the practice remained, in reality it was outmoded. This meant that questions of workmanship, hours, and pay were now determined by competition in an open market. The one exception to this trend in the cloth trade was found in Yorkshire, where the tendency was to follow the older system. Clothiers who actually worked part of the process themselves were still common, although there were the "opulent clothiers" who resembled the entrepreneurs in other parts of the country. Then too, "factory clothiers"

---

worsted warp and woolen weft. Bombazine with a worsted warp and silk or cotton weft was also coming in. In the western Midlands and western counties woolens were still predominant, although around Salisbury fine flannels were more common. Devon was producing serges of worsted warp and woolen weft. In the north, Yorkshire was gradually changing from woolens to worsteds.

were beginning to appear, with shops in which the looms were operated. The new era had begun. Once mechanical power was used, the capitalistic clothier would become the factory owner. Without the intervention of the domestic system, the eventual development of the factory system would have come, as it did in France, only at a much later date.

Other textile industries had their own particular forms of organization, but followed generally the plan of woolen manufacture. The cotton industry never had a gild organization. Using material relatively new and always imported, it immediately fell under the control of the merchant who supplied the raw cotton, bringing it from the seaports. Its principal area of production was the west country, particularly Lancashire and the area around Manchester. As early as 1619 the Chetham brothers, with a joint stock of £10,-000, were employing a good many Manchester folk in weaving and spinning. In 1736 another man in the same area owned over 600 looms. While there were virtually no all-cotton goods produced before 1700, fustians made from a mixture of linen (the warp) and cotton (the woof) were popular. It is estimated that about 40,000 pieces were produced as early as 1621. By 1701 almost 2,000,000 pounds of cotton were being imported, while the value of the exported manufactures reached £23,253. Coupled with the cottons were linens. These were manufactured primarily in Lancashire, Ireland, and Scotland, but it is impossible to estimate their value. As mentioned before, silk throwing and weaving was also increasing in importance: and the setting up of a silk-throwing factory on an Italian plan by Thomas Lombe in 1719 gave the industry a considerable impulse to expansion.

By their very nature, the heavy industries had always been somewhat capitalistic in organization, and as they developed, they moved further in that direction. Coal mining is a good example. Owing to the destruction of the forests, coal during the seventeenth century became important as an industrial fuel. As early as 1621 Dud Dudley claimed that he had learned how coal could be used to smelt iron, although we have no certain knowledge of anyone doing this until 1709, when Abraham Darby discovered the secret. By 1700 the coal pits of the Tyne Valley and Wales were producing about 2½ million tons per annum. A considerable amount was also coming from Fifeshire in Scotland. The pits, meanwhile, were going deeper and were becoming harder to mine and more difficult to drain. This meant a rise in prices. It also forced the owners to seek for a way of removing the water, for which purpose Newcomen set up his first steam engine. The mines were usually exploited by a contractor paying royalties to the owners and selling the coal to the middlemen who took care of the marketing. The latter, known on the Tyne as "hostmen," gained, as distributors, such control of the industry that they became its virtual dictators. Both contractor and middleman conducted business on a large, capitalistic scale.

Iron production continued in its old groove, but as it did not produce nearly enough for local consumption, large quantities of bar iron were imported from Sweden, Russia, and North America. It was to keep up the supply of colonial iron and to provide a market for finished wares that the manufacture of iron goods in the colonies was prohibited. By 1700 the principal centers of production of finished articles were Sheffield, Birmingham, and their surrounding areas. Sometimes there were small working masters, but more frequently the work was done in homes at piece rates for merchants. The latter often owned blast furnaces and forges also, thus controlling the whole process. Not infrequently the operations were so minutely divided that one man gained particular skill in but a single small phase of production. He never saw the finished article but worked for a wage or at a piece rate. This system could be followed only on a capitalistic basis. The Mines Royal and the Mineral and Battery Works, producing copper and brass, which were united in 1689, and which retained their monopoly until 1700, followed much the same plan. Thus, by 1700 the domestic system with its capitalistic organization had become general in industry.

The change in the form and attitude of industry helped to bring about a change in government industrial policy. The opposition to monopolies turned the government from the policy of giving special protection to a group of individuals within the country to that of helping and protecting industry as a whole. Export bans going back to the Middle Ages were continued. After 1617 no wool could be taken out of the country—at least legally—but much of it was smuggled across the Channel. The same policy was tried with leather and a few other commodities. In this way the price of raw materials could be kept down. At the same time, the importation of competing goods, such as cloth, was restricted. Around 1660 silks and cottons began to compete seriously with woolen cloth. This resulted in violent attacks on the East India and Levant companies, but it was not until 1721 that printed or painted calicoes were finally refused entry. Thus, the woolen interests unwittingly obtained protection for the domestic cotton manufacturer. A third way in which home industry was helped was by the prohibition of the emigration of native craftsmen and the export of their machines. A law of 1719 finally made such exports illegal. At the same time, inducements were offered to foreigners to come to England in order that advantage might be taken of their skills. In this way it was hoped that England would be able to attract new workmen and also to keep her own skills to herself, although at times her religious intolerance acted in the opposite direction.

In keeping with the current policy, any attempt on the part of Ireland to build up industries was definitely discouraged. As pointed out above, Irish wool could be sent to England only in order that English merchants and manufacturers might be able to make their profit. Thus, by 1715, except for the northern linen production, Ireland had little industry.

Throughout the century continual efforts were made to stimulate industrial production in Scotland, but the wars in which the country was willingly or unwillingly involved, by destroying its trade, limited its capital for investment. Coupled with this, the older groups of merchants and the landowners were frequently more interested in exporting raw materials than in working them up into processed goods. The Stuart monarchs, on the other hand, did everything they could to encourage industry. To stimulate woolen production, James VI, who was also James I of England, abolished the English customs duties on Scottish cloth. He also granted monopolies on new industrial processes, such as the one for making glass given to Sir George Hay of Nethercliff. After the Restoration various laws were enacted to help industry by prohibiting the importation of foreign luxuries, by restricting the export of raw materials, and by offering encouragement to alien settlers. Some Dutch and Flemings did immigrate but, as in the sixteenth century, did not stay any length of time. The instability of the government as well as the low standard of living did not attract them. Finally, in 1681 a mill for the manufacture of fine cloth was established near Haddington, and others modeled after it soon followed. As these goods began to compete with English manufactures, the English clothing interests heartily endorsed the Union which enabled them to swamp the infant rival. Thus Scotland was left after 1707 with nothing much more than her domestic manufacture of rough plaiding and linen, fishing, and Highland grazing.

Such was the condition of British industry in 1715. Now completely dominant, the domestic system had outgrown the old medieval jacket, which was no longer adequate for the expanding economy. In this was laid the basis for later developments. Yet, at the same time, it deprived the individual producer of protection from exploitation, of pride of craftsmanship, and of freedom to work as he pleased. Children, now more than ever, were being used in industry even from the age of three or four years. Worst of all, with many workers dependent upon foreign trade, fluctuations in the European economy might well bring unemployment and disaster. It was, however, but an interim system, which would have to develop a closer integration if industry were not to fall to pieces from lack of effective organization.

The Beginnings of the New Agriculture

The seventeenth century saw much of the land in the British Isles change hand. One of the causes of this was the rise of the middle class. In both England and Scotland newly rich merchants and industrialists bought lands and manors. The English merchants also invested in land in Ireland. Sometimes they held their properties for only a short time and then resold at a profit. At other times they retained the land and farmed it. Many of the middle class directors of the Bank of England were landowners. This process was also furthered by the Civil War. Cavaliers often forfeited their estates for adherence to Charles I or were obliged to sell in order to pay heavy fines. More fortunate neighbors might buy these properties to round out their own estates, or city magnates might purchase them to obtain landed titles. In Ireland only one third of the land, and that the poorest, was left to royalists. The rest went to Cromwell's army and financial supporters. In Scotland something of the same effect was achieved by Charles I's resumption of the ecclesiastical lands granted to the Scottish nobles at the time of the Reformation. The new owners were usually enterprising men, looking for a profit from their investment. The result during the latter part of the century was a growth of interest in businesslike farming.

The desire for agricultural improvement becomes apparent when one reads contemporary farming literature. William Blith, author of *The English Improver Improved*, and others like him were continually advocating new methods and systems, very often derived from Holland and Belgium. Sir Richard Weston even entitled his work *A Discourse of Husbandrie used in Brabant and Flanders*. Every one favored the total abolition of the old medieval system, with its vestiges of services and its rigidity of method. Each individual should be permitted to do as he thought best with his own land. This would mean, of course, enclosure, a procedure that was always heartily favored. It was felt that on purely economic grounds enclosure was the only possible course to follow.

To a considerable extent because of this publicity, improvements gradually began to take place despite the farmers' conservatism, the open field system, and the risk of having the rent raised. New machines came into use: the double furrow plow, the earliest of drill seeders, and implements for drainage. Then there were such new field crops as turnips and potatoes. Clover, flax, madder, hops, and artificial grasses, such as sainfoin, were also raised. Asparagus and artichokes appeared in the gardens, while greenhouse experiments were carried on with lemons and oranges. Tobacco too was grown until it was banned by the government in the 1650's. Along with the new crops, and partially because of them, improved crop rotations were employed, the old order of wheat, rye, and fallow gradually being superseded. This trend was helped further by an extension of the practice of artificial fertilization of the land with chalk, marl, sea sand, compost, potash, and even old rags. But one must always keep in mind that these changes took place only very gradually and in relatively small areas. Nothing could be done on a large scale until enclosure had become the rule instead of the exception.

Despite the considerable outcry against enclosure during the seventeenth century, by 1750 almost half of the available land had been affected by the new procedure. Before the Restoration there had been great fear that the country's food supplies would not be sufficient. But as improved methods of agriculture gradually increased production, this fear departed, and with it, little by little from 1660 on, the violent opposition to enclosure. The new enclosure was primarily for the grazing of meat cattle, although enclosure for the plow was not uncommon. Indeed, it was for grain production that the Earl of Bedford and his company (1637-51) drained some 400,000 acres of the rich loamy fenland. In the Midlands, however, where the soil is clay, pasturage was more profitable. Usually the land enclosed here and in places such as Devon came from the commons and the waste, upon which already half starved cattle were grazing and equally starved squatters were living. There was a great outcry by the poorer people against such "intakes," but in their existing state the commons and waste lands were unprofitable and useless. As a result, whether by general agreement, by force, or by Act of Parliament, which was a new method, enclosure continued slowly throughout the century. The same thing was taking place in Scotland, although with less resistance, since the tenants had few rights in the land. As a result of the change, there was a general though slow improvement in farming technique. But even by 1715 it had not advanced very far.

The gradual extension of enclosure meant alterations in the size of the farms. As leases fell in, landlords laid fields to fields. Yeomen, who might be copyholders, bought or rented "intakes" from the commons or became tenants on the new farms, which varied in size from 10 to 200 acres. Wealthy landowners, on the other hand, often possessed extremely large farms, particularly if they were devoted to profitable grazing. The other side of the coin is that presented by the poor man, the "husbandman" who held less than ten acres. He usually devoted himself to working for other farmers and, in his spare time, to some phase of the woolen industry. The landless man, even lower in the scale, was usually forced to take to the road, although with the expansion of industry, he could often find work among the cutlers of Sheffield or the cotton weavers of Manchester.

In Ireland there were few yeomen except in the north. Instead, there was usually the absentee landlord, his resident bailiff, and the poor wretched peasants who tilled his ground or cared for his cattle.

The government was very often torn between two opinions, as it has been ever since, regarding the conflicting claims of industry and agriculture. Industry wants low food costs in order that production costs may be low, while agriculture wants high returns in order to buy the products of industry. This situation often leads to trouble. Down to 1660 the export of corn was very spasmodic, but as production increased and prices dropped, the state adopted a new policy. When prices were below a certain level,[5] export was permitted and import was taxed. But as prices rose, export was curtailed and tariffs fell. This helped to stabilize grain supplies. After 1673 bounties were sometimes given in order to keep land under the plow. When barley or malt was selling at 24s. or less, the bounty was 2s. 6d.; rye at 32s. or less received 3s. 6d.; and wheat at 48s. or less was given 5s. By this means grain production was maintained. It was for the same purpose that the importation of Irish cattle and dairy products was prohibited. These had been forcing down the English farmer's prices, with the result that the landlords, who made up Parliament, were having difficulties. At the same time, to help the cloth manufacturers, the export of wool was forbidden, thus keeping this commodity cheap. By these means the government, not always consistently, endeavored to control and to aid farming.

As an index of the conditions of farming during the seventeenth

[5] See page 159, note 2.

century, prices generally rose, although not violently. Increased output was consumed by a growing population, and it is possible that, as a result of the higher demand, food prices climbed more than those of any other commodity. This is indicated by the fact that rents also increased by perhaps 33 per cent, while the value of freehold land may have risen even more, perhaps by 50 per cent. The erection of new brick farmhouses and the improvement of barns and outbuildings also show that to the man who had, even more was being given. But, at the same time, from those who had not was being taken even the little that they did possess.

The New Methods of Finance

Because of the over-all expansion of trade, industry, and agriculture in the seventeenth century, opportunities for investment naturally increased. In the draining of the fens the Earl of Bedford invested some £100,000, while Dutch capitalists put in as much, if not more. Iron works, coal mines, and the like, which required a large capital outlay, also provided opportunities to employ one's money. But, above all other things, trade was the favorite. For instance, the planting of the Massachusetts Bay colony cost some £192,000, while the initial cost of a sugar plantation was around £5,600. Looking to the Orient, the goods exported by the East India Company between 1601 and 1620 amounted to £292,286, although the bullion sent with them came to £548,090. The cargo for one voyage alone was worth £36,000. All this had to be provided by investors, who were the more willing to pay seeing that they would receive a large return on their money. The laws against usury, which had been abolished in Scotland in the late sixteenth century, were finally repealed in England in 1625. Interest on loans was to be kept at 8 per cent. Money could now be made by investment, and men were free to invest as they saw fit. As long as the return was good, that was all that had to be considered.

In the growth of investment, the employment of the joint-stock form of organization was probably of the greatest moment. Between 1560 and 1720 the amount invested in such enterprises has been estimated as increasing from £10,000 to £50 million. The East India Company is typical. At first each voyage was financed separately, the cargo and ship being sold and the profits divided according to the proportion of shares held. But this soon became complicated because there might be five ventures going on at once. Consequently, in 1657 a permanent General Stock was established, paying a dividend which varied between 5 and 10 per cent. The holders of the shares could sell them freely on the open market. It was usually accepted that if such companies had a charter, the shareholders were only liable to the full paid-up value of their shares. If, however, they had no charter, the shareholders were "jointly and severally responsible" for all the company's debt. This tended to restrict investment in unchartered companies, but not greatly, for during the period after the Restoration there was a rapid increase in the number of joint-stock companies formed to finance all sorts and kinds of industrial and commercial ventures, of which, not trade, but coal mining and iron smelting were the most important.

Investment was further encouraged by the growth of credit and banking. As already pointed out, by 1600 a considerable knowledge of the mechanics of these matters had been attained. The scriveners and the goldsmiths during the early part of the seventeenth century continued to do banking as repositories of money and as middlemen for loans. They were greatly helped when Charles I seized for his own use the bullion deposited for safe-keeping by merchants in the Tower of London (1641). Fearing to trust the government, businessmen began dealing more with the goldsmiths, who paid them a small rate of interest. At the same time, these embryonic bankers not only loaned money; they also discounted bills of debt and made payments for depositors on written instructions, now called checks. Most important of all, however, were their relationships with the government. Very necessary to Cromwell as a source of funds, under Charles II, they became even more important. Thus, down into the eighteenth century goldsmiths occupied a leading place in this world of finance. They made large sums of money, often receiving on a poor risk as much as 30 per cent in interest, the rate frequently charged the crown.

Basic to the development of such banking practices was the growth of the use of credit. Even in the sixteenth century clothiers had been obliged to give long term credit, sometimes for fourteen months, to the London drapers. The wool factors often paid off the clothiers and carried the London drapers themselves. But others who began to take the same type of risk, at a price, were the goldsmiths. The risks were very real too, for during the seventeenth century bills of debt were not transferable, and, what was even harder, they could not be protested for nonpayment. Not until 1698 was it made possible for such an obligation to be collected by law with interest and damages. In 1705 promissory notes were given the same position on endorsement. Since 1650 goldsmiths' notes had been circulating as money, but as the goldsmiths gradually gave up their craft to become simply bankers, bank notes in the modern sense came into use. All this meant a great easing of financial transactions. Notes could be discounted, bills paid, and money received without any transfer of coin or goods. But only during the last half of the seventeenth century had this really become normal procedure.

Involved in the matter of credit, and absolutely necessary for later financial evolution, was the founding of the Bank of England. In 1694, a group of London financiers headed by William Paterson, a Scot who later organized the Darien Company,[6] offered to loan to the government £1.2 million in return for a charter as a joint-stock bank with the right to take deposits, make loans, and deal in bills of exchange. In return, the government was to pledge its revenues as security and give 8 per cent interest, plus £4,000 a year for expenses. The government of William III accepted the plan, as it had up to that time been paying 12 per cent and more. In this way the Bank was established, the total stock being subscribed in less than two weeks. In reality, it was an investment in the national debt. At first the Bank issued only £20 notes, but the important thing was that by reducing interest rates, by helping to control the coinage, and by providing government backed banking facilities it gave a sense of financial security both at home and abroad. Its discounting of bills of exchange helped to maintain stability by guaranteeing that such bills could be collected. Such dependability was necessary if investment were ever to grow.

The Bank of England enjoyed one monopoly. It was virtually the only joint-stock bank which had the right to issue notes, and it kept that exclusive power down to the nineteenth century. On the other hand, it did not go in for branch banking. Consequently, local banks soon appeared throughout the country, very often founded by wealthy merchants or industrialists who were depositors in the Bank of England. Commencing by accommodating their friends through having bills discounted in London or providing bank notes, before they knew it they were in the banking business. The first Nottingham bank was founded by a mercer, and the Old Gloucester Bank by a chandler.

In Scotland, where the establishment of joint-stock organization was easier, banking developed even more rapidly owing to the fact that the Bank of England's monopoly did not cross the Tweed. The Bank of Scotland was organized in 1695, the Royal Bank of Scotland in 1727, and the North British Linen Company, organized to encourage linen manufacture, was involved in banking by

1760. These all were chartered. Private banks in Edinburgh were established by a corn dealer, a linen draper, a cloth merchant, and a tobacconist. In this way the foundation of the whole credit and banking system was being laid.

All did not go well, however, with the organization of credit, for in the early years of the eighteenth century came the South Sea Bubble. In 1711 the South Sea Company was founded, supposedly to trade with the Spanish-American colonies, a closed area. Since the company did not do too well owing to Spanish objections, it turned to other fields. It then offered to take over a considerable part of the national debt and received £9.5 million of it at 5 per cent. By dint of great publicity its stock climbed rapidly from £100 a share to £1050 on June 24, 1720. This rise caused a great flurry of speculation, with everybody organizing or investing in joint-stock unlimited liability enterprises of the wildest type. One company proposed to make a machine gun which would fire round ammunition to shoot Christians and square to shoot Turks. Another was floated "for carrying on an undertaking of Great Advantage which shall in due time be revealed." Most of these companies were, in turn, investors in South Sea stock, or their shareholders bought their stock with money borrowed on the security of South Sea shares. When the South Sea Company took legal action against these fly-by-night companies for daring to establish joint-stocks, the Bubble was pricked. Many companies were heavily in debt with few assets. South Sea shares were then thrown on the market to obtain the means of repaying the money borrowed. This caused a panic, forcing the whole structure to collapse, bringing the South Sea Company down with it, to the ruin of hundreds of investors. In an attempt to salvage part of the wreck, the Bank of England and the East India Company had to take over a block of the shares of the South Sea Company. For over a century afterward people were very dubious about the wisdom of investing in joint-stock companies. Only if they held charters of limited liability were they regarded as safe.

One outcome of the South Sea Bubble was the establishment of a number of new insurance companies. In the sixteenth century merchants meeting in Lombard Street or the Royal Exchange had been used to sharing risks on sea ventures. A premium was paid by the owner, and, in return, reimbursement was guaranteed if the ship was lost. After the Great Fire of London a fire insurance business was established by Nicholas Barbon, and by 1688 both marine and fire insurance companies were operating freely. Life insurance, which at the time was more or less a gamble, was also beginning. But as a result of Sir William Petty's studies of the London Tables of Mortality, some idea was obtained of the chances involved. In 1706 the Sun Insurance Company was founded, followed during the Bubble by some seventy other offices dealing in insurance on life, accident, and marriage (both for and against). Most of them failed with the Bubble, but two chartered companies have lasted to the present time: the Royal Exchange and London Assurance. Another beginning had been made.

Taxation and Coinage

Coupled with business finance was the need for paying the government's expenses, a fact which involved the early Stuarts in continual difficulties. The old tax grants of the tenth, fifteenth, subsidy [7] and customs were worth even less than in the sixteenth century. Prices had increased and the Stuarts were inclined to extravagance. Moreover, for various reasons, they could not get along with their parliaments. Their attempts to obtain more revenue without this body's consent was one of the causes of the Civil War. The Commonwealth of Cromwell, however, was in no better condition. The Protector met the problem by increased efficiency of collection, by new taxes, and by a monthly assessment throughout the country. These measures, however, only helped to make the Commonwealth more and more unpopular.

After the Restoration the problem remained, for income was far below even necessary expenditure. Under Charles II feudal dues were abolished by Parliament, depriving the crown of close to £100,000 a year. It was felt, however, that this loss of revenue would be made up by customs duties and an excise on beer. In 1643 Cromwell had abolished "tax farming" by setting up commissioners of customs. These men collected the customs for the government instead of following the old practice of paying a lump sum, albeit less than the expected amount, in return for the privilege of trying to collect for themselves all they could. "Tax farming" was reintroduced in 1660, but was abolished again in 1671. Although this increased efficiency in collection, inefficiency in the valuation of goods remained. Duties were not charged on the basis of real value, but on the value set in the Book of Rates, whose figures were usually out of date. A 5 per cent duty in the Book of Rates might mean 20 per cent ad valorem, making continuous revision necessary if accurate valuations were to be made.

[7] See pages 114, 151.

Excise duties were also carried over from the Commonwealth. These were levied on homemade goods, particularly liquors, eventually being extended to a number of other articles. Another source of income was monopolies, for which high prices were always paid. They had tended to die out with the Commonwealth, but their place as revenue producers was taken by the monthly assessments, which continued to be levied until 1692. In 1662 there was added a "hearth tax" of 2s. per hearth on all except the poorest homes, but it was so unpopular that it was dropped in 1689, to be replaced six years later by a "window tax," which continued down to 1851. Finally, in 1700 a land tax came into existence. Ostensibly a levy on all property, both real and personal, at the rate of 1s. (later 4s.) in the pound, before long it was being reckoned at £500,000, the principal taxpayers being the landowners. Merchants and traders seem to have successfully avoided any obligation.

By 1715 the royal revenues amount to about £5.5 million, the most important items being: excise £2.3 million, customs £1.7 million and land tax £1 million. This may be compared with the total of Queen Elizabeth's income of less than £400,000.

There was, however, the difficulty that these revenues did not meet extraordinary expenses. The crown still had to obtain loans in times of national emergency. James I and Charles I had secured funds from the Merchant Adventurers and the East India Company in return for privileges. Under Cromwell and Charles II the East India Company and also the goldsmiths had come to the rescue, until in 1672 Charles II said he could not pay even the 6 per cent interest on his debts. This bankrupted a number of goldsmiths. In 1675, however, to pay the debt charges, he assigned the revenues from excise duties, which were so employed until 1685. In 1705 this debt was united with the general national debt, and it was later taken over by the South Sea Company. Part of the problem of national debt had been solved by the erection of the Bank of England, which became the government's bank. Interest on the bank's loan was guaranteed by the assignment, first of customs and then of excise duties. The consequent new ease of borrowing for such purposes as war was reflected in the rapid climb of the national debt from £664,000 in 1688 to £54 million in 1714. Still, as the country was expanding economically, it was able to take care of such a load.

Another help to the government was the stabilization of the coinage and the increased use of gold coins. Henry VIII had used a gold sovereign worth 20s. James I had introduced a silver "unite" officially worth 20s., but since all unites were not of a standard weight, some were worth more, some less. In 1661 by proclamation the heavier coins were rated at 23s. 6d., and the lighter at 21s. 4d. Charles II issued a gold guinea nominally worth 20s., but, owing to dishonest clipping and wearing of the silver coins, it increased in value. William III undertook a recoinage in 1696-98, establishing the guinea at 21s. 6d. In 1717 it was lowered by Parliament to 21s., where it has remained ever since. Henceforth the gold guinea was to be the standard coin by which all others, both foreign and native, were tested. Silver was still used for small payments, but gold or notes based on gold became the usual medium of exchange, thus beginning the idea of a gold standard.

The Social and Political Effects

The years between 1600 and 1715 saw very considerable social changes take place in the British Isles, but particularly in England. It was the time of the rise of the big capitalist merchant and, to a lesser degree, of the industrialist. Some clothiers accumulated fortunes of £100,000, while Crowley, the north country ironmaster, was said to have died leaving over £200,000. This put the mercantile and industrial element on an economic level with most of the aristocracy. Such men formed a group which increasingly demanded freedom of action in economic pursuits. Not infrequently, although of Puritan background, they had thrown off the Puritan concepts of social responsibility, thinking only of money. Richard Baxter, the Puritan preacher of the mid-seventeenth century, complained frequently of his trouble with such people. It was they upon whom the government was becoming increasingly dependent for taxes, especially loans. This meant that the capitalistic class was wielding a growing influence upon the political life of the country.

Among the causes of the Civil War and the Glorious Revolution were to be found economic forces. The crown was seeking for greater revenues as well as for power to enforce its religious and social views upon the country. The people who were particularly opposed to the Stuart kings' religious ideas were those who were strongly Protestant and who were also becoming important economically: the urban middle class and the country squires. When opposition to arbitrary taxation was joined with opposition to the imposition of certain religious views, the result was revolution—revolution which had on its side the country's moneyed interests. This goes a long way toward explaining the success of both the Puritans in the 1640's and the Whigs in 1688. The causes of the revolts were not primarily economic, but the economic factor was one of the forces which made them successful. They were victories of the Puritan middle class.

There was no parallel improvement during the century in the state of the lower classes. Although prices did not rise appreciably, it was not until 1660 that wages began to improve. Even then they rose only at a crawl. In Scotland miners were in a state of virtual serfdom. Until 1775 they were bound to the mines and were paid a very small wage. In Somerset they received about 4s. a week (1610), and in Yorkshire about 1s. a day. Even by 1700 there had been no noticeable increase in their pay. Then too, the average agricultural laborer with a small farm never had enough income from the land to support himself and his family. Consequently, he usually went in for weaving at low piece rates, which were made smaller by all sorts and kinds of deductions taken by the clothier. In 1640 he would earn about 3d. a day, and in 1700 perhaps 6d. In Ireland the peasantry lived in even more abject poverty. What was worse, since the small farmers, particularly in England, were becoming increasingly dependent upon industry for their livelihood, foreign tariffs, foreign wars, a crop failure in Europe, or some other misfortune might depress the market and throw them out of work. Consequently, unemployment was becoming a chronic problem. Coupled with this, as enclosure progressed they were not infrequently thrown off the land altogether. Jobs were often hard to find in the neighboring towns, so they were obliged to wander through the land looking for work. It is not surprising that the drinking of cheap gin became a common means of enabling them to forget their troubles.

In order to meet this situation the crown attempted to enforce medieval and Elizabethan laws. Re-establishment and expansion of the gilds was thought to be the solution. The early Stuarts, therefore, granted them wider powers to control and help industry, but after 1650 the gilds were completely obsolete. Attempts were also made to enforce regulations regarding prices and wages. This was the responsibility of the Privy Council, but with its loss of power in the Civil War, it ceased to have much effect. Consequently, the fixing of the price of bread and the wages of farm laborers by the Justices of the Peace was virtually abandoned by 1700. The revival of old rules and regulations was almost completely unsuccessful.

In the Poor Law of 1601 another method of attack was tried. The right to levy a compulsory poor rate in each village was granted, along with the power to erect houses of correction where rogues and vagabonds could be made to work. Provision was also made to have pauper children apprenticed by the overseers of the poor. Under Charles I, who in 1640 issued the Book of Orders, the Privy Council attempted, and in part succeeded, in enforcing this law. With the outbreak of the Civil War, when Justices of the Peace were taking opposing sides, this was no longer possible. During this period, however, some of the towns, such as Aylsham and Hitchin, actually established schools to instruct the poor in spinning and weaving. After the Civil War, with the demobilization of the armies and the unsettled state of trade, conditions deteriorated even further, but still no solution to the problem was found. Under Charles II, instructions were issued to establish a stock of wool or flax upon which the poor could be made to work. This was seldom done. It was cheaper to give the poor and the unemployed small sums of money to keep body and soul together. The one important measure was that of 1662, the Act of Settlement, which enabled parish officials to send back to their original parish within forty days of their entry any migrants who *might* come on the rates. This meant a drastic curtailment in the mobility of labor. It also meant that, rather than helping the poor to find work, the officials were more interested in preventing settlement, even if the town or village was in need of labor for an expanding industry. Many of the people, therefore, went to the larger towns, where they could more easily escape detection. It was under these laws that the poor continued to exist long after 1715.

The only answer which the laboring classes had to such a state of affairs was organization. Gradually during the latter part of the seventeenth century there was an emergence of "friendly societies" among the wage earners. They provided a type of mutual insurance, paying sickness and sometimes funeral benefits. Possibly they grew out of the older yeoman companies. Not infrequently they were also used as a means for trying to obtain higher wages or better conditions of work. Weavers, wool combers, feltmakers and others in some districts became highly organized, furnishing men looking for jobs with tickets of reference when they traveled abroad. Parliament, controlled by the aristocracy and the upper middle class, was against such organizations, but nothing much could be done at the time to stop them. On the other hand, they do not seem to have had any very great permanent effect.

The year 1715 stands at the beginning of a new era. The steam engine had just come into use in the coal mines, banking and finance had recently been set on a firm basis, taxation, somewhat improved, rested on a more stable foundation. In the social and political fields the middle class had risen to new heights of power and influence. Although the worker was not so well off, he was beginning to realize the need of organization. At the same time, with the opening up of colonies, new sources of raw materials and larger markets were becoming available. The modern age had begun. Yet one must always keep in mind that all these improvements and changes, the result of trial and error, took over a century to develop. The beginnings of the modern age can be seen by 1600, but not until after 1715 did it really begin to manifest itself in all its complexity.

Chapter 10

THE REVOLUTIONARY CLIMATE OF OPINION, 1715-1870

THE PERIOD from 1715 to 1870 was one of revolutions. Preparations having been made in the seventeenth century, the eighteenth and nineteenth centuries saw the completion of the change to modern conditions. The way in which the situation altered between these dates may be seen even if one glances only at the changes which took place in the political sphere. During this century and a half France had three revolutions and two empires, changing from a typical despotism to the home of European radicalism. Germany had evolved from a congeries of petty principalities to a large and powerful kingdom, soon to be an empire. Italy was unified, although largely at the expense of Austria, which had fallen to the position of a third-rate power. Thus the continental nations experienced many changes during this period.

An Era of Revolutions in Britain

While not suffering from similar violent upsets, Britain also experienced many political innovations. For one thing, the whole of the British Isles during this period came under one government. In 1707 Scotland and England had achieved political unity, and in 1801 the Irish Parliament was persuaded to vote itself out of existence in return for representation at Westminster. Simultaneously, a new British Empire was being built on the ruins of the old left by the American Revolution, only this time with more wisdom and consideration for the colonial peoples. This, however, was but a reflection of the difference in outlook in Britain itself, which was becoming the example for all democratically minded people. Her political modifications, revolutionary though they might be, following the plan of "broadening down from precedent to precedent," were being achieved without bloodshed. In 1832 the middle class gained the vote, and in 1867 skilled artisans obtained similar rights. Thus, many political changes took place during the hundred and fifty years following the reign of Queen Anne.

But the revolutions of these years were not merely political. Such political manifestations indicate more basic and fundamental alterations. Man's outlook had changed radically. By 1870 Christianity was not only being more and more ignored, it was being replaced by the worship of material things. Religious faith had to some extent been discredited in the popular mind, while science had been elevated to the position of a "sacred cow." Along with this change went a social revolution. No longer were the old gild ideas of the relationship between employer and employee held. No longer was cooperation between the two classes regarded as normal. Instead, they were by 1870 becoming separated into conflicting groups, one representing capital and the other labor. The gap between the two was disconcertingly wide, so wide indeed that some continental writers, such as Karl Marx, were urging the workers to revolt. Below this social change another was taking place, an economic one: the Industrial Revolution. It is this which has dominated the scene since the days of Queen Anne.

The economic revolution was a revolution in production. It came with the introduction of power machinery run by the steam engine, and set up in factories. No longer could the cottager spin his yarn, weave his cloth, or make his pins at home. He had to work in the industrialists's own building, the factory, at the industrialist's machines, and on the industrialist's materials. The laborer became a mere wage earner, owning nothing but his hands, which performed but a small part of the manufacture of the finished article. He was dependent upon the man or men who supplied the capital to build the factories, to buy the machines, to supply the raw material, to sell the goods, and to pay him wages. Thus, not only did the economic revolution consist of the introduction of new methods of production, but, by necessity, also of new methods of finance and distribution. It became both the age of the factory and of the capitalist and, by virtue of the need for improved communications, also of the railway, the steamship, and the telegraph. It resulted in starvation or near starvation for some, and enormous accumulations of wealth for others. It was a period which produced great quantities of goods, but quantities which were not always equitably divided. It is this period in which are rooted many of the present day's troubles and problems.

England was the focal point of the Industrial Revolution, but Scotland also felt its influence very strongly, particularly in the

Lowlands, where there was good farming land and considerable supplies of coal and iron. As a result of the opening up of English colonies to Scotland's exploitation, the latter also developed commercially. Thus, during the eighteenth century the Scottish economy became thoroughly integrated with that of her partner, and, consequently, from this point on, dealing with her as a separate unit is not feasible. Ireland, on the other hand, lacking mineral resources and educational opportunities and suffering from absentee landlordism, did not experience the same economic development. With the exception of a certain amount of industry, dependent upon England and Scotland, which developed around Belfast, she continued in very much her old way throughout the period. Although some modifications in the system of landholding were made during the latter decades of the century, nothing very much was achieved, so Ireland received relatively little benefit from the increase in industrial production.

Why Did the Industrial Revolution Commence in Britain?

Great Britain was the home of the Industrial Revolution, which subsequently spread to the rest of the world. By 1800 British industrialism was increasing apace, and by 1850 it dominated the scene. In Europe and America, on the other hand, it was not really until after the Napoleonic Wars that the new economic methods began to appear. The reason for Britain's head start in this race was that at the time she had certain particular advantages over all other countries.

For one thing, with the exception of two abortive Jacobite rebellions in Scotland (1715 and 1745), she had complete domestic peace throughout the century and a half. Few if any of the other countries had such a blessing.

Added to this was the considerable freedom enjoyed by British society at the opening of the Hanoverian period. By 1715, as we have already seen, government control of the country's economy was beginning to slacken. The gilds were powerless. Trade regulations were unenforced, resulting in a growth of freedom to seek one's own profit as one pleased. This was very different from the rigid control of Colbertism in France, which attempted to reestablish the gilds. Coupled with this, for over a century there had been an extension of religious liberty. True, it had had its expansions and contractions, but, generally speaking, the governments, whether Royalist or Roundhead, had not been, for those days, overly hard on religious dissenters. Consequently, there had been a continuous influx of religious refugees from the Continent, people who brought with them new industrial ideas and techniques. At the same time, from 1688 on many of the dissenters' disabilities had been removed or ignored, with the result that English and Scottish nonconformists, instead of migrating to the colonies, became more satisfied to remain at home. Finally there was greater liberty in the study of science and an extension of education. This was greatly stimulated by the creation of the Royal Society and by the fact that, after the Union of 1707, English nonconformists, who were excluded from Oxford and Cambridge, could attend Scottish universities. It is no accident that many of the inventors and practical scientists of the eighteenth and nineteenth centuries were either Scots or trained in Scottish institutions. Having a close connection with Holland, one of the most intellectual countries of the time, stressing hard work, and interesting themselves in science, the Scottish universities helped greatly in the preparation of those who were later to become innovators in industry and agriculture. These were some of the spiritual foundations of the economic revolution.

On the other hand, there were also economic reasons to explain why the revolution took place first in Britain. For one thing, the population was growing. By 1700 it stood at 5 million, and by 1750 at 5½ million. This meant not only greater productive power, but also an expanded domestic market. Without more capital, however, this would only have led to a declining standard of living. But the period from 1660 on had seen a steady growth in savings and investment. To a much greater extent than before money was becoming available for investment in agriculture, industry, and trade. An indication of this is to be found in the decline in the rate of interest from 8 per cent in 1695 to 3 per cent in 1760. Furthermore, the expansion of the credit system through the wide extension of banking facilities also helped very greatly.

Besides these influences there were the technical innovations already foreshadowed in the sixteenth and seventeenth centuries: the fulling mills, the gig mills, the tilt hammers, and wire drawers, all of them run by water power. Although the gilds had attempted to have them outlawed, their lack of success is indicated by the increasing numbers in use after 1660. Another side of this technical evolution was the division of labor, which Adam Smith reckoned as one of the most important characteristics of industry in his own day. This was the foundation of the whole domestic system. One man would spin, another would weave, still another would shear the cloth; or in the pin making trade there might be eleven or twelve men working, each at some particular phase of the manufacture. This helped to lay the groundwork for factory industry, including the heavy capital investment required before it could work effectively.

The revolution, however, was more than a matter of mere production. The goods had to be sold. The expansion of British trade in the seventeenth century was therefore very important in preparing the way for the Industrial Revolution. Not only was there an expanding home market, but exports also were on the increase. This meant a greater demand for goods, resulting in more capital to help grease the wheels of industry. Moreover, Britain's geographic position at the crossroads of the western world gave her an enormous commercial advantage which she exploited to the full. Thus, from 1715 on all the ground for a radical economic change was prepared. The change, however, came slowly, modified by many different influences and reaching its peak between 1850 and 1870.

That no other country enjoyed such privileges is very clear when one glances over the history of the period. For one thing, war had been endemic on the Continent. Between the years 1530 and 1648 Germany, made up of some 350 sovereign states, had been torn by religious conflicts which invited the interference of such neighboring powers as Spain, France, and Sweden, who participated in the wars of religion for their own ends. Italy had had much the same experience of external intervention, while France also for about seventy-five years (1560-1635) had suffered under the destructiveness of religious conflicts. After the dying down of religion as a cause of international and civil wars, a series of struggles took place largely because of Louis XIV's ambition to dominate Europe. The culmination of this phase was the War of the Spanish Succession (1701-13). After this there was a short lull followed by the wars of the Polish Succession and Austrian Succession, in which all the major powers were engaged. Although Britain usually took part in these conflicts, she, as a rule, contented herself with the granting of subsidies, with naval action and, on occasion, with the despatch of expeditionary forces. She never knew the devastation wrought by actual invasion. At the same time, by the use of her navy she did acquire control of large areas of the globe, such as India, which were of great economic importance. Thus, while wars retarded her possible rivals, they aided in her own development.

Much the same thing can be said regarding liberty. During the seventeenth century, with the exception of the Dutch States General, all the representative political bodies on the Continent tended to disappear, being supplanted by dictatorial bureaucracies which although at first efficient, with the passage of time lost that characteristic, becoming increasingly more oppressive and restrictive. A good example is the system set up in France under the intendant Colbert, who attempted to regulate everything. Coupled with this went the common practice of religious persecution which in the cases of Spain and France forced many members of the industrial and commercial classes to leave the country. Those from France were welcomed, however, in Holland, Prussia, and Britain, the latter being particularly well prepared to use their talents to the utmost. Religious restrictions also tended to curtail scientific development, giving a country such as Britain something of an advantage. Similarly, the desire in many Roman Catholic countries to retain the medieval way of life with the gild organization and widespread regulation also had its influence in hindering industrial and commercial development.

Thus, in economic matters the continental countries were generally somewhat behind Britain. The destruction of war had tended to keep down the accumulation of wealth which might be used to finance new projects. Moreover, the demands of war forced the governments to control industry and commerce more rigidly. Consequently, there was, compared with Britain, relatively little opportunity for the beginning of the Industrial Revolution on the Continent.

From Rationalism to Romanticism

As has been pointed out a number of times before, economic development is never determined solely by economic forces. Those people who are active in the economic sphere are also members of others spheres of activity: politics, the church, the home, etc. The way in which one reacts to economic changes, therefore, depends not merely upon the economic facts themselves, but upon one's interpretation of the facts in the light of a whole philosophy of life. At the same time, it is necessary to remember that man is at no time the mere victim of economic circumstances. His interpretation and understanding of these circumstances may lead him to attempt to alter them, thus changing the course of economic development. This was very clearly demonstrated in the early years of the Industrial Revolution. Consequently, in order to understand the economic history of the period, one must obtain some knowledge of the way in which men thought about the world and life in general and about economic processes in particular.

The eighteenth century was a century of rationalism. This was true of practically all European thought, but particularly of that in Britain. The final court of appeal with regard to everything was man's reason. There was unlimited confidence that man by his thinking could solve all problems. It was therefore a period of great optimism. The German philosopher Leibnitz taught that since this is the best possible world, any trouble in it is entirely owing to man's lack of understanding of the basic rules of Nature. To solve his problems man needs only to learn and to apply these rules, since all things, whether economic, philosophical, artistic, or religious, operate in much the same way. Scientific human analysis could therefore be expected to bring the answer to every question.

In this attitude is found a point of view very different from that of the Middle Ages or the Reformation. In the former the ultimate interpretations or explanations were to be found in the Bible and the teaching of the church; in the latter they were in the Bible, enlightened by the Holy Spirit, dwelling in the Christian. God for the rationalist was no longer a present reality. He had started the universe running, like a clockmaker, and then left it to go by itself. Man, as part of the universe, had been given the ability to understand the world's mechanism. Therefore, by means of his thinking he could discern ultimate truth, so attaining perfection. Condorcet, in his *Progress of the Human Mind*, written shortly before his execution during the French Revolution, proclaimed quite confidently that perfection was just around the corner. Man by his reason would soon solve all his problems.

Rationalism soon broke down under its own weight. For one thing, it stressed the intellectual side of human personality to the exclusion of the emotional, the aesthetic, and the religious. But what is more, by the reasoning of its most rigorous exponents, such as the Scot David Hume, it accepted a purely empirical interpretation of knowledge. All that one could really know of the external world was sensations received through stimuli being applied to the sensory organs. Even the existence of "cause" and "effect" was unprovable. To carry the matter further, one was faced with the serious question of one's knowledge of even sensation. Man was beginning to lose faith in the possibility of knowing anything, the only outcome being complete scepticism. The result was a reaction against the sweeping claims of the rationalists, but at the same time it was a reaction on a rationalistic basis, i.e., romanticism. The other side of man's nature, the emotional and volitional, was now brought into the picture.

Rousseau, Burke, and others of the Romantic school of thought held that man was governed mentally and socially by laws which, in their sphere, were comparable to the law of gravity. Just as the physical law was not something about which man had to think if it was to be effective, so the laws of the individual's being were beyond the requirements of thought. If these laws were allowed to operate naturally, all would be well, but if they were tampered with, perhaps by undue reflection, only trouble would result. Hence, for man to live properly, that is, in accord with his own nature, he must be given freedom to act naturally, for nature, according to Burke, was "reason without reflection." Thus, man, left to express himself as he would, could achieve his own proper end. True, Burke held that one must follow tradition, but that in itself was also the product of nature over a period of years. Others, such as Byron and Shelley, rejected tradition and convention on the ground that each individual nature was a law unto itself. All the romantics, however, felt that action must be based upon feeling, not reason. Even the German philosopher Emmanuel Kant approached close to this view by teaching that knowledge from reason was limited to the things of the senses. That which was beyond the range of the senses, in the area of how one should act, for instance, was a matter of faith and feeling. Religion and philosophy were matters of speculation, while the natural and social sciences were matters of exact investigation, albeit even in these fields one could never come to know essences, or the things in themselves.

Perhaps the best way of indicating the change in thought which resulted from the rise of romanticism is to compare it in one or two points with the so-called Enlightenment. For one thing the rationalists, or representatives of the Enlightenment, were inclined to be antihistorical, sneering at most things which had gone before. They felt that they had reached the apex of human achievement. The romanticists, on the other hand, stressed history and tradition as a guide to such an extent that they were in danger of becoming traditionalists in the worst sense of the term. The rationalists also, believing in the ultimate authority of human reason, felt that the "enlightened" person should have the authority to direct the common herd. They supported the idea of the "benevolent" despot. The romantics, on the contrary, believing in the intelligence and goodness of the common man, were more inclined to favor the removal of controls and restraints. Finally, there was the contrast between the complacency of the rationalists, who seemed to feel that they had almost "arrived," and the sense of struggle involved in romanticism. Only by the free expression of one's feelings and sentiment did the romantics believe that man could gain a true knowledge of the universe.

Rationalism was predominant in intellectual circles during the eighteenth century, but toward the end of the period romanticism began to gain adherents. It grew very slowly, however, until the French Revolution, which greatly enhanced its reputation. During the early part of the nineteenth century its principal advocates were literary men, such as Wordsworth, Coleridge, Byron, Shelley, and Scott. Never did it completely replace rationalism, for both ways of thinking accepted the same premises: man's goodness, his perfectability, and the adequacy of his natural reason. Thus, both schools tended to coalesce into a general philosophy which exercised a considerable influence on British thinking.

The Growth of Materialism

While rationalism and romanticism are particularly characteristic of the eighteenth and early nineteenth centuries, after the Napoleonic Wars the dominant point of view gradually became that of Materialism. Owing to the increased interest in and understanding of natural science, this seems to be a logical outcome of eighteenth century tendencies. Natural law, understood in physical terms, was made the arbiter of all things, being inherent in all existence. The eighteenth century thinker had believed the universe to be created by God, with natural laws imposed upon it. By 1800, however, man had come to assume that nature and natural law were self-existent. When Napoleon asked the scientist Laplace, in 1799, why he had not mentioned God in his theories, he replied: "Sire, I have no need for such an hypothesis." Man had abolished God.

While rationalism had in a sense stressed the idea of unchanging natural law, romanticism, on the other hand, highlighted the concept of progress and development. The German philosopher Hegel, in his pantheism, had concluded that nature was a living force vitally attached to the soul of man. For this reason God was an evolving being who came to self-consciousness in nature and man. Thus, nature and man were both progressing toward understanding. This meant that nature was conceived as developing or evolving by its own inherent forces and laws. This philosophic position became the basis of nineteenth and much twentieth century science. It has been the framework into which scientific facts have been fitted. Laplace, in his *Treatise on Celestial Mechanics* (1799), Lyell, in his *Principles of Geology* (1830), Lamarck, in his zoological writings, and finally Darwin, in his *Origin of Species* (1859) and *Descent of Man* (1871), presented the idea of the gradual development by innate natural law of the whole of the world and its inhabitants from primordial matter. All things were the product of evolution.

By this means God had been relegated to the museums, and matter was man's new deity. Since the fundamental law of all things was evolution and progress, in this light all things were to be understood. No attempt was made, however, to explain the origin of natural law, and what is more, according to this new way of thinking even natural selection and the influence of environment become in reality matters of chance. Consequently, not law, but chance was made the ultimate, although this was only seen some time after the close of the period discussed here.

The important thing is that this whole conception of evolution on the basis of natural law was applied to the thought and development of man. Religion, philosophy, and social relationships were all interpreted in terms of evolution. Economic institutions as well as social organization fell under the spell of materialistic development. Man, it was felt, could not control economic laws; all he could do was understand and obey them. It was this point of view which for a long time dominated the "classical school of economists." They attempted to understand the laws of economic behavior and development, but they were thoroughly convinced that little could be done about them. One can be thankful that there were those who held other views and that even the economists themselves were not prepared to submit fully to their own interpretation. Since this trend of thought lay, and to a considerable extent still lies, at the bottom of much economic thinking, it must be understood if one is to appreciate the economic point of view of the modern world.[1]

While the intelligentsia, at least in part, accepted these views, they were neither believed nor understood by the average man, particularly the factory worker. Throughout the period from 1715 to 1870 the principal intellectual stimulus of the lower classes came from their Christianity. In the eighteenth century, however, it was

[1] J. H. Randall in his *Making of the Modern Mind* (Boston, 1940), points out certain characteristics of this type of thinking: (1) It stressed change as being ultimate. (2) It developed greater interest in biology and psychology as explanations of social evolution. (3) It attempted to set up a new scale of social and moral values, all based on the developmental philosophy. (4) It emphasized the complexity of organization in all life. (5) It reinforced the humanistic and naturalistic attitude already prevalent. (6) It brought in relativism and irrationalism, since even thought itself was regarded as being the product of environment.

not the established churches of England, Ireland, or Scotland which wielded the great influence. These churches, run primarily by and for the upper classes, had become urbane, polished, and ineffectual. The clergymen were very often appointed to their charges by local magnates. Not infrequently, particularly in England, a man might hold five or six cures, albeit serving in none. The Bishop of Llandaff actually visited his diocese once in thirty-four years, while a writer in the *Edinburgh Review* at a somewhat later date described how the Scottish clergy of this period read "cold moral essays . . . to cold and none too moral congregations."

On the Continent, meanwhile, there had grown up what came to be known as the Pietist movement. It was a reaction against the coldness of both the Lutheran and Reformed churches, and it stressed Bible study, personal faith in Christ as Saviour, and the importance of Christian fellowship and morality. This movement, brought to England by the Moravian Brethren, had a mighty influence upon John and Charles Wesley and Charles Whitefield, all Church of England clergymen. Since the new teaching was not popular in the Established Church, these men turned their attention to the lower classes, preaching in houses, barns, and in the open air. Whitefield did much of his work in Wales, Scotland, and the north of Ireland, with amazing effects. The result was the "Evangelical Revival." This movement, which exerted a powerful influence among the British laboring classes, gradually extended to the higher ranks of society, even receiving the patronage of such people as the Countess of Huntingdon. The Wesleys eventually organized the Methodist Church, whose membership by 1800 ran into the thousands, while in Scotland the result was the disruption of the State Church and the formation of an evangelical Free Church. Before long the impact of the Evangelical Revival was felt even by the established churches, resulting in numerous reforms.

The importance of the Evangelical Revival was that, to the lower classes in particular, it gave some meaning to life. Re-emphasizing the doctrines of man's sinfulness and God's all-sufficient redemption in Christ, it placed the individual in a new perspective. What is more, within the movement there was a new fellowship and a new sense of responsibility. The continual emphasis of the evangelicals was upon the importance of all Christians taking part in the church's work. The Methodists held classes of ten or twelve members every week for fellowship and mutual encouragement. A high standard of morality was also inculcated. Honesty, purity, diligence, and sobriety were all regarded as of the greatest importance.

This meant that a new point of view had entered into the life of the average man. While there was no doubt much hypocrisy and sham, nevertheless, the Evangelical Revival did much to form the character of nineteenth century Britain.

Another force in the Church of England which was of some importance was the Oxford Movement, originally organized to protect the church against the attacks of Dissenters. Its stress was placed upon the corporate unity of the church, the importance of ecclesiastical tradition, and such things as the church's liturgy and sacraments. Ultimately, some of its adherents such as John Newman joined the Roman Catholic Church. Unlike the Wesleyan movement, however, it was influential primarily among the clergy, many of whom as a result became interested in improving social conditions among the laboring classes.

Finally, there were the Broad Churchmen in the Church of England, who also had their counterparts in Scotland. These were strongly influenced by the materialism of their own day. For them Christianity had lost most of its supernatural character, and the Bible was regarded as a jumble of folklore and fairy tales, the only important thing being Christian morality. They adopted the humanitarian tradition, which, on a somewhat sentimental basis, had continued to exist throughout the eighteenth century. In a sense they attempted to compromise between materialism on one side and evangelicalism on the other. Before 1870, however, neither they nor the High Church Oxford Movement had achieved great success or popularity.

Social and Economic Thought

Under the influence of such a climate of opinion, it is not difficult to understand why economic and social thought developed along certain lines. With the great expansion of industry and commerce, which brought so many changes between 1715 and 1870, it was natural that men should seek to give an explanation of what was happening and that this explanation should be in conformity with the point of view of their own day.

The one who laid the foundations for economic theory was the Glasgow University professor Adam Smith, who in 1776 published his *Enquiry into the Nature and Causes of the Wealth of Nations*. While a very acute thinker in his own right, Smith based much of his work on French writers, such as Quesnay, on fellow Scots, such as Hutcheson and David Hume, and on English economic writers, such as Davenant, all of whom, since the beginning of the century, had been advocating greater freedom in economic activity. Smith's work was followed by Thomas Robert Malthus's *Essay on Population* (1798), by David Ricardo's *Principles of Political Economy and Taxation* (1817), and by John Stuart Mill's *Principles of Political Economy* (1848). The views set forth in these works, representing the "classical economics," dominated economic thought down to 1870. Adam Smith, however, remained the great high priest of this school, for he laid the foundations, albeit somewhat shaky at times, for the later writers, who introduced numerous modifications into his theories.

Of equal importance with Adam Smith was Jeremy Bentham, who, while not an economist, had considerable influence on contemporary economic thinking. His ambition was to be the Newton of the social sciences. Seeking for the one fundamental law of society, he believed it existed in man's desire for happiness. The individual's happiness, therefore, whatever quality that happiness might possess, was the proper moral objective of man. Supremely confident that the human race was coming close to perfection, he felt that its greatest need was freedom. The individual was the best judge of what would bring happiness. Consequently, he should be allowed to seek happiness as he pleased. Bentham also strongly favored widespread education as a means of guiding people in their pursuit of this golden treasure. His maxim was "the greatest good for the greatest number," implying that the greatest freedom possible should be allowed in order that all, without trespassing on another's freedom, might seek their own pleasure. This social philosophy came to be known as "Utilitarianism" which had as its later advocates James Mill, his son John Stuart Mill, and others, such as Lord Brougham. Throughout the nineteenth century, as the cornerstone of liberal thought, it became the underlying assumption of the thinking of the "classical school of economics." The state's control of, and interference with, the individual was to be kept at a minimum in order that the individual might be free.

Benthamism, romanticism, rationalism, and the expanding economy, all combined to produce new economic concepts. The idea of a natural order and natural harmony was assumed. The whole of economic activity was conceived of as governed by an amoral natural law, the amoral character of the law being stressed in the early part of the nineteenth century by Nassau William Senior. This basic law of economic activity was enlightened self-interest, or "the natural effort of every individual to better his own condition." Furthermore, since each individual by seeking his own profit would benefit all others, the state, while providing protection for the country and the framework of necessary law, must govern as little as possible in order that the individual might be free. To obtain such freedom meant that gild and trade regulations must be abolished in order that one might use his labor and his money as he saw fit. It meant also that competition should be untrammeled by charters of monopoly or by state interference. In this way man, permitted to follow the natural laws of economic activity without let or hindrance, would produce the maximum economic value and wealth. The individual was thus abstracted from society, being made into an "economic man" acting only according to abstract economic laws. This abstraction was probably the greatest mistake of economists, for people seldom act according to the dictates of economic reasoning alone.

The foundation upon which the school of Adam Smith endeavored to build an edifice of general principles was its explanation of *the nature of value*. These economists completely rejected any idea that wealth was based upon gold and silver, although Ricardo held that paper money should always be backed by gold if it were to be a dependable medium of exchange. Real wealth, it was held, consisted in goods which were produced by the land, by labor, and by invested capital. But how to determine the "value" of such goods was not an easy matter.

Adam Smith in discussing this problem talked about "value in use" and "value in exchange," contrasting the usefulness and cheapness of water with the expensiveness, but comparative uselessness, of diamonds. Being mainly interested in the latter type of value, he was inclined to ignore the problem of utility. "Value in exchange" was the important thing. Value, he held, was ultimately determined by the labor cost of production, although in any advanced society the rent of land and the capital invested were also involved. These three determined the "natural price" of goods. He pointed out, however, that when the market was glutted, the market price dropped until it was no longer worthwhile offering the goods for sale. As a consequence, the supply was reduced so that only enough was available to satisfy the effective demand at approximately the "natural price." Thus supply and demand, along with the cost of production, determined exchange value.

Fundamental to the problem of keeping prices down so as to meet a greater demand was the need of lowering costs or, conversely, of increasing labor's productivity. This, according to Smith, could be achieved by division of labor, whereby the making of an article would be broken down into a number of individual operations, each performed by a different person. The individual worker in this system would acquire a skill which would enable him to perform his operation more rapidly, while he would also be saved the bother and waste of time involved in changing from one type of work to another. Smith illustrated this principle of the division of labor by pointing to what it had accomplished for the nailmakers in the neighborhood of Birmingham. Thus, through this change in the use of labor, production costs would be lowered, resulting in an augmentation of the country's wealth. At the same time, he realized that the amount of the division of labor was limited by the requirements of the market. That is, a decline in demand would arrest division where the market price fell far below the natural price. Another limiting factor, he pointed out, was the amount of capital available for investment, since capital was necessary to provide the tools, materials, and wages for labor. Thus, value could apparently be increased in every field of production through the division of labor, the investment of capital, and the extension of the market.

Smith's successors continued to study this question of value. Malthus, who believed that population always increased until production could no longer meet its needs, stressed the importance of supply and demand. The scarcity of goods was the deciding factor in the determination of their market value. Ricardo, on the other hand, was inclined to hold that value was ultimately determined by labor, of which capital was merely one particular form. The wages for labor and the profits for capital, therefore, were the determinants of any article's market price. For this reason it might not be profitable to put the necessary amount of work on certain goods because of the low return which they would command. There was a law of diminishing returns, beyond which it was not profitable to go. Nassau William Senior added a further interpretation by saying that value was determined by both labor and capital, the latter being the fruit of the capitalist's abstinence from use. He, therefore, could expect a return or reward for his self-denial in the form of profits. Finally, John Stuart Mill taught that market value was determined by the cost of production, around which natural value the price oscillated because of variations in supply and demand. Cost of production, in his thought, included Ricardo's two factors increased by taxes, although he held that capital investment had a greater influence than was allowed by his predecessor. Thus the classical economists believed that to make large profits, it would be necessary to keep costs low and demand high. The former could be done by the use of machinery and low wages, while the latter could be achieved by increasing population or by opening up new markets.

In speaking of value the term "rent" was frequently employed, a term which needed to be defined and, consequently, over which much ink flowed. Smith held that it was the gift of the earth's fertility which gave to man more than he had invested. It was the result of nature's cooperation with man. Consequently, the landlord in taking rent was almost parasitical, for he was receiving that upon which he had bestowed no labor. Malthus, however, pointed out that naturally the land never produced enough to satisfy the population, for numbers always increased until they consumed all that was taken from the land. This led Ricardo to deduce his theory of rent, basing it upon the idea, not of nature's cooperation, but of her reluctance to give up her products. All land does not respond to farming in the same way; some fields are less fertile and productive than others. Normally the best land, both from the point of view of fertility and of proximity to markets, is cultivated first. As demand increases, however, more land is brought into cultivation, despite the fact that it is of a lower grade, for it is cheaper to do this than to apply increased labor to the better land. The poorer land, because it requires more labor per bushel of produce, must ask a higher price for its products, thus giving a margin of profit to the better land. This margin is rent. Thus, if one field can produce wheat at 10s. a bushel, while the poorer field can produce only at 15s. a bushel, the rent of the first field would be 5s.

If there were an unlimited supply of land, all the same in quality and all equidistant from the market, there would, of course, be no rent. But, because lands differ in quality and situation and because nature must be coaxed to produce, there must always be rent. Senior went a step farther and applied this to all production. He stated that because there was imperfect competition arising out of natural advantages, monopolies, and the like, one party, as a result of high prices, might obtain in an exchange value far higher than the cost of production. This he termed "rent." It is more than a return for saving or abstinence and forms a large portion of the wealthy individual's riches. Consequently, the landlord and the monopolist were both regarded as profiting from their fellows' difficulties of production, or, in other words, through the high market value of certain goods gaining wealth without doing anything to deserve it.

Most important of the factors which went to determine value, however, was, as we have seen, the cost of labor. The question at this point was, what determined the return which labor should receive for its work. Smith did not believe that this was decided by economic law and continually berated employers for attempting to reduce wages to their lowest possible level, since he held that wages had to be "sufficient to maintain" the laborer. High wages, on the other hand, he recognized to be possible only as the funds available for wages grew, these, in turn, depending upon the employers' surplus revenue. Thus, only with increasing national wealth could there be higher returns for labor.

Certain views held by Malthus, on the other hand, were accepted and developed by Ricardo and John Stuart Mill. According to these writers, wages were determined by supply and demand. Under ordinary circumstances, if wages were raised, the working population would have more children, creating an ultimate surplus of workers. This would mean, in the labor market, more competition which, by the laws of supply and demand, would reduce wages to the lowest possible level, or that of mere subsistence. Since in the return on all production the proportion available for wages was fixed in a so-called "wage fund," the greater the working population, the less each individual would obtain. The reason for the proportion of the return on production which paid wages being so limited was that if it increased, rent and interest on capital would be so reduced that neither land nor industry would attract investors. The only solution, therefore, was the curtailment of population. The government should not interfere to increase the worker's pay, for a raise could not really alter the situation. It would only increase the demand for goods, which would, in turn, raise prices, leaving *real* wages at their old level. Generally speaking, wages always find the level of subsistence, which may be above "mere existing." They will, however, vary up or down, according to the economic condition of the country and the supply of labor. Thus, real wages, it was held, would tend to remain at a steady level without anybody being able to do very much about them, trade unions or governments notwithstanding. This meant, according to such thinking, a fairly stable basis for determining exchange value.

There was, however, a third element in the fixing of market value: the return on capital invested. It was the investor, the enterpriser, that most of this school of economists looked upon as the salt of the earth. The landlord, as we have seen, was regarded as one who "gathered where he had not sown"; while the laborer was more or less the victim of circumstances, condemned to live at a level close to mere subsistence, whose only hope was the curtailment of population and the free import of grain, which might raise his standard of living. The industrialist and the merchant, who saved their money and invested it, who took risks, and who produced or marketed goods, were the real supports of the economic framework. While Adam Smith had some reservations with regard to this middle class element, in his successors' minds there was little doubt that they were the real causes of Britain's prosperity. It was held, however, that owing to the increasing population, which would force up rents, and to the increasing demands by labor beyond the limits of the "wage fund," profits would decline. As a result, the time might come when the capitalist would find it unprofitable to invest his money, economic stagnation being the result. They did not seem to realize that increasing production by means of machinery would cheapen goods, thus providing a higher standard of living, nor did they see the possibilities of such things as joint-stock companies, in which the landlord and artisan could both have a share.

Despite any tendency, however, toward pessimism, the feeling was unanimous that the state must adopt a "hands-off" policy toward economic affairs. It was hoped that "natural" economic laws would solve the problem, but this could only take place if the laws were given freedom to function. Let each man seek his own profit, and all would be well.

This point of view was applied even to international trade. Mercantilist controls must go! Trade should be allowed to follow its natural course. Exchange was "natural" among men, contended Smith, pointing to the division of labor in domestic industry as an example. It was foolish to manufacture goods which could be obtained from abroad more cheaply. At the same time it was foolish for the government, unless for defense or fiscal purposes, to attempt to direct or tax trade. Regulation of commerce had only disrupted it and therefore had tended to decrease the country's wealth. Smith was even opposed to joint-stock companies as well as monopolies, for he felt that in such organizations the individual lost his freedom of action. He could not seek his own interest as Smith desired. Ricardo, following the same line of thought, felt that the specter of rising rents and wages, coupled with falling profits, could only be laid by the free import of such things as foodstuffs. By this means both rents and wages could be kept under control. It was largely this theory which make Britain a "free trade" country. The state should simply let economic affairs take their own course unless they operated to the detriment of the country's security.

It was because of this outlook upon the government's relation to economic matters that the classical policy came to be known as "laissez faire." Let things go as they see fit, for they will follow their natural inherent laws. Man, who is naturally good and tending toward perfection, by following his own interest will always do what is best for society as a whole. This reasoning was weak in many ways, but still, it became extremely popular among the industrial and trading middle class of the nineteenth and early twentieth centuries.

The Opposition to Laissez Faire

While the classical economists tended to become increasingly abstract in their thought concerning "economic man," the social consequences of laissez faire industrialism in other quarters gave rise to misgivings. The poverty, exploitation, and depression of the working class began to be deplored by many. The antagonism to the classical doctrines, however, was not usually based upon economic, but rather on social and humanitarian, grounds. Although very frequently the classical doctrines were accepted unhesitatingly, or at least with slight modifications, at the same time, attacks upon the consequences of following their precepts grew stronger throughout the whole period.

From the Tory party, largely dominated by the landowning interests, came some of the earliest opposition. While the Tories accepted many of the laissez faire ideas, they felt that agriculture should have special protection. Edmund Burke and Sir Walter Scott both spoke for this interest, laying great stress upon the historical and traditional importance of the landed gentry in Britain's development. With their romantic approach they feared for the position of the aristocracy if the industrial middle class were given full and complete freedom. They felt that the state still had certain rights of control and in this they were supported by such economists as Lord Lauderdale and John Rae, both Scots, who criticized many of Adam Smith's concepts. The final defeat of this body of opinion, however, came with the repeal of agricultural protection in 1846.

Another part of the opposition came from the Radicals. Tom Paine, the author of *The Age of Reason* and *The Rights of Man*, attacked any form of oppression or exploitation. He was not exactly consistent, however, for his fundamental anarchism would have led to complete exploitation of the weaker by the stronger. More important than Paine was William Cobbett. He was primarily interested in protecting farm laborers from the social consequences of the enclosure movement. He hated enclosing landlords, businessmen, capitalists, nonconformists, and Malthusians. He seems to have hoped that, in some way, England could be returned to its former condition of imagined economic development and prosperity. Not a Tory, but a Romantic, he had a large reading public for his *Political Register*. Without any real political or economic program, his influence was ephemeral.

More consistent, but not much more effective, were the socialists of the period. Godwin, Shelley's father-in-law, termed by D. C. Somervell a "philosophical gas-bag," [2] held that there should be no government. If everything were held in common, men could live by reason alone. Later socialists such as the mill owner, Robert Owen, held to the idea that association and the cooperative ownership of the means of production would solve the problems of the working class. If only the environment could be changed, everything else would improve, even the profit motive would disappear. Man in his ideal system would trade work for work, without having recourse to money. As one can see, he was definitely optimistic. One socialist who accepted the theory that labor provided all the value in production was William Thompson. He held that the difference between the pay of labor and the selling price of the goods was "surplus value," which rightly belonged to labor. He did not advocate abolition of private property, but he did lay the groundwork for much later thought. Finally came John Stuart Mill. Beginning as an adherent of laissez faire, by the time his *Principles* had reached its seventh edition in 1869 he had so modified his views that he was advocating socialism, many of his ideas having been borrowed from the French writers St. Simon and Fourier. Socialistic ideas, however, obtained no great currency before 1870.

Probably the most effective critics of the ideas of laissez faire during early nineteenth century were those who represented the Evangelical Revival. Frequently, but by no means always, they came from the ranks of the Tories. The important thing was that they were not too impressed by "iron" economic laws, and, above everything else, their deep Christian piety urged on them the necessity of alleviating the lot of the Negro slaves in the colonies, of the children and women working in factories, and of the laborers in the mines. While they accepted many of the current economic views, they were strong advocates of protective legislation for the workers. William Wilberforce, a leading evangelical, for a long time headed the fight against Negro slavery. Robert Peel, the father of the future prime minister and an industrialist, was responsible for the earliest factory act (1802). Later on the leadership of

[2] *English Thought in the Nineteenth Century* (London, 1947), p. 30.

the fight for factory legislation devolved upon the Earl of Shaftesbury, a Low Church Anglican who was supported by Methodists,
Quakers, Presbyterians, Baptists, and Congregationalists. In Scotland the leader of the Free Church movement, the Reverend
Thomas Chalmers, also did much to help understand the need
and methods of relieving poverty. None of these reformers, however, advocated any change in the economic system. Many were
even convinced that the existing order was ordained of God. At the
same time, they realized that no system is better than the people
who make it operate. Consequently, a change of moral and spiritual
outlook was more necessary than a change of the economic organization.

Much the same attitude was adopted by the leaders of the High
Church movement. They did not, however, bother very much with
factory legislation, for they believed that the Christian's duty was
to give charity to those in need. The Broad Church element, on
the other hand, influenced by the growing tendency toward socialism in secular thought, tended to favor collectivism. Their socialism, which was largely of the cooperative variety, caused them
to make many attacks (1848-54) upon the depressed condition of
the working classes, as, for instance, when Kingsley wrote such
books as *Alton Locke* and *The Water Babies*, in which he exposed
current evils. Although workmen's organizations were encouraged
and cooperative movements helped, such aid does not seem to have
had any immediately important effects.

The Spread of Economic Ideas

While at times economic theory may seem very abstract and
very ineffective in economic history, from the days of Adam Smith
on it has wielded a growing influence. The reason is that men are
more aware of its importance both in explaining and influencing
activity and are consequently prepared to understand and discuss it.
The growth of factory towns also played its part, for even the common people, brought close together in common interests, began to
exchange ideas and complaints.

One of the most important aids in this development was the
expansion of educational facilities. The eighteenth century saw a
considerable growth of the effort to instruct even the working
classes. No doubt partially to keep them docile, people such as
Hannah More organized schools among the lead workers in the
Mendip Hills, and Robert Raikes established his Sunday Schools in

industrial towns. But whatever the motive, people were taught to read the Bible and to write, thus opening to them a new world. In Scotland general education had since the Reformation been more widespread than in England. What is more the Scottish universities, because of their close connections with the Continent, were using methods far in advance of those followed by Oxford and Cambridge, where enrollment was still limited to Anglican students. In England, the nonconformists' academies, which were well-attended, stressed practical subjects, such as science, business methods, and the like.

During the early part of the nineteenth century this trend continued. Various private school societies were established. Although many of these did not give an extensive training, they were better than nothing. At length, in 1834 the government was persuaded to grant financial aid to schools. Despite the disputes between the nonconformists and the Church of England over which schools should receive government support, advance now began in earnest. Charity schools, under the leadership of men such as Shaftesbury in England and the Reverend Thomas Guthrie in Scotland, also continued to furnish opportunities. Added to all this, University College, London, was established on a nonreligious basis, and in 1871 Oxford and Cambridge were thrown open to nonconformists. Meanwhile, under the influence of Lord Brougham, mechanics institutes had come into existence to further adult education among the working classes. Thus working class education was becoming an accepted fact with far-reaching results.

Coupled with the growth of education went an expansion of printing and publishing. For the upper classes there were such quarterlies as the *Edinburgh Review* (founded 1802), the *Quarterly Review* (1809) and the *Westminster Review* (1824). In their order of appearance these were Whig, Tory, and Benthamite. At the same time monthlies, such as *Blackwood's* (1817), and by 1840 weeklies, such as *Punch*, were appearing, to be followed by others: *The Economist*, *The Nation*, etc. Papers for the working classes, such as Cobbett's *Political Register* and his *Twopenny Trash*, also had wide circulation. By these means economic and political ideas were passed freely from mind to mind, and before long they began to have important repercussions.

The outcome of such stimuli to thought was very practical. Men started to question the current economic ideas. Those who felt themselves aggrieved began to combine for action, to demand the vote, and to seek reform. All this, in turn, influenced economic development and modified its growth. Therefore, as one studies the economic history of the period, one must continually remember the gradual change which was taking place in economic thought. But even by 1870, despite criticism, laissez faire ideas still predominated.

Chapter 11

AGRICULTURE BECOMES AN INDUSTRY, 1700-1875

Necessary to any understanding of the economic revolution in eighteenth and nineteenth century Britain is a grasp of the fundamental changes which occurred in agriculture. Without an agricultural revolution there could have been no great industrial and commercial development. The reason for this is very plain. With the concentration of industry and commerce in urban centers, many people moved off the land and ceased producing even a part of their own food. Thus, the remaining farmers had to expand production in order that they might feed not only themselves but also the industrial workers in the cities. As the population was growing rapidly at the same time, further pressure was added to the demand for foodstuffs.[1] The farmer, in turn, was helped by businessmen who, seeing his need, were prepared to put money into agriculture. They sought not only a secure investment, but one that would yield both social prestige and profits. In this way a considerable amount of the income derived from the industrial expansion itself was used to increase farm production. At the same time, the improvement of communications, the rise of the machine manufacturing industry, and other industrial advances contributed directly to the agricultural change. In these ways agriculture and industry influenced, stimulated, and cooperated with each other, sometimes for the betterment, sometimes to the detriment, of the common people.

The New Techniques

Basic to the agricultural revolution was the appearance of new farming techniques. These took a number of distinct forms. There

[1] The population probably stood at about 7¼ million in 1751, and 9¼ million in 1781, while by 1821 it was 12 million, in 1851 almost 18 million, and by 1871 almost 23 million.

was first of all the production of new crops. We have already seen how both artificial grasses and turnips were introduced to England in the 17th century. Their cultivation was steadily improved. Jethro Tull in 1733 published his *Horse-Hoeing Husbandry*, advocating in particular the drill sowing of turnips. Lord Townshend also did his utmost to spread turnip culture in Norfolk. Clover, carrots, new types of wheat, and hops were all either introduced or grown more widely during this period. In both England and Scotland potatoes became a favorite crop, while in Ireland between 1776 and 1831 tobacco was successfully cultivated. The planting of forests on nonarable land was also taken up on a scientific basis, particularly in Scotland. One of the reasons for the interest in these new crops was that some were known to return to the land chemicals which others had taken out. Thus, instead of the old medieval fallow system, which annually left one third of the land useless, a system of rotation was adopted, as in the four course rotation of Lord Townshend: wheat, clover, barley, and turnips. In this way the land could be kept continually under the plow, and its fertility not only preserved, but increased.

Along with the new crops and a good system of rotation went the use of new and improved fertilizers. Prior to the eighteenth century little had been used except barnyard manure and some lime. Tull did not favor manure because it so often carried weeds. He thought that deep plowing and a frequent loosening up of the earth around the roots was sufficient. However, bone manure and rape dust came into common use. Then, as a result of the researches of Sir Humphry Davy for the Board of Agriculture in 1803 and succeeding years and the publication of Liebig's *Chemistry in its application to Agriculture and Physiology* (1840), there was an increase in the use of chemical fertilizers, such as nitrate of soda and superphosphates. In the 1840's the droppings of birds, or guano, was imported in large quantities from certain sections of South America. It also became the practice to fold sheep on light and sandy soil in order that their manure might be used. Thus even poor land was made to produce good crops.

Rotation and fertilizers, however, are of little use if the ground is very damp or marshy, a condition common to many areas of the British Isles, especially Ireland, owing to heavy rainfall and poor natural drainage. Although the first attempts at drainage on a large scale had been made during the seventeenth century in the Fenland, it was not until the eighteenth century that the practice really began to spread. At first farmers simply threw the land up into ridges or dug ditches which were filled with brush and then covered over. Joseph Elkington of Warwickshire in 1764 introduced a new technique, using a deep ditch with holes driven through its bottom, to reach the underground water. His practice was followed generally until James Smith of Deanston, Perthshire, about 1831 developed the idea of digging ditches which were filled with stones and covered with sods. He would run a number of parallel drains in order to do the work more thoroughly. The next improvement came in the 1840's with the introduction of tile pipes. The government, very much interested, granted sums at various times to help with this work, and private drainage companies were also organized. Tile drains, however, were not efficient enough for the very low lands of the Fen district. At first windmills had been used to pump out the water, but later, with the advent of steam, mechanical pumps were employed. As a result of all these techniques large tracts of land hitherto regarded as useless were turned into gardens, which brought returns well worth the effort and expense.

Few of these improvements would have accomplished much, had it not been for the invention and employment of machinery. There was Tull's drill plow, by means of which seed could be sown in rows and then cultivated by a "horse hoe" running between the plants. This was a considerable step forward. In 1750 John Small, a Scot, invented the swing plow, pulled by two horses, to replace the old wooden plow using twelve or fourteen animals. Shortly afterward James Meikle, another Scot, brought out the winnowing machine, while his son Andrew produced in 1786 a mechanical thresher. Thereafter new machines of many different types appeared on the market: sowers, harrows, hay makers, tedders, chaff cutters, and turnip slicers. It was not, however, until 1826 that a grain reaper was produced by the Reverend Patrick Bell, a Scottish minister. Although very cumbersome, it had no competition until the appearance in the '50's of lighter American machines. Most important of all was the employment of steam. Threshing machines, as well as many others, soon came to be run by steam engines, while in the 1840's and '50's steam plows made their appearance. The same power helped in another way, for, applied both to trains and ships, it materially aided the farmer in transporting his goods to market. Thus, not only was his work made easier and more efficient, but he was enabled to get his produce to the consumer more quickly and in much better condition.

Side by side with the improvement of arable techniques went an advance in animal husbandry. Since much of the land in Britain is better suited to this type of farming, it is easy to understand its importance. Prior to 1750, with the cattle, sheep, and horses running loose on the commons, there was little chance of scientific breeding, the result being poor, nondescript animals. What was usually taken for scientific classification of cattle or sheep consisted in measuring the length of the horns or listing the color. The man who changed this situation was Robert Bakewell of Dishley, in Leicester, who by means of inbreeding produced a new type of sheep, known as the Leicesters, which unlike the earlier breeds provided not only good wool but was also palatable as food. He also developed the common longhorn cattle for fattening purposes and improved on the current Leicester Black Horse, giving it cleaner, shorter limbs. Bakewell's methods were followed by others. The Collings brothers, for example, originated the Shorthorn breed, which, besides being good beef cattle, surpassed Bakewell's longhorns as milkers. Others, such as the Devons, the Herefords, the Ayrshires, the Aberdeen-Angus, also appeared during this period. Different strains of sheep were likewise established, the most important being the South Downs. In Scotland the Lintons and the Cheviots, because they stood the climate so well, became the favorite breed. So it may be seen that animal husbandry was able to keep step with the improvements in arable farming.

The introduction of new techniques meant a very great increase in farming returns. With scientific methods the productive capacity of the land could be doubled both in grain and animals. Yet, despite this fact, the improvements came in only very gradually, even by 1800 few being widely known, let alone widely followed. Throughout the country the farmers' conservatism tended to keep them in the old rut. It is interesting to note, however, that there were certain areas which did advance quite rapidly. Such districts as Norfolk, the Fens, Leicester, and Lothian were by 1800 considerably advanced beyond the rest of the country. Close behind came certain areas around London and some of the northern industrial centers. In Ireland, on the other hand, there was relatively little improvement. The big stimulus came with the Napoleonic Wars and with the prosperous period subsequent to 1840. By 1875 the new techniques were quite general, but even then not absolutely universal. Yet it is important to remember that, despite the slowness of their adoption, the new techniques were the foundation of all the changes which took place in farming between 1700 and 1875.

The Changes in Landholding

Along with, and largely caused by, the introduction of new techniques went enclosure. As already seen, this movement had taken place on the demesne farms in the Middle Ages and had also been introduced for the purpose of sheep raising in the fifteenth, sixteenth, and seventeenth centuries.[1] The eighteenth and nineteenth centuries, however, saw a new type of enclosure. While the earlier movements had affected only a small portion of the population, this one was to change the face of the whole of the British Isles. It meant that the old "strip farming" and the use of commons were to disappear entirely by 1865. The strips were to be consolidated and fenced, the commons were to be cut up and joined to the arable or pasture. It meant also, particularly in England and Wales, the elimination of the "customary rights" possessed by such people as cottars and day laborers. In Scotland and Ireland this latter problem did not arise, as only a few enjoyed such privileges. Yet, on the whole, it meant a complete change in the old system of landholding.

Why was this necessary? Elsewhere we have pointed out the deficiencies of the old system; the difficulty of common cultivation, the inevitably poor methods in use, and the restraints imposed on the energetic farmer. One could put up with these disadvantages as long as demand for agricultural produce was relatively stationary. Once the need for foodstuffs began to increase, however, something had to be done. Grain production had to be stepped up, and the breed of animals had to be improved. This could be done neither under the strip farming of England nor under the runrig or rundale systems of Scotland and Ireland. Along with this went the growing individualism of the period, which, on a priori grounds, favored the abolition of common effort. Consequently, it was only natural that enclosure should take place.

The method by which enclosure was achieved varied according to the country. In Ireland, because the landlord or the middleman was absolute, he could very easily evict the tenants and enclose the land—unless the Whiteboys Association succeeded in frightening him into leaving his tenants alone. In Scotland an act of 1695 had established that the landowners could have the sheriff enclose the runrig land and apportion it among the various claimants, while land in commonty could be divided by commissioners of the Court of Session. This system facilitated changes, so in the Highlands during the last half of the eighteenth century the landlords cleared out the tacksmen or middlemen who contracted to rent out the land, and brought in their own tenants, usually from the Lowlands. In England, if the owners and tenants were agreed, enclosure might be achieved by consent, but to make it legal one had to obtain a

[1] See pages 86 ff. and 136 ff.

confirmatory letter from Chancery. Usually, however, enclosure took place by means of an expensive private Act of Parliament. The small farmer seldom had any say in the matter, the whole thing being determined by the big landowners. Parliamentary commissioners, appointed to apportion the land, did so without reference to customary rights, insisting that only proven legal claims could be recognized. Some owners, although they were few in number, provided small allotments for those deprived of common rights and similar privileges. To help and also cheapen the process a general Enclosure Act was passed in 1801, to be followed in succeeding years by other acts of the same type. Parliament, being composed largely of men interested in advancing such reorganization, did not exercise itself very effectively on behalf of those too poor to oppose.

The rate of enclosure seems to have been determined by a number of factors: the character of the soil, the type of farming, and, above all, the price of farm produce. Thus we find that before 1760, enclosure for arable and grazing took place only slowly, while after that date it gradually increased in momentum. The great stimulus came during the Napoleonic Wars, when food was scarce. It was then that the number of enclosure acts (1800-1810) reached 906, taking in over 1½ million acres. In the following ten years almost the same area was enclosed under 771 acts. Although these figures apply only to England, the process was also going on in both Scotland and Ireland. In the latter country, since the export of wheat to England was not permitted before 1806, cattle raising had been popular, resulting during the eighteenth century in a very considerable advance of enclosure for pasturage. Speaking of Britain in general, however, it seems that arable land was usually enclosed first, with pasturage following. By 1830 most of the enclosing was completed, and by 1865 it was at an end. In the latter year a society was organized to prevent further enclosing of commons in order that they might be used as parks for the industrial population. Thus, in a little over 100 years, Britain had seen a complete change in both its method of landholding and its ideas of cultivation.

As one looks at the whole process of enclosure, he cannot but admit that, despite the suffering entailed for the small man, it was necessary. If Britain was to provide even a small portion of her growing population with food, the old system had to be abandoned. It was the only way by which the new agricultural machinery could be employed effectively and by which advantage could be taken of other new techniques. Furthermore, as long as the old subsistence method was followed, every farmer, whether it suited his land or not, had to be an arable farmer. But with a more scientific approach lands such as the heavy Midland clays and marls could be laid down to grass, while the loamy soils of such areas as the Fens, East Anglia, Lothian, and other districts could concentrate upon the growing of grain. Thus, it was only with enclosure and the use of the new techniques that the best advantage could be taken of the various types of soil. This was of considerable importance, not only in improving production, but also in the lowering of food prices, a very real necessity for the industrial worker.

The Beginnings of Capitalistic Farming, 1700-1800

In attempting to understand the actual progress of the agricultural changes which took place in Britain during the eighteenth and nineteenth centuries, one finds that the personal element has an important place. Had it not been for a few men and one or two organizations, nothing would have happened. The "improving landlords" of the period were the leaders. Mention has already been made of Lord Townshend and Robert Bakewell, who did much not only to devise new methods, but also to bring them to the public's attention. Under Bakewell's influence, the Smithfield Club was established in 1798 for the improvement of livestock. Even more important was Coke of Holkam, in Norfolk. He not only improved his own farms, but every year held "sheep shearings" to which farmers used to come from all over Europe in order to discuss new methods. In Scotland much the same type of thing took place. It was Thomas, Sixth Earl of Haddington, who about 1707 began to introduce new methods which soon became popular. The Scottish banks also wielded a beneficial influence by making loans to "improving" farmers.

Coupled with the efforts of these individuals went the work of various organizations. In 1723 a number of wealthy Scottish landlords organized The Society of the Improvers in the Knowledge of Agriculture to disseminate the new ideas. In 1787 was established the Highland Society, which offered prizes for new agricultural methods and techniques. During this period also the Royal Dublin Society made its appearance with the same purpose. Finally, to help farmers throughout Britain, in 1793 the Board of Agriculture was set up, the president being a Scot, Sir James Sinclair, and the Secretary, Arthur Young. The latter, although a failure as a practical farmer, was a great success as a promoter and publicist, his writing giving a great stimulus between 1780 and 1820 to the spread of agricultural knowledge.

One other important step was the endowment by Sir William Pulteney, in 1790, of a chair of Agriculture and Rural Economy at Edinburgh University. Real education in the most approved methods thus became possible.

It was somewhat more difficult to persuade the small holder to accept the new ideas. Not only were there psychological reasons, but there were very important economic barriers. This was particularly noticeable in connection with leases and "tenant right." The problem was that of persuading a tenant, holding land on a short lease, to improve the land at his own expense. He was always faced with the fact that his lease might not be renewed, resulting in the loss of the money invested. In England, where year leases were common, this was met during the eighteenth century by a "gentleman's agreement" that as long as the land was properly tilled the tenant would continue to occupy it. In Scotland, particularly in the Lowlands, the nineteen or twenty years' lease became common, thereby enabling the tenant to use up his investment. In the Highlands and Ireland, however, the custom of leasing land through tacksmen and middlemen prevented improvements, for if any were made, the tenant could be evicted or forced to pay a higher rent. Only in Ulster was this system not in vogue. There, the customary "tenant's right" to compensation on his removal for unexhausted improvements was recognized. All these methods could be abused by dishonest landlords or tenants, but it is interesting to note that the least progressive areas were those where insecurity of tenure was most common. Stability of tenure was an incentive to the small man to improve his land.

Besides the leaseholders, there were, of course, still many freeholders usually possessing only small portions of land. Because of lack of funds they found it difficult to improve their methods. Frequently, during the eighteenth century, they continued to farm only because many of them had some other means of livelihood. There was still a certain amount of wool spinning and weaving done in the farmers' cottages, while in Scotland fishing was an important by-industry. Because of this situation, the majority of the freeholders seldom used the new techniques. These they left either to the large tenant farmer or to the gentry.

The farmer's economic position during the eighteenth century varied considerably from year to year, the reason being the very limited importation of foodstuffs, causing prices to fluctuate directly with the weather, a none too stable factor in Britain. If the weather was good and the crops plentiful, the prices dropped; if the weather was poor and the crops short, the prices rose. From 1700-1765 the weather was generally fine, with the result that wheat prices might vary from year to year by only 10s., and that in certain limited areas. After 1765 the climate deteriorated, so prices fluctuated more violently. In 1718 wheat was 27s. a quarter, in 1750 30s., in 1765 42s., while between 1785 and 1794 it averaged 47s. There had been a steady climb in prices even with the considerable fluctuation.

The arable farmer had been aided also by a government bounty on wheat when the price dropped below 48s. a quarter. The sum of 5s. a quarter was granted when crops were good, to help export the surplus grain, while in times of scarcity export was forbidden and importation allowed. From 1765 on, however, this was of no great importance, as prices were rising and population increasing. But this system did tend, when the weather was good, to stabilize prices for the farmer.

Grazing, even more than arable farming, experienced a rise in profits despite heavy frosts, diseases, such as sheep rot and the cattle plague, and a drop in wool prices owing to the improvement of the sheep. After 1707, with an increasing demand for meat, Scottish and Irish cattle were being driven from Galloway to Norfolk, where they were fattened for the London market. At the same time, many farmers were beginning to realize that grazing brought larger returns than arable farming, it being reckoned that the average profits over nine years from twenty acres of arable would be £88 while it would be about £212 from the same area of grazing. Of course, violent fluctuation of prices did sometimes trouble the cattleman, but generally he prospered during the period.

Another factor which influenced the agricultural situation was the state of the roads. They were generally very bad, making the transportation of grain extremely difficult. It was hard for the farmers to get their produce to the market, unless, of course, it could walk by itself. The development of canals at the end of the century helped matters somewhat, while the building of roads in Ireland and Scotland, frequently for military purposes, had a very beneficial effect. Even by 1800 the poor communications hindered the proper distribution of agricultural products. In many cases the situation was complicated by the opposition of farmers near a good market to the improving of the roads or canals, lest prices should be forced down by outside competition.

Thus, by 1793 British agriculture was only beginning to awaken to the situation. The new techniques were still relatively unknown and over 6,000 acres were still unenclosed, yet there were some farmers who were employing the latest knowledge with good results. Writers such as Arthur Young and organizations such as the Highland Society and the Board of Agriculture were spreading information. But what was more important, prices were beginning to rise, thus increasing the possibilities of profits for the farmer. In this way Britain entered the French Revolutionary Wars with a very greatly increased agricultural potential which was to stand her in good stead during the next few years.

The Effect of the Napoleonic Wars, 1793-1836

The Napoleonic Wars gave agriculture its needed stimulus. For one thing, Britain was faced with the necessity of maintaining her army and navy at full strength for long periods. This meant that many men were taken off the land. Coupled with this was the general scarcity of food because of poor weather and Napoleon's blockade, which closed the European ports to British trade. The demand for home-grown produce became very pressing, particularly in times of drought and flood. The outcome was a steady rise of agricultural prices. This acted as a strong incentive to better farming, although prices still varied considerably according to the weather.

A clear indication of the way in which the war altered the situation is the jump in wheat prices from 41s. 9d. a quarter in 1792 to 115s. 11d. in 1801, and to 155s. in 1812. Between 1760 and 1804 the price of wheat trebled, while that of meat, butter, and fowl quadrupled. Thus the farmer was receiving a much higher money return on his crops than ever before. No doubt this was partially owing to wartime inflation, but even more it was caused by scarcity of food arising from a greatly increased demand. This, in turn, brought about, between 1790 and 1815, a violent rise of rents, which has been estimated at about 150 per cent. Farms, instead of selling for the price of twenty years' rent, were going at twice that amount. The farmer was prosperous as long as the war conditions lasted.

The increased prosperity, in turn, had an important effect upon farming practices. For one thing, it meant that capital now became available for improvements which would raise production. There was a wider use of manure and marl and a greater dependence upon machinery. In addition, much land which was never considered profitable when wheat sold at 50s. a quarter, at 100s. became worth cultivating. Consequently, a considerable amount of grazing land both in England and Ireland was put under the plow to raise wheat. This was particularly common in Ireland, once permission was granted in 1806 to export Irish grain to England. Scotland also increased its wheat production rapidly, sending to England in 1816 as much as 106,000 quarters. During the period enclosure also went forward by leaps and bounds, the peak of the movement being reached about 1810. In this way the war forced an acceleration in the pace of agricultural improvement.

Although the farmer seemed to be prospering, his life was by no means one long holiday. Taxation was extremely heavy. While the price of wheat had increased 90 per cent, property taxes had risen 400 per cent and county taxes 700 per cent. Added to this was the fact that at Speenhamland, Berkshire, in 1795 the Justices of the Peace had decided to augment the pay of farm laborers from the Poor Rates, an example which was soon imitated widely. Although only paupers could receive this aid, nevertheless, it very quickly became a heavy burden on those who had any property, increasing the poor rate by about 400 per cent. As a result of all these burdens, many of the small owner-occupiers were put out of business. Those who were not were so heavily loaded with costs that they did well if they were not in debt by the war's end. Few of them, except the biggest farmers and landlords, really made actual profits during the period of hostilities. Most farmers did not understand this, for although, as far as many were concerned, costs completely outran income and they were falling into debt, it was expected that once the war was over taxes and rates would drop, while prices would continue high.

When the war actually did come to a close in 1814, they were sadly disillusioned. Once the blockade was withdrawn, wheat was imported freely from the Continent, bringing an end to the home farmer's monopoly. At the same time, taxes remained high in order to pay for the war. Government expenditures in 1815 stood at almost £107 million, as compared with £20 million in 1790. Coupled with this was the fact that the farmer, who at the end of the war was actually producing foodstuffs on land which could not warrant such use except under great scarcity, was faced with a serious problem. How was he to keep up prices and profits?

In one sense he was for a time not too badly off, for prices during the next few years did not fall to the level which they had reached in 1792. But he could not hope to hold the high peak which he had attained in 1812, when war and weather combined to help. There was no hope of a state bounty because he could not even supply the whole of the home population, except at violently inflated prices which would make a subsidy impossible. Consequently, the only answer was protection from importation except when prices did go very high. As a result of this point of view, a law was enacted in 1815 forbidding the import of wheat unless the price of the home-grown product reached 80s. a quarter. By this Corn Law it was hoped that the farmer would be given a good return on his labor and investment so that he might continue to live in the state to which, during the war, he had grown accustomed.

The Corn Law, however, gave him little help. A succession of good seasons following 1815 brought a drop in prices, although occasional bad seasons caused some violent fluctuations. As prices declined, so did rents, falling about 25 per cent by 1820. But even this decrease was not enough, and there is a continual tale of tenant bankruptcies year after year, particularly in the arable farming districts which were hardest hit. Added to this, the rapid deflation caused by a return to gold payments brought further distress to the farmer. Men who had taken properties at high rents on long leases found themselves totally unable to meet their obligations, so they either failed or decamped, sometimes both. The result was great distress throughout the country, accentuated by the general economic crash in 1825. Unemployment was rife, and discontent flared up continually.

The effect upon agriculture was both good and bad. For one thing, it meant a considerable decline in the numbers of small holders. Frequently unable to stand the pressure, they sold out, going either to the cities or emigrating. Along with this there went a noticeable slowing down of enclosure, for it was a rather expensive business, which men were not prepared to undertake when profits were low. On the other hand, the very pressure of circumstances forced improvement. Not infrequently landlords, finding farms thrown onto their hands, were forced for their own protection to cultivate them themselves, which they could do only if they used the most efficient methods. It is probable that, as a result of this trend, the average size farm was by 1837 about 200 acres. On the other hand, almost half of those still actually holding farms used no hired labor. These were smaller landowners who, although they had been able to keep their heads above water, had given up improving their farms. They did not have the money to buy fertilizers and new machinery, nor were they able to pay for drainage projects. For this reason the small holdings which remained deteriorated, losing much of their fertility. Owing to lack of statistical information, one cannot quote production figures, but it is known that the rise of wheat imports relative to the population increase went up from 1½ gallons per person between 1820 and 1830 to 2¼ per person in the following decade, a jump of 50 per cent. This would seem to indicate that the aftermath of the war was lower production.

While the agricultural decline was fairly general throughout the British Isles, two groups of farmers seem to have stood the strain better than others. One group was made up of the graziers. They had an initial advantage in that they required less labor and less outlay for their production than did the arable farmer. The other group comprised the farmers in Lothian, who, because of their general carefulness and very efficient methods, were able to produce at a figure generally lower than others. Moreover, they had been among the first to employ machinery, it not being unusual for each farmer to have his own 6 h.p. steam engine for threshing and other processes. In this region the introduction of machines and other new methods proved to be of real value, further stirring the farmers' interest in improvements. An example of the development in Scotland was the expansion of a property near Kelso between 1790 and 1836. It grew in size from 21,000 acres to 35,000 acres, and in value from £84,600 to £172,400.

During this period, however, the farmer was not left friendless, for measures were taken to improve his situation. In 1836 the Royal Agricultural Society was founded for the purpose of stimulating agricultural research and disseminating new ideas. Then as the Corn Law of 1815 had not accomplished anything but an accentuation of difficulties in the lean years, a sliding scale was applied in 1828. It permitted wheat importation at 52s. a quarter, but the duty was 34s. 8d. As the domestic price rose, the duty decreased until the price reached 73s., when the duty became only 1s. This did not help very much, as frequently foreign importers inflated the price in order to bring in their grain under a lower duty, thus accentuating the fluctuations.

Probably the most important move, as far as the farmer was concerned, was the reform of the Poor Law. The Speenhamland system had put a premium on poverty. No man who had property of any kind could obtain help from the rates and therefore could not compete on the labor market, for, receiving no subsidy from the Poor Rates, he had to ask more for his work. This had produced a very bad effect upon the laborers as well as upon the employers. While some parishes stopped abuse by severe measures, so that they had little pauperism, others allowed it to go on, with the result that they were often paying a rate of more than 20s. in the pound value. It was a burden such as this which forced many small holders into bankruptcy.[2] The new Act (1833) was very stringent, requiring a

[2] If a man had any land he would be obliged to pay a portion of the Poor Rates, part of which went to subsidize labor in the parish. If the rates demanded of a

workhouse test and also attempting to stop outdoor relief. All paupers were required to live in poorhouses. It was so effective that between 1833 and 1837 the Poor Rate dropped from £7 million to £4 million. Another change came with the commutation of the ecclesiastical tithe. There had been trouble over its collection, frequently involving lawsuits. In 1836 provision was made for it to be turned into a money payment based upon the changing value of money and the cost of living. This aided the farmers greatly. Coupled with this, land taxes by 1837 were reduced about 25 per cent, which gave the farmer further relief.

By the year 1837, when Queen Victoria ascended the throne, the agricultural situation was beginning to improve. The farmers were recovering from the rather deep gloom which had lain over the country for the preceding twenty years. Yet, while one may talk of improvements and new methods, they were still by no means universal. The big farmers used them, but the small farmers, of whom there were still some 133,000, followed older methods, a number indeed employing the antiquated medieval practice of open field cultivation. Even on enclosed land, hand labor for mowing, sowing, and threshing was still the most common form of power. The year 1837, however, saw the opening of a new era.

The Agricultural Boom

The period from 1837 to 1875 was one in which British agriculture enjoyed the greatest prosperity of its history. There were many reasons for this. One was British industrial supremacy with ever expanding foreign markets, bringing a rise in the national income. This, coupled with the growth of population by some 4½ million during the period, meant an even greater demand. Moreover, this was a market in which the British farmer, even after the complete repeal of the Corn Laws in 1846, had no strong competitor, largely owing to the wide extension of railways, which enabled him to send his produce quickly to any part of the country. On the other hand, increased returns invited improvement, which, in turn, stimulated further production. Throughout the period the farmer was growing better off and agriculture was booming. The one exception was Ireland, which knew little betterment of its condition until after 1850, and even then its advance was very slow.

It is difficult to determine exactly how many people were actually employed in agriculture during this period, but it would seem

farmer were 21s. in the £1 value of his land he would be able to make nothing from his land and would have to sell out.

that between 1831 and 1881 the over-all agricultural population remained steady, although in Scotland it dropped from 700,000 to 299,000. The surplus moved to the cities or emigrated. At the same time, the size of the farms increased, although very slowly. By 1851, in England and Wales farms under 100 acres occupied less than 25 per cent of the land, while in Scotland four-fifths were still under 200 acres. By 1875 45 per cent of the English farms were between 100 and 300 acres, probably a good many of them nearer the 300 than the 100 figure. The small holder, particularly in England, was gradually disappearing. In Ireland the tendency toward grazing and the desire to get rid of paupers caused widespread eviction, so there also, the small cultivator was fighting a losing battle for his existence. The increased use of machinery was likewise beginning to have its effect, supplanting the laborer as a worker and forcing him to move out, although this movement was not strong until after 1875.

By 1840 active enclosing was practically at an end. There was still some fighting among shepherds for rights on moorland in the Welsh mountains, but from 1865 no attention was concentrated upon preserving the commons as breathing space for the industrial population rather than upon enclosing them for farming. By 1850 in England and Scotland the policy of "tenant right" was being followed generally, and in 1865 it was given legal standing. In 1870 it was extended to the whole of Ireland by the Land Act, which endeavored not only to protect the tenants from losing their improvements, but also from being evicted or rack-rented. In England the one year lease continued to be common, while in Scotland the nineteen year lease was customary. Thus there was little change in the position of the tenant farmer, except that he was encouraged to improve his farm as much as possible.

Farming continued to improve during the period, under the influence of various societies which were either revived or founded at the time. The Royal Agricultural Society, by its *Journal*, helped to instruct the farmers, as did also the Agricultural Improvement Society, instituted in 1840. In 1842 Lawes and Gilbert set up an agricultural experimental station at Rothamstead because of their interest in Liebig's work on agricultural chemistry. To this team was added the Royal Agricultural College at Cirencester in 1845. Through the work of such organizations farming began to advance technically even more rapidly. In 1850 Ransome and May of Ipswich, manufacturers of agricultural implements, were employing some 800 men. Steam engines were being used more freely for drainage, and the traveling steam thresher was also becoming a more common sight, although no efficient reaper was yet on the market. The breeds of cattle were likewise being continually improved, emphasis being laid on meat and milk rather than draft power. Moreover, all this knowledge of better farming was becoming much more widely spread. In this way the general level of farming practice had advanced a great distance by 1875.

The gradual development in method meant an increase in production. As a result of better manures and fertilizers, the estimated 26½ bushels produced from an acre in 1850 had increased by 1868 to 28 bushels. By 1875 43 per cent of the total farming area was under pasture, which supported between twenty-eight and thirty million sheep and about six million cattle. Yet this growth took place in spite of the difficulties of weather and disease. 1838-41 were bad years for arable farming, resulting in a dearth. In 1844 there first appeared the potato disease from the Continent, while the following year there was such a crop failure that the price of wheat rose to 103s. 5d. a quarter. Graziers were also troubled. From 1839 on there were recurring epidemics of foot and mouth disease. In 1865 over 200,000 head of cattle had to be slaughtered because of rinderpest, and about 8,000 died in 1872 from pleuro-pneumonia. Yet, despite the farmer's difficulties, this was the time of his greatest productivity.

Another factor in this prosperity was the steady level of prices. This was helped materially by various wars on the Continent, which effectively prevented the European wheat areas from competing with the domestic producer. Generally speaking, wheat prices ranged between 54s. and 61s. a quarter. The grazier, however, did even better. Meat, wool, and butter, all rose considerably in price. Beef prices, for instance, were in 1869 some 30 per cent to 40 per cent above those of 1850, and by 1873 they were up another 10 per cent. The prices of the other commodities were rising at the same rate. The natural outcome of this was, as during the Napoleonic Wars, a rise in rent, in England by about 25 per cent and in Scotland by over 40 per cent. Similarly, agricultural wages were rising, although they increased more in the north, where there was industrial competition for labor, than in the south. In the north they averaged 11s. 6d., but in the south only 8s. 5d. per week. While such wages were not very great according to present standards, the cost of living had been on the decline, resulting in a betterment of the laborer's condition. In this way all the farming community was improving.

But the improvement was not destined to last for any length of time. The first sign of this was the repeal in 1846 of the Corn

Laws. Huskisson's sliding scale of 1828 had not been too successful in helping the farmer, and by 1840 many people were very much
opposed to the laws. Peel tried without any effect to modify Huskisson's sliding scale. The result was that opposition grew louder
by the hour. Some held that the Corn Laws placed a tax on the
poor man's food, for the benefit of the farmer. Others stressed the
fact that this was hindering industry, by causing the laborers to
require wages which industry could not bear. Others argued that
Britain could not sell foreigners her manufactures if she would not
take their farm produce in return. The result was the founding in
1839 of the Anti-Corn Law League, controlled mainly by Manchester industrialists. They spent large sums of money in propaganda against the Corn Laws, printing numerous pamphlets and
sending speakers, such as John Bright and Richard Cobden, around
the country to rouse the people against the laws. Finally, the great
dearth in 1845 and 1846 enabled them to press home their attacks.
The only solution, they said, was the repeal of the Corn Laws so
that wheat might enter the country duty free. Sir Robert Peel, the
Tory prime minister, at first somewhat doubtful of the benefit of
such action, was eventually persuaded, and in 1846 moved the Laws'
repeal. But in so doing he smashed his party and forced himself
out of politics. The Tories, largely representing the landed interests, felt that he had turned traitor.

Yet, as shown above, the Corn Law repeal did not spell immediate ruin for the farmer. Indeed, the peak of his prosperity was
reached only some years after the Corn Laws had disappeared
from the statute book. Throughout the period from 1850 to 1875
the farmer did well: his production was up, his prices were rising,
and there was little indication that the situation was going to
change. The repeal of the Corn Laws, however, had prepared the
way for trouble. If one looks at the figures of importation of foreign
grain, he finds that the amounts were gradually rising. In 1852
only about 26 per cent of the wheat available for consumption was
imported, but by 1870 it had risen to 48 per cent. This was the
beginning. As the United States and Canada swung into production on their virgin soils, and as steamships began to operate across
the Atlantic, cheap wheat would become the order of the day. And
if wheat should drop below 50s. a quarter, the farmer was doomed.
But up to this point the farmer did not see what was happening,
so we shall leave him for the moment in his rosy dream of prosperity.

Chapter 12

THE MACHINE AGE IN INDUSTRY

In 1715 industry, on its technical side, remained very close to the Middle Ages. The gilds were still in existence and, in some cases, had considerable influence, but in the staple industries, such as woolen and worsted production, they were unimportant. Yet the larger industries, while they had a new organization, the domestic system, continued to employ medieval techniques such as hand spinning and weaving, even when, on occasion, a number of the workers were under one roof in a workshop. There were really no factories. In Ireland and Scotland, the spinners and weavers were primarily small part-time farmers, and the same was true of most rural industrial workers in England. Attached to their houses were spinning or weaving rooms, pottery sheds, or nail shops. There everything was done by hand, although, as Adam Smith pointed out in the case of pinmakers, there might be a division of labor, with each worker specializing in some particular part of the process. While this was an improvement in that it speeded operations, it was not enough. The demands of Great Britain's expanding markets were beginning to put pressure on the country's productive system which could be met only by the introduction of power machinery.

The Foundation of the Machine Age

During the seventeenth century, industry had experienced most of the changes and innovations in organization which laid the basis for modern developments. In the larger industries, such as woolen, iron, and pottery manufacture, capitalism had appeared. The small independent worker was gradually disappearing under the growing power and influence of the entrepreneur, who was becoming an employer of labor as well as a merchant. The industries were increasingly falling under the control of the large, moneyed interests who provided the raw materials, frequently the machines, and always the marketing facilities. Sometimes, as in the case of some potteries and some weaving organizations, the operatives were gathered together by the employer into workshops to ply their trade. In this way the direct control and supervision of the capitalist was increased, but there was still no factory in the modern sense. The domestic system had merely been housed under a single roof. To have a true factory there must be mechanical power and automatic, or at least semiautomatic, machinery. By 1715 this stage of production had not arrived, although in the large workshop the foundation for modern factory organization had been laid.

It must also be kept in mind at this point that one of the characteristics of British economy in 1715 was government control. Mercantilism was at its peak. The government felt that it had the right to dictate to industry and to rule it for the national good. This meant that for the individual there was no great freedom of action. The statutes on the books regarding economic matters were mostly medieval or Elizabethan in outlook. The Statute of Artificers was still nominally the labor code. Controls, restrictions, and subsidies were numerous. It would not be until a good many of these had been removed that new ideas and techniques could flourish. In fact, one of the great conflicts of the eighteenth century was caused by the rise of the new techniques which brought destruction to the old regulations. These new methods were to be the new wine which would burst the old bottles of medieval practice. This was the situation which prevailed when George I ascended the British throne (1714).

The Development of Machinery

The basic factor in the so-called Industrial Revolution which made the modern economy possible was the advent of power-driven machinery. These inventions, with their roots far back in the past, were not just the work of one or two men, but rather of the society in which they lived. In addition, it was social demand for greater production which stimulated the inventors to experiment. Because of these facts, one must never think that the Industrial Revolution was sudden. The period 1715-60 was one of gathering momentum. From 1760 to 1790 the speed began to pick up, with acceleration increasing during the Napoleonic Wars (1798-1815) owing to demands for war material. While the years immediately following the wars were times of stagnation, from 1830 on increasing foreign trade made greater and greater demands on production, forcing the pace both in invention and in industrial organization. The result was that by 1870 Britain had, relative to the other nations of the world, reached the peak of her industrialization. By this time her civilization was largely mechanized.

While it is difficult to know what order should be followed in outlining the development of machinery, it seems that the most fundamental change came with the introduction of truly mechanical power. As we have already seen, various natural sources of power had been tried. Water power for fulling mills, tilt hammers, and even forges had not been unknown in the fifteenth century. Wind power was also employed, not merely for propelling ships, but also for pumping water from the fenlands. Although both these types of mechanical power were extremely important and dominated all mechanized industry down to 1815, they were not really satisfactory. For one thing, they might very easily fail: the wind might fall, or a river might dry up. Another disadvantage was that in the case of water power one was forced to go to the water. This might mean locating a factory far from the source of raw material. To meet these difficulties one might employ horses or oxen walking on an endless belt which turned wheels. Such methods were often used later in North America before the appearance of the gasoline engine for running farm machines. In 1793 a canny Scot in Glasgow set up the first power loom which was run by a big Newfoundland dog. But none of these forms of power really met the need.

In connection with the use of power the name of the Scot James Watt is the most important. In the late seventeenth century Thomas Savery had invented the steam engine, which Newcomen had made practicable for pumping water out of mines in 1709. The engine was a clumsy affair, however, having a cylinder from four to six feet across, making ten to twelve strokes a minute, and burning about twelve tons of coal a day. It was operated by injecting into the cylinder steam, which forced up the piston to the top of the stroke. The steam was then stopped, cold water being shot into the cylinder and causing a vacuum so that the air pressure on the upper side of the piston was able to force it down. This machine was about 85 per cent inefficient. The man who improved it was Watt, the instrument maker of the University of Glasgow. He closed both ends of the cylinder, allowing the steam to enter alternately at each end. He kept the cylinder hot and by condensing the steam in a separate chamber away from the cylinder was able to increase both the speed and power of the engine. The result was a machine far superior to that of Newcomen. He also discovered the principles of rotary or crank motion and parallel motion. He had, however, great difficulty in producing his new engine in Scotland owing to lack of experienced engineers, but with Boulton of Birmingham as partner he began to manufacture it on a commercial basis. The first engine was built in 1775, and by 1800 over 300 were in use; by 1850 the textile industries were using 105,000 h.p. of steam and only 24,000 h.p. of water.

The steam engine, while it was of vast importance, could not have accomplished nearly as much as it did had there not been a simultaneous improvement in iron production. Down to 1700 iron ore had been smelted in charcoal-burning blast furnaces, the result being cast iron, hard, brittle and full of impurities. To make it malleable the iron then had to be reheated with charcoal and hammered. The use of charcoal, however, was depleting Britain's wood stocks so that by 1700 iron production was becoming a very real problem. Since coal, because of its impurities, could not be used, ironmasters were having to set up their works in the distant but better forested areas in Wales or the Scottish Highlands. As a result of these difficulties iron output fell rapidly, from 180,000 tons in 1695 to 17,350 in 1740. Meanwhile, however, before 1709 Abraham Darby of Coalbrookdale, Shropshire, had been experimenting in smelting iron with coked coal, which did not have the impurities of the ordinary coal. He had no great success as long as he used only a bellows for the blast. It was only when John Smeaton in 1768 invented a cylinder blower and established it in the Carron Iron Works in Scotland that coke could be used efficiently. At first it was run by water, but in 1775 steam was applied to the blower, and the problem of smelting was solved. Thus, when in 1801 David Mushet discovered a mixture of iron and coal near Glasgow, it could be easily smelted. Finally, James Neilson in 1828 introduced the hot blast, making it possible to use the hard splint Lanarkshire coal without coking. By this means Neilson halved the price of iron, completely revolutionizing iron production.

Meantime improvements had also been made in iron refining. Cast iron could not be reheated in contact with coal, as it would take up too many impurities. Therefore, it was a real advance when in 1784 two men, Henry Cort and Peter Onions, took out separate patents for "puddling" iron in a reverberatory furnace. The iron and fire were in separate beds beside each other, and the burning gases from the fire were deflected from the furnace top down onto the iron. By this method the iron became soft and pasty, so that it could be "stirred" or "puddled" to burn out impurities. Cort also brought into use the practice of rolling the iron between grooved rollers. In this way he could squeeze out impurities and at the same time form the bars into any desired shape. To these processes were added Nasmyth's steam hammer in 1840; and in the '60's mechanical puddling. Iron was now plentiful, cheap, and easily worked.

In the field of metalworking there was to be one further improvement before 1870. While wrought or malleable iron was all right for some uses, a harder metal was required for cutlery, tools, and the like. Steel met this need, but it was difficult to make. Wrought iron had to be melted and a proper proportion of carbon added to make it hard. Around 1740 Benjamin Huntsman had developed a system for making crucible steel by melting the iron in a crucible and adding steel scrap. This, however, was not only a long process, but the quantity produced was small.

The big step forward came when Sir Henry Bessemer discovered that if air were blown through molten iron as it came from the blast furnace, all the impurities would be burned out in twenty minutes instead of six hours, as in puddling. Carbon and manganese could then be added immediately to make steel. This process was improved some nine years later when William Siemens introduced the Basic Hearth method, using a "regenerative furnace" which burned heated gases. He kept the iron ore melted, gradually reducing the carbon, silicon, and manganese content until it was below that needed for steel. The required chemicals could then be added in any desired proportion. This method was better than Bessemer's, for, as it was somewhat slower, it could be controlled more exactly. Both processes, however, were limited to the use of nonphosphoric iron ores which were somewhat scarce in Britain. Until the phosphorus could be eliminated, much of the iron used for making steel had to be imported from Spain. Nevertheless, very cheap steel was now available for machines, tools, engines, and building construction.

Although this period saw an improvement in the methods of iron and steel production, something more was needed. These metals had to be worked, and worked exactly. Watts' biggest problems when attempting to manufacture his steam engine had been the lack of skilled mechanics and efficient tools. Each of the early steam engines was made separately, every piece, even each screw, being individually made by hand. The result was that each piece varied according to the workmanship of the particular craftsman. As standard parts were unknown, the early steam engines often took a lot of coaxing before they would operate. To overcome this difficulty many skilled workmen in places such as London or Birmingham wrestled with the matter. Goldsmiths, silversmiths, watchmakers, printers and the like, all were interested. The answer was the perfection of machine tools with which machines could be turned out more rapidly and much more cheaply.

One of the first men to achieve some success in this direction was John Wilkinson (1728-1808) the inventor of a cannon boring machine. This device enabled Watt to obtain for the first time an accurately bored cylinder. Some time later Joseph Bramah (1748-1814) set up a machine for making locks and also employed the force pump to work the hydraulic press. A few years later Maudsley (1771-1831) invented the self-acting lathe, which eliminated all guesswork, and Whitworth (1803-1887) developed the screw lathe, which standardized screw threads. Following these, planing machines, steam hammers, and other machine tools were developed, so by 1830 machinery production was becoming a simple matter. This was the foundation of the machine industry. In the early days spinners, weavers, and others had been obliged to make their own machines, but from 1830 on machine manufacture became an important industry, giving a further stimulus to industrial development.

Strangely enough, coal mining, the process basic to the metallurgical and other industries, advanced much more slowly than the others and even by 1870 was still largely dependent on hand operations. Drainage, haulage, and gas in the mines were the three big problems. The danger of explosion from "firedamp" was largely obviated after 1815 by the use of Sir Humphry Davy's safety lamp, whose flame was protected from the gases by means of wire gauze. Then too, steam engines had been employed in the early eighteenth century, as we have seen, for pumping water out of mines. By 1800 the haulage of coal was being made easier through the use of iron rails, upon which coal carts could run, and by 1850 iron cages on wire cable instead of wicker baskets on ropes were being used to lift coal from the pit. Better methods were also being employed to ventilate the mines: steam jets, furnaces which caused an updraft, and various other appliances. But despite all apparent improvements, even in 1870 coal still had to be won from the ground by hand.

Although the heavy industries were very necessary and were consequently growing in value throughout the period, the most important industrial products were still textiles. As already seen, for many centuries wool had dominated the picture, and it continued to do so into the nineteenth century. For broadcloth, wool had to be carded, since it was usually quite short; for worsted, on the other hand, long wool being employed, it was usually combed. Both types were then spun and woven into cloth. In the production of worsted this was the end of the process. Woolen cloth, however, had also to be fulled (thickened by beating in water), teasled (have its knap raised through being scratched), and sheared (have the knap cut off). Before 1800, with the exception of agriculture, more people were employed in this industry than in any other. Of importance in Scotland and Ireland was linen, made from flax, which had to be heckled (combed) and spun. Cotton needed much the same sort of treatment. It was carded into a roving (a thick loose sort of rope) and then spun into thread, which was woven into cotton cloth. While the wool was either dyed in the yarn or in the cloth, linen and cotton were first bleached, after which they were dyed or printed. These were the processes which occupied so many people in Britain during the eighteenth century.

The first mechanical contrivance to be applied to textile production in the eighteenth century was John Kay's flying shuttle (1733), which enabled one weaver to do the work of two. Instead of the shuttle being thrown from one hand to another, it was cast by a spring which enabled it to travel farther and faster than was possible by hand throwing. While this innovation was first employed in woolen weaving, all the other early improvements appeared first in the manufacture of cotton goods, which was a new industry with no particular traditions. The fiber used was stronger and more uniform than wool, and there was an abundant supply at low cost. Consequently, the cotton industry had more liberty to use new machine techniques.

In the early days of the cotton industry the greatest need was yarn for weaving, since it took six or eight spinners to supply one weaver. Because of this, attention was first turned to the acceleration of spinning. In 1748 Lewis Paul invented a carding machine to speed that process. Nineteen years later James Hargreaves invented the eight-spindle jenny, which, instead of two threads, as the Saxony spinning wheel, could spin eight at a time. By 1784 the number of spindles had been increased to eighty and by 1800 to one hundred and twenty. Meanwhile Richard Arkwright, a barber, had invented the water frame, a water-driven machine to spin cotton by means of rollers. This produced a stronger thread than the jenny, which up to that time could manufacture only the thread used for the warp, the weft still having to be made of hand-spun yarn. Now both could be made by machine. The only difficulty was that water frame cotton was coarse. In 1779 Samuel Crompton combined both jenny and frame into a "mule" which would produce cotton of any fineness desired. His machine was improved by Buchanan of Catrine, Scotland (1807), who invented a self-acting mule. Finally, the first automatic spinning machine in England was set up by Richard Roberts at Manchester in 1825. Cotton spinning had now become very largely mechanized, producing all the yarn needed for weaving.

With the increase in spinning production, weaving had to accelerate its pace. For this, Kay's spring loom was not enough. In 1785, therefore, a clergyman by the name of Cartwright invented a power loom. Although adopted in a few places, it was too clumsy for general use until it was modified and improved twenty-five years later by Horrocks and Radcliffe. After this it became increasingly popular, by 1835 there being some 125,000 employed in the production of various textiles.

Improvements were also introduced into the finishing processes of the cotton cloth. The old method of bleaching had been that of steeping the web in sour milk and then putting it out in the weather to whiten, a process which might take eight months. In 1746, Dr. John Roebuck discovered that a quicker and better result could be achieved with the use of sulfuric acid. Meanwhile, Berthollet, the French chemist, discovered the method of bleaching with chlorine, which was imported to Scotland by James Watt in 1786. Chemistry was also endeavoring to create new dyestuffs which could be used in place of the expensive cochineal or woad. Here was the foundation of a chemical industry. Besides this, another Scot, Thomas Bell, in 1783 commenced printing calicoes by means of copper rollers instead of blocks. To print 28 yards of calico in one color by the old method required 448 applications, while by the new method two or more colors could be printed simultaneously and at a very rapid rate.

The woolen industry because of its conservatism and the nature of its raw material adopted these new methods much more slowly than did the cotton industry, and in most cases its machines were adaptations of those already used for cotton. Nevertheless, the worsted industry soon took up the jenny, the mule, and the flying shuttle. These were used principally in the West Riding of Yorkshire, to the detriment of East Anglia and the West Country: Gloucester, Somerset, and Wiltshire. The first worsted spinning mill was established in Bradford in 1787. A new type of carder invented in 1835 and a German-invented machine comb introduced into the country in 1845 brought about further changes. Yet, despite all the mechanical aids employed, the woolen and worsted industries before 1850 did not experience nearly such radical changes, as had taken place in cotton production.

The linen trade was in somewhat the same situation as wool. Owing to the stickiness and gumminess of the flax when being spun into yarn, the jenny and mule were not very useful until the idea of wet-spinning was introduced in 1826. After that the cotton spinning and weaving machines were adapted more fully to linen production. In the hosiery trade there was no great change until after 1850, when steam was used to run the stocking frame. The same was true of the lace industry of Nottingham and Buckinghamshire.

While the pottery manufacturers had little in the way of machinery, the clothing and boot and shoe industries began to discover its benefits. During the Napoleonic Wars a man named Brunel invented a machine to peg the soles and uppers of boots together. Then in 1850 Singer, an American, produced the first sewing machine. This could be used for sewing both clothing and boots, making greater speed and regularity possible.

All these machines had one primary objective: to increase production without increasing labor. By this means goods could be cheapened, bringing about their wider distribution and more common use. Thus, by 1870 British industry was fast becoming mechanized. But mere machines were not enough. They had to be constructed, housed, and operated. This was the work of the factory system, the inevitable partner of machine production.

The Factory System

The machine could hardly have prospered in Britain, particularly England, had there not been a simultaneous appearance of the factory system. This was a natural consequence of the domestic organization common in textile and metal production. In fact, there had always been in some industries a tendency toward factories. The first one with thoroughly modern characteristics was Thomas Lombe's silk-throwing mill (1719), and by 1800 such establishments were becoming common in other industries. It was the advent of the machine that forced the setting up of factories, since the machine could hardly be used except in such a system. For one thing, the individual worker found the machines too expensive for him to own. Another factor was the need of power, which was very costly unless employed on a mass production or factory basis. The factory was therefore needed for economy, because only there could machine production reach its greatest volume or its lowest costs. On the other hand, since the domestic or putting-out system was about as economical as possible when hand labor predominated, the established industries, such as the woolen trade, were slow to adopt power machines. The capital expenditure and the risk involved were felt to be greater than was warranted by the decreased cost. Not until the cloth trade was faced with the growing competition of cotton did the clothiers seriously adopt cotton's own methods. The operator also hesitated to enter the factory, for it changed his whole way of life, broke down his family solidarity, and took him off the land. Despite all these objections, however, growing markets demanded the increased production which the new machine alone could give. The result was the gradual rise of the factory system.

In the metalworking industries a certain amount of concentration had always been necessary. For one thing, mines, whether of copper, tin, calamine, or iron, had always been controlled by the owners of the land. In the Middle Ages, the owners had been the only persons capable of paying the men and of furnishing the tilt hammers, the forges, and the lime to do the work. Consequently in these industries it was customary for workers to be mere wage earners or sometimes subcontractors, using equipment supplied by the mine owner. In the eighteenth century the Cornish tin mines averaged about 160 wage earners, while the copper mines of Anglesey probably averaged more. It has been reckoned that in 1760 the iron industry employed around 200,000 people, with the number of employees varying according to the size of the unit, which ranged from the small blast furnaces of the Sussex Weald, to Darby's large establishment at Coalbrookdale. By the early part of the nineteenth century the average production unit, usually of more than one blast furnace, would employ between 1000 and 2000 men. Anthony Hill of the Plymouth Works, Merthyr, for instance, had 1500 employees. By 1860, William Baird and Company had forty-one blast furnaces in six different establishments. The factory aspect of the industry was by this time only too apparent.

This tendency was to be found also in the engineering and metalworking industries. When Adam Smith wrote his *Wealth of Nations,* he took the workshop for the making of pins as his typical example of the division of labor. A few years later he would have thought in terms of a factory, the Carron Iron Works being a good example. Heavy machinery such as the cannon borer, the puddling furnace, the rolling mill and similar appliances could be used only in a factory. The same was true of those who specialized in making machinery for the textile industry, since power lathes, power drills, and the like, necessary for producing such equipment, could not be operated in the worker's small shop. In the copper and brass industry a parallel movement existed. Many of the smelting companies, such as the brass works at Warmley, Gloucester, producing vats for distilling and sheet copper for ship bottoms, employed some 800 people in the early years of the nineteenth century. For small wares such as nails, cutlery, ornaments, and copper utensils, on the other hand, the tendency was for the work to be produced on a putting out basis, since it was done largely by hand and on commission. Thus, while large, heavy goods had to come from the factory, small goods such as those made in Birmingham were, as late as 1870 manufactured under the old domestic system.

Coal mining, even in 1715, was still conducted on something of a medieval plan. Frequently a mine would employ no more than fifteen men underground, hired by a "butty," who contracted with the mine owner to take out the coal at a certain price per ton. In Scotland until 1799 the owner so controlled the miners that they were virtually serfs. By 1820, however, with the increasing demand for coal and the introduction of safety devices, the workings were larger, employing around eighty people to the mine, and the number continued to grow. It was usual by this time to lease the mine from the landowner who received a royalty on each ton. The lessee then employed his men and furnished them with the tools necessary for their work. Here again was a type of factory.

The classic example of a factory industry, however, was seen in cotton manufacture. Since it was a hand-worked machine, the spinning jenny brought no great change, although some employers began to establish workshops where the spinner could be supervised. Arkwright's water frame, on the other hand, was definitely a power machine and its adoption resulted in cotton mills. The first in Scotland and one of the earliest in Britain was set up at Penicuick in 1778. Others soon followed and by 1787 in Scotland alone there were some twenty mills. A typical example was David Dale's New Lanark Mills, where each mill was 160 feet long, 40 feet wide, and seven stories high. The machinery consisted at first of water-driven frames and "mules." In 1792, however, Kelly, Dale's engineer applied steam power to Crompton's mule, which from then on became the commonly used factory machine. By 1796 the Scottish cotton industry was well organized. It used 39 water frames with 124,800 spindles, 1200 jennies with 100,800 spindles and 630 mules with 86,400 spindles, representing a total capital investment of £490,000. In 1812 there were some 120 mills with 900,000 spindles, and twenty years later while there were only

14 more mills the number of spindles had increased to 1,600,000, showing the growing size of the individual unit. In England the growth was even greater. By 1820 there were around Manchester 43 mills, with an average of 300 employees each, while two of them actually had over 1,000. Ten years later the average had risen to 401. The power loom also had come into use by 1815, but its adoption was comparatively slow, there still being many hand loom weavers as late as 1850. Very frequently spinners such as Horrocks of Stockport, would employ weavers to make up their yarn into cloth, in which case there might be as many as 7,000 on the payroll. It is probable, however, that most of the factories employed no more than 150 or 200 people, although after 1850 in England, the size of the individual unit grew rapidly. In Ireland and Scotland, on the other hand, cotton manufacture declined owing to the depression of 1857 and the cotton famine during the American Civil War. By 1870 the cotton industry had largely disappeared from Ireland, while the sewing-thread industry was almost all that remained to the Scots.

Since mechanization came to the woolen and worsted industry much later than to cotton, it follows that factory organization was also far behind. Worsted spinning, the first branch to enter the factory, was already being revolutionized in this way by 1800, particularly around Bradford, so by 1850 it was completely mechanized. At the same date the spinning of wool was still largely a hand process, although in a good many cases it was done on the hand-operated jenny in workshops. After 1850 mechanization came rapidly, and by 1870 factory production was almost universal. Much the same story can be told of weaving. In 1835 less than 7 per cent of the total power looms employed in the country were in the cloth industry, most of these being for worsted manufacture, and it was not until 1860 that the factory really took over. In some places in Scotland, particularly in the Western Isles, the home of Harris tweeds and similar cloth, hand weaving has continued even down to the present.[1] In England, a few isolated districts continued to follow the domestic system, being able to compete with factory production by the erection of joint-stock finishing mills.[2]

---

[1] The name tweed itself is of curious origin. Sir Walter Scott popularized the rough cloth used for shepherds' cloaks by having trousers made from it. This cloth was known as tweel, and it was an English clerk in London who mistook the name for tweed, the name of the border river. Ever since, tweed has been the name applied to this cloth. It has been imitated both in England and Ireland.

[2] The proportion of factory workers to domestic workers can be judged from estimates made in 1834. It was reckoned that there was a total of 334,600 people

In the other textile industries much the same pattern prevailed. Silk, of course, had been a factory industry prior even to cotton. By 1760 a few silk manufacturers employed up to 1500 hands, with many of the factories having about 500. Owing to French and oriental competition, however, by 1870 the silk industry was stagnating. Linen on the other hand, never became much of a factory industry. Irish hand workers could be employed at such low wages that it was not worth while. Consequently, the linen industry gradually migrated to Ireland. By 1850, however, even in Ireland there were attempts at the factory organization of the spinning process, weaving continuing to be largely a domestic occupation. The English net and lace industry was also becoming somewhat mechanized by 1860, although domestic production remained predominant. The hosiery industry, once long trousers appeared, suffered from declining demand. Yet it succeeded in adapting itself to the production of underwear on a large frame and by 1870 was almost completely a factory industry. Last, but not least, with the departure of linen manufacture from eastern Scotland, attention there was centered upon the processing of jute and hemp. The fabrication of jute bags became important in Dundee and that of linoleum in Kirkcaldy. By 1850 both these industries were well organized, having been set up from the very beginning under a factory system.[3]

Other industries followed the pattern of the staple manufactures. Pottery making had become a workshop industry by 1800, and by 1850 it was in the factory. The introduction of shoe manufacturing machines, sewing machines, and the like, tended to move the clothing industry in the same direction. Ready-made garments were increasingly common, particularly for the male, whose clothes became more and more drab and uninteresting. Confectioneries adopted a similar plan. In 1826 Huntley and Palmers set up their factory in Reading, and the Cadburys followed suit in Birmingham three years later. In 1850 each of these establishments was employing around 300 people.

---

engaged in the woolen trade in England. Of these 65,461 were employed in 1102 woolen factories. Apparently the others continued to work at home.

[3] The comparative numbers employed in textile factories are as follows:

	Cotton	Wool	Flax, Jute, Etc.	Silk
1835	219,286	55,461	33,212	30,745
1850	330,924	154,180	68,434	42,544
1861	451,569	173,046	94,003	52,429
1870	450,087	238,503	145,592	48,124

L. A. C. Knowles, *The Industrial and Commercial Revolution Great Britain During the Nineteenth Century* (London, 1933), p. 59.

By the year 1870 not only the organization but also the geographical pattern of British industry had undergone a radical change. In 1715 wool spinning and weaving had both been carried on quite generally throughout the country, while iron production had taken place primarily in the south, in the Weald and the Forest of Dean, and coal production around the Tyne Valley. By 1870 this had altered, certain industries being limited to definite localities, individual industries sometimes even being divided into specialized geographic areas. The two primary factors in this change were sources of power and sources of raw materials, although with the improvement of communications after 1850 the latter tended to be of less importance. By that time, however, the pattern had been well determined.

Iron and steel production was centered naturally around the more recently found iron ore deposits of the Black Country, from Birmingham to Sheffield, in Lancashire, near the port of Liverpool, and in southwest Scotland, near the iron deposits discovered by Mushet close to the port of Glasgow. As a result of this contiguity of iron to Liverpool and Glasgow both the Clyde and the Mersey became great shipbuilding rivers, until 1914 the most important in the world. Textile manufacture became localized in somewhat the same areas. Worsted production departed from coal-less East Anglia to settle in the West Riding of York, while woolen manufacture was concentrated around Leeds and worsteds around Huddersfield, Bradford, and Preston. From the Pennines could be easily obtained not only wool, but also power, whether from water or coal. The cotton industry at first centered in Lancashire, southwest Scotland, and Dublin. The famine of raw material caused by the American Civil War hit all of these centers. In Scotland many turned to shipbuilding, which at this date was growing in importance. At the same time, the swamping of the Irish market with cheap English cottons during the depression years 1857-1862 smashed the Irish industry completely. Consequently, by 1870 Lancashire and Cheshire had almost a monopoly of cotton spinning and weaving. Furthermore, the proximity of Liverpool and the damp climate, so suitable for spinning cotton, gave this area a natural advantage. Subdivision of the industry is seen here, with Bolton and Manchester making fine yarns and Oldham and Ashton spinning coarse yarns. Preston and Blackburn specialized in weaving. The potteries continued in their historic county of Staffordshire, while silk remained centered around Macclesfield, Stockport, and Manchester. The south of England, the north of Scotland, and Ireland had relatively little industry, with the consequence that workers were moving into the industrial centers in such numbers that by 1870 the whole population pattern of 1715 had radically altered. Since 1870 it is the industrial sections of the country which have had by far the largest part of the population.

The rearrangement in the population pattern indicates the enormous change which had taken place in the country's economy. There was a steadily increasing flow of people from the agricultural to the industrial counties, so after 1850 the industrial tended more and more to outnumber the rural agricultural population. Between 1851 and 1871 the workers in the textile factories increased from 617,000 to over 800,000. At the same time, the number and size of the factories grew. In 1871 there were 2,469 cotton factories with an average of 177 hands (1838 average, 137), 1,768 woolen factories averaging 70 hands (1838 average, 46), and 627 worsted factories averaging 175 hands (1838 average, 76). Employment in the heavy industries followed much the same line of development. In 1870 there were 78 shipbuilding concerns averaging 570 hands (30 in Scotland averaged 800), primary iron works averaged 209 (26 in Wales had 650 each), while the machinery industry averaged 85 to the factory. By 1870 Britain was no longer an agricultural nation. She was "the workshop of the world," her whole economy being geared to industrial production.

The Growth of Production

The period from 1715 to 1870 was a period of transition from an agricultural to an industrial economy; from hand production in the domestic system to machine production in the factory system; and, therefore, from small scale to large scale manufacture. In 1770 most of the industries, with the exception of cloth, supplied only a limited domestic market. By 1870 all this had changed, for most of Britain's industries were producing for export. In 1851 there was held in the Crystal Palace near London a great exhibition of Britain's industrial prowess, by which she showed to the world at large her wares and her means of making them. This was the living proof that she was the workshop of the world. It has been calculated that, while Britain's population did not double (5.5 million to 8.7 million) between 1690 and 1800, her wealth multiplied almost five times. It has also been estimated that, although her population between 1821 and 1871 was enlarged by 50 per cent, her wealth had risen 300 per cent. Here was an example of unparalleled material development, much of it resulting from a phenomenal expansion of production. In 1871 Britain led the world industrially.

This change is grasped most clearly by glancing at the production figures for the various types of industry. In 1750 iron output was at a rate of 17,500 tons per annum. By 1830 Welsh iron production alone was close to 300,000 tons, the total for the country coming to 650,000 tons. Twenty years later, some two million tons were being produced, and three times that amount by 1870. With the increase in the amount of iron and steel available and the removal in 1825 of restriction on machinery export, the engineering and machinery industry also grew to enormous proportions. Between 1822 and 1849 the value of these goods shipped to foreign and colonial ports rose from £116,220 to over £700,000. By 1875 this total stood at £9 million. Beside this, there were ships, increasingly made of iron or steel, which in 1870 represented particularly the production of the Clyde and the Mersey. At the same time, there was a noticeable rise in the exports of hardware: tools, cutlery, clocks, etc. In 1835 the total value of these goods stood at £1¼ million, but by 1870 it had multiplied more than three times.

Textiles followed the same trend, increasing beyond all bounds of expectation. The consumption of raw cotton, a good index, rose from 11 million pounds weight in 1781, to 144 million in 1820, and to 1,075 million in 1870. Although we do not have reliable figures for this period, the value of cotton goods exported increased between 1785 and 1870 some 65 times. In the woolen and worsted industry the situation is somewhat more complicated. While the amount of domestically grown wool remained about the same, imports by weight increased from 7 million pounds in 1801, to 76 million in 1850, and to 266 million in 1870. The actual value of manufacture cannot be ascertained, and, owing to such international disturbances as the Crimean, American Civil, and Franco-Prussian wars, exports fluctuated greatly. Nevertheless, it would seem to be clear that production of woolen goods expanded appreciably. In the silk industry imports of raw material in 1765 stood at 715,000 pounds, while in 1850 they were 6¼ million pounds, reaching the peak of 10 million pounds in 1865 and thereafter beginning to decline. Exports of silk manufactures in 1820, 1849, and 1870 rose in value from £370,000, to £1 millon, to £1.45 million, respectively. Other textile industries, such as linen and jute, had similar increases, but enough has been said to show the magnitude of the expansion which took place in textile production during this period.

What the output of the coal mines was at the beginning of the nineteenth century cannot be determined. It may have been something between 15 and 20 million tons. By 1850 it stood between 50 and 60 million tons, while by 1870 it was up to 110 million tons. For most of the other industries it is not easy to obtain production figures, but as one studies the pottery, glass, leather goods, and other "minor" industries, he finds that the same increases are apparent all along the line. While the actual increase in British manufactures might vary greatly from industry to industry, it was general in most of the trades.

The expansion of industry had a number of effects on the country's economy. Instead of producing merely a basic minimum to meet the needs of the population, as she had been doing in 1715, owing to the Industrial Revolution, by 1870 Britain was making a large surplus of goods. This meant first of all, a cheapening of many commodities. Goods such as cottons had become very common by 1870, whereas at the beginning of the period they had been regarded as luxuries. There was also a growing quantity of goods available for export, often at lower prices than they could be produced by foreign workers. This gave Britain an opportunity to build up a large export trade in payment for which, and to meet her own needs, she took large quantities of foreign goods. Last of all, with this increase of production, came larger and larger accumulations of capital, whether in the hands of individuals or of groups. Thus, in distinction from the ages which went before, this period became one of industrial capitalism par excellence. Industry rather than commerce became the great source of the country's wealth.

Chapter 13

THE REVOLUTION IN THE
MEANS OF COMMUNICATION,
1715-1870

M<small>EANS</small> of communications in 1715 were very poor, but then nobody worried very much, for everything moved at a slow pace. The roads were usually no more than earthen tracks, in the spring liable to be flooded, in the summer covered with ruts, some even four feet deep, and in the winter impassable with mud and snow. Human hazards in the form of highwaymen, such as Dick Turpin, also played their part. Coaches were few and uncomfortable, even though they could travel on "the wings of the wind" at five miles an hour. It took five days to go from London to Manchester, ten to twelve days from London to Edinburgh, and two days to cover the 44 miles between Edinburgh and Glasgow. Rapid travel could be safely accomplished only on horseback. The rivers, being quite short, were of little use for carrying freight any distance, and, besides, the mouths of many were gradually filling with silt. Most heavy and bulky goods, such as coal, were therefore transported by sea, a slow, tedious process, often accompanied with no little danger. Thus, in 1715, and even in 1745, there was little travel. Goods were conveyed in paniers or bags, slung across horses' backs, or by coasting vessel. Even news, good or bad, traveled slowly.

This state of affairs meant that for inland areas transportation costs were often very high. For instance, wheat carried 100 miles by road had to pay 2½d. a bushel, while coal transported eleven miles by packhorse doubled in price. If some region should experience a crop failure, as did Ireland in 1845-46, it suffered severely, while even in ordinary times districts without coal and other bulky products paid greatly inflated prices. Besides the need for cheap carriage, there was a great demand for transport which would safely convey breakable goods, such as Staffordshire pottery. Moreover, the government, particularly after the Jacobite risings of 1715 and 1745, also felt that improvements should be made. Good roads must be built for the transmission of news and the movement of troops and supplies. Nothing much, however, was actually done. It remained for the eighteenth century growth of industry to create not only a demand for cheaper transportation of bulky goods, but also to provide the capital and the engineering technique to solve the mechanical problems. Industrial development was a prerequisite for the improvement of the means of communication, and as they, in turn, became more efficient and effectual, industry was stimulated to grow. Thus, the growth of industry and the development of the means of communication had a reciprocal effect upon each other.

Such mutual influence becomes apparent when one keeps in mind that there were two tendencies in the history of communications during this period. One was to seek for a means of conveying increased quantities of bulky goods without raising the cost. The progress from the cart, to the canal barge, to the railway train indicates this. The other tendency was to seek for increased ease and speed in handling goods or information. These two objectives were always before those interested in improving communications, for success facilitated the conduct of business, opening up new markets and offering new opportunities.

The Improvement of the Roads

While rivers might, to a certain extent, provide a means of communication, not every place in the British Isles was near a river. Faster, cheaper, and more universal arteries were needed. These came first in the improvement and extension of roads through the Turnpike Trusts. The central government in the eighteenth century took little or no action to develop highways, since each parish was responsible for its own roads. These were constructed and repaired by means of compulsory labor shared by all the parishioners, although one might pay a sum of money instead of working. The actual road work was carried on under an unpaid surveyor. In Scotland and Ireland much the same method was employed. As a result of the rebellions of 1715 and 1745, however, the government itself built a number of good military roads in Scotland to keep the Highlands in subjection. In Ireland the Irish parliament and the Grand Juries also did something to improve the roads, although after the Union of 1800, the main roads throughout the British Isles were placed under the supervision of the Postmaster General. The answer to the demand for secondary and local roads, on the other hand, was found in the activities of private individuals. This resulted in the turnpike. A group of men, usually organized as a joint-stock company, would be given a charter authorizing them to improve a section of road, using parish labor as needed. When the road had been completed, a toll booth, or turnpike, was set up at each end of the improved section, no one being permitted to pass along the road without payment of a fee.

The first English turnpike charter was granted in 1663, and the first in Scotland was dated 1714. After the latter date they became more common, their creation being facilitated by the General Turnpike Act of 1773. Roads radiating from London to Cornwall, to Holyhead, the port connected with Dublin, and to Scotland were all improved. By 1825 there were some 1,100 trusts, taking care of about 20,000 miles of road. This was the period of their great popularity, when coaching had become almost a fine art. The stretches of turnpike were originally quite small, running between ten and twenty miles, each under a different authority, but after 1815 there seems to have been a tendency for the trusts to consolidate into larger units, although this was by no means universal. Even in 1870, after the railways had been in existence for thirty-five years, there were still some 845 trusts controlling parts of the country's roads.

The growth of the turnpike system was a help in developing communications because from it also came a new knowledge of road building. John Metcalfe, the blind engineer who built roads between 1765 and 1800, stressed the importance of drainage. His two successors, Thomas Telford and John Macadam, were even more scientific. Both of these men commenced their work in their native Scotland but, because of their success, were soon given government positions. Instead of dumping cartloads of loose stones on the road in the hope that they would stay, they carefully laid a foundation of rocks. Telford even insisted that they should be placed by hand. Then smaller and smaller stones were laid in successive layers, the whole being topped with gravel. The weight of the vehicles passing over helped to pack the stone into a hard mass. Telford also stressed the importance of widening the crown of the road and of abolishing sharp curves. The examples of these men stimulated the turnpike trusts to pay professional surveyors to do their work. It was largely owing to the surveyors' objections to statute labor as ineffective that in 1835 a parish tax was substituted. By 1840 Britain had an efficient system of main roads, but the coming of the railway, for the time being, virtually put them out of business.

The boom in road building which took place between 1800 and 1835 conferred many benefits upon the country. It not only gave employment to the poor, but, much more important, it provided a faster and easier method of transport and communication. Before the coming of the macadamized road, the government had endeavored to protect the highways by laws, limiting the weight of wagons, prescribing the type of wheel they were to use, and making various other regulations. The new roads did not require such protection. By 1830 the fast mail, or stage coach, was carrying passengers at the whirlwind pace of ten miles an hour, at a cost of 2½d. to 4d. a mile, while freight moved at the more sedate pace of 2½ miles an hour, at a cost of ½d. to ¾d. a mile. By 1800 the trip to Manchester had been cut by a day or so, while the London to Edinburgh journey was down to three days. The recent introduction of an improved "flying" coach, with continuous relays of horses, promised to speed up travel even more.

Yet with all this, transport was still too slow and too limited to meet the needs of growing industry. Although the pace of 10 miles an hour had caused the doctors to have misgivings as to how long the human race would last at such a speed, many men felt that they had to go faster. The continual stopping to pay tolls not only slowed traffic, but also raised prices. Moreover, all the roads were not kept at the same level of efficiency. The Postmaster General actually had to take over the London to Holyhead road for a time in order to put it in proper condition before handing it back to the turnpike trusts. Moreover, the vehicles of those days could not carry large enough loads to meet the increasing demands of the cotton mills, the engineering works, or the potteries. One must also keep in mind that while there were 20,000 miles of improved roads, there were also 100,000 miles of unimproved parish roads maintained after 1835 by pauper labor. Thus, even by 1800 turnpikes were becoming inadequate for the needs of the country.

The Development of Water Transport

The growing demand for such goods as coal, iron ore, raw cotton, and china clay forced men to look for an economical means of bulk transportation. This they found in the use of waterways. At first, efforts were made to improve the existing rivers, the Mersey, the Don, the Trent, and others. But as rivers are not always located most suitably for use as arteries of transportation, they may have to be modified by diversions or supplemented with canals. For this reason, rivers, and particularly canals, became in the late eighteenth century the principal means of bulk transportation. Much larger quantities of goods could be carried by a barge than by a cart, while for breakable commodities, such as chinaware, the canals and water routes were much smoother than the rutted highway. Canals and rivers, therefore, were very important in the early days of the Industrial Revolution.

Canals were not new, for they had been built in the fifteenth century in Italy and Holland, and the Aire and Calder Canal had been completed in the north of England before 1700. The real boom, however, came as the result of the Duke of Bridgewater's disappointment in love. Rejected by the woman he wanted to marry, he left London for his estates in Lancashire, where he became interested in the exploitation of his coal properties. Because of the expense of carrying coal by road from Worsley to Manchester, seven miles away, he employed an engineer, James Brindley, to build a canal between the two places. To do this Brindley actually had to carry the canal on a viaduct over the River Irwell, a project which caused much amazement.[1] The important thing was, however, that, as a result of Bridgewater's venture, the price of coal in Manchester fell 50 per cent. Following this, the Duke had Brindley build a canal from Manchester to the mouth of the Mersey, thus connecting Manchester with the port of Liverpool. The canal era had begun.

Brindley's early successes gave canal building a great stimulus. He and Telford, the road engineer, became the leading canal engineers. The Trent and Mersey (Grand Trunk) Canal was finished in 1766, the Staffordshire and Worcestershire followed soon after, the Birmingham and Coventry was completed in 1768, the Oxford in 1769 and the Grand Junction, connecting London with the Midlands, in 1793. In Scotland the Forth and Clyde Canal was commenced in 1763, but was not finished until 1790. Although a considerable number of these canals turned out to be relatively useless because of their situation, they all had to fight myriads of objections, particularly from the landed interest, who feared that the proximity of a canal would lower the value of their properties.

---

[1] The measurements of the aqueduct were 200 yards long by 12 yards wide, and it was carried 39 feet above the level. The coal mines were dug in the cliffs beside the river, and to save the labor of hauling the coal up to the top of the pit Brindley tunneled into the cliff to the foot of the pit, where the barges could be loaded with a minimum of effort.

The need for such transportation, however, waved aside all attempts at obstruction.

The canals were constructed, in accord with the economic thinking of the day, as ventures of private investment. Only the Caledonian and the Crinan canals in Scotland received any government aid. The companies were granted charters giving them permission to construct the canals and the right to expropriate the land which they needed and limiting them as to maximum charges which they could demand for the canal's use. This last provision was important, since the canal companies did not have their own boats, but, like the turnpikes, they only provided the canal upon which others operated. The companies were generally of the joint-stock variety, and when once their charters were received, they carried on business with complete freedom. With the exception of Ireland, after 1800 there was no real government control. The companies built the canals as they saw fit with regard to both size and material of construction. There was consequently no uniformity, so while canals might be linked with each other, they varied in width and depth to such an extent that the barges operating on one canal often could not move into the one adjoining.

The years 1792-93 were years of "canal mania," but canals continued to be dug until 1830. The greatest of these from the point of view of engineering was the Caledonian Canal, constructed by Telford in 1823, through Scotland's Great Glen, to join Inverness on the east coast with Oban in the west. It cost £1,300,000 and enabled naval vessels to move from one coast to the other, but it was never of much real economic value, although the scenery is magnificent. The really profitable canals were those in the industrial areas of both England and Scotland, around Birmingham, Coventry, Leeds, Sheffield, and Glasgow. The Forth and Clyde Canal's revenues increased from £8,000 in 1790 to £13,500 in 1795, to £48,071 in 1814. By 1816 it was paying a dividend of 25 per cent, and its £100 shares were selling for £650. In England the profits were even greater. In 1824 the Trent and Mersey was paying a dividend of 75 per cent with £100 shares selling at £2,200, and the Loughborough was paying 197 per cent with the share at £4,600. On the other hand, there were many which were paying less than 5 per cent and some nothing at all. Canals were not always built sensibly; sometimes they cost far too much, while others were dug in districts where they were useless. This was particularly true of the Irish canals, which were of relatively little value. By 1830, English and Welsh canals extended to some 2,000 miles, with another 1,300 miles of improved rivers; Scottish canals accounted for 183 miles, and Irish, 848 miles. By 1830, however, the importance of the canals was declining.

Although the canals were decreasing in value by 1830, during their period of development they had accomplished much. First and foremost, they cheapened bulk transport. Estimates have been made that, compared to road haulage rates, their charges were one-half to three-quarters less. This was extremely important to the industrial areas, for it meant that raw materials, coal, and food could be moved at much lower cost. Canals opened up a growing market for the farmer and also facilitated the distribution of manufactured goods, both to the domestic users and the ocean ports. At the same time, they also aided the movement of the population, which, in comparison with earlier days, could now travel with much greater freedom. Along with this, they stimulated construction and engineering, laying the ground work for the railway age. To the slow, uncomfortable, and expensive transportation which then existed, they brought unknown ease and cheapness.

At the same time, it must be recognized that they had very serious defects. For one thing, they were inefficient because of their differences in size. Some canals could carry a 60 ton barge, but a good many could not handle anything larger than a 20 tonner. Goods had to be shipped in small quantities or had to be continually trans-shipped, thus adding to the cost and complications of bulk transportation. Furthermore, by 1815 the canals had a virtual monopoly of transport. Consequently, they became careless about the handling of goods. They were not punctual in delivery, their charges were increased beyond what was necessary, and the bargemen were a very difficult group with which to carry on business. But what may have been even more important, they were too slow in movement. The pace of business was increasing faster than the movement of the barges. From Birmingham to Liverpool a barge had to traverse six canals, and from Birmingham to Hull, ten, all of which meant not only increased costs, but also loss of time. As most of the canals were not built for anything but horse towing, the use of steamboats was out of the question, so there was no real hope of accelerating their movement. It is not surprising, therefore, that by 1830 the coasting steamship was beginning to take over a considerable amount of their trade. When the railways came into common use a few years later, the canal's doom was sealed. Unable to stand the competition, many canals were sold to railway companies, while others were allowed to fall into disuse. By 1850 they had lost nearly all their old importance.

One of the lasting results of the canal era was the growth of the seaports, which were part of the waterway development. Cities such as Glasgow, Liverpool, Hull, and London grew quickly under the stimulus of the industry in the hinterland, which, in turn, had developed when canals made possible the transportation of goods from the interior. At the same time, there was also a growing demand abroad for British products. Increasingly Britain was becoming a nation producing for the whole world. Such a situation required good ports in order that both imports and exports might be handled quickly and efficiently.

Unfortunately, the harbors and port facilities of Britain were not very good until after 1800. Some improvements were made in London during the eighteenth century, but it was not until 1805 that the West India dock was built, the East India docks coming three years later. In 1713 bonding privileges had been granted to plantation rum, the taxes not being paid until it was removed from the warehouse to the retailer, thus constituting a big saving to the importer. Throughout the century the list of goods in this category was increased until the Warehousing Act of 1803 made the practice more or less general. As a result, warehousing soon became a profitable business, and competing companies were organized. The port of London, however, had no real central authority in control of all facilities until the present century. Meanwhile, Liverpool's first dock had been built in 1715, but it was not until the early nineteenth century that the city really became important as the cotton manufacturing district's outlet to the sea. Unlike London, the control of the port was in the hands of the Corporation of Liverpool, until 1857, when it was committed to a central board composed of nominees of the Mersey Conservation Commission and representatives of those who paid rates on ships and goods. At the same time, Glasgow was expanding. The growing Scottish cotton and heavy industries were a great stimulus to activity. The Clyde was dredged so that it could take a vessel of twenty foot draft, docks were built, and by 1861 1½ million tons of goods were passing through Glasgow's customs house. Similarly, Southampton was experiencing a rapid growth. Its natural advantages as a port for American and Indian trade were soon recognized, the result being that 1842 saw the opening of the first big dock as well as the advent of its first railway line. Besides these, smaller ports also were being developed or repaired: Bristol, Hull, Harwich, Newcastle-on-Tyne, Leith, and Aberdeen. By 1870, while inland water transportation had declined sharply, the seaports were booming. Improved and modernized, they were handling the largest stream of commerce in the world.

The Impact of the Steam Engine

By 1830 industry had expanded to such an extent and Britain's commerce had so increased that the older means of transportation were not enough. The slowness, the high prices, and the inefficiency of the canals were again forcing industrialists and merchants to look around for a cheaper and faster method of moving their goods. At the same time, because of the economic growth of the country, the reserves of capital which could be used to develop transportation were much greater than they had been fifty years earlier. Added to this, the scientific and engineering advances since 1800 were encouraging men to look for a mechanical, to replace the "natural," means of transport.

As a result of these various factors, steam as a locomotive power became a subject of great interest and study. To provide a suitable steam system, however, very great modifications had to be made in the existing engine. It had to develop a much greater horse-power per pound weight than the usual factory power plants if the engine were to move. At the same time, it had to be able to maintain a continuous head of steam, for it could not afford to stop every so often along the route to get up more steam to carry it on. Finally, it had to be simple in construction and easy to drive; otherwise, it would be impossible either to construct or operate economically.

Although this was not at first realized, some of the problems of running such a vehicle had been solved as far back as the seventeenth century. At an early date it had been the custom in the mines around Newcastle, in order to make the wagons run more easily, to lay boards in the ruts which they had cut. A little later, the boards were covered with iron. In 1767 an L shaped rail was first employed, with the wheel of the wagon running on the flat part of the L. Finally, by 1800 it was found that the best arrangement was to use flanged wheels on unflanged rails. A horse could often draw fifty times more weight on these than he could on the road. In England, Wales and Scotland such horse-drawn railways, or "tram lines," were in common use in the mines and between the mines and the canals, drastically reducing the cost of coal haulage. Between 1776 and 1802 quite a number of rail lines were also constructed by canal companies to bring goods to their barges. Then in 1801 and 1803 two lines for passenger and freight were laid in suburban London, the country's first real railways. They were not, however, great successes. What was needed was greater power and greater speed of operation than was furnished by the horse.

The answer to this demand was to be found in the moving steam engine. One or two were built experimentally before 1800, but the first which could actually be used was a steam coach produced in 1801 by a Cornishman named Trevithick. He was successful in this because he used a sheet iron boiler in which he generated a head of steam amounting to about 60 lbs. per square inch. He did not use a condenser, as Watt had done on his engine, but simply allowed the steam to escape. It is believed by some that he actually used this exhaust steam as a forced draft in the smoke stack by permitting it to enter the stack a foot or so from the top. Others deny that he did so. Because his coach ran on the roads, he threatened competition with the stagecoach interests, who opposed him bitterly. He was also unpopular with the turnpike trusts, who feared that his invention would ruin their road surfaces. These objections, coupled with the difficulty of handling his coaches, meant that they never achieved any great popularity. Trevithick, however, had laid the groundwork for a workable moving steam engine.

The man who brought together all the elements to form the modern railway train was the self-educated George Stephenson. He was faced, first of all, with the problem of placing a steam engine on rails. Trevithick had tried this in a South Wales colliery but was unsuccessful, as his engine was too heavy for cast iron tracks. Because friction was not properly understood, it was thought that for the engine to pull, it was necessary to have a cogwheel which fitted into slots in the rail. Stephenson, however, showed that a smooth wheel on a smooth rail generated enough friction to enable the engine to haul the train. From this he turned to the problem of the engine itself. Copying the design of a certain Blenkinsop, he used a tubular boiler to obtain a greater head of steam; he employed the steam exhaust to make a forced draft; and he simplified the mechanism by attaching the pistons directly to the driving wheels. In 1814 he drew his first train load of coals weighing 30 tons at 4 miles an hour up a gradient of 1 in 450. From this point he went on to the study of gradients, realizing that, if only the steep hills could be taken out, it would be possible to use the traveling steam engine in any country. In these various ways he laid the foundation of the modern railway.

The first real steam railroad to come into operation was the Stockton and Darlington Railway, built to carry coal to Stockton-on-Tees. It was originally planned to have stationary steam engines to pull the trains up the hills, while horses, carried up and down hill in a "dandy cart" attached to the rear of each train, were used to pull them on the level. Stephenson persuaded the projectors, however, to use a moving steam engine at least for their coal. His first trip was a huge success. At the start of the run he was preceded by a man on horseback carrying a flag, but he soon put him out of the way to drive along at the breakneck speed of twelve miles an hour. The railway company, however, did lease the right to carry passengers to an outside concern which used horses for motive power.

The real change came five years later with the establishment of the Liverpool and Manchester Railway. Stephenson's "Rocket" proved itself to be far superior to all engines competing for a £500 prize. It attained the speed of 29 m.p.h., and its first through run, completed June 14, 1830, was at the average rate of 27 m.p.h. The success of this venture proved beyond doubt that the traveling steam engine was going to be the moving force on the railway, and, because of that, leasing the rail line as the canals and turnpikes had been was of no use. The railway company was obliged to be the carrier, or at least it had to provide the engines and control the traffic. Otherwise the railway would never be satisfactory.

By 1835 the victory of the railways over their opponents was complete. It had been declared that cows would stop giving milk, woods would be burned, birds passing over the smoke stacks would be killed, and little boys would have their morals wrecked by these roaring monsters. Canal companies, landlords, innkeepers, coaching companies, and many others opposed the building of railways. But it was all in vain. The only thing which they could do was force the railways to pay large sums for land on which to build and oblige them to take every precaution in the matter of construction. For instance, the Liverpool and Manchester Railway had to pay £70,000 before it could obtain the consent of the Duke of Cleveland to the granting of its charter, because he was afraid that the railroad would disturb his fox hunting. The demands for care in building, along with the need for tunnels, cuttings, and the like, particularly in the western part of the country, likewise helped to increase expenses. The result was that the amount spent on the building of railways in Britain by 1849 averaged over £50,000 per mile, while they cost only £11,000 in Austria and £5,000 in the United States. The Blackwall Railway actually cost £289,000 per mile. But despite the opposition and the expense, between 1825 and 1835 parliament passed 54 railway acts providing for over 400 miles of line in England and Wales and 50 miles in Scotland. Trains were now traveling at an average speed of around 30 miles an hour, and although private companies could have their own goods wagons, the railway company did the hauling and was in complete control of schedules. But what was of even more importance, to the surprise of everybody, the railways were particularly popular for passenger traffic. While at first they had been regarded as supplementing canal transport, very quickly they became an independent means of locomotion, completely overshadowing the canal barge and putting the stagecoach into the museum.

The period from 1835 to 1847 was one of rapid expansion. The difficulty was, however, that since there was virtually no government control, all of the lines built were short, being interested only in some local need. Fortunately, most of the lines adopted Stephenson's gauge of tracks, 4 feet 8½ inches. The Great Western Railway, however, under the advice of its engineer Brunel, used a 7 foot gauge. This was really a better size, for it was safer, permitting higher speeds; but as all the other lines used the smaller gauge, there was no possibility of running trains from the Great Western Railway on the other lines. This caused trouble, and finally parliament decided to make the small gauge standard. Meanwhile, despite the lack of central control and the shortness of individual lines, the railways were meeting a real need and expanded rapidly. By 1847 some 200 companies had laid in England and Wales 4,000 miles of track. The longest line was that of the London North Western Railway, built up out of a number of smaller lines, amounting in 1846 to 379 miles, a capitalization of £17,000,000, and an annual revenue of £2,000,000. In Scotland the railways had not developed quite as rapidly, but the network was increasing. In 1847 even Ireland had 209 miles, which carried 4⅓ million people annually. Thus, by 1847 the railways were booming. Between 1844 and 1847, 637 railway acts were passed, representing a projected 9,397 miles. Dividends were being paid at the rate of about 15 per cent, so it looked as though everything was all right.

The year 1847, however, saw a considerable change in the situation. A financial panic forced a movement toward amalgamation. Since numerous small lines were inefficient, some of the companies by 1844 were making agreements with each other regarding through traffic, fares, and use of each other's depots. The Railway Clearing House was established in 1842 to facilitate the operation of these agreements. Meanwhile, competition was growing between two main groups: those wanting to carry all the London-to-Scotland traffic via the Midlands and the west coast, and those seeking to do the same via the east coast. As a result of the competition of these groups, a number of western companies came together in 1846 as the London North Western Railway. A number of years later, beginning in 1854, the London North Eastern Railway was organized by a similar group of east coast railways. At the same time parliament, believing in keen competition, had permitted the Midland Railway, which the London North Western Railway had attempted unsuccessfully to absorb in 1853, to extend its services to London and Scotland, thus becoming what was later known as the London, Midland and Scottish Railway. Meanwhile, in the southwest the Great Western and in East Anglia the Great Eastern railways had come into being. Consequently, by 1870 the 200 railways of 1846 had been reduced to one tenth that number, although the length of track had grown to 15,310 miles and traffic had increased by leaps and bounds. By 1870 the average annual number of passengers was 330 million, and by 1880 the annual freight traffic had risen to 235 million tons. Consolidation and amalgamation had resulted in increased efficiency, cheaper rates, and greater revenues.

Because of the growing tendency toward amalgamation, parliament had begun to think that it would have to supervise railway development more closely. It had hoped that the canals would offer enough competition to keep the railways in their place. Since 1845, however, it was quite evident that the canals were doomed, it was frequently asserted that it was the state's duty to maintain competition between railways and to supervise their activities. But parliament, with its strong laissez faire convictions, was very loath to take decisive action. Nevertheless, it was faced with the inescapable fact that the railways had an actual monopoly of land transportation which had to be controlled. The result was the beginnings of the state's interference in private business.

Parliament had, of course, always asserted a certain amount of control over the railways by obliging them to obtain charters of incorporation. This gave an opportunity for the opposition to be heard, and in the case of the London and York Railway the hearing of evidence took seventy days. As the charters included the right to expropriate land, private property was also given a chance to defend itself. In 1842 there was added to this the requirement that the Board of Trade must approve any application for new lines and that all lines must annually report their traffic and their accidents. In 1844 a parliamentary commission was set up to oversee the railways, but as it was without any real power, it lasted only about a year. In 1845 parliament obliged the railways to provide suitable accommodation for third class passengers at 1*d*. a mile. Up to this time the third class passengers had been carried in open cars, without seats, at the rear of freight trains. Now they were to be protected from the weather and were to receive improved service. Two years later another body of commissioners was appointed, but, as they also had few powers, they were abolished in 1851. Parliament could not make up its mind to exercise effective control. In 1845 it had fixed the railway profits at a maximum of 10 per cent and had reserved the right to purchase the lines in twenty-one years time. When the time was up, however, no action was taken. Monopolistic conditions were growing with the forming of larger and larger railway companies, but still parliament would take no direct action. It was not until after 1870 that something concrete was done to regulate the railways and their business.

It might be well at this point to stop for a minute and see how people traveled on the early train. The first passenger carriages were usually open wagons with benches. Provision was also made to carry people in their own coaches set on flat cars. As this was not satisfactory, it soon became the custom to fasten a number of coach bodies on a car permanently and from this developed the present form of British railway car. Second class passengers usually sat in an open car, over which was a canvas tilt to keep off the rain and sun, while the third class passengers stood in the open wagon without any protection against the weather. A sudden stopping of the train might send the third class passengers either into a heap on the floor or over the side on to the roadbed. The railways lost a good many passengers that way! If one missed the train and had influence or money enough, he could always hire an engine to overtake it. In such cases brakes would sometimes not work properly and the engine would crash into the last cars, causing a mild wreck. On the other hand, sometimes a car's couplings would break, resulting in part of the train being left far behind without the engineer's even realizing what had happened. To help solve this problem a man known as "the guard" was stationed on the back of the engine to keep an eye on the rest of the train.

As time passed improvements were introduced. Less difference was to be found between the first, second, and third class accommodations. In 1872 the Midlands Railways finally abolished the second class altogether. Passenger trains were equipped with continuous brakes, smoking cars were introduced around 1870, and some lines were beginning to use dining cars. By 1870 the system of block signals was also employed. Such innovations helped greatly in speeding passenger traffic and in obviating accidents. One could travel quite safely and in great comfort from London to Edinburgh in the space of about twelve hours. Freight trains remained much as they had been. Since about half the cars were owned by private companies, little could be done to introduce improvements such as a continuous brake system. The result was that these trains remained small and slow. Even so, in fifty years there had been a revolution.

What did this change actually mean? How did the application of steam to land transport affect economic development? First, it made the transfer of goods and people much faster, cheaper, and more efficient. Besides delivering goods more punctually than did the canals, the railways cut costs, in many cases by 50 per cent and sometimes by even more. The retailer no longer had to keep large stocks on hand, but could order smaller quantities knowing that he would usually receive them overnight. Distances are short compared with America, so it was cheaper to carry on business in this way. The traveling merchant was also displaced by the traveling salesman, who carried only samples and could have the goods purchased delivered to the customer in a matter of days. Along with this, there was increased mobility for the population. Men could more easily move about to find work or could go where employment was offered. Last but not least, the railways were a new industry. In 1848 they were employing 188,000 men in construction and 56,000 in their regular operations. This was indeed a big business, which, in turn, stimulated big business. The railways could do more rapidly and more cheaply all that the canals had done. By 1870, therefore, they were practically the only means of long distance land transportation.

While steam power was being used on land men were also attempting to meet the special problems involved in its employment in ships. As early as 1786 William Symington took out a patent for a marine engine and in 1789 he performed a number of experiments on the River Clyde with a boat powered by an engine made by the Carron Iron Works. In 1801 the first practical steam boat, *The Charlotte Dundas*, pulled two loaded seventy ton boats on the Forth and Clyde Canal for 19 miles. Robert Fulton soon followed Symington's example in America, while in 1812 Henry Bell's *Comet* commenced regular runs on the Forth and Clyde Canal. From that time on the number of steamships increased steadily. By 1816 there were services operating from Liverpool to Glasgow, Holyhead to Dublin and Greenock to Belfast, while two years later steampackets were running between Dover and Calais. In 1829 they were even entrusted with His Majesty's mails.

All these ships were under 1,000 tons and were fit only for short trips, since the fuel for long journeys would be too bulky. In 1854, however, the compound engine was developed. This new type of power plant used the same steam twice, thereby reducing the coal consumption by from 30 per cent to 40 per cent. But even without this engine, a beginning had been made in transatlantic steamship travel. In 1819 the *Savannah* crossed from the United States with both sail and steam, while the first all-steam voyage took place from Pictou, N.S. in 1833, the trip being made in 20 days. In 1838 three more voyages were completed, the fastest being 13½ days. Finally, in 1839 Samuel Cunard of Halifax, N.S., was granted the contract for carrying the Royal Mail and given a subsidy of £55,000. His ships made the trip from Liverpool to Halifax and New York in about twelve days, the first voyage taking place in 1840. Other contracts were let for the carrying of mail to the Far East and the British West Indies. Although the sailing vessel dominated the scene until after 1860, the steam engine was beginning to take its place in transoceanic traffic.

With the application of steam to ocean transport went also the use of iron in ship building. As early as 1787 John Wilkinson had built a canal barge of iron, and in 1818 a second was made for use on the Forth and Clyde Canal. Iron boats, however, did not attain immediate popularity. Ship owners were suspicious and at first the most they would do was accept ships with iron frames. Only gradually were prejudices broken down. The voyage in 1832 of an iron boat, built by John Laird, from Britain to Nigeria convinced a number, and in 1839 the first East India Company iron boat was launched. Yet the first iron Cunarder did not come off the ways until 1865. Another problem raised by the use of steam in ships was that of propulsion. At first the paddle wheel was the accepted method, but in 1838 a change came when Captain John Ericsson perfected the screw propellor. Although adopted by the British Admiralty in 1843, it really did not become common until the '60's, when the usual type of new vessel was being made of iron and driven by the compound engine. By 1870 out of a total of 26,367 vessels with a combined weight of over 5.5 million tons, there were 3,178 steamers having a net tonnage of 1,112,934 tons. Steamers were beginning to form the majority of the larger ships.

The success of the steamship accelerated a change which had already begun. Ocean shipping is much harder to regulate than railways, since a vessel may be away for years before returning to the home port. As shipping companies do not have to spend money building a right of way, or even docks, ship transportation is cheaper than that of railways. What is more, it is more vulnerable to foreign competition because of its world-wide connections. All these factors forced certain alterations in shipping organization. For one thing, in earlier days the custom had been for merchants or trading companies to own their own ships, but the appearance of the larger iron ship with its greatly increased cargo space made this practice no longer economical. Moreover, the general expansion of world trade meant that frequently more money could be made carrying varied cargoes not necessarily destined for one port. The result was that frequently ship-owning merchant companies sold off their boats or went into the shipping business exclusively. Some became owners of tramp steamers, while others preferred liners which ran between specified ports on fixed schedules. But whichever system was followed, the new method meant cheaper and more efficient freight handling. With Britain's widespread trade connections, this was a great boon, particularly as after 1854 the abolition of the Navigation Acts made export and import completely free. Subsidized by mail contracts and unfettered by mercantilist restrictions, by 1870 British shipping dominated the sea lanes of the world.

Urban Communications

The development of passenger vehicles in the towns during this period was following a line of its own. Before 1800 two types of conveyance were in general use. There was the Sedan chair carried by two men, and there was the hackney coach, which, because of its bulk, found difficulty in negotiating the narrower of the city streets. In 1823 the French two-wheeled cabriolet, which had a folding cover and carried two passengers, was introduced. In the thirties a Mr. Hansom, who had invented certain safety devices to keep the "cab" from tilting backwards or forwards, brought out an improved two-wheeled, two passenger conveyance. A four-wheeled "cab" was also developed for larger numbers. Throughout the period these were the principal vehicles for hire, holding the same place as our modern taxi.

For the less opulent members of society who could not afford an "'Ansom cab," a means of mass conveyance now made its appearance. This was of great importance, as, with the expansion of industrial towns, workers often had to travel long distances to their jobs. In 1829 George Shillibeer brought to London from

Paris the horse-drawn omnibus. He was soon imitated by a number of others who set up competing lines. In 1846 the first 2d. fare was established, and the buses pasted up their first advertisements. The big change came in 1855 however, when a French company, *La Compagnie Generalê des Omnibus de Londres*, began operations. It established what was very close to a monopoly and by 1878 was employing as many as 8,000 horses to convey Londoners to and from work.

The only real competition offered to the buses was that furnished by horse-drawn tramways. These were an American invention, or rather re-invention, which had been tried out unsuccessfully in 1861. In 1868, with an improved type of rail, the tramway succeeded in Liverpool, and the following year it was re-introduced to London. From then on the tramways grew apace, helped on by a general act in 1870 designed to facilitate their establishment.

A word might also be said about town roads. Tolls continued to be levied in London until 1871, when they were abolished. In the meantime, improvement had been made in urban road building. The old cobbles were poor paving material, so in 1824 Telford paved Hanover Square in London with granite blocks, or sets. In 1840 Blackfriars Bridge received the same treatment. The real improvement came, however, in 1869, when the Val de Travers Asphalte Paving Company of Switzerland paved Threadneedle Street. This cheap, long wearing type of material would make it possible for all city streets to be well paved, smooth, and easily cleaned. It meant not only increased ease of travel, but also more sanitary towns.

The Communication of News

Since the communication of news is of as great economic importance as is the transportation of goods, the Industrial Revolution stimulated development in this field also.

In the seventeenth century letters had been carried in many different ways. The Post Office, a royal monopoly, was primarily utilized for the transmission of royal dispatches. In 1760, however, the office was nationalized, becoming a public service operated for the profit of the state. The mails were usually carried by "fast" coach, the charge for letters being according to the number of sheets with the recipient paying the cost. In 1839 it cost 13d. a sheet to send a letter from London to Edinburgh, the high charges naturally tending to restrict letter communication or forcing people to arrange private delivery. To obviate this contravention of the government monopoly and to facilitate postal communications, Rowland Hill headed a crusade for uniform penny postage. In 1840 he was successful, and the new system was set up. Postage stamps, the first being the famous "penny black," were issued, communication by mail thereafter becoming a matter of ease. From the 99 million letters delivered in the United Kingdom in 1839, the number grew until by 1843 there were 265 million and by 1871, 867 million. Total Post Office revenue also climbed from £2 million to over £4.5 million. In 1839 postal money orders were inaugurated; in 1861 postal savings banks; and finally, in 1864, postal life insurance and annuities. In this way the post office became not merely a means of communication but also the financial agent of thousands of British working people.

Letters, however, were not the only way of communicating information. In 1837 an electric telegraph was patented, although it did not come into common use until an American, S. F. B. Morse, in 1844 produced a practical instrument. Two years later the Electric Telegraph Company was formed to work primarily with the railways, public business not being accepted until 1850. Other companies then began to compete, but the service was not particularly good. Consequently, in 1870 the government bought out all the domestic systems, establishing a state monopoly under Post Office direction. During the same period cables had been laid under the sea: to Calais in 1851, to Calcutta in 1865, to New York in 1866, and to Australia in 1871. This resulted in a great change in business methods. News could be flashed around the world in a very short time. In 1847 the Queen's speech from the throne was sent out in a few minutes to the whole of the British Isles, and in 1851 word of the coup d'état in France reached Britain in two hours, while in the sixties news could be brought equally quickly from Asia and America. Not only could orders for goods, reports on the condition of the market, and specifically economic news be obtained, but word of revolutions, wars, or any thing else which might disrupt trade could also be quickly received. Industry and trade could now become geared overnight to the needs and demands of any part of the globe. From this time forward the tempo of business has continually increased.

Another form of communication which has had a very great influence upon British economic life is the newspaper. At first, owing to heavy taxes, circulation was small, but from 1836 on, a change took place. The tax was lowered from 3½d. to 1d. per paper, and in 1855 it was completely abolished. With this change the newspaper became not only a carrier of news, but also an important medium for mass advertising. The producer was able to reach the public directly, brand names started to appear, and some companies began to build up a reputation for certain goods. Lever Brothers, the soap manufacturers, was one of the earliest firms to employ this method of selling goods. At the same time, the newspaper, in keeping people informed about the outside world, helped to create new desires, as well as new fears, just as at the beginning of the Korean war in 1950 the fear of shortages caused a violent increase in demand for certain goods, thus upsetting the economic equilibrium. In these ways newspapers, now coming into common use, played their part also in the economic history of the times.

In summary, on looking back over the period 1715 to 1870, one finds that concurrent with the rise of industry a radical change in communications occurred. The two principal characteristics of this revolution were the increase of speed and the increase of capacity. In terms of transportation, goods in bulk could be shipped at a pace often 10 or 20 times faster than before, markets could be reached more quickly, and raw goods obtained with greater ease. Added to this, by means of the telegraph an order could be sent from New York to London in an hour or two, and the goods landed in New York within two weeks, instead of requiring a six weeks journey each way. Contact could be kept with all the markets of the world, and their orders filled within a matter of days instead of months. Thus it was that Great Britain in 1870, the "workshop of the world," with her communication systems radiating to all parts of the globe, seemed to stand in an unshakable position of dominance.

Chapter 14

BRITAIN'S RISE TO COM-
MERCIAL SUPREMACY

Prior to 1715 trade and commerce meant primarily the exchange of commodities within the country, for while foreign trade was important, it was of relatively less significance than internal trade. The period from 1715 to 1870 saw this situation reversed. Foreign trade increasingly occupied the country's attention until by 1870 it was all-important. This meant of course that Britain's international relations were of the greatest moment to the country, for a war, a revolution, or a famine could completely disrupt her economy. No doubt the Hundred Years' War had its repercussions in England, but they were nothing to the effect of the French Revolutionary and Napoleonic wars. Nor were these nearly so influential on Britain's economy as was World War I or World War II. As Britain's international economic interests increased, so her international relations became of greater moment. Hence, one must glance at the international scene before turning specifically to the subject of Britain's trade.

The International Background

The period from 1715 to 1815 was one of ever recurrent wars, frequently with France. In the 1730's and 1740's Britain was involved in the War of Jenkins' Ear and the War of the Austrian Succession. She faced her greatest challenge, however, when she fought France in the Seven Years' War (1757-63), which eventually brought her Canada. Then came the American Revolution (1775-83), and finally, from 1793 to 1815 she was again at grips with France. In each of these conflicts the economic factor became increasingly important. In both the Treaty of Utrecht (1713) and the Treaty of Paris (1763) Britain benefitted by commercial clauses written at her insistence. The American Revolution was caused, in part at least, by restrictive economic regulation. But the great example of the high place that economic matters had attained is to be found in Napoleon's Continental System, by which he hoped to smash Britain through the exclusion of her goods from continental markets. He was unsuccessful, however, and the succeeding fifty years of peace provided her with the opportunity to build up her trade without either suffering losses or making gains through international conflicts.

While Britain had peace during the last half century of our period, other nations did not. The eighteenth century conflicts had been largely dynastic and territorial. A change came, however, in the nineteenth century. From 1800 on there was throughout Europe a growing sense of nationalism. France, Britain, Spain, and Holland had already experienced this feeling. It was in central and eastern Europe that it now began to appear, resulting in a number of wars. The "Christian" subjects of the Turks endeavored to establish their own kingdoms as in the cases of Greece, Romania, and Serbia. The Italians fought for their unity against the whole Concert of Europe and by 1870 were fairly well knit together as a nation. Most important of all, the founding of the German Empire in 1870 saw the culmination of efforts to unify Germany. Naturally the rise and growth of these nationalities had their economic causes and their effects which influenced Britain.[1] Economic and political nationalism go hand in hand.

Coupled with nationalism went imperialism among the powers already possessing national consciousness and unity. The old imperialism of the eighteenth century was primarily mercantilist in outlook. The colonies existed for the benefit of the mother country. But this attitude, when pushed to an extreme and especially when applied to the same national and racial stock as in the home country, brought revolution. This was what happened, at least in part, in America. One of the causes of the trouble was that the British colonists resented home interference in their economic activities, for they too were British subjects possessing British rights. Thus the United States came to birth, proclaiming its British liberties. For some years afterwards, Britain was very dubious about colonies of predominantly Anglo-Saxon stock. They were inclined to be too independent. Colored men could be more easily ruled.

Yet Britain could not escape from imperialism. For her own protection she added to her possessions in America, Africa, and India, by taking over in 1815, West Indian Islands and the Cape

---

[1] It is well to remember that the movement towards the founding of the German Empire had its origins in a customs union, called the *Zollverein*.

of Good Hope, and in 1819, Singapore. Simultaneously, Canada was being opened up to Loyalists from the United States and displaced Scots, Irish, and English from the home land. From 1788 on Australia received exiled criminals, who, after 1815, were followed by free colonists. Settlers also commenced to move to South Africa. For the next fifty years the Empire expanded. Hong Kong was added, settlements were established on the east and west coasts of Africa, and islands were occupied in the South Pacific. But this was a new kind of imperialism, which finally achieved a definite form with the creation in 1867 of the self-governing Dominion of Canada. Other countries were also extending their imperial aims and rule, but in their colonies self-government came in more slowly.

The reason for the imperialistic expansionism of the nineteenth century was not merely a matter of a worship of force or a search for security. Religious as well as economic or patriotic motives were involved. One of Britain's most potent reasons was the search for raw materials and for markets. As production increased, so it was necessary to find outlets for goods. At the same time, there was an increasing demand for raw materials such as cotton, wool, and lumber. Trade stimulated industry, and industry, trade. This was eventually to lead Britain into rivalry and conflict with other nations. But as she was industrially and commercially on top of the world until 1870, that difficulty would come only at a later date.

Coupled with these factors went the growth and acceleration of communications. In the days of the sailing ship it might take anything from six weeks to four months to go from Britain to United States. Six months was the time required to travel to India. Winds had to be used as best they might, but with the application of steam power to ships a great change was immediately apparent. To this was shortly added the telegraph. International contacts were now much quicker. Countries seemed to draw nearer together. Word of needs in one part of the world could be quickly flashed to another part and almost as quickly met by steamer carried cargo. The world was shrinking greatly by 1870, which meant that producer and consumer were coming closer to each other in point of time and space. With machine production added as a further complicating factor, this meant that commercial practice, because of the revolutions in agriculture, industry, and communications, was itself in for a time of very drastic alteration.

The Changing Organization of Trade

The old method of trading, prior to 1715, had been largely that of the individual "adventurer." If trading in the domestic market, he might be a merchant traveling around with his wares from fair to fair, or he might be a peddler seeking his customers among those who were the consumers of his goods. A merchant dealing in foreign wares, on the other hand, as a member of a chartered company, would conduct his business in distant lands under company supervision. Once factory production became common, however, and travel facilities improved, all this was changed. The commercial traveler, or traveling salesman, with his illustrated catalogues and samples, began combing the country for business. With the introduction of the telegraph a further change took place through the establishment of agencies and foreign "correspondents," who would keep the merchants or industrialists informed of local needs.

The first effect of this upon the organization of domestic trade was that with the rise of factories, the big wholesaler and the individual shop keeper no longer needed to depend upon a middleman who would go around the country collecting small lots of cloth, hardware, or pottery from small producers. They now dealt directly with the manufacturer, at first through his salesman and by 1870 through a manufacturer's agent. Thus the middleman in the "concentration" end of the wholesale trade began to disappear. In the "distributing" end, however, middlemen might even increase in number. For one thing, not all goods, particularly those which were imported, could be bought directly from the manufacturer. Secondly, since people cared nothing for brand names on goods in those early days, one did not feature any particular manufacturer's products, but obtained his food stuffs, spices, or hardware wherever available. To save time and money in this process, it was easier to go to a wholesaler or middleman who, dealing directly with the producer, would have the desired wares on hand. Thus, while one stage of the trade would tend to squeeze out the middleman, the other part would tend to give him greater importance.

Two innovations in the domestic retail trade which helped to alter its character were the beginnings of the use of brand names and the employment of advertising with "customer appeal." Both Josiah Wedgwood and Matthew Boulton in the eighteenth century used these techniques. Wedgwood's Etruria china, for instance, was advertised on the Continent by means of illustrated handbills. In the nineteenth century this method became even more common. Later on Lever Brothers introduced "Sunlight" soap with advertising which warned women that they would become old and haggard over the washtub unless they used "Sunlight" in washing their clothes. This is the foundation of modern "soap opera" advertising. Another novelty was the appearance by 1825 of the "bazaar," a shop for all types of fancy goods, and also of the early departmental shops. J. & W. Campbell of Glasgow and J. M. Morrison & Co., Leaf, Son & Cole, Wynn Ellis, all of London, set up the earliest of these organizations. Here one could buy a great variety of goods in one store and, because of mass purchasing, often at lower prices. Provincial stores followed the metropolitan example by putting in glass display windows and by keeping in close touch with London by fast coach, later by train, in order that their merchandize might always be up to date. Retailing by 1850 had definitely removed its medieval garb.

In other types of domestic commerce, such as the coal trade, there were somewhat similar developments. By 1800 the big London coal merchant was buying through a factor from the collier owner. He, in turn, might sell to "second merchants," who would take the coal inland to large industrial consumers, or to such people as merchants' clerks, who would handle the sale of small lots to domestic users. By 1850 further changes were taking place, with increased amounts of west country coal arriving by rail. Between 1850 and 1870 inland coal sales in London jumped from 55,000 tons to 3.5 million, while at the same time sea coal dropped from 3.5 million to 2.5 million tons. The coal was now shipped direct by the coal owners to the Coal Exchange, where it was bought by merchants who sold direct to the consumer. Attempts to regulate prices had broken down in the early '40's, resulting in fighting competition, which brought lower costs and the elimination of the middleman. There were still a few "second merchants," but they bought at the wharves or in railway yards to sell in small amounts to the poor.

The food trades, particularly in the cities, also saw a change in methods. In the smaller towns and country districts much of the trade was still directly between producer and consumer. In London, Liverpool, Glasgow, and other cities, however, this was not possible. At the beginning of the century dairy maids with pails in their hands could often be seen distributing milk. They might even drive a cow into town to milk it before the customer. About this time big dairies with large numbers of cattle were opened in cities such as London and Glasgow to supply retailers. But the expansion of the cities, and the advent of foot and mouth disease and *rinder-pest* in the '40's and '50's, brought this to an end. Besides, trains were now bringing in more and more of the milk from distant points. Dairies turned to handling this milk on a large scale, selling it directly to the consumer. The trade in meat also experienced similar changes. The railways or steamships brought the live cattle from Ireland and Scotland to the seaport towns. There they were slaughtered and butchered by men who did nothing else, and a salesman sold the meat to the retailer. In the same way potatoes from Cornwall were handled by a London middleman. The retailer was now nothing but a retailer, purchasing his stock from agents or primary processors, who brought in the meat, milk, or vegetables from distant points.

By 1870 the grain trade also had been greatly simplified. From 1815 on imports gradually increased, since the country was not producing all that it could eat. But down to 1870 the British farmer was still meeting most of the demand. Before 1780 the factor had dominated the scene, buying grain for millers or maltsters from the farmers or selling a big farmer's crop on the London Corn Exchange. He might even be interested, in days of plenty, in sending cargoes abroad. With the disappearance of export and the rise of import, the factor's function became less necessary. Speculation in grain now became common. The merchants who forgathered at the Baltic Coffee House would trade cargoes among themselves, sometimes even before the grain was grown. This was known as "trading in futures." When the grain arrived in the country, samples were taken to the Corn Exchange where the load was disposed of, usually being bought by factors or agents of the millers or brewers. Although "the Baltic men" speculated on wheat, they also played a very important part in bringing grain into the country when it was needed. Before restraints on import were removed in 1846, they sometimes even had it stored in bonded warehouses, in the hope that scarcity would create a good market.

One other change which took place in the organization of the country's internal trade was the appearance of the Cooperative Movement. This movement, really based on Robert Owen's ideas, was founded in Rochdale in 1844. The plan was very simple. A number of men each subscribed a certain sum of money to set up and operate a store. At the end of the year, after all bills were paid and a sum reserved for capital, 3 per cent was paid on the subscriptions or stock, and the rest of the profits were divided among the registered customers pro rata according to their purchases. This movement expanded widely through the industrial areas and by 1870 was doing an annual business of £13 million. In 1863 a cooperative wholesale society was organized to buy for the re- tailers, the stock being owned by a number of stores and the "divi" going to them according to their purchases. Within a year this company had bought and sold over £2.5 million worth of goods. The "co-ops" then commenced to go directly to the producer for goods, and even some cooperative factories were started. Scottish cooperatives were also organized about the same time both in the retail and wholesale fields. In this way efforts were made, despite great opposition from outside, to give the consumer a share in the retail business's profits.

Simultaneously with the changes in domestic trade, foreign trade was seeing many innovations. While we do not have reliable trade figures for the eighteenth century, the expansion can be demon- strated by the growth of registered shipping from 317,000 tons in 1700 to 1.95 million tons a century later. It has been estimated that this meant an increase in the annual value of trade from £12 million to over £62 million. While the Napoleonic Wars took their toll by holding trade for some years at the 1800 figure, by 1870 it had risen considerably past the £400 million mark.[2]

As the increase in domestic commerce had forced a change in its organization and methods, so the growth of foreign trade forced corresponding innovations in its activities. For one thing, the old monopolistic chartered company practically disappeared. By 1800 the East India Company and the Hudson Bay Company were the only two left. The East India Company lost its monopoly of Indian trade in 1813 and of the China trade in 1834. Private trade dominated. Added to this, trading by ship owners now disappeared, for ship owning and operating was a full time job, either on a char- ter or on a carriage basis. The merchant might charter the whole ship or rent merely a portion of its carrying space.

One of the fundamental reasons for this change was the im- provement in communications. No longer did a company in foreign trade have to load up a ship with goods which it *hoped* might have a sale on a distant Indian, Chinese, or African market. When the East India Company first came into existence, this was the only possible method, and it was properly known as "adventuring." With the advent of the steamship, bringing faster communications, a new method was introduced. An exporter might take goods on

---

[2] There is a difficulty in estimating the relationship between 1800 and 1870 figures. In 1800 figures were based on "official" valuations, but after 1854, on de- clared value. What is more, the influx of gold after 1850 tended to raise prices. Consequently, we cannot make exact comparisons.

consignment from a manufacturer, paying him a percentage down
and the balance when the goods were finally sold. He could risk
doing this because of his relatively accurate knowledge of the foreign market. The coming of the telegraph and cable systems made
a further change. The industrialist could be contacted by his agent
or correspondent in the foreign country and could be told exactly
what was wanted, thus eliminating more of the element of chance
in production. But the final step had been taken by 1870 when
orders were received either from the agent or directly from the
consumer. The goods to fill these orders were then made and paid
for as soon as received. "Adventuring" had by now almost entirely
disappeared, and consignment dealing had declined greatly in importance.

The expansion of trade and communications forced likewise a
change in methods of financing. As mentioned above, the exporter
would usually make an advance to the manufacturer of a certain
per cent of the price of the goods to be sold. The importer was
obliged to do the same to the producer of cotton, tea, or sugar,
whose goods might not be sold for ten to eighteen months after
their shipment. A broker in the British ports might accept a bill
drawn on the importer by the producer, and when the cargo
arrived, he would be reimbursed by its sale. This was all quite
risky unless the producer was known to be thoroughly honest, for
his goods might be already mortgaged to someone else, or the
quality might be below that specified. But this was the only way
to obtain the goods from certain areas such as Australia or South
America. From other areas foreign goods were bought with profits
made from British sales or investments in the locality. In the
United States, for instance, bills given by American purchasers
could be used to buy cotton for British processing. As all returns
on such sales could not be used in this way, profits were often invested in foreign railways, factories, and the like, the money, in
turn, being employed by the foreigner to purchase rails, engines,
and machines from the British producer. Britain by this means
helped to finance her own sales. At the same time, speculation
increased owing to better communications. A scarcity in one part
of the world could be met by having goods shipped quickly from
another part to take advantage of the resulting high prices. As
this was frequently done on credit, little needed to be invested,
although great profits were reaped. In this way methods of commercial finance adapted themselves to the new conditions.

A subsidiary development in the trading world was the growth
of marine insurance. In insurance Lloyd's was the most impor-

tant organization, although imitators were increasing in number. The commercial importance of the insurance was that it prevented a merchant from being "wiped out" in the case of his goods being lost through shipwreck or, in time of war, by enemy action. It gave added stability to trade, which tended to reduce the "adventuring" aspect. In times of peace the premium rate was usually between 1 per cent and 2 per cent, although in times of war it might rise to 40 per cent. Along with this, Lloyd's was important for fostering the use of safety devices, the use of lifeboats, and the building of light houses. Thus insurance also played its part in the trade development of the period.

Imports and Exports

As has already been pointed out, the period from 1715 to 1870 was one of enormous trade expansion. Imports climbed from about £5.5 million to £72 million in 1850, and then by the new method of estimation used after 1854, to £237 million in 1870.[3] Concurrently, exports increased from £6.5 million, through £60 million, to £181 million. Meanwhile, drastic changes were taking place in the pattern and character of foreign trade. For one thing, from the 1840's onward imports always exceeded exports in value, the loss of funds being made up from British freight charges, insurance, and returns from foreign investments. Then too, the direction of trade changed. In 1715 Europe was Britain's best customer, with America far behind. By 1800 America was closing up the gap, and by 1870 she was Britain's best customer, with a total annual trade of close to £80 million. The Empire also improved its position in the British pattern of trade, Europe becoming less and less important. The third change came in the alteration of the balance of goods exported. Wool was supplanted by cotton as the chief export, while machinery, ships, and hardware increased greatly in volume.

An important part of the cargoes brought to Britain was food, in which sugar had long been the leading item. In 1790 it was by far the most valuable of the imports, rating twice the value of the next commodity, tea. Between 1822 and 1870 the value of sugar tripled, giving some idea of the improvement in living conditions. However, a part, perhaps one fifth, of the sugar was always re-exported to the Continent. Not being popular as a drink, coffee imports were not great. Tea, on the other hand, which had caused considerable trouble in Boston somewhat earlier, and which was

[3] See page 264, note.

sponsored by the East India Company until about 1830, was growing increasingly in demand in Britain, the imports tripling in value during the first seventy years of the nineteenth century. Since tea prices were gradually falling, this meant that the quantity had increased even more than would at first appear. Tobacco was also brought in in greater amounts owing to the increasing popularity of smoking. In 1822 the value entering was £338, and by 1870 it was over £2 million. While wine was not in very great demand, rum from the West Indies and brandy from France were. The import of all liquors increased some six times between 1815 and 1870. Foodstuffs, on the other hand, really began to come in in large quantities only after 1843 when tariff barriers were lowered. By 1847 the amount of imported butter had increased to 15,000 tons, more than four times that of 1822, while cheese imports rose even more rapidly, to 18,000 tons. In the five years between 1842 and 1847 live animal imports jumped from 5,000 to 216,000, and bacon imports from a few tons to 43,000 tons. By 1850 25 per cent of the food consumed was imported; by 1870 the increase had gone so far that about one half came from abroad.

One of the reasons for this rapid general increase was the growing demand for wheat. Between 1660 and 1760 Britain had been more an exporter than an importer of wheat. Only in years of famine was it necessary to bring in foreign grain. During the Napoleonic Wars, through cultivation of the less fertile soil the country was supported by its own land. In order to keep this land under the plow after the wars, parliament, dominated by the agricultural interest, passed the Corn Law forbidding import unless the price was above 80s. per quarter (roughly $2.50 a bushel, 1939). Poor crops, along with a growing population, forced modifications, and, eventually, the law's repeal in 1846. But even before this imports had been expanding. In 1823 13,000 tons were brought in, while in 1827, when crops were particularly bad, the import figure was 700,000 tons. In the famine years of 1845-46 foreign wheat averaged 900,000 tons. From this time on the wheat imports gradually increased until in 1870 they reached the figure of 1.6 million tons. More and more Britain was depending upon trade for her supplies of basic foodstuffs.

It was not only food, however, that she had to bring from abroad. For her manufactures she was largely dependent upon imports of raw materials. This was especially true in the case of textiles. Even the old industry of woolen manufacture was affected, sheep raising in Britain being now more for the butcher than for the spinner. The woolen manufacturers therefore turned to Spain,

Saxony, and in the 1840's to Australia. In 1789 the import came to about 1,000 tons, a quantity which by 1824 had increased some ten times. By 1850 the figures stood at 9.5 million tons, increasing to 307 million tons by 1870. Hemp, jute, and flax were also imported in larger and larger amounts every year. By 1850 the annual average was about 175.5 million tons of flax, 107.6 million of hemp, and 48.4 million of jute, while by 1870 the figures were 255 million, 132.8 million, and 420.3 million tons respectively.

Much more important than all the others was cotton. In the 1780's about 800 tons had been imported annually, in 1800 the quantity stood at 25,000 tons, and by 1830 that figure had quadrupled. In 1850 the imports were 825.6 million tons and in 1870, 1,524.3 million tons. During the American Civil War (1860-63) cotton was scarce owing to the fact that almost three quarters of it came from the southern states, but from 1865 on the situation righted itself, by 1870 cotton being the largest of the imports.

In the heavy industries during the eighteenth century most of Britain's steel had come from Sweden. But with the improvement in metallurgy: the invention of puddling and rolling by Cort, and the discovery of how to make crucible steel by Huntsman, there came a decline of importation after the Napoleonic Wars. In 1800 the British were bringing 40,000 tons into the country, but in 1828 only 14,000 tons, below which figure it remained for the next few years. Not until it was found necessary to obtain non-phosphoric ores for the making of Bessemer steel did iron shipments, particularly from Spain, begin to increase, although even by 1870 these were not large. Some foreign copper and tin in small quantities were also being brought in for use in the brass and tinplate industries.

What was perhaps of more significance was that from 1850 on, imports of manufactured or partially manufactured metal goods were growing, the Belgians in particular being interested in this trade. Even on home ground foreigners were beginning to compete with one of Britain's most important industries. Although the import was not great by 1870, amounting only to about £400,000, it was an indication of what might happen in the future. High quality French manufactures, such as silks, woolens, and gloves, were also appearing on the British market making up between two fifths and one third of the manufactured imports.

Besides these main classifications of imports, there were large quantities of miscellaneous items, the most important being timber. By the eighteenth century most of Britain's forests were exhausted, obliging her to turn to the Baltic and to America for her needs.

Although Scandinavia supplied most of the timber before 1802, during the Napoleonic Wars Britain looked to Canada, to whom she gave a preference on the market. By 1821 the Canadian proportion of the timber import was three to one, and in 1844 out of 1.3 million loads the colonies supplied 922,000. With the growth of free trade ideas in the '50's the colonial preference was cut, and in 1866 duties on timber were completely abolished. From that time on European lumber supplied the British market.

To pay for these imports, which were the life blood of her industries, Britain had to export manufactured goods in return. The raw materials were processed, a large part of the finished products being sent abroad again to pay for further purchases of raw commodities. In this way imports were taken in repayment for exports, and the exports paid for the imports. During this period, however, the character of the exports began to change, for not only did certain new commodities rise to positions of prominence, but there developed also a growing export in men, in capital, and in services. All these helped to pay for the raw materials purchased across the world.

One thing that was notable in the export trade was the relative decline in the position of woolens. In 1700 they headed the list, amounting in value to about £3 million. This had increased by 1833 to £7 million, by 1850 to around £9 million, and by 1870 to something over £25 million. Despite this growth, cottons were by this time the greatest textile export. In 1800 the value of exported cotton goods stood at £4.1 million and by 1830 out of a total export trade worth £38.3 million, cottons accounted for £19.3 million. In 1850 they came to £28 million out of a total £197 millions of exports and by 1870 the ratio was £71 million to £244 million. Although the other textiles also increased their sales abroad, silk exports between 1815 and 1870 increasing from £633,000 to £2.6 million, and linen from £1.8 million to £9.5 million, none of them could approach cotton. Cotton was king, alone forming one third of the total textile exports, which, in turn, accounted for one half of the country's total foreign sales.

Small metalwares formed another considerable part of the goods sold on the foreign market. Throughout the eighteenth century Birmingham had been exporting brass and copper work, toys, swords, and firearms. Many an unsuspecting tourist in India even now buys a monstrous looking god with "Birmingham" stamped upon its base. Principally from Swansea in Wales went tin plates for the manufacture of tin cans. Of greater importance, however, were iron and steel products, such as hardware and cutlery, whose export between 1815 and 1870 tripled in value. By 1870 Britain was the great source of the world's screws, tools, firearms, and other metal goods.

Of supreme importance in the field of metal manufactures was the sale of machinery and steam engines. Down to 1820 the export of machinery was forbidden because of the fear that foreigners would be able to copy British machines and compete with British production. There were also misgivings over a possible shortage of machinery. By 1820, however, it was obvious that despite regulations, machinery, or at least plans for it, was being smuggled out of the country. Furthermore, the fear of shortage was disappearing through the development of more efficient machine tools. Consequently, it was felt that if other nations were going to obtain the machines anyhow, it would be better to make and sell them at a good profit. A gradual relaxation of restraints upon machinery export resulted, until by 1843 there was complete freedom. A great expansion of the machine and engine export business followed. In 1822 legal sales had amounted officially to only £116,000, but by 1842 they were £555,000. In 1845 the figure stood at £905,000, in 1860 at £3.8 million, and 1870 at £5.3 million. Britain was supplying machines, railway locomotives, and railway rolling stock to countries the world over.

Other exports which come under manufactures were pottery and china, which were largely developed through the activity of Josiah Wedgwood, who was not only an artist, but a consummate business man. Toward the end of the eighteenth century Britain became an important source of Europe's and America's pottery. By 1815 Wedgwood had built up a considerable reputation, particularly in the United States, the result being that about five sixths of all his manufactures were sent abroad. By 1870 the total export probably amounted in value to around £2 million.

Britain's exports of raw materials were limited to two commodities: coal and steel or iron. Although the value of the latter rose from £1.2 million in 1815, to £5.3 million in 1850, and £23.5 million in 1870, of much greater importance was the sale of coal. Before 1815 this article of trade was relatively unimportant, and even for the next twenty years it did not amount to a million tons a year. As the industrial revolution spread to the Continent, however, countries with little or no coal were obliged to import it. France, Denmark, Russia, and to a certain extent Germany, all became customers. But even by 1850 the amount sold abroad did not come to much over three million tons. By 1855 this had increased to five million, and by 1870 it had increased to over ten million. Added to the growth of industry on the Continent, two new factors now entered in. Steamships, coming into more common use, demanded fuel, not only at home, but also in the far-distant places where they needed to replenish their supplies. This led to the establishment of coaling stations around the world. Further, there was a demand for coal cargoes on outgoing ships. Since most of Britain's exports were manufactures, usually small in bulk but high in value and as most of her imports were raw materials of which the opposite was true, her ships would frequently leave the country half empty. This meant much waste space, as well as loss of freight charges. The habit developed, therefore, of outbound ships carrying coal as ballast and as a bulk cargo which could be sold in foreign ports. In this way coal became an exceedingly important export, for wherever the ships might go this cargo always had a market.

While Britain was sending her own industrial products and coal to all parts of the world, she was at the same time exporting other commodities. For one thing, from the days of the foundation of the Muscovy and East India companies she had been re-exporting the foreign goods brought in by these traders. Thomas Mun had based his defense of "John Company" on the re-export of Indian cottons and spices. In the nineteenth century the re-export trade grew greatly. The setting up of bonded warehouses, whence foreign goods, landed and stored without paying duties, could be shipped abroad had been proposed in vain by Sir Robert Walpole. Eventually the idea was accepted and Britain became the world's great entrepôt for goods from every quarter of the globe. In 1815, out of a total export worth £58.5 millions, £15.7 million were re-exports. By 1870 the re-exports had about tripled in value. This does not show an increase commensurate with the general sixfold increase in exports. Britain's expanding industrial capacity and population increased her consumption, obliging her to retain a greater proportion of her imports. Nevertheless, £45 million was a respectable part of Britain's sales abroad.

A much less respectable part of British commercial interest was the slave trade. This was a three-cornered type of venture. Ships leaving Liverpool loaded with West African trade goods would purchase from the chiefs of coastal tribes cargoes of natives, which they would then carry across to the plantations both in the West Indies and continental America. There the traders would pick up cargoes of cotton, tobacco, and drugs for sale in Liverpool. At the end of the eighteenth century there were some 190 ships, which, it has been estimated, transported annually about 20,000 Negroes.

Largely on account of the opposition to this traffic by such men as William Wilberforce and other leaders of Evangelical Revival, "The Society for the Abolition of the Slave Trade" was organized in 1787. As a result of their propaganda, in 1807 Britain prohibited her subjects from taking part in slaving. It was not until 1833, however, that throughout the Empire slavery was abolished. The slave-owners, who objected strongly to this action were compensated for their losses and Britain achieved peacefully what was done in the United States only after three years of civil war.

As has already been noticed, throughout the early nineteenth century Great Britain's balance of actual trade gradually became less and less favorable. In terms of the value of goods, she was selling much less than she was buying. How was she paying for her surplus imports? One part of the answer is: by services, the most important of which was the carriage of goods and passengers. This was made possible by Britain's position as the world's greatest shipowner. In the 1850's American Clipper ships began to provide some competition, but the Civil War and westward expansion turned American attention and capital in other directions, leaving the British monopoly secure. In 1815 Britain had some 2.4 million tons of shipping, which by 1849 had risen to 3.5 million tons. Owing to inadequate statistics before 1850, it is not known what proportion was actually in foreign trade, but it is known that in 1850, out of a total of a little over 3 million tons, 2.4 million were either partly or wholly, employed in foreign trade. By 1870 the total tonnage stood at 4.6 million tons, steam accounting for almost 900,000 tons. When one remembers that in 1850 United States sent only 566,000 tons of shipping to Britain, and in 1870, only 629,000, one can obtain some idea of British superiority. Two-thirds of the world's shipping was under the Union Jack. Freight carrying thus became a very considerable part of British exports, the rates obtained helping to pay for imported goods.

Another form of export was insurance. Lloyd's and similar British marine insurance companies began to venture abroad for business. In return for risks taken by these companies, foreign shipowners paid considerable sums in premiums. The funds so obtained were in turn employed to purchase goods which Britain needed for her industrial machine.

Last but not least, was the export of men and capital. As the British population increased in size and as displacement of a part of it occurred through economic and other causes, considerable numbers tended to move out. Although from 1821 to 1831 emigration had amounted to less than 200,000, in the decade of the Irish famines (1841-51) it jumped to 1.2 million. In the next two decades it was 2 million and 1.6 million respectively. Many made homes for themselves in Canada, Australia, and South Africa, while a large number also went to the United States. For instance, between 1830 and 1843 British North America received 440,000 and the United States, 445,000. The emigrants usually took with them money, but what was more important, they took with them the need, at least at first, of British tools, machines, and textiles. Thus, they provided an expanding market for British products. Others went abroad to work in foreign industry, as, for instance, in the building of the Continental railways. Usually a part of their pay came back home in form of money or goods which they purchased. Thus, the export of men also had its importance in Britain's economic operations.

It has been mentioned that a large part of the profits of British trading was often invested in foreign countries. In 1827, according to some estimates, Britain had around £93 million invested abroad, and in the thirties £50 million was in the United States alone. While the total foreign investment is hard to estimate, it has been suggested that £300 million and £600 million represent the figures for 1850 and 1870 respectively. If one calculates the interest at even 3 per cent, it is easy enough to ascertain the amount of income. It was this income that would be employed to purchase goods for Britain, or could be reinvested to produce more profits. Thus Britain was receiving anything from £9 million to £20 million annual income, a sum which represented the surplus of her total exports. She was the creditor nation of the world, who every year, despite a mounting adverse balance of trade was increasing her total profits.

Britain's Foreign Markets

Throughout the whole period colonial trade was very important. When one says "colonial," however, he must keep in mind that, strictly speaking, India was not a colony, the real colonies being The West Indies, America and Australasia. As a result of natural increase and immigration, the Thirteen Colonies increased from 200,000 in 1700 to 2 million in 1760. About that time Canada was added to the list. They all provided raw materials: furs, lumber, tobacco, rice, and a little cotton. At the same time, they demanded British manufactures: tools, shoes, clothing, and the like. Only New England made any real attempt to compete with the mother country. To the south, the West Indies provided sugar, molasses, and rum, while they took slaves, industrial products, and frequently wheat, for they grew little food. Since America was, therefore, the most important of Britain's markets, it is little wonder that every effort was made to keep the trade to British merchants. This was one of the causes of the Revolution. But although the Thirteen Colonies were eventually lost, and many began to feel that the only good colonies were those which had an economy strictly supplementary to Britain's, colonial trade went on. While the West Indian trade fell off after the abolition of slavery, dealings with Canada, Australasia, and South Africa increased. Between 1850 and 1870 the Empire took annually between 25 and 35 per cent of British production.

That it was unnecessary to keep the Thirteen Colonies in leading strings in order to preserve the market for British goods soon became apparent. From 1800 to 1850 the United States' purchases of British goods amounted to about 50 per cent of the total bought by European countries. In some years she took as much as one quarter of Britain's total export. In 1839 American customers bought one third of the woolen cloth, nearly all the carpets, one third of the finer woolen "stuffs," two thirds of the blankets and blanketing, and one half of the cloth made of mixed cotton and wool. They also took large quantities of rough iron goods as well as hardware and cutlery. From 1850 on, however, the quantity of American purchases fell in relation to Britain's whole export, amounting in 1870 to about 12½ per cent, but even then it was still growing in terms of money. Besides, the United States was now supplying about three quarters of the raw cotton used in British manufactures. Thus, the United States and Britain were economically closely bound together. When one adds to this the growth of trade with Central and South America which took place after 1815, the American continent appears as Britain's most important market. The following table gives an opportunity to compare figures (in millions):

Year	Exports to U.S.A.	Exports to South and Central America	Total Exports
1830	£ 6	£ 5.2	£ 38.2
1854	21.4	6	115
1870	28.3	16.5	244

Trade with Europe went through many vicissitudes between 1715 and 1870. For one thing, Europe was not as dependent upon British products as were the more backward countries. Indeed, until 1780 France was more of an industrial country than was Britain, although French production was tied to a "national" gild system. The Continental wars in which Britain sometimes became involved also had the effect of hindering commerce. But despite these conditions, Britain was trading with the Continent on a considerable scale. She even succeeded in making a treaty with France in 1786 whereby restrictions in the markets of each country were reduced so that her producers could compete on equal terms with the French craftsman. All this came to a sudden end with the outbreak of the French Revolution. The leaders of the movement were largely middle class, opposed to the influx of British goods on to the French market. Prohibitions were immediately clamped on British products. Napoleon later continued this policy with his Continental System, banning all British goods from Europe. While he was by no means successful, owing to the need for Britain's products even by his own army, he caused a serious disruption of trade, which was further aggravated by the British Orders in Council, aimed at keeping neutrals from trading with France and her satellites. Out of this came the Anglo-American War (1812-14).

Once the wars with France were over Britain attempted to get back into the European markets, but she was faced with new difficulties. At first the Europeans were too poor to buy, and then, because of rising nationalism, they refused to buy. They desired to foster their own industries. Nevertheless, British sales on the Continent gradually increased, reaching £15 million by 1830. By 1854 this had doubled, and by 1870 it was close to £85 million. Of this total, Germany was taking some £20 million worth, primarily of textiles. By 1854 Europe was exporting to Britain some £63 million of goods, France was sending over £10 million, and Germany, over £15 million. By 1870 this had climbed to £138 millions, with France selling almost £38 millions and Germany over £15 millions. A large part of these purchases were fancy goods: brandy and wine from France; with wheat, eggs, and some manufactures from Germany. For these Britain paid not only with exports but also with the return on her investments in such things as French railways and the German steel industry.

Considerably more important than Europe were the tropical and subtropical countries. Not only did they supply much of the raw material, but they also bought a large part of Britain's manufactures, particularly textiles. Down to 1814 the East India Company maintained a firm grip on the commerce with India and points east, but in that year the trade to India was thrown open, to be followed by the full relaxation of the East India monopoly in 1834. The Company had by this time become more of a ruler than a trader. Under the leadership of such men as Clive in the eighteenth century, it had asserted a claim to control large parts of India, and it was from the taxation it levied that it made its profits. Once the eastern trade was freed, there was a real boom. Although in 1800 little cotton cloth had been shipped to India, by 1855 the export amounted to £4.3 million, and by 1870, to £14.1 million, one sixth of the total amount sent abroad. After 1830 it was difficult to obtain a return cargo from India, until the production of linseed oil, shellac, rum, hemp, and sugar increased. Most of the imports from China consisted of tea, in return for which the Chinese took some woolen cloth, considerable cotton cloth, and, as a result of the Opium War (1839-41), large quantities of Indian opium. Along with the slave trade this is one of the most discreditable aspects of the growth of British foreign trade. Between 1854 and 1870 the import-export situation was as follows (in millions):

	INDIA		CHINA		Total Far East	
Year	Imp. from	Exp. to	Imp. from	Exp. to	Import	Export
1854	£10.7	£ 9	£9.1	£ .533	£21.2	£11
1860	15	17	9.3	2.8	27.8	24.4
1870	25	19.3	9.6	6.1	40.7	33.7

Thus, in 1870 British trade was bound up first of all with Europe, then with America, and thirdly with the East. At this point Africa did not enter too much into the picture, nor was Australasia or Canada of very great importance, although their purchases were increasing in total. But one thing was certain: Britain's trade connections by 1870 extended to all parts and corners of the earth. She had become not only the workshop, but also "a nation of shopkeepers" for the world.

Yet Britain faced certain possible dangers. There was, of course, the danger of complacency and self-confidence which might weaken an interest in advancement and invention. More tangible, however, was the possibility that she would neglect her agriculture to the point of its destruction. Once the wheat from far distant lands was brought close by fast transport, what would happen to the British farmer? Another possible danger was that other nations with greater natural resources and advantages might develop their industry on British lines, eventually undercutting Britain on the world market. In 1870 the British seemed to be unaware of these possibilities. Instead, they were quite satisfied and confident that all was well. Like the United States in the mid-twentieth century, she bestrode the world like a colossus, without fear of any economic rival.

Chapter 15

THE FINANCIAL REVOLUTION

As HAS already been seen, even in prehistoric Britain men came to realize that trade must be more than mere barter. Once it came about that a man could not obtain in exchange for what he had to offer exactly what he wanted when he wanted it, credit or money became necessary. He had to have some medium, economically acceptable to most of his fellows, bringing, in exchange, value equal to what he had originally given. Further extension of the principle took place when there was a time lag between his obtaining the medium of exchange: iron bars, gold, silver, or some other object, and his use of it to obtain other goods. Then too, he might have to travel long distances to buy what he wanted. His medium of exchange in this case would have to be almost universally acceptable. With the advent of the Industrial Revolution, a further need appeared. Men not only had to wait for extended periods of time for returns on their purchases, they not only had to go long distances for trade, but as industry and commerce developed, they were obliged to deal in larger and larger amounts of money. If in the Middle Ages the employment of large sums was difficult, how much more difficult would it be in the nineteenth century, when the sums of money in use were much greater than the total available supply of precious metals!

The Importance of Finance

It was this increasing need for money, or a substitute, which brought about the financial revolution of the nineteenth century. In 1715 the average amount of money involved in individual industrial or commercial operations was relatively small. The individual entrepreneur invested his money in his own business, whether it was cloth trading, iron manufacture, or a bank, and usually he "plowed back" part of his profits. Even in the 16th century, however, it had been discovered that there were some ventures which were either too big or too risky for any one man to attempt.

The result had been that men joined together to share in a joint stock, to be used for trading. No man could afford to sink all his fortune in a single venture to India or Russia. For one thing it would mean ruin if it was a failure; for another, even if successful, he would have all his capital tied up for six months to a year, which was a very great disadvantage. The basic principles of joint-stock enterprise had in this way been laid down before 1715.

With the development of the Industrial Revolution, the need for improved methods of finance was intensified. To provide capital goods, such as machines and factories, large sums of money became necessary. Moreover, such investments would be tied up for a considerable time before bringing in a profit. The expansion of trade to the uttermost parts of the earth also required large amounts of capital to provide ships, cargoes, and crews, with profits coming only much later. Thus there was an increasing demand for long term investment to fertilize the economic development. At the same time, the growth of industry, the improvement of the means of communication, and the expansion of trade helped to provide the capital. At first it came from the "plowed-back" profits of the individual traders and industrialists, but before long it was coming also from the dividends paid on capital invested. This new capital (profits and dividends) sought other new and profitable means of investment, in this way stimulating further production and expansion. Here one can see how the financial growth stimulated industrial and commercial growth, which, in turn, called for greater and more efficient financing. They acted upon each other as "challenge and response."

Money and the Growth of the Banks

Money and banking ever since 1720 have been dominated in Britain by the "Old Lady of Threadneedle Street," the Bank of England. In 1708 she was granted a monopoly of joint-stock banking, a very doubtful honor, for after the South Sea Bubble nobody was willing to trust any joint-stock organization. The Bank itself was interested primarily in managing its note issue and the National Debt. The latter, as a result of the wars of the eighteenth century, by 1790 had risen from £54 million in 1700 to almost £100 million. Of this the Bank held more than £10 million, while it also managed the balance of the rest of the debt in the form of 3 per cent Consolidated Bonds ("Consols" [1]). Its notes promising to pay were backed by the government obligations and by sums deposited with

[1] For the origin of "Consols" cf. page 300.

it by individuals. But, because of its preoccupation with the National Debt and also the issue of large denomination notes, much of the usual banking business, such as taking small deposits and discounting bills, was handled by private banks. This was particularly true in the country, for the Bank of England had no branches. As mentioned before (page 172), many of the private banks traced their origins back to scriveners, goldsmiths, or, latterly, to merchants who kept an account with the Bank of England. To help their friends, such merchants would discount bills which could be remitted to London, or they would issue promissory notes. This was particularly true in the case of some merchants who took the responsibility of paying on credit the employees of iron masters or other local manufacturers. With gold and silver scarce commodities, the notes issued became important in the provinces as a medium of exchange, and before long the merchant was a full-fledged banker. In this way the Bank of England and the private banks went along side by side, supplementing each other's activity.

The problem of a medium of exchange occupied much of the economic thinking of the time. Throughout the period of 1694-1797 the Bank maintained the convertibility of its notes into gold. But as none of its notes until 1759 were even as low as £10, smaller media of exchange were necessary. These were to be found, it was hoped, in gold and silver coins. By the Coinage Act of 1774 the 21s. gold guinea was coined to replace the worn and clipped coinage of the seventeenth century. The following year, in order to curtail the issuance of small denomination provincial banknotes, it was enacted that no notes smaller than £1 should be printed, and in 1777 the restriction was altered to prohibit the use of anything less than a £5 note. At the same time, silver was made legal tender for amounts under £25. This was all done in the hope that "hard money" would be the predominant medium of exchange except in larger transactions. The private banks would in this way also be kept from issuing more notes than they could redeem.

The whole structure, however, came crashing down in 1797 when Pitt, to help finance the war against France, drew too much money from the Bank of England. The Bank had to stop payment of bullion, its notes thereafter remaining inconvertible until 1821. The private banks likewise stopped payment of gold and silver, but they had to be prepared to redeem their own notes in Bank of England notes. The need for small denomination money then had to be met by a return to issuing £1 and £2 notes in the place of the disappearing silver and gold. Bank of England notes now became the basis of the English currency, it being contrary to the law to pay more than 20s. in hard cash. Payment of taxes in paper was also legalized. In this way the credit of the Bank of England, backed by the government, became the basis of the monetary system. Britain was "off the gold standard."

The first thirty years of the nineteenth century saw considerable experimenting with the currency. Both the Bank of England and the private banks during this period issued large quantities of notes over which the government had little control. In 1804, however, the first step towards regulation was taken when all notes, in order to be valid, had to be stamped, while by 1808 all who wished to issue notes had to obtain a government license. Yet despite these efforts, by 1810 the value of the Bank of England notes had declined some 30 per cent. A government committee of investigation which was strongly influenced by David Ricardo, the economist, advocated a resumption of specie payments as soon as possible, a step prevented by the continuance of the war with France.

Once the war was over every effort was made to go back on to the gold standard. Although it was hoped that redemption of notes in gold might be possible in 1816, the paper pound was not completely redeemable until 1821. The return to gold affected quite a number of private banks which had invested poorly or had overissued, the result being that between 1816 and 1830 some 206 of them collapsed. In order to control the situation to a certain extent, in 1826 parliament passed a bank law by which the Bank of England was obliged to make a regular report to the Treasury and to publish weekly the amount of its notes in circulation. It was also authorized, if it saw fit, to open branch banks. By the same act notes worth less than £5 were to be put out of circulation, and private banks with an indefinite number of partners—that is joint-stock banks—were allowed to establish themselves outside a sixty-five mile radius of London and were given recognition as corporations. In this way, while the Bank of England was brought somewhat more under government control, the private banks received greater liberty.

In 1833 further change came in British banking and currency. As a result of the depression of the late twenties, the Bank was authorized to take more than the customary 5 per cent discount on a bill of less than ninety days. This, it was felt, would deter the holders of such bills from causing a run on the Bank and so would halt the outflow of money in times of crisis. Private joint-stock banks of unlimited liability (unlimited partnerships) were also permitted to operate even in London, although they could not issue notes. Outside London, banks could issue notes but had to have an agent in London to deal with the Bank of England. This act was followed by the more famous 1844 Bank Charter Act, which laid down the pattern to be followed for nearly 100 years. Feeling that the notes in circulation should be readily convertible into specie, country banks which had hitherto come under little regulation were now limited in their note issue, to the average amount in circulation during the first quarter of 1844. If a bank, for any reason, stopped issuing, it could never resume, and if two banks amalgamated, they could combine their issues unless they had more than six partners, in which case they could not issue at all. Two thirds of any defunct issue could be taken over by the Bank of England. The latter was now divided into two independent departments: issue and banking, which could not even lend to each other without government permission. The banking department continued its normal banking operations. The issue department could put out £14 million of notes against securities which it held, £11 million being government obligations, and it could print all the paper money it wished as long as it was backed completely by bullion. Peel, the framer of this act, felt that gold and notes should be tied together. An outflow of gold, he reasoned, would bring notes back to the Bank, thus causing a bank note scarcity which would tend to raise their value in terms of gold. This, in turn, would help to bring the gold back once again to the Bank as it increased in value. It was simply applying the principles of free trade to banking.

The chief difficulty with this theory was that from 1840 on the matter of currency in financial dealings became less important owing to the increasing use of checks. A check was as good as a bank note, could be issued for an exact sum, and was not backed by gold, but by credit. At the same time, the discovery of gold in Australia and California increased considerably the quantity available for use. This, however, did not result in an increased note issue. Between 1845 and 1870 the notes remained at about £40 million, while the gold coinage jumped from about £46 million to £80 million. The gold sovereign (20s.), issued at the recoining in 1821, became one of the commonest and most used coins for all smaller transactions, even establishing itself as an almost international currency. It was in very much the same situation as the United States' dollar in Europe after World War II. The important thing was, however, that these two innovations completely offset the well-laid currency plans of Sir Robert Peel. What is more, the inelasticity of the supply of notes in times of particular stringency, when notes were needed, caused trouble, for three times within twenty years the act had to be suspended to stop a panic.

As we have seen, the private bank was something of a problem. Very often unwisely, if not dishonestly, managed, it might overissue notes, might discount unsound bills, or might do something else equally dangerous. Throughout the Napoleonic Wars and the succeeding years the mortality of such banks was very high. Frequently one man alone did not have the requisite capital to carry on proper banking. Yet such banks served a very useful purpose, particularly during the war years, when gold and silver were not available. They furnished notes with which the employer could pay his workers, and they also discounted bills when it would have been difficult for the bills to be sent to London. In addition, the better banks always kept in touch with London, dealing either directly or through an agent with the Bank of England and maintaining their balances in Bank of England vaults.

Within the London area, the private banks were early faced with the problem of settling among themselves for the notes which they cashed. At first clerks used to walk around to the different banks to settle the accounts each day, but eventually they began to meet in a public house, where they paid off their balances. Finally, in 1805 a clearing house was established where direct payment was made between the members. In 1841 they began to make clearances by a single daily cash payment, while in 1845 clearance was made by check drawn on an account in the Bank of England. In 1855 the country banks came into this organization, to be followed by the Bank of England in 1864. The Bank of England further facilitated business by the operations of branches established in centers such as Newcastle, Manchester, Leeds, and Bradford. For the country banks these fulfilled much the same position as the main office did to the London private banks. They held reserves of bullion and could discount the notes of the provincial private banks. In this way the banking system in England, centered around the Bank of England, was becoming more integrated.

From 1826 on, a new movement began to manifest itself. Private banks were disappearing, their place being taken by the joint-stock bank, a trend in which Scottish example had a considerable influence. In a previous chapter mention has already been made of the establishment of the Bank of Scotland, the Royal Bank of Scotland, and the North British Linen Company. These banks were all joint-stock chartered organizations with rights of note issue. There were also local joint-stock banks such as The Banking Company of Aberdeen (1767) and the Banking Company of Dundee (1764).

Private banks were relatively uncommon because of the Scottish lack of capital. In 1819 there were only eight, and by 1844 they had completely disappeared. All of the Scottish joint-stock banks granted interest upon deposits (4 per cent), and most would lend money at 5 per cent to enterprising individuals who could obtain the recommendation of two well-known local citizens, usually the minister and the schoolteacher. In this way a good many Scots set themselves up in business. As a further financial development, from 1776 on the chartered banks began establishing branches throughout the country. By 1826 the Linen Company had twenty-six branches, the Commercial Bank of Scotland (founded in 1810 and chartered, 1831) had thirty-one, and the other two had similar numbers. By means of joint stock organization and their branches the Scottish banks were in a strong position, as shown by their capitalization. In 1820 the Bank of Scotland and the Royal Bank each had a capital of £1½ million, the Linen Bank, of £½ million, and the Commercial, of £450,000. About the same time a share of the Banking Company of Aberdeen, whose par value was £150, was selling on the market for £1,400, and by 1836 it had risen to £3,000. Between 1820 and 1870 a certain amount of concentration of banking took place in Scotland as the number of banks declined from thirty-six to thirteen, but there were practically no failures.

When attempting to regulate British banking, parliament always had to make exceptions for the Scots. Because of the stability of their system, they had never suffered from the violent fluctuations which had affected England; and owing to the scarcity of bullion in Scotland, a curtailment of note issue would work grievous harm. It was for these reasons that Sir Walter Scott and his supporters forced the government in 1826 to except Scottish banks from the prohibition against the issuing of notes of small denominations. In 1844 further exceptions had to be made. While no new issuing banks were to be permitted, the established Scottish banks could issue notes to the value of £3,087,209, the amount then in circulation, and could also issue further amounts equal to their gold reserves. Amalgamations were permitted and issue could be continued no matter how many partners were involved. The outcome of this law was that the Scottish banks expanded and developed. With all their head offices in Edinburgh, they could easily work together. In 1865 they began publishing their financial statements, while at the same time they adopted the practice of keeping a large reserve of gold and Bank of England notes. In this way they developed one of the most stable banking systems in the world.

In England from 1708 to 1826 no bank had been permitted to have more than six partners. As a result of propaganda by Thomas Joplin of Newcastle, however, this restriction was removed from provincial banks in 1826 and by an act of 1833, from London banks also, although the latter could not issue notes. As an outcome of these concessions, by 1840 various joint-stock banks had grown up both in London and the midlands. There were the London and Westminster, the London Joint Stock, and others. The 1844 act permitted these companies to be chartered as corporations, but they were all of unlimited liability. From the protection of limited liability the banks were explicitly excluded by the corporation act of 1855, a right withheld until after the crash of 1857. Subsequent to that date, however, banks could adopt this form of organization, although even then many did not, as it was considered to be an easy method of avoiding the payment of debts. This was partly a result of the propaganda of private banks with whom the joint-stock banks were in active competition. Gradually, however, between 1844 and 1854 a number of the private banks were either absorbed by the latter or themselves became joint-stock organizations. In 1821 there were 781 English private banks, their number having fallen to 436 by 1831. In 1834, on the other hand, there were 32 joint-stock banks. By 1841 the private banks had dropped to 321, and the joint-stock banks had climbed to 115; by 1871 there were 252 private banks and 120 with a joint stock. Coupled with the rise of the joint-stock bank went an expansion of branch banking so that by 1864 the National Provincial of Birmingham had 119 branches, the London and County, 127, the Manchester and Liverpool, 34, and others, similar numbers. This all added to the stability of the British financial structure.

Banking in Ireland did not develop at the same rate as in England and Scotland. For one thing, there was not the capital available, whether from individuals or from joint efforts. Coupled with this, the laws of the country prevented any development. One law enacted in 1745 forbade partnerships of over nine people and a capital of over £10,000, while by a law of 1781, permitting limited liability companies to have a capital of not more than £50,000, banks were specifically excluded. The harshest law of all was enacted in 1759, making it possible for creditors of a banker to seize property given by him to his children even before his debts had been contracted. Moreover, when the Bank of Ireland was chartered in 1783, it was given a very wide monopoly which restrained the formation of other banks. Despite this, some were organized, but they soon fell to the ground. Not until 1845 did the

Bank of Ireland lose its monopoly of joint-stock banking and short-term note discounting. After that, joint-stock banks began to develop very much along Scottish lines, showing remarkable stability down to 1870. Nevertheless, their being tied rather closely to the Bank of England kept them from having the stability of their Scottish examples, for they did not have control of their own policies.

So far we have been speaking in terms of banks of deposit. There was, however, another side to banking. Many of the banks had a beginning through merchants accepting and discounting notes for fellow merchants and industrialists or by permitting others to draw bills of exchange on them. On such bills they would advance money to be repaid from the future sale of goods. Out of this grew commercial banks. Some even began to handle bills of exchange on London houses for foreign merchants, endorsing the bills on behalf of foreigners who had good credit. In this way they developed into "acceptance houses," lending their credit to the foreigner. By 1857 some of the joint-stock banks were also performing these services. In somewhat the same way there grew up, particularly in London, the investment banker. His job was usually that of floating loans, primarily for foreign governments. He would give his backing and promotion to the loan, receiving in return certain fees and perquisites. Business was so good that from 1850, when London was recognized as the world's money center, foreign investment houses also began to establish branches within the City: Huths', Doxats', Raphaels', and Hambros' banks or investment houses were typical, coming from Germany, Denmark, and other European countries. In this way trade, commerce, and government were tied closely together by the commercial banking system.

Most of the banks established to finance industry and trade were not interested in the small depositor. This was true even in Scotland. The factory worker turned, therefore, to his friendly society, which, resembling somewhat the Medieval gild, was a kind of savings association. Each week he could pay in an amount, ranging from 2d. to 1s. or more, to obtain some sort of insurance against sickness or unemployment and to make provision for a decent burial. These societies, given legal standing in 1793, were quite important for the working man. In 1801 it was estimated that there were some 1,000 clubs in England and Wales with 600,000 to 700,000 members. By 1815 the total for Great Britain was put at 925,000. Among them was the Oddfellows of Lancashire, who by 1832 numbered some 31,000. The finances of these organizations, however, were not always well managed, often resulting in loss of funds. From the banking point of view, more important than the friendly societies, was the savings bank movement. For some time before 1800, attempts had been made to have the poor save "for a rainy day." Philanthropists had offered to give interest on their savings, and various other encouragements were brought forward. The man who really started the movement was the Rev. H. Duncan of Ruthwell in Scotland, who in 1810 set up a bank similar to those of the friendly societies. Depositors who did not save regularly were penalized; those who did were given bonuses. Withdrawals were also curtailed somewhat in order that there might be no foolish spending. In 1813 "The Society for the Suppression of Beggars" was organized in Edinburgh with the same aim, although it operated simply as a bank without attempting to control deposits or withdrawals. The movement soon spread to England, Wales, and Ireland. The officers were usually wealthy people who gave their services freely, and the funds were usually held by the chartered banks who gave 5 per cent interest. In 1817 a law was passed for their regulation, providing also that the funds might be invested in 3 per cent Consols. While their history is not always one of prosperity, the savings banks did perform a very great service. In 1861 Gladstone put through a bill establishing the Post Office Savings Bank, which gave 2½ per cent as against the 3 per cent paid by the Savings Banks. The latter had in the meantime organized an association, and in 1863 a consolidated act was passed for their regulation. Yearly deposits were limited to £20 per individual, while total deposits could not exceed more than £150. During the period between 1830 and 1870 the total number of depositors increased from 427,830 to over one million and a quarter. At the same time deposits rose from £14½ million to £38¼ million. This is exclusive of the Post Office, which in 1870 had about a million depositors and a little over £15 million in deposits.

Thus, as one looks back over the period between 1715 and 1870, one cannot but be impressed with the development of the mechanics of finance during the intervening century and a half. Most important remained the Bank of England, issuing most of the notes, managing the national debt, and keeping a watchful eye on industry and commerce. But supporting "the Old Lady" were joint-stock and private banks, commercial and investment banks, friendly societies and savings banks. All of these were playing their parts in receiving the country's savings and redistributing them into channels which led out into the industrial and economic world. The banks were like the heart that pumped the blood out to every part of the economic body. Without their development industry and trade could never have flourished, since the old methods were too cumbersome and unwieldy for the increasing tempo of the middle nineteenth century. The banks in this way played a leading role during the period of the Industrial Revolution.

The Growth of Credit Capitalism

The rise of the banks, however, was not an isolated phenomenon. They could not have developed nearly so far, had it not been for the methods employed to finance industry, trade, and government. As already mentioned, the earlier method of financing industry and trade was reinvestment of profits in the business. If the expansion of the business, on the other hand, was more rapid than the receipt of profits, this would be impossible. The need then would be to bring in capital from outside by obtaining funds from investors, who would receive as security bonds or shares in the business. They gave credit to the business for being able to repay them. In this way savings were converted into investments in securities. As more and more people invested, whether in government bonds or industrial stock, so the ownership of the country's industry and finance would be dispersed ever more widely. True, the personal contact between owner and worker, even between owner and management, would be lost, but profits would be much more widely spread. It was the growth of this type of finance, which we have called "credit capitalism," that became so important during the nineteenth century.

During the eighteenth century there was relatively little demand for investment capital. Industrialists such as Watt, Boulton, and Wedgwood were plowing profits back into business, and since expansion was slow, they did not need any more. On the other hand, there was not very much free capital available. What there was found plenty of scope in the existing joint-stock corporations, such as the East India Company, or in the 3 per cent Consols. From 1815 on conditions changed radically. It was not that British industry and commerce were now seeking funds, but rather that foreign governments and such interests as Mexican gold mines were offering their securities. In 1817 there was the French indemnity loan, in 1818 a Prussian loan floated by Rothschilds, in 1824 a Russian and a Greek loan. In 1820 Colombia floated a loan which it repudiated in 1828, but liquidated in 1845 by means of another loan. Even a loan for the mythical "Kingdom of Poyais" was acceptable to some. Canals, turnpikes, banks, and insurance supplied some stock and bonds, but by 1840 only 20 per cent of those on the London Stock Exchange were corporation stock, as against 80 per cent national and foreign government bonds. Yet despite the increased demand, money was cheap, for the supply of capital was growing. Trade was expanding, industry was booming, and land values were skyrocketing. The Earl of Derby's Lancashire rent roll between 1800 and 1840 jumped from £14,000 to £180,000 per annum. Despite growing demands for credit, the reservoirs of capital for investment were expanding.

Investment took two forms. There was, first of all, the demand for short-term credit which would supply funds to finance trade or to purchase goods such as textile machinery. The return on these investments would be relatively quick, some within a year, some more, some less. They usually had as their object the satisfaction of consumer need. Down to 1850 they were usually met by a bill of exchange which could be discounted by the bank or by one drawn directly on the bank with the understanding that the money would be forthcoming before it was due. By 1850, however, another method was being introduced. A loan would be obtained in the form of a deposit by the bank against which checks could be issued. Because of economic expansion more capital was thus made available through easier and quicker methods of obtaining credit. If too much credit were given to weak concerns, however, there was always the danger of a sudden call, which might put the bank out of business.

The other type of investment was the long-term security, which included not only government bonds, but also such things as railway stock. These did not pay a very high rate, nor did they mature quickly. While the railway stocks were not as important before 1850, after that time, with the influx of foreign gold, the economic expansion, and the growth of railways, this type of investment became much more popular. These long-term securities often had violent fluctuations in value owing to overinvestment or to declining profits of the company. Along with railway stocks went the securities of insurance, mining, gas, and other public utility companies, such as *Lâ Compagnie Generalê des Omnibus de Londres*. In 1865 there were 975 companies, with a total capitalization of £235 million, of which only 10 per cent had been actually paid. This was a great increase over the number existing in 1860, resulting largely from the fact that in 1863 the formation of limited liability companies had been greatly facilitated. Still, even by 1875 company offerings had by no means pushed out government securities. In that year on the London Stock Exchange 68 per cent of the securities represented government paper, 25 per cent was railway stock, 2 per cent was bank stock, and 5 per cent was from other corporations. In long-term investments government bonds, whether national or foreign, still led the field.

That which facilitated the growth of the corporation security market was the gradual removal of restrictions from the joint-stock company. In 1719 the so-called Bubble Act had forbidden all undertakings to act as corporate bodies without the authority of a charter. This restrained joint-stock development until the beginning of the canal boom in the 1780's and '90's, when it became necessary to obtain a government charter before one could expropriate the needed land. Most of these companies were joint-stock ventures. The railways in the early nineteenth century did the same. To facilitate organization, general acts for railways, gasworks, and the like were passed during the 1840's, giving corporate rights and limited liability to the companies organized for such specific purposes. In 1844 any company with a capital of £10,000 and whose shares were worth £100 was allowed to have a charter of incorporation, but it was not until 1855 that it was also granted limited liability. Finally, in 1863, it was enacted that seven men signing a Memo of Association which was registered with the addition of "Limited" to the name of the company, was all that was necessary to set up a limited liability joint-stock company. From this time on joint-stock companies sprang up like mushrooms, organized for every conceivable purpose and seeking money from every available source. Henceforth corporation securities offered increasing opportunities for investment.

The actual mechanism of investment was already operating through the stock exchange. Stockbrokers, or rather "stockjobbers," as they were called in the eighteenth century, were at first disliked intensely. In 1733 a law was passed to curtail their activities, but it was unsuccessful. In 1762, following the example of other commercial operators, they formed a club at Jonathan's Coffee House in Change Alley. There they used to buy and sell stocks. In 1773 they organized the Stock Exchange on Threadneedle Street, and about 30 years later they erected a new building. With the coming of peace in 1815, they increased their activities, so by 1820, when they were becoming respectable, they were dealing in the securities of foreign governments, canals, gasworks, docks, waterworks, bridges, insurance, and by 1824, gold mines. The Continental money centers such as Amsterdam, having suffered heavily during the wars, the London Stock Exchange now had no rival, and from 1820 on, it gradually attained a completely dominant position in the financial world. Although some provincial exchanges were opened, they were all dependent upon London. After 1850 London, the money center of the world, became the best place to float loans, to sell shares, or to obtain money for ventures in any part of the globe.

Merely having a security to sell, however, was not enough. It had to be sold. This led to security sales promotion. As a rule, short-term, fine trade bills, endorsed by commercial banks, would be accepted by bill brokers, such as Overend, Gurney and Co., for the advancing of funds. In this way the bill brokers were heavily involved most of the time in the short-money market, holding no long-term investments. While they made money easily, a sudden drop in the market or a panic would wreck them. Long-term investment promotion was usually in the hands of either the investment bankers or a new type of organization, the "investment trust." The latter was a company which made its profits by investing shareholders' money in various stocks in order to spread the risk. All of these companies faced very great dangers. If they bought too heavily in some poor quality security, if they floated some loan which turned out to be unredeemable, they lost greatly both in money and credit. Besides errors in judgment because of the lack of contact between shareholders and management, there was also frequent managerial irresponsibility, manifested in dishonesty and carelessness, which sometimes brought about a slump. Promotion of stock and bond sales could easily be overdone, introducing into the financial system a new type of instability.

The tendency to fluctuation was often accentuated by the growth of financial journalism. In 1825 both the *Times* and the *Morning Herald* instituted "the city," or financial column, which discussed the current market trends. In the thirties the provincial papers started to print similar features. Then before very long papers and journals began to appear dealing exclusively with certain specific phases of the financial activities of the country: banking, stock-broking, or investing. In 1843 *The Economist* was established to cover the whole range of economic affairs more or less for the layman. While these forms of publicity were on the whole useful, another and less beneficial form of journalism appeared in the stock and bond prospectuses. These publications made alluring promises of high returns, often distorting figures and making false reports. Dishonesty eventually became so prevalent that in 1844 the government required all prospectuses to be registered in the hope of giving a little protection to the often deluded investor. Thus, while journalism tended to open up the whole subject of investment to the general public, it was frequently misused for the purpose of separating the "sucker" from his money. But, whatever its faults, it did facilitate and stimulate investment.

Another form of investment which became prominent during this period was insurance. In an earlier chapter we have seen how it had its beginnings in marine and fire protection policies, some of which go back into the middle ages. Insurance grew, however, very rapidly in the late eighteenth and throughout the nineteenth centuries. The marine underwriters of London, who were meeting at Lloyd's Coffee Shop, in 1769 organized a club possessing at the time a virtual monopoly of private marine insurance, a business which by 1815, owing to the wars, had grown to enormous proportions. The Royal Exchange and the London Marine Insurance Companies had, meanwhile, a government monopoly of joint-stock marine insurance which was not broken until 1824. Lloyd's however, continued to dominate. For fire insurance many companies appeared in England and Wales, but, owing to the prevalence of stone houses in Scotland, such institutions were not in much demand in the northern country. By 1832 England and Wales had 39 fire offices, most of them being either joint-stock or large partnerships. Between 1783 and 1868 the amounts of insurance bought increased from £135 million to £1,430 million. Life insurance on the other hand was but in its infancy, owing to the slow growth of actuarial knowledge. From the 1840's on, with the cooperation of the government a number of men prepared scientific tables which enabled the companies to operate on a sounder basis. By 1840 the Equitable had in force policies totalling some £14 million and this, along with the money of all the other life insurance companies which had grown up since 1800, would indicate a very great volume of investment. Most of the funds in insurance, of course, went into long term securities helping both directly and indirectly to finance economic expansion.

By 1870 Britain's economy was no longer on a "cash and carry" basis. Despite the increased use of gold and notes, credit based upon stocks and bonds formed the financial foundation. No longer was one's surplus income hidden away in a box, nor was it usually loaned to some individual. Instead, one purchased railway shares, Mexican mine stock, French government bonds, or Ohio state bonds. As the investor's savings went into some project, at least hoped to be productive of wealth, the wheels of the economy were kept turning.

"Booms and Busts"

There was, however, the grave danger that if credit contracted, if people lost their faith in the securities they held, there would be an attempt to sell out. This would cause untold financial trouble, probably leading to disaster. It is such fluctuations in credit that occupy much of the history of the first seventy years of the nineteenth century.

The nineteenth century saw the real beginning of a new phenomenon in economic life: the business cycle. There had indeed been rises and falls in economic activity back into the Middle Ages. But they had been gradual and over long periods. In the nineteenth century the movement was different; there were sharp rises and falls which worked in something approaching a pattern. The variations seem to have been based largely on the expansion and contraction of credit, usually reflected in the rate of bank discount. When the rate was low, credit expanded and everything was booming, but when the bank rate rose over 6 per cent, then moved up to 7 per cent, and sometimes even hit 10 per cent, credit contracted, for a break had taken place in the economy. Many forces were involved in these changes: poor or good harvests, wars, pestilence, and the like. But one thing which many fail to notice is the moral aspect, which, one might almost say, was fundamental. Frequently the boom commenced with dishonest promotion. Then human greed for gain and desire to obtain something for nothing would increase sales. After a time, however, someone, realizing that there was something wrong, would begin to sell. Quickly others would follow, and a panic would begin. The dishonestly promoted companies usually went to the wall, carrying others with them, the result being a financial collapse followed by a depression. This seems to be very much the pattern set during the period 1800 to 1870.

It is necessary, however, to distinguish between short- and long-term cycles. The short-term cycles during this period lasted about five years and were usually connected with short-term investment. Actuated by the effort to fill some immediate consumer need, they were not as a rule violent, but they were inevitable. A manufacturer might hear of a market in Australia to which he could sell. As it would take some time for the market to become saturated with his goods, he might keep on producing long after the required quantities had been made, so in Britain there would be over production. Such a situation might have repercussions resulting in a short-term recession. Much more devastating, however, was the long-term cycle, based upon the fluctuations of long-term investment. These usually ran in nine to ten year periods. They seem to have been caused largely by overinvestment in long-term securities which did not bring quick returns as well as by a gradual decline in the quality of the securities purchased. The fluctuations caused by these cycles were usually very much more violent, frequently disorganizing a large part of the financial system. They, in turn, had wide repercussions upon the social, political, and international life of the day.

Throughout the eighteenth century the fear of a debacle such as the South Sea Bubble (1715-20) helped to restrain the British from investment speculation. The wars which brought heavier taxes and curtailed trade also played their part. But, what was perhaps even more important, there was not too much in the way of securities in which to speculate. Apart from Consols and East India Company shares, there were not many securities available until the appearance of the canal companies.

The years from 1790 to 1815 were years of turmoil and change. From 1793 to 1815 war dominated the scene, resulting in much economic production, with the profits of trade going largely to finance the military effort. Yet, despite this, in 1793 there was a canal stock boom which was brought to a sudden halt the next year by a minor panic. The real panic, however, did come in 1797, when there was the run on the Bank. In 1810-11 there was a second boom, this time in South American investments. As the Spanish American colonies had but recently declared their independence, everybody wanted to profit by the new freedom of trade. There was much overpromotion, some flagrant dishonesty and considerable inflation on the part of the private note-issuing banks. The bubble was pricked suddenly in 1811, causing a depression and the collapse of a considerable number of smaller banks and other business houses.

Once the war was over, another boom took place. The continental markets were again open to British goods, while the United States market, which had been closed since 1812, was also available. New machinery being introduced into the textile trades in large quantities was lowering costs so that more goods could be sold abroad. The natural result was a quick growth of trade which helped to expand credit transactions and stimulate investment. Numerous foreign loans were floated without sound backing, so between 1823 and 1825, out of a total of twenty-six placed on the market, only ten did not default. At the same time any number of jóint stock companies were promoted, although many never started operations. Of some 624 schemes offered for sale during these three years, only 127 were still in existence in 1827. Why the great majority of such projects did not survive can be easily understood when it is remembered that one of the companies was established to drain the Red Sea and retrieve the jewels which the Egyptians lost when they were overwhelmed in their pursuit of the Jews. While the faith placed in the historicity of the Scriptures is commendable, at this point a closer adherence to their ethical principles would have been better. Stock in Mexican gold mines was another extremely popular type of security that was being promoted with every art then known to the salesman. Very narrow margin trading was also common, so before long something had to give way. The market began to fall. Some of the country banks collapsed first, being followed quickly by a number of companies. The result was a panic and a crash, resulting in the loss of some £16,000,000 on the London Stock Exchange. Britain had suffered its first major "bust."

From 1827 to 1835, warned by experience, financial affairs continued on the even tenor of their ways. By 1835, however, particular interest was being shown in railway shares, Spanish bonds, and American state bonds. At this time the American government, which had liquidated its national debt, was attempting to set up a gold-backed currency. In order to obtain the gold, United States banks, many of whom were in a very weak condition, commenced selling their holdings in Britain, taking gold from the Bank of England while, at the same time, borrowing from the Continent. The Bank Of England at first let the gold go, but when some of the joint-stock banks which had discounted bad American paper began to present it to the Bank for acceptance, the latter was forced to protect itself by raising the discount rate. It even went so far as to refuse to discount bills already discounted by joint-stock banks. This brought panic, the result being a crash. Some banks failed and a number of acceptance houses in the American trade went to the wall. By January 1837, however, normality had returned, although the momentary panic had exercised a sobering influence on the public, bringing to a temporary halt the flurry of unsound investment.

The years 1839 to 1842 were somewhat difficult. Crops were poor, the American cotton producers were trying to force up prices, and there was a partial collapse of continental banks. The Bank of England had to keep its discount rate at 5½ per cent and to borrow some £2,000,000 from Paris, but with the 1842 harvest, which was much better than usual, the situation began to improve. Food became cheaper. Since there was less need for grain imports, capital was diverted to railway construction. For the next three years railways, both British and foreign, boomed. But in so doing they both froze and wasted so large an amount of capital that prices began to fall. The Irish potato famines of 1845 and 1846, followed by a rise in wheat prices until May, 1847, then caused violent price fluctuations. To this were added in January, 1847, calls to cover margins in railway stock, and, as many of these were foreign railways, money commenced to leave the country. This was followed (March-June) by exports of bullion for grain. To counteract this movement the Bank raised its discount rate, thereby promptly causing trouble for a considerable number of the new British railways which had been paying dividends out of capital, because as yet they were not earning anything. In August came the panic caused by a sudden drop in wheat prices owing to large imports of grain. As the same thing was happening at this time with cotton, the result was an economic debacle. The Bank of England's discount rate rose with a marked restraint upon the discounting of public securities, thereby causing a drastic fall in stock prices and a hoarding of money. After some hesitation, the government authorized the Bank to issue notes in excess of the bullion reserve in order to prevent a money shortage. With this danger averted, the crash was over, but the loss was about £100 million.

Much of the trouble in 1847 had been caused by fraudulent company promotion, but men will not learn. The speculators now turned their attention to railway construction in the United States. Although the Crimean War did cause a certain amount of difficulty, the next real problem was the pouring of British money into American railway building. By 1857 it was estimated that over £80 million of British money were invested in these securities. In the scramble for profits many of the British investment houses became involved in shady promotions without bothering to keep reserves of credit on hand. The consequence was that when the American banks began to crack because of their overinvestment, they could not meet their British obligations. This meant trouble for the British investment bankers who saw their money rapidly disappearing. Again there was a panic. In October of 1857 the Borough Bank of Liverpool failed, and there was a run on the Glasgow banks, which might have been disastrous, had not the Bank of England given aid. In an effort to halt the hysteria the discount rate jumped to 10 per cent, and the Bank of England was permitted to issue an extra £2,000,000 in notes. This, coupled with the arrival of a cargo of gold from Australia, steadied the balances by December. But considerable damage had been done. A number of British houses had crashed, causing great distress to the continental firms with which they were connected.

The succeeding years were troublesome for the cotton manufacturing area because of the American Civil War which brought about a recession in all the country's financial activities. Improvement began only after 1863. The facilitating of the formation of joint-stock limited liability companies in that year began a spate of company promotions. New British firms of all types were formed, domestic investment now being very popular. Not all these companies were by any means efficiently run, but still they were actively promoted, one of the main agents being Overend, Gurney, and Company. This corporation dealt in many poor quality securities, although its reputation, particularly in the provinces, was very high. Therefore, when Germany and other foreign governments began to withdraw funds for war purposes in the spring of 1866, bringing about a rise of the bank rate to 10 per cent, Overend, Gurney, and Company found itself in a difficult position. It could no longer borrow at such a rate to meet its needs, and rumors began to fly that it was insolvent. On May 11th the company crashed with a loss of £5,000,000. If Overend's could not be trusted, nobody could, and a run on the banks resulted. The London Joint-Stock Bank fell along with a good many other "light" joint-stock enterprises. For the last time in the century the Bank raised its rate to 10 per cent, simultaneously seeking the right to issue more notes. This was granted by the Chancellor of the Exchequer, so the panic was brought to a sudden halt. By December economic affairs were back to normal, but the shock had been such that for the next four years investment remained somewhat depressed and quiet. This had been merely a local British "bust" caused largely by overinvestment and misrepresentation. It did, however, have a salutary effect upon the security market, turning the flow of money in the direction of sounder and more solid investments. Long-term securities which would produce a steady revenue, rather than short-time investments with skyrocketing returns, were now the fashion. Stability rather than sudden wealth seems to have become the general objective.

Thus, by the year 1870 one finds that Britain was dominating the financial world. Based upon the wealth derived from improvements in agriculture, industry, and trade, she had been able to build up a strong economic structure. This had been greatly facilitated by the development of the use of credit, the principal instrument being the Bank of England. In this way the economic affairs of the world had become largely controlled by the new finance or credit capitalism. It was now the financier rather than the industrialist or the merchant who ruled the roost. As the man who had much to say about the investment of Britain's capital, the financier was, in a sense, lord of the world's economy. Britain, being the one nation with large surpluses, was the great investing power. In London often lay the secret of the success or failure of a company or a government in far distant lands. This is one of the explanations not only of Britain's economic, but also of her political power throughout the century. It also explains how every fluctuation on the London Stock Market very soon had its impact on such far separated places as the Argentinian pampas, the Canadian prairies, or the Australian bushland. The world's economy was largely centered in London's financial houses.

Britain's financial supremacy, however, depended upon her capacity to produce and sell. If once her primacy in these fields was taken away, there was grave danger that her financial leadership would also depart. Shortly after 1870 signs of such a change began to appear. Thus, one might say that 1870 was the year when Britain reached the highest point in her economic history. At that date she was not only the workshop and the store, but also the bank of the world.

Chapter 16

TAXATION AND TARIFF REFORM

By 1700 important changes had taken place in men's thinking concerning the best method of paying for the costs of government. The old feudal system was finally dead, and it was realized that the king could not meet his own many expenses and pay for the government out of his private revenues along with moderate customs and excise dues. State expenditures were increasing year by year, forcing a rise in the government's demand for money which could be obtained only by borrowing or taxation. The existence of the Bank of England proved that borrowing was being tried. Similarly, the increase and more general application of customs and excise duties showed that taxation was becoming even more important than it had been before. But there was as yet no general system or theory of taxation. If the customs or excise returns began to decrease, what could the government do? New sources would be needed. The period from 1715 to 1870 manifested this very situation. With the economic revolution, the rising costs of government, and the demand for free trade, the state's resulting financial difficulties forced the government into new methods of taxation. This, in turn, seriously affected the economy of the country.

The Weakening of the Old System

Sir Robert Walpole, who helped to clear up the debris of the South Sea Bubble, commenced the work of taxation reform. He had three principal sources of revenue. There was, first of all, the land tax, which had been originated as an income tax but was soon applied only to land. He did his best, landowner that he was, to keep this impost as low as possible. Secondly, there was the excise tax, collected on commonly used commodities at the point of consumption. Cromwell had introduced this system, but Walpole extended and systematized it. The excise returns from salt, spirits, malt, candles, leather, soap, and paper were often applied to specific government debts. In order also to strike at the smuggling of such imports as tea, coffee, and chocolate and so increase the revenues from these commodities, he fell back upon the excise system. Imported freely, these goods were placed in warehouses, the tax being levied only when they were removed for distribution. If the goods were re-exported only a nominal duty was charged. Thirdly, in 1724 Walpole revised the 1660 Book of Rates, bringing the customs duties up to date. Moreover, the duties were placed primarily on luxuries, keeping them low enough to make smuggling unprofitable. By these means he did much to improve the government's finances.

It is well to note, however, that while increasing government revenues, these improvements also benefited trade. Although Walpole was a mercantilist who believed in tariff protection for the home producer, he seems to have felt that a little competition would not hurt, if simultaneously the returns from customs duties were expanded. Competitive goods could be allowed in upon the payment of a fairly stiff duty. In 1721 he abolished import prohibitions, cut prohibitive tariffs, and even made some imports free. He then went on to offer bounties for the production of commodities such as grain, gunpowder, Empire-grown sugar, ribbons, silks, and fish. His warehousing policy was likewise of considerable aid, since it facilitated the collection of duties while, at the same time, it caused the least possible trouble to the importer. If one were re-exporting goods he received a "draw-back" on them, a method of dealing which helped Britain to become an entrepôt for trade between Europe and the colonial world. His downfall came, however, with the attempt to use the warehousing system for imported wines and spirits. Both the smuggler and the purchaser rebelled at this, for the taxes would then assuredly be collected. After a big battle, in 1733 Walpole gave in, ceasing henceforth to experiment with the collection of taxes.

One of the major financial problems of the state during the 18th century was the national debt. Part of it was held by the Bank of England, and the remainder by various private individuals or groups of individuals. In 1742, the year of Walpole's retirement, it stood at £50 million, but by 1783, the year of the younger Pitt's accession to office, wars and poor management had increased it to £273 million. Of this, £238 million were funded, that is in bonds payable only at the option of the government. If the bonds rose over par value, the government could then offer to redeem them at par or could convert them to a lower rate of interest. In 1749 such a conversion took place, reducing the interest rate from 4 per cent to 3 per cent and bringing about a considerable saving in government expenditures for the debt. In 1752 all the 3 per cent bonds were consolidated into one fund, henceforth being known as "Consolidated Annuities" or "Consols." But, even with such a reduction, the cost of the debt stood at about £9 million a year, or approximately two thirds of the government's annual revenue. Thus, by 1785 the problem of the government's debt was becoming a source of worry to those in power. What is more, when the government's credit was poor, 3 per cent bonds were often issued with a greater face value than the money actually loaned. Thus a higher rate of interest was obtained by the investor without the danger that it might be reduced to a lower rate by conversion, for the government could hardly consider paying less than 2 per cent. Consequently, when Pitt came into office the government's financial condition was not good.

William Pitt, the Younger, until 1798 attempted to meet the demands on the Exchequer by a more efficient system of tax collection rather than by tapping new sources. Like Walpole, Pitt was content to increase the amounts collected from indirect taxation such as customs, excise, stamp duties, and the like. He consolidated the recurring expenditures into one block to which he assigned certain fixed revenues, thereby achieving greater efficiency of administration. He also consolidated the tariffs so that on each import there was but one duty and not a number for different purposes. To aid in the customs' collection he drew up a new Book of Rates, with specific duties based on weight and size of the articles, in order to prevent conflicts between official and current values as well as undervaluation. He likewise made sure of duties on such goods as tea by obliging the East India Company to pay 12 per cent ad valorem on all its tea imports. Excise duties he spread as widely as possible, frequently raising the rates. Finally a number of luxury taxes such as those on servants' coaches, race horses, hair-powder, windows, houses, and the like were brought together under the name of Assessed Taxes. In this way he hoped to tax those able to pay, by taxing their expenditures for nonessentials, while at the same time the poorer people went free. One difficulty was that his idea of nonessentials, which included items such as candles, malt, sugar, and similar commodities, might not always coincide with that of the poor man.

Pitt was not content with attempting to meet current expenses but was also interested in liquidating the national debt. He was very much influenced by the writings of a radical nonconformist minister, Richard Price, who thought that the debt could be wiped out by the use of compound interest. Out of his theories came Pitt's Sinking Fund. Submitted to Parliament in 1786, it was briefly this: He expected a surplus in the treasury for the coming year of about £1 million. This sum he planned to turn over to Commissioners of the Sinking Fund, who were to purchase government bonds on the open market. Unlike earlier procedures, however, they were not then to cancel this part of the debt. Instead, they were to hold on to it, drawing the interest from the government until their total holdings reached £4 million, when it could be cancelled if desired. If £1 million could be paid over each year in this way, by holding them and drawing the interest, the debt would shortly cancel itself. In 1792 the government's situation had improved to such an extent that Pitt was able to cut tariffs by £200,000 and, at the same time, add a further £400,000 to the Fund, which would become thereafter an annual first charge on the Budget. Any new loans which might be contracted were to have 1 per cent set aside at compound interest for their redemption so that they would be automatically liquidated. To the eighteenth century mind this was a beautiful system, for it was automatic, operating by "natural law." However, if the government were in difficulties and had to borrow at, say, 4 per cent in order to keep paying money into the Sinking Fund for the redemption of a 3 per cent debt, it would be very unprofitable. The main advantage of the plan was that in good times it forced the government to redeem its debts, while in bad times it made it difficult to stop this process completely. Sad to relate, in 1793 war broke out, bringing disaster to Pitt's and Price's finespun theories.

The war with France which commenced in 1793 seemed likely to be one of short duration. To Pitt, therefore, the proper way of financing it was by means of a small rise in taxes and by loans. Why he should have thought that loans were the proper means it is hard to say. At this time the Consolidated Accounts, which included the Civil List (the Civil Service), requiring £1.5 million and the expenses of the funded and floating debt, amounting to £43.5 million, were already far too large for the revenues. Nevertheless, he depended upon loans issued at anything from 3 to 5 per cent interest, and considerably below par. For instance, to obtain a loan of £18 million the bonds had to bear a face value of £26 million, so the government was actually paying about 11½ per cent. At the same time, the value of the 2½ per cent Consols dropped to less than £50. These the Commissioners of the Sinking Fund were purchasing with money borrowed at anything from 8 to 10 per cent. The situation was further aggravated by Pitt's obtaining parliamentary permission in 1793 to borrow unlimited amounts from the Bank of England. The result was that the resources of the Bank of England were so depleted that it had to suspend gold payments in 1797, resulting in a decline in the value of the pound and inflation. During the period 1793-98 the government's annual deficits grew steadily from £1.5 million to £20 million, while the national debt rose by considerably more than £100 million. To meet the interest alone on this increase, new taxes had to be imposed, which brought in an additional £5.7 millions. Pitt's policy, probably followed in order to keep from disrupting business, had accomplished what it had tried to prevent.

By 1797 Pitt had come to the conclusion that drastic action had to be taken to meet the country's needs. Borrowing could not go on indefinitely and the customs or excise duties were bringing in about all that they could. Between 1793 and 1799 customs revenues doubled (£3.5 to £7 millions), but this was not enough. The Assessed Taxes were also insufficient, and Walpole's old land tax had been made redeemable for a lump sum payment. Pitt therefore introduced the income tax. He did not like this tax because it was inquisitorial, but since it was necessary, he did his best to free it from the taint of unwarranted interference. An exemption for incomes of £60 and under was granted, as well as a partial exemption for incomes between £60 and £200. Abatements were also allowed for children. The average rate came to about 10 per cent. By 1803, despite much dishonesty and a poor system of collection, this tax was producing a revenue of £6 million. During the truce of 1803 the tax was removed, but with the reopening of hostilities, although very unpopular, it was reimposed. It was now collected at the source of payment, an increase in efficiency which helped to raise its annual total to £15 million by the end of the war. Even this, however, did not solve the government's problems, for the Sinking Fund was continued. It is true that for new loans which were contracted the policy of earmarking 1 per cent for use as a sinking fund was temporarily suspended and also that the Commissioners' holdings were no longer limited to £4 million. Apart from these modifications, however, the old sinking fund plan was restored. In spite of all this the debt kept growing, and as the Commissioners bought more stock, the interest paid to them increased. Thus, by 1816 to pay to the Sinking Fund the government was *borrowing* £15.5 million, £13.5 million of which was to pay interest charges on the stock held by the Commissioners. It was an impossible situation.

What made it even more difficult was the effect of the Napoleonic Wars on trade. There was, of course, the usual amount of commerce raiding. More important still, Napoleon, who was a Jacobin in his economic views, hoped to keep Britain out of the continental markets, thereby ruining her trade and, at the same time, building up a European demand for French goods. Britain retaliated with an attempted blockade of the Continent, trying to force all cargoes for Europe to go through British ports and pay duties to the British Exchequer. Neither side was successful in its endeavor, but Napoleon undoubtedly caused Britain much trouble, until she finally began to cultivate the markets in areas such as South America. The mutual blockade also eventually brought Britain and United States to war.

Napoleon was responsible, not only for direct attacks upon the British economy, but also for indirect assaults via the British government itself. The wars forced both a growth of restrictions and a relaxation of mercantilist controls. Restrictions increased because of the serious curtailment of imports, both of food and of raw materials. To keep the income of the farmer up, when wheat prices were below 63s. a quarter, import duty was high; when above 66s., the duty was nominal. Below 48s. a quarter, wheat could be exported under a duty of 5s., but when above 54s., wheat export was forbidden. In 1809, in order to help pay for the war, import duties on unspecified manufactured and partially manufactured goods were set at 37½ per cent plus one third of the duty as war surtax. On cottons the duty was 85 per cent, on cloth, 90 per cent and on glass, 114 per cent, while silk imports were prohibited. This naturally had a very restrictive effect upon trade without increasing government revenues, to the annoyance of the merchant class. Yet, despite the use of tariffs and restrictions, the government was at the same time breaking the Navigation Laws concerning the importation of goods in British ships or in ships of the country providing the cargo. With French privateers scouring the high seas in search of British vessels, the government was prepared to allow ships of any nation to bring in needed goods. Cold facts were forcing a change in the old mercantilist protectionism.

Both the government's restrictions and its ignoring of the Navigation Laws had the effect of strengthening a movement becoming vocal in its advocacy of Adam Smith's views on laissez faire. State restrictions only damaged the country, while freedom of trade was its salvation. Even before the war Britain had been moving gradually in this direction and away from such outmoded monopolies as that held by the East India Company, which brought high profits to a small group but hamstrung the activities of the generality of merchants. This revolt against authority received some support from the landowners, who were opposed to the income tax, on the ground that they were required to divulge to the government the extent of their annual revenues. Manufacturers also opposed regulation because they found that old apprenticeship laws and requirements that cloth should be of a certain width, weight, and length were harmful. Consequently, by 1813 there was a strong movement of protest against government interference. This point of view prevailed at the renewal of the East India Company's charter in 1813, when the Indian trade was made free to all. It was the same pressure which forced the government after 1810 to permit trade with neutrals and to allow British merchantmen to enter European ports. When the Orders In Council which established the continental blockade were repealed in 1812, there were great rejoicings in the Midlands. Trade would now be given a free hand and goods could be exported and sold without restraint. This was the beginning of a policy which would bring great changes.

The end of the war, however, brought little relief either to the government or to the taxpayer. While the Sinking Fund had been paying off pre-1789 debts, others had been contracted at a higher rate of interest. By 1815 the total debt stood at about £850 million, requiring carrying charges of £37 million, which, when the sum annually paid to the Sinking Fund was added, amounted to more than £40 million. This was no small figure when one realized that the total government income was around £56 million. Moreover, there was strong opposition to the income tax. Everybody was against it, and although after Waterloo, Vansittart, the Chancellor, tried to retain it at a reduced rate, he was forced to surrender his money-making device. It had helped to keep down annual deficits to about £2 million during the latter years of the war and would soon have provided a surplus. But nobody wanted it. Consequently, the treasury again had to depend on indirect taxation. Thus, when the war came to an end, taxes had risen steeply, debt charges were heavy, and there was little money available for the meeting of inflated costs.

The situation had changed radically from 1715. In the intervening century income had soared, but so had expenditure, and with the series of wars in which Britain had been involved, her debt was becoming a great burden. Fortunately, the phenomenal increase in production and trade helped to meet the needs, so the

Treasury's difficulties never became quite as great as they threatened to be.

Prelude to Free Trade, 1815-46

With the cessation of hostilities, a radical change took place in the economic situation. Much of the productive power used to make armaments was quickly turned to making consumer goods. The army and navy, on the other hand, were demobilized, throwing thousands of men onto the labor market at the very time that the curtailment of government expenditures on war materiel removed an extremely important stimulus to business. The restriction of the issue of paper money, culminating in the resumption of cash payments in 1821, also had a strong deflationary effect. Added to all this, two or three bumper crops altered the aspect of the agricultural situation by providing substantial grain surpluses. The result was a steady and rather rapid decline in prices.

The first people to feel the pinch were the farmers. Many had invested heavily in marginal land which could not produce profits without artificial protection. They, therefore, because of their hard work during the war and in order to maintain the home-grown food supply, insisted on a high protective tariff. There was no little selfishness in their attitude, but since the landed interests controlled parliament, they succeeded in passing the desired Corn Law. When the home price of wheat dropped below 80s. a quarter, none could be imported; when it rose above that price, it could be imported freely. As domestic wheat never reached this price after the war, the law was really prohibitory. Industrialists and industrial laborers alike, were very bitter about this action. It not only kept up the cost of food, but also prevented agricultural countries from selling Britain their grain, thus preventing them from obtaining the means to buy manufactured goods. Their protests, however, went unheeded.

In the meantime, sentiment in favor of free trade had been growing up in certain political quarters. While the merchants were often rather hesitant about the removal of tariff protection from their *own* manufactures, Liberal Tories, such as Canning, Huskisson, Robinson and Peel, were convinced that a freeing of trade was necessary. For one thing, they desired to change the Corn Law. This may have been partially because of their interest in manufacturing, but they also favored free trade on general principles. Desiring to have other countries make trade freer, they felt that

Britain should lead the way. Freer trade would be to the mutual advantage of all.

To accomplish this purpose Huskisson, President of the Board of Trade, worked hard to modify the Corn Law's prohibitory character. In 1822 he lowered the limit to 70s. and arranged to have a tariff of 15s. which dropped 1s. for each rise of a shilling in the price of wheat until it sold for 85s. a quarter. But as Parliament would not permit this scheme to commence until wheat first rose to 80s. a quarter, it never came into effect. Finally in 1828 a sliding scale was adopted, with free import allowed at 72s. a quarter, the duty rising by jumps as prices dropped. It was not a happy solution, as the gaps were too large. A merchant might withhold grain from the market in the hope of forcing up prices and thereby lowering tariffs. But this was, at least, a step in the direction of free trade.

Another move in the same direction was made by the alteration of many of the tariff and tax laws. In the field of general taxation a good many assessed taxes on windows, servants, horses, and shops were reduced or abolished. Much more important, however, was the modifications made in the laws of trade. Between 1822 and 1825 the taxes on many goods were drastically reduced. Manufactured goods, which had been prohibited, were now allowed in with a 30 per cent duty, while duties on raw materials were reduced to a very low level. For instance, the cotton duty was dropped from 50 per cent to 10 per cent ad valorem. Artisans were also permitted to leave the country freely, and even machinery could be exported under license from the Board of Trade. Furthermore, the tariff laws were codified and systematized to make them easily understood. Then, feeling that the monopoly of colonial trade was bad, Huskisson attacked the Navigation Laws. Permission was given for American ships to trade with the West Indies: the idea of "enumerated articles," being out of date, was discarded. The law restricting foreign ships to carrying goods directly from their own countries was also relaxed. Owing to the protests of the colonies and the shipping interest, colonial and coastwise trade was still reserved to ships of the empire, and imperial preferences were retained. But by 1830 much greater freedom had been introduced into trade. At the same time, the revenues from customs had increased noticeably. Lower duties made smuggling more and more unprofitable, while consumption expanded to such an extent that the resulting growth of trade more than compensated for the lower rates. Free trade was proving itself profitable.

The enlargement of government revenues by no means brought about a release from all financial problems. Great Britain received little or nothing in terms of indemnity from France after the Napoleonic Wars. At the same time, her revenue was cut by £14 million through the loss of the income tax. Therefore the government had to make even greater demands upon the existing tax system. This was opposed by the agricultural element who wanted relief from land taxes and by the industrial interests who favored free trade, particularly in corn. Meanwhile, Huskisson's reorganized tariff system was making up some of the loss by bringing in more and more revenue. In 1827 some £27 million were raised from duties on luxury and semiluxury goods: sugar, £4.5 million; tea, £3.2 million; coffee, £5 million; imported spirits, £3 million; and other similar commodities. On bacon was levied a tax of 3d. a pound, on butter, 2d. a pound, while the duty on cotton was 6 per cent ad valorem on foreign-grown and 4d. per 100 lbs. on Imperial. Excise taxes also were taken from home-manufactured commodities, such as glass, paper, and printed calicoes and muslins. Altogether, customs and excise produced £36 million. All other taxes put together: land tax, assessed taxes, window and house taxes, licenses, stamps, and legal papers produced only £13 million. Nontax revenues came to about £2 million. Thus, through taxation the government received annually a little over £50 million. This has been estimated at about one sixth of the national income.

In the same year (1827) the funded national debt stood at £780 million, which annually cost the country £29 million. The other expenses were: army and navy, £16 million; collection of revenue, £4 million; and civil list, £7 million. Thus, over half the state's income each year went to pay for the debt. To cut this Gordian knot various expedients might be used. Taxation could be increased, but this was difficult without the income tax. Ricardo and some of his satellites advocated a capital levy. There could also be economies, always the cry of those out of power. Last of all, the rate of interest on the debt could be lowered and the Sinking Fund abolished. It was the latter method which was followed. Some of the debt was converted to a lower interest rate. But even more important, in 1829 the Sinking Fund was closed. While this stopped a big drain on the Exchequer, it did not actually solve the problem. The debt continued to be a burden, and with nothing but the old system of indirect taxation there was little hope of the government ever getting out of the financial woods. The only bright spot in the whole matter was that Britain owed practically nothing abroad. The debt was held by her own people, which meant that the government always had control of the situation, a position very different from that of 1951.

The period of the thirties was one of political rather than economic change. The Whigs, who put through the Reform Bill of 1832, did not accomplish much in terms either of improving the government's financial stability or of removing restraints from trade. The need for modifying trade policy was becoming increasingly obvious, for during the thirties trade was certainly in the doldrums. There were various reasons for this, but the merchants felt that the primary one was the tariff system which prevented other nations from selling their wares to Britain. There was, consequently, a growing demand for the reduction of tariffs, particularly upon raw materials, including grain. The principal advocates of this freeing of trade were the Manchester manufacturers who were largely responsible for the founding in 1839 of the Anti-Corn Law League. Dedicated to the removal of all restraints on the corn trade, this body was eventually to have a very great influence on Britain's trade policy.

The Whigs, who dominated the scene during the thirties, can claim the credit for little except the cutting of some taxes and tariffs. The excise duties on leather, calicoes, candles, slates, tiles, and similar goods were removed. At the same time, bounties on some British goods such as linen, herring, and cured fish were abolished. The East India Company's monopoly on the importation of tea, which cost the country about £2 million a year, was likewise brought to an end. Other duties were reduced, and imperial preferences were cut. The result was a decline in the government's income, for there was no corresponding increase in consumption. Althorp, the Chancellor of the Exchequer, was forced to cut taxes, although he was obliged at the same time to increase revenues. Without the income tax this was impossible. The result between 1837 and 1841 was continuing deficits, which varied from £2.5 million to £5 million. Finally in 1841 the Whigs were put out of office, to be succeeded by Sir Robert Peel, who had the difficult duty of restoring the country's finances.

Sir Robert was an honest and upright person who placed his country before party or tradition, willing to change if convinced that a change was for the benefit of the nation. He came to power as leader of the Tories, more or less pledged to agricultural protection, but such a pledge might not mean too much if he believed that protection should go. His chief obligation in 1842, however, was that of increasing the revenues. As far as he could see, this meant a revision in the whole tax system. It required the curtailment, if not actual abolition, of imperial preference, for monopolies in the long run did not stimulate but only hurt trade. A drastic reduction of tariffs was also advisable, since this would increase consumption and so raise revenue. But as it would take some time for these innovations to achieve their objectives, a "carryover" was needed. In the income tax, Peel saw his great hope, and it formed the cornerstone of his tax reforms.

The new scheme of taxation was largely the work of the vice-president of the Board of Trade, William Ewart Gladstone. The first step was taken in 1842 with the removal of import prohibitions and the relaxation of prohibitory duties. Tariffs on raw materials were cut to less than 5 per cent, on partly manufactured, to less than 12 per cent, and on completely manufactured goods to less than 20 per cent. Within the next three years other changes were made. In 1843 and 1844 the duty on slave-grown sugar was almost halved, despite fierce opposition, the export of machinery was relieved of all restrictions, and raw wool imports were given free entry. Further decreases in duties were introduced in 1845, so raw materials imported after that date paid practically no duty. Some excise taxes were also removed and export duties on coal were abolished. When the changes were completed, customs revenues were down by £5 million, and, out of the remaining £22 million received, nine articles alone paid £18.6 million. Peel and Gladstone also altered the sliding scale of corn duties. When the home price was 51s. and 52s., the duty was 20s. Between 52s. and 55s., it stood at 19s., and then as the home price rose, the duty dropped 1s. for 1s. until corn entered free at 73s. or more. Britain was heading towards free trade.

To make up for the drop in revenue caused by tariff reductions, the income tax and death duties were reintroduced. Peel believed that this would be only a temporary measure, since a lowering of tariffs would increase consumption and thus bring revenues back to their old level. Therefore, he asked only that the income tax be applied to incomes over £150 at 7d. in the pound, to run for no more than three years with the option of having it renewed for another two. The Whigs, in particular, were violently opposed, but it became law, and Peel proceeded to collect his tax.

The effect of his tax changes seem to have surprised even Peel. By 1844 his surplus was £4.1 million, with the revenues continuing to rise. As a result, Consols rose above par, so he was able to carry out a big conversion, reducing the interest on £250 million of bonds from 3½ per cent to 3¼ per cent until 1854, and, after that to 3 per cent until 1870. This meant a saving each year until 1854 of £625,000 and thereafter of £1.25 million until 1870. By 1845 the government's annual surplus stood at around £5 million. At this time Peel's income tax was about to expire. He desired, however, to continue it for a time in order that he might further reduce tariffs. He hoped that since the country was booming, if only the tax system could be reformed, it might be possible to abolish tariffs and excise completely.

Then the blow fell. The corn crops of 1845 were very poor and were followed by the total failure of the potato crop in Ireland. Corn had to be imported at low prices in order to meet the need for food. Peel at this point wanted to reduce the corn tariffs drastically in line with his other tariff reforms, but the cabinet could not agree. Lord John Russell, the Whig leader, who was then called upon to head the government, failed to form a cabinet, so Peel was called back to power. On January 19, 1846 he moved the total repeal of the Corn Laws, asking that only a registration duty of 1s. a quarter be levied on grain imports. He won his case in Parliament, but he split the Tory Party, with result that they went out of power for a good many years. The important thing as far as fiscal history was concerned was, however, that the last great hurdle before full free trade had been taken. It remained for others merely to complete the process.

The Completion of Free Trade, 1846-70

The year 1848 did not see the end of all the problems of trade or finance. The Whigs, who succeeded Peel in the government, found life still rather difficult. They had to overcome the effects of the Irish famine, while attempting to offset the effects of the railway "boom and bust" of 1848. Yet despite these problems they took one or two important actions. In 1849, under Gladstone's influence, they repealed the Navigation Laws, feeling that even if Britain were the only nation to throw its colonial trade open to all, such action would be profitable. This move was followed by the removal of duties on a considerable number of commodities although tariffs did not all disappear until the sixties. The Tories meanwhile repeatedly demanded the abolition of the income tax, but when they obtained a precarious hold on power in 1853 they found that they could not dispense with the revenue which it provided. Consequently they had to continue it whether they would or no.

The Tories, of course, were not alone in their attitude, for there was general unanimity on the necessity of getting rid of the income tax as soon as possible. At the Exchequer, Gladstone, hoping that he could abolish it by 1860, was not prepared to discuss such matters as increased exemptions or differentiation between incomes received from investment and those received for work. He added also incomes between £100 and £150 at 2½ per cent, or 5d. in the pound, and restricted exemptions. His position might have been sound had it not been for the fact that Britain did have one rather costly war in the fifties, the Crimean War. This pushed up the rate to 9d. in the pound, effectively killing any hope of the early disappearance of the unpopular impost. Gladstone also introduced a legacy tax, but it was not very successful in increasing revenues.

Simultaneously, he was carrying forward a plan for reducing tariffs. He concentrated on a few articles in general consumption but avoided taxing either raw materials or foodstuffs. He imposed excise taxes only at the final stage of manufacture and felt that if industry could be freed as much as possible from taxation, a general decline in prices might follow, to the benefit of the workingman. As a result, between 1855 and 1860 he slashed tariffs on food imports by at least 50 per cent, freed the import of cotton, equalized the duties on free- and slave-grown sugar, abolished all tariffs on manufactured imports, and removed the excises on soap and paper. Finally, in order to help forward the free trade cause, through Richard Cobden he negotiated a commercial agreement with France (1860). French goods were to come into Britain without payment, or at very reduced rates, while British coal was to enter France free of all duties. The French also abolished their prohibitive tariffs on other goods, lowering them immediately to at least 30 per cent ad valorem, to become after 1864, 24 per cent. Thus, Gladstone did his utmost to free trade from tariff restrictions in the hope that this would so stimulate industry that resulting prosperity would do away with the need for much of the taxation then being levied.

The Crimean War and postwar rearmament, because of French erratic behavior, brought an end to these aspirations. The income tax became more necessary, as customs receipts fell. Although the treaty with France had not brought any revolutionary changes, Britain offered to make similar agreements with other nations, if they so desired. "The most favored nation" clause was introduced in order to entice others to lower tariff barriers. Coupled with this, 1860 saw not only a drop or total abolition of certain customs duties but also a rise of income tax to 10d. The following year brought the end of the excise on paper, but only a drop of 1d. in the pound on income tax, which, however, continued to be reduced until in 1864 it stood at 6d. in the pound. Meanwhile, duties had been considerably reduced on tea and sugar. Thus, increasingly the government, whether it liked it or not, was having to depend upon income tax because of the dwindling returns from its vanishing indirect taxes. Free trade meant the absolute necessity of the income tax.

The period between 1865 and 1870 was one in which, strive as the government might, whether Conservative (Tory) or Liberal (Whig), expenditures could not be reduced. There was the crash of the Gurney firm and the Abyssinian War, which cost £8 million instead of the estimated £3.5 millions. To prevent waste, in 1861 the Public Accounts Committee had been established and in 1866 it was given authority to control government expenditure. But more than this was needed. The Conservatives, when they came into power, raised the income tax from the low 1865 level of 4d. in the pound to 5d., a further rise to 6d. coming in 1868 to meet the costs of the Abyssinian Campaign. During the same period both parties followed the policy of conversion of government debts. For instance, £24 million of Post Office Savings Bank stock were converted into more highly rateable annuities terminable in 1885. This was in reality an untouchable Sinking Fund. Finally in 1869 Gladstone, with Lowe at the Exchequer, cut down expenditures of the armed services, at the same time advancing the collection date of certain taxes for the coming year, and so was able to budget for a surplus of £3.5 millions. But for all his efforts, the problem of finance still dogged the footsteps of the party in power.

By 1870 the general pattern of British taxation had to a considerable degree hardened into shape. It was this pattern which was to continue down into the fourth decade of the twentieth century. A primary characteristic was that it depended upon direct rather than upon indirect taxation to supply the funds. Indirect taxes: customs, excise duties, etc., had been found to hamper and hinder the country's economy, while direct taxation enabled the money to be collected more economically as well as with less damage to trade and industry. Moreover, it was more equitably distributed, coming from the people who were more able to pay. This meant that trade had been freed from vexatious and price-raising imposts, an achievement heartily endorsed on theoretical grounds by all the liberals of the day. Thus, not only theoretical considerations, but also financial necessities had led ultimately to free trade.

Yet, although the government had been withdrawing from direct involvement in economic matters, it was forced to extend its operations in other directions. In imposing the income tax, it had been obliged to interfere in one of the most private matters of the individual: his income. At the same time, because of social inequalities and oppression which resulted from the Industrial Revolution, the government had been forced to restrain individual freedom in other ways. Much of the energy it had formerly employed in controlling trade and commerce was now used to deal with social problems. Therefore, to see the other side of this picture, we must turn to the Industrial Revolution's impact on society.

Chapter 17

GOVERNMENT ASSERTS
CONTROL OVER SOCIETY

W<small>HILE</small> the period 1815 to 1870 was one in which the idea of laissez faire became more generally accepted, there was at the same time a tendency in the opposite direction. On one hand, there was a growing demand for free trade, while on the other, there was an increasing call for government interference in society. This desire for state control arose from labor's gradual realization that it could not stand up unaided against the pressures and demands of employers. To talk about "freedom of contract" was ridiculous when the employer held within his own grasp all the financial power as well as all the opportunity for employment. The government therefore, was obliged to make an attempt to maintain a proper balance by giving protection to those in danger of being exploited. Nevertheless, the state itself, controlled largely by the upper classes, especially in the early days, tended to restrain labor's efforts to obtain better terms of employment. Only gradually, did it begin to feel that it had some responsibilities to the lower classes. The result was often hesitation, vacillation, and uncertainty, but by 1870, even in an age completely devoted to laissez faire, the state was asserting a much greater amount of control over society and its economy. It followed no logical pattern, but as the need arose and as the pressure was applied, it took what it felt to be appropriate action.

The Changing Class Structure

In order to understand the growth of state interference in economic and social life, it is necessary first to see the social changes brought about by the Industrial Revolution, for during this period two new classes came into prominence. It was the conflict between them that really forced state action.

314

On one side was the new industrial middle class. A capitalistic middle class was not something new, for this group had existed even in the days of Edward I. But heretofore the capitalist had been a merchant, not a manufacturer. With the growth of foreign demand for English cloth, however, there had appeared the clothier, operating the domestic system. He was the first of this new capitalist group. With the subsequent development of machinery and the establishment of the factory, the industrial capitalist became a very important economic type. He was the factory owner and the employer, hardly ever seeing his employees, but supplying the capital for and drawing the profits from their production.

The industrial middle class was to a large extent composed of men who had come up from the bottom of the ladder. The typical industrialist had had little capital or financial support to begin with, but by dint of hard work, saving, and reinvesting of profits, he had gradually built up a large business. He was usually energetic, frugal, hard-headed and rather unsympathetic with those who had not done as well, feeling that if he could succeed, others could too. This tended to make him an exacting employer, who demanded the last ounce of production from his workers. Many picture him as a sort of ogre, who enjoyed nothing more than the oppression of the poor, the widow and the fatherless. But such is not the case. He was often a very kind man, a good father and deeply interested in religion, as was Sir Robert Peel, Sr., or in philosophy, like Josiah Wedgwood, or even in social reform, like Robert Owen, and frequently much concerned about his employee's welfare.

One thing, however, which often made him seem utterly ruthless was his acceptance of current economic theory, and there has probably never been an age when the economist wielded such power and influence over men's minds. The eighteenth and early nineteenth centuries saw a steady desertion of mercantilist for laissez faire ways of thinking, a movement accelerated by the writings of Adam Smith, Malthus, Ricardo, and Senior. Since it was believed that all political economy was governed by natural law, legislation could neither hinder nor help a country. The best thing to do, therefore, was to remove all controls. If this meant opppression and degradation for the laboring population, it could not be helped, for the solution was in their own hands. After all, if their lot was improved, they would only have larger families, thus preventing their standard of living from rising above a subsistence level. It was only the poverty, squalor, and disease in their lives which kept them from having too many children. For this reason, labor unions were not only useless but indeed positively bad, for they attempted to dictate to the employer what he should do with his own possessions. In this way the industrialist, holding, of course, with particular fervor to those parts of contemporary economic thought which increased his profits, justified his actions. He was simply obeying natural law.

This point of view can be clearly discerned when one considers the attitudes of this group. For one thing, while they were only too ready to accept the idea that combination among laborers was worse than useless in improving their position, they were quite sure of the efficacy of combining among themselves to raise prices or to keep down wages. One of the best examples of this combination tendency is to be found in the action of the "vend" which controlled the prices of Newcastle coal, but such practices were common in most industrial fields. Not content with combines and agreements, the middle class soon began to demand a part in the government. Largely deprived of the vote and excluded from Parliament, in the late 1820's they raised such an outcry and, backed by the laboring classes, seemed to be bringing the country so close to revolution that the government passed the Franchise Reform Act of 1832, giving them a voice in Parliament. Once in the House of Commons, the middle class then set its face like flint against the admission of the laboring classes but, at the same time, increased its own influence in both the Tory and Whig parties. The final victory came in 1846 with the Corn Law's repeal. This action was both a sign that the middle class had taken away the political supremacy of the aristocracy and a means of keeping labor satisfied without raising wages.

Meanwhile, between 1800 and 1870 the condition of labor changed greatly. It had, to a certain extent become divided into skilled and non- or semi-skilled categories. Skilled labor, having learned from middle class example, in 1867 gained the vote. By various means it was also experiencing a rising standard of living. It believed implicitly in the middle class virtues of thrift, diligence, and self-help, Samuel Smiles, the author of such works as *Thrift*, *Self Help*, and *The Lives of the Engineers*, being one of its patron saints. On the other hand, stemming both from the teaching of Robert Owen and French thinkers such as Saint Simon and Fourière, socialism was beginning to gain some followers, particularly among those interested in the lower ranks of labor. They were coming to the conclusion that the whole capitalistic and "free enterprise" system was wrong. Socialism, involving a greatly increased amount of government control and supervision, was held to be the only answer to the problems of the laborer. To this position even such middle class thinkers as John Stewart Mill were prepared to give their support. Thus by 1870 there was a growing tendency in many quarters to accept government interference in society. Such ideas, unpopular though they were with the middle class and skilled artisans, found their chief proponents amongst the semi- and unskilled workers looking to the state for help and protection.

The Standard of Living

The standard of living of the middle class during the period rose steadily. With the expansion of production, the increase of trade, and the introduction of the joint-stock company, money income for this group increased fairly rapidly, particularly after 1830. Simultaneously, owing to the cheapening of many processes, costs began to decline, thus lowering prices. The result was that real income rose quite steeply. New comforts and luxuries now became commonplace, housing improved, and food was better. At the same time education was improved. Thus from the beginning of the Industrial Revolution down to 1870 the economic position of the middle class was greatly advanced. At the same time, clearly defined differences between the laboring and the middle class appeared—differences as distinct as those formerly existing between the aristocracy and all of inferior rank.

With regard to labor's standard of living between 1715 and 1870 there seems to be considerable difference of opinion. Those who are inclined to be leftist in their sympathies usually hold that it rose between 1700 and 1750, only to decline from 1750 down to 1830. Although they admit that it improved after that date, they hold that the standard never really returned to the old level. It is said, for instance, that prior to the Napoleonic Wars only the man had to work to earn as much as the whole family was earning in 1830. Moreover, in the eighteenth century, twelve hours a day was the maximum period of labor, while in the nineteenth century eighteen hours a day was not uncommon. The fact is, however, that we do not have very accurate knowledge about laboring conditions in the eighteenth century, since even by 1800 most of the industrial production still operated under the domestic system. It is hard, therefore, to determine what were the hours of labor. In any case there is clear evidence that even in the homes of the laborers, children often commenced to work at the age of five years and that they toiled for very long hours. The figures cited by the leftist writers for the nineteenth century are often those indicating the worst possible conditions and are not in themselves typical either as to hours, conditions of labor, or wages. The situation varied radically from industry to industry and from period to period. Consequently, a broad generalization is very dangerous. That the laborer's standard of living was not high in the early nineteenth century is certain, but that it was much lower than that of a laborer in 1720 is impossible of verification. Each group of industries must be taken by itself.

One of those whose lot deteriorated considerably was the agricultural laborer. The enclosure of the fields and commons for intensive cultivation brought him great hardship, since those in charge of the enclosing usually cared little for the small farmer with his few acres and his one cow. Consequently, most of the small freeholders, the leasehold tenants, and the squatters were forced off the land. They either migrated to the towns to become factory hands or, if they stayed in the country, they were reduced to the position of landless day laborers, without even a by-industry such as weaving to supplement their incomes. Many of them took to poaching, for which they were savagely punished. Others tried to organize unions to protest and strike, but they were treated as severely as criminals, often being transported for years. Even in the 1850's housing and living conditions were still extremely bad and wages had not risen appreciably. The farm laborer in the north was in a better situation because he could always leave and go into industry. But in the south, where other employment was scarce, his situation was difficult, for there was no means of escape.[1]

For the industrial laborer throughout the period the standard of living varied very greatly. There was always, of course, the problem of technological unemployment: e.g., the hand loom weavers being put out of work by the power loom. If the weaver was too old to adapt himself to the new machinery, he had no resources to which he could turn. This situation, however, tended to improve as the years went by, with fewer and fewer losing their jobs because of technical innovations. At the same time, the wages of skilled laborers and of the machine operators were climbing. A number of economic historians have estimated that from 1800 to 1870 money wages in most trades rose between 33 per cent and 50 per

---

[1] The variation in wages between 1837 and 1872 was as follows: in the southeast and east Midlands, from 9s. 5d. to 14s. 10d.; in the southwest and west Midlands, from 7s. 2d. to 13s. 1d.; in the north and northeast, from 9s. 1d. to 13s. 2d.; and in the north and northwest, from 11s. to 17s. 4d. G. P. Jones & A. G. Pool, A Hundred Years of Economic Development in Great Britain (London, 1940), p. 154.

cent. This, of course, does not take into account periods of unemployment, nor does it include industries such as building, in which the wages probably went up only about 15 per cent to 20 per cent. Some wage rates, on the other hand, increased by more than the specified 50 per cent. Another general improvement was the gradual disappearance of "truck" payments, whereby the workman received part or all of his wage in goods, a practice very liable to abuse.

Along with the rise of wages there went a fall in the cost of living. The reduction of tariffs on foodstuffs and some other imports helped this movement. For instance, the loaf of bread which sold for 12d. in London in 1855 sold in 1863-65 for 7d. and in 1870 for 8d. Rents for the better built houses probably went up somewhat, but they did not wipe out the improvement in real wages gained through the fall of other costs. It has been estimated that real wages, as opposed to money wages, increased between 20 per cent and 30 per cent for the first seventy years of the nineteenth century. From this point of view, therefore, labor's standard of living was generally on the upgrade. At the same time, there were wide variations between industries, with periodic depressions and bad harvests modifying the picture. Still, taking it as a whole, labor seems to have been receiving for its efforts considerably more in 1870 than it had say, in 1815, or even in 1790.

While real income had increased, had labor's situation really improved? Here again there is considerable difference of opinion. It is acknowledged by all that, although housing did not become much better during the whole period, after 1850 there was some amelioration. Even by 1870, however, overcrowding, poor drainage, and lack of cleaning facilities were the rule rather than the exception. It has also been said that the quality of the food consumed had become worse. Despite the declining death rate, a much larger number of people were suffering from malnutrition. Difficult as this is to prove for labor as a whole, it is possibly true of certain sections of the industrial population. It has also been asserted that while hours of work decreased slowly, the introduction of more complicated machinery brought with it greater physical and mental exhaustion for the worker, causing him to be intellectually and physically retarded. Here again one needs to be careful, since increased profits and increased machines do not necessarily establish such a conclusion. Wide generalizations are very misleading when applied to all industry.

Looking at the state of the industrial worker as a whole, it would seem to be true that throughout the years 1715 to 1870 his situation improved, although there were undoubtedly exceptions to this statement, as for instance in the case of the cotton hand loom weaver. The rise in the standard of living seems to have been proportionate to the amount of skill required in one's work. The skilled worker's lot, therefore, became very much easier, although the Marxist explains this by saying that the capitalist was merely trying to keep him quiet. Those whose economic condition changed least were the unskilled laborers, such as the poverty stricken immigrants from Ireland. But taking the industrial workers as a whole, it would seem that their position was better in 1870 than it had been either in 1820 or in 1750.

The Problem of Poverty

Despite this improvement, poverty continued to be a problem, particularly as the Industrial Revolution brought with it a new type of poverty, or at least one which had previously been relatively rare. With Britain's enormous and rapid economic expansion she became bound to her foreign supplies of raw materials and to her foreign markets. Consequently, a war, a famine, or a plague in some distant part of the globe might disrupt her whole economic organization. This was given dramatic demonstration during the American Civil War, when lack of cotton practically ruined Lancashire. Cotton mills closed down in large numbers, and the workers were laid off. True, it was only a temporary problem, but the cotton worker did not have a plot of land which he could cultivate, nor was there, because of his lack of training, a chance of turning to some other industry for employment. Thus, with the fluctuations of the trade cycle, there arose the problem of people who were out of work temporarily through no fault of their own, but because there was no market, at the moment, for their labor. This was the new type of poverty, considerably different from that found in the earlier, predominantly agricultural economy.

Under the old system the Elizabethan Poor Law had operated with moderate effectiveness. Parish rates had been levied to supply the poor with necessities and to provide them with materials upon which they could work. Although the Civil War of the seventeenth century had permanently disrupted the system, it continued haltingly. After the Restoration (1660) another law had been enacted which enabled parishes to return to his home parish any person resident for less than 40 days who was liable to become a charge on the poor rates. For vagabonds, prostitutes, and the semicriminal, parishes also, with or without the approval of parliament, during the seventeenth century began to set up houses of correction. These institutions, however, soon lost their popularity with parish authorities, their places being taken by workhouses for the poor. London opened the first in 1647, to be followed by Bristol, Hull, Crediton, Lynn, and other towns. By 1800 there were probably some 60 urban workhouses, while there were around 900 similar establishments in the rural parishes, often with two or three neighboring parishes participating. Organized as refuges for the poor, they were also equipped with workrooms and sometimes even with plots of land which could be tilled by the residents. The biggest of these houses was built by the corporation of Norwich. In 1770 it had 1200 inmates, 600 ablebodied, and the remainder children and impotent. Poorhouses, which were merely refuges for the poor without any corrective or economic objective, were also being built in the hope of lowering the rates. By forcing the poor into these establishments it was believed that they could be cared for more cheaply. By 1790 the whole problem of poverty was of growing importance, but not by any means understood.

In the eighteenth century those who suffered from the worst poverty were the agricultural laborers. While the Justices of the Peace were supposed to fix wages in relation to the price of bread and ale, most of them did not bother. After all, they were the employers. But the laborers had to be kept alive. Consequently, in 1795 a group of Justices of the Peace meeting at Speenhamland, in Berkshire, devised a plan for augmenting wages from the poor rates. They decided to use the rates to bring weekly wages up to a minimum of three gallon loaves for a man and one and a half loaves for his wife and each child. This system was unfair and demoralizing. It relieved the large farmers of the necessity of paying a decent wage to their laborers, while, at the same time, it obliged the small freeholders, who did not hire laborers but who paid rates, to help pay for the servants of their wealthy neighbors. Poor rates rose as a result of this policy, often forcing many of the small farmers to sell out. The effect upon the laborers was also bad, since without working they would receive almost as much from the poor rates as they did if serving some local landowner. Moreover, it placed a premium on immorality, for the more children, whether legitimate or not, one had, the greater was the amount of relief available. This plan, therefore, became an unmitigated evil, particularly in the south, where it was very common.

It was not long before the Speenhamland system, along with the whole poor law administration, came under fire. Malthus set forth the view that poor relief of any kind was fundamentally bad.

After all, it provided living for the poor, who then had larger families, so increasing their own misery. Others felt that the current method of relieving poverty was wrong since it did not penalize the needy, who, they held, were basically lazy. Did not their poverty prove their laziness? Again, others saw the settlement laws as the real causes of the trouble. But, whatever their view of causes or needs, all were agreed that the more than £6 million expended on poor relief in 1831 was too much. They felt it to be an unwarranted burden which was inefficiently and wrongly managed. What is more, they believed, and in this they were quite correct, that the current policy was having an exceedingly bad effect upon the agricultural laborers. Thus, by 1832 there was a growing demand for poor law reform.

As early as 1817 a special inquiry had been made into the question of poor relief, but nothing happened. Finally in 1832 a Royal Commission was appointed, with Edwin Chadwick, a militant Benthamite as its main driving force. After two years of investigation the Commission produced an historic report. Accepting the presuppositions that poverty was usually caused by laziness and big families, the commissioners laid down certain principles. They were opposed to a centralized national poor relief system, preferring to leave the matter in the hands of the parish authorities. They were also convinced that no poor relief should be given to people who lived outside the workhouses. Outdoor relief, as it was called, was to be abolished, all the poor being forced to move into workhouses where conditions would be made as uncomfortable as possible in order that they might be encouraged to go out to find work. It was also advised that segregation of the sexes as well as of adults from minors should be the rule. The workhouses were to be built by parishes organized in groups so that they could afford large establishments. The whole system was to be placed under three poor law commissioners in London. These suggestions were adopted by Parliament as the proper solution to the problem of poverty. The poor were to be made uncomfortable, to be prevented from breeding, and to be kept in their proper station.

Theorizing about poor relief and putting it into effect were two very different things. By 1847 most of the parishes had been organized into groups each with a central workhouse. The only difficulty was that the plans did not work. For one thing, much of the poverty, then as now, was temporary, being more effectively dealt with by outdoor relief. Added to this, the administrative machinery was not efficient. The parish authorities were usually incapable, and although the Poor Law Commissioners appointed assistant commissioners for the 12 districts into which the country was divided, they could not force action. Those who were the subjects of the law's tender mercies were also somewhat reluctant to avail themselves of their privileges. In the north particularly, there was violent hatred of the new workhouse, the workers being supported in their opposition by most social reformers. The laborers felt that they had been betrayed by the middle class whom they had supported in their efforts to obtain the vote. If the law had been enforced, it might have led to violence, and in some places where strict application was attempted there was considerable trouble.

In view of the opposition and also of the physical difficulties of making effective the provisions of the 1834 Poor Law, modifications, particularly in administration, were bound to come. The segregation according to sex and age was not carried out. Vagrants, petty criminals, poor, impotent, and young, all lived together, often with disastrous results. At length, in 1861, a new commission was appointed to study the whole matter. This body recognized that certain changes which had taken place were all for the good. For example, union, interunion, and even district rating had been set up for unemployment relief, while loans had been made by the government for the erection of public works as relief measures. These practices were now incorporated into the poor relief system, with the addition that funds were made available to Poor Law Guardians in order that they might provide special quarters for vagrants, asylums for the insane, and some free medical care, such as smallpox vaccination. Since 1847 the whole system had been under the direction of a Poor Law Board, with the president sitting in Parliament. This was continued. The new system also allowed the continuance of general outdoor relief. The failure of the 1834 plans had forced widespread modifications.

The changes in poor law administration in England and Wales did not affect Scotland. Poor relief north of the Tweed had, since before the Reformation, been supplied by parish collections, charitable bequests which were invested, and personal charity. The Presbyterian Church had stressed such charitable giving, which seems to have been sufficient while Scotland was largely agricultural. The impotent poor were enrolled, often receiving licenses to beg. The ablebodied poor, on the other hand, were faced with the need of working or starving. When there was a general manpower shortage this was not too harsh; but once industrialization entered Scotland the situation changed. The strain on private charity became great. What is more, the old idea of the ablebodied being refused help no longer applied. Thomas Chalmers, minister of St. John's

Church in Glasgow, organized a parish system which worked well, but which was not applicable to the whole country. The Scots, however, both the rich and poor were not greatly smitten with the idea of English poor relief. It was only very gradually that circumstances forced the establishment of poor houses, compulsory parish poor rates, and similar English innovations. By 1870 Scotland had gradually fallen into line, although her system of poor relief was not as efficiently run or as effective as that of England.

It was in such ways that attempts were made to meet the problem of the new type of poverty, but these efforts did not really get to the root of the difficulties. There was still much insecurity and misery arising from trade recessions and industrial depressions. Something more was needed in terms of government action to help solve the problem not only of those who were permanently incapable of working, but also of those who had temporarily lost their capacity to earn.

The Government and Labor Organizations

As has already been mentioned, the problem raised by periodic economic recessions and booms brought to light a relatively new type of poverty caused by temporary unemployment. This was aggravated by the distress resulting from extremely low wages and poor conditions of work. Economic insecurity became a very concrete problem for an ever increasing part of Britain's population. To meet these needs the government did very little in the eighteenth century, and, consequently, the workers themselves began to take action. They organized their friendly societies, which were kinds of mutual insurance associations. Weekly contributions might assure one of a decent burial, might bring in a shilling a week during sickness, or might simply furnish an excuse for periodic social gatherings. Not infrequently these organizations led to combinations of workmen for the purpose of forcing up wages. This, of course, had been done in the Middle Ages, but, given the closer bond of working in the same factory and a common grievance, the workman's organization now became a formidable weapon.

The masters and factory owners were much disturbed over the trend towards combination, which, coupled with the French Revolution in the 1790's, brought them to the verge of panic. As a consequence, acts were passed in 1799 and 1800 banning any workmen's organizations that attempted to raise wages. Although masters were also forbidden to combine, that clause was never enforced, the workingman being the only one who suffered under the rigorous application of the law. But despite all the efforts of the government, labor organization could not be stopped. If attacked, it usually went underground to burst forth in mob violence, as when workers under a mythical "King Ludd" began smashing gig mills and stocking machines and even burning factories. The government then resorted to the use of the military and the transportation of the rioters to Australia. This, however, simply provoked further disturbances, such as the Peterloo Massacre (1819), in which a good many workers were killed or injured. At the same time, radical political clubs began to appear, organized along the lines of the Methodist Churches and agitating for an improvement in the worker's legal position. The Whig party, shocked by Peterloo, also began demanding reform. Finally, after a long investigation largely engineered by two radicals: Francis Place and Joseph Hume, Parliament consented in 1824 to repeal the obnoxious combination laws. There was an immediate flood of strikes, which brought the reimposition of many restrictions, although workingmen's combinations or trade-unions were now legalized. The first victory had been won.

From 1824 on, as mentioned above, there was continuous agitation for reform of the House of Commons. In this labor took an important part, largely through the radical political clubs; workingmen rioted, burnt hay ricks, and generally disturbed the country, but despite all their efforts they achieved nothing. Once the middle class gained admission to the Commons, labor had the door slammed in its face. Meanwhile, others, suspecting that this would be the case, had turned to trade-unionism as the one great hope. Little could be done via this route, however, as there was a depression between 1826 and 1828. Unions were organized in Northumberland among the miners who struck in 1829 but were defeated by the use of police and troops. Because the cotton spinners had the same experience, they held a conference in 1829 on the Isle of Man for the purpose of organizing a "Grand General Union" of all the spinners in order to have more strength. This attempt was no more successful, but it did lay the foundation for the National Association for the Protection of Labour (1831), which blossomed and died, as did William Lovett's "National Union of the Working Classes." None of these bodies possessed the funds, the organization, or the leadership necessary for success, although they did prepare the ground. Therefore, when Robert Owen proposed his "Grand National Consolidated Trades Union" in 1834, it received wide support. Over half a million members joined in a few weeks. The employers, however, attacked it savagely, often having its members transported for illegally administering oaths. Along with this, Owen, who always had a new idea before he finished with his last one, now turned to cooperative production and merchandising. The result was that the union went down nearly as fast as it had arisen. By 1838 trade-unionism, while not dead, was at least sleeping.

Because of unionism's failure and also because of the treatment received in the Reform Bill of 1832, labor turned back to political action. In 1836 Lovett drew up a "People's Charter" for the London Workingman's Association. It contained such points as: manhood suffrage, payment of members of parliament, voting by ballot, annually elected parliaments, equal electoral districts, and the abolition of property qualifications for members. The idea was received with great acclaim by the working classes, who now began a great agitation for the charter. However, the leadership was poor, the organization was ineffective, and the government hostile, jailing some 700 and transporting 87 others who were involved. Chartism, too, seemed to flourish only in times of distress. Three great petitions were presented to Parliament in favor of the Charter (1839, 1842, 1848), but nothing happened. Poverty and misery prevented effective action, and the movement split over the methods to be employed. Finally, helped by the repeal of the Corn Laws, the prosperity which appeared around 1848 brought Chartism to an end. If labor was to obtain better treatment, it would have to be by other means.

Much more effective than all the grandiose union schemes or political agitations of the workers were the friendly societies. Quietly, but steadily they had grown. The Unity of Oddfellows, the teetotal Rechabites, and the Hearts of Oak were nationwide and federal. Alongside these there existed many local organizations. The latter were of various types, the smaller usually being sociability societies, with the larger emphasizing health, accident, and burial insurance. In many towns there still stand friendly society halls which are used today primarily for local social gatherings. That the growth was gradual but solid is shown by a typical organization, The Blackburn Philanthropic Burial Society. Founded in 1839, by 1850 it had 45,000 members and by 1870, 127,000. The big concentration of such societies was among the mill workers in Lancashire, of whom some 258,000 had by 1850 joined the Oddfellows alone. It has been estimated that in 1870 the total enrollment in these organizations came to more than 2 million. Here was a very important form of working class organization which might lead to bigger things.

At the same time, trade-unionism had again been growing. After the collapse of the Owenite movement a few small unions, numbering perhaps a couple of thousand members, had continued. Usually local and limited to one trade, such as spinning, machine making, or something similar, these unions were not very successful. Frequently mismanaged and prone to employ violence to achieve their ends, they often called poorly organized strikes, which were easily smashed by employers who had the support of the government. Consequently, in the later 1830's, while the unions remained free of Chartist ties, they met with increasing public suspicion and dislike.

In the 1840's the character of trade-unionism, particularly among the skilled laborers began to change. Instead of adopting a "class warfare" attitude, under the influence of the current laissez faire philosophy they turned to cooperation. Rather than thinking in terms of conflict, they stressed cooperation with the employer, avoiding strikes like poison. Another reason for their changed point of view was that they also emphasized the friendly society aspect of the unions. They opposed paying out funds as strike benefits when the same money might be used for sickness or unemployment relief. One of the unions which gave the lead in this movement was the Manchester Steam Engine, Machine Makers, and Mill Wrights Friendly Society, which, under the leadership of William Allan, its paid secretary, brought about a nationwide union of similar bodies. This organization, known as the Amalgamated Society of Engineers, had some 110,000 members contributing about £550 per week. It soon had many imitators among the labor aristocracy. Other crafts likewise formed large unions according to varying plans. They all, however, had paid secretaries and sometimes even retained lawyers to give them proper and efficient leadership.

It was not long before the well-organized unions began to draw together. As a result of a building-trades' dispute in London in 1859, this trend was accelerated. The Amalgamated Society of Engineers contributed some £3,000 to the builders' strike fund, and throughout the country trade-union representatives began to consult together on common action. These meetings soon became permanent local trades councils. Moreover, they were all directed from London where the secretaries of five of the leading unions: engineers', carpenters', ironfounders', bricklayers', and ladies' shoemakers', had a standing consultation committee which has come to be known as "The Junta." Composed of solid, careful men, The Junta did much to improve the reputation of the unions, to extend the franchise to the urban workers in 1867, and to help in the organization of the first Trades Union Congress held in 1868. To all intents and purposes, by 1870 trade-unionism had achieved a very favorable position.

The legal status of the unions, however, was not by any means settled. From 1855 on they had come under the Friendly Societies Act which gave such organizations corporate status. Four years later they had gained the right of peaceful picketing, to which was added the following year the right of the coal miners to have a checkweigher at the pit head, to see that they were not cheated on the amount of coal they dug. Employers, however, were doing all they could to rouse public opposition to the unions. Therefore, when a bomb was exploded in a nonunion worker's home in Sheffield in 1866, Parliament, becoming worried, appointed an investigating committee. The next year the courts ruled that while unions were not illegal, they were in restraint of trade and so could not come under the act of 1855. These two things, coming at the same time, caused consternation in labor circles. Evidence was produced before the parliamentary committee to show that they were not the old fighting unions, but concentrated on friendly society activities. Largely as a result of this proof of their respectability, a considerable part of urban labor now received the vote (1867), and the following year the Trade Union Congress was formed. It was, however, only after much pressure that in 1871 the unions' funds were given legal protection against defaulting officials. The unions still had not achieved corporate status. What is more, the Criminal Law Amendment Act of the same year so limited their action that even peaceful picketing became a crime. Legally, by 1872 they were worse off than they had been in 1860.

One other type of labor organization already referred to was the cooperative movement. In 1850 there were 130 stores, or "co-ops," with 15,000 members; by 1872, the number had grown to 1,266, with 437,000 members, a capital of £4.4 millions, and annual sales of £13 millions. In the '60's cooperative wholesale societies were organized in both England and Scotland. So successful were they that their sales rose from £54,000 in 1864 to £1.5 million ten years later. The important thing about these organizations was that here the laborer owned his own means of distribution, effectively bringing one important economic activity under his own control.

Thus, when the year 1870 arrived, the position of organized labor was, generally speaking, considerably improved. There had been setbacks for the unions, but they were on the way up. The one group which had not improved its position, despite the endeavors of a Methodist lay preacher, Joseph Arch, was that of the farm laborers. On the whole, however, labor's efforts had been quite successful, for notwithstanding much opposition, labor organizations had won their way to a position of importance and influence in the country.

The Movement for Factory Reform

Another result of the Industrial Revolution was the gradual growth of feeling during this period that the government must take steps to control conditions of labor. In the old days the gilds had attempted something like this on a local basis; in the nineteenth century it became a national matter.

The earliest factories had usually been run by waterpower, which was generally far from urban centers. As adult workers would not move to the factory sites unless they were paid high wages, factory owners turned to the parish guardians of the poor, who were persuaded to turn over to them the parish pauper children. These youngsters were then taken as "apprentices" to the factories, lodged in foul barracks and worked some sixteen hours a day. By the time they reached maturity they were often crippled or diseased, good for nothing but to be cast adrift. With the advent of steam the factories moved to the cities where children living at home could be employed at less cost than "pauper" children who had to be fed and lodged. The "free" children could still be maltreated and overworked in the same manner, since their parents, who themselves received a starvation wage, had to send them to work in order to keep the family alive. Some attempts were made to ameliorate the conditions of the pauper "apprentices" when Sir Robert Peel, Sr. had enacted in 1802 a "Health and Morale of Apprentices Act" establishing a twelve hour day and providing for better housing and proper training. In 1819, another act originated by Owen, and again sponsored by Peel, was passed to protect the "free" children, reducing their hours and providing for more cleanly buildings. Neither of these laws, however, was effective. Not only did the industrialists fight them tooth and nail, claiming that the government was interfering with private property and freedom of contract, but, what was more important, no machinery for enforcement was set up. Consequently, nothing was accomplished.

Despite the opposition to factory reform, the pressure continued. Political radicals, along with Anglican and Dissenting Evangelicals, took up the cry in the name of humanity and Christianity. Investigations showed clearly the prevalent conditions. A boy of fourteen might work forty hours between 1 A.M. Monday and 11:30 P.M. Tuesday, and then start in again at 5 A.M. on Wednesday. Although the youngsters were often beaten to keep them awake at their work, the incidence of accidents owing to children falling into the machines while drowsy was appalling. Besides all this, the bad ventilation of the factory often led to tuberculosis, or, if that was escaped, the continual performing of one operation, frequently brought lifelong deformity. At length, in 1831 Michael Sadler introduced a reforming Ten Hour Bill, but before he could carry it through, he was defeated in the 1832 election, so Lord Ashley, later the Earl of Shaftesbury, took charge of the measure. After a bitter fight and many modifications, it became law. Applied to all textile mills except lace, it forbade those under eighteen years of age to work at night; it interdicted the employment of any children under nine years of age, except in silk, and it limited the hours of those between ten and thirteen years to nine and of those between thirteen and eighteen to twelve. Two shifts of children were permitted, but they were limited to eight hours each. Most important of all, four inspectors were appointed to see that the law was enforced.

While it is possible that this law did not make very much difference to the working classes, it was a beginning.[2] Shaftesbury was unwilling to let matters rest with the 1833 victory. In 1840 he succeeded, without effect, however, in having an investigation of nontextile industries. Much more successful was the move for an investigation of conditions in the mines. The evidence, and the picture presented of the conditions of the children and women in the mines, was appalling. Children, often under the age of seven were sitting all day in the dark, opening connecting doors, or were pulling coal wagons, while women frequently worked with picks on the coal face. The moral and intellectual results of such a life were disastrous. Consequently, a bill was passed in 1842 which banned all women and boys of less than ten years from underground work. Although the mine owners' opposition was strong, it was ineffectual. A little later (1844) came laws calling for the fencing of machinery, followed by others designed to safeguard such people as the "climbing boys," the chimney sweeps about whom Kingsley wrote in his *Water Babies*. Thus the state gradually established a system of protection for those considered too weak to care for themselves.

[2] For a discussion of the innovations of the bill, see J. H. Clapham, *Economic History of Modern Britain* (Cambridge, 1938), Vol. I, pp. 565 ff.

One particular aspect of governmental interference in industrial relations was that relating to hours of work. Every attempt to shorten hours was opposed with the argument that it would ruin British industry. In 1815 Peel had suggested a ten hour day for children. This idea soon took hold and eventually led to the passing of the 1833 Factory Reform Bill, which established the right of the government to set such limitations. By 1840 children were restricted to nine hours in the day and forty-eight in the week, while in 1844 women and children were lumped together, their day to commence at nine in the morning. Carrying the matter further, in 1847 Fielden pushed Shaftesbury's Ten Hour Bill for women and young persons through the Commons over very determined opposition. It was hoped that this would force a curtailment of the men's hours, but the hope was doomed to failure, since the shift system was permitted for children. In 1849 other limitations were applied to child employment but it was not until the next year that working children in shifts was ruled out, women being limited to a 60 hour week with Saturday afternoon off. While this was still a long work week, the hours were being controlled and gradually reduced.

From 1850 on the government gradually extended its control over other fields of industry. As a result of a complaint by textile manufacturers that they were suffering from discrimination because of these laws, similar regulations were applied to lace factories and to bleaching and dying works. In 1860 a new law was enacted limiting the age of boys in mines to twelve years or over. Then in 1867 the factory legislation was applied to all industries having units with fifty or more workers, and three years later it was extended to include all workshops. Home Office Inspectors enforcing the law were to see that the local Sanitary Authority kept a careful check upon factory health conditions. Parliament even attempted to regulate agricultural labor, protecting people who worked in gangs picking stones, turnips, or the like.

Thus by 1870, largely through government interference, the hours of work of the average laborer had been reduced while his conditions of labor had greatly improved. Some writers feel that the advancement would have come about even without government action, since, through the use of automatic machinery, the exploitation of the workers could be achieved less painfully and more unobtrusively than formerly. Some, such as J. Kuczynski, have even gone so far as to state that the employers were quite willing to see these reforms introduced, as they gave an appearance of moral progress while, all the time, they were inevitable. This theory, however, gives no explanation of the violent opposition to every change by the majority of the industrialists, nor does it explain why automatic machinery was installed after the reforms, and not before. What is more, increased production per operative through the use of the automatic machinery, does not prove increased exploitation, unless one accepts Kuczynski's view, which can be justified only with a Marxist interpretation of "exploitation." On the other hand, looking at the general condition of the laborer in 1870 as compared with what it was in 1800 or even 1830, it would seem to have improved considerably, although it still was by no means ideal.

The Government Supervision of Health and Education

Besides wage levels and conditions of work, one of the other major problems of the laborer is always that of housing. In the period 1715-1870 it was very bad in Britain. While many would try to show the superiority of life under the domestic system, the fact of the matter is that the country worker in his thatched cottage often lived in filth and squalor equal to that of the slums of Liverpool or Glasgow. By 1850, however, about half of the population had become urbanized, living around the factories in jerry-built houses. Usually poorly constructed, put up back to back, with windows few and small, they were always overcrowded. It has been estimated that in 1850 the average number of people per house was 5.5. In some cases the number was far above the average, particularly in the slums, where one might find four families in one room, separated from each other only by chalk lines on the floor.[3]

Such living conditions naturally had a very bad effect on the health of the people. Their position was made even worse, by the complete lack of sewage and water systems. Since no urban group had the responsibility of laying sewage pipes, paving the streets, or collecting garbage, if one local authority attempted to take action, it usually came into conflict with some other jurisdiction. The result was that garbage, ashes, and other refuse were frequently dumped into nearby vacant lots. If the sewage pipes were actually laid, they usually ran into open ponds or poured their filth into the rivers from which the people drew their drinking and washing water. Little provision was made for the piping of water to the houses of the people, so much of it had to be carried or to be

---

[3] In 1840 in Liverpool 39,000 people were living in 7,800 cellars. P. Gregg, *A Social and Economic History of Britain* (London, 1950), pp. 192 f.

bought from a carrier. Under such circumstances, it is not strange that the people did not wash frequently. Thus, down to 1850 the actual living conditions of the working classes were both uncomfortable and extremely unsanitary. It was no wonder, therefore, that plagues of cholera, typhoid, and the like repeatedly swept through the cities, carrying off a large part of the inhabitants. In Manchester it has been reckoned that the average expectation of life for the laborer was 17 years. A short life, but not a very merry one!

To meet the need for better living conditions, as early as 1840 the government began to take an interest in sanitation. A commission report on the health of towns was prepared in that year, but nothing much was done until the 1847 cholera epidemic. In 1848 a Public Health Act set up commissioners who could give permission to municipalities to take the necessary precautions for safeguarding public health. The difficulty was that their powers were only permissive, except in special cases of unusually high mortality. While some 200 towns availed themselves of powers given in the act, many did not. Vested interests were opposed to improvements, while the public resented being forcibly scrubbed into good health. Consequently, the Board was abolished in 1854. However, from 1855 on the Metropolitan Board of Works began to employ its recently acquired wide powers and authority to develop the London drainage system. The Local Government Act of 1858 gave all local authorities similar increased powers of control. By an Act of 1866 these were made mandatory. If the local authorities refused to carry out their duties, the Home Secretary could force them to provide proper sewage systems and water supplies. The outcome of this was that by 1870 the death rate was down to about twenty in the thousand and the expectation of life had greatly increased. Coupled with attempts to prevent the adulteration of food, all these improvements tended to raise the laborers' standard of living.

Just one more thing should be said about state interference in the economic and social life of the period. Education also became the interest of the government, which prior to 1833 took no part in the matter, considering it to be a private affair. Thus different types of schools grew up, some for the middle class and others, of a cheaper variety, for the workers. It was to the latter that the government in 1833 made its first educational grant, of £20,000. By 1839 the amount paid was £30,000, allocated on the advice of government inspectors. Twenty years later the sum expended on education had reached £813,000, all being distributed through private schools. Attempts were also made to have all the young factory workers provided with educational facilities, but as the schools were entirely voluntary, nothing much was accomplished. Finally, in 1870 the government introduced a bill which endeavored to provide universal education. Wherever possible, it was to operate through private schools run either by the Church of England or the Dissenters. If there were no such schools in the district, the school boards could establish their own. The local boards also had the right to determine whether education was to be compulsory and whether it was to be free. In this way instruction was extended to the working classes, a measure considered very necessary, since in 1867 skilled labor had received the vote.

Thus, by 1870 the economic developments had succeeded in greatly altering the whole social structure. Industrialism was supreme in Britain, bringing numerous intellectual, social and political changes. Materialism grew apace among all classes. Social divisions became deeper and wider, while everyone sought increasingly for freedom to do as he pleased. It was in accordance with the philosophy of laissez faire that the trading element sought free trade, the laborer desired labor and factory legislation, and the industrialists, with all their strength, opposed government interference in industry. For the same reason the middle class sought and gained the vote in 1832, a privilege attained by urban labor in 1867. By 1870 Britain had reached the peak of her economic development, dominating the world like an economic master. The problem then was: could she keep that position? At the same time, she had to ask herself: could she continue to press her economic social and political reforms? These were some of the problems with which she had had to wrestle during the succeeding seventy years.

Chapter 18

GREAT BRITAIN IN THE CHANGING WORLD ECONOMY

THE PERIOD between 1870 and 1914 saw a radical change in Great Britain's economic position. In 1870 she ruled the economy of the world. She was the biggest manufacturer, the biggest exporter, the biggest investor, and the biggest carrier the world had ever known. By 1914 this was all changed. While she was still a great economic power, while her production had risen greatly and her exports were much increased over 1870, she was no longer the dominant power of forty years earlier. In some respects both United States and Germany had surpassed her. Indeed, she was even importing the manufactures of those two industrially young countries. At the same time, others, such as France, Japan, and India, were creeping up on her. They were entering her markets and stealing her customers. An indication of something of Britain's position is also given in the increasing excess of imports over exports which was appearing. By 1914 Great Britain was faced with serious economic problems, most of them arising out of her changed position in the economic world.

The fundamental cause of this change would seem to be the spread of industrialization beyond Britain's borders. Prior to 1870 Great Britain was really the only nation which was a highly developed industrial power. Other nations, however, soon began to desire to follow her example, an ambition aided by British investors who were ready to finance railroads, factories, and mines in the undeveloped countries. With money received from the British investor British machinery was purchased for these industrial developments. This, in turn, produced profits for those who had loaned their money, and so the financier, the merchant, and the industrialist reaped a plentiful harvest. But while the British were taking their large profits, they were also preparing trouble for themselves. As these nations developed industrially, so they tended to become competitors of Great Britain, thus creating for her the

greatest problem she had to face during the last quarter of the nineteenth and the first decade of the twentieth centuries.

The Rise of Great Britain's Competitors

The new economic powers came to the problem of industrialization with knowledge gained from British example and British mis-
takes. While the older country had to develop its industries by
trial-and-error, they could use British experience to avoid pitfalls
and thus make short cuts. Because of the lateness of their rise, they
also had the advantage of being able to use the newest British
machinery, which a good many British manufacturers could not
afford because of the large sums invested in what were becoming
obsolete methods and processes. Another advantage was that these
young countries, because of their very youth, were more conscious
of themselves, were more nationalistic. They felt that they had to
take every means possible to catch up with the more mature British
economy. This frequently meant government aid of various types.
Finally, they were usually helped by a rapidly expanding population,
which provided a growing domestic market for industrial goods,
as well as a rapidly increasing labor force.[1] Consequently they were
able to make very rapid strides and in some cases within thirty years
to outdistance Great Britain herself.

The period 1868-73 was important because it was during these
years that a great change took place in the United States, Germany,
and France. In the United States a tremendous westward expansion had come in the wake of recovery from the Civil War, giving
impetus to investment and production. Within the same five years
Germany became a united empire. The influx of the 5 billion
francs taken from France as reparation after the Franco-Prussian
War (1870-71) provided the funds for a very considerable industrial expansion. Along with the money came an equally important
industrial asset, namely, the rich French lands of Alsace-Lorraine,
supplying Germany with both deposits of iron ore and a well-developed textile industry. Despite her losses in the war, France, on the
other hand, was also in a better position. With a more democratic
government demanding less in taxation and giving more political

[1] Population figures:

	1870	1914
Germany	38.5 millions	64.9 millions
France	36.4	39.6
U.S.A.	38.2	91.9
Great Britain	24	40.7

stability, she was able to devote herself to economic expansion, an important point, particularly as she was now concentrating on the amassing and exploiting of an empire both in Africa and Asia. For these reasons, by 1873 all three nations were prepared to enter the race for industrial supremacy.

One asset which both the Americans and the Germans possessed was an abundant supply of raw materials, especially of foodstuffs. The United States, with her vast untouched prairie lands only just coming into use, was able not only to provide all that she needed for herself but also to export large quantities, principally to Britain.[2] While not in quite such a good position, Germany was almost as well off. In 1912 it was estimated that she needed to import only 15 per cent of her grain and 7 per cent of her meat. Thus, food was not a worry. To become strong industrially, however, a nation needs raw materials for manufacture: coal, iron, and cotton, as well as many others. In all these commodities the United States was very rich, while Germany fell behind her only in cotton growing. Coal and iron were plentiful in both countries; indeed, much more plentiful than they ever had been in Great Britain. Along with these, they possessed large quantities of potash and other necessary commodities. Therefore, neither the United States nor Germany (except for cotton) had to look abroad for raw materials with which to supply their own industries. Both were, to a large extent, self-sufficient.

From what has been said, it was to be expected that one of the first phases of the industrial development would be a spectacular growth of the iron and steel industry. World pig iron production rose from 11.8 million tons in 1870 to 64.7 million tons in 1910, while, at the same time, that of steel increased from 510,000 to 59.3 million tons. In this the United States led the way, raising her pig iron manufacture from 1.6 million tons in 1870 to 27.3 million in 1910, with a corresponding increase in steel from 39 tons to about 26 million tons. During the same period Germany experienced a similar trend, pig iron jumping from 1.2 million to 12.9 million tons and steel from 1.1 million tons to over 13 million tons. While Britain had commenced in 1870 with a very considerable advantage, by 1910 the United States was producing 170 per cent more pig iron and 400 per cent more steel. The comparable percentages for Germany were 30 per cent and 85 per cent. Thus, by

[2] Britain's average annual imports of wheat rose from 106.2 million bushels in 1870-80, to 215.7 million in 1901-14, most of it coming from the United States. E. L. Bogart, *The Economic History of Europe, 1760-1939*, p. 262.

1910 Britain had been largely surpassed in the field which had been her specialty.

In the production of textiles Britain had not been left quite so far behind. Consumption of cotton in American manufacture jumped from 893 million pounds in 1870 to 4,273 million in 1908, while for the whole of the continent of Europe it rose from 1,570 million to 5,720 million pounds. In this manufacture Germany was definitely the leader. Meanwhile, in Britain the increase had only been from 2,410 million pounds to 3,690 million. It must, however, be kept in mind that Britain concentrated upon the finer types of cotton, in which field she was still well ahead of any of her competitors. Yet, despite this, in total production she was again lagging behind.

One of the primary reasons for this great industrial expansion, in both Germany and United States was that the very latest machinery and techniques were being employed. With a great demand in the domestic market for their goods, but with only a small body of skilled labor, they had to turn wherever possible to labor-saving devices. Inventiveness was stressed. This resulted in all sorts of new technical improvements which helped to speed the wheels of industry and lower costs. Although at the beginning of the period the machinery and machine tools came largely from Great Britain, by 1900 both countries were producing most of their own. Moreover, they were developing new industries. Germany was particularly active in the chemical and electrical fields. She had a virtual monopoly of the production of coal-tar dyes and other coal-tar products such as aspirin. By 1913 she produced about one third of the world's electrical equipment, her exports of such commodities amounting to approximately one half that of the world's total. The United States also was very much interested in electrical production, but at the same time went in for such manufactures as sewing machines and typewriters, of which she sent over £4 million worth to Britain in 1901. She even attempted to catch up with Britain in the weaving of fine worsteds. Thus, not only in Britain's staple industries was the competition becoming keen, but new industries were also being developed and expanded.

Some indication of the total competition which faced Britain is given in the figures of the other countries' increasing output. Between 1850 and 1914 the value of American manufactures grew from $1 billion to over $20 billion. While this surprising increase in terms of money is partially owing to inflation, it has been estimated that the real increase was about eighteen fold. In comparison with the United States, German production in 1914 could be reckoned at over $12 billion, while Britain's hardly reached to the $10 billion mark. Thus, by 1914 the latter was definitely outclassed by her two principal rivals.

But the problem was not merely in the field of industrial production. Britain was likewise facing growing competition in investment. With their increasing wealth, Germany, the United States, and France were coming to the position where they were able to make loans by investing in foreign stocks and bonds. For instance, by 1900 American financiers' loans abroad were estimated at the high figure of $100 million. These investments were principally in foreign government and municipal bonds, although continental shipping and commercial concerns were also included. At the same time they were buying up American bonds and stocks held in Europe. Germany, attempting to do much the same thing, totaled its foreign investments in 1914 at about $8 billion. Under the leadership of their various banking houses, France and Belgium were also active, although to a lesser extent.

In the field of industrial exports, as over against capital exports, Germany was of much greater importance than the United States, since the latter country consumed about 90 per cent of her own products. Germany, however, had a much larger share of her manufactures for sale, the value of her trade rising from 5,600 million marks in 1872 to 22,000 million marks in 1912. During that period her exports mounted in value from 2,318 million marks to almost 11,000 million marks, the value of the manufactures included in these sums having increased seven times. What is even more significant, the manufactures were nearly all in direct competition with those of Great Britain: iron and steel goods, chemicals, drugs, cottons, woolens, machinery, and coal. Belgium, with her expanding heavy industries, was also growing as a rival, but not as noticeably as was Germany. France, on the other hand, was concentrating primarily on luxury goods which gave little competition to British produce. Consequently, by 1914 Germany was second only to Britain as the world's greatest exporter of manufactures.

In the carrying trade Britain was for a large part of the nineteenth century absolutely supreme and down to 1914 continued to be predominant. However the shipbuilding industry was being accelerated in both Belgium and Germany, with the result that the German merchant marine especially, with considerable government help, was growing rapidly. In 1871 Germany had a total shipping of 982,355 tons, of which over 900,000 tons were sailing vessels. By 1910 this situation had changed radically, the total tonnage now coming to almost 3 million, with well over 2¼ million driven by steam. Although Germany was by no means near the figure of British tonnage, nevertheless, she was beginning to catch up on her great competitor.

Probably the most characteristic feature of the economic development in both the United States and Germany was the trend towards big business. This was true in the case of individual concerns and also of industries as a whole. For instance, between 1895 and 1907 the number of German textile factories decreased in number by 50 per cent, while the number of people employed in textile production increased 100 per cent. In 1907 there were in Germany more than 1400 establishments employing more than 1000 persons, one combine having 70,000 on the payroll. By 1909 Germany had more than 200 concerns with a capital valuation of over 10 million marks, the biggest being the Krupp Corporation, capitalized at 180 million marks. In the United States the average manufacturing plant between 1850 and 1910 multiplied its capitalization thirty-nine times, its wage earners seven times, and its production nineteen times.

Along with the increased size of the individual unit went the growth of industrial combinations. In Germany there appeared cartels, based upon agreements between producers for the purpose of controlling the market either for purchasing raw materials or for the selling of products. This included also price fixing and sometimes even the allocation of orders. The system depended primarily upon the cutting of costs to a minimum. To facilitate this there appeared *konzerns*, which were both vertical and horizontal combines, to control the whole process, say, of iron manufacture, from the coal and iron mines to the finished rifle, needle, or stove. In the United States one finds the same sort of thing was going on: pools, including agreements as to rates, territory, and prices; trusts, in which the stockholders of a number of companies gave a group of trustees the controlling interests in their companies; and holding companies, which had purchased a majority of shares in many different concerns. The Standard Oil Company was one of the best examples of a trust; the United States Steel, with a capitalization of $682 millions, of a holding company. In all these cases the objective was that of gaining a monopoly of the market in order that costs might be cut while profits were maintained at a high level.

Despite opposition to this growth of monopolies in the United States, government policy in America as well as Germany actually favored them. The rise of tariff walls in many countries, but particularly in those trying to build up their industries, was very important. In 1861 the Morrill Tariff began the American policy of high duties. By 1897 American tariffs stood at 57 per cent, a rate which was pushed even higher by the Payne-Aldrich Act in 1909. From 1879 on, Germany also tended towards protection. Although the provision of the "most-favored-nation" clause, guaranteeing favorable treatment to other countries willing to give her special concessions, tended to mitigate the effects of her tariffs, by 1914 her economy was surrounded by a high wall. France also sought tariff protection after 1881, setting up an average rate of 24 per cent, which was gradually pushed higher because of pressure from various economic interests. It was behind these tariff walls that the big combines, trusts, cartels, and syndicates were able to develop. Without foreign competition they could charge such high prices and make such large profits on the home market that they could afford to undercut their competitors on the world market by selling below cost.[3]

Monopolies and tariffs, however, would not have been effective had it not been for the enterprising character of the businessmen in these countries. Faced with the preponderance of Great Britain in the world market, they had to be enterprising or fail. The Germans, in particular, studied their customers' needs, trained their travelers in any languages which might be useful, gave them courses in commercial law, and also attempted to attract interest by packaging their goods with the idea of an appeal to the eye. German banks gave long-term credits to foreign customers, the government gave special rates to export goods on the government railways, and everything was done to forward the export trade. Helped on by a high tariff wall and a virtual monopoly of the home market, the German export industries were able to expand their sales at an astonishing rate.

One other factor in this growth of German, French, and American economies was the new interest manifested in colonies. In 1870 Great Britain had by far the largest colonial empire, and by 1914 she was still well ahead of all others. Yet in the intervening years France had gathered up an empire of 4 million square miles with 62.4 million inhabitants, Germany had acquired ten colonies covering 1.2 million square miles and 13.1 million inhabitants, and Italy had four colonies with 591,000 square miles and 1.4 million inhabitants. While the United States had not gone in for "old world" imperialism, by 1914 she held Porto Rico (now Puerto Rico), the Panama Canal Zone, the Hawaiian Islands, the Philippines, and a number of smaller islands in the Pacific. What was

[3] See page 348.

even more important, she was attempting to dominate South and Central American markets by swinging them into her economic orbit. In fact, she had even been willing to risk a war with Great Britain to prevent the latter from collecting debts and settling boundary disputes with Venezuela by force of arms. By these nations, colonies were regarded as their own special preserves of raw materials and markets. In fact, that was the primary reason for their existence. Consequently, as these colonial areas were taken over, Britain found that her economic interests in them were curtailed and limited in favor of the businessmen of the country in possession.

The outcome of all these various factors working together was an enormous growth of trade and commerce altogether apart from Britain. If one looks first at the United States, he finds that while her exports in 1870 stood at $392.7 million and her imports at $453.9 million; by 1910 they had climbed to $1,744.9 million and $1,556.9 million respectively. In 1870, 83.3 per cent of her exports were agricultural goods, but by 1900 these had dropped to 60.9 per cent, while in 1910 Europe was taking 70 per cent of all American exports. France had also increased her foreign trade by about three times in the forty years under consideration. But, from Britain's point of view, the German development was by far the most dangerous, for she had experienced a great trade expansion. In 1870 her imports had been worth 3,258 million marks and her exports 2,318 million marks, which figures expanded by 1913 to 11,366 and 10,882 million marks respectively. Foreign countries were well on the way to becoming independent of Britain's trade and industry, thereby posing a serious threat to her predominance.

To see the actual situation in summary, it is necessary to look at it in terms of percentages. Between 1870 and 1913 world trade had increased in value 173 per cent. Britain's share of this, however, had dropped from 23 per cent to 17 per cent while the United States had increased hers from 10 per cent to 15 per cent and Germany hers from 9 per cent to 12 per cent. This is perhaps the best indication which can be given of Britain's changed position in the world's economy. Although her actual trade had risen greatly in money value, relative to other nations she was not doing as well in 1914 as she had been in 1870.

Great Britain and Her Competitors

To say that Britain was in 1914, because of new competition, in a different economic position from that which she held in 1870 does not give the whole story. How was it that the competitors were able to do so well despite Britain's very great head start? What effect did this growing competition have upon Britain's own internal economy and her foreign trade? These questions must be answered before it will be possible to understand the revolution which took place in Britain's economic standing in the world market.

Fundamental to the change was the fact that Britain now had to compete with countries which possessed much greater supplies of raw materials. While she still had large deposits of coal, they were harder to mine; iron ore was beginning to run out and other metals, such as copper, zinc, and nickel, were practically nonexistent in the country. She was also obliged to import all her raw cotton and most of her raw wool. On top of all this, she was not nearly self-sufficing in food-stuffs, being obliged to bring them from far-distant lands, America and Australasia. Thus, to a much greater extent than her competitors, she was dependent upon imports if she would export. This obliged her, in turn, to cling to free trade as long as possible, but the time would eventually come when here also there would have to be a change. Between 1870 and 1914, however, no modification in point of view took place. Free trade brought cheap raw materials, and cheap raw materials and food-stuffs Britain had to have.

As important as the need for raw materials was the need for a change in the attitude of the British manufacturers and exporters. From 1825 to 1870 they had dominated the world of industry and trade. They had not been obliged to consider their customers' wishes and desires, because if the customer did not accept what he was offered he would have to go without. Moreover, the customer had to buy it at the seller's price and terms and to receive it packaged according to the pleasure of the British agent. Such an attitude led to complete self-complacency on the part of the British businessman. Everybody knew and recognized that Britain produced the best goods which could be obtained. Therefore, there was no need to adopt the new techniques of the Germans and Americans, nor was it necessary to accept small orders, give long credits, conform to changes in style or demand, or pay for expensive representatives to travel around the world seeking customers. A well-illustrated folder in the English language was all that was necessary. British superior workmanship and honesty would counteract all the other attractions offered by competitors. It was this supreme self-satisfaction and complete disregard of its rivals which was so characteristic of and so disastrous to British foreign commerce. British consuls all over the world were complaining bitterly about this attitude. Manufacturers would not exert themselves to hunt for business, nor would they endeavor to meet the needs of the market. Instead, they had a "take-it-or-leave-it" attitude which lost them much of their trade. This outlook, which was very common, must always be kept in mind when we are thinking of how Britain's competitors crept up on her in the race for world markets.

The period between 1873 and 1896 has been known as "The Great Depression." The peculiar thing about it is, however, that in some ways it was a time of considerable expansion in certain quarters. For one thing, it saw a very rapid economic advance in Germany and United States, so for them the "Depression" was not very noticeable. What is more, in many ways it was a time of improvement for British industry. Although prices fell to a considerably lower level, wages did not have the same experience, so the wage earner obtained a real increase in his income. Similarly, in industrial production, it was noticeable that average output increased from £69.3 per person (1870-76) to £105.4 per person (1894-1903).

Why then call it a period of depression? The answer would seem to be that the British industrial and trading classes during this period experienced their first real recession in fifty years. Prices fell without a compensating increase in volume of sales. Exports, standing at £256.25 million in 1872, had by 1879 dropped to £191.5 million, thereafter increasing only enough to keep the manufacturers from complaining of "overproduction." This situation, in turn, resulted in a considerable reduction in profits, helping to bring about three definite periods of depression: 1872-79, 1883-86, and 1890-96. Interspersed with years of buoyancy these periods affected the country as a whole. During the "down" periods Britain experienced fairly heavy unemployment, an increase in business failures, and a contraction of bank credit. There was, however, no catastrophic break in the economy, so the time was one of stagnation rather than of actual depression.

The question then arises as to the reasons for this stagnation of prices and profits. There were a good many. One was that British overseas investment, which formerly had been very active, now tended to taper off. The Franco-Prussian War (1870-71) began a period of political instability in Europe which had its counterpart in America. Consequently, British investors were somewhat reluctant to risk their money in projects which might be wiped out through political upheavals. At the same time, overinvestment both at home and abroad before 1873, had fostered such industrial expansion that the result was overproduction in the following years. All this brought economic fluctuations which forced a decline in profits.

The most potent factor in Britain's difficulties, however, was that for the first time in her history Great Britain really faced strong industrial rivals. While in their earlier days the Germans and the Americans were dependent upon Britain for such things as machinery, railway rails, and rolling stock, by 1880 they were beginning to produce these in their own factories. They no longer needed British help. Similarly, other countries who were now able to meet part, but not all, of their own requirements were becoming limited markets, where Britain could sell decreasing quantities of steel and iron goods. But not only were newly industrialized countries able to forego British goods, they were tending to lose interest in British investment. As their production increased, the company promoters, the governments, and other bodies needing money more frequently turned to their own financial institutions rather than to London. Consequently, Britain from 1873 to 1896 was losing the opportunity to sell and invest in her old markets.

It was not, however, merely a matter of the loss of old markets. The countries which were rising: Germany, France, Belgium and the United States, with their neo-mercantilist ideas, were endeavoring to close new markets to the British. These countries, seeking for both raw materials and buyers for their manufactures, were inclined, by means of tariffs and other restrictions, to keep British goods not only out of the home countries, but also out of their colonies. Therefore, if Britain was to expand economically, she must turn in other directions, either to her own empire or to non-colonial countries still interested in British commodities.

In all this procession of difficulties the British businessman was given very little help by the state. According to the views of laissez faire, the government which ruled best was the one which ruled least. It was only under considerable pressure, therefore, that the government in 1887 introduced the Merchandizing Marks Act, which promised to invoke penalties against foreign firms forging British trademarks. As a consequence of this step being taken, the foreign customer who had been buying German or American goods through a British agent, on discovering where the goods were made, frequently went directly to the foreign producer. In this way the act helped to short-circuit the British entrepôt trade which was one of the reasons why between 1870 and 1896 the value of re-exports remained stationary. It was not until 1908 that holders of patents in Britain were forced either to produce in the country or to license others to do so. Prior to this Germans had taken out patents in

Britain for industrial processes but had refused to allow any production by means of these processes except in their own factories in Germany. This had forced Britain to "buy German." Thus it was only in very unusual circumstances that the government ever felt that it could and should do something to control trade.

As a result of this situation, there was a change in the direction of Britain's trade and investment. Since it was becoming increasingly difficult to sell goods to the developed countries, their colonies and the lands within their spheres of influence, the British were limited to investing in home and empire industries and in the noncolonial semicivilized areas. Both lines of action were followed. There was considerable investment in British industries after 1880, although many believed that it led to further overproduction. The solution, therefore, seemed to be a program of investment in South Africa, Australasia, and South America. One difficulty was, however, that such a plan did not bring in quick returns. Moreover, in the early days it concentrated on the financing of the production of raw materials which only gradually created a demand for manufactures. Consequently, not until the middle nineties did the investments of the eighties begin to provide a market for manufactured goods such as machinery and railway supplies. Thus, while exports of manufactures to India rose 65 per cent and to Australasia 95 per cent between 1885 and 1911, those to the United States showed a slight decline. In the case of Germany, on the other hand, although exports showed a rise from £16 million to £39 million, these were offset by British purchases of German goods which grew from £25 million to £43 million. The pattern of British trade was being completely altered, a matter of no little significance, since it took Britain some time to adapt herself to the new situation. It was during the period of adaptation that Britain experienced the so-called Great Depression.

One other factor which has been stressed by a number of writers was the world gold situation. Between 1870 and 1890 precious metal seems to have been scarce, a fact which, it has been held, curtailed financial activity. But when one considers the rapid expansion of the credit system which took place during these two decades, this is a little hard to accept, for gold was no longer an absolute necessity in financial transactions. It may be, however, that it is correct to say that discovery in the 1890's of gold in large quantities in South Africa and Australia helped to stimulate world economic activity. Gold mining boomed, not only furnishing large supplies of the metal, but also extending opportunities for investment which promised quick returns. Much of the gold which was dug, it is true, was either hoarded in lands such as India or disappeared into the vaults of countries going onto the gold standard, but the enlarged supplies, along with the effort of winning them, no doubt did influence the economic situation. With more gold in use and with gold mining stimulating investment, prices began to climb, demand for goods became stronger, and world economic activity increased.

In Great Britain from 1896 on, there was an ever-quickening tempo of activity. Foreign investment, which had been gradually building up, was now yielding a rising income to pay either for imports or to be used for reinvestment.[4] The result was a renewed demand for British goods in the newer lands, encouraging production and increasing employment. Thus after 1896 the economic outlook for Britain began to brighten.

During the period from 1896 down to the Great War, Britain actually had a considerable economic boom. There were recessions and periods of stagnation, but, on a general view, there was a real acceleration of activity. Her exports, rising from a yearly average of £239 million between 1895 and 1899, reached £453 million in 1910, while imports followed the same trend, climbing from £452 million to £679 million. Textile exports increased also, particularly cottons, which stood at £69.3 million in 1896 and at £127 million in 1913. Woolens, on the other hand, rose only from £27 million to £31.5 million. Iron and steel exports were up about 90 per cent in 1910, and machinery exports, a little over 100 per cent. The sale of new ships also grew during the period by 100,000 tons a year. At the same time, there were other industries which were not doing so well; railway supplies, for instance, were experiencing a considerable fall in demand. Moreover many of the goods sold abroad, such as machine tools, cotton machinery, and the like, were of the type which would tend to build up Britain's rivals. These were the goods purchased especially by the Germans and the Japanese. Thus, despite trade expansion, there was uneasiness on the part of many that perhaps all was not well.

To others, however, any uneasiness was quite unwarranted. Trade was expanding and revenues and investment were increasing, so all had to be well. The fact of the matter was, however, that, despite the apparent improvement, the situation was actually becoming worse. The factors which had caused the Great Depression were still present. There was the greater pressure of foreign competition in the world market. American, and notably German, selling

---

[4] C. K. Hobson, *The Export of Capital* (London, 1914), p. 200, estimates that the increase of income from abroad rose from £49.5 million in 1890 and to £166 million in 1910.

methods were very much ahead of those of the British merchant. While the British were still sending out well-printed folders, the Germans were being represented by persuasive commercial travelers who succeeded in taking over a considerable number of Britain's foreign customers. With combines, syndicates, and trusts, the Americans and Germans were prepared and able to undercut the prices of the British producer. For instance, in 1904 steel joists manufactured in Germany at 89 marks and selling on the home market for 95 marks were being offered in Antwerp f.o.b. at 82½ marks less 2½%. At the same time, billets of pig iron were being produced in Pittsburgh for $19.50 (81s. 2d.) a ton, sold on the home market at $24 (100s.) and delivered at a British port at 75s. ($18). The British scorned such methods but, because of high costs and lack of tariff protection, were unable to meet them. Foreign tariffs were also going higher and higher. The consequence was that Americans, and to a greater extent Germans, were beginning to cut into Britain's markets, competing strongly for her customers in India, Canada, the West Indies, Australasia, Japan, and South America. But what was even worse, by 1900 they were beginning to invade Britain herself. The American Tobacco Company tried to monopolize the British market but was beaten off by a British combine, the result being a division of the world into spheres of influence. Other industries were not so fortunate, and they were forced to face increasing competition.

Added to this, the procurement of raw materials was becoming more difficult and costly. With a growing demand in the manufacturing countries, the prices of these goods were being forced upwards. Along with this, manufacturing costs in Britain were relatively higher than in Germany, America, or Belgium. These countries were using newer and more efficient machinery, a possibility not readily available to the British producer owing to his heavy investments in now obsolete equipment and the strong objection of the trade-unions to labor-saving devices, obstacles unknown to the continental competitor. For these reasons, Britain found it difficult to stand up against the competition from without. While, on one hand, her raw materials cost her more, on the other, she had to sell her manufactures at a price considerably enhanced because she was not producing efficiently enough to make up the difference.[5]

[5] As an example of declining efficiency, the production of coal per man in the British coal pits fell from 403 tons per annum to 309 tons. Thus, although output rose, so did the costs. J. H. Clapham, *Economic History of Modern Britain* (Cambridge, 1938), Vol. III, p. 60.

Although Britain was developing and expanding her trade after 1896, she was not doing so nearly as rapidly as Germany and the United States. Her trade between 1880 and 1913, despite a 200 per cent increase in value, fell by 20 per cent in proportion to the world total, which was now three times the 1880 volume. The United States, on the other hand, increased her share of world trade by 50 per cent, and Germany by 33⅓ per cent. Perhaps a few added figures will give even greater clarity to the picture. A comparison of export figures in millions of pounds is as follows:

Annual Average	United Kingdom	Germany	United States	France
1880-84	234	153	165	138
1885-89	226	151	146	132
1890-94	234	153	185	137
1895-99	238	181	213	144 [6]

Coupled with this, Britain was finding that while her trade with Germany, for instance, was continuing to grow, she was selling an ever larger amount of raw materials and half-finished goods. If the goods were finished, they were usually of the machine tool category, while Germany, at the same time, was sending to her a growing quantity of fully manufactured consumer goods. Industrially and commercially Britain was not advancing at a pace comparable with that of her rivals.

Another portion of this picture lies in the relationship between Britain's imports and exports. The annual average exports for the years 1885-89 stood at £226 million, while the imports were £380 million. By 1905 the exports had increased to £329 million, a rise of £103 million. The imports, on the other hand, had jumped from £380 million to £560 million, a difference of £160 million. In 1911 the same disproportionate increase was again shown: exports £453 million, and imports £679 million. Britain was able to pay her way under these circumstances only because of the money income derived from investments, shipping charges, commissions, insurance, banking, and government services: an income standing at £91.5 million in 1890, and twenty years later, at £166 million. According to Hobson's estimate, the surplus from this source, after deducting the adverse balance of trade was £8.9 million in 1890. In 1900 it had risen to £67.8 million, reaching a peak of £81 million in 1904 and falling again to £15.2 million by 1910. Thus, it was primarily by means of her investments and services that Britain was able to main-

[6] H. L. Beales, "The Great Depression in Industry and Trade," *Economic History Review* (1934-35), Vol. V, p. 73.

tain a narrow margin of profit after meeting her bills for raw materials.

There was considerable difference of opinion in Britain over the country's economic position. Some felt it to be an entirely satisfactory condition of affairs, while others were very worried. Britain's loss of foreign markets and her increasingly adverse balance of trade placed her in the position where she was dependent for economic survival upon the income derived from international services and foreign investments. This was extremely dangerous. Moreover, since much of her export was in the form of coal, amounting in 1913 to 10 per cent (by value) of the total, she was selling a raw material vital to her industrial survival. In the same way, while her machinery exports in the form of gold dredges and the like did not equip possible rivals, the sale of cotton machinery to Japan and of machine tools to Germany helped to build up competitors who were even then causing trouble. In addition, as an industry, rivals had already appeared who, given enough time, would be able to compete also in offering services to the world. In fact, this was now taking place in the competition offered by German merchant shipping, which between 1890 and 1913 was partially responsible for the decrease from 50 per cent to 40 per cent in Britain's share of the world's carrying trade. To add to all this, if Britain were suddenly faced with an expensive war, she might lose much of her merchant navy, or she might have to sell large amounts of her foreign securities. As this would take a big slice out of her income from foreign sources, she would then be faced with the possibility of national economic disaster.

Many suggestions were offered for the solution of this pressing problem. One was that the British manufacturer should improve his methods of production and merchandising. The British consuls in various foreign ports were almost unanimous on this point, forever telling the exporters that they must remember that they were now facing heavy competition. One industrialist, Joseph Chamberlain of Birmingham, took the advice, and by lowering the cost of manufacturing his screw nails, as well as by standardizing them and packaging them attractively, he succeeded in making considerable inroads into the European hardware market. But few followed his example. Instead, there was a growing demand that the government should do more to help. It was urged that the consuls might give greater aid, and, to the consternation of the aristocratic Foreign Office it was even suggested that diplomats should be instructed to apply pressure on foreign governments to obtain contracts for British interests.

Although these ideas caused some ineffective discussion, there was one proposal which resulted in violent controversy without obtaining any real success. This was the suggestion that Britain should make use of tariffs. Although free trade had dominated the thinking of the commercial part of the country from 1846 to about 1885, the idea of "protection" had never completely died out. Consequently, when new tariffs began to rise on all sides, many felt that Britain should follow the same procedure, if only for bargaining purposes. Such was the theme of the Fair Trade Association, organized in the 1880's. The real leader of the protectionist group, however, was Joseph Chamberlain, Birmingham industrialist, radical, and imperialist. Having split the Liberal party in 1886 on the subject of Irish Home Rule, he joined the Conservatives, whom he almost split over protection. It was only the astuteness of J. Arthur Balfour which prevented this denouément. During the nineties and the first decade of our own century the controversy raged. Chamberlain wished for an imperial customs union which would bring free trade within the Empire, largely to the advantage of the British producer. Labor opposed this, since it was held that it would raise the price of food. The dominions were also lukewarm, since it would expose their infant industries to British competition. Many others were against it simply because protectionism was economic heresy. The real reason that the agitation collapsed, however, would seem to have been that, because of the expanding trade, industry was fully occupied. Nobody among the Liberals felt that tariffs were necessary, and since they were in power, nothing was done.

Thus, at the commencement of Germany's second war on France (1914) Britain was in a very different economic position from that which she held at the beginning of the Franco-Prussian War. While she still had by far the largest trade of any country in the world, carried half the world's commerce in two fifths of the world's ships, and received an increasing revenue from her foreign investments, her position in the world market had deteriorated seriously. No longer "the workshop of the world," she was finding great difficulty in keeping up the pace set by her younger German and American competitors. What really helped her along at this period were her invisible exports of services and capital which brought in good returns. In a sense, however, the revenues from these sources were like an old age pension. Should they have to be liquidated, should the companies paying fail, or should there be a drastic change in the value of money, disaster might result. This in 1914 was Britain's position, seen by some, but understood by few: a situation which was soon to become only too well-known. Before continuing this part of the story, however, it will be necessary to examine more closely certain aspects of the British economy in the years preceding World War I.

Chapter 19

BRITISH AGRICULTURE IN DECLINE

PART of the changed economic position of Great Britain between 1870 and 1914 is revealed in the story of what happened to her farmers. They had reached the peak of their prosperity by 1870, the year which was the climax of "high farming," and from then on there came a downward trend. The Franco-Prussian War's (1870-71) curtailment of European food production had kept British prices high, but once the war came to an end, the situation changed. Between the years 1872 and 1896, as shown in the last chapter, there was a country-wide depression. Although agriculture did not feel its effects at first, from 1875 to 1884 farming was in a trough. There was some recovery during the following six years, but from 1890 to 1894 the position of agriculture again began to grow worse, no improvement being really noticeable until about 1896. From then on there was a gradual rise in agricultural prosperity until the outbreak of World War I. Even by that date, however, the farmer was in a much less favorable position than he had been in 1870. British farming by 1914 had become a secondary industry, relatively unimportant in the country's economy.

The Change in Agriculture

Probably the clearest indication of what was happening to the farmer can be seen in the history of agricultural income. Bogart has estimated that between 1860 and 1894 wheat dropped in price from $1.90 to 70 cents a bushel.[1] By 1895 it was selling in Britain at around 23s. a quarter, the lowest price in one hundred and fifty years. The 1895 price of wheat represented a decline since 1870 of 50 per cent, paralleled by a fall in barley of 39 per cent and in oats of 38 per cent, while meat and animal products such as butter went

[1] E. Bogart, *Economic History of Europe* (New York, 1942), p. 261.

353

down about 25 per cent. The natural consequence of this situation was that the tenant farmers found it increasingly hard to pay the high rents of the late 1860's, and even those who owned their own lands were faced with a relatively higher demand for rates and taxes which could not now be met from a steadily declining income. The Duke of Richmond's Commission, which sat from 1879-82, estimated that rents in England and Wales dropped about £5.5 million in four years. A new Royal Commission investigating conditions in the 1890's pointed out that in thirteen years eight estates in Essex had had their rents reduced by 52.6 per cent, while eleven in Lincolnshire averaged a decline of 48 per cent, one actually having dropped 67½ per cent during the same period. Usually the English landlords were slower in lowering rents than were their counterparts in Scotland. Consequently, their tenants were in continual difficulties. In Scotland the rents were cut before the tenants were bankrupted, which probably explains why the decrease in Scotland was only between 25 and 30 per cent. All told, it was estimated that British agricultural income between 1876 and 1886 fell by £42.8 million.

From 1896 onwards prices began to rise slowly, bringing about a gradual increase in rents and also in the number of farms purchased. Grain began the upward movement in 1896, although it was not until after 1903 that wool began to improve. Meat and meat products tended to come back generally to the level of the 1870's, but grain never recovered completely, wheat rising only 22 per cent, barley 13 per cent, and oats 19 per cent, while potatoes rose only 10 per cent. Because of the relatively small increment in grain prices, the general agricultural increase amounted to no more than 33 per cent. Thus, even by 1914 British agriculture was receiving one-third less from its labor than it had in 1870. Wheat was the hardest hit, for although it never went lower than 30s. per quarter, after 1907 it was still 40 per cent below the 1871 price. It is not surprising, therefore, that the total taxable agricultural income in 1914 stood at £37 million as against £52 million in 1880. Even at the beginning of World War I agriculture had not recovered from its difficulties.

Another indication of the change which took place was rural depopulation. From 1871 to 1901 the number of men employed on farms declined at the rate of about 10,000 a year, the total numbers involved in agriculture in England and Wales decreasing from 1.2 millions to 971,708 in 1911, the lowest figure reached being that of 1901, when employment stood at 923,644. The total decline for the whole of the United Kingdom was from 2.7 million to 1.9 million, about a million having left the land. These migrants came principally from the three groups which suffered most. The first were the tenants, particularly on land encumbered with mortgages which prevented the landlords from coming to their aid with lowered rents. Secondly, there were the small farmers who had no ready market for their produce. Last of all, there were the farm laborers who had been replaced either by machinery or by cattle. In the eighteenth century these three classes had been forced off the land in order that farming might be improved; now they were being forced off because farming was becoming less profitable. While wages actually rose during the period, opportunities for employment contracted until 1901, so fewer and fewer people obtained these better wages. With the rise of prices after 1900 the situation improved somewhat, but even by 1914 the number occupied in farming was still far below that of 1871.

A third sign of agricultural difficulties was the decline in arable farming. For the whole of the British Isles the acreage under the plow contracted between 1887 and 1905 from 21.1 million acres to 18.8 million, only 600,000 being restored by 1914. In England the decline was the greatest, falling from 13.7 million acres in 1870 to 10.3 million in 1914, and Wales had much the same experience, although Scotland lost only about 200,000 acres. The grain which contracted most in acreage and in production was wheat, decreasing during the whole period about 45 per cent in area, and between 1884 and 1914 from 25 per cent to 30 per cent in output. With the exception of oats, potatoes, and turnips, all the other major crops suffered similarly, although not so drastically. Those which were hardest hit failed to achieve anything of a return to 1870 standards, some showing no signs of recovery whatever. The only really important improvement was the rise of hay production by about a million tons. This did not, however, offset other losses.

The land taken from the plow was turned over to animal raising, but that change did not by any means make up the difference with increased output. While the area under permanent grass rose by 30 per cent, meat and animal products climbed only 5 per cent. The sheep of the country actually declined by 6 million for the whole of the British Isles, while pigs decreased by about 500,000. The only element of the animal population which experienced something of a boom was that of cattle, whose numbers were augmented by almost 3.5 millions (40 per cent), the principal growth taking place in England, although Irish cattle also added about a million. This explains the expansion of production in such commodities as milk, butter, and cheese which, along with a rise in egg output, helped to compensate a little for the losses in other directions. But these improvements, confined to certain localities, were not enough to make any great difference. In the 1860's Britain was raising 89 per cent of the meat which she ate, but by 1908 the percentage had dropped to 54 per cent.

This all led to a very noticeable change in land utilization. Instead of grain growing, the principal occupation was becoming grazing, which brought better prices for less work and at less cost. Grazing requires relatively small amounts of such expensive capital equipment as machinery, for there is little need for sowing and harvesting. Moreover, such things as dairy products are always in demand. The outcome was that during periods of depression, the land experienced a rather rapid changeover from arable to cattle farming. In England, Wales, and Scotland the arable acreage dropped from 18.4 to 14.3 million acres, while permanent grass rose correspondingly from 12.4 to 17.6 million acres. Thus there was a general transformation from an intensive and relatively costly type of farming to a more extensive and cheaper variety. "High farming" was no longer characteristic of British agriculture.

That this was so is also manifested by the concurrent deterioration in farming methods. Britain, who had taught the western world new methods of agriculture a century earlier, now fell behind Germany, France, and the United States. With lower revenues, farmers tended to forego draining and fertilizing their land. Much of the old permanent grassland was allowed to fall to rough grazing. The animals themselves were not as carefully watched and bred as previously. There was also a cut in the system of rotation, crops which did not pay, such as swedes and turnips, being dropped. Thus, from 1870 to 1896, although those who had plenty of money were able to employ improved methods of farming, increasing the average output per acre, many could not. This spelled declining efficiency. In addition, although in certain cases there might be something of an increase in production, the crops, by reason of higher wages, more expensive machinery, and the like, were more costly to raise, nullifying the effect of any rise in output. The British farmer needed better fertilizers, more machinery, and cheaper means of transportation, aids which began to come in only after 1900, but which were never universally adopted, even by 1914. Only in areas such as Lothian in Scotland or in some of the districts near Liverpool, Manchester, and London where there was something of a ready market, did farming during this decade again begin to prosper.

Perhaps the fate of the old type farmer is best revealed by the growth of the small market gardener. There were still a great many large farms throughout the country in the first decade of the twentieth century, but they were decreasing in number. Between 1881 and 1911 the farm labor population declined 25 per cent, and although farmers and graziers had remained steady at around 279,000, seedsmen, gardeners, and florists, on the other hand, had increased by 77 per cent. The latter, often tenants rather than owners, occupied small farms, many of them under 5 acres, and catered to a local market. This meant that the farmer was changing over, not only from grain to meat, but even more from grain and meat to vegetables, fruits, and flowers.

To sum up, it is sufficient to say that while in the 1840's Britain was raising enough food to feed 24 million inhabitants, by 1906 she was raising sufficient for only a little over four million. This perhaps indicates most graphically the extent of the intervening decline.

Thus, by 1914 Britain's whole agricultural picture had altered. No longer producing as large quantities of staple foods as in 1871, she had become largely dependent upon imports. Her agriculture, having suffered from a general depression, had by no means recovered, although there were a few signs of improvement, largely resulting from the radical changes introduced into farming practice. By 1914 there was a semblance of stability, despite the fact that the farmer was not in nearly the happy situation which he had enjoyed in the 1860's. Moreover, there was always the possibility of another upset which might spell his ruin.

The Causes of the Change

Having seen the nature of this transformation in the status and condition of British farming, it is now necessary to glance at the forces which caused the change. Why did British farming suffer in this way? Why was it that from about 1872 onward the British farmer experienced a depression from which he had by no means recovered even in 1914?

To understand what happened one must always keep in mind the contemporary fluctuations of the world market. As a result of these Britain had experienced periods of unemployment, the first reaching its nadir in 1879 and the second in the early nineties. They had caused a drop in the amount of money which laboring people had to spend, resulting in a decrease in the demand for agricultural goods and thus forcing prices down. This, in turn, discouraged the farmer, the cost of whose crops was relatively high. He began to turn to cheaper lines or to lines for which there might be greater sale and, consequently, a better return for his work. Added to this, the period saw a general drop in prices both at home and abroad, intensifying the distinctive British problems, so it is easy to understand how the farmer's position might become rather difficult.

Along with this went the declining efficiency in farming which has already been mentioned as one of the signs of the depression. The fall of prices in the late seventies resulted in a serious decline of income. As most landlords, particularly in England, did not reduce rents except under pressure, many of the tenants very quickly became involved in financial difficulties. In order to pay their rents their capital was often used up, so when the first phase of the depression was over, even if still on their farms, they had little or no money left with which to buy machinery, fertilizers, or materials for drainage. This meant that from 1884 down to 1890 much of the land was left unimproved. When the second drop in prices came during 1891, they had no cushion of capital upon which to fall back. Many were bankrupted, rents tumbled to new low levels, and any improvement which was being carried on stopped. Many farms were deserted, and those that were not were cultivated as cheaply as possible, which usually meant a decline in efficiency.

On top of this came the weather. While the majority of the early analysts of the situation placed most of the blame on this factor, it is not regarded now as being of such great influence. Nevertheless, a wet summer, such as that of 1879, had a depressing effect on agriculture. Largely owing to the excessive rainfall in that year, foot and mouth disease, liver rot, and pleuropneumonia carried off large numbers of sheep and cattle. Added to that, the productivity of the soil deteriorated, the acre producing only about fifteen bushels of wheat instead of the usual twenty-four. The resulting losses to the farmers were heavy, causing a decline in capital reserves and making it more difficult to pay rents.

While this was going on, rising costs were causing trouble. The tide of emigration began to swell, drawing its main elements from the country, to the detriment of the available supply of labor. The towns also exercised an attraction because they could provide higher pay, more social life, and generally better chances for comfortable living. Thus, when wages fell in the country, the consequent exodus very quickly brought about a fall in the quantity of labor, particularly in that which was employed temporarily at special seasons such as the harvest. This brought about a rise in the farmer's costs either for wages or for the purchase of labor-saving machinery. At the same time, local taxation and railway charges were beginning to mount. The net result of all this was that the average farmer was faced with growing expenses which effectually cut into any possible profits.

All these influences played an important part in the disaster which overtook British agriculture between 1872 and 1896. The general economic recession, the rising costs, the declining efficiency, and the poor weather, all had their share in causing trouble. Still, it is quite possible that the British farmer, who had faced such problems before, given time and sunshine, would have been able to overcome them and regain his old prosperity. But this time there was an entirely new factor which turned the tide of battle from a gradual resurgence to victory to a virtual rout. This factor was foreign importations. American and Canadian wheat, American, Argentinian, and Australasian meat, New Zealand and European eggs and butter, all began to pour into the country. It was this which finally changed the British agricultural picture.

The reason for the sudden success of these countries was, first of all, their rapid development and expansion during the last quarter of the nineteenth century. Between 1870 and 1903 the wheat acreage of United States expanded from 18.9 million to 49.5 million and that of European Russia from 28.7 million to 45.1 million. During the same period western Canada was being settled and laid down to wheat, while in Australasia and Argentina cattle farming and sheep ranching, financed by British capital, were expanding by leaps and bounds. What is more, the land so used being virgin land, it required little fertilization and because of its "wide-open spaces," particularly in America, was very responsive to the efficient use of machinery. Mass production was the keyword of the new farming lands. Because of their natural advantages their production costs were much lower than those of the British farmer, who had to give intensive cultivation to every foot of ground. With their mass production and more efficient methods, the farmers on the new lands could afford to undersell the British farmer who had to meet high costs and bad weather. Lower production costs abroad resulted in drastically lowered prices at home.

One might feel that, despite all this, the British farmer still had an advantage. Since he was not working for export, his real interest was the sale of his produce on the home market which was close at hand. This might have had some influence had it not been for the improvement in the means of long distance transportation. Railroad lines were being laid in all directions over most of the world's land masses. Between 1870 and 1890 railway mileage in the United States rose from 57,000 to 156,000, and although this was not equaled elsewhere, the increases throughout the world were great. The outcome was the speeding up and cheapening of freight carriage. Then came the steamship, which could handle grain rapidly and in large quantities. After 1880 refrigeration ships appeared on the seas, moving meat, eggs, and butter to the port of London from as far away as Australia and New Zealand. The consequence of such changes can perhaps be best understood by realizing that from 1869 to 1905 the cost of transporting a bushel of wheat from Chicago to Liverpool fell from 36.75¢ to 9.69¢, or by nearly 75 per cent. Wheat was typical of all the other agricultural imports.

The fall in transportation costs meant that the foreign farmer could now unload his surplus produce in Britain at a price lower than could be accepted by his British competitor. At this point the weather intervened to cause further trouble by ruining the home-grown crops and flocks. The resulting shortage of domestic foodstuffs would normally have raised prices, but the opening up of new lands and the lowering of freight rates placed the British farmer in a position where he was absolutely powerless. The foreign producer now had an opportunity of which he was not slow to take advantage. Added to this, the British railways had adopted the custom of giving preferential rates to imported goods, particularly if they were raw materials. While this might help the industrialist, it meant disaster to the farmer whose rival's produce was carried at a rate lower than that which he paid. What is more, wedded to the idea of free trade, particularly in food, since 1846 Britain would tolerate no suggestion of a protective tariff. The British farmer, therefore, had to get along as best he might, with little sympathy and no help from any other part of the population.

What the farmer had to face, and how unsuccessful he was in warding off the blow, is revealed in the ever-increasing imports of foreign-grown food stuffs. Grain rapidly became the biggest import, the quantity of wheat rising from 8.6 million quarters in 1870 to 27.5 millions in 1914. During the same time barley rose from 1.7 million to 4.4 million quarters and oats from 3.8 million to 5 million quarters. Instead of only one harvest a year, there was one every month somewhere on the globe, creating a greatly augmented surplus of grain. Meanwhile, the imports of animal products were also growing. It has been estimated that their total annual value during this period rose from £7.6 million to £63.2 million per annum. After 1882 frozen and chilled meat began to come in in rapidly increasing quantities, mutton imports, for instance, climbing from 181,000 cwts. in 1882 to 3.5 million cwts. in 1899. Along with these, cheese imports were up 33 per cent, butter 100 per cent, and wool 200 per cent. Reckoned in money the total increase in foodstuff imports has been estimated as expanding from £124 million in 1875 to £205 million in 1905. While this may not seem to be as great as expected, it must also be kept in mind that prices were dropping, enabling one to purchase considerably more for a pound in 1905 than he could in 1875. It has been said that, in volume, the imports at the end of the period were 130 per cent larger than they were at the beginning.

By 1914 the market for foodstuffs in Britain was dominated by the foreign producer. The weather had improved, prices were rising, and there was less real threat of disaster, but it was still impossible to slacken the grip of foreign graziers and wheat growers. The British farming population was maintaining its place on the land only by means of drastic alterations in the old agricultural organization. For one thing, methods of agriculture had been improved, providing higher efficiency and lowering costs. But what was even more successful was the turn to the cultivation of foodstuffs which, on the home market, had a comparative advantage over similar products raised across the sea. By these and other means, British farming, although not booming, had at least become stabilized and was enjoying a comfortable, if not a rising level of prosperity.

The Efforts to Revive British Agriculture

The history of British farming between 1870 and 1914 is largely the story of the farmer's efforts to overcome the obstacles and competition which were threatening to bring him to ruin. Even at the end of the period he was not entirely secure, but he was not giving up. Without much help from the government, and without any sympathy from the city dweller, he fought a battle which, while it did not rout the enemy, at least forced him to leave the British farmer in peaceful possession of a part of his own home market.

The first line of defense was that of increased efficiency. If the farmer was to maintain himself, particularly in grain growing, he had to increase production without raising costs. This meant, to start with, the improvement of the land, although few men except the wealthy had enough money left after 1882 to invest in expensive fertilizers. About the end of the '70's it was discovered that basic slag from steel mills, if finely ground, contained enough soluble phosphorus to make it valuable as a fertilizer. From 1885 on this was employed widely, while, at the same time, the use of manure also became more common. After the turn of the century, it was noted that farmers generally were carrying on their work more carefully, using every available means to improve the land and its crops.

Another method of attaining efficiency was by the use of machinery. As wages, particularly after 1900, began to rise, this trend became even more noticeable. From 1878 onward American machinery such as the McCormick binder had been appearing more frequently in the fields of large farms. Hay-making machinery, the mower, the tedder, and the sweep raker, also grew in popularity, as did such cultivating implements as the spring-tined harrow. In the dairy industry the big mechanical advance was made by the introduction of the Swedish de Laval cream separator and by milking machinery which appeared about 1913. Along with these aids, mechanical power was gradually put to more use. While there were few tractors, there was a great number of stationary engines driving grinding mills, threshing mills, butter churns, and saws. There were also some steam plows, but they represented less than five per cent of the steam power employed in farming. Altogether, the number of engines (water, wind, gasoline, and steam) increased from over 17,000 to well over 28,000, between 1908 and 1913 in the effort to lower the cost of production.

Another important means employed to help agriculture was the change in crops. Wheat growing declined more than any other single commodity. Green crops also fell off by about one-seventh owing to the removing of roots from the Essex rotation. Instead the rotation now included grasses: clover or sainfoin, often being sown for two years at a time because hay, not being easily imported, did not fall in price. Of equal importance was the swing to vegetable raising. Reference has already been made to the increase in the numbers of seedsmen, gardeners, and florists, which was caused by the growth of market gardening. The importation of fresh vegetables was so expensive that here the British farmer had a decided advantage. Potatoes became important, new breeds being developed on a large scale in the Lothians and Ayrshire in Scotland and in Lincoln, Yorkshire, West Lancashire, and Cheshire in England, as well as in most of Ireland. Asparagus was grown widely in the Vale of Evesham, the Fens, Wisbech, and a number of other places, while Cornwall grew broccoli, planted after the early potato crop. Besides all these, the usual root crops: turnips, carrots, and the like, were also being raised in larger quantities. Many of the farmers turned to this type of production in order to escape foreign competition.

Keeping pace with the growth of market gardening, went fruit growing. Small fruits, such as raspberries and strawberries, grown particularly for the jam industry, were raised all over the United Kingdom. Whether it was up through the Tay valley or near Glasgow in Scotland or farther south in Sussex and Surrey, these fruits were grown in large quantities. Currants and gooseberries also were important. More valuable than the small fruits were the orchards of apples, plums, and pears. For centuries apples had been grown throughout the country, but, to a large extent, they had been neglected as a commercial crop. Between 1873 and 1914 the situation changed, with the orchard areas registering an increase of 63.9 per cent, those in Kent alone doubling in acreage between 1895 and 1905. One reason for this was that in places such as Devon and Kent the growers were turning to cider production. This was just another way in which the farmer was attempting to raise a crop which could be easily disposed of on the British market.

A type of gardening closely related to open-air market gardening was the raising of fruits and vegetables under glass, which also saw a great expansion. As an example of what was happening between 1874 and 1899, Pet and Kay of Finchley built up a greenhouse covering over 19 acres for the purpose of growing grapes and tomatoes. By 1899 in and around Chesham some 125 acres were under glass, while the same technique was being carried out in Scotland as far north as Moray Firth. Besides grapes and tomatoes, sub- and semitropical fruits such as peaches and figs were being raised for the home market. Flowers also were becoming important as a vendable product, many of them being grown under artificial conditions.

To the cattleman a real lifesaver was the rising demand for milk, which throughout the depression had declined in price less than 20 per cent. At the same time, the introduction of improved methods of dairy farming helped to lower costs and open up more distant markets. Wire fencing took the place of bulky hedges, the cream separator was introduced and, the employment of milk coolers enabled the farmer to ship his milk to more distant cities. Since dairy farming prospered greatly in Ayrshire, it was not long before some of the Ayrshire farmers, seeking a wider market, began to move south into the London area where, in Essex, Hereford, and Suffolk, the tenants who had followed more traditional methods had been forced to leave the land. The Scot, who was made very welcome, introduced a new system of rotation, cutting out unnecessary crops. He worked harder and lived harder than the former tenants and, with London near at hand ready to buy all his products, contrived to do quite well. A similar movement from Cornwall, Devon and Wales into counties such as Somerset, Gloucester and Warwick was also taking place. In this way dairying received considerable stimulus, the milch herds of the country during the 45 years increasing by more than half a million animals.

While British dairy farming was struggling for its life, butter and cheese were flooding the market from Denmark, Australasia, and other areas. At first the British farmer could not compete with the standardized foreign products, but by the beginning of the twentieth century methods of production had so improved that he was able to meet non-British competition without flinching. The greatest advance in this line took place in Ireland, where, as a result of a concerted effort, methods were radically modernized, enabling Irish butter to hold its own on the British market. By 1914 the dairy industry as a whole had so improved both the quantity and the quality of its output that it was able to stand on its own feet.

Along with the growth of dairy farming went the expansion of stock breeding. This, however, was not general, but took place only in several specialized lines. The reason for this was that ordinary meat imported from the Argentine or from Australia was so much cheaper than the similar type raised in Britain. The British farmer, therefore, concentrated on raising high grade animals which would bring correspondingly high prices. From 1880 on various societies, such as The Gurnsey Breeders Society and the Holstein Society, were organized to aid in the breeding of better quality animals. The Ayrshire became the most popular general purpose dairy breed, but others, such as the Devon, the Guernsey, and the Jersey, were also widely favored. Probably even more valuable was the work done on beef cattle, a phase of farming in which the Scots were particularly interested. The Polled Angus became very famous, while equally popular were the Galloways and Herefords, both rugged types. The two latter have formed the basis for a good many American and Argentinian herds, large numbers of them being purchased in Britain and shipped to the new countries to improve the existing breeds. Not infrequently as much as 500 guineas ($2500) would be given for one animal of this type. For the home market the farmers were beginning to concentrate on "baby beef," animals matured rapidly so that they could be slaughtered when about two years old, to give the finest quality meat. Improvements in the breed of sheep were also being worked out to raise the quality of the stock both for the home market and for export. In these ways the farmers, despite a drop of 15 per cent in beef prices, were able to withstand some of the shock administered by the influx of foreign meat. The new practices did not solve the problem, but they were a help, as is indicated by the increase in the cattle population from 10.7 million in 1895 to 12.1 million in 1914 and by the increase of sheep from 29.7 million to 31.8 million between 1895 and 1909. For the next few years the number of sheep dropped, but by 1914 it was again beginning to rise. By 1914 grazing was commencing to prosper.

Although all these efforts at detailed improvement did have a good effect upon the farmer's situation, many believed that the trouble was more fundamental: that there should have been a complete reorganization of land owning. When foreign competition, bad weather, and other forces struck Britain, the tenant farmers had been hard hit because of the demand for high rents. It was felt that by the system of landlordism much of the real estate in the country had to support two people: the landlord and the farmer. To meet the exigencies of the time, therefore, outright ownership by the tenant was the only solution. The man who worked the land should own it. Only then would the situation be properly adjusted, and to prove their point those desiring land reform pointed to France, where despite American and Australasian production, peasant farming flourished.

As a result of such thinking, a survey was made of the system of land ownership in England and Wales. After some revision of the original findings, it was estimated that, out of a total of 37.3 million acres, 4,000 persons holding 1,000 acres or more owned more than 19 million acres. There were also 147,657 who owned between one and one thousand acres. Thus, roughly 150,000, or $\frac{1}{170}$ of the population, owned most of the land. France, with an area 33 per cent larger, had 5.6 million owners, and Belgium, with a population of 7 million, had 1 million owners. In order to change this state of affairs it would be necessary to force the breakup of the big holdings. This was a difficult proposition, as the custom had grown up in many quarters in England for the owner to make a "settlement" with his heir who received only the *use* of the property for life, the real heirs being the succeeding generations from whom the land could not be legally alienated. In Scotland the common practice was that of "entailing" land, by which the land was left to the heir and his descendants, so no one owner could sell, since this would deprive his successors of their rightful possessions. In this way the big estates had been protected from dissolution, making the possibility of purchasing land in freehold somewhat difficult. To facilitate the breaking of these "settled" and "entailed" lands, parliament in 1884 enacted an enabling law. But much more would have to be done before a solution could be found.

The lot of the tenants, meanwhile, despite all the propaganda, was considerably ameliorated. This was partially the result of the demands made by the Irish peasants. Prior to 1870 they had been "precarious tenants" who could be evicted at will, any improvements they had made becoming the landlord's property. To remove this injustice, after lengthy agitation, the Irish Land Act of 1870 applied the Ulster custom of compensating a tenant for his unexhausted improvements to all Ireland. At the same time, efforts were made to protect the tenants from unwarranted disturbance. While much has been written about the Irish peasant's uncertain position, it must be remembered that the English and Scottish tenant farmer was not much better off. From 1883 onward, however, this began to change with the passing of various laws designed to protect him, to compensate him for improvements, and to give him the right to kill game which ate his crops. Such measures were a help, no doubt, but in reality, while they made things easier for the farmer, they came no nearer establishing a freehold peasantry. As far as the reformers were concerned this was but a drop in the bucket.

One partial solution which was offered was the creation of allotments. By 1800 enclosure had caused the disappearance of many cottages with their small garden plots. It was felt that this situation might be remedied by giving farm laborers and town dwellers alike the opportunity to have their own small holding, upon which they could grow part of the vegetables which they ate. By 1850 quite a number of large farmers had adopted this idea, but it was not until 1882 that official action was taken. In that year, and again five years later, the local sanitary authorities were given the right to purchase land which they could rent as allotments, usually in quite small parcels. In 1894 this duty was taken over by the parish councils, and by the next year there were 579,133 such holdings as compared with 246,398 in 1873. In 1907 another act (Small Holdings and Allotments Act) ordered the councils to provide allotments as needed, giving them authority if necessary to expropriate. The outcome of this was that by 1912 the 2,000 councils which had acted held 31,089 acres let to 117,562 individuals and 21 associations. In this way many people were able to have some interest in the land. The chief difficulties were that the allotments were exceedingly small and usually were held only as tenancies rather than in full ownership. They did not satisfy the demand for the enlarging of the number of landowners.

The only answer to this demand was thought to be an increase in the number of small holdings, that is, holdings which could be worked by a farmer and his family. The truth of the matter was, however, that small holdings could only be developed where they could be operated for a specialized market. Certain types of products, such as grain, cattle, or sheep, cannot be raised profitably for the market on small farms, for mass production is the one element which makes these commodities cheap. Small holdings were, on the other hand, particularly useful for market gardening. For instance, in the Evesham district there were some 10,000 acres held in lots varying from one to eight acres, while in Bedfordshire there were a large number varying from seven to ten acres. These holdings produced carrots, cabbages, turnips, beans, and Brussels sprouts. Still, even such market farms as these did not solve all problems, for in the time of a depression they might be very hard hit. Nor did small holdings always guarantee that the farmer owned his land, for in Evesham renting was the custom. Consequently, such a system does not seem to have been necessarily the solution to agriculture's problem.

Despite any misgivings which might have been held that small holdings would provide a means of counteracting the agricultural depression, a Select Committee of the House of Commons in 1888 reported in favor of peasant ownership, and Parliament, accepting the plan, gave county councils permission to buy up land for this purpose. The act, however, was a failure, for by 1907 only 812 acres had been bought and only 200 sold. By a further act of 1907 county councils were given powers to force sales, and the Board of Agriculture was given the authority to put the pressure on the councils. As a consequence, by 1914 some 14,000 holdings had been leased, principally in the Fens, Bedfordshire, and Worcestershire, where market gardening was already common. Still, this was only moderate success, for the small holders often tried to increase the size of their holdings while, at the same time, they refused either to enter cooperative undertakings with others or to buy their own properties. In fact, during the seven years preceding World War I the total number of small farms under 50 acres actually decreased. The Liberals laid great plans for forcing the wholesale breakup of large properties and for the state erection of 125,000 cottages with garden plots. These, however, were never implemented owing to the outbreak of war, but, even so, it is doubtful whether they would really have achieved their purpose.

The policy of establishing small holdings was more effective in Scotland and Ireland. In the Scottish Highlands crofting was very important, but most of the crofters were tenants. In 1883 a Committee of Enquiry recommended that state aid be given to enable these occupants to buy their holdings. This was done, so between 1897 and 1912 640 new freehold farms were created and 1,138 were enlarged, totaling 72,000 acres. Even more drastic steps were taken in Ireland, where the agitation of the Land League, organized by Michael Davitt, had been given emphasis by outrages, boycotting, and forcible resistance to eviction. In 1885 the first Land Purchase Act was passed, by which the government agreed to advance to the peasant the money necessary for the purchase of his land, the peasant, in turn, to repay the loan to the British government in 49 annual payments. Further help was given in later years, as well as a bonus being offered in 1903 to landlords who were willing to sell. The result was that by 1921 two thirds of Irish holdings were in peasant hands. By such means the Celtic inhabitants of the British Isles to a considerable extent reverted to their primitive agricultural organization, but whether in an industrial age this would be satisfactory was by no means certain.

What was the effect of all these efforts? To sum up, one can say that between 1880 and 1914 there was a certain amount of change in land ownership. Under the 1907 Small Holdings Act in England and Wales 154,977 acres had been bought by 1912 or were in the process of being acquired. Of these, 124,709 acres had been let to 8,950 holders, 6,094 acres to 49 associations, and 212 acres had been sold to 20 owners. Two years later 46,660 individuals and 96 associations had made application for some 782,286 acres. Besides this, small landlords were following the same plan in either renting or selling their land. Yet ownership was unusual, for the average English farmer did not enjoy its responsibilities. In Scotland and Ireland it was much more popular, the latter country showing in 1921 600,000 small holders with farms averaging 30 acres. Yet while this process was going on, big farms were also developing owing to the cheapness of land in the mid '90's. Men with initiative built up holdings of 12,000 to 20,000 acres on which they raised one or two special products such as hay or sheep, handled on a mass production basis and aided by modern methods and machinery. These, however, were the exceptions, for the size of farms generally was tending to shrink although, at the same time, the smallest holdings were tending to disappear. Farms between 20 and 300 acres saw the greatest increase in numbers, which, while not startling, were substantial.[2] Despite all the efforts to establish

[2] In England and Wales, while holdings from 1 to 20 acres declined from about 240,000 acres in 1885 to 214,000 acres in 1913, those between 20 and 300 acres

peasant ownership, the usual farm was of medium size, held more frequently in tenancy than in freehold.

Meanwhile, the government was doing something to aid the farmer directly. This took the form of money grants to help lighten local taxation. At the same time, ecclesiastical tithes were made a rent charge which was the responsibility of the owner rather than the tenant. An act was also passed to equalize railway freight rates for foreign and home-grown produce. Further protection for the farmer came with the passing of laws to prevent the adulteration of oil cake for fodder, fertilizers, and dairy products.[3] Action was also taken, particularly after a number of epidemics, to prevent the introduction of cattle diseases into the country. Finally, the Improvement of Land Act (1899) gave landowners the right to make improvements on borrowed money. All these laws facilitated the work and activity of the farmer but did not go far enough.

Probably the most important action was the creation of the Board of Agriculture. In the early years of the nineteenth century such an organization had existed, but it had been allowed to die. The Board of Trade, however, in 1866 had set up a Committee on Agriculture which a few years later became a committee of the Privy Council. At length (1883), a Minister of Agriculture was appointed, and six years later, a Board of Agriculture. This body had the responsibility of making statistical studies of farming in Britain, of seeing to the enforcement of the various agricultural laws, many of which it proposed, and of aiding agricultural education. This was positive action which was bound to have a good effect.

Of all the Board's activities, the most important was the fostering of agricultural education by cooperating with local authorities and private bodies interested in spreading information concerning farming. County councils were authorized in 1890 to provide technical instruction in agriculture, and these bodies frequently set up colleges or founded chairs of agronomy in local universities. Although the Royal Agricultural College, Cirencester, was, prior to 1890, the only incorporated institution for agricultural education, a number of others soon appeared upon the scene. In 1888 the Agricultural Department of the Privy Council was given £5,000 to spend on agricultural education, this amount being gradually increased with the result that soon there were established institutions such as the Royal Veterinary College and the British Dairy

---

had risen from 195,000 to 206,000 acres. Much the same situation prevailed in Scotland.

[3] The Fertilisers and Feeding Stuffs Act (1893) and the Sale of Food and Drugs Act (1899).

Institute besides the regular educational bodies. Farm institutes were also founded to give courses during the winter to those unable to attend day and evening classes in the country schools or colleges.

These efforts were ably seconded by the activities of various private associations. Not only were there the breeding societies mentioned above, there were also other organizations such as the eighteenth century Highland Society. The latter offered prizes, held agricultural shows, and did much to stimulate improved farming in Scotland. In 1868 it promised £150, a figure which the government agreed to match, for the establishment of a chair of agriculture at Edinburgh. Three years later it created a Board of Examiners in Forestry, and in 1877 it leased farms in East and West Lothian to do experimental work on such subjects as manures and new types of rotation. In these activities it was eminently successful. Much less encouraging, however, were the fortunes of farmers' cooperatives. The British farmer was too individualistic to be willing to join with others either in the purchase of farm machinery and materials or in the marketing of his produce. Thus, by 1913, while there were 478 cooperatives, with 48,000 members doing about £2 million worth of business, actually only one in seven of the country's farmers had any connection with a cooperative society.

While discussing the efforts to improve the lot of the farmer one should perhaps mention the demand for agricultural tariffs. Germany from 1879 onwards steadily raised a protective wall around the farmer, an example followed by France after 1885. Britain, however, was wedded to a free trade policy. Joseph Chamberlain, on the other hand, who was not very much impressed by the old tradition, felt that the one hope of the farmer was tariff protection. He maintained that this was the only way to raise agricultural prices so that the farmer could receive decent returns and pay decent wages. In answer to the argument that this would raise the price of food, he said that the improved position of the farming population would mean an increased domestic market for British manufactures which would help the position of industry in general and the industrial worker in particular. His plan, however, was never given a trial for the Liberals, led by Lloyd George, who hated the big landowners, felt that this was merely a wall to protect privilege and would have none of it.

Thus, as we look back over the years which intervened between 1870 and 1914, it becomes clear that there had been a great revolution in agriculture. The primary factor in this change had been the importation of food cheaply produced in the newly opened lands.

For twenty-five years (1870-96) farmers had struggled, but without avail, against this overwhelming onslaught. It was not until new methods, new implements, and new techniques were introduced, and a relative improvement in the whole British economic situation increased demand for high-grade farm produce that the situation improved. But even though the first decade of the new century saw an advance, farming could not be said to be booming. It was stabilized but not much more. Still, this was an improvement over the conditions prevailing in the last quarter of the nineteenth century, an improvement for which the farmers were duly thankful.

Yet while the farmers were feeling happier about their lot the total picture was not very good. With an expanding population and agricultural production stationary, if not declining, the country as a whole was becoming more and more dependent upon foreign food supplies. This meant that an increasing quantity of Britain's industrial production and of her foreign investments went to pay for food imports. While this was not necessarily bad, there lay in it a very real danger. If Britain's foreign investments should be curtailed, if her industrial output should be drastically cut or her markets lost, she would be in an exceedingly dangerous position. Any radical change of the world economic equilibrium might well bring disaster. It was with this before her that Britain entered World War I.

Chapter 20

THE DECLINE OF BRITISH INDUSTRIAL PREDOMINANCE

IN 1870 Great Britain had reached her industrial peak in relation to the rest of the world. The preceding twenty years had seen her expand industrially far more rapidly and far more widely than any other nation. From 1870 on, however, as has already been seen, the British position began to change, at first slowly and then more rapidly. Rivals appeared in the person of the German and the American manufacturer. By 1914 Great Britain was no longer the workshop of the world and what is more, she was even adopting some of the German and American techniques to improve her own now outmoded processes. Having invested heavily in methods developed during the '60's and '70's, she could not afford to change to the newer machines and processes of the '80's and '90's. Moreover, she had become so accustomed to being in a position of prominence that she tended to refuse recognition to foreign improvements and developments, regarding them as being of no really permanent value. Thus, Britain often helped her rivals indirectly by her unwillingness to change. Simultaneously, the rivals themselves often beat Britain in her former markets, taking from her the customers who would ultimately pay for the improvements. In these ways Britain's old industrial supremacy was gradually destroyed.

Yet one must not carry away the idea that Britain's industry remained stationary during the forty years before World War I. Its expansion is marked by the increasing numbers of the population involved in industrial production, in 1870 some 62 per cent of the people being urban dwellers, while in 1914 the proportion had risen to 78 per cent. These were located in clearly defined areas of the country. Coal mining was carried on in Glamorgan and Flintshire in Wales, in the North Midlands and northwest and northeast shires of England, and in Lanark and Fife in Scotland. Cotton was manufactured primarily in Lancashire, Cheshire, York, and Derby, where the damp climate was particularly suitable. Woolens and worsteds came from the West Riding of Yorkshire, Lancashire, and southern Scotland. Metal goods, primarily of iron and steel, were produced in and around Birmingham, Coventry, and Sheffield in England, and Glasgow in Scotland. Thus there was a very clear geographic pattern of population and industry throughout the whole period. Set by 1870, it experienced practically no change until after World War I.

Yet, while the general geographic pattern remained the same, the industrial pattern itself changed rapidly during the period, largely owing to physical factors such as coal and iron deposits or climate. In 1870 the average factory was a relatively small affair of 100 to 300 hands, but by 1914, 800 to 1,000 employees was becoming a common figure. Some plants employed many more. At the same time, from 1890 on industrial combinations of various kinds were being established. The vertical combination, which attempted to control every process connected with its business, from the growing or mining of the raw material to the sale of the finished article, became increasingly common. For instance, John Brown & Co. of Sheffield amalgamated with the Clydebank Engineering and Shipbuilding Co. In this way a producer of rolled and heavy steel turned to the manufacturing of its own products into ships. Cammell and Laird, and Vickers and Maxim were two other companies formed in the same way and for the same purpose. Horizontal amalgamation also took place, whereby one particular process in an industry was brought under the control of one particular organization. This was common in the textile industries, where there is the example of J. & P. Coats & Co. monopolizing the manufacture of sewing thread. The Bradford Dyers' Association and the Calico Printers' Association are two other examples, being made up of thirty and sixty firms respectively. Developed largely for the purposes of economy in order to meet competition, the combinations expanded their factories, improved their methods, and increased their production.

Along with the old stand-bys, new industries were also introduced. Metals such as aluminum, textiles such as artificial silk, and commodities such as rubber were all processed and exported in increasing quantities every year. In this way Britain developed her economy on diversified lines.

Despite all her industrial growth, her new as well as her expanding old products, Britain did not keep up with the rest of the world. She depended too much on the industries, such as heavy metal manufactures and textiles, which had already given her wealth and success. These were now being surpassed in other countries, and although she was developing the newer industries, she was doing so much more slowly than others, with the result that many of her rivals, Germany, the United States, and even France were far ahead. To see this clearly it is necessary to glance at some of the principal industrial changes which were taking place. Only then can one have a proper appreciation of Britain's strength and weakness.

The Course of Industrial Change

Characteristic of the industrial change and development in Britain between 1870 and 1914 was the increased use of mechanical power. While the British had pioneered in this field, in the fifties and sixties the rate of their advance tended to slacken. But with the growing size of factories after 1870, there was a constant demand for larger engines of all types. Concurrent with this went a similar growth even in small units of production. As workshops (containing less than 50 laborers) began to use power driven machinery, small engines also became popular. This demand helped to turn the manufacturers to search for engines and motors which were not as bulky or cumbersome as the old steam engine. The result was the gas engine, the electric motor, and finally the internal-combustion gasoline engine. Thus, by 1914 the use of mechanical power had increased greatly on all sides, and this power was being produced in many different ways.

Throughout the period steam continued to dominate as the chief type of motive power. Coal was still the cheapest form of fuel, and with the improvements introduced in the steam engine its efficiency was so increased that its consumption per horse power hour dropped by about 50 per cent. This was a very real help, since it meant that costs would drop even though wages would not. One of the greatest improvements in steam engine design was in the more common use of the expansion engine, whereby the steam went from one cylinder to another of smaller size where its lower pressure could be employed. Quadruple expansion engines became quite common for the propulsion of ships. Another innovation was the building by Sir Charles Parsons of the first steam turbine, by which the revolutions per minute of the average engine were increased from 300 to 18,000, making it possible to produce electricity by means of steam power. The growth of the use of steam can perhaps be appreciated when it is realized that between 1870 and 1907 the available horse power for industry rose from 900,000 to

8 million, for railways from 2 million to 8 million and for shipping from 1 million to 13½ million, the total increase being about 600 per cent.

The use of coal for the production of steam was not, however, the only way in which it was employed to supply power. Coal gas during this period became very important. Made either directly from the coal or obtained from coke ovens, it was used both for illumination and for the running of gas engines. By 1890 the Bunsen burner was in common use, having obtained a virtual monopoly of artificial lighting. For this reason gas pipes were everywhere, so it was easy for the owner of a small work shop to connect up a gas engine to run his machines. Consequently, down to 1914, for the small producer by far the most convenient form of mechanical power was the gas engine.

Much slower to be adopted was electricity. The gas companies fought hard to maintain their monopolies, while the municipal authorities often involved in gas production were not much more favorable. Besides, there were various difficulties in getting permission to produce electricity, since before an electrical plant could be set up, a private bill had to be passed by Parliament. Probably the greatest obstacle was, however, the lack of water power. It was only after the invention of the steam turbine, therefore, that it became feasible to produce electricity on a commercial basis, and even then it was still relatively expensive. The '90's saw some development, the Manchester Corporation's plant commencing operations in 1894 with 74 customers. By 1900 heavy industry was becoming interested, while, at the same time, electrical power was supplanting horses and steam on tramways and underground railways. Thus by 1914 the use of electricity had increased very considerably, although even by that date the amount produced was only one-third that of Germany. What is more, most of the equipment was of foreign origin. Electricity had not yet come into its own.

As can easily be seen, when it came to providing power, it was still a case of "old King Coal." But the mines were going deeper, the shafts were becoming longer, and consequently the raising of coal was increasingly difficult. The mine engineers, however, were developing new techniques and labor-saving devices to help in bringing the "black diamonds" to the top of the ground as cheaply as possible. Steel girders and concrete pillars were being used increasingly between 1900 and 1913, although the growth of the annual import of wooden pit props by one-third shows that they were still popular. Electricity was employed more commonly in the first decade of the present century for hauling and ventilation, but the fact that in 1903 there were only 231 electric cutters throughout the whole country indicates that it was neglected for actual mining. At the same time, methods of sorting and grading were still far behind those in Germany and the United States. To the British coal owner, however, these refinements did not seem necessary, since between 1905 and 1913 he saw a rise of 40 per cent in exports. Similarly, there had been an increase in production from about 117 million tons to 287 million, owing to the opening up of new mines in Kent, Lincoln, southern Yorkshire, and Fifeshire. It was estimated that, despite the ever-increasing exploitation, there was still enough coal left for about 400 years. So coal mining went on in the same old way, a profitable business which, because of its success, did not seem to require much improvement or reform.

The same thing could not be said about most of the other mining in Britain, for the old minerals were gradually disappearing. Between 1894 and 1914 the production of lead dropped from 29,000 to 19,000 tons. Tin and zinc at the same time declined from about 8,000 tons to less than 5,000 each, while copper seems to have disappeared from the list entirely. Either the mines were petering out or they were so uneconomical that they could not stand the competition of foreign producers who had rich and easily worked deposits. In this way one of Great Britain's earliest industries was coming to an end.

In the case of iron the story of production was somewhat similar, but by no means identical. Between 1875 and 1885 some of the older iron-producing areas were decreasing in output: Wales, southwest Scotland, Yorkshire, and Shropshire. At the same time, other areas were expanding: Staffordshire, Cumberland, Lancashire, Lincoln, and Northampton. The trouble with most of the British ores was, however, that they contained phosphorus which prevented their use in the Bessemer process of steel making. Consequently, nonphosphoric ores had to be imported from Scandinavia, Algeria, and particularly Spain in ever-increasing quantities. By 1913, of the Bessemer ores 87 per cent were imported, amounting to 45 per cent more than the total iron ore raised in Britain itself. This was indeed a dangerous situation. In fact between 1880 and 1913 the total drop in the amount raised within the country was 40 per cent. Britain was becoming increasingly dependent upon foreign sources for the basic raw material of one of her most important industries.

In the smelting of iron the British industrialists introduced a number of improvements, but only very slowly. Before 1870 practically nothing was done to save and use the gases which came from the coking ovens making the fuel for the blast furnaces; nor was much heed paid to the waste gases of the blast furnaces themselves. The furnaces had increased output from about 450 tons to 550 tons per day by the building of taller stacks, but it was not until about 1885 that the ironmasters began to employ the latest coking and blast furnace methods, long since introduced in Germany and the United States. Gradually such practices as the preheating of fuel, the use of waste gases for heating, the employment of escaping steam in low pressure engines, and the extraction of sulphur and other chemicals from coke-oven gas were adopted. Between 1885 and 1913, with these improvements being more widely applied, production rose slowly from around 7.8 million tons per annum to around 10.5 million tons. The increase both in production and in efficiency had been much slower than that of either the Americans or the Germans.

It was during this period that iron, as iron, began to lose much of its old importance. Made into steel, however, it became more valuable. Therefore, as the output of steel rose, that of wrought iron fell, until in the first years of the twentieth century the production of the latter was hardly a million tons a year. The reason for this was that steel could now be produced very cheaply and was more useful. Both the Bessemer and the Siemens methods had been discovered before 1870, but no way of using phosphoric ores was known until 1878. In that year Gilchrist Thomas, a London clerk, found that the phosphorus could be removed by adding lime to the molten ore. Once this was discovered, nations rich in phosphoric ores were able to turn their resources to good use. Germany was one of these, and by 1900, in steel production she had surpassed Britain, who, while making 55 per cent of the world's total in 1870, by 1910 accounted for only 15 per cent. Having invested heavily in Bessemer converters in the early 1860's, when the more efficient Siemens method came into use the British steel companies found it too expensive to change over. Nor were they willing to switch to the electrical steel-making technique which was being employed on the Continent in the '80's. It was only very gradually that the new methods were brought into use. Thus, from 1890 on Great Britain was very rapidly outstripped by both Germany and the United States, as is shown by the relative production figures: Great Britain, 10 million tons; Germany, 15 million tons; the United States, 35 million tons (1913).

Steel making was not, however, limited to the matter of quantity produced. There was the matter of processing. Both Bessemer and Siemens had hoped to make steel directly from the iron as it came from the blast furnace. This was not practicable, since steel is spongy, the ingot requiring to be heated and hammered to make it solid. Andrew Carnegie in the United States tried running together steel from different converters, and in Britain Whitworth tried to solve the problem by compressing the steel while still molten, but this practice died out after his death in 1887. It was ultimately found that the only satisfactory method was the use of a heavy press on the heated ingot, and by 1900 British steel makers were using this technique widely.

One of Britain's greatest contributions to steel making during this period was the discovery of the steel alloy. While manganese had long been known as a means of making steel more forgeable at all degrees of heat, by 1870 R. F. Mushet had found also that silicon and tungsten increased the metal's usefulness. Before long other alloys were made, using aluminum, chromium, tungsten, and nickel to strengthen steel and prevent rust. Here again the United States very soon took the lead, stressing these new steels for tools, knives, guns, and similar articles. Britain made the discoveries, but she did not always exploit them.

From 1870 on advances were also taking place in the manufacture of machinery. Whitworth had stressed the use of measurement in manufacture and also advocated the standardization of bolts and screws. Through his influence this idea gained favor, but much more slowly than in Germany and the United States. The latter country was also considerably ahead of Britain in the making of foolproof machinery and portable power tools such as pneumatic drills and riveters. Machine riveting, for instance, was becoming common on the Clyde only by 1903, a number of years after its general acceptance in American shipyards. From 1885 on, however, more and more foreign methods and techniques were imported, including machinery for grinding basic slag, for making seamless tubes, as well as American lock-making methods and German techniques for making files and cutlery. Most important of all was the gradual introduction of the use of interchangeable parts. The increasing use of measurement and of patterns aided this, resulting in mass production. Here again however, Britain trailed both her chief rivals.

Some may wonder why it was that Britain seems to have been behind other countries in new methods of production, but the reasons are not hard to find. For one thing, British industry, with large sums invested in the obsolete equipment, was loth to throw out its old for new and expensive machinery. Labor also was opposed to changes. Unions which had become quite strong were by 1870 always suspicious of innovations which tended to eliminate the need for human action. With their ideas of craft work, the introduction of automatic machinery was to them a threat to skilled workers. On the other hand, after 1896 there was a considerable expansion of foreign demand, particularly for heavy metal goods such as rails, steam engines, and heavy machinery. This meant that since United States and Germany were consuming most of their own production at home, the British manufacturer could easily sell his goods abroad. Prices therefore kept up without the new machinery and methods, so profits and wages tended to rise. Consequently, neither capital nor labor felt that there was any great need for change.

The great difficulty with this position was that increasingly Britain was becoming dependent upon imported machinery for techniques of production which were new. American and German industrialists stressed the need for the application of recent scientific discoveries to their work. British industry, on the other hand, did not encourage experimentation and new ideas, with the result that there was little attempt to use the latest discoveries in order to lower costs. While this might be all right when there was a large demand for goods, if the competition should become keen, Britain would find herself at a very great disadvantage.

While Britain from 1885 on was thus behind her competitors in most forms of heavy industry, in one, shipbuilding, she was still on top. Before 1885, steel was not commonly used in the building of ships nor their engines, since the ship builders considered steel too erratic in its action. By that year, however, it was coming into use for nearly all steam boilers, and even the hulls themselves were increasingly made of the same material. Thus, from 1885 on steel steam vessels gradually displaced the old sailing ships. New multiple engines were being used more widely, and after 1903 the steam turbine became popular. A further change was the introduction of oil for fuel, while electricity was employed more generally for the lighting of the ships and for the operation of auxiliary machinery. Throughout the last ten years of the period Britain was exporting between 350,000 and 500,000 tons of shipping each year, a total which no other nation was able to match.

In the various branches of the light metals industries Britain maintained her position, although at times only with difficulty. Partially owing to the activity of Joseph Chamberlain, it became the common practice to standardize screws and to package them in small clearly labelled quantities. This helped greatly to stimulate export between 1894 and 1914, from a little over 14,000 tons annually to about 30,000 tons. The manufacture of bicycles also became important. By 1885 some 170 firms were making about 40,000 cycles a year, while by 1914 her annual export of cycles stood close to 15,000. Sewing machines, typewriters, and the like were also being made, but in small quantities only, since most of these goods were imported from the United States.

Although, generally speaking, the lighter manufactures were produced in factories by large firms, there were a few exceptions. In the screw and nail industries, even in 1870, there was still a considerable amount of manufacturing done in the homes of outworkers on the old domestic basis, but by 1914 these workers had largely disappeared. The factory was supreme.

While the metal industries were developing more slowly than their American or German counterparts, the cotton industry seems to have been somewhat more enterprising. There was a certain amount of improvement in machinery: ring spinning, self-acting mules and automatic looms were increasingly employed, although most of the new machines were of American manufacture. Automatic looms, however, were never very popular, as they were good only for coarse cloth, which was not the chief product of Britain's cotton mills. In 1914 Britain had only about 15,000 automatics to the American 400,000. Yet, while she did not go in for the new machinery as much as she might have, by 1900 British mills were producing 14,000 miles of cotton cloth a day, more than all Europe put together. By the opening of the Great War (1914), however, this lead had decreased considerably, for although between 1885 and 1913 the number of her spindles had jumped 43 per cent and of her looms 39 per cent, Europe and America combined, to say nothing of Japan, were manufacturing a good deal more than Britain. The result was a gradual contraction of the market for British cottons.

For the most part, the cotton spinning industry in Britain was located in South Lancashire close to the ports of Liverpool and Manchester, in an area of damp climate advantageous for its work. Bolton and the surrounding country concentrated upon fine cotton yarn, while Oldham and its environs were interested in coarser types. Cotton weaving, along with bleaching and dyeing, was centered in North Lancashire. During the years 1905-07 there was a boom in cotton production resulting in the building in these areas of some 95 new spinning mills containing 8.5 million new spindles, which brought the total number for the whole country to 48 million. Weaving mills also increased in comparable numbers. Thus Britain, with a greatly increased production potential, was beginning to face other countries' competition.

The woolen industry had somewhat better fortune than did cotton. While it had not developed as rapidly as its sister industry prior to 1870, it did not face the same competition in later years. After 1870, there was a gradual swing away from the old type woolen broadcloth to worsteds, which were lighter and more easily handled. The latter industry had by 1870 been pretty thoroughly mechanized, an example soon followed by the remaining woolen producers. With the exception of the makers of such materials as Harris tweeds, whose attraction was their hand weaving, by 1900 woolen and worsted production was almost entirely carried on in factories. At the same time, the manufacture of these goods had so increased that the British import of wool had risen from 263 million pounds in 1870 to over 800 million pounds in 1914, four-fifths coming from Australia. In this field Britain seems to have held her lead, since other countries were not able to produce such high grade materials. On the other hand, with the development of many new types of fabrics, there was not the old demand for woolen goods. Yet, despite this, the value of woolen yarns and cloth exported, rose between 1894 and 1913 from £21.1 million to £35.7 million, representing a substantial increase.

While cotton and wool had their difficulties, other textiles, with one exception, were not improving very greatly. The jute manufacturing industry, centered mainly in Dundee and producing cordage, bags, burlap, and similar commodities, seems to have continued without much change. The same was true of the linen industry, now concentrated almost entirely in Northern Ireland. Both industries by 1914 were pretty well mechanized. The one commodity which did experience a revolution was silk. Through the work of foreign chemists the manufacture of rayon from cellulose had been developed, with disastrous results to the processors of natural silk. By 1900 the first artificial silk factory was established in Britain, and by 1913 her output was topped only by that of Germany, while far outdistancing all other countries.

In such trades as the manufacture of clothes, boots, and shoes the years following 1870 saw considerable mechanization. Formerly industries working to order, they now turned to mass production, "store clothes" becoming the usual, instead of the exceptional, wearing apparel. The making of boots and shoes by means of machinery was also perfected. Thus, by 1900 a large part of the clothing industry in all its various phases, had entered the factory. Although, as a result, there was a drop in prices, men, in particular, paid for this by a general standardization of cut and a drabness of color which has characterized their clothing down to the present time.

The food industry had much the same history. The preparation of food became a factory industry. Flour milling was done by means of engine driven steel rollers, and the preservation of meat and other foods became a matter for refrigeration or canning companies. Crosse and Blackwell, Tucker, and others were making jams, candies, and similar delicacies for the average man's table. Even the preparation of biscuits, cookies, and cakes was being carried on by firms such as Huntley and Palmer, and Gray's, while in the big cities bakeries operating on a large scale were appearing. Even the fishing industry was coming under the control of mass production, working on a factory system, with refrigeration ships picking up the catch while the trawlers were still at sea.

From what has been said, it can be seen that by 1914 the older industries, many of them tracing their origins back before the eighteenth century, having dropped their handicraft characteristics, were tending to become mechanized and located in factories. Just because they had such deep historical roots, they were inclined to move much more slowly than did the industries of such countries as the United States. At the same time, because of her former success with these long established industries, Britain was loth to turn to the new types of manufacture which were being exploited by other industrial nations. Yet the pressure of circumstances eventually obliged her to do so, and from 1891 on a number of new industries began to appear on the scene.

The New Industries

One of the most important of the new types of industry was the German-fostered commercial chemistry. Although existing in some form or other from the beginning of the century, it never really became big business in Britain until after 1890. Between that date and 1911 it had doubled the number of its employees. The heavy chemicals, such as soda and chlorine, had for some twenty-five or thirty years been made by the Leblanc process, which by 1887 was outmoded. Therefore, to meet new demands the more efficient Solvay method was gradually introduced. It was in the matter of coal tar products however, that Britain was farthest behind Germany. Although a British chemist, W. H. Perkins in the early 1860's perfected a method of making dyes from the waste products of coking ovens, his ideas were neglected in Britain. The Germans, on the other hand, took them up, before long becoming the great producers of industrial and medical chemicals from the same source. The Germans also concentrated on improved methods of coking coal which enabled them to derive larger quantities of sulphates and similar materials. Only after 1891 did the British show much interest in these products, increasing their output slowly from about 3 million tons of sulphates to the 1914 figure of 34 million. The dyes from the coal tar were still relatively unimportant even by 1907, when Britain manufactured £373,000 worth and imported £1.7 millon. Yet if one compares Britain's export of all types of chemicals with her imports, a real growth of production becomes immediately apparent. The annual import for 1901 stood at about £9 million and the export at around £12 million. By 1913 the import had increased to £12 million, but the exports were up to some £21 million. The chemical industry was on its way.

A second new industry which was eventually to become of the greatest importance was the manufacture of automobiles. In this case also Britain was rather slow in starting. The first cars to arrive in the country (1894) were of German or French make, a situation which gradually changed when British bicycle firms and a sheep-shearing machine company (Wolseley) entered the field. By 1907 others, such as Leylands, Crossleys, Maudslays, and Morcoms, were manufacturing particularly the heavier type of vehicle, such as buses. Meanwhile, Daimler had moved his factory from Berlin to England which was a help. The result was that while in 1904 the import of cars and parts had been almost eight times the export, by 1913 it was not twice as large. A further point to be noted is that the export of bicycles and motorcycles more than paid for all imports.

Closely allied to the automotive industry, owing to the demand for tires, was the manufacture of rubber. Prior to 1880, Britain had been importing each year 7,500 tons of raw rubber, of which she re-exported half, but thereafter the balance slowly began to tip in the other direction. The perfecting of the pneumatic tire by J. B. Dunlop in 1888 increased the domestic demand, so by 1901 Britain was importing over 9,000 tons, of which she now used more than half. This figure increased by 2⅓ times before 1913. Rubber manufacture was now an important and prospering industry.

The third of the important industries was the production of electricity and electrical appliances. Before 1880 electricity was not popular, as mentioned above, for it competed with the gas companies, many of which had municipal backing. There was also the conflict between private and municipal interests over the question of who should control electrical traction such as tramway lines. One obstacle was overcome by the Electric Lighting Act (1882), which permitted local authorities to take over companies after 21 years. The obstacle caused by Britain's shortage of hydro-power disappeared with the introduction of Parson's steam turbine for the manufacture of electricity. The invention of the Ediswan electric light was also of very great importance, as it provided a good means of turning power into illumination. Still, the British were slow to produce much electrical equipment, the outcome being that American and German companies, such as Westinghouse, set up factories in the country to exploit the local market. Similarly, much of the heavy electrical equipment was imported from America, Germany, or even France.

The expansion of the use of mechanical power, at the same time, tended to revolutionize a good many of the older industries almost beyond recognition. Laundries operated by steam or electricity, sprang up in all the large centers. In the making of pottery, in printing, and in a dozen other trades, the use of electricity as the motive power brought about a complete revolution. Yet here again the average Briton would have to admit with some regret that nearly all his new gadgets and machines were either *Made in U.S.A.* or were manufactured under American licenses. The British, by concentrating on their older industries, had been reluctant to diversify their economy by introducing the new industries.

Thus, generally speaking, by 1914 Britain had lost her proud position as the industrial leader of the world. Other nations had either caught up with or surpassed her in her own particular field.

The Expansion of Communications

The industry employing the probably largest number of people in Britain by 1914 was communications, including both transport and the transmission of information. It has been estimated that around 750,000 were occupied in moving goods from one part of the country, or of the world, to another.

The principal domestic means of conveyance was the railroad. There had been a gradual increase of the mileage from 15,537 in 1870 to 23,701 with the greatest per cent of multiple track in the world, in 1914. As has been seen earlier, it had been costly to lay, averaging $225,000 a mile, as compared with $60,000 in the United States. At the same time, the speed of the trains was being raised, the average express running at about 42 m.p.h. as early as 1883. As a result of this higher speed, various safety devices, such as the block system and continuous brakes on passenger trains, were made compulsory in 1889. In the case of goods trains, however, since there were so many privately owned freight cars, the continuous brakes could not be used, they being still connected up by means of a mere chain and hook. In 1872 third class carriages were made compulsory for all passenger trains, with the result that everybody thereafter travelled third, soon causing the second class to disappear. By 1885, first class corridor, restaurant, and sleeping carriages had also been added, along with bigger and more powerful engines. Various railways began to compete in offering service, the chief contest being as to which could make the fastest trip between London and Edinburgh, with the record being established in 1888 at 7 hours and 32 minutes.

Yet, with all the development of the railways, there were practically no new companies established after 1870. The trend was all toward improvement or extension of the old lines. These were grouped into about seven major "alliances," usually in competition, yet at the same time, frequently trying to amalgamate. Many people protested against amalgamations of any kind because of the danger of monopoly, while others, because the railways, through agreements for pooling profits and for running on each other's lines, frequently had a virtual monopoly, were advocating the nationalization of the railways. The government repeatedly investigated the possibility of taking over the lines but did nothing apart from making an effort to control rates and terminal charges. Parliamentary committees and commissions of supervision were set up at various times, but with few powers, until finally in 1888 a Railway and Canal Commission was established with the authority of a court of record. At the same time, the railways were called upon to revise their rates, but there was so much confusion among the companies themselves that eventually in 1894 Parliament had to attempt to complete its control by setting up fixed schedules of rates. This was not satisfactory, since, although passenger traffic increased by 9 per cent, general merchandise by 10 per cent, and minerals by 12 per cent between 1904 and 1912, costs also rose steeply. A burden added in 1911 was a demand for increased wages. The old rates, therefore, no longer met the need, so Parliament had to authorize an increase in charges. By this means the companies increased their revenues sufficiently to meet the new demands and, at the same time, to augment their profits by about £1 million. The railways were thus prospering when war broke out.

One of the most important effects which the increased use of the railways had upon business was that, because of the short average hauling distance (less than 50 miles), merchants stopped keeping large stocks of goods on hand. A telegram to a port warehouse or to a manufacturer would bring a consignment the next day. At the same time, the improvement in the comforts of travel as well as the relatively low fares enabled people to move around the country with comparative ease, greatly increasing the mobility of labor.

Meanwhile, the use of canals had been dying out, in spite of great efforts to keep them alive. Only those which went through coal country or which had one terminus at a port were at all active. The railways were too fast and dependable for the waterways to offer much competition, although the Weaver Navigation, the Aire and Calder Canal, and a few others continued to prosper. Various grandiose plans were submitted to Parliament for the rehabilitation of the whole canal system, but they were never very practical and usually came to naught. The one exception was the Manchester Ship Canal. Built between 1887 and 1893 to bring ocean-going ships to Manchester, it has proved a considerable boon to the inland city despite Liverpool's disapproval. Canals generally, however, are now mainly pleasant places for sailing and fishing without very much economic value.

Although inland waterways were of relatively little importance in the British communication system, this was not the case with the harbors and ports of the country. From 1885 on dock building was taking place on all sides. Many of the smaller ports such as Hull, Grimsby, Cardiff, and Harwich enlarged their facilities, while, at the same time, big advances were made in the larger, transoceanic termini. Liverpool kept extending her long line of floating quays until by 1914 she had 420 acres of docks, compared to the 120 acres of her rival Manchester. To the north, Glasgow had been improving and dredging the Clyde so that ocean going vessels might sail farther up the river. Across the Irish Sea, Belfast had been carrying out the same type of improvement. Equally important as these developments had been the establishment in 1908 of the Port of London Authority, which took over all the various docks, controlled the dredging of the river, licensed lighters, and did various other routine jobs, including the establishment of an efficient police. Greater than all these, however, was the development of Southampton. Beginning about 1885, docks were built, railways were brought in, and facilities were improved so that full advantage could be taken of the wonderful landlocked harbor provided by the Isle of Wight. The result was that between 1887 and

1914 Southampton's traffic had risen from £14 million to £54 million in value and in tonnage had increased about five times. All these additions to the country's ports were of great value to Britain's trade, upon which her industry so largely depended.

Subsidiary to the main forms of public transport were various types of local carriers. Among these, the most important during this period was the tramway, the earliest, drawn by horses, appearing in Liverpool about 1868 and a year later in London. Between 1870 and 1886, such tram lines appeared in different parts of the country, increasing their mileage by about 45 miles each year, until in 1886 there were some 779 miles of track, with 23,000 horses pulling the cars. As time went on, however, other forms of locomotion were introduced. Steam appeared as early as 1877 but was not popular. The advent of electric traction really gave the great impetus to expansion. Large companies, such as the British Electric Traction Co. and the South Yorkshire Traction Co., began to develop electric tramway systems. By 1914 the municipalities had taken over many of these lines, about 60 per cent of the country's 2,530 miles of track being then in their hands.

By 1914 tramway expansion had reached its limit, the reason being the advent of motor busses. The old horse omnibus, which had been popular particularly in London, very quickly evolved into a new bus once the gasoline engine had been substituted for the horse. In many localities authorities resisted the buses as competing with their trams. But in a place such as London, where the police licensed the buses, and the London County Council the trams, the municipal authorities were able to do very little. The result was that the London busses increased steadily in number, until by 1914 there were some 3,600 altogether. Buses also began to take to the open road, thus giving competition to the railways, although it did not become serious before 1914.

While the trams and busses were the principal means of transporting the general public, other vehicles were employed by private individuals. The Hansom cab was the taxi of those days. A two-wheeled affair, with the driver sitting up behind the passengers, it was the customary means of quick conveyance for one or two people. The Brougham, a four-wheeled light coach, was used for larger groups. It has been reckoned that in 1881 London had some 15,000 cabs, most of them owner-driven.

The privately owned means of transportation for the working and middle-class part of the population was the bicycle. Of very great importance not only in enabling people to move around quickly and easily, but also in giving many the opportunity to get out of their industrial surroundings into the country in a very short time, it helped to make their lives more pleasant. For the upper classes from 1890 onwards, automobiles took the place of the horse-drawn coaches or Broughams. Built high and wide something like sight-seeing buses, they were not very comfortable. Still, in spite of difficulties, they did get around at the relatively fast pace of 15 m.p.h., thus making them useful and a decided improvement upon a horse drawn vehicle. By 1914 there were some 200,000 licensed in Britain.

It was the automobile which faced Britain with a new and very real problem. Because of the rapid expansion of the railways in the mid-nineteenth century, roads had generally fallen upon evil days. Consequently, only when the automobiles began to tear them up was it realized that something had to be done. By an early law all horseless machines on the road had to travel at no more than 4 m.p.h. with a man preceding them on horseback with a red flag. In 1896 this regulation was removed, cars under three tons being permitted to travel at 14 m.p.h. Even these concessions, however, were ineffective, for the young blades of the day often raced from London to Brighton at a speed of 30 to 35 m.p.h.! How they did it on the roads then in existence defies imagination. In 1903 a further act was passed, raising the speed limit to 20 m.p.h. and imposing a license. Six years later it was decided that to finance road building the returns from the licenses and a tax on gasoline should be used, these two items providing by 1914 the annual income of about £400,000. One of the chief advocates of the development of the roads' system was the Roads Improvement Association, founded in the 1890's. By its propaganda it succeeded in having a Road Board appointed in 1909 to help supervise improvements. This body, however, had relatively little success owing to the fact that the roads were under various local managements: Urban and Local District Councils, often involving too much management and not enough action. The result was that roads in Britain in 1914 were not in a very good condition.[1]

For the transmission of information, the Post Office was the chief medium. In 1875 Britain became a member of the Universal Postal Union and established a rate of 2½d. for letters to Europe, a rate later extended to the whole world. In 1881 the postal money order was introduced, followed two years later by parcel post. In 1870 the Post Office also took over all the telegraphs in the country. Meanwhile the telephone had appeared. Financed

---

[1] On the 303 miles of road from London to Carlisle there were 72 different managing authorities.

largely by private capital, in the 1890's, there was a good deal of competition out of which one company, the National Telephone Company, in 1900 came to the top. At this point the Post Office successfully claimed that its monopoly of telegraphs gave it the right to all telephones also. At first it took over only the trunk (long distance) lines, leaving the National to run the exchanges and local lines until 1911, when all telephones finally came under state control. At this time there were 774,000 telephones with 62,000 miles of trunk line. Wireless was also coming into use, primarily on ships, but nothing of any account was done with it before 1914. It is interesting to notice that it was the wireless in 1913 which brought ships to the rescue of the Titanic as she sank in mid-Atlantic, and by the next year 879 ships are registered as being equipped.

One further means of communication might be mentioned: the newspaper. While there had been newspapers in the country for two centuries, most of them had catered only to the upper classes. True, there had been cheap publications for the laboring classes, but they had never lasted very long. The dean of newspapers, owned by the family of Walters, was the London *Times* which, particularly under the editorship of Delane in the middle of the nineteenth century, had expanded both its circulation and its news coverage. It was, however, despite this, still an upper class organ. It rested with A. C. W. Harmsworth, later Lord Northcliffe, to change the situation. He believed that a cheap paper with news of "human interest" was what was needed. In 1888 he founded *Answers*, which offered prizes for competitions and contests. Then in 1894 he purchased the *Evening News*, following this in 1896 with the founding of the *Daily Mail*, in 1903 by the purchase of the *Daily Mirror*, and, finally, in 1908 by the acquisition of the now almost defunct *Times*. His great stress was upon timeliness, succinctness, and human interest, an example which was followed by others, even the labor element when it set up its own organ, the *Daily Herald*. The political and social influence of this cheap popular press was incalculable. From the economic point of view it was also of great importance, for out of it came the growth of another great industry employing hundreds of thousands of people and calling for the investment of millions of pounds in capital.

Looking back over the period 1870-1914, one cannot but be impressed with the change which had taken place in British industry during these forty odd years. The common characteristics seem to have been, increased mechanization and the growth of mass production, bringing with them steadily expanding output. Yet all was not well. For one thing, Britain's greater production meant greater dependence upon foreign countries for raw materials and food stuffs. For another thing, although production was rising, it was not rising as rapidly as it had before 1870, nor as rapidly as the production of such countries as the United States or Germany. Indeed, much of the new technical improvement in Britian's industry had actually to be imported from those countries. Thus, while outwardly prospering and expanding, in actuality Britain was heading into difficulties owing to her reluctance to change her ways, to the rise of potentially much wealthier rivals, and to the growing competition for raw materials. Here was her economic danger which a great war would only accentuate. Consequently, although few seemed to realize the nature of her critical situation, in 1914 Britain's industrial position was in reality very insecure.

Chapter 21

LONDON, THE WORLD MONEY MARKET

Between 1870 and 1890 London became "the financial metropolis of the world,"[1] a position it continued to hold down to the opening of World War I. The fundamental reason for this was that Britain still dominated world trade. Others might be developing as rivals in the industrial and commercial fields, but Britain up to 1914 was still regarded as the leading economic world power. With a much longer tradition of industrialism than any other nation, coupled with the outlook this engenders in the "captains of industry and finance," she had a world rather than a national viewpoint. Not that the British industrialists had any philanthropic motives, but rather they thought in terms of a world instead of a local economy. This was necessary because of the wide ramifications of British trade. Added to this, while opportunities for investment at home expanded to a certain degree, far greater opportunities for profitable investment were to be found outside the limits of the British Isles. For this reason the British investor became increasingly interested in foreign government and industrial offerings as sources of income. Since he also had the money, more than the investor in any other country, he attracted to London those who needed financial backing for their various plans. By this means London became the arbiter of financial matters around the globe.

Joint-Stock Companies and Amalgamations

This growing preponderance of the power of London was closely linked with a change which took place in business organization. It consisted of the expansion of the joint-stock principle into all kinds of business, and the rise of increasingly large corporations.

[1] G. W. Edwards, *The Evolution of Finance Capitalism* (New York, 1938), p. 32.

The joint-stock principle was not new, for it had been known in the sixteenth century. What was new was that after 1863 it became much easier to establish a joint-stock company of limited liability, and even more important, such companies were now regarded as respectable. The result was that increasingly the small man could put his savings into business in order to participate in the profits. Thus joint-stock ventures became not only respectable, but popular as well.

It was not, however, in order to help the small man that the new form of organization was devised. It was a result of the logic of the situation. By the expansion, both at home and abroad, of the market for various types of commodities, particularly in the field of heavy industry, there was a growing need for larger and larger plants, warehouses, docks, and the like. These things were not only costing increasingly larger sums, but they made it necessary for the investor to wait a longer time for returns on his money, particularly if it was being used to finance projects in central Africa or Borneo. Along with this, there was the heavier pressure of foreign competition, often aided by foreign governments. The big corporation was about the only organization which could meet the challenge. Finally, foreign competition was often responsible for forcing down prices, a trend stimulated by labor-saving devices in manufacturing. Since British costs in the form of wages, however, remained the same and sometimes even rose, every effort was made to achieve greater economies in production by increasing the size and activity of the industrial unit. Here again there was the demand for the big corporation which could exist only on the joint-stock, limited liability basis.

From 1870 on a larger number of joint-stock companies was registered each year. In 1863 there were 691, but between 1881 and 1883 the yearly average stood at 1600, and by 1914 the new joint-stock companies were being registered at the annual rate of about 7,000. Nearly all of these were of limited liability, the shareholder being liable to lose, if the company failed, only the money he had invested. It has been estimated that a large number of these companies did not last very long, about 20 per cent folding up within five years of their founding. As is usual in times of great speculation, dishonesty was often involved, which meant that many were not bona fide from the beginning. But by 1914 there were over 54,000 joint-stock companies in operation with a total paid-up capital of £2,531.9 million.

Many of these companies had originally been firms owned by one man, by a partnership, or by a family. They had perhaps found that they lacked the capital to make the necessary expansion for their growing volume of trade. Therefore, they would set up a joint-stock company to offer shares to the public for purchase. This was particularly true in the heavy industries, where we have the example of Bolckow, Vaughan and Whitworths. On the other hand, some of the old firms decided to take advantage of the limited liability clause without letting in any new members. The result was the private company, where the family or the partners held all the shares with certain restrictions on their transfer so that no breach would be made by the public in the dyke. Such companies were those formed by the Harland and Wolff shipbuilding partnership, by Huntley and Palmer, the biscuit manufacturers, or by Crosse and Blackwell, the jam and candy makers. Usually having less than 10 shareholders each, by 1890 private companies made up one third of the registrations and one half of the actual company formations. These organizations were usually more solid and effective than many of the new public joint-stock companies. It was not until 1907, however, that the private company was actually recognized in law. By that time it was so common that the legislation was hardly necessary.

The same form of organization was also adopted during this period by the banks. Joint-stock banks were becoming more common even by 1870, but none of them were "limited." It was felt that shareholders in the banks should be responsible for all the banks debts. This attitude changed somewhat radically after 1878, when the City of Glasgow Bank failed through mismanagement, leaving each of the shareholders responsible for six times the amount he had invested. Hundreds were beggared by the crash. The result was that shareholders began to demand and to obtain limited liability. In England and Wales many private banks also sought the protection of limited joint-stock organization, although in Scotland, with its eight or ten joint-stock banks, the addition of limited liability was all that was necessary. Gradually the unlimited liability private bank disappeared from the picture.

Concurrent with the extension of the joint-stock idea went amalgamations. Private firms were usually very loth to submerge their identity and lose their names in a new combine. Joint-stock companies, on the other hand, had no such sentimental scruples. Being much more impersonal organizations, increased efficiency and profits were their interests. Consequently, there were many large amalgamations throughout the whole period, but especially after 1890. In the heavy industries, particularly in armament production, such amalgamations were extremely common. Commencing with 1902, Vickers, the product of a number of early unions, joined up with Beardmores of the Clyde and then with Cammell Lairds of Birkenhead. John Brown, the shipbuilder, followed the same course, eventually obtaining a controlling interest of Harland and Wolff. In textiles, J. & P. Coats of Paisley gradually took over various manufacturers of sewing thread until they had a virtual monopoly, with factories spread all over the world: the United States, Canada, Russia, Hungary, and India, and a profit in 1906 of almost £3 million. Courtaulds, the silk manufacturers, were assuming control of artificial silk production, while Lever Brothers were expanding their capital from £4 million in 1906 to £30 million in 1913. So it went on throughout the various industries.

Such amalgamations were not limited to British firms, for there were similar international combines. Eastmans Limited, of New York, a meat-exporting firm, combined with Bells, its London and Glasgow agents. Oil companies also began to link up, as in the case of the Royal Dutch Shell which was a British-Dutch corporation. One of the biggest organizations, the Imperial Tobacco Company, was that in which all the British tobacco companies joined together to fight an invasion by Duke's American Tobacco Company. This resulted in the two interests dividing the world between themselves and jointly forming the British-American Tobacco Company. In 1914, the Imperial Tobacco Company was capitalized at £18 million and the British-American at £14.5 million. This was a virtual monopoly very much in the same style as the Nobel Dynamite Trust, into which Nobel brought all those who held his licenses for manufacture. While each unit retained its own identity, there was a super directorate, appointed by the subsidiaries, in control of policies. Here was an almost perfect monopoly.

Amalgamations were not limited to manufacturers, for financial institutions were following the same plan. Insurance companies were increasing in size, partially by expanding business, partially by the absorption of smaller concerns. Between 1891 and 1902 the English banks showed an even greater trend in that direction, with 114 amalgamations. The largest of these was the formation of Barclay's Bank in 1896, when fifteen institutions united. The result was that between 1886 and 1910 the private banks declined in number from 250 to about 12, nearly all being absorbed into limited joint-stock organizations. Thus, by 1910 individual banking organizations, although fewer in number, had greatly increased in strength. They had realized the advantages of the Scottish system, which possessed only a few banks (eight in 1910), all of which were thoroughly sound.

The growth of the large joint-stock bank on the Scottish plan led to another development similar to that used north of the Tweed: branch banking, which soon became the rule rather than the exception. The Bank of England made no attempt to extend its facilities, but the other banks did. Between 1872 and 1908 the number of banking offices in Great Britain grew from 2,924 to 7,861. The London and County Bank had 165 branches as early as 1886, the National Provincial coming second with 158, and the Capital and Counties coming third with 99. By 1914 the number of branches was much larger, although the Scots still had more banks per capita than either England or Wales.

Parallel to branch banking was the growth of the multiple food shop, or what the American calls the chain store. Even before 1870, the Civil Service Supply Co. and the Aereated Bread Company had adopted this form, but from 1880 on it experienced a great growth. Thomas Lipton, starting in 1879 as a Glasgow grocer, by 1890 had seventy tea and grocery shops which he organized as a limited company in 1898. Other retailers, such as dairies, meat dealers, and restaurants, followed the same plan, Lyons being a good example, with its restaurants scattered all over Britain. By 1914 some of these companies had as many as 400 to 600 branches.

Another type of store which developed rapidly was the department store. By no means new in 1870, it gradually became important after that date, with more and more departments added, until it could provide anything one required. While Harrods' commenced in 1889 as a grocery store, nine years later Selfridge's on Oxford Street was established as a complete departmental store from its beginning. Harrod, in founding his store, provided the original contributors with "founders' shares" which received an increasing percentage of the profits as the company grew. By 1914 their value had increased ten times over what they had been at the beginning. Thus, even the retail business had adopted the principle of joint-stock ownership and bigness in size.

Probably one of the earliest types of retail organization to follow this plan had been the cooperative stores. Since their founding in the early 1840's they had grown rapidly, reaching by 1870 what might well have seemed the maximum size, but even after that date, while not at the same rate, their progress continued. Patronized principally in the industrial northern towns by the working classes, they were a real means of helping to keep down the laborers' cost of living. Usually the stores limited the value of the shares to be held by any one person to £200, although the limit might be lower. The fixed rate of interest was established at 4 per cent or 5 per cent and the annual "dividend" on the purchases made by the members, averaged, between 1896 and 1910, something around 2s. 6d. on the pound. In 1885 their sales stood at about £20 million, while the total wages of British industry is estimated to have been around £480 million. By 1912 sales had risen to about £80 million out of some £700 million in wages, indicating the cooperatives' relative expansion. The cooperative stores were aided by the growth of the Cooperative Wholesale Societies in England and Scotland. These organizations helped to reduce the costs of production, the savings being passed on to the customer. By 1913 there were probably about three million members belonging to about 1400 cooperative retail societies. Some £46 million were invested in the organizations, and, out of the trade of £80 million in 1913, about £13 million were net profit. The two wholesale organizations had a trade of about £40 million, while in the bank organized by the co-ops, the annual turnover was almost £170 million. Thus, a section of labor had applied to its own problems the techniques of big business, with very profitable results.

By the beginning of the year 1914 the limited liability joint-stock company was, therefore, the most usual form of business organization. There were still many private firms, but they were no longer the predominant type. For various reasons which will be discussed later, the total capital invested in new joint-stock companies during the first decade of the twentieth century declined from its peak in 1897. But what is of more importance, the average capitalization of the individual company declined from around £65,000 in 1896 to £26,500 in 1910. Many were still being formed with much higher capitalization, but these figures would indicate that the smaller type of business as well as the larger one was increasingly being made into a joint-stock enterprise. Many, of course, remained private joint-stock companies, their shares not being for sale; 6,328 were of that character in the 7,321 new registrations of 1913. But the general change is only too clear. It is true that it brought with it disadvantages, particularly in the public companies where the owners became separated both from management and labor. But, for good or ill, the development took place and exercised a very great influence on the financial as well as industrial history of the time.

The Position of the Government in British Finance

The government always has some influence on a country's economy, the national debt, taxes, war, and the like being bound to influence industry and trade, if for no other reason than because they require part of the national income. From 1870 to 1890 the British Parliament did its utmost to exert as little influence as possible upon the country's economy. Wedded to the principles of laissez faire, it desired to act as a policeman and nothing else. During the '90's, however, there took place a gradual change, which had become quite noticeable by 1906. The Liberal and Labour Parties were by that time both committed to state interference in economic and social affairs. National social services were being demanded on all sides, while, at the same time, the country was arming against possible external attack. Both of these demanded larger and larger amounts of money, which could come only from taxes. Consequently, from 1890 on there was a gradually increasing tendency on the part of the government to interfere in the country's economic affairs.

Leaving the various social aspects of government activity to a later chapter, at this point our interest in its influence on the national economy is purely financial. This side, however, was fundamental and basic to its social and military program, for only as its finances were in proper order could the bills for social reforms and armaments be paid.

The first consideration in studying the government's financial position is the national debt. It is important because throughout the period, Consols were one of the best securities on the market and because much of the national revenue went to pay debt charges. In 1870 this debt stood at £747 million and in 1879 at £778 million. Every effort was made by succeeding Chancellors of the Exchequer to reduce it, thereby curtailing a continual drain on the treasury. The size of this drain can be realized when it is remembered that in 1870 the debt charges took over one third of the treasury's receipts (£27 million). Gladstone, from 1866 on, attempted to liquidate the funded debt by turning much of it into terminable securities to be paid off by 1885. He did this principally, by converting the government stock held by the Savings Banks. In 1875 Northcote set up a New Sinking Fund into which the government each year was to place money for debt reduction. The Old Sinking Fund of 1829 was to continue as before, and both were to work for the same end. The usual fate of sinking funds, whether new or old, was, however, that when the government was hard up, it raided them so that they could no longer meet the debt. While Gladstone's plan was partially successful, probably one of the best moves was made by Goschen in 1888, when he converted 3 per cent government stock to 2¾ per cent, to be reduced to 2½ per cent in 1903. This meant large savings, and by 1899 the debt was down to £635 million.

The period from 1870 to 1900 was thus very bright from the point of view of debt reduction. The services of handling it had declined by almost 60 per cent, while its capital amount was decreasing at the same time that the national income was climbing. The end of this favorable development came with the Boer War (1899-1901). Not at first appreciating the seriousness of this conflict, the government attempted to finance it by borrowing instead of by increasing taxes. The consequence was that of the £217 million which the war cost, less than one third had been paid off by the time peace came. Simultaneously, £92 million were added to the funded debt, the total national indebtedness by 1905 having reached the figure of £797 million, while the Sinking Funds had been raided repeatedly, thus destroying their effectiveness. Asquith, Chancellor of the Exchequer 1906-1908, tackled the problem vigorously, reducing the debt to around £708 million, where it stayed until 1914. The per capita debt in that year amounted to £15.3, as over against £22.7 in 1879. There had been an improvement, although it was not very noticeable to the tax payer.

While Asquith succeeded to a certain extent in reducing the national debt, it was not brought down in proportion to the increasing wealth of the country. There were a number of reasons for this. In the first place, the flood of government bonds sold on the security market during the Boer War tended to reduce the value of government stock, bringing a rise in the rate of interest. At the same time, the advent of the Liberal Government in 1906 saw an increase in government social services. These took revenues which could have been devoted to debt reduction. Coupled with these requirements were those of the Army and Navy for greater and greater expenditures to meet the threat of an armed Germany. Consequently, the reduction of the debt by about £90 million was, under the circumstances, surprisingly good.

As can be seen from what has just been said, the period 1900-1913 was one of mounting expenditures, but this was generally characteristic of the whole forty years prior to World War I. Before 1900 the great ambition of both the Liberals and Conservatives had been to reduce taxes. So, whenever they had a surplus they favored the idea of applying it to tax rather than debt reduction. Simultaneously, however, disbursements continued to rise. In 1870 they were less than £70 million, but by 1892 they were almost £90 million, and by 1900 they were well over the £100 million mark. The tendency towards inflation after 1894 facilitated this move upward, but there were other causes, such as the introduction of free primary and secondary education and the increasing activity of local authorities in dealing with the problems of poverty. In the next ten years expenditures almost doubled, reaching in 1914 the all time high of £197 million. Old Age Pensions, introduced in 1908, were by 1913 costing over £12 million; education costs had more than tripled since 1890, while armaments, as well as government investment in and aid to certain industries, were demanding increasing sums.[2] It was not surprising, therefore, that a greatly expanded tax system was needed to meet growing government costs.

From the earliest days, as we have seen in the foregoing chapters, one of the most usual ways of increasing government revenue was to raise customs duties. But this was now all changed. Ever since the repeal of the Corn Laws in 1846 Britain had become more and more enamored of free trade. Consequently, taxes on food, drink, and raw materials, although never abolished, were kept at a minimum, certain duties remaining on tea, coffee, wine, and tobacco. There was also an excise tax on alcoholic liquors made within the country, while those who retailed them had to pay for a license. In the 1890's the average annual return from all these taxes came to over £40 million, a sizable sum for the Exchequer. As this was about the limit of what they could produce, however, it was necessary, as expenditures increased, to look elsewhere for funds. By 1895 it had become quite clear that the whole tax structure had to be revised and modernized to meet the growing demands made on the government.

The first change attempted was in connection with death duties and inheritance taxes. In 1870 there were four extremely cumbersome types of taxes which were levied on each estate. What was worse, they were really not very profitable, producing in 1886 only a little over £8 million. In 1894 Sir William Harcourt commenced a reorganization by abolishing the old distinction between real and personal property and by substituting two new for the four old taxes. Henceforth there was to be a graduated tax from 1 per cent to 8 per cent on all estates according to size. Another tax was also to be levied according to the kinship of the heirs to the deceased. It was estimated at the time of their institution that these reforms

[2] For an outline of these, see page 401.

would enlarge the returns by about £4 million, whereas the first year saw the total amount actually come to over £14 million. In 1907 Asquith raised the rates to 10 per cent, while two years later Lloyd George put a further tax on estates of over £5,000, making their rates vary between 4 per cent and 14 per cent. Thus, by 1914 the Death Duties were actually bringing in £27.4 million a year, a tidy increase over the £8 million of twenty years before.

While the revenue from inheritance taxes was gratifying, it was not enough. It was not long, therefore, before the income tax came under the Exchequer's scrutiny. Gladstone, although he had always disliked this tax as interfering with a person's private property and curtailing his initiative, had never been able to abolish it. Between 1870 and 1900 its rate had varied from time to time but had tended gradually to climb. During the Boer War it reached 1s. 6d. in the pound, but by 1904 it had again fallen to 11d. With the advent of the Liberals a change took place, for Asquith, holding that it was a permanent tax, in his budget of 1907 established a system of graduation. Harcourt in the 1890's had moved in this direction by increasing exemptions for lower incomes and by allowing something off for houses and land. It was Asquith, however, who made the final move, adding to the plan of graduated taxes a distinction between earned and unearned income. In 1909 Lloyd George made further radical changes. He set the rate at 1s. 2d. in the pound but allowed those with incomes under £3,000 to pay only 9d. in the pound for the first £2,000 and 1s. for the amount between £2,000 and £3,000. He also clamped on a super-tax on incomes over £5,000, while increasing abatements and exemptions to the lower income brackets. By 1914 these taxes were producing altogether over £47.2 million annually for the treasury.

The year 1909 also saw another change in the system of taxation. Lloyd George, who was not only trying to meet a possible deficit of £16 million but was also out to "get" the big landed interests, brought in two new land taxes. One was a tax on the "unearned increment" of land whose value had increased owing to the growth and activities of the community. Whenever land was sold or inherited, after a fixed date the tax was to be 20 per cent of the increase, while on the reversion of a lease, the lease-holder was to pay 10 per cent of any increased value. At the same time, an annual tax of ½d. in the pound was placed on the site value of undeveloped land, along with 1s. in the pound on mining royalties. While the tax on undeveloped land was of relatively little economic importance, it caused a considerable political upheaval, ultimately leading to the severe curtailment of the power of the House of

Lords. The mining royalty, on the other hand, did produce considerable amounts. All told, however, the taxes were of no great economic value, most of them being repealed after World War I.

While national taxation was rising, the same thing was true of local rates. It has been estimated that for England and Wales the latter in 1881 amounted to £53.8 million, while by 1914 it stood at £169 million. With the need for new water works, electrical or gas-producing plants, tramways, and other utilities, local authorities were both offering increased numbers of bonds for sale on the market and making greater demands on the taxpayers.

Similar to the local governments' investment in public utilities was the national government's increasing involvement in ordinary commercial transactions. In order to save the Cunard Steamship Line from being bought up by the International Mercantile Marine Company of New Jersey, the government was forced to loan Cunard considerable sums, as well as to give it an annual subsidy of £150,000. Britain's growing interest in the oil industry was manifested in the government's willingness to help finance the Anglo-Persian Oil Company by subscribing for 50 per cent of the companies shares. In both these cases and a number of others, despite much talk of laissez faire and an avowed adherence to free trade principles, the government was spending an increasing amount of the taxpayers' money in ordinary business ventures. This also tended to raise national expenditures.

When we attempt to assess the importance and influence of the government on the financial affairs of the country, one thing is clear. Year by year an ever-increasing amount of the country's wealth was being funnelled into government coffers. The government was no longer interested primarily in floating long-term loans in which men with spare cash could invest. Instead, it was taking that money in taxes. Indeed, taxation had increased more rapidly than had the country's wealth. It has been estimated that the nominal capital wealth of Great Britain rose, between 1890 and 1913, from £9,400 million to £14,310 million, the annual national income climbing in the same period from £669 million to £951 million.[3] When one remembers, however, that prices were also going up, this increase in income is not as great it would at first seem to be. To place over against the 50 per cent increase in national wealth and the 45 per cent increase in annual national income, the more than 120 per cent increase in government taxation makes clear how the government policies influenced the financial

[3] M. Dobb, *Studies in the Development of Capitalism* (London, 1950), pp. 300 f.

activities of the country. At the same time, the new taxation system was making considerable effort toward redistributing the wealth of the country. As a result, it becomes evident that by 1914 governmental taxation policies were bound to have a very considerable influence upon the availability of capital for investment, in this way controlling a large part of the economic activities of the country. There were, on the other hand, countervailing forces, such as armament contracts and the like, which hid much of this until after World War I.

The Expansion of British Investment

Against the background of joint-stock companies, amalgamations, and government finance, it is now possible to understand a little more easily the actual financial organization and history of the period. With the expanding foreign market, the demands for the building of railways in South America and India, for the erection of oil refineries in Persia, and for the establishment of cotton mills in Japan, increasingly large amounts of capital were required. Moreover, while the home government was forever taking more in taxes, foreign governments were, at the same time, seeking larger and larger loans. It was not long, therefore, before the possibility of financing these projects was far beyond the capacity of individuals or of the smaller joint-stock enterprises. The result was amalgamations of corporations and enterprises, calling, in turn, for greater amounts of capital, which, because of its very quantity, had to be organized and channeled into the areas whence it would bring forth the best returns. Profits of finance were greater than before, but by the very size of the business deals now being carried out the dangers were equally great. A war or a drought might bring ruin to millions. Therefore, sound financial organization was of the greatest importance.

The foundation of the whole British structure of finance was the banking system. As has been already pointed out, it had been strengthened very greatly after 1870 by the growth of amalgamations, and after the Glasgow City Bank debacle, by a great increase in the number of limited joint-stock banks. From 1870 on there was also a general convergence on London by Scottish, provincial, and foreign houses. The Scots alone succeeded in keeping both their London offices as well as their right to issue notes. Provincial, European, and American banks increasingly established connections with the London money market by setting up branches to handle their business. The only place on earth where one could find such a gathering of the financial clans, London became the money market and banking capital of the world.

At the very center of London financial circles stood "The Old Lady of Threadneedle Street," the Bank of England. Still the banker's bank, she held a considerable part, although by no means all, of the other banks' gold reserves. By 1900 she was getting to the position where she also issued most of the notes in use in England and Wales. They were, however, of relatively little importance, since gold and silver were still the common media of exchange. Notes were used only for payments over £5, while for large sums the inland bill, or more commonly the check, was employed. In Scotland bank notes of denominations from £1 up were still common. The Bank of England gave relatively little direct help to industry, except that it had begun to loan money on safe marketable securities. Its really important function was that of attempting to control the money market by raising or lowering the discount rate or by buying and selling gold and securities. If there was a danger of gold leaving the country in large quantities, the raising of the bank rate above 6 per cent usually brought it back. In this way the Bank maintained Britain's and the world's financial stability with a minimum of trouble.

Yet the Bank was dependent in this whole matter of finance upon the ordinary banks, both commercial and savings, along with the insurance companies as they were the agents who accumulated funds for investment. At this point the Scottish banks took the lead in venturing into new fields. Although the old idea of giving small loans to worthy, hard-working people had disappeared, the Scottish banks were advancing credit for security purchases. About the same time they began "accepting" bills drawn by exporters on their foreign creditors. The Scottish banking houses were also particularly interested in colonial banking companies, to whom they advanced money for purchases in Britain and who, in return, gave them the work of handling their London business. In this practice they were soon followed by the provincial and foreign houses. One other general duty which all the banks were beginning to perform was the collecting of dividends and clipping of coupons for individuals fortunate enough to be holding stocks and bonds. Thus the banks were increasing both their services and their activities.

The banks also took over business from the bill brokers, those men who had been interested in bringing the buyer and seller of a bill of exchange together, or who had been accustomed to buy bills to hold until maturity. Checks were largely displacing the inland bill, while the foreign bill was being discounted increasingly by the bank. Thus short-time investments fell almost entirely into the banks' hands.

Long-term investments, on the other hand, were usually handled by investment banks or investment trusts. Barings, Rothschilds, and others, were investment banks which specialized in floating loans, primarily for foreign governments. Taking over a whole issue of securities, they would sell them in small quantities at a profit. If they could not sell the securities, however, they might experience serious loss. Some banks dealt in industrial securities only, but this type was not so common until after 1880, and when they did become very active, they tended to show more interest in foreign industrials which produced higher profits than in domestic issues. One exception to this rule was the British brewing industry, which always paid well. British industrial securities, however, were usually handled on a somewhat different plan, which will be described later.

Investment trusts appeared in the 1880's and 1890's. These organizations bought up stocks and securities with the proceeds received from the sale of their own stock. The profits which accrued from their investments were then paid out to their own shareholders.

By and large, the whole of this investment activity centered around the London Stock Exchange, the world's chief stock market. There were exchanges also in Edinburgh, Glasgow, Birmingham, Manchester, and other provincial cities, but London dominated the scene. The provincial and Scottish exchanges tended to deal primarily in local securities, Birmingham Gas Works and the like, or in securities sent down from London. London, on the other hand, dealt mostly in national and foreign securities, in which industrials by no means predominated. Railways, public utilities, and foreign government bonds were by far the most common type of security. These were being bought and sold on the market by between 4,500 and 5,500 brokers and jobbers, who through the use of the telephone and cable were developing arbitrage, or the buying of stocks in one market with the idea, at the same time, of selling them in another for a profit. Thus, throughout the period stock market activity expanded, becoming increasingly important in financial affairs.

As mentioned above, the London Exchange did not deal to any extent in British company shares, partially because so many of the

British joint-stock companies were private concerns and partially because people were only gradually getting used to the idea of investing in joint-stock industrial and commercial enterprises. Perhaps even more influential was the fact that the stock of British companies was very seldom backed by one of the big investment banks. Instead, the domestic corporation's issue was usually floated by an agent, who had perhaps persuaded a private firm to become a public company. He would contact a number of wealthy people whom he would ask, for a consideration, to underwrite the sale of a certain block of the stock. These investors would thereupon become the company, whose shares would be offered publicly for sale. When they were nearly all sold, the company would then be registered. This method was also employed for the floatation of new companies. The one trouble was that there was the same danger which beset the South Sea Bubble: dishonest promotion. The art of writing prospectuses was highly developed, so security journalism in Britain became of very great importance as well as of some danger. But, despite the failure and disappearance of many joint-stock companies, the agents continued to flourish, making and losing large sums of money both for themselves and for others. Although a growing number of the companies had their shares sold on the provincial exchanges, only those at the very top ever succeeded in reaching London.

At the same time that London was consolidating her position as the financial capital of the world, the investment tide was rising in other countries such as Germany, France, and the United States. Yet London dominated the scene, for they were all bound to her, not merely because of the large British foreign investments but also because they had all gone on to the gold standard during this period and their money was quoted in terms of the pound sterling. For more than sixty years Britain had been on the gold standard, prepared to redeem her notes with gold. Now that discoveries of that metal in South Africa and Australia in the early 1880's made it much more plentiful, the other nations gradually adopted the same standard. This meant stable currencies with a fixed relationship to the British pound. By 1900 the currency of practically every large country except China was based on gold. France held reserves valued at £120 million, while Russia's gold was estimated at £100 million. By this means commercial transactions between countries were greatly facilitated, and Britain dominated because her gold market was the easiest and freest in existence, the gold sovereign being "chief coin of the world," acceptable everywhere because of its stability and dependability.[4] Thus, as far as money was concerned, the years 1885 to 1914 were years of steadiness without the violent currency fluctuations experienced after World War I.

The Financial Movements

In concluding this study of the financial organization of Britain during the period 1870-1914, we would do well to glance at the main events which took place. Only then can one really see the meaning of these changes.

From 1870 to 1890 there was a period of relative calm. As the profits of British industry were declining, the investors began to look abroad for better returns on their money. In the '70's two small disturbances tended to restrain somewhat this interest in investment: the crash of 1873 in the United States, and the failure in 1878 of the Glasgow City Bank. In the case of the former the Bank of England actually raised its rate to 9 per cent to protect its reserves, but from neither upset were there any serious consequences. The year 1879 saw considerable depression, but from then on for the next ten years there was a steady rise. Between 1881 and 1885 the average amount available for investment abroad was around £30 million, between 1886 and 1890 it was £50 million, and by 1890 it reached £82 million. Indeed, there was more money seeking investment than could be used. Investment companies developed rapidly and dishonest promotion was by no means uncommon. The result was what Clapham calls a "widespread madness of greed."

The bubble was suddenly pricked in 1890 with the near collapse of Barings, the investment bankers. In the previous two years there had been a large amount of company floatation, of which some had been highly speculative. There was too much money with little except low return securities in which to invest. Consequently, the Argentine, which was just being developed at this time, was a great attraction. Argentinian banks were giving mortgages on the security of land and were then turning them over to British investors. At the same time, all the South American countries were establishing public utilities at a great rate. Their mortgages and stocks were usually underwritten by one or two British investment houses, primarily Barings. In 1890, however, people suddenly became suspicious. The sale of the shares of Buenos Ayres Water

---

[4] In the 1890's the author's father traveled all over Europe and the near East paying for his expenses from a pocket full of gold sovereigns purchased before he left Britain.

Works began to fall, and along with them went other South Americans securities. The result was that by November, 1890, Barings, while having securities worth £3 million more than their liabilities, did not have the liquid assets to meet their obligations. It looked as though the firm might fail. The bank rate was raised to 6 per cent, and various bankers were called in by the Bank of England to help guarantee the Barings' solvency. In this way the crisis was met. Barings eventually met all their obligations, but for safety, became a joint-stock company. Their trouble, however, had put a definite damper on the flurry of speculation, bringing it to a rather sudden stop.

After the set-back experienced in 1890, the rate of investment picked up only very slowly, although by 1900 it was again getting into its stride. From 1904 on there was a boom in the export of capital. In 1906 the amount invested abroad stood at £104 million, and by 1913 it had reached £225 million; in that year the total British foreign holdings stood at something like £4,000 million. On the other hand, there was relatively little investment at home, for the highest profits were always paid by the foreign venture. To attract the unwary to invest in their securities, promoters employed all the latest tricks. "Special offers" were made. Boards of directors of companies were dignified by a number of titled members. Great promises were lavishly set forth. The result was that, despite the government's tightening up on the requirements for registering companies, there were a good many fraudulent promotions foisted upon the public. Or, if it was not a matter of doubtful companies, it was one of poor quality bonds from colonial or foreign governments, frequently advertised with inflated prospectuses. Still, people kept on buying just the same. Even the American collapse of 1907 did not destroy confidence sufficiently to stop the upward swing which reached its highest point in 1914. Even if war had not intervened, it could not have gone much further, however, for by that time about one half of the national savings were being sent abroad annually. The war brought all this to a sudden halt.

At the same time, it must be kept in mind that it was by no means a peaceful world in which expansion was taking place. The period between 1895 and 1905 saw three wars: the Spanish-American, the Boer, and the Russo-Japanese. They were followed by threats of war, culminating in the Balkan conflicts of 1912 and 1913 which led directly into the World War. Besides these influences there was the fact that the British were investing at a faster rate than they were saving. This was bound to cause a maladjustment of the money market. With rising prices and taxes, Britain's ability to save was clearly on the decline. On the other side of the Atlantic, however, the production of wealth was growing by leaps and bounds in the United States. Savings were rising rapidly, so the Americans were beginning to enter the investment market, financing their own companies and even buying back foreign-held American bonds, or investing in British and European firms. It is true that as yet the American investors were not very important outside their own country, but they had great potentialities. All these facts portended future difficulties for Britain's continued financial predominance.

In 1914 Britain was still the world's financial dictator. She was the world's greatest investor, with the world's most stable currency. Yet, to one who examined the situation carefully, there were signs that this was a very uncertain position. Britain's foreign markets for her manufactures were being restricted, while she was facing increased foreign competition in the industrial, the shipping, and the financial fields. Her imports of goods were rising more rapidly than her exports, the difference being made up by the return on her investments. Let competition become much stronger, let a war intervene to wreck her trade, and Britain would be in very serious straits. While all seemed to be flourishing and booming, in truth her situation was extremely precarious, one of the best indications of this being the rising number of unemployed and another, the social problems which were appearing in Britain itself. The end of British economic supremacy would seem to have been in sight.

Chapter 22

THE GOVERNMENT ASSUMES
NEW RESPONSIBILITIES

THE YEAR 1870 is, in a sense, a dividing line between two types of economic and social thinking. Before that date it was usually taken for granted that the government's chief duty was to act as an impartial referee in the world of fighting competition. Whether the conflict was between company and company or between employer and employee, the state was not to interfere unless someone took an unfair advantage of his opponent. In the conflict between employer and employee, however, the employer was customarily given the benefit of any doubt which might arise as to who should obtain a favorable judgment. To such thinking there had always been, of course, some opposition, as in the case of the radicals and the Christian reformers. From 1870 on the situation began to change. The concept of laissez faire itself began to experience a modification owing to the impact of the Darwinian theory of evolution upon social thought. This was very much helped by the growing materialism in people's thinking.

The Changing Attitude to Government Activity

Darwin had shown to the satisfaction of many that there is probably a gradual rise in biological existence from the lower to the higher forms of life. The question then was: is not this also true of social existence. Those who are now in the worst condition might be raised to an immensely improved position through social evolution. The contemporary situation, however, prevented such a rise because of the inequality prevalent in the economic sphere. The best solution, therefore, would seem to be that of state intervention to bring about a redistribution of wealth with the aim of making men equal in all spheres of existence. In this way laissez faire would be effectively applied to all classes. Following this line of thought, by 1914 the people of Britain generally had come to a view of the state's functions very different from that held by their forefathers.

The man whose ideas best represent the beginning of this change which led to the breakdown of classical economics was John Stuart Mill. Although at first a devoted follower of Malthus and Ricardo, in the late '50's his position began to change. While still holding to the Malthusian view of population, by 1870 he had rejected the Ricardian "wage fund" theory. Moreover, influenced by French writers such as St. Simon and Fourier, he had become extremely favorable to socialism, feeling that it might well be better than the contemporary economic maldistribution. He advocated the abolition of the wage system, substituting cooperatives and peasant ownership of the land. Believing also that rent was a monopoly of the landowners, he wished to tax the land so that the rent would be entirely absorbed, the tax increasing as the rent rose. Even inheritance did not escape his attack, for while he agreed that a man should be allowed to bequeath his property as he pleased, the government should, in his opinion, control the inheritance, making sure that no one could have more than the "means of a comfortable independence." All this was to be done in order that every individual should have as much freedom as possible. It was really the application of laissez faire on a greatly extended scale. Thus, even at his death (1873), Mill had not entirely reconciled himself to a full-fledged socialism, but he had gone a long way.

Although Mill's earlier classical views tended to dominate economic thinking for the twenty years after his death, his successors, such as Stanley Jevons and Alfred Marshall, gradually forsook the doctrines of Smith, Malthus, and Ricardo. Both these representatives of the newer thought were much influenced by current conditions and thinking, as can be seen by their statements of economic principles.[1]

Jevons tended to follow a materialistic utilitarian philosophy, holding that utility was decided entirely by the balance between pain and pleasure. At the same time, these two factors were largely determined by physical forces. He pointed out that sun spots might ruin crops in India, thereby forcing the natives to import increased quantities of goods from British merchants, in turn stimulating British production. Thus, economic matters were ultimately quite dominated by material considerations alone. Marshall, who in his youth had received a thorough Christian training,

---

[1] Stanley Jevons, *The Theory of Political Economy* (1871); Alfred Marshall, *The Principles of Economics* (1890).

was not nearly so inclined to such simplifications. He believed that man had many other needs besides those which were economic. Every man has a character and no two characters are alike; consequently, men have differing needs and react in different ways to the influences of society. Yet, while holding that there are these variations between individuals, he also thought that society was developing through the evolution of desires and that to measure these desires the only proper yard stick was money. It could be used as the measurement, since it did not indicate motives but only objectively observed desires. Here also was a tendency, despite all his efforts, to a rather materialistic outlook.

Such thinking brings up the fundamental question of what is value? Ricardo and Mill both felt that value was determined by the cost, particularly of labor, involved in production. Jevons, however, held that utility was the final criterion. Total utility was the ability of any good to meet a specific need. The marginal utility of the article, on the other hand, was determined by the relation of the supply to the demand. He pointed out that there are many things upon which one spends labor but which have no utility, such as the ship the *Great Eastern*, wrecked before it was properly launched. There are other things which are very useful but which cost little or no labor, such as water. The one thing which will make water valuable is its scarcity. Two weaknesses in this theory were that he forgot that cost is a factor in supply and also that the price paid is not always an indication of utility.

Marshall had another approach to the matter. He held that, although over a short period value was determined by supply and demand, over a long period the determining factor was eventually cost of production. Yet even cost of production is not easy to define, for it not only includes the cost of the labor, but also the sacrifices involved. Consequently, the relationship between money prices and the real costs are difficult to ascertain. This weakens his claim that money is the measurement of the force of motives. He did point out, however, that in understanding economic affairs abstraction is not enough; concrete reality must be studied in order to find the meaning of anything as vague as value.

With regard to the distribution of economic goods, Jevons stated that wages equalled the value of the goods produced after rent and interest had been paid. Thus, any attempt to decrease hours of labor would inevitably lower wages, for rent and interest would continue to take the same percentage of the profits. This was coming perilously close once again to the wage fund idea. Marshall, on the other hand, held that labor, capital, and land were all factors of production which must have their returns, and the bigger the net earnings, the bigger would be each one's share. At the same time, the actual rate of wages was determined by the laborers' standard of comfort, coupled with the supply and demand of labor. Thus, if the standard of comfort were raised, the wages of themselves would have to be increased, although if labor were plentiful, that would tend to force wages down. Out of this would come, as in the determination of value, a state of equilibrium which would be the level of wages.

While these leading lights of the newer school were discussing economic laws, they did not hold that their theories were as permanent as the Law of Gravity. With an evolutionary outlook, they felt that laws might change and develop. For this reason they were not prepared to dogmatize concerning the position of the state. Jeremy Bentham in his later years had gradually come to the conclusion that the state must increasingly exert its power and influence over social and economic matters. Mill, with his growing socialism, had held much the same opinion. Jevons was not prepared to be absolutely certain, but he felt that the state's duty was to act for the best interests of the majority, each case being decided on its own merits. The state might be called in to coordinate a number of scattered enterprises or actually to control when processes involved were routine, when they were under the public eye, or when little capital was involved. Marshall seems to have held much the same position. Thus the two leading economists of the day, while not becoming in any way socialistic, were prepared to allow the state a much greater influence and say in the economic affairs of the country.

This position was considerably reinforced by the work of the historical school of thinking. Influenced by the German writers, Bagehot, Ingram, Leslie, Toynbee, and Rogers, all turned to historical studies. They felt that, after all, an understanding of economic processes could be gained only by investigating concrete facts. The result was that they rejected most of the old definitions of wages, rent, and cost of production. Instead, because economics was a historical subject, all such definitions and all laws governing economic activity were regarded as purely relative. Therefore, one could not lay down eternal economic principles which must be followed under all circumstances, since they were dependent upon time and place. Such ideas, of course, fitted in well with evolutionary thinking and likewise opened the door to any new ideas regarding the place and economic function of the state.

Another type of thinking which came to somewhat the same conclusion regarding the state was that of the Christians who were interested in these matters. In the earlier days of the century Shaftesbury, Oastler, and others had been anxious to call in the state to protect oppressed workers. The Christian Socialists under Kingsley and Maurice had also favored considerable state interference. The most controversial figure of all the Christian social reformers, General Booth, founder of the Salvation Army, was even more strongly opposed to the ideas of laissez faire. The poor and destitute, he held, were oppressed by such a philosophy. What was needed was homes for the unfortunate, work at which they might be employed, and colonies to which they might be sent. He maintained, moreover, that spiritual rehabilitation of these unfortunates must be brought about by a return to the Christian faith, which alone would give them the proper outlook on life. Such measures were to be carried out by the Christian community, not primarily by the state. None of these reformers were very much interested in abstract economic theory, nor were they socialists. They might, on the other hand, be termed collectivists, for they believed that society had a collective responsibility which could be exercised efficiently only by the government.

Much the same point of view was held by many of the so-called "radicals." Usually middle class, they believed firmly that the gross inequalities of economic well-being observable in the country could be eradicated only by state action. This had been the point of view of Thomas Carlyle and Matthew Arnold, while Charles Dilke and Joseph Chamberlain, the later radical leaders, tended in their early days even to republicanism. Chamberlain, in particular, as the radical mayor of Birmingham, succeeded in having many public services taken over by the municipality, even going so far as to build working men's houses. Finally, in 1885 Chamberlain published his radical "unauthorized programme" for the Liberal Party, in which he called upon private property to "pay a ransom" for the profits it had made by industry, the money to be used to improve the conditions of the lower classes. These improvements would consist of free education, good housing, fair rents, payment of members of Parliament, abolition of plural voting, church disestablishment, and security of farm tenure. T. H. Green, the Oxford philosopher, would seem to have had much the same sort of plan for securing "the good life" to all. These, however, were the ideas of middle-class collectivist radicals. Labor was much more conservative, with the result that radicalism died for lack of support.

A radical of a different type who helped to prepare the way for more socialistic thinking was the American land-reformer Henry George. While accepting most of the views of the classical school, he introduced an innovation in the theory of rent. He held that the real producers of value were labor and capital only. Rent was an unearned increment which took the produce of the other two, thus reducing their returns without contributing anything. The proper way to treat rent, therefore, was to tax it virtually out of existence. If this were done, no other taxes would be needed. What is more, this revenue would come from the place which should pay, because the land is in reality the property of the people as a whole. His book *Progress and Poverty* containing these ideas passed through ten editions between 1881 and 1884, a revelation of the interest it aroused. Yet its theories, which were more applicable to California than to Britain, were never taken too seriously. Its one important effect was that it stimulated interest in ideas of land nationalization which were developed further by socialist groups of his own and succeeding generations.

While Henry George was crusading for his theory of single tax, the doctrines of another writer first began to make their influence felt in Britain. This writer was the German Jew, Karl Marx. At an early age he had become something of a radical, editing a reformist newspaper. As a result of his advocacy of radical social and political theories he had been obliged to leave his homeland and to migrate to Paris, where he came into touch with revolutionary groups who were involved in the uprising of 1848. He also began a study of the works of Prudhon, through which he was converted to socialism. Having to flee Paris because of his activities, he moved to London, where he lived for the rest of his life on the bounty of his industrialist friend, Friedrich Engels. There he studied and wrote much on social subjects, although his two best known productions are *The Communist Manifesto* (1848) and *Capital*, the first volume of which was published in German in 1867 and the two others posthumously by Engels. Although he quickly became known on the Continent, until his works were translated into English in the eighties, his influence on British thought was relatively small. Thereafter however, there was a gradual growth of knowledge of and interest in his theories.

Marx believed that he was able to set forth a rigorously scientific system of socialism by means of an abstract and deductive method. He was done with "utopian" socialisms which he felt were largely made up of wishful thinking. To accomplish his objective he made certain basic assumptions which, by their very nature, are themselves incapable of proof. In the first place, he adopted a completely materialistic philosophy holding that "the ideal is nothing else than the material world reflected by the human mind." This means that religion, art, morals, economics, and all other such concepts owe their ultimate origin, in Marx's thought, to the modes of economic production and exchange. By changing these forms, therefore, from capitalistic to socialistic ownership *all* else would be changed in society.[2] Adopting the Hegelian concept of history developing by means of a dialectic movement from thesis to antithesis to synthesis, he held that society, through the agency of the changing economic organization and of the conflict of one economic class with another, was evolving from the feudal, through the bourgeois, to the communistic form of production. Thus, by an evolutionary-revolutionary dialecticism, communism would eventually result, bringing with it peace, quiet, and perfection. Since everybody would then own everything, there would be no classes and, consequently, no conflict. The materialist ended by becoming a complete idealist. At the same time, he failed to realize that his claim that all views, because of their ultimate origin in economic forces, are purely relative also reflected upon his theory. On his own premise, Marx must admit that his fundamental ideas have no validity beyond his own situation and his own day. Thus, on his own showing, his economic and historical views are without any real scientific or eternal validity.

The cornerstone of Marx's whole system of thought was his concept of value. Adopting the view of Ricardo, he held that all real value is derived from labor, no real influence being exerted by supply and demand. At the same time, the worker is paid by the capitalist only enough for subsistence. Therefore, if only five hours' labor will supply the worker's food, clothing, and housing, but he actually works ten hours a day, the surplus value is taken by the capitalist. In this way he robs the worker of the value of his work. At the same time, the capitalist, according to Marx, is always attempting to reduce the subsistence level by employing cheaper labor and cheaper methods so that he will have to pay out less for

[2] "In the social production which men carry on they enter into definite relations that are indispensable and independent of their will; these relations of production correspond to a definite stage of development of their material powers of production. The sum total of these relations of production constitutes the economic structure of society—the real foundation on which rise legal and political superstructures and to which correspond definite forms of social consciousness. *The mode of production in material life determines the general character of the social, political, and spiritual processes of life.*" *Critique of Political Economy*, p. 11, quoted in H. W. Laidler, *A History of Socialist Thought* (London, 1927), p. 201.

costs, thus increasing his profits. One of the chief criticisms of Marx's whole view is that he sets up an abstract thing known as "labor." He does not differentiate between intensity of the work or the differences in the utility of the various products. Moreover, he commences with the assumption that value is determined by labor alone. Marx was perhaps not quite as scientific as he would like to think.

When dealing with the nature of capital, Marx taught that it was something which had really appeared only in the sixteenth and seventeenth centuries when it had begun to employ propertyless labor—a claim of doubtful historicity. Capital is, according to Marx, of two types: *fixed*, which is used for the purchase of machinery and plant, and *variable*, which pays for labor. It is the latter alone which can be manipulated to increase the capitalists' gains, since it alone gives surplus value. Now, if this were really the case, it would be in the interests of capitalism to oppose machinery. The opposite, however is true, for increased mechanization certainly cuts the costs of labor. What is more, the rates of profit on capital, whether variable or fixed, are usually about equal. The fact of the matter is that Marx forgot that profits, as well as exchange value, are based both upon utility and the supply and demand of the market.

Marx also held that there would be a gradual concentration of capital in fewer and fewer hands, the middle class generally being forced down into the ranks of the proletariat or workers. This would result in a revolution, which might or might not be peaceful according to the nature of the government. The monopolistic capitalists would be expropriated, all industry and production falling into the hands of the people, to be used for the general benefit. Here again Marx's prophecies have by no means been fulfilled, for while monopolies certainly have arisen, they usually generate enough opposition to destroy their control without a revolution.

On the Continent, from 1848 on, Marx had a very considerable influence. He came at the right time, providing doctrines, slogans, and a pseudo-scientific basis for the current revolutionary theories. In Britain, however, the situation was somewhat different. It was not until 1886 that his first volume of *Capital* was published in English, and even when his doctrines were understood most people were dubious. An evolutionary concept of the rise of socialism predominated, resulting in dislike of revolution. Marx's outspoken materialism also did not receive any great support from a nation whose basic concepts had been formed under the influence of the Evangelical Revival. It is true that one socialistic body, the Social

Democratic Federation organized by H. M. Hyndman in 1881, adopted his views, although even they concentrated on his theory of value and his philosophy of history. Another socialistic group, the Fabian Society, formed about the same time (1883), was not committed to materialism and stressed the "inevitability of gradualness," rather than revolution. Labor, if socialistic at all, was much more inclined to follow Mill than Marx.[3]

The general trend, therefore, in British economic thought between 1870 and 1914, while not revolutionary, was favorable toward increasing the interference of the state in economic affairs. It was, in a sense, an intensification of the older collectivism manifested in the early factory legislation rather than a flowering of socialism. The latter point of view was growing in influence and in appeal, but it was by no means dominant even among the more radical labor elements. The important factor in bringing about this change of attitude toward government control was the increasing concern of people with the social welfare of the working classes. In the '80's a wealthy manufacturer of Liverpool, Charles Booth, financed a survey of the living conditions of the laboring people in London, and the result was shocking. It revealed that below the top level of those employed in industry and commerce the situation was very bad. Underlined by such events as the London match-girls' and dockers' strikes, the need for reform was brought home to the average man. Many came to feel that the state was the only body which could take the necessary action. By government control and direction alone could a more equitable distribution of the fruits of industry be obtained. For this reason, when the state did take action, it had the support of a large part of the population.

Social Conditions

Reference has been made to appalling social conditions, but before one can grasp the situation properly, it is necessary to see exactly what they were like between 1870 and 1914.

An important factor in any understanding of social conditions is the realization that Britain's population had been growing throughout the forty years preceding World War I. Rising from 26 million in 1870, by 1911 it reached the total of 40.8 million. Although the rate of increase slowed down after 1890, it did not cease, largely owing to the fact that although the birth rate was dropping, so also was the rate of deaths. In the 1870's the birth

---

[3] For a detailed criticism of Marx, see L. H. Haney, *The History of Economic Thought* (New York, 1949), chap. xxiv.

rate for England and Wales had been close to 36 per 1,000, with Scotland a little behind at 35, but by 1911 the ratio for the whole of the United Kingdom was down to 24 per 1,000. Yet, while births had declined, deaths had dropped from about 21 per 1,000 to 14, still leaving something of a balance on the side of those who were entering into life. At the same time, immigration was tending to make up for losses through emigration. Naturally, the numbers on both sides of this ledger varied according to economic conditions, but during the first decade of the new century Great Britain said goodbye to 3.3 million of her native sons and welcomed some 1.3 million newcomers. It must be added, however, that the new-comers were usually Jewish refugees from Russia, Poland, or other eastern European countries, who often came in on the lowest level of industrial labor, while so many of those who left the country were either farmers or skilled artisans. From an economic as well as a social point of view the exchange was perhaps not as profitable as it might have been. Nevertheless, the population was growing, entailing increasing responsibilities for the state in its part as universal intervener.

Closely related to this question of population was that of public health. Generally speaking, this was improving throughout the period, although it was far from perfect even by 1914. In London, as a result of better sanitation and the completion of the Thames embankment, there was a decline in the danger of epidemics. Other towns were following London's example. Special attention was also being paid to the welfare of the children. Vaccination was becoming more common, and meals were now being provided as well as regular medical examinations for many school children. Despite all this, epidemics of plague or cholera sometimes did break out in the port towns, but they were soon brought to a halt. What was less cheering, infant mortality was still relatively high, although it had dropped in London from 162 per 1,000 to 113 by 1913. The average for the whole country at the latter date was 108. The important thing to note, however, is that the improvement had come principally among the lower classes.

One of the reasons for this was that the same economic and social group also experienced some betterment in their housing. In 1891 11 per cent of the population of England and Wales and 20 per cent of that of London lived more than two persons to a room. By 1911 these percentages had dropped to 8.5 per cent and 16.7 per cent respectively. In Scotland the overcrowding was much greater, being more than four persons to a room. The traditional Scottish "but and ben" of two rooms was still very common and was still being built. On the other hand, throughout the British Isles the planned suburb was gradually becoming the place where many middle-class people lived, while even in the more crowded districts better types of apartments which let in more light and air were being erected for the working classes. After 1907 building slowed down very noticeably, and there was a continuing shortage of suitable dwellings, but, even so, a considerable advance had been made.

Some of the improvement in working-class housing came as a consequence of the general rise in wages before 1900. It has been calculated that in 1886 labor was receiving about one half of the national income as over against one third in 1850. This was better than it had been but was still not enough. Estimates show that from 1850 to 1900 the average man's wage had risen some 50 per cent. Between 1880 and 1906 the lower paid wage earners had an increase of about 16 per cent while wage-rates of the higher paid rose by 26 per cent. This, however, is not the whole picture because not infrequently lower paid workers moved up into the higher paid jobs, bringing an increase proportionately greater. On the other hand, with considerable spells of unemployment, as in 1878 and following years, the average rate would not give a complete picture of earnings. Moreover, in hard times, while industry might not lower wages, it might shorten time with the same result. After 1900 wages generally ceased to rise, although it does not look as if profits did. Not until 1911, when labor forced capital's hand, did another upsurge of wages take place. This trend was brought to an abrupt stop by the demands of war.

The whole story, however, is not given in terms of money wages. While these had been rising prior to 1900, in a good many different ways the cost of living had been falling. Some have said that it came down by 20 per cent during this period, while others claim even more of a decline. But whatever figure one accepts, it is probable that the real wages of the average workman who stayed in the same job between 1870 and 1900 rose unevenly by about 40 per cent. Chapham has calculated that food which cost 17s. 8½d. in 1850 had dropped to 16s. 2½d. in 1886 and 13s. 8½d. in 1897. Although rents were rising as buildings were improved and the cost of labor rose, these did not entirely offset the decline in foodstuffs, so the increase in real wages was more than that shown by the rise in money received. After 1900 the cost of living commenced to climb once more, and since in most industries there was a general leveling off in money wages, there must have been a general decline in real wages. It did not, however, by any means destroy the gains already made—gains which were further consolidated by the increase between 1911 and 1913 in the wage rates of many of the basic industries.

Meanwhile, what was happening to the middle class? By some writers of socialistic leanings it is held that profits were rising throughout the period even more rapidly than wages. It is very difficult to be exact in such estimates, for the totals cannot be ascertained accurately. That there was an increasing amount of investment abroad has already been indicated. Such investment undoubtedly brought in large revenues, something like £185 million a year by 1913. At the same time, it has been claimed that profits generally increased between 1899 and 1913 by 55 per cent, a large portion being invested overseas in foreign enterprises which were potential rivals to British industry. Thus, it would seem that, while undoubtedly the position of the working class improved vastly between 1870 and 1914, that of the middle class advanced even more rapidly. The only qualification of this generalization which must be made is that many of the upper ranks of labor were beginning to invest in stocks and bonds, thus themselves becoming, in one sense, members of the middle class.

Turning from the question of the increase in wages and real income, it is necessary to note that labor also experienced decided improvements in the conditions of employment. This is indicated, for instance, in the gradual shortening of hours. In 1870, the sixty hour week was normal. This was brought down by 1886 to fifty-four hours, and in some trades by 1900 to forty-eight, while at the same time there was the introduction of the week-end holiday beginning at noon Saturday. Along with this shortening of hours went a general rise in numbers employed. In 1886 the highest figure of the period for unemployment was reached, amounting to 10.2 per cent of those in trade-unions. From 1887 to 1900 the figure stood at 5 per cent and from 1901 to 1913 at 4.5 per cent. True, in some industries, such as ironfounding and blacksmithing, the percentage was considerably higher, but while this was so, new industries were employing a larger part of the growing population. The electrical industry, automobile manufacture, and chemical production all played their part as well as older industries, such as coal mining and cotton, which were expanding. Women were also finding employment on a much larger scale as teachers, nurses, clerks, and the like. It is for this reason that, in spite of the fact that the population was increasing and wages were rising, unemployment was relatively low. Thus, although the average wage earner might have to work somewhat harder at his job, and even this is doubtful, he was working for shorter hours, higher pay, and with less chance of unemployment. Therefore, he was considerably better off in 1914 than he or his father had been in 1870.

What had caused the improvement? Economic factors had, of course, been important. Trade and commerce had expanded, prices had fallen with increased and cheapened production. At the same time, there had been a growing feeling generally that the worker should receive a larger part of the national income. To force a consideration of his needs he had organized into trade-unions, while through the extension of the franchise he had been given an opportunity for direct influence upon the government. The upshot of all this had been an improvement in his way of life.

Working-Class Organization

In order to understand how it happened that the state was prepared to aid in the redistribution of wealth despite a long laissez faire tradition and why it was that employers were prepared to grant increases in their workers' pay, it is necessary to see what the workers themselves were doing. Although by no means socialist, they were prepared to organize in order to make their demands effective.

The basic form of organization was still the friendly society, which was, as in earlier days, more an insurance club than a trade-union. A means of strengthening had been the Friendly Society Act of 1875, which had laid down numerous regulations for their protection. By 1887 there were nearly 4 million members of the federations or individual societies, while twenty-three years later this number had risen to over 6 million, with assets totalling between £40 and £45 million. Particularly important were the Independent Order of Odd Fellows and the Foresters. Besides these, there were the so-called collecting societies of industrial insurance companies, and the burial societies, whose membership by 1910 had reached nearly 7 million. The working class was organizing financially to meet such emergencies as sickness, unemployment, old age, and burial when they should arise.

Much the same type of activity was carried on by the trade-unions during the fifteen years after 1870. Composed of over a million of the higher paid workers who were respectable imitators of the middle class, the unions, generally speaking, were primarily interested in insuring their members. The larger unions, in particular, were very conservative, as can be shown by the attitude of the Trade Union Congresses of the period, a result, no doubt, of their growing wealth. For instance, in 1889 the Amalgamated Society of Engineers received £183,651 and paid out, largely in sickness, old age, and death benefits, £132,642; the United Society of Boilermakers and Iron Shipbuilders received £104,513 and spent £56,655. It has been estimated that in 1895 the unions received, all told, an income of around £1.2 million in dues. Having a careful regard for their treasuries, they were not interested in strikes, for these cost money, and anyhow real wages were rising rapidly.

The respectability of the trade-unions was further increased by legislation passed during the 1870's giving them a better position before the law. In 1871 Gladstone had Parliament pass a Trade Union Act which gave protection to their funds by enabling them to take legal action as a corporation. His Criminal Law and Amendment Act, on the other hand, restricted their freedom to picket or even to persuade men to go on strike. In fact, some women were later arrested under it for saying "bah" to strike-breakers. When the Conservatives came into power in 1874, they promptly changed the law by passing the Conspiracy and Protection of Property Act and the Employers and Workmen Act. The first statute defined the unions' position, protecting them from being sued for doing that which was perfectly legal for an individual. The other act made masters and servants equal before the law, so not only a master's breaking of a contract, but also the same action by his employee should be but a civil offense. Thus, unionism became respectable and recognized by the law. At the same time, the unions could be registered and so given special recognition, although this was not required in order for them to be legal.

The depressed state of trade between 1875 and 1880 both restricted union activity and caused a decline in membership. From 1880 on, however, the unions grew and expanded. Trade-unionists also began to find their way into Parliament as Liberals, thus bringing further prestige to the movement. In fact, one of the political unionists, Henry Broadhurst, a bricklayer, in 1880 became an Under Secretary of the Board of Trade, while another, John Burns, in 1893 became one of the newly formed Department of Labor. Throughout the country laborers were also being appointed to the office of Justice of the Peace and were being elected to County and Town councils. It is not surprising that, with their interest in conserving their benefit funds, their settled legal position, and their growing influence in both local and national politics, the trade-unions, particularly those of the labor aristocracy, were at this time quite content to maintain the status quo in the belief that nothing more was needed.

What shattered the calm was the rise of a "new unionism." This was based on the revolt of the unskilled worker against the conditions under which he had to labor. Instead of desiring to have merely craft organizations, the demand now was for "general workers' unions." At the same time, there was a drive to amalgamate the craft unions already in existence into larger organizations. This was none too popular in the old, conservative union ranks. There was also a feeling in many quarters that labor should have a living wage, not one determined by the state of the market, and that it should not have to work for more than eight hours a day. In this latter point one can see the influence of socialistic thought of the Marxian variety. Labor, it was held, has the first claim on industry's production, for which it should not have to work more than a set time. As socialism was spread by the Social Democratic Federation, the Fabian Society, and labor leaders such as Keir Hardie, Tom Mann, John Burns, and Benn Tillett, the new unionism was stimulated to become more pugnacious and more demanding.

The new type of unionism really had its first fling in the attempt of Joseph Arch, a Methodist lay preacher, to organize the agricultural laborers. Between 1872 and 1874 his union was very active, but after that time it fell to pieces as a result of the landowners' opposition. The first successful effort on the part of unskilled labor was the strike in 1888 of the London match girls demanding higher pay and better working conditions. Organized by Tom Mann and Benn Tillett, they obtained much popular support which helped them to win their demands. In the following year the Gasworkers and General Labourers' Union forced the gas companies to grant an eight hour day to their employees. A few months later the dockers of London, who were largely casual labor, went on strike for 6d. an hour, 8d. for overtime, and no hiring for less than four hours. Led by Burns, Mann, and Tillett and supported financially by contributions from all classes in Britain, as well as by the Australian labor unions, they won. The first big step had been taken; the lower grades of labor were uniting for action.

The effect of these victories was noticeable almost immediately in the trade-unions themselves. Many of them began to expand rapidly, some growing by as much as 40 per cent between 1888 and 1890. The membership of the Miners' Federation actually rose from 36,000 to 147,000. This federation, whose counterpart could be found in other trades, was composed of a number of unions which had come together because of their inability to meet the requirements of the situation individually. Some of the unions about this time began to accept semi- and unskilled labor into their ranks, thus greatly augmenting their membership, the Engineers being a case in point. These unions then began demanding a greater share of industry's profits. In 1893, by the Brooklands Agreement, the wages of cotton workers were tied directly to profits, an arrangement which lasted for twenty years. Similarly, the miners in 1903 gained a guarantee of minimum and maximum wages. The employers were none too happy about this, but labor felt that it had the first claim and was going to make it effective.

As has already been mentioned, these views were strengthened by the socialist propaganda which was being disseminated by various agencies. The Social Democratic Federation published a number of works in which an undiluted Marxism was advocated, while The Fabians circulated some 750,000 copies of pamphlets setting forth a gradual evolutionary type of socialism. These groups, between them, reached many, particularly among the ranks of the labor leaders, although the Social Democratic Federation publications were too revolutionary for general acceptance. Robert Blatchford, editor of the *Clarion* and author of such books as *Merrie England*, not only preached socialism through the press but had vans touring the country to give lectures. While most of the propagators of these views were middle class in the beginning, very soon a section of labor was converted and began to demand the application of their ideas.

Down to 1890 there was relatively little action which could be called really socialistic, for the Trade Union Congress was definitely Liberal in its outlook, as were most trade-unionists. In that year, however, Keir Hardie, who in 1888 had organized a Scottish Labour Party, succeeded in having the Congress accept a socialist platform. As this was not generally popular, it was revoked the following year. Despite this set-back, in 1893 Hardie, Burns, and J. H. Wilson succeeded in obtaining a certain amount of T.U.C. support for the organization of the Independent Labour Party. While before this there had been some independent "labor" members of Parliament who had refused to be Liberals, this was the first attempt to form a real "labor" party. The platform was specifically socialist, calling for "the collective ownership and control of the means of production, distribution, and exchange." Along with this were demanded various other reforms, such as a universal eight hour day, free non-sectarian education of all grades, and government care of the ill and aged. Such a radical program received little backing. The T.U.C. rejected it, and Keir Hardie could be sure of obtaining a parliamentary seat only in a Welsh coal-mining constituency.

The I.L.P., therefore, had no great success, its membership falling from 20,000 in 1893 to 16,000 in 1900.

The real change came when in 1899 the T.U.C. called a conference of all labor and socialist groups to form a true "labor party" in Parliament. Although the Marxist Social Democratic Federation pulled out, a "Labour Representation Committee" was formed with J. Ramsay MacDonald, Philip Snowden, and other later prominent parliamentarians, dominating its policies. The I.L.P. continued to exist as a separate entity within the organization. No great success was achieved until the Liberals, in 1905, came into power by a landslide which also placed twenty-nine Labour members in the Commons. These immediately formed the Labour Party, receiving the support of labor representatives in the Liberal ranks, known as "Lib-Labs." In 1907 the new party came out for a socialist program of public ownership. Yet, while this was its official position, there were still many within the party who were not socialists and were not too favorable to the idea. It was this step which probably slowed down the party's progress in gaining electoral support. But, owing to the need of the Liberals for labor votes in 1910 and 1911, the Labourites along with the Irish Nationalists held positions of much greater power than their size would warrant. Political socialism was on its way.

Meanwhile, trade-unionism was developing along its own lines. Although in 1874 the unions had around a million members, by 1885 that figure had been cut in half. From then on, however, their numbers began to climb rapidly; 1890, 1.5 million; 1910, 2.5 million; 1913, 4.1 million. By 1907 their annual income amounted to around £2.4 million, with £5.6 million in reserve. Simultaneously with the growth of union membership and wealth went the tendency to consolidate the smaller organizations, causing a decline in the total number of unions. Yet all was not peaceful and quiet, for there was still considerable conflict within labor's ranks between the conservatism of the larger unions and the pugnacious radicalism of the smaller organizations. In 1895 a change was made in the Congress' constitution by altering the system of voting. No longer was it to be a matter of counting delegates' hands but rather of voting according to the membership of the unions. This gave the slower moving and more lethargic unions control. The election of the chairman was also placed on a more limited basis. In protest against this there was the formation of a fighting General Federation of Trade Unions which, however, never made much progress because of its peculiar regulations. By 1906 it was supported by only 116 organizations. Generally speaking, trade-unionists were still very conservative and antirevolutionary.[4]

How long this state of affairs would have lasted is hard to say, but a change in the picture was brought about by two judgments handed down by the House of Lords. The first was in the Taff Vale Case, in which the Taff Vale Railway sued the railway union for destruction caused by its members when on strike. The Lords awarded the company £23,000 damages, thereby wrecking the union's finances. Labor was very much roused over this, forcing the Liberals in 1906 to pass a law which exempted Trade-Unions from corporate liability for any acts of its members, even though committed under orders of the union's officers. By this they were freed from corporate responsibility without losing the privilege of being corporate bodies. The second decision was given in 1909 in the Osborne Case. It was ruled that the unions could not use their ordinary funds to support political representatives. Since this would make it virtually impossible for the Labour M. P.'s to continue at Westminster, it would practically destroy the Labour Party. Again, the Liberals met the situation by passing a law paying all members annual salaries of £400. Finally, in 1913 the unions were given the legal right to use their funds as they liked, even for political purposes if they saw fit. All expenditures, however, must be agreed to by secret ballot, and no compulsion was to be placed upon the members to contribute to political funds even though the union decided to so use its money. While in both cases the demands of labor were met, the Lords' decisions had given the whole class a new feeling of solidarity and common interest. What is more even the older trade-unions were forced to adopt a more belligerent attitude than heretofore.

Another reason for a growth of pugnacity among unions was the introduction of "syndicalism" from the Continent. This particular type of thinking was opposed to political action. Instead, it held that the only thing for labor to do was to stage strike after strike until the unions could take over their own industries. This point of view was greatly aided by the growth of nationwide unions, such as the Railway Brotherhood or the Amalgamated Textile Workers, which covered a whole industry. Furthermore, in 1899 Ruskin College had been founded to bring education of a socialist variety to the working classes. This was followed in 1903 by the Marxist Central Labour College, an offshoot of Ruskin, while in the same

---

[4] 1896-1907 expenditures of 100 unions averaged 13.4 per cent for disputes; 22.1 per cent for unemployment; 42.5 per cent benefits; 22 per cent administration. Ogg and Sharp, *Economic Development of Modern Europe,* p. 372.

year the Socialist Labour Party, a strictly Marxist group, was organized. All these movements had their influence upon working class thinking and were partially responsible for the rash of strikes which broke out between 1908 and 1914. In 1910, 30,000 miners of the Rhondda and Aberdare valleys came out, in 1911 there was a nation-wide railway strike for union recognition and higher pay, and this was followed the next year by a strike of 850,000 miners for a minimum wage. In each case, the strikers achieved their objectives. While there was no attempt to seize industry, direct action was paying dividends in raising wages to meet the ascending cost of living.

In all of this the employers were by no means passive. In some cases, during the nineties, Boards of Conciliation composed of workers and employers were organized to keep the peace. Generally, however, and particularly after 1886, employers tended to organize on a fighting basis, some of the groups actually dating back to 1865. Organization on a national scale had been attempted in 1873, but nothing was achieved until 1895, when the Employers' Federation came into existence, a parliamentary committee being set up three years later to scrutinize legislation. Very foolishly, the employers refused whenever possible to budge an inch in granting concessions to their workers, not infrequently trying to starve them into submission. This was not too difficult as long as the Conservatives were in power (1895-1905), but with the advent of the Liberals, supported by a Labour Party, the situation changed. Lacking the aid of the government, the employers usually had to accede to the strikers' demands. The Tories by now represented the "capitalistic" class both landowning and industrial, while the Liberals stood generally for the workers and the lower middle class. Thus, it looked as though it would not be long before the issue would be joined both on the political and industrial fronts. The conflict was only halted by the outbreak of war.

The Extension of Government Power

As a result of the growing influence of both collectivism and socialism, the old laissez faire ideas were breaking down. The steady improvement in the workers' economic condition down to 1900, followed by a leveling off of wages while profits continued to increase, tended to gain stronger support for the new philosophies. The resulting conflicts between employers and employees brought the whole matter into sharp focus. Consequently, after 1895 the government was gradually obliged to assume added responsibilities in order to preserve peace and to achieve a more equitable distribution of the national income.

As has been pointed out, prior to 1893 there were no official labor representatives in Parliament; nevertheless, the fact that a number of laboring men sat in the House obviously had its influence. Likewise, the extension of the franchise in 1884 to provide virtual manhood suffrage made both parties feel that they must do something to meet the needs and demands of the working classes.

The outcome of this situation can be seen in the growing amount of legislation designed to this end. Indirectly, a great many laws had the effect of improving labor's position. Education for children up to twelve years was first made compulsory in 1870 and finally made free in 1891. In 1871 Oxford and Cambridge were thrown open to Dissenters. In 1888 County Councils were set up on an elected basis, providing opportunities for workers to obtain a share in local government. The consequences of this statute were seen after 1890, when municipalities were given the right to undertake slum clearance. Towns began to pull down condemned areas, a greater interest was manifested in public health and sanitation, and municipal funds were spent on meals and milk for school children. Added to these measures went the extension of the inheritance dues and income taxes to achieve some redistribution of wealth. There were also laws which had a direct bearing on labor conditions. For one thing, trade-union legislation gave those bodies full corporate status and greater freedom to carry on strikes. The Factory Acts were extended and expanded until they took in practically every factory and workshop except those without mechanical power. Dangerous trades were regulated; the mine acts were extended. In 1896 employers in most industries were forced to insure themselves to provide compensation for any accidents which their employees might suffer. The idea of a "just price" for the use of money was also restored by the enactment in 1900 of a law limiting the rate of interest allowable under circumstances which might put the borrower at a decided disadvantage. Between 1870 and 1900 great steps had been taken by the government to aid the lower classes. The state was becoming the body to solve all problems.

The appearance in Parliament after 1895 of a specifically labor element accelerated the trend. Although its influence before 1905 was relatively slight, it was a continual reminder to all parties of the labor vote. When campaigning for votes in 1905, the Liberals consciously took this situation into account by making their great appeal for support to labor. The logical outcome of this was further pro-labor legislation.

It was for this reason that the Liberal landslide in 1906 opened up the way for increased social legislation, thereby vastly extending the state's influence. For one thing, taxation was made to bear more heavily than ever upon the wealthy with the increase and steeper graduation of income tax and death duties as well as the tax on unearned increment and undeveloped land. More immediately influential on the workingman's way of life were the laws of 1909 which gave the municipalities greater power to control town planning and to regulate the erection of dwellings. Meanwhile, a demand was being made for old age pensions in imitation of the German plan. Although New Zealand had introduced a scheme in 1898, nothing was done in Britain until Lloyd George, as Chancellor of the Exchequer, brought in his plan in 1908. Everyone at 70 years was to receive 5s. per week if his annual income were less than £21, the amount being graded down to 1s. as the income rose to £31. It was estimated that, by 1913, this would cost the country about £12.6 million. The important thing was that it constituted the first step in the breaking up of the old poor law system. The second step came the following year with the introduction of "National Insurance," which provided sickness and invalidity benefits to the lower-paid classes and also unemployment benefits to certain industrial groups, such as those employed in construction and shipbuilding, industries affected by seasonal unemployment. Employee, employer, and state, all contributed to the fund.[5] This plan was really an experiment, the first step towards the formulation of a scheme for general unemployment insurance. It was ostensibly to finance this that Lloyd George introduced taxation objectionable to the Lords, who attempted to amend the bill. It was passed, however, despite the upper house's obstructionist tactics, which only gave the Liberals an excuse to limit the Lords' power of veto.

More directly related to labor's conditions of work were other laws passed during this decade. In 1901 the Conservatives had consolidated the regulations regarding factories into a Factory and Workshop Act which gave the Home Office power to control conditions of work in practically every manufacturing institution. In 1911 this was further extended to those serving in shops.[6] In 1906

---

[5] Employees paid weekly; 4d. if a man, 3d. if a woman; employers paid 3d., and the state 2d.

[6] The administration of the labor laws was under the Secretary of State for Home Affairs. A permanent under-secretary was in charge of the Factory Inspection Department. There were six inspection divisions with a total of 51 districts in each of which was a district inspector and his assistant. By 1913 the total staff numbered 224 at a cost of £98,926, inspecting 117,275 factories and 155,697 workshops employing 5.1 million people. Ogg and Sharp, *op. cit.*, p. 372.

the laws of 1894 protecting the health and governing the employment of seamen were broadened. Two years later further regulations were introduced to govern the work of miners, limiting them
to eight consecutive hours' labor per day. Along with these very
specific statutes went the establishment of Labour Exchanges.
Started at first by the London authorities, by 1910 the Board of
Trade had taken control, establishing them in all parts of the
country. In 1913 these bodies found jobs for more than a million
people. Finally, there was the ticklish question of wage regulation.
As early as 1888 there had been repeated complaints about conditions in certain "sweated" trades such as custom tailoring and shoe-
making. Pay was low, working conditions were poor and hours
were long. At length, in 1909, after much agitation, the Board of
Trade established machinery for fixing minimum wages by means of
committees of employers and employees. Somewhat the same policy was followed when, in 1912, the government provided for the
setting of minimum wages for the coal miners by district committees composed of labor and management. Thus the state had
assumed the right to take a greater part in directing the economic
and social affairs of the country, usually on behalf of the working
man.

While the national government had in these ways been extending its power, the same pattern was being followed, albeit somewhat
more slowly, by a number of municipal governments. In 1888
London was made a county, but its council had only very limited
powers over such concerns as streets, gas, water, and health. Therefore, the Progressive Party, which was influential in the county
government, campaigned for an extension of the council's authority.
So strong was the opposition that it was not until 1899 that a
compromise was reached whereby a considerable number of boroughs were set up, each responsible for local improvements and
sanitation. The rich in this way did not have to pay for the poor.
In other English cities public utilities, such as tram lines and gas
and water supplies, were gradually acquired by the local administration, while in Scotland, since all these services had originally been
established by the local authorities, no change was needed. Thus,
it was also at the municipal level that the growing tendency towards
collectivism, if not to actual socialism, was being manifested.

As one looks back over the forty years preceding World War I,
it can be seen that there was a gradual but very clearly indicated
trend towards much greater government activity in the economic
sphere. The Conservatives had taken some of the steps in this
direction, largely, one might suspect, for the same reason that

Bismarck had instituted reforms in Prussia: to undermine the socialists and radicals. Toward the end of the period, however, the Conservatives had become weary in well-doing. Labor, on the other hand, thoroughly convinced of the need of more state action, had formed its own party advocating clear-cut socialistic policies. Between these two groups stood the Liberals in imminent danger of losing the working-class vote, if not also that of the lower middle class. At the same time, led by one or two crusading reformers whose motives are not always clear, they seem to have had a genuine interest in giving the state more power for reform. Thus, by 1914 the Conservatives had become quite reactionary, and Labour was committed to socialism, while the Liberals, trying to keep a middle of the road position as well as their power, were supporting collectivism or interventionism, but definitely not entering into truly socialist activity. The trend was indeed in the direction of socialism, but it would require two world wars and a world wide depression before this would be accepted by a majority of the British people.

Chapter 23

WAR ECONOMY CHANGES BRITAIN'S POSITION

THE GREAT impact of any war upon a country's economy is that of the destruction of both material and invisible assets. In this World War I was no exception. While Britain did not experience an invasion and felt the blast of only a few bombs, nevertheless, the war's physical destructiveness had a great influence upon her. For one thing, she lost nearly a million of her men between the ages of seventeen and forty-five. Added to that was the sinking of over one half of her tonnage of shipping. But even more important than either of these items, from an economic point of view, was the destruction on the Continent, indeed all over the world, impoverishing the countries which had at one time been Britain's best customers. The resulting breakdown of the economies of France, Germany, Russia, Italy, and such far off places as Africa and the Near East was disastrous for Britain, up to this time the great merchant of the world.

Of even greater importance than the physical destruction, however, was the loss of Britain's immaterial assets. As A. L. Bowley has said, "the dislocation was worse than the destruction." The war changed the whole pattern of Britain's foreign trade. During hostilities her contacts were broken with her best Continental customer, Germany, while other countries were lost as British markets owing to her inability to supply them with goods. The result was the building, either by the former customers or by neutrals, of factories to replace British goods. Government wartime control of industry was also extended in many lands—control which, after the war, was employed to maintain the new factories by means of tariffs and monopolies, keeping out British goods. To add to the difficulties, the whole structure of world finance disintegrated. In Britain herself the stable gold sovereign disappeared, being replaced by currency notes which even a loyal Englishman distrusted. In the rest of the world the economic situation was even worse. With the exception of North America, most of the national currencies were so inflated that Britain lost much of the benefit of her foreign investments. In the case of investments in Russia, after the revolution they simply disappeared, confiscated by the Bolshevists. Last but not least, there was the great loss of normal production by virtue of Britain's industrial resources being turned to manufacturing engines of destruction. All these losses are directly attributable to the impact of World War I.

One other influence of World War I was the change which took place in the British population. The war itself accounted for the death of nearly one million men. Yet, despite this, the population actually increased between 1911 and 1921 by about two million, or by 5 per cent. The important fact is, however, that the proportions of the population changed. For one thing, in 1921 there were 1.75 million more females than males. This made it harder to get a husband, with the result that more women than ever before were looking for jobs. While the employment of women had helped the war effort, it was sure to depress the labor market after the war was over. At the same time, between 1911 and 1921 there was a movement toward the city, continuing that of the nineteenth century. The comparative percentages of urban population in the two census years were 78 per cent and 79.3 per cent, so by 1921 the city population had increased by about one million. Last but not least, since most of those killed had been young people, the average age of the population had risen. Britain was becoming a nation of older men and women.

Up to this point, we have been talking in general terms of the dislocation and destruction wrought by World War I upon British economy. It is now necessary to examine systematically and in detail the actual changes which took place in British economic life and organization during this first holocaust of the twentieth century.

The Government Takes Over

When the war began the prevailing attitude among both business men and government officials was one of economic laissez faire. "Business as usual" was the watchword, for most people believed that the war could be fought as a kind of side show. It was necessary of course for the government to assume enlarged powers of control and authority. This it did by the Defence of the Realm Acts (known unpopularly as DORA), but nobody thought at first that the state would really require much greater authority. Everybody was opposed to controls. It was only as the war continued, disaster being piled upon disaster, that the British people began to realize that this was a total war and that to fight a total war the government needed much greater power of control. The acquisition of this authority was perhaps one of the most significant developments in the economic life of the country during these four hectic years.

The first controls had been instituted right at the beginning of the war, with the government taking over the railways and about twenty per cent of the country's shipping. At the same time, in order to keep marine insurance rates down to a practicable level, the state also set up a marine insurance office which, by selling cheap policies, brought the premiums down to under 5 per cent. In all three cases, however, the government was thinking primarily of its own military and naval needs. It wanted the railways and shipping for transporting troops and supplies. The purpose of lowering marine insurance rates was to protect itself, as well as private concerns, from having to pay too much. So far nothing was done in terms of the general economy of the country.

Another form of control introduced (December, 1916) was the regulation of prices. Usually the method employed was that of establishing minimum and maximum wholesale and retail prices, within which limits lay a reasonable profit. Frequently the minimum price was entirely ignored, the seller, particularly the farmer, obtaining the top price permitted. Such controls, while not so necessary at the beginning of the war, became increasingly important as the war progressed. But price fixing was not enough. If prices were to be kept down, other controls were required. So, before very long, the government found itself faced with the necessity of instituting a new and greatly extended supervision over every phase of economic activity.

The war had not been going many weeks before it was discovered that if food prices were to be kept at a sensible level, the government would have to go into food buying. In cooperation with the French therefore, and largely financed by British credits, "La Commission Internationale de Ravitaillement" was established for the joint purchasing of foodstuffs. The principal commodities acquired at first were sugar and wheat, for they were in short supply at a very early date. Thus, almost from the beginning of the war the government was forced to undertake a certain amount of bulk purchasing.

Despite these tentative moves toward control of the country's economy, however, it was only as a result of the pressure of threatened defeat that any really decisive action was taken. At first, with no conscription for the army and navy and no allocation of essential materials to producers, there was a very serious drain on the country's resources. Highly skilled men needed for the armament industries were enlisting and were being killed on the fields of Belgium and France. In agriculture, the farmer was having a difficult time obtaining sufficient labor to harvest his precious crops. Added to all this, as the German U-boat campaign got underway, food and war materiels were becoming scarcer, and a general allocation became absolutely necessary. At last, as a result of demands from all quarters, the government did step in, but then only with the greatest diffidence.

The first move was made after the Liberal prime minister, Asquith, had formed a coalition government. The spring of 1915 had revealed a terrible shortage of munitions, the artillery being limited to firing a few shells a day. To meet this need, in June of 1915 a Munitions Act was passed, setting up a Ministry of Munitions headed by the fiery Welshman, David Lloyd George. This body, armed with extensive powers of coercion and control, immediately commenced to take over mills, supplies, warehouses, and the like for the purpose of munitions production. The government had greatly extended its power over the property of the country, and this was but the beginning.

Meanwhile, prices were rising, and the cost of living was mounting steadily, while wages and salaries lagged behind, entailing severe hardship upon many. Furthermore, despite government bulk purchasing and control of the whole of the merchant fleet, the increasing effectiveness of German submarine warfare, which had destroyed over 100,000 tons by May 1915, threatened to send prices even higher. Therefore, as a result of the desperate needs of the army and navy, and also of the increasing demands of the civilian population, by the end of 1915 strong government action was forthcoming.

The first thing needed was greater agricultural production. The 1916 crops throughout the world had been poor. Besides, before the war Britain had been raising only enough food for 125 days in the year, and with 250,000 farm laborers now in the army, the level of production was even lower. Efforts had been made to persuade the farmer to change over from grazing to arable farming, since the latter type would support four times as many people. Farmers are, however, notoriously impervious to propaganda. Definite state action, therefore, had to be taken. During the autumn of 1916 the Board of Agriculture was given power to control farming in order to obtain better supply. With this authority, it proceeded to establish County Agricultural Committees to direct in all matters regarding cultivation, machinery, labor and finance. Groups of districts were placed under commissioners who could take over a farm if it were not properly run and who also received the right to force an owner to cultivate unoccupied land. Furthermore, by the Corn Production Act of August 1917 they were empowered to fix the price of produce between a guaranteed minimum and a maximum. Similarly, the Board of Agriculture was given the power to allocate fertilizers and machinery to the various producers. Finally, in 1918 the county boards were made responsible for selecting those laborers who were to be exempted from the now universal military conscription. Thus farming, which had been so long ignored by the government, now became one of its chief concerns.

The reason for this changed attitude was the growing scarcity of food. Starvation was Germany's chief weapon. While this was to be met partially by increased agricultural production, there was still much food which had to be imported. Therefore, in December 1916 a Ministry of Food was set up to regulate and direct the production, consumption, transportation, and storage of all foodstuffs, to requisition any article on its own terms, to require information as to amount of prices and quantities of food any one had on hand, to fix prices, to control exports, and, if necessary, to ration goods. Although rationing was approached only with the greatest reluctance, by the middle of 1917 even that had to be accepted by the British. Not only was the farmer brought under control, but even the private citizen's food could now be eaten only with government permission. And the end had not been reached. By 1918 85 per cent of all food supplies were being bought by the Ministry of Food.

At the same time that agriculture and food were being brought under government control, identical plans were being worked out in connection with other industries. Coal mining had been hit very early in the war by the loss of man power to the army, one third of the labor force having volunteered before March, 1916. The result was that the annual production of coal had dropped by 30 million tons, while prices soared. Some people were advocating government control of the mines, but the owners were opposed lest their dividends should decline. In February, 1915 an Advisory Coal Mining Organization Committee was established to stimulate production, but even that failed to stop the downward trend. Moreover, despite the rising cost of living, miners' wages remained at the 1914 level. The outcome of this situation was that in December, 1916 the South Wales miners came out on strike, forcing the government to seize the mines and run them until the end of the war. The industry was placed under a Controller of Coal Mines, assisted by a committee of seven owners and seven employees. Profits equal to prewar levels were guaranteed, although an increase of more than 5 per cent over those levels would be taken by the government. Wages and pithead prices were also under regulation. In this way, by giving a fair deal to all, it was hoped to increase production.

Another move in the direction of maintaining a large volume of necessary materiel was the assumption by the government during December, 1916 of almost total control over all industrial commodities. Wool was placed under the regulation of the War Office, which in 1916 took over the country's total wool clip. Coal, timber, petroleum, and similar materials were placed under the Board of Trade. There was a controller for practically everything usable. In 1917 the War Trade Department and the Departments of National Service and Reconstruction were organized to extend the government's regulation of the country's economic life. Most of the personnel staffing these various departments were businessmen summoned to the aid of the nation. Those left to run their businesses were in charge of technical processes but nothing more. The manufacturer no longer did any buying, selling, or even hiring, for the state now ran everything. It even lent its influence to large amalgamations in industries such as steel in order that control might be facilitated. Added to this, in the latter part of 1917, Britain, by becoming a member of various international councils dealing with food and munitions, placed both her industry and agriculture to a certain extent under the control of authority which was not even British. This indeed was a far cry from the days of laissez faire!

The years 1916 and 1917 also saw a great extension of the government's control over shipping. When the war started, Britain owned about 40 per cent of the world's 49 million tons, but by 1917 she had lost over 7 million tons and, as building was not keeping pace with sinkings, cargo space was becoming alarmingly scarce. Consequently, early in 1916 controls were placed on imports, shipping being allocated to only the most needed goods. In this way many commodities were prevented from entering the country. Although this helped, it was not enough, so later in the same year a controller of shipping was appointed to allocate space for the various supply ministeries. In January of the following year the whole problem was placed on an international footing by the establishment of the Inter-Allied Shipping Committee. This body did not wield any effective power until it was reorganized in November as the Allied Maritime Transport Council, with a permanent executive of ministerial rank and authority to direct the whole of allied shipping, allocating space to various countries as it was needed.

The last phase of government control during the war went beyond goods and services to deal with people. Despite much opposition, the government found it necessary to enforce nationwide and rigid controls over all labor. At first, with a completely voluntary army, recruiting was indiscriminate, taking many key individuals out of industry. The result was a shortage of labor which was only partially met by the dilution of the working force with women. To solve part of the problem, in 1915 limitations were set on recruiting, those kept in industry being given badges to show that they were needed at home. Only gradually was it realized that much greater regulation had to be employed. First of all, the population was registered, and then, in 1916, conscription was introduced. By 1917 further controls were imposed: strikes and lockouts were banned, trade union restrictions on output were abolished, and the right to leave a job or to hire a worker was severely restricted. By this means strikes were kept down to a minimum, and production increased. But the trade-unions were not happy. They felt that labor was not receiving a proper proportion of profits. They were also afraid that after the war they would not be able to return to the old freedom of prewar days. While all in favor of restrictions on the employer and his profits, they resented any attempt to control wages. Consequently, by the end of the war, labor was becoming distinctly restive. Nevertheless, the controls stood the strain, being largely responsible for Britain's weathering the storm.

Government Production and Distribution of Goods

As has already been seen, the over-all impact of the war was to change production and distribution from a peacetime to a wartime footing and direction. It was for this purpose that the government controls were employed. Natural laws such as those so confidently accepted by Adam Smith and his early followers would never have brought about the necessary changes in the time required. The government therefore had to step in with its coercive powers and force a change, despite what men felt to be their own particular interests. In this way alone was it possible to gear the whole economy to a total war effort. The figures of production and distribution are indications of this effort's achievements.

When one endeavors to understand the influence of the war on agricultural production, it is necessary to call to mind that by 1914 British agriculture was more a luxury than a staple industry. The arable area was 4.75 million acres less than it had been in 1870, while the labor force had declined in about the same proportion. The stress was being laid principally on fancy types of beef and greenhouse production of such items as tomatoes and small fruits for the table and for jam. Wheat and other cereal grains were no longer the prime interest of the farmer, a fact which meant that a considerable change had to be made if he was to help meet the need for wartime provisions. Thus, government controls became necessary and, as shown above (pages 435 ff.), were extensively applied.

While the success of these regulations was by no means phenomenal, they at least helped the situation. For instance, between 1914 and 1918 there was a considerable extension of arable farming, over 3 million acres of grassland being plowed up. Wheat acreage rose from 2 million to 2.7 million, and that of oats, from 4.1 to 5.6 million. At the same time, the yield per acre rose in the case of wheat by over one bushel, and in that of barley by two bushels. Production at the end of the war, as compared with that of 1913, showed an increase in wheat of 60 per cent, in oats of 50 per cent and in potatoes of 40 per cent. The result was that over a million more tons of food was being raised in Britain in 1917 than in 1914. This total was, of course, helped by the devoting of flower gardens to vegetables as well as by the creation of 870,000 allotments. The result of all these efforts was that Britain at the close of hostilities was supplying herself with 155 instead of 125 days of food. Controls had helped but had by no means solved the problem.[1]

Much less successful than the government's attempts to increase agricultural production was the effort to mine more coal. In 1913 the output of the mines had been 287 million tons, a phenomenal figure. By the end of 1914 this had dropped to 266 million tons, and by the end of 1915, to 253 million. As a result of concessions made to the miners by the government in 1916, the downward

[1]   Wartime Agricultural Production (million quarters)

Crops	1918	1916	1904-13	% of 1916	% of 1904-13
Wheat	10.5 m. qtrs.	6.8m.	6.6m.	+54%	+58%
Barley	6 m.	5.1m.	6.2m.	+17%	− 2%
Oats	14.3 m.	10.4m.	10.5m.	+38%	+36%
Mixed corn	620,000	—	—	—	—
Potatoes	4.2 m. tons	2.5m.	2.6m.	+68%	+59%

+ = increase; − = decrease

Source: Lord Ernle, *English Farming,* p. 407.

trend was stopped for a short period, during which the production actually rose to 256 million tons. But this was only a temporary improvement. Even the seizure of the mines by the government did not change the situation, 1917 seeing only 249 million tons raised, and 1918 a further decrease of 22 million tons in production. Thus, by the end of the war British coal production had dropped, notwithstanding all efforts to stop the decline, by 60 million tons. Herein lies the root of much of the trouble which came upon Britain in the following decade.

Other forms of industrial production also suffered, which was only natural in a nation involved in a total war. At first even armament manufacture was down. However under the dynamic leadership of Lloyd George, that situation was rectified by mid-1916. The voluntary method of production having proved to be a failure in 1914 and early 1915, the government took over industry, employing flour mills to roll out cordite and converting all kinds of factories to the manufacture of shells, rifles, and bombs. As a result, between June 1915 and June 1916 the output of rifles had increased three times, machine guns fourteen times, bombs thirty-three times and high explosives sixty-six times. Simultaneously, steel had maintained its level of production at about 10 million tons a year. Thus, as far as munitions were concerned, by 1916 government controls had shown marked success.

The war, however, played havoc with other industries. Textiles were hard hit, with the exception of wool, which maintained its level of output only because it was employed for the manufacture of uniforms. Cotton consumption, on the other hand, declined, the annual average (1914-1916) of 1,854 million pounds dropping between 1917 and 1919 to 1,623 million. For the same period, the consumption of flax dropped from 225 million pounds to 121 million. Other industries, unless they were directly engaged in war production, frequently suffered even more severely. Government controls had the effect of stopping the production of any goods which were not deemed essential to victory.

The influence of government regulation, along with enemy action, upon the distribution of British goods was also very profound, whether in domestic trade or export. In the case of the latter, the sinking of shipping was of prime importance, although government restrictions also played a great part.

It is hard to estimate exactly what happened to Britain's balance of trade, owing to factors such as rising prices, exports to forces overseas, and the like, but a general calculation seems to point to the fact that British imports rose from £696 million in 1914, to

£1,316 million in 1918, while her exports rose from £526 to £532. The trouble in all of this was that, owing to her curtailment of production, she lost many of her best customers. For instance, the decline in her export of cotton piece goods to India amounted to 57 per cent, and although her trade with South America between 1913 and 1922 rose from £48 million to £49 million in value, owing to inflated currency, it actually decreased greatly in volume. Altogether, the export of British cottons between 1913 and 1918 dropped from 7,000 million yards to 3,700 million, of woolens, from 168 million to 98 million yards, of iron and steel, from 5 million to 1.6 million tons, and of coal, from 73 million to 25 million tons.

Added to this, Britain's inability to supply her old customers meant that either they themselves or a neutral nation attempted to provide the goods. Factories were built in India, Canada, Australia, and South America. At the same time, American productive capacity was greatly expanded so that it was able to supply former British markets such as South America, where, in ten years time United States trade volume more than doubled. Britain not only had to fight, to turn her industrial potential to profitless production, but she also lost many of her best markets to those who remained out of the war.

At home, the market, while not shrinking, was very seriously undersupplied. For this reason, rationing was introduced in order to achieve equality of sacrifice. Many have held that the plan was not successful in this regard, but it seems to have accomplished as much as might be expected. Practically all the basic foodstuffs except bread, as well as many other commodities, came under government control. Thus, an effort was made to guarantee that the best possible advantage would be taken of the small amount of goods available.

As one studies the effects of the war and the resultant government controls on British economic life, one sees a nation converted in a relatively short time from a trust in the eternal efficacy of individualism and natural processes to dependence upon government regulation. The success of these attempts of the government to direct economic life was only moderate in the case of agriculture, although in industry of a certain type state controls were of considerable value, as they were also in the distribution of goods. On the other hand, in coal mining, despite all efforts, production continued to fall steadily. It must be recognized, on the other hand, that without these controls and the measure of success which they attained, the war could hardly have been won.

Financing the War

One very important part of the economic aspects of the war was the question of finance. There were, as there had been during the Napoleonic wars, only two methods of paying the bills: by loans and taxes. As usual, the government endeavored to use that which was less painful, namely loans. But in a short time it found that taxes had to be increased if any semblance of financial stability was to be maintained. Along with this, Britain was faced with the necessity of paying for her imports from foreign countries. Since she was not exporting, she had to find some other method, a necessity which led to a serious impairment of her oversea investments. Thus, at the end of the war she was much weaker financially than she had been in 1913.

Even before the entrance of Britain into the war, her finances had been somewhat shaken. The threat of war in the middle of July, 1914 and its actual outbreak at the end of the month had caused a freezing of all British assets on the Continent. Acceptance houses in London were caught with large quantities of unredeemable foreign bills on hand and this, in turn, hit banks and other houses holding short term commercial bills. Moreover, many people began to feel that they should convert what paper money they had, into gold. This caused a run on the banks, who met the difficulty by handing out Bank of England notes. When the resulting run started on the "Old Lady of Threadneedle Street," the bank rate climbed steeply to 10 per cent without much effect. The government thereupon authorized the Bank to pay acceptance houses in notes for their foreign bills and permitted it to stop paying gold. Simultaneously the Treasury began to issue notes in denominations of 5s., 10s., and £1 to ease the pressure for small change. Although these were regarded as merely temporary, they remained and were added to, so by 1918 the total note issue was £1,700 million. This resulted in inflation, which reduced the ratio of bullion to currency by about 30 per cent, all metal coins but those of very small denominations disappearing from circulation. Thus, although the currency problem was dealt with at the very beginning of the war, it helped to cause the inflation which, coupled with the shortage of supplies, raised the price index from about 100 in 1914 to 295 in 1920.

Meanwhile, the war had to be financed. At first this was done largely by borrowing, a method which is not good, since it creates a liability on future production and helps to cause inflation. The government issued (Aug. 6, 1914) £100 million in Treasury Bills which were taken up by the banks. As these bills were only short-term, however, the debt had to be funded on a long-term basis, which was done with the raising of the First War Loan in November, 1914. Bonds were issued at £95 for 3½ per cent, redeemable in 1928. The total amount raised in this way came to £331 million, but in the same month a further credit was voted amounting to £225 million. Something much more drastic than the raising of loans was needed. Heavier taxation was the only answer, although this was not realized until March 1915.

The fact was that Lloyd George would take no steps which might make him unpopular with the country. His budget of November 16th increased the existing tax on earned income by 1s. in the pound, raising it to 2s., and on unearned income by 1s. 8d. Taxes on beer and tea were also raised, but that was all. It was expected that these measures during the last four months of the fiscal year would increase revenue by £15 million. Since estimated expenditures were well over £300 million, however, the balance would have to be borrowed. The same policy was followed in the second budget. In the hope of a sudden end to the war, borrowing was held to be the best method. Out of an estimated expenditure of £1,132 million only £267 million was to come from taxes. At the same time, prices and wages were rising, and the government was spending money lavishly. As no attempt was made to be realistic about the situation, the actual deficiency for 1914-15 amounted to £333 million, promising to be much higher for the fiscal year 1915-16.

Fortunately for everybody concerned, in June Lloyd George was given the post of Minister of Munitions, his place being taken by MacKenna. By September 1915 daily expenditure was running at around £4 million, a fact which forced the submission of a new budget. Income tax was increased by 40 per cent, exemptions were lowered, farmers were required to pay for the first time, and excess profits taxes of 50 per cent were applied to businesses. By this means revenues were increased more than £100 million to £336.7 million. Even this was not nearly enough, so further increases were made in taxes on incomes, profits, and various commodities, until the government receipts were up to £573.4 million. In 1917, Bonar Law took over the portfolio of the Chancellor of the Exchequer and raised the excess profit taxes to 80 per cent but did not increase the others correspondingly. During his first year he obtained an income of £707 million, while for 1918-19, by raising income taxes and customs and excise duties and by lowering exemptions, he raised £889 million. The country, consequently, at the end of the war was paying almost four times the taxes of 1914.

Yet, with all his efforts, government expenditures, for various reasons, had far outstripped income. For one thing, partially owing to the government policy of borrowing, prices had risen sharply. Then too, there had been a tremendous increase in the cost of the war simply through the ever-growing expenditure of materiel. Finally, there was governmental extravagance, which had become something of a byword in the land. By March, 1918 the annual disbursements of the country had reached £2,696 million, £1,988 million of it borrowed. Because the war ended in 1918, by March, 1919 the total expenditure had dropped a little, to £2,579 million, with borrowings standing at £1,690 million. These vast sums of money were loaned to the government, to a large extent, by the British people themselves. For instance, £1,000 million were subscribed in the third and last War Loan, which, at that time, was the biggest financial operation in history. Besides the loan drives, there were steady sales of war savings certificates, and after the Third Loan, bonds were sold continuously at the rate of £450 million for the year 1918-19. Thus, out of Britain's total expenditures of £9,593 million for the war, 28 per cent or £2,733 million were raised by taxes, and all the rest by loans, leaving her at the end of the war with an annual interest charge on the war debt of £246.3 million. Britain's whole financial situation had altered drastically in five years.

Had the indebtedness of the British government been only to its own people, the situation might not have been too grave. This, however, was not the case, for Britain was heavily in debt to the United States. Since she needed far greater quantities of materiel than she herself could produce, Britain had been obliged to turn to the American continent for help. Increasingly she had to depend upon American guns, munitions, and civilian supplies. Yet, at the same time, she was not manufacturing very much for export, with the result that she could give little or nothing in the way of goods as repayment. She was therefore dependent upon the returns from her foreign investments, amounting in 1914 to about £4,000 million. Since, even at 5 per cent, this sum was not sufficient to meet her needs, something further was required.

The answer was loans from the United States. Early in 1916, Britain sought an American loan of £1,000 million, but the bankers, many of whom were pro-German, would handle nothing larger than £50 million. However, after much negotiation, in August 1916 Great Britain and France together obtained $254 million at 5 per cent, and two months later another loan of $300 million also at 5 per cent. Even that was not enough, for by March 1917 expenditures had soared to around £6.6 million a day, so Britain had to obtain another loan of $250 million. Added to these obligations was another, for the American financiers usually endeavored to have her back any loans which they gave to her allies.

Since loans are not given without collateral, measures were also necessary in order to stabilize her international financial position. The British government gradually took over from private individuals their holdings of American securities. For these, they were reimbursed either by payments amounting to ½ per cent over the usual dividends or, if it was found necessary to dispose of the securities, with government bonds. While there is no certain knowledge as to how large an amount of British holdings in the United States was sold, it has been estimated that it came to about 25 per cent of the total. Securities not sold were put up as collateral for the loans. Along with these moves, in order to protect her currency and so stabilize the value of the loans, she arranged with J. P. Morgan and Company to peg the pound sterling at $4.765, buying in when it tended to drop and selling when it rose. In this way Great Britain carried on to the end of the war.

The cessation of hostilities found Britain in a serious financial plight. For one thing, her currency was greatly inflated, increasing prices and wages. At the same time, taxation was high; at least it was much higher than it had ever been before, the per capita payment having risen between 1914 and 1919 from £5 5s. to £19, or from 11.29 per cent of the national income to 23.56 per cent. The reason for this enormous increase was that the war alone had created a national debt of £6,300 million, raising the prewar debt by 1,000 per cent. Of this amount, she owed the United States £842 million, a fact which at first was not too alarming, since the Continental allies owed Britain over £1,700 million. A radical change in the situation came, however, when it was discovered that the allies could not pay. Britain, therefore, was left as a debtor to the United States. With a considerable part of her holdings of United States securities dissipated, London's position as the creditor of the world, the controller of world financial destinies, had to a large extent been taken by New York.

Added to all of this, Britain's trade and industry had been so affected by the war that she was in no condition to regain her old place with any ease. While the loans she obtained in the United States had been spent there, many of the loans which she had given to her allies had not been spent in Britain and so had not helped to develop her industry. At the same time, growing nationalism abroad, both economic and political, was beginning to build up barriers against British goods, meaning that she would have a much harder task to regain her old markets. Thus, at the end of the war, in terms of finance as well as of industry and commerce, Britain found herself in very greatly reduced circumstances.

The Economics of British Society

The impact of World War I upon the British economy naturally had a very considerable influence on the country's social structure. Many of the relationships between social classes had been based upon an economic structure the underpinnings of which were now being shaken. Therefore, in considering the economic influence of the war it is necessary to examine, at least generally, how it affected British society.

As has been seen, the production of consumer goods decreased steadily throughout the war. Many foodstuffs, such as sugar, fats, and eggs, were in short supply, as were also nearly all items of clothing and furniture. The consequence was that essential commodities were rationed, while items considered to be less necessary were allowed to remain in short supply. This brought about a certain amount of black-marketing, and hardship for those who did not have the money with which to buy.

Coupled with, and partially caused by, the shortages was the rise in prices. *The Economist*, Britain's principal business weekly, estimated that the price index, which it took as 100 in July, 1914, rose to 140 in December, 1915, to 226 in December, 1917 and to 235 in December, 1918. This meant that the pound of 1914 bought only 8s. 3d. worth of goods four years later. To those who were being paid wages, or who were making profits, this was no real hardship, for as prices rose, they increased their incomes proportionately. At the same time, investors of new money also profited, for they were able to obtain higher rates of interest. The wage-earning class was also helped by controlled rents, which remained steady, although wages advanced. There were others, however, who suffered severely: for instance, those who were living on fixed pensions or on the returns from such things as government stock or on the rents, now frozen, of houses or real estate of other types. Prices rose, but the income of these unfortunates remained at a steady, unchanging level. The result was that many older people who had retired from business suffered, as did a good many of the middle class whose income was largely made up of fixed returns.

Much the same thing might be said with regard to the operation of taxation. Here the proportion paid by the upper brackets of income was much greater in 1918 than it had been in 1913. With the placing of a supertax upon incomes over £2,500, reduction in exemptions for family and the increase of excess profits tax on business to 80 per cent, a much larger proportion of revenue was coming from the wealthy section of the population. The imposition of indirect taxes upon certain commodities, such as beer and tea, did have its effect upon the lower classes, but not to nearly the same extent. The result was a very real change in the distribution of income throughout the country. A. L. Bowley [2] has endeavored to show what happened by making a study of the higher income brackets. He points out that those receiving an annual income of £10,000 in 1913 were 4,000 in number, while those receiving the equivalent in purchasing power in 1924 numbered only 1,300. At the same time, he points out that the supertax on incomes over £5,000 in 1913 was applied to a total of £176 million, bringing in a revenue of £3.3 million, whereas in 1924, the same tax, applied to £326 million, brought in £66 million. Taxation was clearly achieving the aims of many social reformers, namely, the redistribution of wealth.

The economic changes and disruption brought about by the war also had a decided effect upon labor, giving it a new sense of strength and importance. Whether they gave labor a sense of responsibility as well, is hard to determine. The workmen realized as never before that they possessed great power to influence and even control the destinies of the country. This idea was fostered not only by experiences in the army, but also by the spread of unionism, which by 1918 had reached even into the country to include agricultural workers.

Along with this came a change in the position of women. Having taken a very considerable part in the manufacture of the instruments of war as well as filling the places of tram conductors, railway guards, and the like, they gained a new acceptance as workers. Once in industry, it was not long before they began to take part in labor organizations. While many entered the regular unions, a National Federation of Women Workers was established whose membership increased between 1914 and 1919 from 11,000 to 60,000. These figures give some idea of their growing importance and influence. By 1919 they were accepted as holding a very crucial place in the economic life of the country.

[2] A. L. Bowley, *Some Economic Consequences of the Great War* (London, 1936), p. 131.

Thus, on looking back over the four years of war, one cannot but be impressed with the fact that World War I brought great and widespread changes in the economic life and conditions of the British people. Yet, these changes were not entirely new. The War made them come more rapidly then they would have in the ordinary course of events, but much of that which took place was already in the program before the war broke out. The war acted as a speeding-up agency, in scientific terms—as a catalyst. The radical changes which had taken place in Britain's economic position and organization between 1870 and 1914 presaged many of the difficulties which would have come anyway. The rise of new competitors, the decline of industrial predominance, and even the decrease in foreign holdings had probably all commenced before 1914. The war, however, stimulated the movement already in progress, leaving Britain in a considerably impoverished position with many difficulties to be solved in the postwar world "fit for heroes."

Chapter 24

THE GOVERNMENT AND POST-
WAR PRODUCTION

A<small>LTHOUGH</small> Great Britain suffered little in
terms of actual material destruction during World War I, by 1918
the country's trade and industry were completely dislocated. Tariff
barriers, new industries, rival producers, and similar phenomena had
all appeared in such great force that throughout the '20's Britain
never really recovered her old position. Before she could become
accustomed to these changing conditions, the early '30's brought
a depression which effectively wiped out any success at adaptation
to the new situation. Once again a new environment had to be
faced, but hardly was it well understood before there appeared
over the horizon the menace of Nazi Germany and Fascist Italy.
Rearmament was now added to other problems. British trade was
not nearly as prosperous as it had been before World War I, yet,
in spite of rising prices and costlier weapons, for self-preservation,
Britain had to turn much of her income to the making of munitions. Rearmament helped to meet the problem of unemployment,
but it also gave rise to many others. With these still unsolved,
Great Britain was plunged in September 1939 into another holocaust of war.

The Slow Death of Laissez Faire

To a very large extent a result of World War I and of the continual twenty-year effort at postwar rehabilitation was the growing
disrepute of the doctrines of laissez faire. For instance, completely
free competition now lost its character as a panacea for all economic
problems. Monopolies were no longer regarded as, of themselves,
necessarily evil. They were rebaptized as "rationalized planning"
and given government blessing. Mercantilism came back into the
picture. The principle that the government possessed the right to
control the economic life of the country for the benefit of all

449

to many became axiomatic. After all, during the war the government had successfully run the country's economy so that victory resulted; could the government not do the same even more easily in times of peace? It is not surprising, therefore, that the '20's and '30's saw the rise of an attitude to the government very different from that of the prewar era. That a Labour government should twice be elected to power between 1920 and 1930 is indicative of the changed outlook.

Such thinking was whole-heartedly supported by a considerable number of economists. One group active immediately preceding the War, was known as the "welfare" school. Its leading representative, J. A. Hobson, published in 1914 a book entitled *Work and Wealth*, in which he frankly rejected the old laissez faire ideas, spurning free competition and also evaluating everything on a monetary basis. The ideas of "real" value and "real" wealth expressed by the classical economists were set aside, to be replaced by "vital" value. It was this which dealt with the standard of living. What was needed was a balance between human costs and human utilities. He pointed out that saving, along with sacrifice, is the source of capital. To the middle and upper classes this was relatively easy, and their work was relatively pleasant. For the laborer, on the other hand, there was monotonous toil plus the difficulty of saving, which meant that his work cost him much more than it did the upper classes. Moreover, much of the work spent on luxuries should be turned to socially productive projects. As a result, the state should step in to control production and distribution, taking "from each according to his ability and giving to each according to his need" as a consumer. The professions should be considered government services, industry should be largely socialized, and the surplus product obtained used for giving people "the good life."

Although there were a considerable number of difficulties in Hobson's theories: for instance, in his evaluating everything in terms of money, his talking in terms of human costs and human utilities, and his rather subjective decision as to what was useful and what was not, still, in the early '20's quite a number of people were prepared to accept his theories. Soon, however, their attention was taken by another economist, John Maynard Keynes.

Keynes had studied and written on economic problems before and during the war, but he first gained a reputation by his *The Economic Consequences of the Peace*, in which he attacked the plans of the peacemakers to keep Germany in economic bondage. He insisted that a prosperous Germany was necessary for world economic stability. His next major work was his attack upon Churchill for restoring the gold standard in 1925, *The Economic Consequences of Mr. Churchill*. His two principal writings, however, were produced in the thirties: A *Treatise on Money* (1930), appearing at the commencement of the Slump, and *The General Theory of Employment, Interest and Money*, published in 1936. In the last work he effectively broke with the old optimistic outlook, particularly of the "neo-classical" school (Marshall and others) and its faith in laissez faire. Instead, he strongly advocated government intervention in economic matters. Only by the state's activity could the economy be stabilized.

In order to understand Keynes's point of view, it is necessary to remember that the "classical" economists dealt only with special cases. Rent, wages, and interest were analyzed as the factors which made up value. It was taken for granted that supply and demand, allowed to operate freely, would automatically bring equilibrium in all prices and values as well as stimulate the full use of all the factors of production. This was the laissez faire of Adam Smith and his successors who assumed the automatic working of economic laws. The only difficulty was that Britain, the most economically "liberal" of all the nations, did not prosper after World War I, and in the early thirties she suffered greatly, experiencing especially the effects of widespread and prolonged unemployment. It was partially to meet this situation that Keynes propounded his theories.

Rejecting the temptation to follow the old paths, Keynes held that since the economy was a whole, it must be treated as such. Periods of unemployment were the result of an unbalanced economy whose equilibrium could be restored only by government controls and influence exercised through financial institutions. If the fiscal policy of the government were properly directed, it would be possible to overcome economic difficulties and to maintain employment always at the highest level.

From this it can be seen that Keynes's thought was occupied with the problem of the relations between income, expenditure, and employment. He believed that income and expenditure will be in equilibrium when the aggregate demand equals aggregate supply; *i.e.*, when people are spending all that they earn on all the goods available. It will, however, be purely accidental if at this time everyone is fully employed. Let the production now change to another level and the equilibrium will be destroyed. Should supply (production) fall below the level of demand, with more money seeking less goods, the result will be inflation, which can be arrested only by cutting incomes through such measures as increased taxation. If, on the other hand, production rises, bringing increased incomes, people will commence saving part of their incomes, and aggregate demand will soon fall short of aggregate supply. For this situation there are two possible solutions. The first is that a lower relative demand would force a cutback in production, bringing about also a corresponding decline in employment. The alternative is that the gap between demand and supply might be closed by means of investment from either private or public sources. Only if this takes place will the higher level of production and employment be maintained.

The question then arises as to how investment may be stimulated so that effective demand will rise. Until this is achieved, "underinvestment" and "oversaving" will lead to economic stagnation. This situation will be changed only when the returns on investment exceed the returns on loaned, or saved, capital; that is, when the expected return on investment is greater than the interest rate. The latter is determined, according to Keynes, by two things: how much people prefer to keep their assets in money rather than in goods, and the quantity of money available. As income rises, there is a tendency to prefer goods, but as it falls, the preference is for money, at the actual time when people should be spending and investing. Therefore, to Keynes, a low rate of interest on money was a constant necessity in order that people might find it more profitable to invest rather than merely to save. This, he felt, could be accomplished largely through government control of bank credit, but most of all by a system of government financed public works. By such government action investment would be increased, calling for more goods, consumption would expand, income would rise, and employment would climb to higher levels.

One of the reasons for Keynes's confidence in the effect of investment is his belief that money, when spent, had "a multiplier effect"; that is, that it resulted in much greater return than the actual value of the amount of money invested. He felt that the multiplier would be about three times, so the original investment had something of the effect of a stone dropped into water causing ever widening ripples over the whole economic pool.

Keynes feared, on the other hand, that as capital assets increased, production would surpass possible consumption at a rate profitable to the producer. In such an eventuality the result would again be stagnation. This reminds one a little of the Mercantilist "fear of goods," and many economists have rejected this so-called "bogey of economic maturity." Keynes felt, however, that the antidote for the trouble was government action, whereby, through control of bank credit, interest rates, and quantity of money in circulation and by manipulation of the national budget deficit and taxation, the economy could be further stimulated.

Thus Keynes helped to popularize a new attitude towards the economic functions of the government. No longer was it to be merely a big policeman to see that the rules of the game were observed and to help those damaged in the play. The government was consciously to have a part in the direction and planning of the economy in order that income and employment might be kept at the highest possible levels. Yet it must be pointed out that Keynes never went as far as many of his would-be disciples. While he insisted on the government's obligation to keep national income high, he very definitely did not hold to the idea of economic planning in any detailed manner. He believed that since the "classical" automatism was by no means correct, the state, by judicious spending and control of bank credit, had to take some action to give general direction. He was, however, equally convinced that if this were done, the system of free enterprise and the capitalistic economy was by far the best yet devised.

It was principally in the ranks of the Labour Party and among those farther to the left, and to a certain limited extent also among the Conservatives and Liberals, that Keynes's views were carried to unexpected lengths. "Central planning" became the watch word of men such as Harold Laski, Maurice Dobbs, and even Sir William Beveridge. It was held, for instance, that there should be a central investment board to control and direct private investment into the "proper" channels. This would result in close government control of all industry involving even the allocation of raw materials and the direction of labor. For this reason, Keynes has often been regarded as an actual socialist when such a point of view was very far from his liking.

There have been many attacks upon the Keynesian ideas. Some critics have held that Keynes's views of consumption simply do not conform to the facts of the case. Individuals do not follow his supposed pattern, nor does he make the necessary differentiation between the actions of individuals and classes. Others point out that, although effective demand may be stimulated by increased amounts of available money, under such conditions prices will not remain steady but will rise, absorbing much of the increased monetary supply without increasing production. It has also been pointed out that when the government commences to invest heavily, for instance, in public utilities, private investors become fearful of what will happen to their investments, the consequence being that they stop. The outcome will then be only heavier government invest- ment until the government eventually takes over everything. Like- wise, the means used to reduce the interest rate on money available for investment might, at the same time, reduce demands for that money in investment. Yet, despite any shortcomings, Keynes was and is extremely popular amongst many British radicals and econo- mists. His ideas also spread to the United States, exercising a very great influence over President Franklin D. Roosevelt and his "New Deal" policies.

While other groups were not too certain that Keynes was correct and even disliked his neo-mercantilist views, they still were not able to stem the main current of economic thinking. With unem- ployment generally high throughout the twenties and rising during the early thirties, there was a great demand on all sides for the government to do something. Consequently, the state, whether controlled by Conservatives, Labour, or a National Coalition, grad- ually took over more and more power to regulate economic life. This trend was further accentuated by the need for rearmament from 1937 on, when the government began to take a larger part of the national income and productive facilities to build up national defenses. Thus, by 1939 laissez faire was dead, with government control securely seated in the saddle, dominating most phases and aspects of economic life and activity.

The Farmers Are Protected

The postwar period for the farmer was one of difficulty and discouragement, but, at the same time, he began to regain some of the state protection denied him in 1846 by the repeal of the Corn Laws. As a result of state action, when the war came to a close in 1918, Britain had 1.3 million more acres of land under the plow than in 1913. Many hoped that Britain would now become agri- culturally self-supporting, but their hopes were doomed to disap- pointment. Prices generally began to fall rapidly in 1921 from almost 200 per cent over those of 1913, until in 1931 they were only 12 per cent over 1913 prices. Feed and fertilizers, fortunately for the farmer, also dropped in price until they were 10 per cent less than they had been in 1913, but, to offset this, wages were going up. The result was that, as farming costs rose, more and more arable land went out of cultivation. Farming fell back into its old hand- to-mouth existence. The government at first tried to change the situation by informal aid and encouragement, but with little real

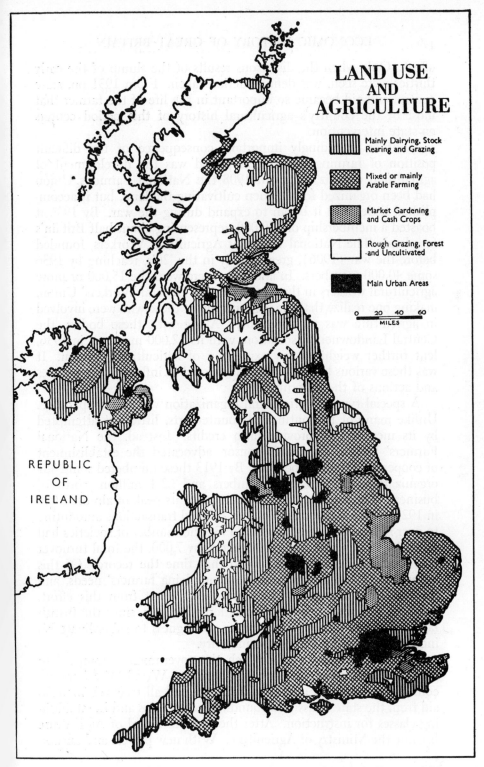

LAND USE
AND
AGRICULTURE

Mainly Dairying, Stock
Rearing and Grazing

Mixed or mainly
Arable Farming

Market Gardening
and Cash Crops

Rough Grazing, Forest
and Uncultivated

Main Urban Areas

0   20   40   60
MILES

REPUBLIC
OF
IRELAND

(By permission from *Britain, A Reference Handbook*, 1952. British Crown copyright.
Modified. Comparable data for the Republic of Ireland not available.)

effect. Only when the disastrous results of the slump of the early thirties were seen, was definite action taken. From 1931 on, state control and aid became so important in the life of the farmer that most of the country's agricultural history of this period centers on state intervention.

Another exceedingly important consequence of the difficult position of farming during this period was the development of agricultural organizations. In 1908 the National Farmer's Union had been organized for the men cultivating the land, but it accomplished little until it began to expand during the war. By 1936 it boasted a membership of 130,000, representing about half Britain's farmland. The National Union of Agricultural Workers, founded before the war (1906), grew rapidly in the '20's, reaching by 1936 some 40,000 members. In addition, there were the 15,000 or more agricultural workers in the Transport and General Workers' Union, making one realize that the organization of those who were involved in agriculture was now a reality. Along with these bodies, the Central Landowners Association, with its 12,000 members in 1936, lent further weight to any expression of agricultural opinion. It was these various bodies which endeavored to influence the policies and actions of the government.

A special type of agricultural organization was the cooperative. Unlike many of its continental counterparts, little was attempted by its members to provide farm credits. Instead, the National Farmers' Union, the chief sponsor, advocated the establishment of cooperative trading societies. By 1913 these numbered some 381 organizations, with 37,000 members and £2.4 million worth of business. The number of societies reached its peak of almost 1,000 in 1923, with a membership of 145,270 and transactions amounting to over £11 million. Although by 1936 the number of societies had fallen by 50 per cent, and of members, by 7,000, the total turnover had touched £16.5 million, up to that time the record. Of this latter sum, £9.5 million came from supplying farmers' needs, and the rest from the sale of farm produce. Apart from this effort, however, little other cooperative action was taken, since the British farmer has never been noted for his willingness to subordinate his individuality to the will of the majority.

One of the first ways in which the government attempted to help the farmers was by education. Prior to World War I county councils, universities, and farm institutes had all received financial aid from the state to assist in founding lectureships and in establishing classes for instruction. After the war the Board of Agriculture became the Ministry of Agriculture. With new powers and authority, it proceeded to organize the country into provincial areas, each with an agricultural college or a university department as the center of instruction. These institutions provided not only two or three year courses leading to a diploma or a degree, but they also advised local farming communities and by extramural lectures instructed the farmers on the best ways of cultivating their land. At the same time, agricultural research was carried forward at experimental farms such as Rothamsted and in the universities, noticeably at Cambridge and Aberdeen. All this was of very great help, the only difficulty being that when a man had a degree he did not usually want to go back to the farm. Consequently, despite government financed education, there were few well-trained farmers actually on the land.

The situation at the close of the war, however, forced the government to do more than merely try to expand facilities for agricultural education. In 1917 the Corn Production Act had fixed minimum prices for wheat at 60s. a quarter and for oats at 38s. 6d., while, by means of Agricultural Wages Boards, wages were set at a minimum of 25s. a week. When the war was over, the Ministry of Agriculture established a Council of Agriculture composed of representatives from all interested parties. It was really this organization which produced the Agriculture Act of 1920. Minimum wheat prices were set at 68s. and oats at 46s. a quarter, with provision being made for yearly revision, and the Ministry was given the power to enforce good cultivation, if necessary by seizing the land. Unfortunately, however, when in the following year prices commenced to tumble rapidly, the government found that it could not keep up the high minima established.[1] The financial provisions of the act were therefore repealed and the Wages Boards abolished, to be replaced a little later by Conciliation Committees. In 1924 the Boards were re-established but there was no minimum wage. Quite naturally, when the farmers saw the promised aid and support disappearing, they were angry, feeling that they had been deserted in the crisis.

When the Slump came in 1930, the farmer suffered severely. Faced with very low priced agricultural imports, he could not meet the competition, so the government was obliged to take action in the Agricultural Marketing Act (1931-32). It was hoped that this statute would stabilize domestic agricultural prices at a fairly high level, that it would strengthen ties with agricultural countries within the Empire, and that it would give the home farmer protec-

[1] Wheat prices dropped from 86s. 4d. a quarter in 1920 to 49s. in 1921 and 40s. 9d. in 1922, while oats dropped between 1920 and 1922 from 45s. 7d. to 26s. 6d.

tion against cutthroat foreign competition. The core of the Act
was the establishment of marketing boards to see to the sale of
produce and, if necessary, the subsidization of production. These
boards, covering various types of production, were patterned on the
Permanent Joint Milk Commission, established in 1922. Their
formation was not to be held back by a small dissident minority,
for the Ministry of Agriculture had the authority to organize them
as long as two thirds of the producers agreed. When functioning,
the boards had complete control over the selling of all the output.
They had power to fix prices, to limit production, to control all
marketing, and to regulate the methods of packing. In 1933 the
boards' authority was extended to give them control over imports
by means of tariffs and quotas. In this way controls were set up
over pork, bacon, milk, hops, potatoes, and other commodities.
Sometimes boards, such as those for pork and bacon, came into
conflict with each other, working at cross purposes, while at other
times the plans and policies of the boards were insufficient. Nevertheless, they do seem to have helped to ease the farmers' rather
desperate situation.

Although direct action on the part of the government had
tended to fall into abeyance after 1922, a certain amount of help
had been given the farmer in the form of financial credits. By the
Agricultural Credits Act of 1923 the Public Works Loan Commissioners were authorized to make long-term loans to farmers who
purchased their lands under the Corn Production Act, 1917-21.
This prevented a considerable number of farmers who had paid
high prices for their properties from losing them. Five years later,
in 1928, another Agricultural Credit Act made the joint-stock banks
the means of giving long-term loans on land, for a period up to
sixty years, or short-term loans on farm assets. To implement this
plan the Treasury actually put out some £650,000, most of it over
extended periods, helping many farmers to tide over difficult times
and enabling others to purchase their own farms.

The agreements reached at the Ottawa Imperial Conference in
1932 were another aid to the farmer. Imports of foreign meat were
cut by one-third, while Australia and New Zealand also agreed
to a reduction in their Britain-bound exports. Following these
arrangements came government subsidies, tariffs, and minimum
prices, particularly for sheep. In this way every effort was made to
strengthen the farmers' hands.

As mentioned above, part of the problem which faced the farmer
throughout the period was his increased costs. By 1933 average
prices were only 6 per cent higher than those of 1913, while in the

case of fat cattle they were lower by 7 per cent. Yet there was some compensation in the fact that feed was 10 per cent less than it had been before the war. The real blow came, however, with the rise of wages which went up by about 100 per cent between 1913 and 1936. As wages normally formed anywhere between 25 and 40 per cent of the farmer's normal costs, this meant that he suffered very severely, for while his income was declining, his expenses were steadily mounting. Thus, until rearmament caused a rise in agricultural prices, the farmer found himself in serious difficulties. The result was a gradual but steady decline of the farming population from 1.4 million in 1913 to 1.2 million in 1931.

One of the best means of offsetting the scarcity of labor was the introduction of mechanical power, which, however, was profitable only on the larger farms. Between 1913 and 1930 the number of gas or oil engines increased four times, while electric motors rose in number from 314 to 2,896. Tractors, which were at first regarded with suspicion as being undependable, gradually became more common, until in 1939 there were 50,000 in use, as over against 18,000 in 1925. Along with these went a growing number of other machines, such as an adapted version of the American harvesting combine, mechanical milkers, and the like. Thus, by the introduction of power the farmer hoped to make a stand against rising production costs.

After 1918 there was a growing belief that many problems would be solved if there were an increase in ownership by those cultivating the land. Small holdings were encouraged by various government measures, such as the Land Settlement Act of 1919, for the benefit of "returned" men, and the Small Holdings and Allotment Acts of 1926. By the first act some 254,000 acres divided into 16,700 holdings—55 per cent of them bare land—were set aside for ex-soldiers. Of these, 24,319 settled on the land, but only 18,915 stayed, since the cost of starting such a farm was usually around £2,000, a sum which many could not afford. At the same time, the County Councils were finding that they had either to raise the rents on county owned small holdings or to take a loss. Actually, the small holdings had not proved very successful, since they could be profitable only if utilized for market gardening. Consequently, by 1930 only 15 per cent of the agricultural land was owned by farmers having less than 50 acres. On the other hand, the occupant-ownership of the larger farms was increasing. High postwar prices for land and the forceable breaking up of large estates through high taxation tended to force more land onto the market. In England and Wales the proportion of the land farmed by owners increased from 20 per cent to 30 per cent between 1921 and 1927, while in Scotland between 1914 and 1931 it jumped from 11 to 32 per cent. Thus the individual farmers were increasingly obtaining possession of their own property, gaining more independence but also facing greater difficulties in times of depression.

Yet even with government aid, the growth of individual ownership, and the much more general use of power machinery, British farming during this period, suffered many setbacks. Arable farming, for instance, declined by some three million acres reverting to pasture. Although improvements were made in types of grain and other crops, the farmer still found it very hard to make both ends meet. The one part of arable agriculture which did progress was the sugar beet industry, but did so largely because it received considerable protection and was relieved of most of its taxes. As the result of expenditures on sugar beet amounting to about £40 million between 1924 and 1934, the acreage increased from 22,000 to 404,000. Then, in 1935 the industry was reorganized, with all the factories being made into a semipublic corporation. After this took place, even the sugar beet acreage began to shrink falling to 345,000 acres in 1939.

Arable farming, however, was not alone in its trouble, for meat raising also suffered considerably. The government tried to improve the country's herds by distributing pedigreed sires to various clubs, and, in 1934, by requiring the registration of all bulls used for breeding. Yet despite these efforts, beef prices fell drastically, in company with those of sheep and pigs, resulting in a decline of production. Only with the introduction of protection in 1933 and subsidies in 1934 did profits rise, bringing with them an increase in the output of beef from an annual average of 22.9 million cwt. (1927-31) to 25.8 million cwt. (1935-36). While this was better, it was still quite low.

Dairy farming was the only section of animal husbandry which really showed any expansion. The number of registered cows grew between 1918 and 1935 from 20,000 to 140,000, the average annual production of milk per cow rising at the same time from 450 to 540 gallons. Improved feeding and tuberculosis tests, along with restriction on imports resulting in less foot and mouth disease, all helped to improve the dairy farmer's fortunes. Thus, by 1939 he was considerably better off than most of his fellows.

In some other parts of the agricultural picture things were also a little brighter. Fruit farming experienced an improvement with the introduction of new practices such as spraying and new methods of packaging. The canning industry, which was putting out over 100 million cans a year by 1936, gave a considerable stimulus to the production of garden and orchard fruits. Greenhouse growing was also on the increase, one company having in 1936 over 1.5 million square feet under glass, while private landowners such as the Earl of Moray, owner of Donnibristle Castle, were investing in similar ventures. Egg production was likewise increasing. Between 1913 and 1939, the number of fowls rose from 33 million to 69 million, the average annual production of eggs per hen at the same time climbing from 75 to 120, largely as the result of more careful breeding and improved feeding.

As one looks at the fortunes of agriculture during the interwar period, it becomes apparent that prior to 1931 farming found itself in serious difficulties. After that date, owing to government help, things improved considerably, but even then the improvement was not general. While milk, fruit, poultry, and egg production was expanding, grain and meat output either improved only very slightly or not at all. After 1937, with rearmament stimulating industry, prices tended to rise, helping the farmer, but even by 1939 he was by no means out of the woods. Although government aid was greater than ever, he was depending upon it more than before. Government controls, unless applied absolutely, could not make people buy the British farmer's expensive produce. Consequently, another depression or a relaxation of government control might bring a final collapse.

Industry in Fluctuation

As has been pointed out, one of the most damaging results of World War I in British industry was the dislocation of trade. Another consequence, almost as bad, was that by the end of hostilities much of British industrial equipment was worn out, or at least outdated, while other countries had frequently developed more efficient processes as well as new labor-saving machinery. What is more, there had also been a concentration on certain types of industry, such as armament production, so that Britain was not immediately ready for peacetime competition. With the rise of industry in other countries, there was also a much greater demand for raw materials, forcing up prices, which, in turn, because of the shrinkage of markets, made industry much more speculative than formerly. The speculation largely ended in the slump of the thirties, a period in which British industry reached a lower point than it had known for a hundred years. Only with the subsequent revival of trade, partially owing to rearmament, did it once again begin to regain its health.

Yet even such generalizations as those made in the preceding paragraph must be somewhat qualified. An analysis shows that industry was of two types. There were the old staple industries, such as textiles, machine manufacture, and the like. These generally had a very difficult time of it throughout the whole of the interwar period. Then there were the new industries, manufacturing such things as automobiles and electrical goods, involved in entertainment and sports, or providing other services such as laundrying. These experienced an expansion. The same thing was true of the older trades, such as building construction or goods distribution, which were affected by the growth and distribution of population as well as by a higher standard of living. Thus the prospering industries were primarily those which catered to the home market, while those dependent upon oversea customers tended to lag behind. This was particularly dangerous for a country such as Britain which is so utterly dependent upon foreign trade for her very existence. Nevertheless, such was the situation, and pre-World War II rearmament only aggravated it.

One of the characteristics of postwar industry was a growth in the size of industrial corporations. Prior to World War I there had been some large semi-public corporations owning public utilities such as docks. During the war, however, the government found that it was much easier to control industry if there was some central body in charge; consequently, when the war came to an end, the government favored the continuation of these large industrial or commercial organizations. Out of this came public corporations organized by the government to administer certain public utilities and subject to Parliament: the British Broadcasting Corporation, the Central Electricity Board, and the London Passenger Transport Board. At the same time, the government also supported the idea of other industries being controlled by large private combinations to obtain economies of operation and to facilitate state control. The result was that by the middle of the '20's base metals, chemicals, tobacco, wall papers, salt, cement, and even textiles, coal, and heavy industry had all come largely under the direction of such large combines. These groups were permitted to fix prices, regulate output, and direct marketing. In some cases they even went so far as to destroy out of date equipment, as when the cotton industry between 1930 and 1938 did away with nearly 20 million redundant spindles, reducing the total by 33 per cent. Both in government and industry there was a grave suspicion that competition had failed. Experiments were now to be made with state supported industrial self-control.

Along with the disappearance of the traditional laissez faire point of view in industry went the idea that American mass production methods should be introduced. This was attempted in some of the new industries, notably in automotive plants. Rigid standardization was not, however, entirely practicable, for in attempting to get back into the world market Britain had to keep her production rather flexible. At thc same time, the British manufacturer and worker did not take kindly to the new methods, which they considered too impersonal and also too "American." This led to a mild conflict within the British economy. There were those who talked in terms of mass production in order to sell goods cheaply abroad. There were, on the other hand, those who maintaincd that Britain must keep to quality production, albeit at higher prices. The British never seemed quite able to make up their minds which line they would follow.

In prewar days, Britain's most important manufactures had been those of her looms, especially woolen goods. Before the war the annual production of this commodity had been about 550 million square yards; by 1924 it was 443 million, and by 1939 was around 400 million. Exports fell in comparable measure. Most of the producers of woolens or worsted were small firms; in the woolen industry each establishment handled all the processes from carding to finishing the cloth, while in the worsted industry, a firm was accustomed to deal with only one process. But whichever method they used, they were hard hit in the postwar world. Fashions were changing, demanding lighter wools with more intricate patterns, and, at the same time, Continental competition was becoming more intense. Along with this, the people in Britain were tending to spend their money for luxury goods rather than staid woolens. The result was that this industry suffered, for with its small units, it could not bring about the complete reorganization which was necessary to change the picture. In 1939 therefore, it was in much the same position as it had been in 1920, only it was producing less.

Even harder hit than wool was cotton. Production of yarn declined between 1912 and 1919 from 1,983 million lbs. to less than 1,200 million lbs., the reduction of piece goods between 1912 and 1935 dropping from 8,050 million square yards to 3,386 million. This decline was largely owing to a decrease in the export of yarns by more than one-third and of piece goods by more than two-thirds. The problem, therefore, was primarily the shrinkage of the export market. The solution seemed to be a reduction of costs by the reorganization of the 3,000 relatively small uneconomic firms into a few large companies, each covering a section of the industry. Only then could the needed efficiency be attained by the introduction of new methods. Mule spinning, which was slower and less efficient than the American ring spinning, was still common, while there were few automatic looms in use. In 1927 the American section of the trade organized the Cotton Yarn Association to control prices and production, but it failed. It seemed to be thinking in terms of more profits rather than of more output. Then in 1929 the Lancaster Cotton Corporation (American section) was organized, as was also the combined Egyptian Spinners and Quilt Manufacturers Association. The Lancaster Cotton Corporation attempted to help matters by scrapping about 140 inefficient mills. This action was followed in 1936 by the Cotton Industry Reorganization Act, which enabled a Spindles Board to buy up redundant spindles. As the market was still shrinking, however, another act was introduced in 1939, but before it could be put through, war had once again hit Britain. Thus during the interwar period nothing had really been accomplished for the cotton industry.

Another industry whose condition had not improved but had rather become worse during the twenty years after World War I was coal mining. The year 1913 saw the peak of production reached with 287 million tons, but by 1939 this had dropped to around 230 million tons, while, concurrently, the export of coal had dropped 50 per cent. Continental customers were purchasing their requirements from German or Polish mines or were employing oil and electricity to drive their machinery.[2] The new fuels were also cutting into the home market. By 1936 half of the ships on Lloyd's registry were oil-fired, while even the steel industry was powering its mills on an increasing scale with electricity.

At the close of the war it was realized that something drastic had to be done to protect the coal industry. Therefore, to investigate the situation the government appointed a Coal Industry Commission, which recommended in 1919 that the mines be nationalized, a solution rejected by the government adherents of laissez faire. However, provisions were made for the increase of wages and the shortening of hours. But even this did not settle matters, for the wage increases were not enough, with the result that a strike called in 1921 was settled only by means of state subsidies. When the subsidies were taken off in 1925, the owners'

[2] Between 1913 and 1936 Italy's imports of British coal declined from 900,000 tons a year to 60,000 while German imports dropped 40 per cent.

demand for a wage reduction brought forth another strike, joined this time, for some nine days, by the adherents of the Trade Union Congress. Again, a Commission was appointed, and it recommended that many of the inefficient mines be closed while the others be amalgamated. Something along this line was done, but not much. In 1930 an act was passed enabling the government to force the unification of mines while, at the same time, it gave local boards the right to fix quotas and prices. The owners accepted the latter plan gladly, but fought the former, thus virtually nullifying the law. As a result, in 1938 a Coal Act provided for nationalization by 1942, with compensation of £66.5 millions to the owners. That something drastic had to be done was obvious from the fact that, in 1937, 77 per cent of the coal mined in 1,000 undertakings came from only 127. Reorganization was long overdue, but little had been accomplished by the time Britain entered the second World War.

A somewhat different story is that of the iron and steel industry. While the production of pig iron in 1939 did not quite equal the 9.64 million tons of 1913, the 15.1 million tons of steel produced in that year was an all-time record, although it was not much when compared to the output of United States or even Germany. The iron and steel industry during the interwar period experienced greater prosperity than did most of the other older industries. True, the production of iron in 1931 and 1932 dropped to less than 4 million tons a year, but that was only a temporary setback. The explanation for this relative resiliency of the industry would seem to be that during World War I there had been a great extension of the vertical combine, making it easier for the companies to obtain supplies. Along with this went cooperation, amalgamation, and specialization. For instance, in 1933 Colvilles took over from Stewarts and Lloyds their steel plate business in Scotland, and a year later they took over the same from Beardmores. Very frequently rival firms set up jointly controlled companies to deal with certain phases of the business. As an example, in 1934 Firth-Vickers Stainless Steels, Limited, was organized from the English Steel Corporation, controlled by Vickers-Armstrong Limited and Cammell Laird, and the stainless steel department of Thomas Firth and John Brown Limited. In this way competition was cut to a minimum, efficiency was stressed, and the benefits of large scale organization were obtained. Thus, Britain entered the war of 1939-45 with her iron and steel industry in good condition. Granted, she was still heavily dependent upon Spain for nonphosphoric ores;

but, despite this handicap, her heavy industry was better off than most of the other sections of the economy.

While the iron and steel industry had experienced little in the way of government regulation, one of its principal offshoots had found government aid very necessary. At the close of the war there was a redundancy of shipping and a contraction of trade. This caused trouble enough, but when foreign governments began the policy of subsidizing their own merchant marines, British ship-building was hard hit; nor would the British government do anything to help. Therefore, in 1930 the National Shipbuilders' Security was organized with the aid of the Bankers' Industrial Development Company. Primarily interested in getting rid of "redundant companies," up to March 1935 it put twenty-seven of them out of business. Many Scots have claimed that most of the yards closed were Scottish which helped to raise unemployment in Scotland's industrial areas.[3] From 1935 on, however, no more yards were shut down owing to the need for war vessels. In the same year another important step was taken when the government agreed to subsidize the building of two giant passenger vessels for the Cunard Line. These were the *Queen Mary* and the *Queen Elizabeth*, which played such important parts in wartime transportation. Shipbuilding was thus by 1939 on the way up, production since 1935 having more than doubled.

Production also rose greatly in the manufacture of the newer types of goods. Between 1913 and 1938 the number of automobiles made in Britain was multipled about ten times. The increase in the production of rayon was even greater, rising from about 3 million lbs. in 1913 to around 160 million lbs. in 1939. Between 1913 and 1935 the value of electrical goods manufactured went from £14 million to £83 million. Thus, although the older industries had their difficulties, the new types of manufactures grew and expanded by leaps and bounds, with relatively little government interference.

The Growth and Regulation of Communications

Government regulation not only increased in agriculture and the declining industries, it was extended also to the field of communications. This was, in a sense, not new, for before the war the Post Office had taken over the telephone and telegraph services. Railway nationalization, however, never received much support until the time of World War I, when the government took charge. At

[3] See Neil Gunn's *The Shipbuilders* for the Scottish attitude to this policy.

the close of hostilities, although many advocated complete nationalization, the government decided to hand the trains back to private ownership, after first making certain modifications in the system. For one thing, there was consolidation. In 1914 there had been 214 separate companies, 121 of which were now combined into four main systems: the London Midland and Scottish, with 7,750 miles; the London North Eastern, with the same, the Southern, with 2,150 miles; and the Great Western, with 3,750 miles. Many Scots were very much annoyed by the fact that their lines had been given to an English company which concentrated control in London and was accused of ignoring the Scottish needs for services. In this connection, one cannot deny that there was a considerable deterioration of railway service in Scotland after the amalgamation. Through the Railway Rates Tribunal the government also planned to control such things as rates and regulations, and while monopolies were given in certain districts, competition was allowed to continue in the heavy traffic areas. This was a typical British compromise between nationalization and private ownership.

The freight rates schedule of 1891 was altered by the Rates Tribunal in order to produce £50 million, the aggregate net revenue received in 1913. Although they were allowed by this to raise their freight rates by 60 per cent, the railways were never able to reach the hoped-for figure. One reason for the low returns was the difficulty of standardizing either equipment or services. For instance, different railways had their engineers sitting on different sides of the engines; they had different types of signals, different heights of platforms, and different sizes of loading gauges. By 1939 some of these variations had been abolished. Platforms were being built at a standard height; the Great Western Railroad had introduced automatic signalling, and automatic continuous air brakes for passenger cars were in use. One of the big problems was that such brakes could not be used on freight trains, since, out of almost 1.3 million freight cars, 638,000 were still privately owned. Furthermore, most of these were older types, unsuited for rapid haulage and too old to be worth equipping with air brakes. As a result, freight trains are still joined together with chains and hooks. Thus, while passenger service was considerably improved, freight service remained much as before.

Partly a cause and partly a result of this situation was the rapidly growing use of road transport. Private automobiles in the country increased between 1922 and 1939 from 294,000 to over 2 million, while trucks rose from 159,000 to 492,000, and buses in similar proportions. The effect of this development upon the railways can be easily seen when one realizes that between 1913 and 1937 the number of passengers carried by the railways fell from 1332.4 million to 1295.4 million, while the freight hauled, excluding coal and fuels, declined from 138.8 million tons to 109 million. Road transport could afford to haul at cheaper rates than the railways because of lower overhead in equipment, roads, and maintenance. The railways, even by offering special rates and services, could not beat their rivals.

The railways then demanded the right to invest in road transport for both passengers and freight, a demand acceded to in 1928. They thereupon invested in bus lines to the amount of £9.5 million and by 1939 owned over 10,000 motor vehicles. Coordination of road and rail passenger services was achieved by the provision of inter road and rail tickets. In the field of road haulage, they purchased a number of the big trucking firms, such as Pickford's and Carter Patterson's. Then, in 1933, by the Road and Rail Traffic Act, they were permitted to levy an "agreed charge," or a flat rate per ton, as long as the consignor sent all his goods by rail. By 1939 two thirds of the railway-handled freight was being carried at such exceptional rates. In that year also a bill was prepared to give the railways complete freedom in quoting charges, but before it could go through the war was in progress. Thus, while government control of the railways was intended for their benefit, they seemed generally to have felt that greater freedom would have enabled them to deal more effectively with competition.

It must not be thought that road transport, on the other hand, was completely uncontrolled. Down to 1930, it is true, this had largely been the case. By the Road Traffic Act of that year, however, three Traffic Commissioners were appointed to each of thirteen traffic areas with power to grant or withhold licenses both to buses and trucks, depending upon the suitability of proposed routes, the need for services, and the services already being provided. This policy very definitely limited the possibility of new lines, particularly as the railways used their power to object whenever new routes or lines were envisaged. This meant that from 1930 on bus and truck line extension slowed down perceptibly.

In 1933 London saw the same type of organization set up to control her transportation facilities. The London Passenger Transport Board, composed of representatives from various public bodies, was given authority over all passenger transportation except that of the four railways, and even in their case the revenues from suburban traffic were pooled with those of the Board. A fixed dividend had to be paid by the Board, while its charges were subject to the Railway Rates Tribunal. The result of this plan was an expansion of the tube railways, the removal of many tramlines, and the substitution of trolley or motor busses. Thus the traffic situation in London, while congested, is not nearly as bad as it might have been.

Besides the bus and truck lines, the railways had also a rival in the private car. As has already been pointed out, these increased about eight fold between 1922 and 1939. The road mileage, however, did not grow to any great extent. In 1900 there were 175,000 miles, and by 1939 this had grown merely to 178,900, of which only 44,000 were main roads. Improvements were hard to obtain mainly because of the fact that road maintenance was in the hands of small administrative units. Nevertheless, because of high-pressure salesmanship and instalment buying, an increasing number of motorists were traveling the roads, to the detriment of railway revenues and all too frequently to the damage of themselves.

Older than either the railways or the automobiles were the canals. They had been taken over by the government on the outbreak of the war, but when handed back to the owners in 1919, they were felt to be a very doubtful asset. Between 1913 and 1937 the annual flow of traffic fell from 32 million tons to 18.5 million. The canals had, therefore, lost most of their importance in the country's transportation of freight.

The shipping industry, like the railways, also faced serious difficulties. When the war came to an end, it was found that, owing to rapid construction during the war and the decline of postwar trade, the world had a surplus of tonnage. Added to this, foreign governments had begun to subsidize their shipping lines. Britain, on the other hand, not believing in such a policy, saw her own shipping suffering from the competition. In many cases ships were simply laid up, while others, when they became too old for service, were not replaced. Consequently, although United States shipping tonnage almost tripled between 1914 and 1939, British tonnage dropped around 15 per cent, to 18 million tons. To counteract the trend, subsidization of tramp steamers was commenced in 1935 and at the same time the government gave its support to the building of the Cunarder queens. In this way shipping was aided, but only to a very limited extent, by the state.

Air transport was the principal innovation in communications during the interwar period. It was not important for domestic travel, since distances are so short in the British Isles that it would not normally pay. The exception is to be found where there are some large bodies of water to cross, such as flights between the United Kingdom and Ireland, or between the mainland and the Western Isles. Much more important was the development of services to the Continent and beyond. In 1919 the first regular oversea services were established between London and Paris, to be gradually expanded across the Continent of Europe to Asia and even to Australia. In the summer of 1939 a flying-boat mail service was established between London and Montreal, Canada. Air travel and transportation was now coming into its own. In 1919, 104,000 miles were flown in the carrying of 870 passengers and 30 tons of cargo. And twenty years later 13.4 million miles were covered in the transportation of some 210,000 passengers and 4,858 tons of cargo. Most of the lines were under the control of Imperial Airways Limited, a combine of various companies which had pooled their resources in 1924 and which received considerable government aid. Other smaller lines were also functioning, with airports springing up on the border of every metropolis. The world was becoming increasingly bound together both for better and for worse.

As one looks back over the twenty years between the two wars, one cannot but be impressed by the speed with which the worship of laissez faire declined. Many working-class people had had strong doubts about this philosophy before 1914, but practically all classes threw it overboard in the postwar years. Britain was facing competition the like of which she had never known before. Other nations had rejected free trade, and Britain could do nothing but follow suit. Yet even then she did not go in wholeheartedly for state controls. Where industries were expanding and developing, she was prepared to leave them alone to achieve their own success. Where, on the other hand, they were not prospering, as was the case with most of the older staple industries, the state did step in with controls, aids, and protection in order to help them face the increasingly stringent competition. This meant that the government, particularly in the '30's, assumed greater and greater powers of economic control. Still, it was not only in the field of industry that this was true. The government was obliged to extend its direction into the fields of trade, finance, and social relationships, and to this we must now turn.

Chapter 25

THE SEARCH FOR POSTWAR PROSPERITY

In the preceding chapter we have discussed the ways in which the government increasingly extended its influence into industrial fields. In the present chapter it is necessary to examine the reasons for and the results of these actions, for they represented a considerable reorientation of the British outlook and approach to economic affairs.

The period between the two wars was one of trade difficulties. Although by 1924 international commerce was back to the 1913 level, and by 1929 it was 30 per cent higher, Britain's trade tended to decrease.[1] New nations coming into the picture were taking away her markets, so throughout the twenties Britain was faced with declining sales. Then came the Great Depression, known in Britain as the Slump, which dealt an even harder blow. Labor troubles, changes in economic policy, and government involvement in economic direction resulted. It was these factors that led to the developments noted in the previous chapter.

The Ups and Downs of Trade

When World War I came to an end, Britain found herself in a new commercial position. She had, of course, replaced none of her prewar machinery with new equipment during the war, so most of her capital goods were old and relatively outmoded. Besides, there was also the persistence of tradition and a rigidity of organization which tended to restrict the search for new ideas. Much more important, however, was the fact that many of her markets

[1] In 1913 Britain's share of world imports was one sixth and her exports one seventh. For the twenty postwar years the imports were frequently below this and the exports, always. The percentage exported of her total production was 30.5 per cent in 1907, 22 per cent in 1930 and it fell steadily thereafter. E. Lipson, *Growth of English Society* (New York, 1950), p. 420.

had disappeared, while others were now protected from her by high tariff walls. Besides all this, she owed the United States nearly $5,000 million, which could not be paid in goods, but only in gold. This made heavy taxation necessary, cutting down on the funds available for investment at home and abroad. Finally, there was the general world poverty resulting from the wartime destruction. Thus Britain was faced with very great problems when she turned once again to peaceful pursuits.

The true situation was obscured, however, by the fact that there was at first a noticeable postwar boom caused by an increased demand for the replacement of goods worn out or destroyed. This increased demand was not from the old customers in Europe or Asia, but was rather to a certain extent from the dominions and colonies and even more from the home consumer. It has been estimated that, making allowance for the advance in prices between 1913 and 1922, British exports had actually fallen by 25 per cent, notwithstanding the fact that world trade was getting back to normal. While some may feel that this did not necessarily imply disaster, the fact that British coal exports were down 60 per cent, resulting in 33 per cent unemployment in the mines, and that cotton exports were down 75 per cent, with approximately the same result, told its story. Until 1921 it had looked as though things were returning to normal, but by the middle of 1922 Britain was in the grip of a depression. In the preceding two years imports had fallen from around £1,900 million to £1,000 million, while exports and re-exports dropped from £1,500 million to £800 million.

Any optimism as to the future was at this point a little strained. Nevertheless, Britain once again girded up her loins to deal with the problem. The Conservatives had by now become the protectionist party, looking to government regulation for help and demanding that the war time policy of selective tariffs be extended. Under their influence, in 1921 the Safeguarding of Industries Act was put into force, giving key industries, primarily those connected with war production, the protection of a 33⅓ per cent duty. Four years later it was extended to apply to goods coming from countries enjoying the advantage of depreciated currencies and to goods receiving government subsidies. While the act was to last for only five years, in 1926 it was renewed for another ten.

Despite these measures, others, such as increasing taxation and the return to the Gold Standard, tended to raise British prices so that, in reality, they were burdened with an export duty. Efforts to aid industry by government protection and stimulation were not noticeably successful. It has been estimated that between 1924 and

1929, while the volume of imports increased by about 10 per cent, the volume of exports fell some 16 per cent, in both cases the value being down by nearly 25 per cent. With regard to exports, those trades which suffered most were the old staple industries. For instance, the quantities of steel bars, rods, angles and the like fell from 5.4 million tons in 1923, to 4.3 million in 1929, while steel plates and sheets decreased from 8 million to 5.9 million tons during the same period. The cotton industry did not succeed in expanding to any extent, while both woolen and worsted exports declined from 100 million to 75 million square yards. On the other hand, electrical equipment, wireless sets, and chemicals were being exported in much greater quantities, although the increase was not nearly enough to offset the decline in the formerly important trades. This was the situation in Britain during the same years that United States and a number of other countries were enjoying the biggest boom in their histories. Britain's position had improved, but not to nearly the extent noticeable elsewhere.

Then came the Slump. This was caused not so much by trade conditions as by errors in financial judgment. The general situation in Britain also tended to aggravate the disease. Because of the collapse of the financial structure, first in United States and then in Austria and Germany, Britain found that her trade suffered a severe blow. Added to this, her foreign investments brought in an ever-declining return, while her shipping, which was now only about 25 per cent of the world total, obtained fewer and fewer customers. The result was that in 1931 she had not only a trade deficit of £408 million but a total adverse balance of payments amounting to £104 million.

To recover from this situation was doubly difficult, partially because it was beyond Britain's control, but also partially because the rigidity of Britain's industrial system prevented rapid adjustments to new conditions. The result was that other nations, protected by high tariff walls, began to dump goods onto the relatively unprotected British market. Such competition, along with its resultant increase in unemployment, threatened a fall in the standard of living which immediately brought forth an outcry for protection. Britain had to insulate herself from the shocks of foreign economic disasters by a sort of economic nationalism similar to that already in vogue both in America and Europe. Generally speaking, the old Free Trade principles went overboard, with nearly everybody accepting the view that tariffs and similar defences would solve the problem.

The resulting mercantilism was two-sided. There were, first of all, the defensive policies, represented by a tariff system. The Safe Guarding of Industries Act was now extended widely by the Import Duties Act (1932), which provided for a 10 per cent import duty upon all goods except food and some raw materials. This percentage could be increased further on the recommendation of the Import Duties Advisory Committee, which in some cases permitted the rates to rise to 33⅓ per cent, between 1930 and 1932 the percentage of imports paying duties growing from seventeen to seventy-five. Along with the tariffs went the granting of subsidies to help certain infant industries, while wheat growers were given a guaranteed price. Last of all, quotas were placed on certain foodstuffs to help protect the farmer. None of these measures were unanimously accepted in their entirety both because of the continuing free trade tradition, particularly among the Liberals and Labourites, and because of the serious conflicts which frequently arose between the interests of producer and consumer. But the country was in something of a panic, and the measures of defense were forced through.

The second part of the mercantilist strategy was the adoption of offensive measures. The first line of attack was "Imperial Preference." In 1919 a one-sixth ad valorem preference had been given to all imperial goods liable to duties, a plan extended widely by the Ottawa Agreements of 1932. While tariffs were not lowered appreciably within the Empire, they tended to be hoisted against the outside world, in part an attempt to teach the mercantilists of United States a lesson. The result was that inter-imperial trade increased, Britain's imports from the Empire by 5 per cent and her exports to the Empire by 7 per cent, although in actual fact Britain gave a good deal more than she received in terms of preference. At the same time she took action to implement part of the 1932 tariff act which gave the government power to work out bilateral agreements with other nations willing to reduce trade barriers. While this was a help, it also manifested a tendency to work out trade balances on the basis of relations between two countries instead of encouraging multilateral dealings. Still, there was always the hope that such arrangements could be expanded into multilateral agreements. It was, at any rate, a step back in the direction of free trade.

A third measure, which was both defensive and offensive, was Britain's departure from the gold standard in 1931. After going off it in 1914, she had returned to it in 1925. Since many blamed the restoration of the gold standard at an overvalued level for holding up British commercial expansion, when the economic situation became very dark, she promptly gave up gold for a managed currency. This brought the price of British goods in terms of nongold currencies down, cheapening them on the world market. At the same time the lower value tended to protect British goods from dumping, for it raised the costs of purchasing goods in gold standard countries such as France and United States.

Partially as a result of these measures, from 1933 on, a gradual change in the economic situation was noticeable. Britain experienced a gradual improvement which by 1936 was receiving further stimulation through accelerating rearmament. Many feel that the policy of protection had good results. Britain's share in world trade rose from 12 per cent in 1930 to 14 per cent in 1938, although close to 50 per cent of that was imperial. While this does not sound too bad, the fact remains that her increased trade was due largely to growing imports, for her exports were not expanding nearly so rapidly. Imports in 1937 had increased 15 per cent beyond those of 1930, to fall back to 10 per cent in 1938, but exports increased only 3 per cent by 1937 and the following year were back to the 1930 level. At the same time, her exports of capital and services had also dropped, so Britain was faced with an adverse balance of payments nearly every year between 1931 and 1939. She remained continuously in debt to the rest of the world.

Thus, in 1939 Britain was not in a satisfactory position. Exporting only half as much in value as she imported, rearming as fast as possible, and suffering serious shortages in certain basic raw materials, such as iron and cotton, Britain was in much greater difficulty than she had been in 1920 or 1931. At the same time, the trade situation was deteriorating progressively, since Hitler was attempting to increase his hold on the economy of central and eastern Europe for the benefit of "the greater Reich." Added to this, while outwardly sound, Britain's financial situation had really never recovered from the effects of World War I. When all these factors are combined, one has an explanation for many of Britain's problems at the opening of World War II.

Financial Problems Between the Two Wars

It is very difficult to understand the fortunes—or misfortunes— of trade in the modern world apart from finance. The complexity of the present economic organization links the two indissolubly. Therefore, in order to see many of the reasons for Britain's commercial problems between 1918 and 1939 it is necessary to understand something of her financial difficulties. One must realize that her position had changed radically from what it had been in 1913. In that year she was the world's financial center, but by the time the war was over, her situation was very different. The world creditor was now the United States, Britain being a borrower as a result of four years of hostilities. It is true that while she was in debt to the United States for just under £1,000 million, she was owed considerably more than that by European nations, but most of them were poverty-stricken because of the war. Besides this, Britain had spent far more than any other ally on the war, so, while her factories and towns had not been destroyed, she was as poor as the rest of Europe. Only the United States had actually made money out of the conflict. Thus Britain's whole financial position had been radically altered.

It was partially because of this, and also because there was much less money available for investment and saving, that the banking system experienced considerable changes during the twenty post-war years. The national debt, which was reduced slightly, between 1918 and 1931 took for its services alone 42.8 per cent of the government's income, as compared with 13.2 per cent in 1913. By 1931 it stood at £7,413 million, while local government debts had jumped in the period 1921-31, from around £865 million to £1,470 million. This meant greater demand for funds to meet debt charges. Taxation increased so greatly that, instead of only 20 per cent of the national income being swallowed by the government's coffers as in 1913, by 1931 over 32 per cent was taken. Local government expenditures also increased nearly three times, requiring a corresponding rise in local rates. Thus, in 1931 less than 17 per cent of the national income was being saved, as compared with 27 per cent in 1913, and individuals no longer had the same amount of funds with which to contribute to the support and refurbishing of industry.

This condition of affairs was very clear on the stock market, for although a large number of companies were being organized every year, it was becoming increasingly difficult to obtain purchasers for their stocks. This led, without too much success, to all sorts of devious practices to persuade people to invest their money. Consequently, demands began to be made on the banks which up to this point had never taken a very active part in investment and had, in fact, been frequently accused of favoring foreign securities at the expense of domestic issues. The banks, however, were by 1925 in a position to give very considerable help, since there had been large-scale bank mergers during and just at the close of the war, which resulted in an extremely strong banking organization. This was dominated by the "big five": the Midland, Lloyds, Barclays, National Provincial and Union, and the Westminster banks. Over all presided the Bank of England which from 1928 on had, except in Scotland, a monopoly of note issue.

The outcome of this situation was that gradually after 1925 the banks began to feel some sense of responsibility toward home industry. In 1926 the government guaranteed exporters against loss up to 75 per cent of the credits granted to approved foreign purchasers, and the banks agreed to accept such bills for advances to exporters. Then, in 1928 the Agricultural Credits Act enabled them to give aid to farmers, both for short- and long-term improvements. Most important of all, however, in 1929 the Bank of England organized the Securities Management Trust to advise banks and financial houses on industrial reorganization. Such organization was further extended by the setting up in 1930 of the Bankers Industrial Development to provide capital, supplied by the banks and the Trust, to help in financing "rationalization" of industries. As this organization worked particularly in connection with such large industries as the steel, shipbuilding, and similar concerns, another organization was set up in 1934, Credit for Industry, to help small and medium sized producers. In this way a considerable amount of capital, unobtainable through the flotation of bonds or stocks, was made available to stimulate and strengthen the financial condition of Britain's producers.

Meanwhile, steps had been taken to stabilize the currency by a return to the gold standard. It has been estimated that the increase of the issue of bank notes in 1919 over 1913 was about 500 per cent, this being one of the reasons for prices rising during that period by about 200 per cent. The question of what to do about it was committed to the Cunliffe Commission, appointed in 1918 by the Treasury and Ministry of Reconstruction. This body recommended in its report that government borrowing should be stopped and the floating debt reduced, that the bank rate should be used to check expansion of credit and drain of gold, and, finally, that the gold standard should be restored. This latter measure was to be accomplished by the reduction of the uncovered treasury note issue, until the Bank of England's reserve should stand at a minimum of £150 million. When the gold reserve and fiduciary note issue should reach a balance at £150 million, the treasury notes would be replaced by Bank of England notes. Following this plan, in 1919 the pound was unpegged so that it could find its own level. It promptly dropped to $3.22 (U.S.). At the same time, the bank rate was raised to 7 per cent, cutting credit drastically. The result was deflation, so the price index fell between March, 1920 and December, 1921, from 323 to 168. Many feel that this helped to bring on the depression of 1922. But, whether it did or not, the volume of treasury notes was drastically cut, and the value of the pound by 1923 had reached $4.69 (U.S.). The bank rate then dropped to between 3 per cent and 5 per cent, and on April 28th, 1925, England went back on to a gold bullion standard. Henceforth, any issue of fiduciary notes over £260 million had to be backed by an equivalent in gold. Britain felt that the economic situation was now well in hand and that stability had at last been achieved.

The action of Winston Churchill, at that time Chancellor of the Exchequer, in restoring the gold standard has been strongly criticized. With only about £150 million reserve, credit was sharply limited, curtailing the possibility of expanding industry. At the same time, the restoration of the prewar rate is held to have overvalued the actual purchasing power of the pound by about 10 per cent. This meant that while it was easier for Britain to buy goods from America and those other countries with currencies of high value, she found it much harder to sell to countries whose currency, in prewar terms, was of low value. The franc, for instance, was now worth only 2 cents compared to the prewar 20 cents. Since much the same thing was true of many other currencies, it is often said that the return to gold made it difficult for foreigners to buy British exports. A large number of financiers at that time, on the other hand, felt that it was a sound move. It demonstrated Britain's financial solvency and would encourage other nations to stabilize their currencies to the general improvement of trade. Instead of governments manipulating their currencies as they saw fit, a return to the gold standard would enable them to react naturally to trade movements. Probably the truth is somewhere between these two positions. A return to the gold standard at a lower rate might have been the solution.

Still, whatever the answer may have been, it would seem that the strict deflation, in truth, caused certain difficulties. Between 1919 and 1929 there had accumulated in the financial world about £2,000 million, whose movement from center to center in the form of short-term credits was determined by such things as fear of government interference, high rates of interest, and other factors. This upset the normal action of the gold standard by causing frequent fluctuations in various national exchanges. The London financiers, however, took a considerable portion of this money and placed it

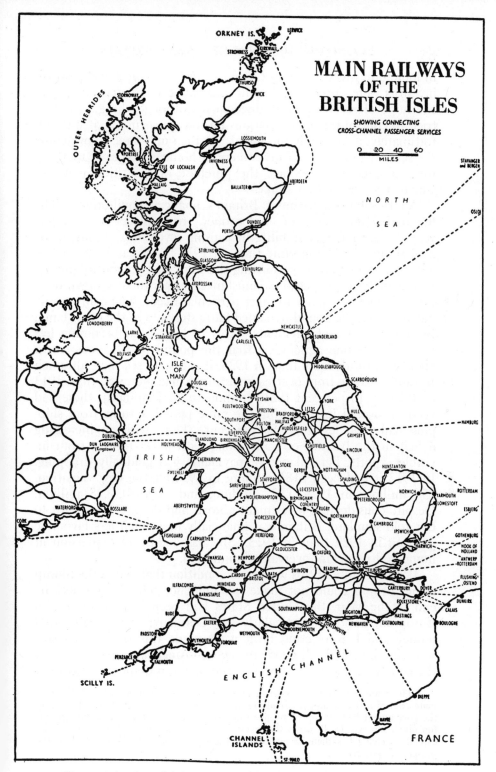

MAIN RAILWAYS
OF THE
BRITISH ISLES

SHOWING CONNECTING
CROSS-CHANNEL PASSENGER SERVICES

0   20   40   60
MILES

479

in long-term investments in Germany, just as many private British investors were purchasing highly speculative German securities in the hope of receiving large dividends. Although the government tried to control this by restrictions on foreign spending, it was, unfortunately, not entirely successful. At the same time, to overcome the scarcity of money for investment at home, all types of methods were adopted to encourage the purchase of securities, many of which were also rather shaky.[2]

All this tended to upset Britain's financial equilibrium. The fluctuating movement of "hot money" from place to place prevented real monetary stability by causing severe disruptions in the gold standard. At the same time, in 1928 the Treasury tended to get away from gold by permitting the Bank of England to alter its note issue to meet special circumstances; either to keep down overexpansion or to expand to meet particular needs. Generally speaking, however, the pound remained fairly steady. On the other hand, Britain's balance of payments seems to have been becoming less favorable. If one remembers that the pound in 1913 was worth about two thirds more than in 1925, it is easy to see that, although Britain's income from oversea investments had increased from 1913 to 1925 by 10 per cent (£210 million to £235 million), there had been an overall loss. During the same period, returns from shipping had risen less than 50 per cent. Thus, with an increasing deficit in the balance of trade along with lower returns from invisible exports, her balance of payments was gradually dropping. In 1913 it had been £181 million; in 1924, at the new valuation, £56 million; in 1928, £137 million; and in 1930, £28 million. Despite considerable investment abroad and despite the return to the gold standard, Britain was financially in a much less favorable position in 1929 than in 1913. She had industrial depression at home and monetary overvaluation abroad.

It was because of this weakened condition that, when the Slump came, Britain could not make her influence felt. Ever since the end of the War, the United States had been loaning money to European nations, particularly to Germany. Her high-priced money and her towering tariff walls made this the only means whereby she could sell goods to the non-American world. Toward the end of the twenties, however, the boom in domestic expansion

[2] There was usually wide diffusion of the holding of these stocks, but the ultimate control of the company usually rested in the hands of a very few. Here again the government had attempted to give some protection to the investor, but without too much success. In 48 issues the investing public contributed 98 per cent of the capital, receiving less than 22 per cent of the equity and only 21 per cent of the prospective profits.

was attracting increasing amounts of American capital, so the stream to Europe gradually dried up. Then came the crash of the New York market in October, 1929, putting the final touch on the situation. American investors tried to get their money out of Europe, but it was tied up in factories, buildings, and the like which could not be easily turned into cash. The result was that the economy of Europe began to shake. Germany and Austria had been paying off reparations largely with borrowed dollars, but even when these dollars stopped coming, the payments had to go on. What is more, American and British investors were demanding repayment of the money loaned but now unavailable. At this point, it was suggested that the nations might agree to freeze all credits in order that there might be a breathing time for the Austrian and German banks. This, however, was not enough, and they began to collapse. The Hoover Moratorium (June 20, 1931) then stopped all payment on reparations and interallied debts for a year. As far as Britain was concerned, this was of little help, since a very considerable part of her foreign investments were, for the moment at any rate, paying her nothing. Therefore, with declining trade bringing unemployment at home and a rising adverse trade balance abroad, Britain looked disaster in the face.

In May of 1931 Great Britain held approximately £400 million of foreign credits in London, while all that she had abroad in short-term loans was £150 million. Then at the end of July, the "May Committee," appointed to study the matter, reported that there would probably be a deficit in the budget of £120 million unless drastic action were taken to curtail government spending. This resulted in the withdrawal of about £200 million by frightened foreigners, the gold reserve of the Bank of England falling by September to £130 million. The Labour Government, under Ramsay MacDonald, had in the meantime passed out of the picture, to be succeeded by a predominantly Conservative "National Government." This government thereupon proceeded to cut unemployment relief allowances and the pay of government employees. Some sailors at Invergordon walked off their ship as a result, and the papers, already panicky, declared that the fleet had mutinied. The result was a second scare, causing the flight of more capital. Despite loans from Paris and New York, it was felt that nothing more could be done and on September 21, Great Britain once more departed from the gold standard.

The British flight from gold had an immediate impact upon the countries who were tied to her financially. They followed suit. Gradually, still other nations were forced to take the same action, even the United States succumbing in 1933, to be followed in 1935 by France and her small group of gold currency states. Henceforth, automatic action on the part of currencies disappeared; instead, governments now manipulated their monetary systems for their own protection. Britain met the situation by establishing the Exchange Equalization Account to control noncommercial fluctuations in foreign exchanges. Provided with a fixed amount of Treasury bills the EEA would buy sterling and sell it again for gold-backed foreign currencies. In this way it could prevent an untoward rise in the price of the pound. On the other hand, by selling foreign currencies it could prevent the pound from dropping too much in value. Until 1933 the currency usually dealt with was American dollars, and from then until 1936, francs. When France finally went off gold, it was arranged that the three countries, each with similar mechanisms operating, would buy their own currencies from the other two with gold, thus maintaining the three currencies roughly on a par. As Holland, Switzerland, and Belgium also eventually came in on this arrangement, by 1936 a moderate amount of stability had been achieved.

The effect of the Slump on Britain's economic, and especially her financial, situation was generally adverse. From 1932 to 1939 she had only one year in which her balance of payments was favorable. This, however, may not give the full picture, for while in 1938 her debit on foreign account was £55 million, at the same time, she invested some £376 million at home, giving her a net investment of £321 million. The achievement of the latter sum was probably due to the fact that money was much cheaper once the gold standard was forsaken. The bank rate dropped because of the conversion of the national debt from a rate of 5 per cent to 3½ per cent, which resulted in a saving in debt services. At the same time, increased bank deposits stimulated banks to purchase securities, thus helping industry. Simultaneously, as foreign trade began to pick up, prices stopped falling, although the sterling cost of raw materials also began to increase. Some feel that Britain might now have gone back on to gold at a low parity, but this was not done. It was hoped that by means of a managed currency the problem would be solved.

At this point, the threat of Hitlerite imperialism was beginning to appear over the horizon, bringing a warning that rearmament must be undertaken. While nothing very much was done until 1937, in that year the government really commenced to pour money into the armaments industry,[3] so it began to expand, and

[3] British expenditures on rearmament were: 1932, £105 million; 1936, £170 million, and 1939, £400 million.

imports began to rise, although exports did not. Retained imports increased from £701 million in 1935 to £858 million in 1938, while exports of United Kingdom produce during the same period rose only from £426 million to £471 million. Thus, in 1938, while the gross capital formation at home has been estimated at £700 million, Britain's adverse balance of payments abroad was represented by a deficit of £70 million, and the following year, which saw the beginning of the war, by £250 million.

The year 1939 brought a rather frustrating period to a close. Britain had come out of World War I with high hopes of building a land fit for heroes. Something, it is true, had been accomplished in general social amelioration, but the end of the two decades also saw her going increasingly into debt, a debt caused not merely by rearmament, but by her economic situation in the world. With falling returns from exports of capital, goods, and services, and with rising costs because of expensive imports, she was in economic straits. This was by no means apparent in Britain, however, for with industry booming in rearmament, there seemed to be increasing prosperity. This, however, was largely artificial, for it was producing neither capital or consumers' goods, but war material whose very purpose was self-destruction. Prosperity had appeared, but prosperity turned out to be a devil and not an angel of light.

Labor's Improving Position

Labor, forming a very considerable part of British society, was, of course, deeply affected by the ups and downs of the nation's economy. Periods of slump meant hardship, and periods of boom meant prosperity. Because of the difficulties experienced during the periods of slump, efforts were made to cushion the fall, bringing about general progress in the condition of the laboring man. Since most of the advancement came under Conservative, or Conservative-dominated governments, Labour has never been anxious to acknowledge much improvement, but, speaking generally, improvement was there.

In considering the matter of standard of living, particularly among the laboring class, an important factor which must be taken into account is the growth in population. During the interwar period the number of people resident in the United Kingdom rose by about 9 per cent, reaching a total of over 47.5 million. The increase was caused, not by a rise in birth rate, which actually dropped from 23.1 per thousand in 1921 to 15.3 per thousand in 1939, but by a steady decline in the death rate from 12.2 per thousand to 11.8. Thus, as the number of births gradually declined, so the population in general tended to become older, raising the problem of supporting a larger percentage of people who as time went on, would find it hard to adapt themselves to new conditions or who would be unable to supply their own needs. Simultaneously the urban population was expanding in comparison with the rural areas, resulting in the towns holding 80 per cent of the people by 1931. Thus there was not only an increase in population, along with a rise in its age, but also a movement of about 2 per cent from the country to the town.

This urbanization may have been one of the reasons for the labor's growing self-consciousness. More important, however, in this connection were two other forces. One was the propaganda of Continental Syndicalism, which advocated that by direct action the workers should take over and run industry. The English version of this theory was known as Guild Socialism, preached by H. S. Hobson and G. D. H. Cole before the war, whereby the workers were to form guilds to run each industry for the workers in the industry. The whole system was to be coordinated in a national guild congress, while Parliament was to continue as the representative of the consumers and also to deal with such matters as foreign affairs, defence, and education. Where ultimate control of the state was to lie was not explained. After World War I this type of thinking became strongly tinged with Communism. The other factor was the self-consciousness of labor, engendered by war activities both on the fighting and the industrial fronts. Why could labor not run things—even the government? Such an attitude was reflected in the Trade-Union Congress, which increasingly claimed the right to speak on behalf of all labor. A new social force was showing its face on the British scene.

Probably one of the best indications of the influence of "laborism" was the increase in the trade-union membership. Between 1913 and 1918 the numbers grew from 4.1 million to 6.5 million, two years later reaching the peak at 8.3 million, although, because of troubles and difficulties experienced later on, they fell to about half that number by 1932. With the return of moderate prosperity after 1935, the numbers again rose until in 1939 they totaled 6.2 million. What was even more important, however, was the fact that this period was marked by a great expansion of unions among nonskilled workers. For instance, between 1913 and 1921, the number of organized agriculturial laborers increased about ten times. Concurrent with this development went the trend toward big unions. Those such as Ernest Bevin's Transport and General

Workers Union were typical, and were most noticeable in the new rayon, electrical equipment, and automotive industries. At the same time the Trade-Union Congress was reorganizing itself with a General Council, whose job was that of initiating labor legislation as well as of preventing measures which might be detrimental to the working class. It was this growing assertiveness of labor which led to one of the most dramatic episodes of the middle twenties: The General Strike.

At the close of the war various efforts had been made to set up machinery to facilitate cooperation between the employer and his employees. These, however, had not been too successful, with the result that labor was rather restive. "The world fit for heroes" had not materialized and the workmen wanted to know why. According to some labor leaders, the reason was that labor had little or no say in the control of industry. To meet this situation during the war the "shop steward movement" had come into existence, but it was not popular, since it was leftist and tended to drift toward Communism. Neither the employers nor the workmen were very much impressed. Another attempt to meet the situation was embodied in the Whitley Committee's Report (1916) which advocated joint industrial councils. In the well-organized industries, joint councils of labor and management were to be set up to discuss problems. In the industries which were less advanced, the government was to appoint advisers to such councils, and in the unorganized trades, Trade Boards on the 1908 model were to be established. Finally, a permanent, but voluntary, Industrial Court was to be created, to which disputes might be referred. In practice it was only the Trade Boards which really succeeded, for neither labor or management favored the Whitley council idea.

The result of these failures to bring industrial cooperation was most plainly manifested in the General Strike of May 1926. The basic cause was the sick condition of the coal industry. Although it had been more or less paying its way while German coal production was low, particularly during French occupation of the Ruhr, once the French moved out, German production rose and world prices fell. Thereupon, the British coal owners decided to lower wages or increase hours of work. The miners, headed by the radical James Arthur Coop, opposed the move. The government tried to solve the problem by appointing an investigating committee and by giving a temporary subsidy of £24 million to the industry. The committee's report was rejected by both sides, so the government could do nothing but stop the subsidy. The result was that the miners went out on strike, demanding that the Trade Union Congress call a General Strike. This it did, but only very reluctantly. The full strike lasted only nine days (May 4 to 12), being broken largely by volunteer labor and the other unions' unwillingness to follow through. The miners continued their strike alone, but were forced to submit by November.

The General Strike was a landmark in the history of British trade-unionism. Parliament attempted to stop any repetition of this move by banning "sympathetic" strikes or strikes aimed at compelling Parliament to take political action. At the same time, it forbade civil servants to ally themselves with the T.U.C. Whether or not this law was of real value is debatable, but there was certainly a change in labor's attitude from this point on. Instead of acting against capital and management, it tended much more toward cooperation, always, of course, demanding its share of profits. At the same time, the unions' numbers tended to decrease, as did their political funds. On the other side, the government also changed its attitude somewhat. For instance, in 1934 collective bargains, for the first time, were made enforceable at law, thus strengthening the unions' legal position. Generally speaking, unionism had become less radical, thereby easing the country's fear of labor action.

This change in attitude can be seen most clearly in connection with the history of the Labour Party during the postwar years. At the close of the war it forsook the coalition coming out on a clear-cut socialist program: minimum standard of living, the nationalization of most of the industries, more steeply graded taxation, and the use of the national surplus for the benefit of the people. Postwar feeling, however, put the coalition back into power. The next four years were years of Labour Party consolidation and expansion so when Baldwin went to the country in December, 1923, on the issue of tariffs, labor was ready with a fairly efficient machine. When all election returns were in, 192 seats had fallen to Labour representatives, who, supported by 158 Liberals, came into power. Since the Liberals had put Labour in, Ramsay MacDonald, the prime minister, and his followers could do little about establishing socialism. What is more, the Labour and Liberal attitudes to Russia differed so widely that finally the Liberals forced Labour out over the question of the recognition of and trade with the new U.S.S.R. Not until 1929 did Labour come back to power, but when it did, it was again by grace of the Liberals. This time, however, the Labourites had to face the Slump which was too much for them. Ramsay MacDonald formed a National Government which was predominantly Conservative, most of his former colleagues being thenceforward permanently in the opposition until the outbreak of war.

With the growing political power of labor, the tendency towards direct action was disappearing, the General Strike being the last violent gasp. The Trade-Union Council, with its eight departments and nine advisory councils, emphasized the importance of state regulation of hours, working conditions, and wages. This point of view was adopted by the Labour Party, which began to insist increasingly that nationalization, particularly of public utilities, was the solution to most of Britain's economic problems. The Bank of England, which Labour blamed for the Slump, was a special target. At the same time, influenced by Keynes, Labour also advocated a board of national investment to prevent the misdirection of funds. Along with this, the Party also strongly advocated free trade, even in the depression. Philip Snowdon, the Labour Chancellor of the Exchequer, would give no credence to cries that tariffs were needed. Thus, throughout most of the period socialism was widely expressed in Parliament, although usually from the opposition. On the two occasions when Labour was in power it was so hampered by its Liberal allies that it could do little or nothing. It was, however, biding its time until it could gain complete power to carry out its principles.

In the meantime, largely through labor pressure both inside and outside of Parliament, the length of the working day had been reduced. Having consciously or unconsciously accepted Marx's dictum that after the worker had earned his own keep, any further work only gave surplus value to the capitalist, shorter hours became a major objective. By 1919 the 47- or 48-hour week was extremely common. The steel industry, for instance, had reduced its shifts from twelve to eight hours, while the average work-week for over 7 million employees had declined about six hours by this time. Finally, in 1937 the Factories Act wiped out all distinctions between factories and workshops and set the maximum for women and young persons at 48 hours a week, children under sixteen being limited to 44. The resulting average, including male workers, who were still unregulated, was 47.8 hours. This was a far cry from the long-drawn-out day of the nineteenth century worker.

While hours were decreasing, wages were generally improving. In March, 1920, the cost of living was about 200 per cent higher than in 1914, but by 1922 it had dropped to only 50 per cent above the base figure. From then on it dropped even farther, until it was down to around 140 per cent of the 1914 level. At the same time *money* wages fell, but not nearly as much, so it has been reckoned that between 1924 and 1933, *real* wages were actually about 18 per cent higher than at the outbreak of World War I. The improvement was not general for all trades and industries, however, since the unskilled laborer and the piece worker improved their returns much more than did the skilled worker paid at fixed wages. From 1933 on there was again general improvement in the money wage level, but this was offset by the rising cost of living. Still, even taking this into account, real wages continued to rise. If one was able to hold one's job throughout the Slump and to carry on through the rest of the decade, one found that one's position in 1939 was greatly improved over what it had been in 1920. Hours were shorter, and pay was higher. The one black spot on the picture was the unemployment, which from 1925 to 1933 was so widespread that labor did not improve its situation as generally as one might at first suppose.

There were, however, other factors which must be taken into account. For one thing, the Cooperative Movement had expanded in all directions, so by 1939 its organizations were far larger than any private company. They produced more goods, employed more workers, and owned more land than any others, except perhaps a very few landlords. Between 1913 and 1936 their membership tripled, their sales doubled, and their production rose probably 200 per cent. This was one way in which the laboring classes were themselves able to help to lower the cost of living.

Another factor in changing the position of labor was the alteration in taxation and its relation to income. In 1911 the working class received about 35 per cent of the national income, while salaried individuals received 14 per cent, and those dependent upon profits and interest, almost 41 per cent. By 1932 the relative figures stood at 40 per cent, 27 per cent, and 23 per cent, while 1938 saw the same classes receiving 41 per cent, 25 per cent, and 33 per cent of national income. The wage earner was thus obtaining a much larger share, while salaries, although they had increased, had not risen proportionately. In the meantime, the steeper grading of income taxes in the higher brackets and the application of a surtax on all incomes over £2,000 increased the ratio of taxes paid by the wealthier classes. Although the national percentage of income taken in taxes had jumped from 12 to around 33 in 1938, the percentage paid by wage earners seems to have actually fallen from 34.3 to about 33. By far the larger part of the taxes was paid by salaried and professional people. Thus, since the wage-earning group was receiving 41 per cent of the national income and paying only 33 per cent of the expenses, it is obvious that their monetary position was definitely improving. The salaried group, on the other hand, had lost 2 per cent of its share of national income, while its proportion of tax obligations had risen by about 25 per cent.

The same was true of the distribution of social services which were aimed directly at the laboring class. These included such items as health and unemployment insurance, old age pensions, public assistance, and free education. In 1925 the national pension scheme was widened greatly by the establishment of contributory pensions for widows of men insured for unemployment, for minor children, and for the laboring man and his wife at the age of 65. At the same time, the noncontributory old age pension of 5s. a week, established in 1908, was raised to 10s. In 1937 white collar workers were permitted to participate if the men's incomes were below £400 per annum and the women's less than £250. During the period 1923 to 1939 the numbers insured against unemployment had risen from 11.5 million to 15.5 million. At the same time, those coming under national health insurance had increased from 14 million to 22 million, and those receiving old age pensions had risen from 17 million in 1926 to 22.8 million in 1939. This all meant much larger state expenditures. In 1910 the costs of social services, including education, stood at £63 million, by 1935 it was £260 million, and by 1939, £275 million. It has been estimated that while in 1913 the wage earners received £75.5 million in services, they paid out £90 million in taxation. By 1936, while paying out £338 million, they actually obtained in services around £430 million including their portion of such things as defence, judiciary, and the like. Thus, national wealth was experiencing a rather radical redistribution.

With the improvement in real wages and a great expansion of government services, it is only natural that the general standard of living of the wage-earning class tended to rise. For one thing, housing was improved. While between 1925 and 1929, about 203,000 houses were built each year, between 1934 and 1939 the average annual construction figure was around 348,000. At the same time, slums were being cleared away, council apartments being erected in their places to provide suitable dwelling quarters for the wage-earning classes. This helped to develop many of the new industries, such as those involved in electrical equipment production. The resulting stabilization of rent freed money for the purchase of commodities such as rayon and other semiluxury goods. Cars also were being purchased by the workers, although never to the same extent as in America. Probably even more important was the improvement in the quality of the food consumed. While the eating of staples such as flour and potatoes increased only very little, the consumption of butter rose over 50 per cent, of sugar 25 per cent, of fruit 80 per cent, and of vegetables over 100 per cent. All this indicated a much greater degree of comfort in the life of the working man.

The one fly in the ointment at this point is that the improvement in the conditions of the working classes was real only in the case of those who were able to maintain steady employment. Such a favorable state of affairs, however, was by no means universal. While it is impossible to deal with all the changes which took place in the question of handling unemployment during this period, one or two facts have to be kept in mind. For one thing, prior to the Industrial Revolution 5 per cent had been the usual unemployment figure, although in times of depression during the nineteenth century, this sometimes rose to 10 per cent. In the period following World War I the situation deteriorated seriously. For one thing, there had been a great wartime expansion of productive capacity which could not be immediately put to peacetime use. This had its effect in causing temporary unemployment. At the same time, there was the contraction of overseas trade which struck hard at the exporting industries, causing considerable unemployment. On the other hand, in the industries catering to the home market, unemployment was relatively low. Coupled with the Slump of 1930-33, all these factors tended to increase people's sensitivity, and with good reason, to this problem. If one takes the January figures, it appears that there was a steady rise of unemployment to January, 1922, when 17.7 per cent of the insured workers were out of jobs. There was then a fall to between 10 per cent and 12 per cent, until it started to climb again in 1931, reaching a high of 23 per cent in January, 1933. From that time on the figure improved steadily until the opening of the World War II.

The government attempted to meet the problem, first of all by extending the pre-World War I insurance provisions to all workers. This raised the number of those protected from 2.5 million to 12 million. The depression of 1921-22, however, hit the insurance funds so hard that they began to face a deficit. Therefore, a "means test" was brought in, supplemented by a test of "genuinely seeking work" in 1924. At the same time, "extended" benefits were given beyond the fifteen weeks allowed by law. Even this was not enough in some cases, so payments were made more or less on an unlimited basis to those who needed them. When the Slump of the early thirties came, the necessity of cutting unemployment benefits roused much opposition but was carried through, a 10 per cent reduction being applied until 1934. In that year the insurance plan was further extended, raising the number of workers involved to 13 million. "Unemployed Assistance" (the dole) was also given to those who had no contributory claims upon the unemployment insurance funds. The old poor law function of caring for paupers was thus largely turned over to the Unemployment Assistance Board. By these means the government succeeded to a certain extent in mitigating the effect of unemployment, but it by no means struck at the root causes, which were involved in Great Britain's general economic situation.

As one looks back, therefore, over the period between the two wars from the vantage point of the post-World War II period, one can see that, while Great Britain was by 1939 coming out of the Slump, her position was really not good. Her balance of payments was still adverse, and her trade had by no means come back to the level needed. While her industry and agriculture were undoubtedly hard at work, they were largely so because of government regulation and protection and because of the threat of war. The old days when Britain, economically, could stand against the world were gone, the place of economic leadership having been largely taken by another. Added to this, Britain was on the threshold of a second major conflict. What would be the result?

At the same time there is little doubt that, speaking from the point of view of the wage-earning class, the situation in 1939 was vastly improved. Labor had been through difficult times during the period since World War I, but there had been a general amelioration of its condition. Compared to what was being paid in, taxation was certainly taking less out of the workman's pay envelope. Besides, social services were continually expanding at the expense of the upper classes. The improved standard of living, however, did not mean increased production at a lower cost. Output was probably down slightly, but the cost was considerably higher. To reduce expenses was the first of Great Britain's needs. The second was an increase of trade, the attainment of which partially depended upon a lowering of trade barriers. With the world hurling itself into another maelstrom, there was little indication that these changes would take place. Thus Britain's progress towards settling her problems, economic and social, by 1939, while apparently considerable, was in actual fact largely illusory.

Chapter 26

ANOTHER WORLD WAR AND ITS CONSEQUENCES

IF World War I and the Slump had struck two hard blows at the British economic position, World War II came close to being the knockout. Britain found herself unable to recover completely from the two earlier disasters before the third came, and there was a considerable acceleration of previous trends whose ultimate point cannot yet be seen. Thus, as one studies the economic history of Britain during World War II and the postwar period, he is inclined to wonder what the end will be.

The War itself fell into three distinct divisions. There was, first of all, the period known in America as "The Phony War," lasting from September, 1939, to June, 1940. This was the period during which the Germans overran Poland, but did little to disturb France or Britain. The two allies, depending on the naval blockade, at the same time did nothing to upset Germany. The second period was one of Allied disaster beginning with the fall of France, the evacuation of Dunkirk, and the Battle of Britain. Defeat piled upon defeat, with the loss of Crete, Libya, and Italy. During most of this period Britain and the Commonwealth stood alone against the might of Hitler's Germany. A sudden change took place, however, with the German attack upon Russia, forcing that nation to fight for its life. But this did not directly improve Britain's position, for she had to send supplies to her new-found ally. It was not until December 7, 1941, with the Japanese attack upon Pearl Harbor that the third period began. The United States then became involved, altering the whole aspect of the struggle, for with her industrial potential and her large population, the balance of power leaned very much in the favor of the United Nations. From this point on, victory, although not certain, was much more probable. It finally arrived with the collapse of Japan in August, 1945, and the war was over.

In the preceding chapter, mention has been made of the impact of rearmament upon the British economy between 1935 and 1939. Down to the beginning of this four year period, Britain's arms production as well as the condition of her armed forces had been allowed to deteriorate. It had been taken for granted that there could be no war for at least ten years. In 1935 this attitude changed. Owing to the threat of Germany, and, to a lesser extent of Japan, rearmament commenced, but only very slowly. The Royal Navy began working on a three power standard: Germany, Italy and Japan, while the Royal Air Force endeavored to build "in depth," concentrating on bombers. Simultaneously, the army was restrained in its expansion, since it was thought to have only "limited liabilities" in case of war. Along with all of this went the effort to continue business as usual. The total result was little progress on all fronts. In 1935-36 Britain spent on defenses £137 million which had increased to £400 million by 1939. When this is compared with the German expenditures, which amounted to £1,710 million, or 23 per cent of her income, one can see that, even in 1939, Britain's expenditure of 7 per cent of her income was not nearly enough.

With the outbreak of the war, Britain was in no position to cope with the German onslaught. As a consequence, the economic aspect of the conflict was, at least in its early days, very much a mad rush to make up for lost time. The history of the succeeding periods was one of rationing and budgeting resources. For convenience, however, we shall endeavor to cover the various phases of the economic problems throughout the whole conflict, making our interrelations between these phases as we cover the ground.

Organization of the War Effort

When it was quite obvious that war was coming, tentative steps were taken to set up an organization for the directing of the war effort. Both the Cabinet and Parliament, however, despite the need, were somewhat dubious about giving too much power to the Cabinet. Consequently, much was left undone, although the situation was considerably better than in August, 1914. At the apex of the organization stood the War Cabinet of about ten men meeting every day.[1] This body set up a number of subcommittees to deal with details concerning various phases of war activity. At the

---

[1] It was made up of the Prime Minister, the Chancellor, Lord Privy Seal, the Foreign Secretary, Minister for the Coordination of Defence, the ministers of the three fighting services and one minister without portfolio.

same time, some new ministries were being established; Home Security, Economic Warfare, Food, Shipping, and the like. In this way it was hoped that some coordination could be accomplished, but the achievement was not nearly great enough to meet the need.

The advent of Winston Churchill as successor to Prime Minister Chamberlain saw a considerable change in this situation. Faced with the near disasters of Norway, Holland, and Belgium, the Cabinet sought and attained very greatly extended powers. During his tenure of office Mr. Churchill also organized new ministries when needed, and combined others. In May, 1941 the Shipping and Transport ministries were combined into that of War Transport, while somewhat later a Minister of Production was appointed. Most of the important cabinet committees were continued, but the ministers directly responsible for carrying out their recommendations were given more influence in their deliberations. As a sort of super-committee, the Lord President's Committee was set up to direct the actions of all the civilian committees and also to formulate general economic policy. Fundamental to all the cabinet's action was the Secretariat of the War Cabinet, with its Central Statistical Office and its Economic Secretariat. These bodies were found to be very important, since the statistics available at the beginning of the war were so inaccurate as to be a hindrance rather than a help in the formulation of plans.

Subordinate to these top level bodies were a number of other committees, usually under the supervision of the Lord President's Committee. The most important were the War Agricultural Executive Committees, made up of unpaid volunteers nominated by the Minister of Agriculture and endowed with large powers of supervision, even of compulsion, over the farmers. Committees were also set up to deal with matters such as shipping, production, and manpower. The Ministry of Fuel and Power had controllers appointed to supervise the use of those precious commodities, as well as a committee to study methods of improving coal production. Controllers for various other commodities were also appointed. Thus, by June of 1940, efficiency and control had been greatly increased through these numerous committees and executive bodies.

Organization and coordination were needed, however, not merely within the country, but also to help to facilitate common action with Britain's allies, in the first instance, France. Prior to the war some plans had been laid for Anglo-French cooperation, but nothing had been really achieved because of the lack of pressure and also because of the lack of adequate statistics upon which to base forecasts and estimates. M. Jean Monnet pushed the work of coordination as far as possible but it was not until September, 1939, that a Supreme War Council was created, and not until December that the Anglo-French Coordinating Committee became an actuality. Its work was that of checking on available resources and planning their use as well as arranging joint purchasing of supplies from neutrals. Here again, lack of accurate statistics was a serious handicap. Yet, even with the difficulties, much was accomplished in various fields. Arthur Purvis, a Canadian, as head of the Anglo-French Purchasing Board in Washington, coordinated the allies' buying, and when in June, 1940 France collapsed, he bought from the French representative all France's undelivered purchases in the United States for $1, thus saving both Britain and United States much trouble later.

Aided by Monnet, Purvis, subsequent to France's collapse, continued to act for the British Government, gradually winning the closer cooperation of the American officials. This movement in 1941 was further stimulated by the Atlantic meeting of President Roosevelt and Prime Minister Churchill. Joint Anglo-American committees now began to work together, albeit unofficially, to gear Britain's war effort and United States' rearmament for greater efficiency. Statistics were by this time more accurate, so, after Pearl Harbor, there were possibilities of much more effective cooperation. Joint boards were set up to deal with the production and use of munitions and with shipping and raw materials, as well as a board for purchasing. Gradually, by much trial and error, a well-integrated system of supply was established, providing for the needs of the fighting forces of all the United Nations.

From what has been said above it will be easily recognized that organization was one of the most important weapons for victory. The war was conducted on such a tremendous scale that without effective and careful coordination nothing could have been achieved. Rather painfully, and at very great cost, the organization was completed, so by the end of 1942 most of the major problems had been solved.

The Drive for Production

Almost as important as the fighting front was the production front, for without it the armed forces were helpless. Here Britain was the very keystone of the war effort, particularly until June, 1942. France did not even provide enough to meet her own needs; consequently Britain and the Commonwealth had not only to supply themselves, but also to make up any deficiencies on the part of the allies. After France's collapse, this burden might have been eased somewhat had it not been for the tremendous loss of materiel at Dunkirk. The pressure, therefore, was applied primarily to Britain, with her great industrial potential, and to the end of 1940 she was furnishing 90 per cent of the manufactured war supplies of the Commonwealth, while in the following year she was still producing 81.8 per cent. When Russia came into the struggle in 1941, she immediately called for aid, whereupon Britain, in spite of her shortages, dispatched 450 aircraft, 22,000 tons of rubber, and many other commodities. For the first few months, she was sending as much to Russia as was the United States. After Pearl Harbor, however, the balance quickly changed. All told, between October, 1941, and April, 1946, Britain supplied Russia with £108 million worth of military materiel and £120 million worth of raw materials, food, and machinery. From this it is easy to see the importance of production if Germany and her allies were to be defeated.

Fundamental to production was manpower. While Neville Chamberlain was prime minister no drastic action was taken to provide needed workers. Between September, 1939, and June, 1940, the numbers in the armed forces increased from 1 million to 2.2 million, while the labor force rose by 926,000. The armed forces, however, lacked arms, and the labor force was not increasing as rapidly as it should, nor were the requisite number of shifts from civilian to military production taking place at a rapid enough pace. Even by April, 1940 there were over 1 million unemployed, while the Minister of Labour, the Trade Unionists, and the employers were all opposing stringent labor regulations. Only with the defeats in Norway and the Low Countries was the picture changed, and finally Ernest Bevin, Minister of Labour in Churchill's government, brought in a bill which gave him legal powers to direct labor to necessary work. Here was the beginning of really effective manpower controls.

The reason for these controls was that Britain had to have larger armed forces and greater production. It was estimated that by June, 1942, fifty-five divisions should be under arms. The plan to have 8.5 million people in the armed forces and munition plants by the end of December, 1941 meant that even women had to be called in to help. Of these, there were over 10 million officially, although not actually, available. The result was the National Service Act which conscripted everyone. Military service age for men was lowered to 18½ years and raised to 50 years, while all unmarried women between 20 and 30 years were also summoned to the colors. At the same time the employment of skilled labor was rigidly controlled.

Even then 2 million more were needed, resulting in manpower budgeting: the switching of workers from industry to industry as the need arose. By June of 1944 when the attack upon the Continent was developing, Britain had 55 per cent of her working population either in the army or in munitions production.[2] By this time the manufacture of civilian goods had been cut to the bone, as had even civil defense. Britain had reached her peak of employment, every man and woman possible being used directly in the war effort. This was something of a record, bringing immediate results but posing problems for the future.

In the matter of production itself, probably the most immediate concern of the government was that of getting more for its people to eat. Because of the threat of submarine warfare to Britain's food supplies, it seemed advisable to increase the home output to its greatest possible capacity. Only in this way could space for valuable raw materials and machinery be increased in the holds of the ships coming from other parts of the world. Consequently, everything had to be done to improve the productivity of the land. This meant planning as to what should be grown, how it should be cultivated, and where it should be used. Regulations and controls had to be introduced, and farmers had to be guided, cajoled, and even compelled to follow government instructions and policies.

The fall in the standard of living which took place after Dunkirk was largely owing to the constriction of cargo space available for foodstuffs. The government found it necessary, therefore, to lay down a very clear policy in the matter of food production. The principal question was whether land should be used for wheat or for pasturage. It was realized that land when employed for growing grain, could support many more people than when used for feeding animals. Therefore, animal raising was curtailed in favor of wheat growing. Orders were issued to reduce the numbers of pigs and poultry, although dairy cattle were permitted to increase in number. At the same time, there was a demand for the extension of plowed land to the extent of 2½ million acres. It was hoped that in this way the food shortage might be alleviated.

A number of methods were employed to attain this improvement. In the first place, there was a great effort made to increase the agricultural labor force. Women were urged to join the Land Army, which, eventually 90,000 strong, was taking over much of the work left by men who had joined the forces. Unskilled male labor was also recruited in order to do the heavy work connected with

---

[2] At the same time the United States had 40 per cent similarly employed, although the actual numbers were, of course, much greater.

such tasks as drainage. Along with this movement went a "plow-up campaign" to have as much usable land as possible put under cultivation. This was aided greatly by the increased use of machinery. During the war almost 140,000 Fordson tractors alone were added to the country's agricultural equipment. These could very often handle more than one implement at a time and could cultivate heavy land much more rapidly than could horses. Stress was also laid upon the necessity of using fertilizers more widely in order that the land might produce the maximum quantities.

The outcome of this concentrated effort was that, while in 1938 the British farmer was producing only enough food for two days out of seven, by 1944 he had doubled the quantity. Moreover, he was providing most of his livestock's feeding stuffs. This improvement was accomplished by a 50 per cent increase in the arable area, raising the acreage from 12.9 million to 19 million, while the area under permanent grass fell from 18.7 million to 11.8 million acres. Simultaneously there occurred a rise in the number of cattle from 6.1 million to 9.6 million head, while sheep, pigs, and poultry declined. In this way, not only did the vegetable content of the diet increase, but also such things as beef and particularly milk were being produced in much larger quantities. Thus, by the end of the war Britain, while by no means agriculturally self-supporting, was in a greatly improved situation, the farmer having taken a new lease on life.

The coal production picture was not nearly so attractive. The winter of 1941 saw the country running into difficulties because of the severe weather, the demands of industry, and declining production. Between June, 1939 and January, 1942 the number of miners fell from 773,000 to 707,000. Efforts were then made to bring the men back from the army and from other industries into the pits, but they were not successful. What is more, not only was the remaining force of miners made up generally of the older men, but there was also no little discontent over the question of wages. As a result, production fell steadily from 227 million tons in 1938 to 183 million tons in the final year of the war. The old problem of the coal industry was still a very real one and demands for nationalization were again heard.

In contrast to the coal industry's weakness, there was a tremendous growth of the industries producing instruments of war, while those catering to civilian needs almost disappeared. The total iron ore produced increased from 14.5 million to 18.5 million tons between 1939 and the peak year, 1941. At the same time, the total steel production varied around the 13 million ton mark, with an expansion from 646 to 820 in the number of steel furnaces in operation between 1939 and 1944. Textile production, on the other hand, dropped steadily along with a good many other industries producing civilian goods.[3] Firms producing bicycles, automobiles, chinaware, household appliances, and the like were either turned to war production, were closed down, or were combined with others producing the same types of goods. By this means the country's industry as a whole was devoted to making the tools of war.

Such a change was natural and necessary under the circumstances. By 1942 unemployment had virtually disappeared, only the very minimum of civilian goods was coming on to the market, and everything was being devoted to producing for victory. This was particularly true once Lend Lease came into operation, for then Britain no longer had to manufacture for export in order to obtain exchange with which to buy. With Lend Lease, Britain was also freed of the fear that she would not be able to obtain the raw materials necessary for the production of her defense weapons. The outcome was that more and more, industry was geared to war production alone.

Production, however, was not the only problem which had to be solved. There was the question of transportation. Great Britain was not self-sufficient—has not been for centuries—consequently, she had to look to the rest of the world for both finished goods and raw materials. While in one way this was a means of strength, in another, it was a source of weakness. Her strength was only as great as her system of transportation. As long as the raw iron, wheat, meat, and the like could be brought in, Britain could fight on, but break the connections with the outside world, and she would be finished.

At the beginning of the war Britain and France had tried to determine the amount of shipping space that would be required, but they were very sadly mistaken in their calculations. They estimated that British and neutral ships could bring in a minimum of 48 million tons per annum which was considered to be enough. Owing to lack of statistics and serious thought, however, they were, from the start, short by over 1 million tons. The Ministry of Shipping was faced with the demands of the ministries of Food and Supply for far more space than was available. At the same time, France's requirements caused something of a strain. Then, after the fall of France, submarines became the real problem, particularly as Britain

[3] Raw cotton consumption fell from 607,000 tons to 338,000 tons between 1939 and 1945, while raw wool production fell from 69 to 58 million pounds, and consumption from 481 to 272 million pounds.

could not use the ports of Eire as bases for her convoys. During 1942, owing to the difficulties of escorting ships laden with aid for the Russians, to Murmansk, the situation deteriorated rapidly. Between December, 1941 and June, 1942, 4.5 million gross tons of United Nations shipping were lost, 70 per cent through submarine action. Between January and April of the following year the average monthly sinkings were about 400,000 tons. Of this, Britain's share was 72 per cent, which made a very serious hole in her carrying capacity. The result was that imports fell in 1941 to 30 million tons, in the next year to 23 million tons, and by 1944 had risen to a mere 26 million—a far cry from the estimated 48 million tons of prewar days. Even the rise was obtained only by stringent economies and the careful allocation of space, along with the United States' turning over in Lend Lease some fifteen to twenty ships each month for ten months, to help Britain to replace her lost freighters.

If shipping had been the sole problem, something might have been accomplished quickly to restore the balance. Britain, however, had a problem of ports and also of inland transportation, both of which were entirely inadequate for the wartime needs. By the middle of 1940, to any but escorted ships, the threat of air attack had virtually closed the east coast ports. By January, 1941, raids on Glasgow, Liverpool, and Bristol had damaged their facilities sufficiently to slow up the movement of goods. Coupled with this, the railways were being bombed, throwing them into confusion worse even than that which they were already experiencing from the tremendous increase in demand. The rationing of gasoline curtailed road haulage, which could no longer carry its former cargoes, let alone supplement the railways. Congestion was everywhere, increased by the closing of the Suez Canal and by the time lost in repairing damaged ships. At length, in May, 1941, a Minister of War Transport was appointed to direct both sea and internal transport. Controls were increased, some railway building was done, coal dumps were established, and various other measures taken, with the result that by 1944 there was general improvement and the increasing imports, both of goods and American troops in preparation for the final blow, could be handled speedily. A great effort had brought success.

By these various means Britain succeeded in changing her economy to meet the demands of war. She ceased exporting practically everything except war materiel, many of her civilian factories being either converted to munitions production or strictly limited in output. To meet the demand for arms and military equipment, her imports of the necessary raw materials, tools, and finished goods increased apace at the expense of civilian supplies. At the same time, her shipping was hard hit losing over 11 million tons, about 60 per cent of the total. Thus, when the war came to an end, Britain's position as an industrial and maritime power had been severely shaken.

Financing the War

Had Britain's misfortunes been limited to the field of industry and shipping alone, the situation might not have been so disastrous. The trouble was that when she obtained goods from abroad, she had to pay for them. To do this she could raise money by taxing her own people, and this she did, as will be shown later; but unless Britain had either foreign holdings or was making large exports, the value of her money on the foreign market would fall perilously low. Prices would consequently rise against her, so she would not be able to make purchases to meet her needs. It was for this reason that war finance became one of Britain's biggest headaches.

When the war broke out, the costs to Britain stood at £29.7 million a week; by the end of 1942, they had risen to £95.6 million; but by December, 1944, had dropped back to £91.1 million. This rise was not caused entirely by an increase in the amount of goods being used, but much of it was the result of a rise in costs of production, particularly of labor, and inflation. Although the government attempted to solve the problem after 1941 by price control, rationing, and subsidies, it was not entirely successful. During the war wages rose on an average over 50 per cent, while the general cost of living climbed over 30 per cent. Coupled with this, foreign supplies were becoming scarce, shipping costs were rising, and sterling had fallen by 14 per cent on the American market. As a result of all this, between 1938 and 1945, government spending increased five and one-half times, from £1,000 million to £5,500 million. The big question was how, with her efforts devoted to wartime production, Britain was to get the money to foot the bills?

At the beginning of the war the government did not take immediate steps to try to balance the budget. Its taxation policy was one of proceeding slowly, for no one seemed to take the war too seriously. The standard income tax rate was raised from 5s. 6d. to 7s. 6d. in the pound, and an Excess Profits Tax of 60 per cent was established. Simultaneously, indirect taxes on tobacco, beer, entertainments, and the like were increased. Once the war became hotter, however, the attitude changed. In April, 1941, the standard income tax rate was pushed up to 10s. in the pound with decreased exemptions, while the E.P.T. was set at 100 per cent. In the case of incomes of £2,000 and over, the surtax was raised so stiffly that those in the highest brackets were paying sometimes as much as 95 per cent. A purchase tax was also applied in order to keep down inflation. Yet, with all these efforts, not enough was being done. This may seem strange when one considers that while in 1938, 21 per cent of the national income was being taken in taxes, by 1945, 30 per cent was going to the government. Nevertheless, there was still a serious gap between government income and expenditure.

That heroic measures were desperately needed is obvious, in view of the fact that while, in 1938, the government was meeting 86 per cent of its expenditures from revenue, in 1940 that proportion had dropped to 39 per cent. By 1944 it had risen to 55 per cent, and the year following to 59 per cent, with total expenditures of £6,000 million and £5,500 million respectively, over against revenues of only £3,300 million and £3,200 million. The budgetary gap was large, but, considering the income, this could not be avoided. The only way to solve the problem was to borrow. National Savings Bonds and Defence Bonds were put on the market, the main loan in the early part of the war being issued in March, 1940 for £300 million, at 3 per cent. This was not successful, as less than £200 million were subscribed. Keynes suggested the introduction of compulsory savings, but the government was slow to take his advice. Instead, every effort was made to stimulate voluntary savings and, by controlling the loan market, to obtain loans at a low rate of interest. In this way the government succeeded in going through the war on yearly borrowings varying between £2,000 million and £3,000 million, which, of course, would have to be repaid when peace returned. The total national debt, as a result, grew from £3,800 million in 1939 to £17,800 million in 1945, against total dollar and gold assets of £668 million. If to these figures one adds the interest payments on the debt, which rose during the war from £231 million to £491 million, it is possible to obtain some idea of Britain's financial problems.

This, however, is not the complete picture. Britain was faced with the need for keeping up the value of her money outside her own borders in order to purchase goods, particularly from the United States. She might do this in three ways. She might, first of all, export goods and services in return for imports, an impossible feat owing to her desperate need for the use of all her own productive capacity. Another method was to export gold and to sell off foreign investments. Her limited supplies of both these commodities, however, made this ineffective. Then too, there was the possibility of borrowing the money abroad, a process which would lead her into further and deeper debt. Finally, if all these failed, only one other hope was left; namely, gifts from allied or sympathetic nations.

When the war opened, Britain was faced with the need of obtaining American supplies, but, owing to the Neutrality Act (August, 1938), she was prevented from placing any orders. The United States, in a vain isolationist hope, was committed to the policy of refusing to sell arms to anyone. Although this law was repealed in November, 1939, the Johnson Act prohibiting the floating of loans in the United States by powers who had defaulted on their previous war debts, imposed certain limits. The policy was to be strictly "cash and carry." Britain had to pay cash for her purchases and transport them in her own ships. To meet her needs she had assets of $4,385 million, of which $2,455 million were in gold and dollars, $1,295 in marketable securities, and $635 million in direct loans. At the rate of her continually rising weekly expenditure, such assets were not sufficient to meet her needs over any extended period, particularly as she was frequently called upon to advance funds to American companies to pay for the expense of retooling, or for the addition of facilities to their plants.

While "cash and carry" undoubtedly helped Britain, her position to start with was very much worse than it had been in 1914. For some years prior to the opening of World War II she had suffered from a deficit in the balance of payments, while, at the same time, her foreign investments were of a much poorer quality than they had been at the earlier date. To facilitate financial operations, however, by September 1, 1939 the government had assumed control of all Foreign Exchange transactions, establishing its right also to take over British holdings of foreign securities. At this point the "Sterling Area" came into existence, being made up mainly of Commonwealth and Empire members (Canada and Hong Kong excepted) for whom Britain held the pool of balances through the Exchange Equalization Account. To augment the sterling balance Britain made a considerable export drive, which between September 1, 1939 and December 31, 1940 brought in $345 million. At the same time, she sold Empire commodities such as rubber to gain $670 million, while newly mined and dishoarded gold brought in another $965 million. But even with this $2,000 million addition to her resources, it was calculated that she would still be short some £400 million. To close this gap she would have to sell her foreign investments. These, taken over from the individual holders in February, 1940, turned out to be greatly overvalued, bringing in much less than originally calculated. Moreover, since less than one half of the British holdings were saleable in the United States, the total returns in American funds from these holdings would amount to only about £200 million. The Viscose Corporation, a subsidiary of Courtaulds, was at this point sold for $54 million. But with all the efforts which Britain could make, by December, 1940 her net reserves were down to a total of $2,500 million, made up of $2,155 million in gold and dollar reserves and $334 million in securities. Had it not been for the credit extended by countries such as Argentina and Canada, there is no knowing what might have happened.

By the end of 1940 the situation was becoming desperate, for Britain estimated that from this point on she could spend not more than between £150 million and £200 million a year, and that for only a short time. She would then be at the end of her resources. Meanwhile, however, opinion in the United States was beginning to change. Churchill pointed out early in 1941 that if the United States was not prepared to help Britain, she would eventually have to fight Germany alone, an eventuality that was gradually becoming obvious to even the isolationist elements. Some, however, maintained that Britain was too far gone to be worth helping. Attempts, therefore, were made by certain Americans to force the sale of British rubber interests in Malaya, and her oil interests in Iran as well as various gold interests. It was at this time that the Courtauld subsidiary, the Viscose Company, was sold, while in January, 1941 a United States cruiser took $149,633,653 in gold to America to help pay Britain's bills. Up to this time she had received from the United States munitions, some World War I rifles, overage tanks, and the like, for all of which she had paid cash. Airplanes were also being flown directly to Canada, while some R.A.F. pilots were receiving flight training in Florida. But while Britain was indeed grateful for this help, it did not nearly solve her problem. It seemed that Britain was to be stripped bare before she was to receive enough aid.

At length, on November 23, 1940, the British ambassador, Lord Lothian, set forth Great Britain's pressing needs. Roosevelt, just re-elected as president, now introduced a new type of aid which he named Lend Lease. By this plan Britain and others fighting Germany were to obtain gifts of materiel, which were to be returned, if still in existence, at the end of the war. The United States, however, would not take over and pay for Britain's existing contracts, with the result that by June, 1941 Britain owed $940 million, and her gold reserves were below $12 million. This was temporarily met in July by a Reconstruction and Finance Corporation *loan* of

$425 million. At the same time, Lend Lease did not solve the problem of Britain's need for manufactures, since the United States was rearming not only herself but China and Russia as well. The most valuable contributions made by the Americans at this point were raw materials such as sugar, steel, and impounded enemy shipping. These goods totalled some $1,000 million before Pearl Harbor, although they were given only under very serious restrictions. Despite the fact that Britain still had to export to pay for goods from other countries, she was not permitted to sell goods abroad which even resembled those she obtained from the United States, and she was to keep strict control of the use of those goods in short supply in America. Upon Russia and China were placed no such limitations. But even with the controls, Lend Lease meant Britain's salvation.

From the middle of 1941 Britain could go forward with the confidence of knowing that her supplies were assured. After Pearl Harbor there was a gradual expansion of Lend Lease, so by the end of the war Britain had received over $27,000 million in ships, munitions, gasoline, food, and machinery, in addition to services in the United States. Yet, throughout the war Britain was subjected to restrictions applied to no other nations. For instance, in November, 1943 capital goods such as heavy machinery, were taken off the free list; then, in 1944, civilian supplies, to be followed in January, 1945 by goods which might be components of British exports and by raw materials such as steel and iron. Concurrently, however, restrictions on Britain's freedom to export were also removed. Meanwhile, British gold and dollar reserves had improved owing to annual gold imports from South Africa of around $450 million, and the spending of American troops in the Sterling Area of some $1,200 million. This led some United States officials to demand that Lend Lease be cut until the gold and dollar reserves should fall from their $17,100 million (December, 1944) to a considerably smaller figure. Apparently they did not realize that Britain was having to import large quantities of goods from other lands such as Argentina and that she was also furnishing various necessary commodities at a cost of over $6,000 million in Mutual Aid to the United States. Although Britain was indeed willing to admit that Lend Lease was the one thing which kept her going, it was by no means a completely free gift.

While Britain was receiving help from the United States, she was at the same time giving reciprocal aid, as well as furnishing supplies to other countries. Indeed, in the early part of Russia's campaign, Britain sent her as much as did the United States. All told, Russia was given some £325 million worth of goods, while other nations, apart from the Empire, received materials valued at over £380 million. Thus, Britain not only endeavored, as far as possible, to meet her own needs, she also did much to meet those of her allies.

In September, 1945, when the war was over, a British mission, led by Lord Keynes, went to the United States to negotiate a final settlement of obligations. It was at this point that United States showed herself most generous. Although the net balance was $21,000 million in United States' favor, it was written off in return for a British payment of $650 million. Of this sum, $118 million went to the United States in offsetting Mutual Aid given after the collapse of Japan, $60 million in repayment for United States assets in the United Kingdom, originally costing about $350 million, and $472 million for civilian goods, acquired on Lend Lease and now bought outright. Ships on Lend Lease were returned to the United States, while installations built for American forces reverted to Great Britain in return for British installations in United States. American munitions still in Britain were subject to the right of claim, but they were seldom taken back. At the same time, the United States gave Britain a loan of $3,750 million, free of interest until 1951, when it was hoped that she would be back on her feet economically.[4] This was the final touch. The United States had proved to be willing in the end to help Britain very substanially, but this aid was by no means a cure-all.

The reason for Britain's need of more than a few palliatives was that her financial position by the end of the war had seriously deteriorated. Between December, 1939 and December, 1945 her foreign assets had dropped from $4,385 million to $2,747 million. Although she had reduced her Reconstruction and Finance Corporation loan to $272 million, she still had annually to put aside from her United States holdings a reserve with which to pay the debt. When this had been done, her total annual income from these United States holdings was reduced to around $15 million. Coupled with this was the fact that her gold and dollar reserves stood at only $1,897 million. Furthermore, having lost a considerable part of her shipping and having been unable to replace her factory equipment during the war, she was in no position to earn large sums by exports of either goods or services. Thus, by the end

---

[4] From 1951 on, the loan would be repaid at the rate of $140 million a year, $88 million in interest and $52 million principal. Only the principal, however, would be paid if Britain's total overseas income between 1945 and 1950 averaged less than £1,750 million.

of 1945 Britain's financial position was infinitely worse than it had been when the war opened.

What, then, was the financial cost of the war to Britain? It has been estimated that, in terms of dollar assets, she spent $9,000 million, which, at the 1938 rate of purchase, would have paid for imports from the United States for sixteen years. The depreciation of her industrial equipment has been set at around £1,700 million, a loss mitigated somewhat by improvements in agricultural and heavy industry. Her external disinvestment between September, 1939 and June, 1945 came to £4,198 million, £1,118 being sale of capital assets, £2,879 in increase of external debt and £152 million in decrease of dollar and gold reserves. Added to all this, the buying power of the U.S. dollar dropped almost 50 per cent during the war years, raising her costs enormously. Britain in 1945 faced national bankruptcy.

The Cost in Hardship

Costs, however, cannot always be reckoned in cash. The war years witnessed a great expansion in military production, with more and more civilian factories being turned over to the making of armaments. Manufactures for civilian use, as a result, were severely curtailed. Similarly, imports of nonmilitary goods were greatly restricted in order that essential war supplies might be brought into the country. The natural outcome was a scarcity of civilian commodities and high prices. What is more, earnings had risen about 50 per cent over the 1939 figure, so 50 per cent more money was seeking considerably less than 50 per cent of the normal supply of goods.

For many, this condition of affairs meant a serious decline in their standard of living while for others it meant improvement. A great many high-priced foods became almost unobtainable. Furniture, gasoline, electrical equipment, and other consumer goods virtually disappeared from the market. Many of the middle class, dependent upon fixed salaries, pensions or returns from investments, were faced by definite financial problems owing to the rise in prices. Wage earners, on the other hand, working in munitions plants or on the railways and ships, found their incomes so inflated that they could buy many things hitherto reserved only for the rich. Their food, for instance, improved, since they could now afford more of the better variety. Thus, the war's effect upon the general standard of living was extremely varied.

The principal reason for this was that government controls tended to equalize the absolute fall in the standard of living. Consequently, it did not fall for everyone at the same rate or to the same relative level. To accomplish this the government used certain techniques. The first was taxation, by which purchasing power was to be rigidly controlled. Between 1939 and 1945, the returns from the income tax rose from £335 million to over £1,300 million, while the excise tax income rose £114.2 million to £496.9 million. Simultaneously, the government made every effort to increase the people's savings through various bond issues and war savings certificates, the latter increasing during the war years from £381 million to £1,500. Keynes at the very beginning had suggested compulsory savings, but the idea had not been popular. Therefore, voluntary savings continued to be the order of the day, the actual amount laid aside annually rising from £30 million in 1939 to over £625 million in 1945. At the same time, annual deposits in the Post Office Savings Bank grew from £119 million to £201 million. In this way something was done toward preventing a runaway inflation.

Other methods employed to this same end were those of rationing, subsidies, and controls. While rationing came in only very gradually, it was eventually forced upon the country. At first applied only to machinery and building, by August, 1940, sugar, butter and bacon were added to the list, followed by clothing, furniture, and similar goods. Although the Cabinet tried to keep rationing down to a minimum, it was gradually forced to widen the scope of the regulations. This was necessary partially to distribute goods evenly, but also to keep down prices and wages, which were threatening to go wild. A direct attack was also made on the price problem through price control, supplemented by subsidies. Although the latter increased from £72 million to £215 million per annum, between 1940 and 1944, they did help to keep down the demand for higher wages. Wage and price demands, however, were not entirely obviated, for both the farmers and the miners felt they should receive considerable increases. Since they were in strategic positions they were given what they wanted, miners' wages rising over 100 per cent and the farmers' incomes by £35 million. Yet even with these increases, the advance in the general level of wage rates was kept down to about 50 per cent. As there was considerable overtime, however, actual earnings rose by about 70 per cent. Prices climbed about the same as wage rates, roughly 50 per cent, which meant that with the greater earnings, and continuous employment, the wage earner during the war was between 20 per cent and 30 per cent better off than in 1938.

Looking at the inflation picture as a whole, one finds that while the price index rose from 100 in 1938 to 153 in 1945, during the same period the national real income, on the 1938 basis, increased from £4,671 million to £5,194 million. Thus, while there was a certain amount of inflation, considering Britain's actual war effort it was not nearly as great nor as disastrous as it might have been. On the other hand, even making all allowances necessary, the restrictions in consumption meant a general decline of 16 per cent in the standard of living, a very real sacrifice on the part of the British people. Government policies were only moderately successful in maintaining a level wartime economy.

The final reckoning of the war's cost to Britain has been worked out as follows: external disinvestment amounted to £4,198 million, shipping decreased 30 per cent, exports were reduced to 40 per cent of the 1938 total, 360,000 civilians and military personnel were killed or missing, only 2 per cent of the population was working on exports and 8 per cent on capital equipment, internal disinvestment and destruction amounted to 10 per cent of the prewar total, and capital depreciation amounted to £1,700 million. In all, Britain's losses amounted to 25 per cent of her prewar wealth. Economically, the five years of war had been disastrous.

Britain's primary needs when the war ended were the means of paying for occupation costs on the Continent and rehabilitation at home. To supply these she had, above all else, to get back her trade and to increase it by 50 per cent over what it had been in 1939. Only then could she prevent her gold reserves from almost entirely disappearing. Simultaneously, she had to take steps to build some 300,000 houses for her own people, as well as to meet her responsibilities in connection with foreign rehabilitation under the United Nations. Britain's postwar position, therefore, was one fraught with gigantic problems. She had lost much in every way as a result of her stand against Germany, and now without a breathing space, she had to buckle down, still on short rations, in an attempt to make an economic "come back."

Chapter 27

RECONSTRUCTION ONCE AGAIN

B<small>Y</small> THE time that World War II had come
to an end it was obvious that, for Britain, considerable changes were
in the offing. People were "fed up" with war and yet, at the same
time, were very fearful of what the new era would bring forth. This
attitude was further strengthened by the decline of religion which
had become increasingly apparent during the war years. The
pressure of wartime living, added to the uncertainty, had led many
who had never possessed very great religious faith to conclude
that, even if there were a God, His existence was unimportant.
The events of recent years seemed only to confirm the teachings
of the materialists and the skeptics who had been holding forth in
Hyde Park long before 1939. Those, of course, who had a really
vital faith were not shaken, but they seem to have been in the
minority. The majority of the British people seem to have come
out of the war feeling that they were living in a completely irra-
tional world, in which there was neither sense nor meaning. Consequently, man had to interpret the world on his own authority.
This he could do by his study and planning, at least in so far as it
affected his own life in time and space.

There was not, however, entire agreement as to how the world
should be explained and the problems solved. This was indicated
very clearly by the British election which took place immediately
after the collapse of Japan. During the campaign preceding the
voting, the attitudes of the two major parties were clearly stated.
While the Conservatives under Winston Churchill did not wish to
return to a policy of absolute laissez faire, they wanted to have as
much freedom as possible. Incentives should be offered so that
men would do things on their own initiative. At the same time,
they felt that it was clearly not the time for social experimentation.
Labour, on the other hand, led by Clement Attlee, felt that this
was the proper time to take socialist action. Everything was in
flux, so it would be relatively easy to work out a plan by which
the major industries could be nationalized, incomes would be

equalized, at least to a certain degree, and production and trade would be improved by the application of a master plan under the direction of experts. Proposals were offered for the nationalization of the Bank of England, fuel and power, inland transport, and iron and steel. At the same time, greater measures of social service were promised. If socialism were thus introduced, Labour seemed to believe that a sort of religious conversion would take place which would solve all fundamental problems.

Although the Labour Party campaigned vigorously, it did not seem to have had any great expectancy that it would be elected. Therefore, there was considerable surprise and some confusion in the ranks when, in July, it found itself in power with a majority of 4 million votes and almost two hundred seats in the House of Commons. For the first time in the history of the party it now had a clear mandate to go ahead and change the economy of Britain, and to save her from disaster by the new methods of socialism.

The Postwar Problems

Before describing the policies and actions of the Labour government, it is necessary to gain some understanding of the problems with which the government was faced. This is very difficult to do, since the problems were, in a sense, one, various strands being closely intertwined with each other and going to make up the biggest threat which Britain has faced in her modern history: that of national and international bankruptcy. Therefore, while we attempt to unravel the various strands, it must be kept in mind that they are closely bound together. In dealing with problems which are so near to us in point of time, it is almost impossible to see the full implications of everything, to have a proper perspective on the various relationships involved, and to be able to bring in *all* the facts to everyone's satisfaction. Consequently, in this last chapter, an attempt will be made to give only a very general and tentative interpretation of what has taken place under the Labour regime.

The first problem with which Britain had to deal on the war's cessation was that of rehabilitation and maintenance. It has been estimated above, that all told, Britain lost during the war about one quarter of her national wealth. The destruction had been very considerable through bombing raids, submarine attacks, and loss of material in the ordinary course of the war. At the same time, the war had caused serious shortages, for many goods were either not imported, or were not available for their ordinary peacetime use. Furniture, clothing, cars, and the like practically disappeared from the market. Along with this went the neglect of industrial plants, so by the time the war was over, much of Britain's industrial equipment was either worn out or was completely outmoded. On top of all this, Britain had been obliged to sell a very considerable portion of her foreign investments, particularly in America, so that she could not use the interest on those funds to re-equip herself for the purpose of regaining her old economic position. The only industry which had really improved was agriculture, but even here the farmer was worried lest the wartime boom would leave him overexpanded and unable to meet foreign competition.

Coupled with the problem of rehabilitation went that of redistribution. One thing which had to be done was that the factories had to get back on to a peacetime production basis as fast as possible. This meant moving many people who had been transferred to munitions plants during the war back to their old jobs. But it meant even more than that. Most wage earners could remember the situation in the 1930's, during the Slump, when for weeks on end they had lived on "the dole." The bogey of unemployment was ever before them, coupled with the feeling that they had a right to better living quarters and a better way of life. In trying to meet the situation, the government was faced with demands for protection against unemployment and for much greater security against the expense of ill health and the hardships of a poverty-stricken old age. Thus, the state was obliged, whether it liked or not, to deal with the question of the distribution, not only of the population, but also of the national income, in order that all citizens might have a more equal share.

There was little, however, which could be done about this unless Britain *had* a national income; and that was fundamentally dependent upon international trade. Britain's commercial position had to be restored if she were to get back on to her feet and if she were to raise the standard of living within her own islands. The abolition of Lend Lease as of September 1, 1945 was a hard blow, for it gave the country no time to regain its balance. Added to that, the conditions of the loan of $3,750 million increased her difficulties. The United States demanded that imperial preference should be abolished and that complete convertibility of sterling should be restored within one year, not in five years, as stated in the Bretton Woods Agreement! [1] This meant that Britain's remaining

---

[1] Bretton Woods Agreements were signed on December 28, 1945, with the objective of stabilizing the world monetary system, in particular the dollar, the pound, and the franc. The plan was that: (1) On entry into the Fund each coun-

markets should be thrown completely open to the United States, although the American market was protected by tariffs, and that those nations holding sterling balances should be at entire liberty to turn them into dollars at will, thus reducing Britain's dollar and gold reserves even more drastically. Britain was in a position rather like that of Germany after World War I: she had a heavy debt to meet, but was being deprived of the means of doing so. In such circumstances she would need all the competitive acumen and resiliency of which she was capable if she were to survive.

Survival, furthermore, was becoming an even greater problem since more and more of the nations of the world had developed industrially. During World War II, nations unable to obtain British goods had turned to manufacturing their own, so, with the war's end, they were not prepared to "buy British" any more. Instead, they wanted to protect the manufacturers who would give employment at home and who could very often produce the goods at a lower price than Britain. But even if their prices were not lower, they were at least giving employment to their own people. At the same time, American manufacturers had taken over many former British markets and were not prepared to give them up. On the other hand, if Britain were to get back on her feet economically, she had to increase her exports by 75 per cent over the value of 1938.

The crux of this whole problem lay in the relationship between the Sterling and Dollar Areas. The Sterling Area is composed of the Commonwealth members (except Canada and Hong Kong) and a number of others, all of whom have their currencies linked to the pound sterling. Great Britain holds their balances of sterling and, in consultation with them, releases these as necessary for the purchase of dollars. About half of the non-Soviet controlled world

---

try's monetary system was to be stabilized in relation to gold at the rate of $35 (U.S.) per ounce. The Fund was to provide a means of preventing currency fluctuations of more than 10 per cent on current operations. Only if there were a fundamental disequilibrium in the balance of payments would a deviation of more than 10 per cent be permitted. If a country's currency, on the other hand, became very valuable owing to a favorable disequilibrium, the Fund might declare it scarce and ration it to the members in an effort to restore the equilibrium. (2) To make the Fund work satisfactorily, all Fund members had to make their money freely convertible within five years. (3) To carry out this plan for freeing multilateral trade, a fund of $8,800 million was set up to provide the member countries with currencies which they might need because of a temporary disequilibrium in their balance of payments. Britain's contribution to the fund amounted to $1,300 million, Russia's to $1,200 million and the United States' to $3,175 million. Britain also contributed the same amount to the International Bank for Reconstruction and Development, established with a capitalization of $9,100 million for long-term investment and reconstruction.

carries on its trade in sterling, so the Sterling Bloc holds a very important place in world commerce.

Britain did not worry too much over the conditions of the American loan. She felt that the nations who were in Sterling Area had more to lose than to gain by causing her trouble through exchanging large amounts of sterling for dollars. If the drain on the sterling dollar reserves were too great, Britain would be forced into bankruptcy, which would mean that the others in the Bloc would lose the whole of their balances. If, however, the problem were to be solved, the United States would have to be prepared to take increasing amounts of goods from the Sterling Area to pay for the American goods purchased. In British thinking, the trade between the two areas should balance if the world were not to remain forever dependent upon American charity.

Into the midst of all this came a complicating factor, the threat of imperialistic communism. Events in the Security Council of the United Nations, the refusal of Russia and her satellites to have anything to do with the Marshall Plan, and the seizure of power in Czechoslovakia and Hungary by Communist minorities, all began to impress upon the western nations that they had better be prepared to protect themselves by force. The result was the formation of the North Atlantic Treaty Organization, including the western European nations and a good many of those on the American continent. At the same time, there was the problem of Asia. In China, Communists gradually took over the country, while in Burma, Malaya, and French Indo-China, Communist forces kept thousands of troops in continuous action. Finally, in June, 1950 the Korean conflict broke forth in full flame. Political factors now began to dominate the scene.

The change in the international political situation had immediate and serious repercussions on the British economic position. With a growing fear of Russia, increased numbers of troops had to be shipped to the Continent, while in 1950 men and supplies were rushed to the Korean fighting. Out of a total revenue of

→

THIS MAP shows the present-day concentration of population in the major industrial areas. Until the early part of the nineteenth century the population of England and the Lowlands of Scotland was spread fairly evenly, with some concentration in the London area and in the more fertile southern and eastern sections. Wales and the Scottish Highlands and Islands were less densely populated, especially after the eighteenth-century clearances of the Highland crofters to make way for sheep runs and deer parks. Industrialization led to new concentrations of population in South Wales, the industrial Midlands, Yorkshire, Lancashire, Tyneside, and the Scottish Central Valley. The industrial development of these areas was due to their possession of coal, raw materials, suitable climate, or port facilities.

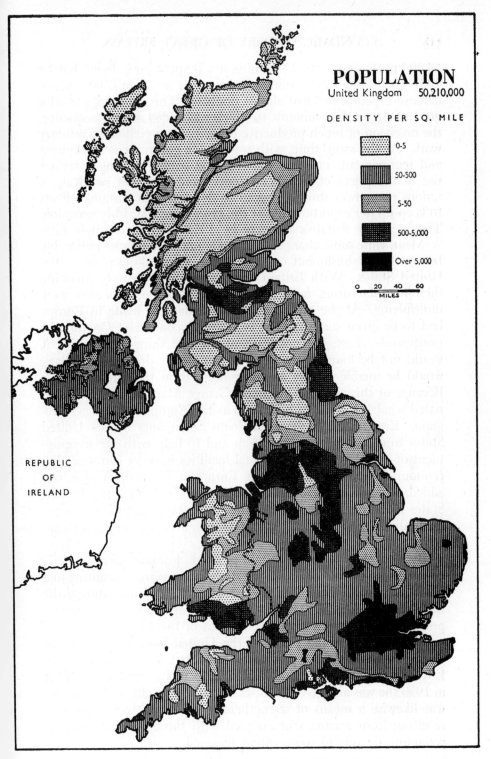

POPULATION
United Kingdom 50,210,000

DENSITY PER SQ. MILE

	0-5
	50-500
	5-50
	500-5,000
	Over 5,000

0   20   40   60
MILES

REPUBLIC
OF
IRELAND

(By permission from *Britain, A Reference Handbook*, 1952. British Crown copyright.
Modified. Comparable data for the Republic of Ireland not available.)

£4,000 million in 1948, £753 million was spent on defense, but by 1951-52, although the revenues had risen by less than £200 million, defense expenditures had almost doubled. This, in turn, placed a great strain on the economy, to which was added as a consequence, the diversion of much productive capacity from civilian to military work. At the same time, with world-wide government stockpiling and rearmament, raw materials became scarce, causing a serious rise in the prices of Britain's imports, and, last, but not least, a serious manpower shortage began to develop with Britain's efforts to keep up her exports, while at the same time feverishly rearming. The hopes of Britain's recovery by 1951 grew increasingly dim.

Meanwhile some changes in attitude not unlike those noticeable before the establishment of Lend Lease, were taking place in the United States. With Britain and Europe progressively diverting their manufacturing facilities to war production, problems were multiplying. At the same time, the standard of living in Europe had to be given some support in order to counteract Communist propaganda. Last, but not least, at the rate things were going it would not be long before Europe, completely drained of dollars, would be unable to buy anything more from the United States. Because of this situation, General George Marshall in 1947 originated what has come to be known as the European Recovery Program. Europe was to be given loans and grants by the United States to aid in her reorganization and to help with the re-equipment of industrial and agricultural facilities in order to restore her economic stability. In 1950 the European Payments Union was added, a grant of $150 million being received from the United States to provide credits for the European nations and thus facilitate the periodical settlement of their accounts amongst themselves.

By all of these agencies Britain profited. For one thing, in 1947, on American insistence, she made sterling convertible, resulting in a heavy run on the pound, to the extent of $237 million during the third week of August. This forced the suspension of convertibility, preventing fulfillment of the conditions of the 1945 loan. At the same time, with rising prices in the United States, the loan was worth much less than previously estimated. Consequently, the E.R.P. grant of $1,093.4 million in 1948 was a great help. That in 1950 she was also given 26.9 per cent of the credits in the E.P.U. was likewise a means of strengthening her hand, so the pressure resulting from rearmament coupled with the attempt to recover economically was to some extent lessened.

Yet, at the same time, Britain was not only receiving, she herself was doing her utmost to help others. From the close of World War II until December, 1951 she had given £616 million in loans and recoverable aid to various European and Asiatic countries, with gifts of over £668 million to international agencies, foreign countries, and the E.P.U., totaling almost £1,300 million. Britain also committed herself to aid in developing southeast Asia through the Colombo Plan which would cost her some £300 million more. When one adds this all up: rearmament, rehabilitation, and an attempt to get back into the world's markets, it is easy to see that Britain has been faced with problems which cannot be settled by platitudes nor even by best wishes. Something very concrete and definite had to be done.

The Labour Government's Policies and Actions

At the close of the war many people, particularly labor and the lower middle class, were feeling that the government must step into the economic picture more fully and completely. They had seen that, during the twenties and thirties, industrial management had been neither active nor enterprising. Instead, there had always been a tendency to limit output in order to keep up prices, while efficiency had been disregarded. During the war, on the other hand, industry had prospered and expanded enormously under government control, leaving the impression that government control was capable of solving most of the problems. Added to this, the Labour Party really produced a program which was a plan for detailed control of the country's economy, while the Conservatives relied upon Winston Churchill's prestige to return them to power. The result was a Labour victory. But it was not a victory for pure unadulterated socialism. The old tradition of nonconformity and respect for the crown prevented anything like a Communist revolution. Instead, it was very largely a practical matter of increasing production and of distributing the national income more evenly. The Labourites disagreed amongst themselves on various measures and on the length to which they should go, but, with the exception of a few "left-wingers," they were mainly moderates headed by Clement Attlee, Ernest Bevin, and Herbert Morrison. They desired to place most of the basic industries and utilities under public control through the establishment of public corporations made up of government appointees, who would occupy their positions because of their abilities, rather than because of party or personal loyalties.

The first step in the program of nationalization was the taking over of the Bank of England. The Labourites generally blamed the Bank for helping to wreck the MacDonald government in 1931, so the first action was to pay off old scores. But, in reality, it made little difference. The Bank had been paying a 12 per cent dividend on the £100 share of stock, so that for each £100 share, £400 of government 3 per cent bonds were given to the shareholders. The government had the duty of appointing the Court of Governors, one third of whose members retire each year, and the new court turned out to be much the same as the old, with a few trade-union men added. The only big alteration was that, "in the public interest," the Treasury might control the Bank's use of short-term money, as, for instance, in instalment buying. This was part of the campaign to give the government more power to control peacetime spending. Actually, there was little opposition to this move, since the Bank was already virtually a state-controlled institution.

In somewhat the same category were the electricity and gas industries, taken over in 1948 and 1949 respectively. Both had been very strictly controlled, and 60 per cent of the electricity distributors were already publicly owned. Consequently, there was little question of the destruction of free competition. Rather, there was the feeling that now it would be possible to direct these two basic utilities on a more rational basis, and perhaps at a cheaper rate.

There was considerably more discussion over the question of the nationalization of the means of communication. Here again, much had already been done. The railways had been consolidated into four main lines after World War I, giving the government ample opportunity for regulation and, in reality, destroying any real competition. In fact, the only competition had come from the road haulage which had been partially brought under railway control when the lines were permitted to invest in bus and truck lines. Even with this help, however, some of the railway lines had been making an annual profit of less than 2 per cent. Nationalization seemed to be the most sensible way to deal with the problem.

By the Transport Act of 1947 the government took over all the railways, railway hotels, canals, and bus and truck lines, giving the shareholders in these concerns government stock in return for their holdings. The original stock was paid for at market prices, the railways and canals, for instance, being purchased for £1,065 million. The first to be taken over were the railways and canals which came under the control of the Railway and Canal Executive of the British Transport Commission. Although the Road Transport Executive came into existence at the same time, it proceeded more slowly because of the complexity of the problem. Gradually, either by compulsion or by negotiation, it took over all the bus lines and all those truck lines carrying goods more than twenty-five miles. The short haul lines were left in individual's hands, but were made subject to government regulation. Those running trucks merely for their own businesses were left completely unregulated. Added to these moves was the nationalization of the oversea cable services, and the airways, although plans for the establishment of the British Overseas Airways Corporation had been laid down before the Labour Government came into power. Thus, by 1950, with the exception of the docks, the government controlled all the means of communication in the country. They were now government instead of, as formerly, private monopolies.

More important than any of the other nationalization projects, was that of coal. By the end of the war it was obvious to all that something had to be done to put the industry back on its feet. It needed to be reorganized, unified, and re-equipped. The Reid Report, published at the close of the war, showed that the whole system of taxation, ownership, and management had to be changed. There had been too little foresight in the planning and exploitation of the mines. Many of the workings were uneconomical, being kept going only by virtue of price fixing and other similar devices. It was felt that through government ownership alone could be made the large capital investments which would bring back efficiency. Production had dropped to alarming depths (190 million tons by 1946), and something had to be done.

Nationalization seemed to be in order. In December, 1945 the necessary bill was introduced to establish the National Coal Board composed of nine members, to be aided by two advisory councils, one representing the consumers and the other the distributors. The Board was to take over all the coal companies' workings, including plant and service installations, such as coal preparation plants, electric power plants, etc. All that the companies had left in their hands was their cash and liquid assets, along with such things as workmen's homes, which, however, could be turned over by agreement between the two parties. Compensation was based upon the average earnings between 1923 and 1938, amounting to £6.9 million. As a result of this act the Board became the owner of more than 800 companies as well as plants for the preparation of fuel, coke ovens, brick works, lands, and houses. For these, compensation was paid to the owners to the amount of £164.6 million. Some 480 mines employing less than 50 were left out of the plan to work under license from the Board. Here again, there was relatively little opposition, except that the owners had hoped to receive higher compensation. Under the circumstances, however, they did not have too bad a bargain.

Most controversial of all the socializing measures was that affecting iron and steel. Even within the Labour Party itself there was considerable doubt expressed as to its advisability. Although this had been one of the planks of the party's platform, no one had ever expected Labour to get into power. Consequently, the Cabinet was somewhat dubious about going ahead with this measure. As a result, however, of difficulties within the party, Attlee had to make some concessions to the more radical element led by Aneurin Bevan, and so preliminary steps were taken. Even then, nothing much was done, particularly as the Iron and Steel Confederation, the principal labor union concerned, seems to have been indifferent to the move. Meanwhile, to head off criticism, the Iron and Steel Federation, an association of owners, had produced a report which set forth plans for large improvements which would raise production to 16 million tons. This project, extending over a period of seven and one-half years would require £168 million, of which the industry itself would provide one half of the annual £22.5 million needed, while new money or the government would provide the other half. The Federation also proposed to concentrate some processes in particular plants and close non-economic firms. To look into these matters and to supervise the industry, in 1947 the government set up an Iron and Steel Board. This, the companies claimed, was quite sufficient, no more government control or ownership being necessary.

Although many of the Cabinet would have been quite satisfied to leave matters at this point, the radical element pushed for further action. If anything was to be done before another election, the House of Lords' veto power, which could postpone action for three years, now had to be cut to one year; otherwise it would be too late, since an election had to be held before the end of 1950. In November, 1947, therefore, the necessary constitutional bill restricting the Lords was introduced, and by December 1949 the Iron and Steel Nationalization Act was on the statute book. The Conservative opposition did succeed in holding up its implementation until January 1, 1951, and by that time the Conservative Party was back in power.

The Act set up the Iron and Steel Corporation of Great Britain, which was to take over the stocks and securities of ninety-six companies, controlling 90 per cent of the total production. The companies would continue to exist, but now for a new shareholder: the

State. Other companies were also to be taken over, but those producing less than 5,000 tons of steel a year were not to be touched. Those producing more than 5,000 tons of pig iron or steel but not more than 50,000 tons of pig iron or 20,000 tons of steel were to operate under license. All subsidiaries except automobile companies were also nationalized. The Corporation had general control, but left the day to day operation in the hands of the companies. It could, however, fix prices, provide subsidies, and either take the profits or make good the losses of the industry's operations. The battle over this bill was loud and long, largely because the industry was booming at the time. But the truth was that here again there had not been too much foresight, nor had efficiency been nearly as important as profits. Consequently, there was considerable support for the plan to take over the industry, although, as with all nationalization projects, the question eventually arose as to whether government is any more efficient than private ownership.

Apart from nationalization, the government also tried to stimulate production by means of controls over those parts of the economy remaining in private hands. One of its first moves in this direction was the Agriculture Act (1947). The basic purpose of this legislation was to provide a means whereby the government could maintain stability of demand and prices, while, at the same time, the farmers would keep up efficiency so as to meet any food shortages. An inefficient farmer could be removed, with compensation, if he proved either unwilling or incapable of cooperation. The whole system, under the direction of the Minister of Agriculture, was based upon the County Agricultural Committees, mainly composed of practicing farmers or landowners. They were to advise, help, and, if necessary, direct farmers, many of whom seemed to appreciate this aid. On the other hand, some felt that the bill tended to ossify agriculture by protecting the poor, but not actually useless farmer, and also by making it difficult for a landowner to take over his land from his tenant except for inefficiency. This has tended to make the landlords keep their land in their own hands, resulting in a decline of tenant farming. But, for good or ill, such was the government's plan.

Two days after the Agriculture Act was introduced into the House of Commons, the Town and Country Planning Act, 1947, was brought in. This act was largely noncontroversial, as its roots went back to 1941, when the Minister of Works and Buildings appointed the Scott Committee to investigate the loss of rural land to nonagricultural uses. The reason for such an investigation can easily be understood when it is realized that between 1918 and

1939 over one million acres of rural land were lost to agriculture.
In 1943 the Ministry of Works and Planning (originally, of Works
and Buildings) became the Ministry of Town and Country Planning, to work out, along with the Ministry of Agriculture, a system
whereby the expansion of towns into the agricultural lands would
cause as little trouble as possible. The act of 1947 stated its objective clearly, setting up a master plan in order that towns should be
permitted to develop only in directions which would inflict the
least damage upon agriculture. It was hoped that in this way the
needs of both the town and country would be met. Many felt that
the system was artificial and would only hinder rather than help
development, but as the measure was generally accepted by all parties it became law.

Even more important than controlling agricultural production
were the efforts to stimulate industry in general. In 1947 American
production was some 75 per cent to 100 per cent ahead of Britain's.
The reasons for this were many: the effect of two world wars, the
British lack of electrical power, and the unwillingness of management and trade-unions to adopt new methods as long as the old
brought in profits, to mention only a few. Government red tape
also played its part with out-of-date statistics and outworn regulations. Equally important was the general attitude that industry
existed for the purpose of supplying jobs rather than for efficient
production. Over the opposition of both labor and management, a
government-sponsored joint Anglo-American committee on production was formed to give Britain new ideas. With the same end
in mind, American companies, with British subsidiaries, often sent
over experts to help increase the output by the introduction of new
techniques as well as by the reorganization of management. These
pressures, coupled with the British realization that something had
to be done, resulted in such improvements as the recasting and reorganization of jobs, particularly in the textile industries. At the same
time, the government, through a network of controls sometimes
more hampering than helpful, endeavored to allocate raw materials
to key industries and thus to facilitate their work for the overseas
market.

Of even more dramatic character were the financial measures,
culminating in the devaluation of the pound sterling. The collapse
of convertibility in August, 1947 put Britain in a difficult position.
It was obvious that the pound was not worth the $4.00 at which it
had been pegged. For one thing, there were Britain's heavy debts,
such as £760 million to India, which had to be paid back gradually
over the years by exports of unrequited goods. On the other hand,

if the pound dropped in value abroad, it would be easier to sell goods, although perhaps harder to buy, especially in dollars. The result of this was that Sir Stafford Cripps in 1950 reduced the value of the pound to $2.80. By this move he hoped to be able to increase exports to the United States by virtue of low prices and, at the same time, to cut imports from dollar countries because of the lower sterling purchasing power. In this way the non-Dollar Area and the Dollar Area would be able to trade as equals. This, however, was not to be.

How did these plans affect the ordinary man? The postwar years in Britain will probably be known as "The Age of Austerity," not morally but economically. While Dalton, the first Labour Chancellor of the Exchequer, had been in office, austerity had been played down, but after his resignation in November, 1947, because of his release of unauthorized information, Cripps took his place. The new Chancellor was austerity personified. In opposition to the European idea of using Marshall aid to raise the standard of living, he felt that it should be employed only for improving capital equipment. Consequently, he introduced, or reintroduced, widespread rationing, covering not only staples, but also candy and other luxuries. He directed the purchase of as many commodities as possible from soft currency rather than hard currency areas, and when they could not be obtained except in America, the British had to go without. He also pushed for the freezing of wages in order to stop useless buying, which could only lead to inflation. In this, after some hesitation, the Trade-Union Congress gave him support on condition that dividends were also cut and taxation raised. Here he was only too willing to cooperate, with the result that taxation up to more than 75 per cent of net income was not uncommon. Food prices and rents were also controlled by means of subsidies and direct ceilings. Costs were thus kept down, but, at the same time, the standard of living began to decline. Many individuals complained that they were having a harder time than they had had during the war. The middle class, particularly those on fixed incomes, suffered greatly, not through absolute want, but in that their standard of living fell relatively much farther than that of either the upper or lower classes. This is part of the reason for the Conservative victory in 1951.

Yet, while living standards were falling, at least in some sections of society, certain measures were being taken by the government to counteract the effect of the decline. The first part of the plan was the improvement of housing, particularly for the working classes. Anyone who has seen the living conditions of people in

Liverpool, Airdrie, Motherwell, and similar areas will realize the need for such action. To this end, in 1945 a Distribution of Industry Act was passed, which enabled the Board of Trade to "persuade" private owners to build or operate factories in what were called during the Slump, "depressed areas," but are now known as "development areas." The persuasion was exercised informally by means of the allocation of building supplies and similar commodities. This law was followed in the next two or three years by statutes which provided for the building of new towns in which to house the industrial populations around London and the development areas. They gave local authorities power to condemn and pull down slums, to build low rent homes for the laboring classes, and to control the sale of farm lands for housing projects, by preventing the owner from profiting through the expansion of a neighboring urban area.

To add to the effect of these measures, the government went in for national insurance on a large scale, basing its laws primarily on the Beveridge Report issued during the war. Protection in case of industrial accidents was increased, the whole matter being tied up with the health insurance plan. Unemployment insurance was extended, sickness benefits were augmented, old age pensions for all men at 65 years and all women at 60 years were introduced, while family allowances of 5s. a week for each child except the first were provided. Finally, Aneurin Bevan, Minister of Health, after much conflict with the British Medical Association, put through a national health plan, providing free medical treatment to everyone who wished it. Each doctor on the plan received a basic salary of £300 plus a capitation fee for each patient, the number of whom could not exceed 4,000. He could also carry on a private practice if he desired. There were other stipulations which caused some trouble, but the difficulties were eventually ironed out. All hospitals and clinics were taken over by the government, while even medicine, eye glasses, and false teeth were provided free of charge. The removal of this latter benefit by the Chancellor of the Exchequer, Hugh Gaitskell, in his last budget (1951) brought about Bevan's resignation from the Cabinet. He had, however, achieved much in his drive for free medical and dental treatment for all. Finally, a National Assistance Act (1947) was introduced to replace the old Poor Law, and a Legal Aid and Advice Act (1949) was passed to help poor people in their law suits.

This was the Labour program and its implementation. To many it was a violent attack on individual initiative and private property. It was declared to be entirely doctrinaire, without any real rhyme or reason. More specifically, it was held by a good many that, by such interference, the government was coming into conflict with basic economic laws. It was attempting to raise the wages of labor without expanding production, thus increasing costs, while at the same time it was endeavoring to keep prices down. With the resultant increasing demand, the effort to arrest inflation was doomed to failure. Therefore, the only thing which the government could do was tax profits in order to obtain funds to subsidize labor above the market wage level. Such taxation, however, must inevitably limit the capital available for investment. This in turn would curtail output, making labor even less productive and, consequently, again more costly. Many could not see any outcome to the Labour Party's policy but bankruptcy or totalitarian absolutism.

There were, of course, also those who went to the other extreme, claiming that only a minimum had been attempted owing to the cowardice and bourgeois-mindedness of the Labour Party leaders. Ernest Watkins' description of it as a "cautious revolution," however, would seem to be most apropos. There was little which was absolutely new and for which the groundwork had not been laid down by previous Liberal or Conservative governments. The principal difference was that Labour carried out the ideas more thoroughly and more completely. At the same time, they made it obvious that they were doing for the working man, something which could and would be done only by the Labour Party. Along with this went the growing pressure on the middle class standards of living, forcing many who had voted Labour in 1945 and 1950, to cast their votes in 1951 for the Conservatives, who promised relief from the Labour created "oppression." It was a revolution, but one which had traditional roots going back to the early days of the Industrial Revolution.

The Labour Party's Success

The question which must now be answered is: how successful was the Labour government in solving Great Britain's problems? How far was it able to bring about a real postwar rehabilitation of the country industrially, commercially, and socially?

There is little doubt that production during the six years following the close of the war increased very rapidly. Its peak, however, seems to have been reached in 1950, a fall taking place thereafter owing to the rising of prices at home and abroad, the scarcities of strategic materials, and the gradual satiation of the foreign market. In the matter of foodstuffs, for instance, wheat which was worth 5s. 9d. a quarter in 1931, was by 1948 up to 23s. 8d., and by 1950 even higher; simultaneously, coal rose by almost 5s. a ton, and other commodities in a similar ratio. As defense production began to grow, more and more of the imported raw materials, such as steel, wool, oil, and the like, became scarce. The supply of manpower was also becoming short, with increasing numbers being called into the services or into munitions production. Although the total labor force was expanding at the rate of about 250,000 a year, this number or more was being drained off into such non-productive activity. Civilian jobs were going begging, one instance being the 18,000 vacancies on the railways at the beginning of 1952. This was bound to have violent repercussions on all production.

The following table can perhaps best sum up the production situation during the Labour government's term of office.

	1938		1946		1951	
Agriculture:						
Bread grains	2,040	thou. tons	2,006	thou. tons	2,246	thou. tons
Potatoes	5,115	thou. tons	10,116	thou. tons	7,973	thou. tons
Milk	1,249	mn. gals.	1,495	mn. gals.	2,025	mn. gals.
Beef and veal					609	thou. ton
Coal	226.0	mn. tons	190.06	mn. tons	222.2	mn. tons
Metals:						
Pig iron	6.76	mn. tons	7.76	mn. tons	9.67	mn. tons
Steel	10.3	mn. tons	12.6	mn. tons	15.6	mn. tons
Textiles:						
Cotton yarn (single)	952	mn. lbs.	661.7	mn. lbs.	968	mn. lbs.
Cotton cloth (lin. yds.)	3,640	mn. lbs.	1,623	mn. lbs.	2,202	mn. lbs.
Misc. Mfrs.:						
Automobiles			219,162		475,919	
Steam locomotives			796		719	

According to the production index, whose basic year is 1946 (100), 1947 was 108; 1949, 129; 1950, 140; and 1951, 144. But again it must be emphasized that a considerable amount of the production of 1951 went, not for export or home consumption, but for military needs. Production generally had increased, but not sufficiently to cover rearmament and the balance of trade.

While considering production, it is also necessary to obtain some idea of the amount of saving and capital formation which took place. Estimates of personal savings are very hard to obtain and are always largely guesswork. It has been calculated, however, that while savings in 1938 stood at £218 million, in 1947 they were £61 million, in 1950, £177 million, and in 1951, £98 million. As for capital formation, such as the erection of factories or the making of machinery for the manufacture of goods, with a certain amount of allowance for faulty estimation, the figures are for 1938, £700 million, for 1945, £336 million, for 1947, £363 million, for 1949, £1,599 million, and for 1951, £1,862 million. At the same time, it must always be kept in mind that since the buying power of the pound had decreased drastically during the war, the amounts recorded after 1945 are not actually nearly as large as they might seem.

All of this had its bearing on the question of Britain's exports. She was in desperate need of greater sales to the dollar market. These sales, however, were becoming harder to negotiate because the hard currency countries were beginning to raise tariffs against her. Along with this, the British manufacturer and exporter, finding that it was much easier to sell to the East Indian or the African market, were making little effort to earn dollars. Meanwhile, the United States was pushing for multilateral trading, but was not willing to abolish her discriminatory tariffs. The first postwar years saw a great boom, the total value of Britain's exports, which had been £470.8 million in 1938, standing in 1948 at £914.7 million and in 1951 at £2,708 million. The only difficulty with these figures is that prices had doubled in that time, so the expansion was not as great as would seem, although the 1951 volume was 67 per cent above that of 1947. Industries such as those engaged in metal manufacturing were by far the most important. The value of vehicles exported (including automobiles, ships, and aircraft) rose from £44.5 million in 1938 to £447 million in 1951, while machinery concurrently increased from £57.9 million to £365 million. Textiles also rose from £92.2 million to £537 million. The value of exports in 1951 was thus well up. This favorable condition was spoiled somewhat by the fact that the value of the pound was down, so imports cost even more.

The problem of imports was very serious because, with Britain's increase in population between 1938 and 1950 from 47 million to 50 million, more mouths had to be fed and more bodies had to be clothed at a much higher cost. From 1936 to 1938, out of an average annual import bill of £866 million, £403 million went for foodstuffs, drink, and tobacco, £237 for raw materials, and £222.5 million for manufactured or semi-manufactured goods. In 1951 the total imports, valued at £3,914 million, were broken up into £1,299 million for food and drink, £1,715 million for raw materials, and £885 million for manufactured articles. Even between 1947 and 1951, while the volume of imports had increased only 32 per cent, prices had more than doubled.

The situation, therefore, was not good. Import prices in 1952 stood about 160 per cent higher than they did in 1938, while export prices were up only 145 per cent. In 1938 Great Britain had a trade deficit of about £300 million, but this was offset by revenues from shipping, foreign investments, and various services, so the net adverse balance of payments amounted to some £70 million. In 1946 the trade deficit alone was £202 million, which, when added to the restricted returns from shipping, depleted foreign investments, and heavy government expenditure abroad, showed an over-all deficit in the balance of payments of £370 million, to be followed in 1947 by one of £630 million. It was shortly after this that the pound was devalued. By 1950 the trade deficit had been cut to around £150 million, while the surplus from invisibles had risen to £391 million, leaving a balance of £244 million, so that Marshall aid could be stopped and Britain could commence to pay back her hard currency loans. It looked as though all was well.

Then came Korea. There was an immediate demand for raw materials and food, which brought in rising returns for British colonial products and manufactures. The trouble was that the money so earned from the dollar area was not held but was spent on imports, so by June 1951 North American goods were coming into the Sterling Area twice as fast as they had in 1950. At the same time, there was a break in prices for Sterling Area goods, which resulted in a 50 per cent fall in returns. Anti-inflationary measures in Canada, the United States, and other countries did the trick, with the result that Britain's dollar imports doubled and her income was halved. Prices of non-sterling commodities on the other hand did not fall nearly as far, the result being that Britain was forced to pay more and get less. Although at the end of 1951 she had a favorable balance of £239 million with the rest of the Sterling Area, her unfavorable balance with the non-Sterling Area was £760 million, leaving a net deficit of payments of £521 million. It is the old story of wartime: rearmament and export cannot be carried on simultaneously. Largely through events beyond her control Britain's temporary balance had been snatched from her, to be replaced by a deficit more than twice as large. At the same time, with the return of her dollar deficit, her balance of credits in the European Payments Union began to diminish. Something had to be done to stop the drain of gold and dollars out of the country. It was at this point that the election took place, resulting in a slim Conservative majority.

The election results were not caused directly by the adverse balance of payments and the drain of gold, but rather by the effect of the Labour government's policies with regard to rationing and taxation. Because of the latter, large net incomes had generally disappeared, although the number of those receiving increased smaller incomes had grown rapidly. In reality, the average workingman was much better off. Those who suffered were the middle class, who were losing a much larger percentage of their incomes in taxes and who were able to purchase less of their usual type of food, as well as being restricted on clothing. Rationing of food, of course, bore on all the people, but since the laboring classes generally had never known a very high standard of living, to them it was not so great a hardship. Moreover, their staples were all subsidized. The middle class, on the other hand, not only could not purchase many of the foods they regarded as essential, but found that many other things which they were used to, were too high in price for their restricted incomes.

It was the feeling that they were having to do most of the belt-tightening, as well as the attacks upon them by such men as Aneurin Bevan and Emmanuel Shinwell, who have repeatedly shown a great disregard for the middle class, that finally turned a good many erstwhile Labourite votes towards the Conservatives.

Labor, however, remained solidly behind the party. Many were happy because employment was steady and earnings had climbed so greatly that between 1938 and 1948 the number of those receiving incomes between £250 and £499 per annum had risen from 1.8 million to 8.7 million. Between October, 1938 and April, 1949 average weekly earnings had gone up some 124 per cent, working time had dropped by about one hour, and the cost of living had increased only 76 per cent. Coupled with this, the great number of homes either built or repaired, amounting to 1.1 million, had its influence. Private building was kept to a minimum, making up less than 10 per cent of the total, the rest being erected under local authorities or government contract. It is true that many of the homes were extremely unattractive in appearance, but they were undoubtedly much better than the quarters formerly occupied. Furthermore, unemployment benefit for a single man over eighteen years of age was now 26s. a week and for a couple with a child, 49s. 6d., and the old age pensions were meeting a long-felt need, as was free medicine. In total, payments for social security had climbed between 1938 and 1950 from £267 million to £630 million, subsidies for food and milk for mothers (welfare foods), from £1 million to £35 million, and general subsidies had gone up from £14 million to £460 million. This meant that, on the whole, the average working man was eating more and better quality food than before the war, besides having better clothing and housing. True, the meat, egg, fruit, and tea consumption was down, but dairy products and fats were certainly more plentiful. Consequently, he was not feeling the pressure but could see the improvements. He therefore continued to vote Labour, while the uncertain middle and lower middle class turned back to the Conservatives.

The Conservatives Again

To many dyed-in-the-wool Conservatives in Britain and to many Americans, Churchill's victory at the polls (1951) meant a return to sanity and British old time prosperity. The trouble was, as has already been shown, that the old time prosperity was very far off. The Conservatives faced exactly the same problems as had the Labourites, a fact which the former do not seem to have recognized until they came into power. They felt, however, that they might overcome the difficulties not only by harder work, more austerity, and certain other restrictions, but also by the restoration of strength to the pound. Of less interest to them was the matter of social reform. By these means they hoped to bring about the recovery of Britain's position in the economic world.

This is the problem which they face. Possessed of a population of over 50 million whose average age is gradually rising, with their economic resources at home sadly depleted and their foreign investments very much reduced, the British must endeavor to pay off a debt of almost £3,000 million while, at the same time, they must try to maintain a favorable balance of payments on current transactions. Can this be done? The answer lies in the hand of God, and only time will reveal what the future holds. It would seem to be safe to say that, under present circumstances, the one hope for Britain is an era of peace coupled with a general freeing of trade restrictions. If this should happen, Great Britain would then have an opportunity to use her undoubted skill and capacity to produce manufactures which the world can use.

In the past fifty years Britain has twice stood as the guardian and defender of democratic freedom, the last time for some months practically alone. But she had to finance this stand with her great accumulated wealth. It would now seem rather hard if she were forced into bankruptcy by the refusal to trade of those very nations whose liberty she fought to defend. If she should collapse, it would mark the end of a historical epoch which traces its roots back to prehistoric times, and of a country which has had a continuous history for more than three thousand years.

BIBLIOGRAPHY

FOR FURTHER READING

General bibliography containing material dealt with in a large number of chapters:

General Works

ASHLEY, W. J. *An Introduction to English Economic History and Theory.* London, 1931, Vol. I, Parts 1 and 2.

BOWEN, E. G. *Wales, a Study in Geography and History.* Cardiff, 1943.

BROWN, P. A., BLAND, A. E., and TAWNEY, R. H. *English Economic History: Selected Documents.* London, 1919.

CHEYNEY, E. P. *An Introduction to the Industrial and Social History of England.* New York, 1931.

CLAPHAM, J. H. *A Concise Economic History of Britain from the Earliest Times to 1750.* London, 1949.

CUNNINGHAM, W. *The Growth of English Industry and Commerce.* 3 vols. London, 1938.

DARBY, H. C. *An Historical Geography of England Before 1800.* Cambridge, 1936.

DIETZ, F. C. *An Economic History of England.* New York, 1949.

DOBB, M. *Studies in the Development of Capitalism.* London, 1950.

GRANT, I. F. *The Economic History of Scotland.* London, 1934.

———. *The Social and Economic Development of Scotland Before 1603.* Edinburgh, 1930.

LIPSON, E. *The Growth of English Society.* New York, 1950.

———. *Introduction to the Economic History of England.* 3 vols. London, 1926-31.

USHER, A. P. *An Introduction to the Industrial History of England.* New York, 1920.

General Works on the Modern Period

BOGART, E. L. *The Economic History of Europe (1760–1939).* London, 1942.

CLAPHAM, J. H. *The Economic History of Modern Britain.* 3 vols. London, 1935–38.

COLE, G. D. H., and POSTGATE, R. *The British Common People.* New York, 1947.

531

FAY, C. R.   *Great Britain from Adam Smith to the Present Day.* London, 1950.

HALÉVY, E.   *A History of the English People in the Nineteenth Century.* 6 vols. London, 1949–52.

JONES, G. P., and POOL, A. G.   *A Hundred Years of Economic Development in Great Britain.* London, 1940.

OGG, F. A., and SHARP, W. R.   *Economic Development of Modern Europe.* New York, 1936.

General Works on Agriculture

CURTLER, W. H. R.   *A Short History of English Agriculture.* London, 1909.

ERNLE, LORD.   *English Farming, Past and Present.* London, 1936.

General Works on Banks

ANDREADES, A.   *The History of the Bank of England, 1640–1903.* London, 1935.

CLAPHAM, J.   *The Bank of England.* 2 vols. London and New York, 1945.

General Works on Trade

ATTON, H., and HOLLAND, H. H.   *The King's Customs.* 2 vols. London, 1908-10.

DAY, C.   *History of Commerce.* New York, 1947.

CHAPTER 1

DEMANGEON, A.   *The British Isles.* Translated by E. D. Laborde. London, 1952, chap i.

FOX, C.   *The Personality of Britain.* Cardiff, 1947, pp. 1-54.

OGILVIE, A. G.   *Great Britain, Essays in Regional Geography.* London, 1930. Chap. i.

STAMP, L. D., and BEAVER, S. H.   *The British Isles.* London, 1946.

STAMP, L. D.   *The Face of Britain.* London, 1940, chaps. i-iii.

———.   *The Land of Britain.* London, 1950.

CHAPTER 2

AULT, N.   *Life in Ancient Britain.* London, 1920.

CHILDE, V. G.   *The Prehistoric Communities of the British Isles.* London, 1940.

———.   *Prehistoric Scotland.* London, 1940.

CLARK, G.   *Prehistoric England.* New York, 1941.

COLLINGWOOD, R. G.   *Roman Britain.* London, 1945.

Fox, C. *The Personality of Britain.* Cardiff, 1947, pp. 55-84.

Green, A. S. *The History of the Irish State to 1014.* London, 1925, chaps. i-iii.

Hawkes, J. and C. *Prehistoric Britain.* London, 1947.

Martin, C. P. *Prehistoric Man in Ireland.* London, 1935.

Piggott, S. *British Prehistory.* London, 1949.

CHAPTER 3

Clapham, J. H., and Power, E. *The Cambridge Economic History.* London, 1941, Vol. I, chap. iv.

Collingwood, R. G., and Myers, J. N. L. *Roman Britain and the English Settlements.* London, 1949, chaps. xx, xxi, xxiv.

Green, A. S. *The History of the Irish State to 1014.* London, 1925, chaps. iv-xxi.

MacKenzie, D. A. *Scotland, The Ancient Kingdom.* London, 1930, chaps. xi-xv.

Orwin, C. S. and C. S. *The Open Fields.* London, 1938, chaps. ii-v.

Sayles, G. O. *The Medieval Foundations of England.* London, 1950, chaps. ii, iv, vi, x, xi, xii.

Stenton, F. M. *Anglo-Saxon England.* London, 1943, chaps. viii, ix, xiv.

Tait, J. *The Medieval English Borough.* Manchester, 1936, chaps. i-v.

CHAPTER 4

Baldwin, S. *Business in the Middle Ages.* New York, 1937.

Bell, J. F. *A History of Economic Thought.* New York, 1953, chap. v.

Carlyle, A. J. "The Theory of Property in Medieval Theology," in *Property, Its Duties and Rights.* London, 1922.

Cunningham, W. *An Essay on Western Civilization in Its Economic Aspects.* London, 1910, Vol. I, chap. ii.

The Encyclopaedia of the Social Sciences. New York, 1948, articles on "Just Price," "Usury," etc.

Haskins, C. H. *The Normans in European History.* London, 1916, chap. iii.

O'Brien, G. *An Essay on Medieval Economic Teaching.* London, 1920.

Parkes, J. *The Jew in the Medieval Community.* London, 1938.

Randall, J. H. *The Making of the Modern Mind.* Boston, 1940, chap. v.

Troeltsch, E. *The Social Teaching of the Christian Churches.* London, 1931, chap. ii.

CHAPTER 5

Clapham, J. H., and Power, E. *The Cambridge Economic History.* London, 1941, Vol. I, chaps. iii, iv, vii, viii.

Curtis, E. *The History of Medieval Ireland.* London, 1938, chap. viii.

Gray, H. L. *English Field Systems.* Cambridge, 1915, chaps. v, vii.

MAITLAND, F. W. *Domesday Book and Beyond.* London, 1897.

ORPEN, G. H. *Ireland Under the Normans, 1169–1216.* London, 1911, Vol. I, chap. iv.

POWER, E. *The Wool Trade in English Medieval History.* London, 1941, chap. i.

STEPHENSON, C. *Borough and Town, a Study of Urban Origins in England.* Cambridge, 1933.

CHAPTER 6

COCHRAN-PATRICK, R. W. *Medieval Scotland.* Glasgow, 1892, chap. vii.

CURTIS, E. *The History of Medieval Ireland.* London, 1938, app. iii.

POWER, E. *The Wool Trade in English Medieval History.* London, 1941, chaps. i-vi.

TAIT, J. *The Medieval English Borough.* Manchester, 1936, chaps. vii-ix.

WEINBAUM, M. *British Borough Charters, 1307–1660.* London, 1943.

CHAPTER 7

CUNNINGHAM, W. *An Essay on Western Civilization in Its Economic Aspects.* London, 1910, Vol. II, Bk. v.

FANFANI, A. *Catholicism, Protestantism and Capitalism.* New York, 1935.

HANEY, L. H. *History of Economic Thought.* New York, 1949, chaps. vii, viii.

HECKSCHER, E. F. *Mercantilism.* London, 1935, Vol. II.

HORROCKS, J. W. *A Short History of Mercantilism.* London, 1925, chaps. iii-vi.

ROBERTSON, H. M. *Aspects of the Rise of Economic Individualism.* London, 1935, chaps. i-iii.

SCHLATTER, R. *Private Property.* London, 1951, Vol. V, chap. vi.

SÉE, H. E. *Modern Capitalism, Its Origin and Evolution.* New York, 1928, chaps. ii-v.

TAWNEY, R. H. *Religion and the Rise of Capitalism.* London, 1948.

TROELTSCH, E. *The Social Teaching of the Christian Churches.* London, 1931, chap. iii.

WOOD, H. G. "The Influence of the Reformation on Ideas Concerning Wealth and Property," in *Property, Its Duties and Rights.* London, 1922.

CHAPTER 8

ASHLEY, W. J. *The Economic Organization of England.* London, 1949, chap. iv.

CLARK, G. N. *The Wealth of England, 1496–1790.* London, 1947.

HECKSCHER, E. F. *Mercantilism.* London, 1935, Vol. I, chaps. vi, vii.

HORROCKS, J. W. *A Short History of Mercantilism.* London, 1925, chap. iv.

MacKinnon, J.   *The Social and Industrial Development of Scotland Before the Union.* London, 1920, chap. iv.

Maxwell, C.   *Irish History from Contemporary Sources, 1509–1610.* London, 1923, Sections LXXI, LXXII.

Price, W. H.   *English Patents of Monopoly.* Cambridge, Mass., 1913, chap. i.

Rees, J. F.   *Studies in Welsh History.* Cardiff, 1947 chap. iii.

Robertson, H. M.   *Aspects of the Rise of Economic Individualism.* London, 1935, chaps. iv, vii.

Sée, H.   *Modern Capitalism.* London, 1928, chaps. ii, iv.

Shakespeare's England. London, 1916, chaps. xi, xii.

Tawney, R. H., and Power, E.   *Tudor Economic Documents.* 3 vols. London, 1951.

Unwin, G.   *The Gilds and Companies of London.* London, 1908, chaps. xiii-xvii.

————.   *Industrial Organization in the 16th and 17th Centuries.* London, 1904.

CHAPTER 9

The Cambridge Modern History. London, 1903-1908, Vol. IV, chap. xviii; Vol. V, chap. x; Vol. VI, chap. xiv.

Clark, G. N.   *The Wealth of England.* London, 1947, chaps. iv-viii.

MacKinnon, J.   *The Social and Industrial History of Scotland Before the Union.* Glasgow, 1920, chap. v.

Saw, R.   *The Bank of England, 1694–1944.* London, 1944, chaps. i-vii.

Warner, G. T.   *Landmarks in English Industrial History* (7th ed.). London, n.d. chaps. xii, xiii.

CHAPTER 10

Ashton, T. S.   *The Industrial Revolution.* London, 1940, chap. v.

Barnes, H. E., and Becker, H.   *Social Thought from Lore to Science.* Boston, 1938, Vol. I, chaps. xii-xvi.

Bell, J. F.   *A History of Economic Thought.* New York, 1953, Part III.

The Encyclopaedia of the Social Sciences. New York, 1948, "Laissez Faire," "Thomas Robert Malthus," "David Ricardo," "Adam Smith."

Gide, C., and Rist, C.   *The History of Economic Doctrines.* New York, 1950. Bks. i, ii.

Hammond, J. L., and B.   *The Bleak Age.* London, 1947, chaps. viii-x.

Haney, J. L.   *History of Economic Thought.* New York, 1949, chaps. ix-xxiii.

Morris, W. D.   *The Christian Origins of Social Revolt.* London, 1949, chaps. xi, xii.

Randall, J. H.   *The Making of the Modern Mind.* Boston, 1940, chaps. xiii, xix.

Somervell, D. C.   *English Thought in the Nineteenth Century.* London, 1947, chaps. i, ii.

TOYNBEE, A. *Lectures on the Industrial Revolution of the 18th Century in England.* London, 1928, chaps. vii-xiii.

CHAPTER 11

HAMILTON, H. *The Industrial Revolution in Scotland.* London, 1932, chaps. i-iii.

LECKY, W. E. H. *A History of Ireland in the 18th Century.* London, 1913, Vol. I, chap. ii.

MACKINNON, J. *The Social and Industrial History of Scotland from the Union to the Present Time.* London, 1921, chap. i.

MANTOUX, P. *The Industrial Revolution in the 18th Century.* New York, 1937, Part I, chap. iii.

O'BRIEN, G. *The Economic History of Ireland from the Union to the Famine.* London, 1921, Part I.

PORTER, G. R., and HIRST, F. W. *The Progress of the Nation.* London, 1912, chaps. x, xi.

CHAPTER 12

BEARD, C. *The Industrial Revolution.* London, 1921, chaps. i, ii.

DIETZ, F. *The Industrial Revolution.* New York, 1927, chaps. i, ii.

HAMILTON, H. *The Industrial Revolution in Scotland.* London, 1932, chaps. iv-viii.

KNOWLES, L. C. A. *The Industrial and Commercial Revolutions in Great Britain During the 19th Century.* London, 1933, Part II.

MANTOUX, P. *The Industrial Revolution in the 18th Century.* London, 1937, Part I, chap. i; Part II.

O'BRIEN, G. *The Economic History of Ireland from the Union to the Famine.* London, 1921, chap. x.

REDFORD, A. *The Economic History of England (1760–1860).* London, 1936. Chaps. i-iii, ix.

CHAPTER 13

Encyclopaedia Britannica. 11th ed. London, 1911, "Railways." Vol. 22, pp. 819f.

HAMILTON, H. *The Industrial Revolution in Scotland.* London, 1932, chap. xi.

KIRKALDY, A. W., and EVANS, A. D. *The History and Economics of Transport.* London, 1915. Introduction, Part I.

KNOWLES, L. C. A. *The Industrial and Commercial Revolutions in Great Britain During the 19th Century.* London, 1933, Part V.

O'BRIEN, G. *The Economic History of Ireland from the Union to the Famine.* London, 1921, chap. xiii.

REDFORD, A. *The Economic History of England (1760–1860).* London, 1936, chap. xiv.

Sherrington, C. E. R. *A Hundred Years of Inland Transport.* London, 1934, chaps. i-vi.

CHAPTER 14

Mantoux, P. *The Industrial Revolution in the 18th Century.* New York, 1937, Part II.

Parkinson, C. N. *Trade Winds.* London, 1948, chap. i.

Redford, A. *The Economic History of England (1760–1860).* London, 1936, chap. vii.

Williamson, J. A. *The British Empire and Commonwealth.* London, 1948, Part III.

CHAPTER 15

Edwards, G. W. *The Evolution of Finance Capitalism.* New York, 1938, chaps. i-iii.

Gregory, T. E. *Select Statutes, Documents and Reports Relating to British Banking (1828–1928).* 2 vols. London, 1929.

Horne, H. O. *A History of Savings Banks.* London, 1947, chaps. iii, iv, xii.

Rostow, W. W. *British Economy of the 19th Century.* London, 1948, chaps. i, ii.

Saw, R. *The Bank of England, 1694–1944.* London, 1944, chaps. vi-viii.

CHAPTER 16

Fisk, H. E. *English Public Finance from the Revolution of 1688.* New York, 1920, chaps. xvi-xxii.

Knowles, L. C. A. *The Industrial and Commercial Revolutions in Great Britain in the 19th Century.* London, 1933, Part iii.

Rees, J. F. *A Short Fiscal and Financial History of England, 1815–1918.* London, 1921, chaps. i-vi.

CHAPTER 17

Cole, G. D. H. *A Short History of the British Working Class Movement.* New York, 1927, Vols. I-II, chaps. i-v.

Duffy, J. "Early Factory Legislation: A Neglected Aspect of British Humanitarianism," in S. C. McCulloch (ed.), *British Humanitarianism.* Philadelphia, 1950.

Gregg, P. *A Social and Economic History of Britain, 1760–1950.* London, 1950, chaps. i, ii, vi, viii-x, xv, xvii.

Kuczynski, J. *A Short History of Labour Conditions Under Industrial Capitalism.* London, 1944, Vol. I, Part 1, chaps. i, ii.

McConagha, W. A. *The Development of the Labour Movement in Great Britain, France and Germany.* Chapel Hill, 1942, chap. i.

Rayner, R. M. *The Story of Trade Unionism.* London, 1929, chap. i-iii.

WEARMOUTH, R. F. *Some Working-Class Movements of the Nineteenth Century.* London, 1948.

WEBB, SIDNEY and BEATRICE. *The History of Trade Unionism.* London, 1920, chaps. ii-vi.

CHAPTER 18

BEALES, H. L. "The 'Great Depression' in Industry and Trade," *The Economic History Review,* V (1934-35).

FAULKNER, H. U. *American Economic History.* New York, 1943. chaps. xx, xxi, xxiv.

HOBSON, C. K. *The Export of Capital.* London, 1914.

HOFFMAN, R. J. S. *Great Britain and German Trade Rivalry.* Philadelphia, 1933, chaps. i-iv.

HUTCHISON, K. *The Decline and Fall of British Capitalism.* New York, 1951, chaps. i-vi.

RAYNER, R. M. *Recent Times.* London, 1949, chap. xv.

ROSTOW, W. W. *British Economy of the Nineteenth Century.* London, 1948, chaps. iii, vii, viii.

CHAPTER 19

CURTLER, W. H. R. *The Enclosure and Redistribution of Our Land.* London, 1920, chaps. xviii-xxii.

Encyclopaedia Britannica. Chicago, 1946, "Ireland: Land Reform." Vol. 12, p. 612.

MACKINNON, J. *The Social and Industrial History of Scotland from the Union to the Present Day.* London, 1921, Part II, chap. ii.

CHAPTER 20

ASHLEY, W. J. (ed.). *British Industries.* London, 1903.

RAYNER, R. M. *Recent Times.* London, 1949, chaps. xv, xxii.

The Times, Past, Present and Future. London, 1932, chap. iii.

CHAPTER 21

EDWARDS, G. W. *The Evolution of Finance Capitalism.* New York, 1938, chaps. iii, iv.

ELLIOTT, S. R. *England, Cradle of Cooperation.* London, 1937, chap. iii.

REES, J. F. *A Short Fiscal and Financial History of England.* London, 1921, chaps. vi, vii.

SAW, R. *The Bank of England, 1694–1942.* London, 1944, chaps. x-xiii.

SAYERS, R. S. *Bank of England Operations, 1890–1914.* London, 1936.

CHAPTER 22

COLE, G. D. H. *British Working Class Politics.* London, 1946, chaps. vi-xviii.

————. *A Short History of the British Working Class Movement*. New York, 1927, Vol. II, chaps. vi-x; Vol. III, chaps. i-v.

ELTON, G. E. *The Life of James Ramsay MacDonald.* 1939.

Encyclopaedia of the Social Sciences. New York, 1948, articles on "Henry George," "Alfred Marshall," "William Stanley Jevons," "Socialism."

GIDE, C., and RIST, C. *History of Economic Doctrines.* New York, 1950, Book III, chap. ii; Book IV: chap. iii.

HANEY, L. H. *History of Economic Thought.* New York, 1949, chaps. xxiii, xxiv, xxvi, xxx, xxxii.

SOMERVELL, D. C. *English Thought in the Nineteenth Century.* London, 1947. Part III, chap. ii.

STEWART, W. *J. Keir Hardie's Biography.* London, 1925.

CHAPTER 23

COLE, G. D. H. *A Short History of the British Working Class Movement.* New York, 1927, Vol. III, chap. vi.

BOGART, E. L. *The Direct and Indirect Costs of the Great World War.* New York, 1919, pp. 3-43.

————. *War Costs and Their Financing.* New York, 1921, chap. vi.

BOWLEY, A. L. *Some Economic Consequences of the Great War.* London, 1931, chaps. iii, iv, vi.

GRAY, H. L. *War Time Control of Industry.* New York, 1918, Introduction.

HIRST, F. W. *The Consequences of the War to Great Britain.* ("Economic and Social History of the World War—British Series.") London, 1934, Part II, Book III, chap. i.

REES, J. F. *A Short Fiscal and Financial History of England, 1815–1918.* London, 1921, chap. viii.

CHAPTER 24

BELL, J. F. *A History of Economic Doctrines.* New York, 1953, chap. xxv.

JEWKES, J. *Ordeal by Planning.* London, 1948.

NEFF, F. A. *Economic Doctrines.* New York, 1950, chaps. xxx, xxxii.

OAKLEY, C. A. *Scottish Industry Today.* Edinburgh, 1937.

PIGOU, A. C. *Aspects of British Economic History 1918–1925.* London, 1947, Parts IV, V.

PLUMMER, A. *New British Industries in the Twentieth Century.* London, 1937, chaps. i, vi, vii.

CHAPTER 25

BENHAM, F. *Great Britain Under Protection.* New York, 1941.

COLE, G. D. H. *British Working Class Politics.* London, 1946, chap. xix.

————. *A Short History of the British Working Class Movement.* New York, 1927, Vol. III, chaps. vii-x.

Edwards, G. W. *The Evolution of Finance Capitalism.* New York, 1938, chap. viii.

Marsh, D. B. *World Trade and Investment.* New York, 1951, Book I.

Pigou, A. C. *Aspects of British Economic History 1918–1925.* London, 1947, Parts I-III.

Plummer, A. *New British Industries in the Twentieth Century.* London, 1937, chaps. ii-v.

Somervell, D. C. *British Politics Since 1900.* New York, 1950, chap. ix.

CHAPTER 26

Beacham, A. "The Efficiency and Organization of the British Coal Industry," *The Economic Journal,* LV (1945), pp. 206-16.

Chester, D. N. (ed.). *Lessons of the British War Economy.* Cambridge, 1951.

Hancock, W. K., and Gowing, M. M. *British War Economy.* London, 1949.

McCurrach, D. F. "Britain's U. S. Dollar Problems, 1939–45," *The Economic Journal,* LVIII (1948). pp. 356-72.

Prest, A. R. "The National Income of the United Kingdom," *The Economic Journal,* LVIII (1948). pp. 31-62.

Stamp, L. D. "Wartime Changes in British Agriculture," *The Geographical Journal,* CIX (1947). pp. 39-54.

CHAPTER 27

Britain, 1950–51, A Reference Handbook. London.

Economic Survey, 1945–51, published each year in British Parliamentary Papers.

Cole, G. D. H. *World in Transition.* New York, 1949, chaps. xiv, xv.

Encyclopaedia Britannica, Book of the Year, 1949–1951. Chicago, n.d., "European Recovery Program."

Marsh, D. B. *World Trade and Investment.* New York, 1951, Book iii.

Watkins, E. *The Cautious Revolution.* London, 1950.

INDEX

Acceptance houses, 285, 442

Accounting, 121

Acts of Parliament; *see also* Laws; Statutes

Agricultural Credits (1923), 458, 477

Agricultural Marketing (1931-1932), 457

Agriculture (1947), 521

Bank Charter (1844), 281

Coal (1938), 465

Coinage (1774), 279

Combination (1799 and 1800), 324-25

Conspiracy and Protection of Property (1874), 422

Corn Production (1917), 436, 457

Cotton Industry Reorganization (1936), 464

Defence of the Realm (1914-1915), 433

Distribution of Industry (1945), 524

Electric Lighting (1882), 384

Employers and Workmen (1874), 422

Enclosure (1801), 208

Factory (1802, 1833, 1901, 1937), 200, 331, 428, 429, 487

Franchise Reform (1832), 316

Friendly Society (1875), 421

General Turnpike (1773), 240

Health and Morals of Apprentices (1802), 329

Import Duties (1932), 474

Improvement of Land (1899), 369

Irish Land (1870), 218, 366

Iron and Steel Nationalization (1949), 520

Land Settlement (1919), 459

Legal Aid and Advice (1949), 524

Local Government (1858), 333

Merchandising Marks (1887), 345

Munitions (1915), 435

National Assistance (1947), 524

National Service (1942), 496

Public Health (1848), 333

Reform (1832), 308, 326

Road and Rail Traffic (1933), 468

Road Traffic (1930), 468

Safeguarding of Industries (1921), 472, 474

Small Holdings and Allotments (1907, 1926), 366, 459

Ten Hour (1847), 330, 331

Town and Country Planning (1947), 521

Trade Union (1871), 422

Transport (1947), 518

Advertising, 257, 261-62, 343, 348

Agriculture, 6ff., 318, 439; *see also* Farms and farming

Anglo-Saxon, 41ff.

areas of, 6ff.

beginnings of the new (1600-1715), 168-71

Board of (1793), 210

Board of (1889), 369, 436, 456

boom (1837-1875), 217ff.

Celtic, 24-25

commissions on, 354

crops, 362, 436

Middle Ages, 82, 139

rotation of, 44, 169, 205, 356

downward trend in (1870-1914), 353-71

education and research, 210-11, 216, 369-70, 456-57

food production, World War II, 497-98

foreign competition in, 220, 359-61, 458

government regulation, 366-71, 438-39, 494, 521-22

enclosure, 170, 212, 366

to increase production, 435-36

to increase small holdings, 366-67

post-World War II, 454-61

imports, 267

Ireland; *see* Ireland

Land Army, 497

mechanization of, 459

medieval, 76ff.

Middle Age, 136-41

Minister of (1883), 369

Ministry of, 456, 522

modern, 204ff., 353ff., 454-61, 497-98, 512